The Apostolic Fathers
By Various
Originally Edited by Philip Schaff
This Edition Edited by Anthony UYl

Woodstock, Ontario, Canada 2018

The Apostolic Fathers

The Apostolic Fathers
By Various
Originally Edited by Philip Schaff (1819-1893)
This Edition Edited by Anthony UYl

Originally Publisehd by:
Wm. B. Eerdmans Publishing Company

Originally Published as:
Ante-Nicene Fathers: Volume 1, The Apostolic Fathers, Justin Martyr, Irenaeus

The text of The Apostolic Fathers is all in the Public Domain. The covers, background, layout and Devoted Publishing logo are Copyright ©2018 Devoted Publishing. This edition is published by Devoted Publishing a division of 2165467 Ontario Inc.

What kind of philosophies do you have?
Let us know!

Visit our online store: www.devotedpublishing.com
Contact us at: devotedpub@hotmail.com
Visit us on Facebook: @DevotedPublishing

Published in Woodstock, Ontario, Canada 2018

For bulk educational rates, please contact us at the above email address.

ISBN: 978-1-77356-194-3

Table of Contents

PREFACE 5
    Footnotes: 5
    Introductory Notice 6
Clement of Rome 8
    Introductory Note to the First Epistle of Clement to the Corinthians 8
    The First Epistle of Clement to the Corinthians[2] 10
        Footnotes: 24
Mathetes 29
    Introductory Note to the Epistle of Mathetes to Diognetus 29
    The Epistle of Mathetes to Diognetus .. 30
        Footnotes: 34
Polycarp 36
    Introductory Note to the Epistle of Polycarp to the Philippians 36
    The Epistle of Polycarp to the Philippians [337] 37
        Footnotes: 39
    Introductory Note to the Epistle Concerning the Martyrdom of Polycarp 42
    The Encyclical Epistle of the Church at Smyrna Concerning the Martyrdom of the Holy Polycarp 42
        Footnotes: 47
Ignatius 49
    Introductory Note to the Epistles of Ignatius 49
        Footnotes: 51
    The Epistle of Ignatius to the Ephesians Shorter and Longer Versions 53
        Footnotes: 60
    The Epistle of Ignatius to the Magnesians Shorter and Longer Versions 63
        Footnotes: 67
    The Epistle of Ignatius to the Trallians Shorter and Longer Versions 69
        Footnotes: 73
    The Epistle of Ignatius to the Romans Shorter and Longer Versions 76
        Footnotes: 79
    The Epistle of Ignatius to the Philadelphians Shorter and Longer Versions 81
        Footnotes: 86
    The Epistle of Ignatius to the Smyrnæans Shorter and Longer Versions 87
        Footnotes: 91
    The Epistle of Ignatius to Polycarp Shorter and Longer Versions 93
        Footnotes: 96
    Introductory Note to the Syriac Version of the Ignatian Epistles 97
        Footnotes: 97
    The Epistle of Ignatius to Polycarp [1131] 98
        Footnotes: 99
    The Second Epistle of Ignatius to the Ephesians 100
        Footnotes: 101
    The Third Epistle of the Same St. Ignatius 102
        Footnotes: 103
    Introductory Note to the Spurious Epistles of Ignatius 104
        Footnotes: 105
    The Epistle of Ignatius to the Tarsians 106
        Footnotes: 108
    The Epistle of Ignatius to the Antiochians 109
        Footnotes: 111
    The Epistle of Ignatius to Hero, a Deacon of Antioch 112
        Footnotes: 114
    The Epistle of Ignatius to the Philippians 115
        Footnotes: 118
    The Epistle of Maria the Proselyte to Ignatius 120
        Footnotes: 121
    The Epistle of Ignatius to Mary at Neapolis, Near Zarbus 122
        Footnotes: 123
    The Epistle of Ignatius to St. John the Apostle 124
        Footnotes: 124
    A Second Epistle of Ignatius to St. John 125

Footnotes: 125

The Epistle of Ignatius to the Virgin Mary 126

Footnotes: 126

Reply of the Blessed Virgin to this Letter 127

Footnotes: 127

Introductory Note to the Martyrdom of Ignatius 128

The Martyrdom of Ignatius 128

Footnotes: 131

Barnabas 132

Introductory Note to the Epistle of Barnabas 132

The Epistle of Barnabas [1444] 133

Footnotes: 143

Papias 149

Introductory Note to the Fragments of Papias 149

Fragments of Papias 149

Footnotes: 151

Justin Martyr 153

Introductory Note to the Writings of Justin Martyr 153

Footnotes: 154

The First Apology of Justin 156

Epistle of Adrian in behalf of the Christians 177

Epistle of Antoninus to the common assembly of Asia 177

Epistle of Marcus Aurelius to the senate, in which he testifies that the Christians were the cause of his victory 177

Footnotes: 178

The Second Apology of Justin for the Christians Addressed to the Roman Senate 184

Footnotes: 189

Dialogue of Justin, Philosopher and Martyr, with Trypho, a Jew 190

Footnotes: 260

The Discourse to the Greeks 270

Footnotes: 271

Justin's Hortatory Address to the Greeks 273

Footnotes: 290

Justin on the Sole Government of God 292

Footnotes: 297

Fragments of the Lost Work of Justin on the Resurrection 298

Footnotes: 302

Other Fragments from the Lost Writings of Justin 304

Footnotes: 306

Introductory Note to the Martyrdom of Justin Martyr 307

The Martyrdom of the Holy Martyrs Justin, Chariton, Charites, Pæon, and Liberianus, who Suffered at Rome 307

Footnotes: 308

PREFACE

This volume, containing the equivalent of three volumes of the Edinburgh series of the Ante-Nicene Fathers, will be found a library somewhat complete in itself. The Apostolic Fathers and those associated with them in the third generation, are here placed together in a handbook, which, with the inestimable Scriptures, supplies a succinct autobiography of the Spouse of Christ for the first two centuries. No Christian scholar has ever before possessed, in faithful versions of such compact form, a supplement so essential to the right understanding of the New Testament itself. It is a volume indispensable to all scholars, and to every library, private or public, in this country.

The American Editor has performed the humble task of ushering these works into American use, with scanty contributions of his own. Such was the understanding with the public: they were to be presented with the Edinburgh series, free from appreciable colour or alloy. His duty was (1) to give historic arrangement to the confused mass of the original series; (2) to supply, in continuity, such brief introductory notices as might slightly popularize what was apparently meant for scholars only, in the introductions of the translators; (3) to supply a few deficiencies by short notes and references; (4) to add such references to Scripture, or to authors of general repute, as might lend additional aid to students, without clogging or overlaying the comments of the translators; and (5) to note such corruptions or distortions of Patristic testimony as have been circulated, in the spirit of the forged Decretals, by those who carry on the old imposture by means essentially equivalent. Too long have they been allowed to speak to the popular mind as if the Fathers were their own; while, to every candid reader, it must be evident that, alike, the testimony, the arguments, and the silence of the Ante-Nicene writers confound all attempts to identify the ecclesiastical establishment of "the Holy Roman Empire," with "the Holy Catholic Church" of the ancient creeds.

In performing this task, under the pressure of a virtual obligation to issue the first volume in the first month of the new year, the Editor has relied upon the kindly aid of an able friend, as typographical corrector of the Edinburgh sheets. It is only necessary to add, that he has bracketed all his own notes, so as to assume the responsibility for them; but his introductions are so separated from those of the translators, that, after the first instance, he has not thought it requisite to suffix his initials to these brief contributions. He regrets that the most important volume of the series is necessarily the experimental one, and comes out under disadvantages from which it may be expected that succeeding issues will be free. May the Lord God of our Fathers bless the undertaking to all my fellow-Christians, and make good to them the promise which was once felicitously chosen for the motto of a similar series of publications: "Yet shall not thy teachers be removed into a corner any more, but thine eyes shall see thy teachers."

A. C. C.

January, 6, 1885.

N.B.--The following advertisement of the original editors will be useful here:--

The Ante-Nicene Christian Library is meant to comprise translations into English of all the extant works of the Fathers down to the date of the first General Council held at Nice in a.d. 325. The sole provisional exception is that of the more bulky writings of Origen. It is intended at present only to embrace in the scheme the Contra Celsum and the De Principiis of that voluminous author; but the whole of his works will be included should the undertaking prove successful.

The present volume has been translated by the Editors.[1] Their object has been to place the English reader as nearly as possible on a footing of equality with those who are able to read the original. With this view they have for the most part leaned towards literal exactness; and wherever any considerable departure from this has been made, a verbatim rendering has been given at the foot of the page. Brief introductory notices have been prefixed, and short notes inserted, to indicate varieties of reading, specify references, or elucidate any obscurity which seemed to exist in the text.

Edinburgh, 1867.

Footnotes:

1. This refers to the first volume only of the original series.

Introductory Notice

[a.d. 100-200.] The Apostolic Fathers are here understood as filling up the second century of our era. Irenæus, it is true, is rather of the sub-apostolic period; but, as the disciple of Polycarp, he ought not to be dissociated from that Father's company. We thus find ourselves conducted, by this goodly fellowship of witnesses, from the times of the apostles to those of Tertullian, from the martyrs of the second persecution to those of the sixth. Those were times of heroism, not of words; an age, not of writers, but of soldiers; not of talkers, but of sufferers. Curiosity is baffled, but faith and love are fed by these scanty relics of primitive antiquity. Yet may we well be grateful for what we have. These writings come down to us as the earliest response of converted nations to the testimony of Jesus. They are primary evidences of the Canon and the credibility of the New Testament. Disappointment may be the first emotion of the student who comes down from the mount where he has dwelt in the tabernacles of evangelists and apostles: for these disciples are confessedly inferior to the masters; they speak with the voices of infirm and fallible men, and not like the New Testament writers, with the fiery tongues of the Holy Ghost. Yet the thoughtful and loving spirit soon learns their exceeding value. For who does not close the records of St. Luke with longing; to get at least a glimpse of the further history of the progress of the Gospel? What of the Church when its founders were fallen asleep? Was the Good Shepherd "always" with His little flock, according to His promise? Was the Blessed Comforter felt in His presence amid the fires of persecution? Was the Spirit of Truth really able to guide the faithful into all truth, and to keep them in the truth?

And what had become of the disciples who were the first-fruits of the apostolic ministry? St. Paul had said, "The same commit thou to faithful men, who shall be able to teach others also." How was this injunction realized? St. Peter's touching words come to mind, "I will endeavour that ye may be able after my decease to have these things always in remembrance." Was this endeavour successfully carried out? To these natural and pious inquiries, the Apostolic Fathers, though we have a few specimens only of their fidelity, give an emphatic reply. If the cold-hearted and critical find no charm in the simple, childlike faith which they exhibit, ennobled though it be by heroic devotion to the Master, we need not marvel. Such would probably object: "They teach me nothing; I do not relish their multiplied citations from Scripture." The answer is, "If you are familiar with Scripture, you owe it largely to these primitive witnesses to its Canon and its spirit. By their testimony we detect what is spurious, and we identify what is real. Is it nothing to find that your Bible is their Bible, your faith their faith, your Saviour their Saviour, your God their God?" Let us reflect also, that, when copies of the entire Scriptures were rare and costly, these citations were "words fitly spoken,--apples of gold in pictures of silver." We are taught by them also that they obeyed the apostle's precept, "Let the word of Christ dwell in you richly in all wisdom; teaching and admonishing," etc. Thus they reflect the apostolic care that men should be raised up able to teach others also.

Their very mistakes enable us to attach a higher value to the superiority of inspired writers. They were not wiser than the naturalists of their day who taught them the history of the Phoenix and other fables; but nothing of this sort is found in Scripture. The Fathers are inferior in kind as well as in degree; yet their words are lingering echoes of those whose words were spoken "as the Spirit gave them utterance." They are monuments of the power of the Gospel. They were made out of such material as St. Paul describes when he says, "Such were some of you." But for Christ, they would have been worshippers of personified Lust and Hate, and of every crime. They would have lived for "bread and circus-shows." Yet to the contemporaries of a Juvenal they taught the Decalogue and the Sermon on the Mount. Among such beasts in human form they reared the sacred home; they created the Christian family; they gave new and holy meanings to the names of wife and mother; they imparted ideas unknown before of the dignity of man as man; they infused an atmosphere of benevolence and love; they bestowed the elements of liberty chastened by law; they sanctified human society by proclaiming the universal brotherhood of redeemed man. As we read the Apostolic Fathers, we comprehend, in short, the meaning of St. Paul when he said prophetically, what men were slow to believe, "The foolishness of God is wiser than men; and the weakness of God is stronger than men .. But God hath chosen the foolish things of the world to confound the wise; and God hath chosen the weak things of the world to confound the things which are mighty; and base things of the world, and things which are despised, hath God chosen, yea, and things

which are not, to bring to nought things that are."
    A. C. C.
       December, 1884.

Clement of Rome

Introductory Note to the First Epistle of Clement to the Corinthians

[a.d. 30-100.] Clement was probably a Gentile and a Roman. He seems to have been at Philippi with St. Paul (a.d. 57) when that first-born of the Western churches was passing through great trials of faith. There, with holy women and others, he ministered to the apostle and to the saints. As this city was a Roman colony, we need not inquire how a Roman happened to be there. He was possibly in some public service, and it is not improbable that he had visited Corinth in those days. From the apostle, and his companion, St. Luke, he had no doubt learned the use of the Septuagint, in which his knowledge of the Greek tongue soon rendered him an adept. His copy of that version, however, does not always agree with the Received Text, as the reader will perceive.

A co-presbyter with Linus and Cletus, he succeeded them in the government of the Roman Church. I have reluctantly adopted the opinion that his Epistle was written near the close of his life, and not just after the persecution of Nero. It is not improbable that Linus and Cletus both perished in that fiery trial, and that Clement's immediate succession to their work and place occasions the chronological difficulties of the period. After the death of the apostles, for the Roman imprisonment and martyrdom of St. Peter seem historical, Clement was the natural representative of St. Paul, and even of his companion, the "apostle of the circumcision;" and naturally he wrote the Epistle in the name of the local church, when brethren looked to them for advice. St. John, no doubt, was still surviving at Patmos or in Ephesus; but the Philippians, whose intercourse with Rome is attested by the visit of Epaphroditus, looked naturally to the surviving friends of their great founder; nor was the aged apostle in the East equally accessible. All roads pointed towards the Imperial City, and started from its Milliarium Aureum. But, though Clement doubtless wrote the letter, he conceals his own name, and puts forth the brethren, who seem to have met in council, and sent a brotherly delegation (Chap. lix.). The entire absence of the spirit of Diotrephes (3 John 9), and the close accordance of the Epistle, in humility and meekness, with that of St. Peter (1 Pet. v. 1-5), are noteworthy features. The whole will be found animated with the loving and faithful spirit of St. Paul's dear Philippians, among whom the writer had learned the Gospel.

Clement fell asleep, probably soon after he despatched his letter. It is the legacy of one who reflects the apostolic age in all the beauty and evangelical truth which were the first-fruits of the Spirit's presence with the Church. He shares with others the aureole of glory attributed by St. Paul (Phil. iv. 3), "His name is in the Book of Life."

The plan of this publication does not permit the restoration, in this volume, of the recently discovered portions of his work. It is the purpose of the editor to present this, however, with other recently discovered relics of primitive antiquity, in a supplementary volume, should the undertaking meet with sufficient encouragement. The so-called second Epistle of Clement is now known to be the work of another, and has been relegated to another place in this series.

The following is the Introductory Notice of the original editors and translators, Drs. Roberts and Donaldson:--

The first Epistle, bearing the name of Clement, has been preserved to us in a single manuscript only. Though very frequently referred to by ancient Christian writers, it remained unknown to the scholars of Western Europe until happily discovered in the Alexandrian manuscript. This ms. of the Sacred Scriptures (known and generally referred to as Codex A) was presented in 1628 by Cyril, Patriarch of Constantinople, to Charles I., and is now preserved in the British Museum. Subjoined to the books of the New Testament contained in it, there are two writings described as the Epistles of one Clement. Of these, that now before us is the first. It is tolerably perfect, but there are many slight lacunæ, or gaps, in the ms., and one whole leaf is supposed to have been lost towards the close. These lacunæ, however, so numerous in some chapters, do not generally extend beyond a word or syllable, and can for the most part be easily supplied.

Who the Clement was to whom these writings are ascribed, cannot with absolute certainty be determined. The general opinion is, that he is the same as the person of that name referred to by St. Paul (Phil. iv. 3). The writings themselves contain no statement as to their author. The first, and by far the longer of them, simply purports to have been written in the name of the Church at Rome to the Church at Corinth. But in the catalogue of contents prefixed to the ms. they are both plainly attributed to one Clement; and the judgment of most scholars is, that, in regard to the first Epistle at least, this statement is correct, and that it is to be regarded as an authentic production of the friend and fellow-worker of St. Paul. This belief may be traced to an early period in the history of the Church. It is found in the writings of Eusebius (Hist. Eccl., iii. 15), of Origen (Comm. in Joan., i. 29), and others. The internal evidence also tends to support this opinion. The doctrine, style, and manner of thought are all in accordance with it; so that, although, as has been said, positive certainty cannot be reached on the subject, we may with great probability conclude that we have in this Epistle a composition of that Clement who is known to us from Scripture as having been an associate of the great apostle.

The date of this Epistle has been the subject of considerable controversy. It is clear from the writing itself that it was composed soon after some persecution (chap. i.) which the Roman Church had endured; and the only question is, whether we are to fix upon the persecution under Nero or Domitian. If the former, the date will be about the year 68; if the latter, we must place it towards the close of the first century or the beginning of the second. We possess no external aid to the settlement of this question. The lists of early Roman bishops are in hopeless confusion, some making Clement the immediate successor of St. Peter, others placing Linus, and others still Linus and Anacletus, between him and the apostle. The internal evidence, again, leaves the matter doubtful, though it has been strongly pressed on both sides. The probability seems, on the whole, to be in favour of the Domitian period, so that the Epistle may be dated about a.d. 97.

This Epistle was held in very great esteem by the early Church. The account given of it by Eusebius (Hist. Eccl., iii. 16) is as follows: "There is one acknowledged Epistle of this Clement (whom he has just identified with the friend of St. Paul), great and admirable, which he wrote in the name of the Church of Rome to the Church at Corinth, sedition having then arisen in the latter Church. We are aware that this Epistle has been publicly read in very many churches both in old times, and also in our own day." The Epistle before us thus appears to have been read in numerous churches, as being almost on a level with the canonical writings. And its place in the Alexandrian ms., immediately after the inspired books, is in harmony with the position thus assigned it in the primitive Church. There does indeed appear a great difference between it and the inspired writings in many respects, such as the fanciful use sometimes made of Old-Testament statements, the fabulous stories which are accepted by its author, and the general diffuseness and feebleness of style by which it is distinguished. But the high tone of evangelical truth which pervades it, the simple and earnest appeals which it makes to the heart and conscience, and the anxiety which its writer so constantly shows to promote the best interests of the Church of Christ, still impart an undying charm to this precious relic of later apostolic times.

[N.B.--A sufficient guide to the recent literature of the Clementine mss. and discoveries may be found in The Princeton Review, 1877, p. 325, also in Bishop Wordsworth's succinct but learned Church History to the Council of Nicæa, p. 84. The invaluable edition of the Patres Apostolici, by Jacobson (Oxford, 1840), with a critical text and rich prolegomena and annotations, cannot be dispensed with by any Patristic inquirer. A. C. C.]

The First Epistle of Clement to the Corinthians[2]

Chapter I - The salutation. Praise of the Corinthians before the breaking forth of schism among them

The Church of God which sojourns at Rome, to the Church of God sojourning at Corinth, to them that are called and sanctified by the will of God, through our Lord Jesus Christ: Grace unto you, and peace, from Almighty God through Jesus Christ, be multiplied.

Owing, dear brethren, to the sudden and successive calamitous events which have happened to ourselves, we feel that we have been somewhat tardy in turning our attention to the points respecting which you consulted us; [3] and especially to that shameful and detestable sedition, utterly abhorrent to the elect of God, which a few rash and self-confident persons have kindled to such a pitch of frenzy, that your venerable and illustrious name, worthy to be universally loved, has suffered grievous injury. [4] For who ever dwelt even for a short time among you, and did not find your faith to be as fruitful of virtue as it was firmly established? [5] Who did not admire the sobriety and moderation of your godliness in Christ? Who did not proclaim the magnificence of your habitual hospitality? And who did not rejoice over your perfect and well-grounded knowledge? For ye did all things without respect of persons, and walked in the commandments of God, being obedient to those who had the rule over you, and giving all fitting honour to the presbyters among you. Ye enjoined young men to be of a sober and serious mind; ye instructed your wives to do all things with a blameless, becoming, and pure conscience, loving their husbands as in duty bound; and ye taught them that, living in the rule of obedience, they should manage their household affairs becomingly, and be in every respect marked by discretion.

Chapter II - Praise of the Corinthians continued

Moreover, ye were all distinguished by humility, and were in no respect puffed up with pride, but yielded obedience rather than extorted it, [6] and were more willing to give than to receive. [7] Content with the provision which God had made for you, and carefully attending to His words, ye were inwardly filled [8] with His doctrine, and His sufferings were before your eyes. Thus a profound and abundant peace was given to you all, and ye had an insatiable desire for doing good, while a full outpouring of the Holy Spirit was upon you all. Full of holy designs, ye did, with true earnestness of mind and a godly confidence, stretch forth your hands to God Almighty, beseeching Him to be merciful unto you, if ye had been guilty of any involuntary transgression. Day and night ye were anxious for the whole brotherhood, [9] that the number of God's elect might be saved with mercy and a good conscience. [10] Ye were sincere and uncorrupted, and forgetful of injuries between one another. Every kind of faction and schism was abominable in your sight. Ye mourned over the transgressions of your neighbours: their deficiencies you deemed your own. Ye never grudged any act of kindness, being "ready to every good work." [11] Adorned by a thoroughly virtuous and religious life, ye did all things in the fear of God. The commandments and ordinances of the Lord were written upon the tablets of your hearts. [12]

Chapter III - The sad state of the Corinthian church after sedition arose in it from envy and emulation

Every kind of honour and happiness [13] was bestowed upon you, and then was fulfilled that which is written, "My beloved did eat and drink, and was enlarged and became fat, and kicked." [14] Hence flowed emulation and envy, strife and sedition, persecution and disorder, war and captivity. So the worthless rose up against the honoured, those of no reputation against such as were renowned, the foolish against the wise, the young against those advanced in years. For this reason righteousness and peace are now far departed from you, inasmuch as every one abandons the fear of God, and is become blind in His faith, [15] neither walks in the ordinances of His appointment, nor acts a part becoming a Christian, [16] but walks after his own wicked lusts, resuming the practice of an unrighteous and ungodly envy, by which death itself entered into the world. [17]

Chapter IV - Many evils have already flowed from this source in ancient times

For thus it is written: "And it came to pass after certain days, that Cain brought of the fruits of the earth a sacrifice unto God; and Abel also brought of the firstlings of his sheep, and of the fat thereof. And God had respect to Abel and to his offerings, but Cain and his sacrifices He did not regard. And Cain was deeply grieved, and his countenance fell. And God said to Cain, Why art thou grieved, and why is thy countenance fallen? If thou offerest rightly, but dost not divide rightly, hast thou not sinned? Be at peace: thine offering returns to thyself, and thou shalt again possess it. And Cain said to Abel his brother, Let us go into the field. And it came to pass, while they were in the field, that Cain rose up against Abel his brother, and slew him." [18] Ye see, brethren, how envy and jealousy led to the murder of a brother. Through envy, also, our father Jacob fled from the face of Esau his brother. [19] Envy made Joseph be persecuted unto death, and to come into bondage. [20] Envy compelled Moses to flee from the face of Pharaoh king of Egypt, when he heard these words from his fellow-countryman, "Who made thee a judge or a ruler over us? wilt thou kill me, as thou didst kill the Egyptian yesterday?" [21] On account of envy, Aaron and Miriam had to make their abode without the camp. [22] Envy brought down Dathan and Abiram alive to Hades, through the sedition which they excited against God's servant Moses. [23] Through envy, David underwent the hatred not only of foreigners, but was also persecuted by Saul king of Israel. [24]

Chapter V - No less evils have arisen from the same source in the most recent times. The martyrdom of Peter and Paul

But not to dwell upon ancient examples, let us come to the most recent spiritual heroes. [25] Let us take the noble examples furnished in our own generation. Through envy and jealousy, the greatest and most righteous pillars [of the Church] have been persecuted and put to death. [26] Let us set before our eyes the illustrious [27] apostles. Peter, through unrighteous envy, endured not one or two, but numerous labours and when he had at length suffered martyrdom, departed to the place of glory due to him. Owing to envy, Paul also obtained the reward of patient endurance, after being seven times thrown into captivity, [28] compelled [29] to flee, and stoned. After preaching both in the east and west, he gained the illustrious reputation due to his faith, having taught righteousness to the whole world, and come to the extreme limit of the west, [30] and suffered martyrdom under the prefects. [31] Thus was he removed from the world, and went into the holy place, having proved himself a striking example of patience.

Chapter VI - Continuation. Several other martyrs

To these men who spent their lives in the practice of holiness, there is to be added a great multitude of the elect, who, having through envy endured many indignities and tortures, furnished us with a most excellent example. Through envy, those women, the Danaids [32] and Dircæ, being persecuted, after they had suffered terrible and unspeakable torments, finished the course of their faith with stedfastness, [33] and though weak in body, received a noble reward. Envy has alienated wives from their husbands, and changed that saying of our father Adam, "This is now bone of my bones, and flesh of my flesh." [34] Envy and strife have overthrown great cities and rooted up mighty nations.

Chapter VII - An exhortation to repentance

These things, beloved, we write unto you, not merely to admonish you of your duty, but also to remind ourselves. For we are struggling on the same arena, and the same conflict is assigned to both of us. Wherefore let us give up vain and fruitless cares, and approach to the glorious and venerable rule of our holy calling. Let us attend to what is good, pleasing, and acceptable in the sight of Him who formed us. Let us look stedfastly to the blood of Christ, and see how precious that blood is to God, [35] which, having been shed for our salvation, has set the grace of repentance before the whole world. Let us turn to every age that has passed, and learn that, from generation to generation, the Lord has granted a place of repentance to all such as would be converted unto Him. Noah preached repentance, and as many as listened to him were saved. [36] Jonah proclaimed destruction to the Ninevites; [37] but they, repenting of their sins, propitiated God by prayer, and obtained salvation, although they were aliens [to the covenant] of God.

Chapter VIII - Continuation respecting repentance

The ministers of the grace of God have, by the Holy Spirit, spoken of repentance; and the Lord of all things has himself declared with an oath regarding it, "As I live, saith the Lord, I desire not the death of the sinner, but rather his repentance;" [38] adding, moreover, this gracious declaration, "Repent, O house of Israel, of your iniquity. [39] Say to the children of My people,

The Apostolic Fathers

Though your sins reach from earth to heaven, and though they be redder [40] than scarlet, and blacker than sackcloth, yet if ye turn to Me with your whole heart, and say, Father! I will listen to you, as to a holy [41] people." And in another place He speaks thus: "Wash you, and become clean; put away the wickedness of your souls from before mine eyes; cease from your evil ways, and learn to do well; seek out judgment, deliver the oppressed, judge the fatherless, and see that justice is done to the widow; and come, and let us reason together. He declares, Though your sins be like crimson, I will make them white as snow; though they be like scarlet, I will whiten them like wool. And if ye be willing and obey Me, ye shall eat the good of the land; but if ye refuse, and will not hearken unto Me, the sword shall devour you, for the mouth of the Lord hath spoken these things." [42] Desiring, therefore, that all His beloved should be partakers of repentance, He has, by His almighty will, established [these declarations].

Chapter IX - Examples of the saints

Wherefore, let us yield obedience to His excellent and glorious will; and imploring His mercy and loving-kindness, while we forsake all fruitless labours, [43] and strife, and envy, which leads to death, let us turn and have recourse to His compassions. Let us stedfastly contemplate those who have perfectly ministered to His excellent glory. Let us take (for instance) Enoch, who, being found righteous in obedience, was translated, and death was never known to happen to him. [44] Noah, being found faithful, preached regeneration to the world through his ministry; and the Lord saved by him the animals which, with one accord, entered into the ark.

Chapter X - Continuation of the above

Abraham, styled "the friend," [45] was found faithful, inasmuch as he rendered obedience to the words of God. He, in the exercise of obedience, went out from his own country, and from his kindred, and from his father's house, in order that, by forsaking a small territory, and a weak family, and an insignificant house, he might inherit the promises of God. For God said to him, "Get thee out from thy country, and from thy kindred, and from thy father's house, into the land which I shall show thee. And I will make thee a great nation, and will bless thee, and make thy name great, and thou shall be blessed. And I will bless them that bless thee, and curse them that curse thee; and in thee shall all the families of the earth be blessed." [46] And again, on his departing from Lot, God said to him, "Lift up thine eyes, and look from the place where thou now art, northward, and southward, and eastward, and westward; for all the land which thou seest, to thee will I give it, and to thy seed for ever. And I will make thy seed as the dust of the earth, [so that] if a man can number the dust of the earth, then shall thy seed also be numbered." [47] And again [the Scripture] saith, "God brought forth Ἀβραμ, and spake unto him, Look up now to heaven, and count the stars if thou be able to number them; so shall thy seed be. And Ἀβραμ believed God, and it was counted to him for righteousness." [48] On account of his faith and hospitality, a son was given him in his old age; and in the exercise of obedience, he offered him as a sacrifice to God on one of the mountains which He showed him. [49]

Chapter XI - Continuation. Lot

On account of his hospitality and godliness, Lot was saved out of Sodom when all the country round was punished by means of fire and brimstone, the Lord thus making it manifest that He does not forsake those who hope in Him, but gives up such as depart from Him to punishment and torture. [50] For Lot's wife, who went forth with him, being of a different mind from himself and not continuing in agreement with him [as to the command which had been given them], was made an example of, so as to be a pillar of salt unto this day. [51] This was done that all might know that those who are of a double mind, and who distrust the power of God, bring down judgment on themselves [52] and become a sign to all succeeding generations.

Chapter XII - The rewards of faith and hospitality. Rahab

On account of her faith and hospitality, Rahab the harlot was saved. For when spies were sent by Joshua, the son of Nun, to Jericho, the king of the country ascertained that they were come to spy out their land, and sent men to seize them, in order that, when taken, they might be put to death. But the hospitable Rahab receiving them, concealed them on the roof of her house under some stalks of flax. And when the men sent by the king arrived and said "There came men unto thee who are to spy out our land; bring them forth, for so the king commands," she answered them, "The two men whom ye seek came unto me, but quickly departed again and are gone," thus not discovering the spies to them. Then she said to the men, "I know assuredly that the Lord your God hath given you this city, for the fear and dread of you have fallen on its inhabitants. When therefore ye shall have taken it, keep ye me and the house of my father in safety." And they said to her, "It shall be as thou hast spoken to us. As soon, therefore, as thou knowest that we are at hand, thou shalt gather all thy family under thy roof, and they shall be preserved, but all that are found outside of thy dwelling shall perish." [53] Moreover, they gave her a sign to this effect, that she should hang forth from her house a scarlet thread. And thus they made it manifest that redemption should flow through the blood of the Lord to all them that believe and hope in God. [54] Ye see, beloved, that there was not only faith, but prophecy, in this woman.

Chapter XIII - An exhortation to humility

Let us therefore, brethren, be of humble mind, laying aside all haughtiness, and pride, and foolishness, and angry feelings; and let us act according to that which is written (for the Holy Spirit saith, "Let not the wise man glory in his wisdom, neither let the mighty man glory in his might, neither let the rich man glory in his riches; but let him that glorieth glory in the Lord, in diligently seeking Him, and doing judgment and righteousness" [55]), being especially mindful of the words of the Lord Jesus which He spake, teaching us meekness and long-suffering. For thus He spoke: "Be ye merciful, that ye may obtain mercy; forgive, that it may be forgiven to you; as ye do, so shall it be done unto you; as ye judge, so shall ye be judged; as ye are kind, so shall kindness be shown to you; with what measure ye mete, with the same it shall be measured to you." [56] By this precept and by these rules let us establish ourselves, that we walk with all humility in obedience to His holy words. For the holy word saith, "On whom shall I look, but on him that is meek and peaceable, and that trembleth at My words?" [57]

Chapter XIV - We should obey God rather than the authors of sedition

It is right and holy therefore, men and brethren, rather to obey God than to follow those who, through pride and sedition, have become the leaders of a detestable emulation. For we shall incur no slight injury, but rather great danger, if we rashly yield ourselves to the inclinations of men who aim at exciting strife and tumults, so as to draw us away from what is good. Let us be kind one to another after the pattern of the tender mercy and benignity of our Creator. For it is written, "The kind-hearted shall inhabit the land, and the guiltless shall be left upon it, but transgressors shall be destroyed from off the face of it." [58] And again [the Scripture] saith, "I saw the ungodly highly exalted, and lifted up like the cedars of Lebanon: I passed by, and, behold, he was not; and I diligently sought his place, and could not find it. Preserve innocence, and look on equity: for there shall be a remnant to the peaceful man." [59]

Chapter XV - We must adhere to those who cultivate peace, not to those who merely pretend to do so

Let us cleave, therefore, to those who cultivate peace with godliness, and not to those who hypocritically profess to desire it. For [the Scripture] saith in a certain place, "This people honoureth Me with their lips, but their heart is far from Me." [60] And again: "They bless with their mouth, but curse with their heart." [61] And again it saith, "They loved Him with their mouth, and lied to Him with their tongue; but their heart was not right with Him, neither were they faithful in His covenant." [62] "Let the deceitful lips become silent," [63] [and "let the Lord destroy all the lying lips, [64]] and the boastful tongue of those who have said, Let us magnify our tongue; our lips are our own; who is lord over us? For the oppression of the poor, and for the sighing of the needy, will I now arise, saith the Lord: I will place him in safety; I will deal confidently with him."[65]

Chapter XVI - Christ as an example of humility

For Christ is of those who are humble-minded, and not of those who exalt themselves over His flock. Our Lord Jesus Christ, the Sceptre of the majesty of God, did not come in the pomp of pride or arrogance, although He might have done so, but in a lowly condition, as the Holy Spirit had declared regarding Him. For He says, "Lord, who hath believed our report, and to whom is the arm of the Lord revealed? We have declared [our message] in His presence: He is, as it were, a child, and like a root in thirsty ground; He has no form nor glory, yea, we saw Him, and He had no form nor comeliness; but His form was without eminence, yea, deficient in comparison with the [ordinary] form of men. He is a man exposed to stripes and suffering, and acquainted with the endurance of grief: for His countenance was turned away; He was despised, and not esteemed. He bears our iniquities, and is in sorrow for our sakes; yet we supposed that [on His own account] He was exposed to labour, and stripes, and affliction. But He was wounded for our transgressions, and bruised for our iniquities. The chastisement of our peace was upon Him, and by His stripes we were healed. All we, like sheep, have gone astray; [every] man has wandered in his own way; and the Lord has delivered Him up for our sins, while He in the midst of His sufferings openeth not His mouth. He was brought as a sheep to the slaughter, and as a lamb before her shearer is dumb, so He openeth not His mouth. In His humiliation His judgment was taken away; who shall declare His generation? for His life is taken from the earth. For the transgressions of my people was He brought down to death. And I will give the wicked for His sepulchre, and the rich for His death, [66] because He did no iniquity, neither was guile found in His mouth. And the Lord is pleased to purify Him by stripes. [67] If ye make [68] an offering for sin, your soul shall see a long-lived seed. And the Lord is pleased to relieve Him of the affliction of His soul, to show Him light, and to form Him with understanding, [69] to justify the Just One who ministereth well to many; and He Himself shall carry their sins. On this account He shall inherit many, and shall divide the spoil of the strong; because His soul was delivered to death, and He was reckoned among the transgressors, and He bare the sins of many, and for their sins was He delivered." [70] And again He saith, "I am a worm, and no man; a reproach of men, and despised of the people. All that see Me have derided Me; they have spoken with their lips; they have wagged their head, [saying] He hoped in God, let Him deliver Him, let Him save Him, since He delighteth in Him." [71] Ye see, beloved, what is the example which has been given us; for if the Lord thus humbled Himself, what shall we do who have through Him come under the yoke of His grace?

Chapter XVII - The saints as examples of humility

Let us be imitators also of those who in goat-skins and sheep-skins [72] went about proclaiming the coming of Christ; I mean Elijah, Elisha, and Ezekiel among the prophets, with those others to whom a like testimony is borne [in Scripture]. Abraham was specially honoured, and was called the friend of God; yet he, earnestly regarding the glory of God, humbly declared, "I am but dust and ashes." [73] Moreover, it is thus written of Job, "Job was a righteous man, and blameless, truthful, God-fearing, and one that kept himself from all evil." [74] But bringing an accusation against himself, he said, "No man is free from defilement, even if his life be but of one day." [75] Moses was called faithful in all God's house; [76] and through his instrumentality, God punished Egypt [77] with plagues and tortures. Yet he, though thus greatly honoured, did not adopt lofty language, but said, when the divine oracle came to him out of the bush, "Who am I, that Thou sendest me? I am a man of a feeble voice and a slow tongue." [78] And again he said, "I am but as the smoke of a pot." [79]

Chapter XVIII - David as an example of humility

But what shall we say concerning David, to whom such testimony was borne, and of whom [80] God said, "I have found a man after Mine own heart, David the son of Jesse; and in everlasting mercy have I anointed him?" [81] Yet this very man saith to God, "Have mercy on me, O Lord, according to Thy great mercy; and according to the multitude of Thy compassions, blot out my transgression. Wash me still more from mine iniquity, and cleanse me from my sin. For I acknowledge my iniquity, and my sin is ever before me. Against Thee only have I sinned, and done that which was evil in Thy sight; that Thou mayest be justified in Thy sayings, and mayest overcome when Thou [82] art judged. For, behold, I was conceived in transgressions, and in my sins did my mother conceive me. For, behold, Thou hast loved truth; the secret and hidden things of wisdom hast Thou shown me. Thou shalt sprinkle me with hyssop, and I shall be cleansed; Thou shalt wash me, and I shall be whiter than snow. Thou shalt make me to hear joy and gladness; my bones, which have been humbled, shall exult. Turn away Thy face from my sins, and blot out all mine iniquities. Create in me a clean heart, O God, and renew a right spirit within me. [83] Cast me not away from Thy presence, and take not Thy Holy Spirit from me. Restore to me the joy of Thy salvation, and establish me by Thy governing Spirit. I will teach transgressors Thy ways, and the ungodly shall be converted unto Thee. Deliver me from blood-guiltiness, [84] O God, the God of my salvation: my tongue shall exult in Thy righteousness. O Lord, Thou shalt open my mouth, and my lips shall show forth Thy praise. For if Thou hadst desired sacrifice, I would have given it; Thou wilt not delight in burnt-offerings. The sacrifice [acceptable] to God is a bruised spirit; a broken and a contrite heart God will not despise." [85]

Chapter XIX - Imitating these examples, let us seek after peace

Thus the humility and godly submission of so great and illustrious men have rendered not only us, but also all the generations before us, better; even as many as have received His oracles in fear and truth. Wherefore, having so many great and glorious examples set before us, let us turn again to the practice of that peace which from the beginning was the mark set before us; [86] and let us look stedfastly to the Father and Creator of the universe, and cleave to His mighty and surpassingly great gifts and benefactions of peace. Let us contemplate Him with our understanding, and look with the eyes of our soul to His long-suffering will. Let us reflect how free from wrath He is towards all His creation.

Chapter XX - The peace and harmony of the universe

The heavens, revolving under His government, are subject to Him in peace. Day and night run the course appointed by Him, in no wise hindering each other. The sun and moon, with the companies of the stars, roll on in harmony according to His command, within their prescribed limits, and without any deviation. The fruitful earth, according to His will, brings forth food in abundance, at the proper seasons, for man and beast and all the living beings upon it, never hesitating, nor changing any of the ordinances which He has fixed. The unsearchable places of abysses, and the indescribable arrangements of the lower world, are restrained by the same laws. The vast unmeasurable sea, gathered together by His working into various basins, [87] never passes beyond the bounds placed around it, but does as He has commanded. For He said, "Thus far shalt thou come, and thy waves shall be broken within thee." [88] The ocean, impassable to man, and the worlds beyond it, are regulated by the same enactments of the Lord. The seasons of spring, summer, autumn, and winter, peacefully give place to one another. The winds in their several quarters [89] fulfill, at the proper time, their service without hindrance. The ever-flowing fountains, formed both for enjoyment and health, furnish without fail their breasts for the life of men. The very smallest of living beings meet together in peace and concord. All these the great Creator and Lord of all has appointed to exist in peace and harmony; while He does good to all, but most abundantly to us who have fled for refuge to His compassions through Jesus Christ our Lord, to whom be glory and majesty for ever and ever. Amen.

Chapter XXI - Let us obey God, and not the authors of sedition

Take heed, beloved, lest His many kindnesses lead to the condemnation of us all. [For thus it must be] unless we walk worthy of Him, and with one mind do those things which are good and well-pleasing in His sight. For [the Scripture] saith in a certain place, "The Spirit of the Lord is a candle searching the secret parts of the belly." [90] Let us reflect how near He is, and that none of the thoughts or reasonings in which we engage are hid from Him. It is right, therefore, that we should not leave the post which His will has assigned us. Let us rather offend those men who are foolish, and inconsiderate, and lifted up, and who glory in the pride of their speech, than [offend] God. Let us reverence the Lord Jesus Christ, whose blood was given for us; let us esteem those who have the rule over us; [91] let us honour the aged [92] among us; let us train up the young men in the fear of God; let us direct our wives to that which is good. Let them exhibit the lovely habit of purity [in all their conduct]; let them show forth the sincere disposition of meekness; let them make manifest the command which they have of their tongue, by their manner [93] of speaking; let them display their love, not by preferring [94] one to another, but by showing equal affection to all that piously fear God. Let your children be partakers of true Christian training; let them learn of how great avail humility is with God--how much the spirit of pure affection can prevail with Him--how excellent and great His fear is, and how it saves all those who walk in [95] it with a pure mind. For He is a Searcher of the thoughts and desires [of the heart]: His breath is in us; and when He pleases, He will take it away.

Chapter XXII - These exhortations are confirmed by the Christian faith, which proclaims the misery of sinful conduct

Now the faith which is in Christ confirms all these [admonitions]. For He Himself by the Holy Ghost thus addresses us: "Come, ye children, hearken unto Me; I will teach you the fear of the Lord. What man is he that desireth life, and loveth to see good days? Keep thy tongue from evil, and thy lips from speaking guile. Depart from evil, and do good; seek peace, and pursue it. The eyes of the Lord are upon the righteous, and His ears are [open] unto their prayers. The face of the Lord is against them that do evil, to cut off the remembrance of them from the earth. The righteous cried, and the Lord heard him, and delivered him out of all his troubles." [96] "Many are the stripes [appointed for] the wicked; but mercy shall compass those about who hope in the Lord." [97]

Chapter XXIII - Be humble, and believe that Christ will come again

The all-merciful and beneficent Father has bowels [of compassion] towards those that fear Him, and kindly and lovingly bestows His favours upon those who come to Him with a simple mind. Wherefore let us not be double-minded; neither let our soul be lifted [98] up on account of His exceedingly great and glorious gifts. Far from us be that which is written, "Wretched are they who are of a double mind, and of a doubting heart; who say, These things we have heard even in the times of our fathers; but, behold, we have grown old, and none of them has happened unto us." [99] Ye foolish ones! compare yourselves to a tree: take [for instance] the vine. First of all, it sheds its leaves, then it buds, next it puts forth leaves, and then it flowers; after that comes the sour grape, and then follows the ripened fruit. Ye perceive how in a little time the fruit of a tree comes to maturity. Of a truth, soon and suddenly shall His will be accomplished, as the Scripture also bears witness, saying, "Speedily will He come, and will not tarry;" [100] and, "The Lord shall suddenly come to His temple, even the Holy One, for whom ye look." [101]

Chapter XXIV - God continually shows us in nature that there will be a resurrection

Let us consider, beloved, how the Lord continually proves to us that there shall be a future resurrection, of which He has rendered the Lord Jesus Christ the first-fruits [102] by raising Him from the dead. Let us contemplate, beloved, the resurrection which is at all times taking place. Day and night declare to us a resurrection. The night sinks to sleep, and the day arises; the day [again] departs, and the night comes on. Let us behold the fruits [of the earth], how the sowing of grain takes place. The sower [103] goes forth, and casts it into the ground; and the seed being thus scattered, though dry and naked when it fell upon the earth, is gradually dissolved. Then out of its dissolution the mighty power of the providence of the Lord raises it up again, and from one seed many arise and bring forth fruit.

Chapter XXV - The phoenix an emblem of our resurrection

Let us consider that wonderful sign [of the resurrection] which takes place in Eastern lands, that is, in Arabia and the countries round about. There is a certain bird which is called a phoenix. This is the only one of its kind, and lives five hundred years. And when the time of its dissolution draws near that it must die, it builds itself a nest of frankincense, and myrrh, and other spices, into which, when the time is fulfilled, it enters and dies. But as the flesh decays a certain kind of worm is produced, which, being nourished by the juices of the dead bird, brings forth feathers. Then, when it has acquired strength, it takes up that nest in which are the bones of its parent, and bearing these it passes from the land of Arabia into Egypt, to the city called Heliopolis. And, in open day, flying in the sight of all men, it places them on the altar of the sun, and having done this, hastens back to its former abode. The priests then inspect the registers of the dates, and find that it has returned exactly as the five hundredth year was completed. [104]

Chapter XXVI - We shall rise again, then, as the Scripture also testifies

Do we then deem it any great and wonderful thing for the Maker of all things to raise up again those that have piously served Him in the assurance of a good faith, when even by a bird He shows us the mightiness of His power to fulfil His promise? [105] For [the Scripture] saith in a certain place, "Thou shalt raise me up, and I shall confess unto Thee;" [106] and again, "I laid me down, and slept; I awaked, because Thou art with me;" [107] and again, Job says, "Thou shalt raise up this flesh of mine, which has suffered all these things." [108]

Chapter XXVII - In the hope of the resurrection, let us cleave to the omnipotent and omniscient God

Having then this hope, let our souls be bound to Him who is faithful in His promises, and just in His judgments. He who has commanded us not to lie, shall much more Himself not lie; for nothing is impossible with God, except to lie. [109] Let His faith therefore be stirred up again within us, and let us consider that all things are nigh unto Him. By the word of His might [110] He established all things, and by His word He can overthrow them. "Who shall say unto Him, What hast thou done? or, Who shall resist the power of His strength?" [111] When and as He pleases He will do all things, and none of the things determined by Him shall pass away. [112] All things are open before Him, and nothing can be hidden from His counsel. "The heavens [113] declare the glory of God, and the firmament showeth His handy-work. Day unto day uttereth speech, and night unto night showeth knowledge. And there are no words or speeches of which the voices are not heard." [114]

Chapter XXVIII - God sees all things: therefore let us avoid transgression

Since then all things are seen and heard [by God], let us fear Him, and forsake those wicked works which proceed from evil desires; [115] so that, through His mercy, we may be protected from the judgments to come. For whither can any of us flee from His mighty hand? Or what world will receive any of those who run away from Him? For the Scripture saith in a certain place, "Whither shall I go, and where shall I be hid from Thy presence? If I ascend into heaven, Thou art there; if I go away even to the uttermost parts of the earth, there is Thy right hand; if I make my bed in the abyss, there is Thy Spirit." [116] Whither, then, shall any one go, or where shall he escape from Him who comprehends all things?

Chapter XXIX - Let us also draw near to God in purity of heart

Let us then draw near to Him with holiness of spirit, lifting up pure and undefiled hands unto Him, loving our gracious and merciful Father, who has made us partakers in the blessings of His elect. [117] For thus it is written, "When the Most High divided the nations, when He scattered [118] the sons of Adam, He fixed the bounds of the nations according to the number of the angels of God. His people Jacob became the portion of the Lord, and Israel the lot of His inheritance." [119] And in another place [the Scripture] saith, "Behold, the Lord taketh unto Himself a nation out of the midst of the nations, as a man takes the first-fruits of his threshing-floor; and from that nation shall come forth the Most Holy." [120]

Chapter XXX - Let us do those things that please God, and flee from those He hates, that we may be blessed

Seeing, therefore, that we are the portion of the Holy One, let us do all those things which pertain to holiness, avoiding all evil-speaking, all abominable and impure embraces, together with all drunkenness, seeking after change, [121] all abominable lusts, detestable adultery, and execrable pride. "For God," saith [the Scripture], "resisteth the proud, but giveth grace to the humble." [122] Let us cleave, then, to those to whom grace has been given by God. Let us clothe ourselves with concord and humility, ever exercising self-control, standing far off from all whispering and evil-speaking, being justified by our works, and not our words. For [the Scripture] saith, "He that speaketh much, shall also hear much in answer. And does he that is ready in speech deem himself righteous? Blessed is he that is born of woman, who liveth but a short time: be not given to much speaking." [123] Let our praise be in God, and not of ourselves; for God hateth those that commend themselves. Let testimony to our good deeds be borne by others, as it was in the case of our righteous forefathers. Boldness, and arrogance, and audacity belong to those that are accursed of God; but moderation, humility, and meekness to such as are blessed by Him.

Chapter XXXI - Let us see by what means we may obtain the divine blessing

Let us cleave then to His blessing, and consider what are the means [124] of possessing it. Let us think [125] over the things which have taken place from the beginning. For what reason was our father Abraham blessed? was it not because he wrought righteousness and truth through faith? [126] Isaac, with perfect confidence, as if knowing what was to happen, [127] cheerfully yielded himself as a sacrifice. [128] Jacob, through reason [129] of his brother, went forth with humility from his own land, and came to Laban and served him; and there was given to him the sceptre of the twelve tribes of Israel.

Chapter XXXII - We are justified not by our own works, but by faith

Whosoever will candidly consider each particular, will recognise the greatness of the gifts which were given by him. [130] For from him [131] have sprung the priests and all the Levites who minister at the altar of God. From him also [was descended] our Lord Jesus Christ according to the flesh. [132] From him [arose] kings, princes, and rulers of the race of Judah. Nor are his other tribes in small glory, inasmuch as God had promised, "Thy seed shall be as the stars of heaven." [133] All these, therefore, were highly honoured, and made great, not for their own sake, or for their own works, or for the righteousness which they wrought, but through the operation of His will. And we, too, being called by His will in Christ Jesus, are not justified by ourselves, nor by our own wisdom, or understanding, or godliness, or works which we have wrought in holiness of heart; but by that faith through which, from the beginning, Almighty God has justified all men; to whom be glory for ever and ever. Amen.

Chapter XXXIII - But let us not give up the practice of good works and love. God Himself is an example to us of good works

What shall we do, then, brethren? Shall we become slothful in well-doing, and cease from the practice of love? God forbid that any such course should be followed by us! But rather let us hasten with all energy and readiness of mind to perform every good work. For the Creator and Lord of all Himself rejoices in His works. For by His infinitely great power He established the heavens, and by His incomprehensible wisdom He adorned them. He also divided the earth from the water which surrounds it, and fixed it upon the immoveable foundation of His own will. The animals also which are upon it He commanded by His own word [134] into existence. So likewise, when He had formed the sea, and the living creatures which are in it, He enclosed them [within their proper bounds] by His own power. Above all, [135] with His holy and undefiled hands He formed man, the most excellent [of His creatures], and truly great through the understanding given him-- the express likeness of His own image. For thus says God: "Let us make man in Our image, and after Our likeness. So God made man; male and female He created them." [136] Having thus finished all these things, He approved them, and blessed them, and said, "Increase and multiply." [137] We see, [138] then, how all righteous men have been adorned with good works, and how the Lord Himself, adorning Himself with His works, rejoiced. Having therefore such an example, let us without delay accede to His will, and let us work the work of righteousness with our whole strength.

Chapter XXXIV - Great is the reward of good works with God. Joined together in harmony, let us implore that reward from Him

The good servant [139] receives the bread of his labour with confidence; the lazy and slothful cannot look his employer in the face. It is requisite, therefore, that we be prompt in the practice of well-doing; for of Him are all things. And thus He forewarns us: "Behold, the Lord [cometh], and His reward is before His face, to render to every man according to his work." [140] He exhorts us, therefore, with our whole heart to attend to this, [141] that we be not lazy or slothful in any good work. Let our boasting and our confidence be in Him. Let us submit ourselves to His will. Let us consider the whole multitude of His angels, how they stand ever ready to minister to His will. For the Scripture saith, "Ten thousand times ten thousand stood around Him, and thousands of thousands ministered unto Him, [142] and cried, Holy, holy, holy, [is] the Lord of Σαβαωθ; the whole creation is full of His glory." [143] And let us therefore, conscientiously gathering together in harmony, cry to Him earnestly, as with one mouth, that we may be made partakers of His great and glorious promises. For [the Scripture] saith, "Eye hath not seen, nor ear heard, neither have entered into the heart of man, the things which He hath prepared for them that wait for Him." [144]

Chapter XXXV - Immense is this reward. How shall we obtain it?

How blessed and wonderful, beloved, are the gifts of God! Life in immortality, splendour in righteousness, truth in perfect confidence, [145] faith in assurance, self-control in holiness! And all these fall under the cognizance of our understandings [now]; what then shall those things be which are prepared for such as wait for Him? The Creator and Father of all worlds, [146] the Most Holy, alone knows their amount and their beauty. Let us therefore earnestly strive to be found in the number of those that wait for Him, in order that we may share in His promised gifts. But how, beloved, shall this be done? If our understanding be fixed by faith towards God; if we earnestly seek the things which are pleasing and acceptable to Him; if we do the things which are in harmony with His blameless will; and if we follow the way of truth, casting away from us all unrighteousness and iniquity, along with all covetousness, strife, evil practices, deceit, whispering, and evil-speaking, all hatred of God, pride and haughtiness, vainglory and ambition. [147] For they that do such things are hateful to God; and not only they that do them, but also those that take pleasure in them that do them. [148] For the Scripture saith, "But to the sinner God said, Wherefore dost thou declare my statutes, and take my covenant into thy mouth, seeing thou hatest instruction, and castest my words behind thee? When thou sawest a thief, thou consentedst with [149] him, and didst make thy portion with adulterers. Thy mouth has abounded with wickedness, and thy tongue contrived [150] deceit. Thou sittest, and speakest against thy brother; thou slanderest [151] thine own mother's son. These things thou hast done, and I kept silence; thou thoughtest, wicked one, that I should be like to thyself. But I will reprove thee, and set thyself before thee. Consider now these things, ye that forget God, lest He tear you in pieces, like a lion, and there be none to deliver. The sacrifice of praise will glorify Me, and a way is there by which I will show him the salvation of God." [152]

Chapter XXXVI - All blessings are given to us through Christ

This is the way, beloved, in which we find our Saviour, [153] even Jesus Christ, the High Priest of all our offerings, the defender and helper of our infirmity. By Him we look up to the heights of heaven. By Him we behold, as in a glass, His immaculate and most excellent visage. By Him are the eyes of our hearts opened. By Him our foolish and darkened understanding blossoms [154] up anew towards His marvellous light. By Him the Lord has willed that we should taste of immortal knowledge, [155] "who, being the brightness of His majesty, is by so much greater than the angels, as He hath by inheritance obtained a more excellent name than they." [156] For it is thus written, "Who maketh His angels spirits, and His ministers a flame of fire." [157] But concerning His Son [158] the Lord spoke thus: "Thou art my Son, to-day have I begotten Thee. Ask of Me, and I will give Thee the heathen for Thine inheritance, and the uttermost parts of the earth for Thy possession." [159] And again He saith to Him, "Sit Thou at My right hand, until I make Thine enemies Thy footstool." [160] But who are His enemies? All the wicked, and those who set themselves to oppose the will of God.
[161]

Chapter XXXVII - Christ is our leader, and we His soldiers

Let us then, men and brethren, with all energy act the part of soldiers, in accordance with His holy commandments. Let us consider those who serve under our generals, with what order, obedience, and submissiveness they perform the things which are commanded them. All are not prefects, nor commanders of a thousand, nor of a hundred, nor of fifty, nor the like, but each one in his own rank performs the things commanded by the king and the generals. The great cannot subsist without the small, nor the small without the great. There is a kind of mixture in all things, and thence arises mutual advantage. [162] Let us take our body for an example. [163] The head is nothing without the feet, and the feet are nothing without the head; yea, the very smallest members of our body are necessary and useful to the whole body. But all work [164] harmoniously together, and are under one common rule [165] for the preservation of the whole body.

Chapter XXXVIII - Let the members of the Church submit themselves, and no one exalt himself above another

Let our whole body, then, be preserved in Christ Jesus; and let every one be subject to his neighbour, according to the special gift [166] bestowed upon him. Let the strong not despise the weak, and let the weak show respect unto the strong. Let the rich man provide for the wants of the poor; and let the poor man bless God, because He hath given him one by whom his need may be supplied. Let the wise man display his wisdom, not by [mere] words, but through good deeds. Let the humble not bear testimony to himself, but leave witness to be borne to him by another. [167] Let him that is pure in the flesh not grow proud [168] of it, and boast, knowing that it was another who bestowed on him the gift of continence. Let us consider, then, brethren, of what matter we were made,--who and what manner of beings we came into the world, as it were out of a sepulchre, and from utter darkness. [169] He who made us and fashioned us, having prepared His bountiful gifts for us before we were born, introduced us into His world. Since, therefore, we receive all these things from Him, we ought for everything to give Him thanks; to whom be glory for ever and ever. Amen.

Chapter XXXIX - There is no reason for self-conceit

Foolish and inconsiderate men, who have neither wisdom [170] nor instruction, mock and deride us, being eager to exalt themselves in their own conceits. For what can a mortal man do? or what strength is there in one made out of the dust? For it is written, "There was no shape before mine eyes, only I heard a sound, [171] and a voice [saying], What then? Shall a man be pure before the Lord? or shall such an one be [counted] blameless in his deeds, seeing He does not confide in His servants, and has charged [172] even His angels with perversity? The heaven is not clean in His sight: how much less they that dwell in houses of clay, of which also we ourselves were made! He smote them as a moth; and from morning even until evening they endure not. Because they could furnish no assistance to themselves, they perished. He breathed upon them, and they died, because they had no wisdom. But call now, if any one will answer thee, or if thou wilt look to any of the holy angels; for wrath destroys the foolish man, and envy killeth him that is in error. I have seen the foolish taking root, but their habitation was presently consumed. Let their sons be far from safety; let them be despised [173] before the gates of those less than themselves, and there shall be none to deliver. For what was prepared for them, the righteous shall eat; and they shall not be delivered from evil." [174]

Chapter XL - Let us preserve in the Church the order appointed by God

These things therefore being manifest to us, and since we look into the depths of the divine knowledge, it behoves us to do all things in [their proper] order, which the Lord has commanded us to perform at stated times. [175] He has enjoined offerings [to be presented] and service to be performed [to Him], and that not thoughtlessly or irregularly, but at the appointed times and hours. Where and by whom He desires these things to be done, He Himself has fixed by His own supreme will, in order that all things being piously done according to His good pleasure, may be acceptable unto Him. [176] Those, therefore, who present their offerings at the appointed times, are accepted and blessed; for inasmuch as they follow the laws of the Lord, they sin not. For his own peculiar services are assigned to the high priest, and their own proper place is prescribed to the priests, and their own special ministrations devolve on the Levites. The layman is bound by the laws that pertain to laymen.

Chapter XLI - Continuation of the same subject

Let every one of you, brethren, give thanks to God in his own order, living in all good conscience, with becoming gravity, and not going beyond the rule of the ministry prescribed to him. Not in every place, brethren, are the daily sacrifices offered, or the peace-offerings, or the sin-offerings and the trespass-offerings, but in Jerusalem only. And even there they are not offered in any place, but only at the altar before the temple, that which is offered being first carefully examined by the high priest and the ministers already mentioned. Those, therefore, who do anything beyond that which is agreeable to His will, are punished with death. Ye see, [177] brethren, that the greater the knowledge that has been vouchsafed to us, the greater also is the danger to which we are exposed.

Chapter XLII - The order of ministers in the Church

The apostles have preached the Gospel to us from [178] the Lord Jesus Christ; Jesus Christ [has done so] from [179] God. Christ therefore was sent forth by God, and the apostles by Christ. Both these appointments, [180] then, were made in an orderly way, according to the will of God. Having therefore received their orders, and being fully assured by the resurrection of our Lord Jesus Christ, and established [181] in the word of God, with full assurance of the Holy Ghost, they went forth proclaiming that the kingdom of God was at hand. And thus preaching through countries and cities, they appointed the first-fruits [of their labours], having first proved them by the Spirit, [182] to be bishops and deacons of those who should afterwards believe. Nor was this any new thing, since indeed many ages before it was written concerning bishops and deacons. For thus saith the Scripture in a certain place, "I will appoint their bishops [183] in righteousness, and their deacons [184] in faith." [185]

Chapter XLIII - Moses of old stilled the contention which arose concerning the priestly dignity

And what wonder is it if those in Christ who were entrusted with such a duty by God, appointed those [ministers] before mentioned, when the blessed Moses also, "a faithful servant in all his house," [186] noted down in the sacred books all the injunctions which were given him, and when the other prophets also followed him, bearing witness with one consent to the ordinances which he had appointed? For, when rivalry arose concerning the priesthood, and the tribes were contending among themselves as to which of them should be adorned with that glorious title, he commanded the twelve princes of the tribes to bring him their rods, each one being inscribed with the name [187] of the tribe. And he took them and bound them [together], and sealed them with the rings of the princes of the tribes, and laid them up in the tabernacle of witness on the table of God. And having shut the doors of the tabernacle, he sealed the keys, as he had done the rods, and said to them, Men and brethren, the tribe whose rod shall blossom has God chosen to fulfil the office of the priesthood, and to minister unto Him. And when the morning was come, he assembled all Israel, six hundred thousand men, and showed the seals to the princes of the tribes, and opened the tabernacle of witness, and brought forth the rods. And the rod of Aaron was found not only to have blossomed, but to bear fruit upon it. [188] What think ye, beloved? Did not Moses know beforehand that this would happen? Undoubtedly he knew; but he acted thus, that there might be no sedition in Israel, and that the name of the true and only God might be glorified; to whom be glory for ever and ever. Amen.

Chapter XLIV - The ordinances of the apostles, that there might be no contention respecting the priestly office

Our apostles also knew, through our Lord Jesus Christ, and there would be strife on account of the office [189] of the episcopate. For this reason, therefore, inasmuch as they had obtained a perfect fore-knowledge of this, they appointed those [ministers] already mentioned, and afterwards gave instructions, [190] that when these should fall asleep, other approved men should succeed them in their ministry. We are of opinion, therefore, that those appointed by them, [191] or afterwards by other eminent men, with the consent of the whole Church, and who have blamelessly served the flock of Christ in a humble, peaceable, and disinterested spirit, and have for a long time possessed the good opinion of all, cannot be justly dismissed from the ministry. For our sin will not be small, if we eject from the episcopate [192] those who have blamelessly and holily fulfilled its duties. [193] Blessed are those presbyters who, having finished their course before now, have obtained a fruitful and perfect departure [from this world]; for they have no fear lest any one deprive them of the place now appointed them. But we see that ye have removed some men of excellent behaviour from the ministry, which they fulfilled blamelessly and with honour.

Chapter XLV - It is the part of the wicked to vex the righteous

Ye are fond of contention, brethren, and full of zeal about things which do not pertain to salvation. Look carefully into the Scriptures, which are the true utterances of the Holy Spirit. Observe [194] that nothing of an unjust or counterfeit character is written in them. There [195] you will not find that the righteous were cast off by men who themselves were holy. The righteous were indeed persecuted, but only by the wicked. They were cast into prison, but only by the unholy; they were stoned, but only by transgressors; they were slain, but only by the accursed, and such as had conceived an unrighteous envy against them. Exposed to such sufferings, they endured them gloriously. For what shall we say, brethren? Was Daniel [196] cast into the den of lions by such as feared God? Were Ananias, and Azarias, and Mishael shut up in a furnace [197] of fire by those who observed [198] the great and glorious worship of the Most High? Far from us be such a thought! Who, then, were they that did such things? The hateful, and those full of all wickedness, were roused to such a pitch of fury, that they inflicted torture on those who served God with a holy and blameless purpose [of heart], not knowing that the Most High is the Defender and Protector of all such as with a pure conscience venerate [199] His all-excellent name; to whom be glory for ever and ever. Amen. But they who with confidence endured [these things] are now heirs of glory and honour, and have been exalted and made illustrious [200] by God in their memorial for ever and ever. Amen.

Chapter XLVI - Let us cleave to the righteous: your strife is pernicious

Such examples, therefore, brethren, it is right that we should follow; [201] since it is written, "Cleave to the holy, for those that cleave to them shall [themselves] be made holy." [202] And again, in another place, [the Scripture] saith, "With a harmless man thou shalt prove [203] thyself harmless, and with an elect man thou shalt be elect, and with a perverse man thou shalt show [204] thyself perverse." [205] Let us cleave, therefore, to the innocent and righteous, since these are the elect of God. Why are there strifes, and tumults, and divisions, and schisms, and wars [206] among you? Have we not [all] one God and one Christ? Is there not one Spirit of grace poured out upon us? And have we not one calling in Christ? [207] Why do we divide and tear to pieces the members of Christ, and raise up strife against our own body, and have reached such a height of madness as to forget that "we are members one of another?" [208] Remember the words of our Lord Jesus Christ, how [209] He said, "Woe to that man [by whom [210] offences come]! It were better for him that he had never been born, than that he should cast a stumbling-block before one of my elect. Yea, it were better for him that a millstone should be hung about [his neck], and he should be sunk in the depths of the sea, than that he should cast a stumbling-block before one of my little ones." [211] Your schism has subverted [the faith of] many, has discouraged many, has given rise to doubt in many, and has caused grief to us all. And still your sedition continueth.

Chapter XLVII - Your recent discord is worse than the former which took place in the times of Paul

Take up the epistle of the blessed Apostle Paul. What did he write to you at the time when the Gospel first began to be preached? [212] Truly, under the inspiration [213] of the Spirit, he wrote to you concerning himself, and Cephas, and Apollos, [214] because even then parties [215] had been formed among you. But that inclination for one above another entailed less guilt upon you, inasmuch as your partialities were then shown towards apostles, already of high reputation, and towards a man whom they had approved. But now reflect who those are that have perverted you, and lessened the renown of your far-famed brotherly love. It is disgraceful, beloved, yea, highly disgraceful, and unworthy of your Christian profession, [216] that such a thing should be heard of as that the most stedfast and ancient Church of the Corinthians should, on account of one or two persons, engage in sedition against its presbyters. And this rumour has reached not only us, but those also who are unconnected [217] with us; so that, through your infatuation, the name of the Lord is blasphemed, while danger is also brought upon yourselves.

Chapter XLVIII - Let us return to the practice of brotherly love

Let us therefore, with all haste, put an end [218] to this [state of things]; and let us fall down before the Lord, and beseech Him with tears, that He would mercifully [219] be reconciled to us, and restore us to our former seemly and holy practice of brotherly love. For [such conduct] is the gate of righteousness, which is set open for the attainment of life, as it is written, "Open to me the gates of righteousness; I will go in by them, and will praise the Lord: this is the gate of the Lord: the righteous shall enter in by it." [220] Although, therefore, many gates have been set open, yet this gate of righteousness is that gate in Christ by which blessed are all they that have entered in and have directed their way in holiness and righteousness, doing all things without disorder. Let a man be faithful: let him be powerful in the utterance of knowledge; let him be wise in judging of words; let him be pure in all his deeds; yet the more he seems to be superior to others [in these respects], the more humble-minded ought he to be, and to seek the common good of all, and not merely his own advantage.

Chapter XLIX - *The praise of love*

Let him who has love in Christ keep the commandments of Christ. Who can describe the [blessed] bond of the love of God? What man is able to tell the excellence of its beauty, as it ought to be told? The height to which love exalts is unspeakable. Love unites us to God. Love covers a multitude of sins. [221] Love beareth all things, is long-suffering in all things. [222] There is nothing base, nothing arrogant in love. Love admits of no schisms: love gives rise to no seditions: love does all things in harmony. By love have all the elect of God been made perfect; without love nothing is well-pleasing to God. In love has the Lord taken us to Himself. On account of the Love he bore us, Jesus Christ our Lord gave His blood for us by the will of God; His flesh for our flesh, and His soul for our souls. [223]

Chapter L - *Let us pray to be thought worthy of love*

Ye see, beloved, how great and wonderful a thing is love, and that there is no declaring its perfection. Who is fit to be found in it, except such as God has vouchsafed to render so? Let us pray, therefore, and implore of His mercy, that we may live blameless in love, free from all human partialities for one above another. All the generations from Adam even unto this day have passed away; but those who, through the grace of God, have been made perfect in love, now possess a place among the godly, and shall be made manifest at the revelation [224] of the kingdom of Christ. For it is written, "Enter into thy secret chambers for a little time, until my wrath and fury pass away; and I will remember a propitious [225] day, and will raise you up out of your graves." [226] Blessed are we, beloved, if we keep the commandments of God in the harmony of love; that so through love our sins may be forgiven us. For it is written, "Blessed are they whose transgressions are forgiven, and whose sins are covered. Blessed is the man whose sin the Lord will not impute to him, and in whose mouth there is no guile." [227] This blessedness cometh upon those who have been chosen by God through Jesus Christ our Lord; to whom be glory for ever and ever. Amen.

Chapter LI - *Let the partakers in strife acknowledge their sins*

Let us therefore implore forgiveness for all those transgressions which through any [suggestion] of the adversary we have committed. And those who have been the leaders of sedition and disagreement ought to have respect [228] to the common hope. For such as live in fear and love would rather that they themselves than their neighbours should be involved in suffering. And they prefer to bear blame themselves, rather than that the concord which has been well and piously [229] handed down to us should suffer. For it is better that a man should acknowledge his transgressions than that he should harden his heart, as the hearts of those were hardened who stirred up sedition against Moses the servant of God, and whose condemnation was made manifest [unto all]. For they went down alive into Hades, and death swallowed them up. [230] Pharaoh with his army and all the princes of Egypt, and the chariots with their riders, were sunk in the depths of the Red Sea, and perished, [231] for no other reason than that their foolish hearts were hardened, after so many signs and wonders had been wrought in the land of Egypt by Moses the servant of God.

Chapter LII - *Such a confession is pleasing to God*

The Lord, brethren, stands in need of nothing; and He desires nothing of any one, except that confession be made to Him. For, says the elect David, "I will confess unto the Lord; and that will please Him more than a young bullock that hath horns and hoofs. Let the poor see it, and be glad."[232] And again he saith, "Offer [233] unto God the sacrifice of praise, and pay thy vows unto the Most High. And call upon Me in the day of thy trouble: I will deliver thee, and thou shalt glorify Me." [234] For "the sacrifice of God is a broken spirit." [235]

Chapter LIII - *The love of Moses towards his people*

Ye understand, beloved, ye understand well the Sacred Scriptures, and ye have looked very earnestly into the oracles of God. Call then these things to your remembrance. When Moses went up into the mount, and abode there, with fasting and humiliation, forty days and forty nights, the Lord said unto him, "Moses, Moses, get thee down quickly from hence; for thy people whom thou didst bring out of the land of Egypt have committed iniquity. They have speedily departed from the way in which I commanded them to walk, and have made to themselves molten images." [236] And the Lord said unto him, "I have spoken to thee once and again, saying, I have seen this people, and, behold, it is a stiff-necked people: let Me destroy them, and blot out their name from under heaven; and I will make thee a great and wonderful nation, and one much more numerous than this." [237] But Moses said, "Far be it from Thee, Lord: pardon the sin of this people; else blot me also out of the book of the living." [238] O marvellous [239] love! O insuperable perfection! The servant speaks freely to his Lord, and asks forgiveness for the people, or begs that he himself might perish [240] along with them.

Chapter LIV - He who is full of love will incur every loss, that peace may be restored to the Church

Who then among you is noble-minded? who compassionate? who full of love? Let him declare, "If on my account sedition and disagreement and schisms have arisen, I will depart, I will go away whithersoever ye desire, and I will do whatever the majority [241] commands; only let the flock of Christ live on terms of peace with the presbyters set over it." He that acts thus shall procure to himself great glory in the Lord; and every place will welcome [242] him. For "the earth is the Lord's, and the fulness thereof." [243] These things they who live a godly life, that is never to be repented of, both have done and always will do.

Chapter LV - Examples of such love

To bring forward some examples from among the heathen: Many kings and princes, in times of pestilence, when they had been instructed by an oracle, have given themselves up to death, in order that by their own blood they might deliver their fellow-citizens [from destruction]. Many have gone forth from their own cities, that so sedition might be brought to an end within them. We know many among ourselves who have given themselves up to bonds, in order that they might ransom others. Many, too, have surrendered themselves to slavery, that with the price [244] which they received for themselves, they might provide food for others. Many women also, being strengthened by the grace of God, have performed numerous manly exploits. The blessed Judith, when her city was besieged, asked of the elders permission to go forth into the camp of the strangers; and, exposing herself to danger, she went out for the love which she bare to her country and people then besieged; and the Lord delivered Holofernes into the hands of a woman. [245] Esther also, being perfect in faith, exposed herself to no less danger, in order to deliver the twelve tribes of Israel from impending destruction. For with fasting and humiliation she entreated the everlasting God, who seeth all things; and He, perceiving the humility of her spirit, delivered the people for whose sake she had encountered peril. [246] .

Chapter LVI - Let us admonish and correct one another

Let us then also pray for those who have fallen into any sin, that meekness and humility may be given to them, so that they may submit, not unto us, but to the will of God. For in this way they shall secure a fruitful and perfect remembrance from us, with sympathy for them, both in our prayers to God, and our mention of them to the saints. [247] Let us receive correction, beloved, on account of which no one should feel displeased. Those exhortations by which we admonish one another are both good [in themselves] and highly profitable, for they tend to unite [248] us to the will of God. For thus saith the holy Word: "The Lord hath severely chastened me, yet hath not given me over to death." [249] "For whom the Lord loveth He chasteneth, and scourgeth every son whom He receiveth." [250] "The righteous," saith it, "shall chasten me in mercy, and reprove me; but let not the oil of sinners make fat my head." [251] And again he saith, "Blessed is the man whom the Lord reproveth, and reject not thou the warning of the Almighty. For He causes sorrow, and again restores [to gladness]; He woundeth, and His hands make whole. He shall deliver thee in six troubles, yea, in the seventh no evil shall touch thee. In famine He shall rescue thee from death, and in war He shall free thee from the power [252] of the sword. From the scourge of the tongue will He hide thee, and thou shalt not fear when evil cometh. Thou shalt laugh at the unrighteous and the wicked, and shalt not be afraid of the beasts of the field. For the wild beasts shall be at peace with thee: then shalt thou know that thy house shall be in peace, and the habitation of thy tabernacle shall not fail. [253] Thou shall know also that thy seed shall be great, and thy children like the grass of the field. And thou shall come to the grave like ripened corn which is reaped in its season, or like a heap of the threshing-floor which is gathered together at the proper time." [254] Ye see, beloved, that protection is afforded to those that are chastened of the Lord; for since God is good, He corrects us, that we may be admonished by His holy chastisement.

Chapter LVII - Let the authors of sedition submit themselves

Ye therefore, who laid the foundation of this sedition, submit yourselves to the presbyters, and receive correction so as to repent, bending the knees of your hearts. Learn to be subject, laying aside the proud and arrogant self-confidence of your tongue. For it is better for you that ye should occupy [255] a humble but honourable place in the flock of Christ, than that, being highly exalted, ye should be cast out from the hope of His people. [256] For thus speaketh all-virtuous Wisdom: [257] "Behold, I will bring forth to you the words of My Spirit, and I will teach you My speech. Since I called, and ye did not hear; I held forth My words, and ye regarded not, but set at naught My counsels, and yielded not at My reproofs; therefore I too will laugh at your destruction; yea, I will rejoice when ruin cometh upon you, and when sudden confusion overtakes you, when overturning presents itself like a tempest, or when tribulation and oppression fall upon you. For it shall come to pass, that when ye call upon Me, I will not hear you; the wicked shall seek Me, and they shall not find Me. For they hated wisdom, and did not choose the fear of the Lord; nor would they listen to My counsels, but despised My reproofs. Wherefore they shall eat the fruits of their own way, and they shall be filled with their own ungodliness." .. [258]

Chapter LVIII - Blessings sought for all that call upon God

May God, who seeth all things, and who is the Ruler of all spirits and the Lord of all flesh--who chose our Lord Jesus Christ and us through Him to be a peculiar [259] people--grant to every soul that calleth upon His glorious and holy Name, faith, fear, peace, patience, long-suffering, self-control, purity, and sobriety, to the well-pleasing of His Name, through our High Priest and Protector, Jesus Christ, by whom be to Him glory, and majesty, and power, and honour, both now and for evermore. Amen.

Chapter LIX - The Corinthians are exhorted speedily to send back word that peace has been restored. The benediction

Send back speedily to us in peace and with joy these our messengers to you: Claudius Ephebus and Valerius Bito, with Fortunatus: that they may the sooner announce to us the peace and harmony we so earnestly desire and long for [among you], and that we may the more quickly rejoice over the good order re-established among you. The grace of our Lord Jesus Christ be with you, and with all everywhere that are the called of God through Him, by whom be to Him glory, honour, power, majesty, and eternal dominion, [260] from everlasting to everlasting. [261] Amen.[262]

Footnotes:

2. In the only known ms. of this Epistle, the title is thus given at the close.

3. Note the fact that the Corinthians asked this of their brethren, the personal friends of their apostle St. Paul. Clement's own name does not appear in this Epistle.

4. Literally, "is greatly blasphemed."

5. Literally, "did not prove your all-virtuous and firm faith."

6. Eph. v. 21; 1 Pet. v. 5.

7. Acts xx. 35.

8. Literally, "ye embraced it in your bowels." Concerning the complaints of Photius (ninth century) against Clement, see Bull's Defensio Fidei Nicænæ, Works, vol. v. p. 132.

9. 1 Pet. ii. 17.

10. So, in the ms., but many have suspected that the text is here corrupt. Perhaps the best emendation is that which substitutes συναισθήσεως, "compassion," for συνειδήσεως, "conscience."

11. Tit. iii. 1.

12. Prov. vii. 3.

13. Literally, "enlargement"

14. Deut. xxxii. 15.

15. It seems necessary to refer αὐτοῦ to God, in opposition to the translation given by Abp. Wake and others.

16. Literally, "Christ;" comp. 2 Cor. i. 21, Eph. iv. 20.

17. Wisdom ii. 24.

18. Gen. iv. 3-8. The writer here, as always, follows the reading of the Septuagint, which in this passage both alters and adds to the Hebrew text. We have given the rendering approved by the best critics; but some prefer to translate, as in our English version, "unto thee shall be his desire, and thou shalt rule over him." See, for an ancient explanation of the passage, Irenæus, Adv. Hær., iv. 18, 3.

19. Gen. xxvii. 41, etc.

20. Gen. xxxvii.

21. Ex. ii. 14.

22. Num. xii. 14, 15. In our copies of the Septuagint this is not affirmed of Aaron.

23. Num. xvi. 33.

24. 1 Kings xviii. 8, etc.

25. Literally, "those who have been athletes."

26. Some fill up the lacuna here found in the ms. so as to read, "have come to a grievous death."

27. Literally, "good." The martyrdom of St. Peter is all that is thus connected with his arrival in Rome. His numerous labours were restricted to the Circumcision.

28. Seven imprisonments of St. Paul are not referred to in Scripture.

29. Archbishop Wake here reads "scourged." We have followed the most recent critics in filling up the numerous lacunæ in this chapter.

30. Some think Rome, others Spain, and others even Britain, to be here referred to. See note at end.

31. That is, under Tigellinus and Sabinus, in the last year of the Emperor Nero; but some think Helius and Polycletus

are referred to; and others, both here and in the preceding sentence, regard the words as denoting simply the witness borne by Peter and Paul to the truth of the gospel before the rulers of the earth.

32. Some suppose these to have been the names of two eminent female martyrs under Nero; others regard the clause as an interpolation. Many ingenious conjectures might be cited; but see Jacobson's valuable note, Patres Apostol., vol. i. p. 30.
33. Literally, "have reached to the stedfast course of faith."
34. Gen. ii. 23.
35. Some insert "Father."
36. Gen. vii.; 1 Pet. iii. 20; 2 Pet. ii. 5.
37. Jon. iii.
38. Ezek. xxxiii. 11.
39. Ezek. xviii. 30.
40. Comp. Isa. i. 18.
41. These words are not found in Scripture, though they are quoted again by Clem. Alex. (Pædag., i. 10) as from Ezekiel.
42. Isa. i. 16-20.
43. Some read ματαιολογίαν, "vain talk."
44. Gen. v. 24; Heb. xi. 5. Literally, "and his death was not found."
45. Isa. xli. 8; 2 Chron. xx. 7; Judith viii. 19; Jas. ii. 23.
46. Gen. xii. 1-3.
47. Gen. xiii. 14-16.
48. Gen. xv. 5, 6; Rom. iv. 3.
49. Gen. xxi. 22; Heb. xi. 17.
50. Gen. xix.; comp. 2 Pet. ii. 6-9.
51. So Joseph., Antiq., i. 11, 4; Irenæus, Adv. Hær., iv. 31.
52. Literally, "become a judgment and sign."
53. Josh. ii.; Heb. xi. 31.
54. Others of the Fathers adopt the same allegorical interpretation, e.g., Justin Mar., Dial. c. Tryph., n. 111; Irenæus, Adv. Hær., iv. 20. The whole matter of symbolism under the law must be more thoroughly studied if we would account for such strong language as is here applied to a poetical or rhetorical figure.
55. Jer. ix. 23, 24; 1 Cor. i. 31; 2 Cor. x. 17.
56. Comp. Matt. vi. 12-15, Matt. vii. 2; Luke vi. 36-38.
57. Isa. lxvi. 2.
58. Prov. ii. 21, 22.
59. Ψ. xxxvii. 35-37. "Remnant" probably refers either to the memory or posterity of the righteous.
60. Isa. xxix. 13; Matt. xv. 8; Mark vii. 6.
61. Ψ. lxii. 4.
62. Ψ. lxxviii. 36, 37.
63. Ψ. xxxi. 18.
64. These words within brackets are not found in the ms., but have been inserted from the Septuagint by most editors.
65. Ψ. xii. 3-5.
66. The Latin of Cotelerius, adopted by Hefele and Dressel, translates this clause as follows: "I will set free the wicked on account of His sepulchre, and the rich on account of His death."
67. The reading of the ms. is τῆς πληγῆς, "purify, or free, Him from stripes." We have adopted the emendation of Junius.
68. Wotton reads, "If He make."
69. Or, "fill Him with understanding," if πλῆσαι should be read instead of πλάσαι, as Grabe suggests.
70. Isa. liii. The reader will observe how often the text of the Septuagint, here quoted, differs from the Hebrew as represented by our authorized English version.
71. Ψ. xxii. 6-8.
72. Heb. xi. 37.
73. Gen. xviii. 27.
74. Job i. 1.
75. Job xiv. 4, 5. Septuagint.
76. Num. xii. 7; Heb. iii. 2.
77. Some fill up the lacuna which here occurs in the ms. by "Israel."
78. Ex. iii. 11, Ex. iv. 10.
79. This is not found in Scripture. They were probably in Clement's version. Comp. Ψ. cxix. 83.
80. Or, as some render, "to whom."
81. Ψ. lxxxix. 21.
82. Or, "when Thou judgest."
83. Literally, "in my inwards."
84. Literally, "bloods."
85. Ps. li. 1-17.
86. Literally, "Becoming partakers of many great and glorious deeds, let us return to the aim of peace delivered to us from the beginning." Comp. Heb. xii. 1.
87. Or, "collections."
88. Job xxxviii. 11.
89. Or, "stations."
90. Prov. xx. 27.
91. Comp. Heb. xiii. 17; 1 Thess. v. 12, 13.
92. Or, "the presbyters."
93. Some read, "by their silence."
94. Comp. 1 Tim. v. 21.
95. Some translate, "who turn to Him."
96. Ps. xxxiv. 11-17.
97. Ps. xxxii. 10.
98. Or, as some render, "neither let us have any doubt of."
99. Some regard these words as taken from an apocryphal book, others as derived from a fusion of Jas. i. 8 and 2 Pet. iii. 3, 4.
100. Hab. ii. 3; Heb. x. 37.

101. Mal. iii. 1.
102. Comp. 1 Cor. xv. 20; Col. i. 18.
103. Comp. Luke viii. 5.
104. This fable respecting the phoenix is mentioned by Herodotus (ii. 73) and by Pliny (Nat. Hist., x. 2) and is used as above by Tertullian (De Resurr., §13) and by others of the Fathers.
105. Literally, "the mightiness of His promise."
106. Ψ. xxviii. 7, or some apocryphal book.
107. Comp. Ψ. iii. 6.
108. Job xix. 25, 26.
109. Comp. Tit. i. 2; Heb. vi. 18.
110. Or, "majesty."
111. Wisdom xii. 12, Wisdom xi. 22.
112. Comp. Matt. xxiv. 35.
113. Literally, "If the heavens," etc.
114. Ψ. xix. 1-3.
115. Literally, "abominable lusts of evil deeds."
116. Ψ. cxxxix. 7-10
117. Literally "has made us to Himself a part of election."
118. Literally, "sowed abroad."
119. Deut. xxxii. 8, 9.
120. Formed apparently from Num. xviii. 27 and 2 Chron. xxxi. 14. Literally, the closing words are, "the holy of holies."
121. Some translate, "youthful lusts."
122. Prov. iii. 34; Jas. iv. 6; 1 Pet. v. 5.
123. Job xi. 2, 3. The translation is doubtful. But see Septuagint.
124. Literally, "what are the ways of His blessing."
125. Literally, "unroll."
126. Comp. Jas. ii. 21.
127. Some translate, "knowing what was to come."
128. Gen. xxii.
129. So Jacobson: Wotton reads, "fleeing from his brother."
130. The meaning is here very doubtful. Some translate, "the gifts which were given to Jacob by Him," i.e., God.
131. MS. αὐτῶν, referring to the gifts: we have followed the emendation αὐτοῦ, adopted by most editors. Some refer the word to God, and not Jacob.
132. Comp. Rom. ix. 5.
133. Gen. xxii. 17, Gen. xxviii. 4.
134. Or, "commandment."
135. Or, "in addition to all."
136. Gen. i. 26, 27.
137. Gen. i. 28.
138. Or, "let us consider."
139. Or, "labourer."
140. Isa. xl. 10, Isa. lxii. 11; Rev. xxii. 12.
141. The text here seems to be corrupt. Some translate, "He warns us with all His heart to this end, that," etc.
142. Dan. vii. 10.
143. Isa. vi. 3.
144. 1 Cor. ii. 9.
145. Some translate, "in liberty."
146. Or, "of the ages."
147. The reading is doubtful: some have ἀφιλοξενίαν, "want of a hospitable spirit." So Jacobson.
148. Rom. i. 32.
149. Literally, "didst run with."
150. Literally, "didst weave."
151. Or, "layest a snare for."
152. Ps. l. 16-23. The reader will observe how the Septuagint followed by Clement differs from the Hebrew.
153. Literally, "that which saves us."
154. Or, "rejoices to behold."
155. Or, "knowledge of immortality."
156. Heb. i. 3, 4.
157. Ps. civ. 4; Heb. i. 7.
158. Some render, "to the Son."
159. Ps. ii. 7, 8; Heb. i. 5.
160. Ps. cx. 1; Heb. i. 13.
161. Some read, "who oppose their own will to that of God."
162. Literally, "in these there is use."
163. 1 Cor. xii. 12, etc.
164. Literally, "all breathe together."
165. Literally, "use one subjection."
166. Literally, "according as he has been placed in his charism."
167. Comp. Prov. xxvii. 2.
168. The ms. is here slightly torn, and we are left to conjecture.
169. Comp. Ps. cxxxix. 15.
170. Literally, "and silly and uninstructed."
171. Literally, "a breath."
172. Or, "has perceived."
173. Some render, "they perished at the gates."
174. Job iv. 16-18, Job xv. 15, Job iv. 19-21, Job v. 1-5.
175. Some join κατὰ καιροὺς τεταγμένους, "at stated times." to the next sentence. 1 Cor. xvi. 1, 2.
176. Literally, "to His will." Comp. Rom. xv. 15, 16, Greek.
177. Or, "consider." This chapter has been cited to prove the earlier date for this Epistle. But the reference to Jerusalem may be an ideal present.
178. Or, "by the command of."
179. Or, "by the command of."
180. Literally, "both things were done."
181. Or, "confirmed by."
182. Or, "having tested them in spirit."
183. Or, "overseers."
184. Or, "servants."
185. Isa. lx. 17, Sept.; but the text is

here altered by Clement. The LXX. have "I will give thy rulers in peace, and thy overseers in righteousness."
186. Num. xii. 7; Heb. iii. 5.
187. Literally, "every tribe being written according to its name."
188. See Num. xvii.
189. Literally, "on account of the title of the oversight." Some understand this to mean, "in regard to the dignity of the episcopate;" and others simply, "on account of the oversight."
190. The meaning of this passage is much controverted. Some render, "left a list of other approved persons;" while others translate the unusual word ἐπινομή, which causes the difficulty, by "testamentary direction," and many others deem the text corrupt. We have given what seems the simplest version of the text as it stands. Comp. the versions of Wake, Chevallier, and others.
191. i.e., the apostles.
192. Or, "oversight."
193. Literally, "presented the offerings."
194. Or, "Ye perceive."
195. Or, "For."
196. Dan. vi. 16.
197. Dan. iii. 20.
198. Literally, "worshipped."
199. Literally, "serve."
200. Or, "lifted up."
201. Literally, "To such examples it is right that we should cleave."
202. Not found in Scripture.
203. Literally, "be."
204. Or, "thou wilt overthrow."
205. Ψ. xviii. 25, 26.
206. Or, "war." Comp. Jas. iv. 1.
207. Comp. Eph. iv. 4-6.
208. Rom. xii. 5.
209. This clause is wanting in the text.
210. This clause is wanting in the text.
211. Comp. Matt. xviii. 6, Matt. xxvi. 24; Mark ix. 42; Luke xvii. 2.
212. Literally, "in the beginning of the Gospel." Comp. Phil. iv. 15.
213. Or, "spiritually."
214. 1 Cor. iii. 13, etc.
215. Or, "inclinations for one above another."
216. Literally, "of conduct in Christ."
217. Or, "aliens from us," i.e., the Gentiles.
218. Literally "remove."
219. Literally, "becoming merciful."
220. Ps. cxviii. 19, 20.
221. Jas. v. 20; 1 Pet. iv. 8.
222. Comp. 1 Cor. xiii. 4, etc.
223. Comp. Irenæus, v. 1; also Mathetes, Ep. to Diognetus, cap. ix.
224. Literally, "visitation."
225. Or, "good."
226. Isa. xxvi. 20.
227. Ps. xxxii. 1, 2.
228. Or, "look to."
229. Or, "righteously."
230. Num. xvi.
231. Ex. xiv.
232. Ps. lxix. 31, 32.
233. Or, "sacrifice."
234. Ps. l. 14, 15.
235. Ps. li. 17.
236. Ex. xxxii. 7, etc.; Deut. ix. 12, etc.
237. Ex. xxxii. 9, etc.
238. Ex. xxxii. 32.
239. Or, "mighty."
240. Literally, "be wiped out."
241. Literally, "the multitude." Clement here puts words into the mouth of the Corinthian presbyters. It has been strangely quoted to strengthen a conjecture that he had humbly preferred Linus and Cletus when first called to preside.
242. Or, "receive."
243. Ps. xxiv. 1; 1 Cor. x. 26, 28.
244. Literally, "and having received their prices, fed others." Comp. Rom. xvi. 3, 4, and Phil. ii. 30.
245. Judith viii. 30.
246. Esth. vii., viii.
247. Literally, "there shall be to them a fruitful and perfect remembrance, with compassions both towards God and the saints."
248. Or, "they unite."
249. Ps. cxviii. 18.
250. Prov. iii. 12; Heb. xii. 6.
251. Ps. cxli. 5.
252. Literally, "hand."
253. Literally, "err" or "sin."
254. Job v. 17-26.
255. Literally, "to be found small and esteemed."
256. Literally, "His hope." It has been conjectured that ἔλπιδος should be ἐπαύλιδος, and the reading, "out of the fold of his people." See Chevallier.
257. Prov. i. 23-31. Often cited by this name in primitive writers.
258. Junius (Pat. Young), who examined the ms. before it was bound into its present form, stated that a whole leaf was here lost. The next letters that occur are ιπον, which have been supposed to indicate εἶπον or ἔλιπον. Doubtless some passages quoted by the ancients from the Epistle of Clement, and not now found in it, occurred in the portion which has thus been lost.
259. Comp. Tit. ii. 14.
260. Literally, "an eternal throne."
261. Literally, "From the ages to the

ages of ages."

262. Note St. Clement's frequent doxologies. N.B.--The language of Clement concerning the Western progress of St. Paul (cap. v.) is our earliest postscript to his Scripture biography. It is sufficient to refer the reader to the great works of Conybeare and Howson, and of Mr. Lewin, on the Life and Epistles of St. Paul. See more especially the valuable note of Lewin (vol. ii. p. 294) which takes notice of the opinion of some learned men, that the great Apostle of the Gentiles preached the Gospel in Britain. The whole subject of St. Paul's relations with British Christians is treated by Williams, in his Antiquities of the Cymry, with learning and in an attractive manner. But the reader will find more ready to his hand, perhaps, the interesting note of Mr. Lewin, on Claudia and Pudens (2 Tim. iv. 21), in his Life and Epistles of St. Paul, vol. ii. p. 392. See also Paley's Horæ Paulinæ, p. 40. London, 1820.

Mathetes

Introductory Note to the Epistle of Mathetes to Diognetus

[a.d. 130.] The anonymous author of this Epistle gives himself the title (Mathetes) "a disciple [263] of the Apostles," and I venture to adopt it as his name. It is about all we know of him, and it serves a useful end. I place his letter here, as a sequel to the Clementine Epistle, for several reasons, which I think scholars will approve: (1) It is full of the Pauline spirit, and exhales the same pure and primitive fragrance which is characteristic of Clement. (2) No theory as to its date very much conflicts with that which I adopt, and it is sustained by good authorities. (3) But, as a specimen of the persuasives against Gentilism which early Christians employed in their intercourse with friends who adhered to heathenism, it admirably illustrates the temper prescribed by St. Paul (2 Tim. ii. 24), and not less the peculiar social relations of converts to the Gospel with the more amiable and candid of their personal friends at this early period.

Mathetes was possibly a catechumen of St. Paul or of one of the apostle's associates. I assume that his correspondent was the tutor of M. Aurelius. Placed just here, it fills a lacuna in the series, and takes the place of the pseudo (second) Epistle of Clement, which is now relegated to its proper place with the works falsely ascribed to St. Clement.

Altogether, the Epistle is a gem of purest ray; and, while suggesting some difficulties as to interpretation and exposition, it is practically clear as to argument and intent. Mathetes is, perhaps, the first of the apologists.

The following is the original Introductory Notice of the learned editors and translators:--

The following interesting and eloquent Epistle is anonymous, and we have no clue whatever as to its author. For a considerable period after its publication in 1592, it was generally ascribed to Justin Martyr. In recent times Otto has inserted it among the works of that writer, but Semisch and others contend that it cannot possibly be his. In dealing with this question, we depend entirely upon the internal evidence, no statement as to the authorship of the Epistle having descended to us from antiquity. And it can scarcely be denied that the whole tone of the Epistle, as well as special passages which it contains, points to some other writer than Justin. Accordingly, critics are now for the most part agreed that it is not his, and that it must be ascribed to one who lived at a still earlier date in the history of the Church. Several internal arguments have been brought forward in favour of this opinion. Supposing chap. xi. to be genuine, it has been supported by the fact that the writer there styles himself "a disciple of the apostles." But there is great suspicion that the two concluding chapters are spurious; and even though admitted to be genuine, the expression quoted evidently admits of a different explanation from that which implies the writer's personal acquaintance with the apostles: it might, indeed, be adopted by one even at the present day. More weight is to be attached to those passages in which the writer speaks of Christianity as still being a new thing in the world. Expressions to this effect occur in several places (chap. i., ii., ix.), and seem to imply that the author lived very little, if at all, after the apostolic age. There is certainly nothing in the Epistle which is inconsistent with this opinion; and we may therefore believe, that in this beautiful composition we possess a genuine production of some apostolic man who lived not later than the beginning of the second century.

The names of Clement of Rome and of Apollos have both been suggested as those of the probable author. Such opinions, however, are pure fancies, which it is perhaps impossible to refute, but which rest on nothing more than conjecture. Nor can a single word be said as to the person named Diognetus, to whom the letter is addressed. We must be content to leave both points in hopeless obscurity, and simply accept the Epistle as written by an earnest and intelligent Christian to a sincere inquirer among the Gentiles, towards the close of the apostolic age.

It is much to be regretted that the text is often so very doubtful. Only three mss. of the Epistle, all probably exhibiting the same original text, are known to exist; and in not a few passages the readings are, in consequence, very defective and obscure. But notwithstanding this drawback, and the difficulty of representing the full force and elegance of the original, this Epistle, as now presented to the English reader, can hardly fail to excite both his deepest interest and admiration.

[N.B.--Interesting speculations concerning this precious work may be seen in Bunsen's Hippolytus and his Age, vol. i. p. 188. The learned do not seem convinced by this author, but I have adopted his suggestion as to Diognetus the tutor of M. Aurelius.]

The Epistle of Mathetes to Diognetus

Chapter I - Occasion of the epistle

Since I see thee, most excellent Diognetus, exceedingly desirous to learn the mode of worshipping God prevalent among the Christians, and inquiring very carefully and earnestly concerning them, what God they trust in, and what form of religion they observe, [264] so as all to look down upon the world itself, and despise death, while they neither esteem those to be gods that are reckoned such by the Greeks, nor hold to the superstition of the Jews; and what is the affection which they cherish among themselves; and why, in fine, this new kind or practice [of piety] has only now entered into the world, [265] and not long ago; I cordially welcome this thy desire, and I implore God, who enables us both to speak and to hear, to grant to me so to speak, that, above all, I may hear you have been edified, [266] and to you so to hear, that I who speak may have no cause of regret for having done so.

Chapter II - The vanity of idols

Come, then, after you have freed [267] yourself from all prejudices possessing your mind, and laid aside what you have been accustomed to, as something apt to deceive [268] you, and being made, as if from the beginning, a new man, inasmuch as, according to your own confession, you are to be the hearer of a new [system of] doctrine; come and contemplate, not with your eyes only, but with your understanding, the substance and the form [269] of those whom ye declare and deem to be gods. Is not one of them a stone similar to that on which we tread? Is [270] not a second brass, in no way superior to those vessels which are constructed for our ordinary use? Is not a third wood, and that already rotten? Is not a fourth silver, which needs a man to watch it, lest it be stolen? Is not a fifth iron, consumed by rust? Is not a sixth earthenware, in no degree more valuable than that which is formed for the humblest purposes? Are not all these of corruptible matter? Are they not fabricated by means of iron and fire? Did not the sculptor fashion one of them, the brazier a second, the silversmith a third, and the potter a fourth? Was not every one of them, before they were formed by the arts of these [workmen] into the shape of these [gods], each in its [271] own way subject to change? Would not those things which are now vessels, formed of the same materials, become like to such, if they met with the same artificers? Might not these, which are now worshipped by you, again be made by men vessels similar to others? Are they not all deaf? Are they not blind? Are they not without life? Are they not destitute of feeling? Are they not incapable of motion? Are they not all liable to rot? Are they not all corruptible? These things ye call gods; these ye serve; these ye worship; and ye become altogether like to them. For this reason ye hate the Christians, because they do not deem these to be gods. But do not ye yourselves, who now think and suppose [such to be gods], much more cast contempt upon them than they [the Christians do]? Do ye not much more mock and insult them, when ye worship those that are made of stone and earthenware, without appointing any persons to guard them; but those made of silver and gold ye shut up by night, and appoint watchers to look after them by day, lest they be stolen? And by those gifts which ye mean to present to them, do ye not, if they are possessed of sense, rather punish [than honour] them? But if, on the other hand, they are destitute of sense, ye convict them of this fact, while ye worship them with blood and the smoke of sacrifices. Let any one of you suffer such indignities! [272] Let any one of you endure to have such things done to himself! But not a single human being will, unless compelled to it, endure such treatment, since he is endowed with sense and reason. A stone, however, readily bears it, seeing it is insensible. Certainly you do not show [by your [273] conduct] that he [your God] is possessed of sense. And as to the fact that Christians are not accustomed to serve such gods, I might easily find many other things to say; but if even what has been said does not seem to any one sufficient, I deem it idle to say anything further.

Chapter III - Superstitions of the Jews

And next, I imagine that you are most desirous of hearing something on this point, that the Christians do not observe the same forms of divine worship as do the Jews. The Jews, then, if they abstain from the kind of service above described, and deem it proper to worship one God as being Lord of all, [are right]; but if they offer Him worship in the way which we have described, they greatly err. For while the Gentiles, by offering such things to those that are destitute of sense and hearing, furnish an example of madness; they, on the other hand, by thinking to offer these things to

God as if He needed them, might justly reckon it rather an act of folly than of divine worship. For He that made heaven and earth, and all that is therein, and gives to us all the things of which we stand in need, certainly requires none of those things which He Himself bestows on such as think of furnishing them to Him. But those who imagine that, by means of blood, and the smoke of sacrifices and burnt-offerings, they offer sacrifices [acceptable] to Him, and that by such honours they show Him respect, --these, by [274] supposing that they can give anything to Him who stands in need of nothing, appear to me in no respect to differ from those who studiously confer the same honour on things destitute of sense, and which therefore are unable to enjoy such honours.

Chapter IV - The other observances of the Jews

But as to their scrupulosity concerning meats, and their superstition as respects the Sabbaths, and their boasting about circumcision, and their fancies about fasting and the new moons, which are utterly ridiculous and unworthy of notice,--I do not [275] think that you require to learn anything from me. For, to accept some of those things which have been formed by God for the use of men as properly formed, and to reject others as useless and redundant,--how can this be lawful? And to speak falsely of God, as if He forbade us to do what is good on the Sabbath-days,--how is not this impious? And to glory in the circumcision [276] of the flesh as a proof of election, and as if, on account of it, they were specially beloved by God,--how is it not a subject of ridicule? And as to their observing months and days, [277] as if waiting upon [278] the stars and the moon, and their distributing, [279] according to their own tendencies, the appointments of God, and the vicissitudes of the seasons, some for festivities, [280] and others for mourning,--who would deem this a part of divine worship, and not much rather a manifestation of folly? I suppose, then, you are sufficiently convinced that the Christians properly abstain from the vanity and error common [to both Jews and Gentiles], and from the busy-body spirit and vain boasting of the Jews; but you must not hope to learn the mystery of their peculiar mode of worshipping God from any mortal.

Chapter V - The manners of the Christians

For the Christians are distinguished from other men neither by country, nor language, nor the customs which they observe. For they neither inhabit cities of their own, nor employ a peculiar form of speech, nor lead a life which is marked out by any singularity. The course of conduct which they follow has not been devised by any speculation or deliberation of inquisitive men; nor do they, like some, proclaim themselves the advocates of any merely human doctrines. But, inhabiting Greek as well as barbarian cities, according as the lot of each of them has determined, and following the customs of the natives in respect to clothing, food, and the rest of their ordinary conduct, they display to us their wonderful and confessedly striking [281] method of life. They dwell in their own countries, but simply as sojourners. As citizens, they share in all things with others, and yet endure all things as if foreigners. Every foreign land is to them as their native country, and every land of their birth as a land of strangers. They marry, as do all [others]; they beget children; but they do not destroy their offspring. [282] They have a common table, but not a common bed. [283] They are in the flesh, but they do not live after the flesh. [284] They pass their days on earth, but they are citizens of heaven. [285] They obey the prescribed laws, and at the same time surpass the laws by their lives. They love all men, and are persecuted by all. They are unknown and condemned; they are put to death, and restored to life. [286] They are poor, yet make many rich; [287] they are in lack of all things, and yet abound in all; they are dishonoured, and yet in their very dishonour are glorified. They are evil spoken of, and yet are justified; they are reviled, and bless; [288] they are insulted, and repay the insult with honour; they do good, yet are punished as evil-doers. When punished, they rejoice as if quickened into life; they are assailed by the Jews as foreigners, and are persecuted by the Greeks; yet those who hate them are unable to assign any reason for their hatred.

Chapter VI - The relation of Christians to the world

To sum up all in one word--what the soul is in the body, that are Christians in the world. The soul is dispersed through all the members of the body, and Christians are scattered through all the cities of the world. The soul dwells in the body, yet is not of the body; and Christians dwell in the world, yet are not of the world. [289] The invisible soul is guarded by the visible body, and Christians are known indeed to be in the world, but their godliness remains invisible. The flesh hates the soul, and wars against it, [290] though itself suffering no injury, because it is prevented from enjoying pleasures; the world also hates the Christians, though in nowise injured, because they abjure pleasures. The soul loves the flesh that hates it, and [loves also] the members; Christians likewise love those that hate them. The soul is imprisoned in the body, yet preserves [291] that very body; and Christians are confined in the world as in a prison, and yet they are the preservers [292] of the world. The immortal soul dwells in a mortal tabernacle; and Christians dwell as sojourners in corruptible [bodies], looking for an incorruptible dwelling [293] in the heavens. The soul, when but ill-provided with food and drink, becomes better; in like manner, the Christians, though subjected day by day to punishment, increase the more in number. [294] God has assigned them this illustrious position, which it were unlawful for them to forsake.

Chapter VII - The manifestation of Christ

For, as I said, this was no mere earthly invention which was delivered to them, nor is it a mere human system of opinion, which they judge it right to preserve so carefully, nor has a dispensation of mere human mysteries been committed to them, but truly God Himself, who is almighty, the Creator of all things, and invisible, has sent from heaven, and placed among men, [Him who is] the truth, and the holy and incomprehensible Word, and has firmly established Him in their hearts. He did not, as one might have imagined, send to men any servant, or angel, or ruler, or any one of those who bear sway over earthly things, or one of those to whom the government of things in the heavens has been entrusted, but the very Creator and Fashioner of all things--by whom He made the heavens--by whom he enclosed the sea within its proper bounds--whose ordinances [295] all the stars [296] faithfully observe--from whom the sun [297] has received the measure of his daily course to be observed [298] -- whom the moon obeys, being commanded to shine in the night, and whom the stars also obey, following the moon in her course; by whom all things have been arranged, and placed within their proper limits, and to whom all are subject--the heavens and the things that are therein, the earth and the things that are therein, the sea and the things that are therein--fire, air, and the abyss--the things which are in the heights, the things which are in the depths, and the things which lie between. This [messenger] He sent to them. Was it then, as one [299] might conceive, for the purpose of exercising tyranny, or of inspiring fear and terror? By no means, but under the influence of clemency and meekness. As a king sends his son, who is also a king, so sent He Him; as God [300] He sent Him; as to men He sent Him; as a Saviour He sent Him, and as seeking to persuade, not to compel us; for violence has no place in the character of God. As calling us He sent Him, not as vengefully pursuing us; as loving us He sent Him, not as judging us. For He will yet send Him to judge us, and who shall endure His appearing? [301] .. Do you not see them exposed to wild beasts, that they may be persuaded to deny the Lord, and yet not overcome? Do you not see that the more of them are punished, the greater becomes the number of the rest? This does not seem to be the work of man: this is the power of God; these are the evidences of His manifestation.

Chapter VIII - The miserable state of men before the coming of the Word

For, who of men at all understood before His coming what God is? Do you accept of the vain and silly doctrines of those who are deemed trustworthy philosophers? of whom some said that fire was God, calling that God to which they themselves were by and by to come; and some water; and others some other of the elements formed by God. But if any one of these theories be worthy of approbation, every one of the rest of created things might also be declared to be God. But such declarations are simply the startling and erroneous utterances of deceivers; [302] and no man has either seen Him, or made Him known, [303] but He has revealed Himself. And He has manifested Himself through faith, to which alone it is given to behold God. For God, the Lord and Fashioner of all things, who made all things, and assigned them their several positions, proved Himself not merely a friend of mankind, but also long-suffering [in His dealings with them]. Yea, He was always of such a character, and still is, and will ever be, kind and good, and free from wrath, and true, and the only one who is [absolutely] good; [304] and He formed in His mind a great and unspeakable conception, which He communicated to His Son alone. As long, then, as He held and preserved His own wise counsel in concealment, [305] He appeared to neglect us, and to have no care over us. But after He revealed and laid open, through His beloved Son, the things which had been prepared from the beginning, He conferred every blessing [306] all at once upon us, so that we should both share in His benefits, and see and be active [307] [in His service]. Who of us would ever have expected these things? He was aware, then, of all things in His own mind, along with His Son, according to the relation [308] subsisting between them.

Chapter IX - Why the Son was sent so late

As long then as the former time [309] endured, He permitted us to be borne along by unruly impulses, being drawn away by the desire of pleasure and various lusts. This was not that He at all delighted in our sins, but that He simply endured them; nor that He approved the time of working iniquity which then was, but that He sought to form a mind conscious of righteousness, [310] so that being convinced in that time of our unworthiness of attaining life through our own works, it should now, through the kindness of God, be vouchsafed to us; and having made it manifest that in ourselves we were unable to enter into the kingdom of God, we might through the power of God be made able. But when our wickedness had reached its height, and it had been clearly shown that its reward, [311] punishment and death, was impending over us; and when the time had come which God had before appointed for manifesting His own kindness and power, how [312] the one love of God, through exceeding regard for men, did not regard us with hatred, nor thrust us away, nor remember our iniquity against us, but showed great long-suffering, and bore with us, [313] He Himself took on Him the burden of our iniquities, He gave His own Son as a ransom for us, the holy One for transgressors, the blameless One for the wicked, the righteous One for the unrighteous, the incorruptible One for the corruptible, the immortal One for them that are mortal. For what other thing was capable of covering our sins than His righteousness? By what other one was it possible that we, the wicked and ungodly, could be justified, than by the only Son of God? O sweet exchange! O unsearchable operation! O benefits surpassing all expectation! that the wickedness of many should be hid in a single righteous One, and that the righteousness of One should justify many transgressors! [314] Having therefore convinced us in the former time [315] that our nature was unable to attain to life, and having now revealed the Saviour who is able to save even those things which it was [formerly] impossible to save, by both these facts He desired to lead us to trust in His kindness, to esteem Him our Nourisher, Father, Teacher, Counsellor, Healer, our Wisdom, Light, Honour, Glory, Power, and Life, so that we should not be anxious [316] concerning clothing and food.

Chapter X - The blessings that will flow from faith

If you also desire [to possess] this faith, you likewise shall receive first of all the knowledge of the Father. [317] For God has loved mankind, on whose account He made the world, to whom He rendered subject all the things that are in it, [318] to whom He gave reason and understanding, to whom alone He imparted the privilege of looking upwards to Himself, whom He formed after His own image, to whom He sent His only-begotten Son, to whom He has promised a kingdom in heaven, and will give it to those who have loved Him. And when you have attained this knowledge, with what joy do you think you will be filled? Or, how will you love Him who has first so loved you? And if you love Him, you will be an imitator of His kindness. And do not wonder that a man may become an imitator of God. He can, if he is willing. For it is not by ruling over his neighbours, or by seeking to hold the supremacy over those that are weaker, or by being rich, and showing violence towards those that are inferior, that happiness is found; nor can any one by these things become an imitator of God. But these things do not at all constitute His majesty. On the contrary he who takes upon himself the burden of his neighbour; he who, in whatsoever respect he may be superior, is ready to benefit another who is deficient; he who, whatsoever things he has received from God, by distributing these to the needy, becomes a god to those who receive [his benefits]: he is an imitator of God. Then thou shalt see, while still on earth, that God in the heavens rules over [the universe]; then thou shall begin to speak the mysteries of God; then shalt thou both love and admire those that suffer punishment because they will not deny God; then shall thou condemn the deceit and error of the world when thou shall know what it is to live truly in heaven, when thou shalt despise that which is here esteemed to be death, when thou shalt fear what is truly death, which is reserved for those who shall be condemned to the eternal fire, which shall afflict those even to the end that are committed to it. Then shalt thou admire those who for righteousness' sake endure the fire that is but for a moment, and shalt count them happy when thou shalt know [the nature of] that fire.

Chapter XI - These things are worthy to be known and believed

I do not speak of things strange to me, nor do I aim at anything inconsistent with right reason; [319] but having been a disciple of the Apostles, I am become a teacher of the Gentiles. I minister the things delivered to me to those that are disciples worthy of the truth. For who that is rightly taught and begotten by the loving [320] Word, would not seek to learn accurately the things which have been clearly shown by the Word to His disciples, to whom the Word being manifested has revealed them, speaking plainly [to them], not understood indeed by the unbelieving, but conversing with the disciples, who, being esteemed faithful by Him, acquired a knowledge of the mysteries of the Father? For which [321] reason He sent the Word, that He might be manifested to the world; and He, being despised by the people [of the Jews], was, when preached by the Apostles, believed on by the Gentiles. [322] This is He who was from the beginning, who appeared as if new, and was found old, and yet who is ever born afresh in the hearts of the saints. This is He who, being from everlasting, is to-day called [323] the Son; through whom the Church is enriched, and grace, widely spread, increases in the saints, furnishing understanding, revealing mysteries, announcing times, rejoicing over the faithful, giving [324] to those that seek, by whom the limits of faith are not broken through, nor the boundaries set by the fathers passed over. Then the fear of the law is chanted, and the grace of the prophets is known, and the faith of the gospels is established, and the tradition of the Apostles is preserved, and the grace of the Church exults; which grace if you grieve not, you shall know those things which the Word teaches, by whom He wills, and when He pleases. For whatever things we are moved to utter by the will of the Word commanding us, we communicate to you with pains, and from a love of the things that have been revealed to us.

Chapter XII - The importance of knowledge to true spiritual life

When you have read and carefully listened to these things, you shall know what God bestows on such as rightly love Him, being made [as ye are] a paradise of delight, presenting [325] in yourselves a tree bearing all kinds of produce and flourishing well, being adorned with various fruits. For in this place [326] the tree of knowledge and the tree of life have been planted; but it is not the tree of knowledge that destroys-- it is disobedience that proves destructive. Nor truly are those words without significance which are written, how God from the beginning planted the tree of life in the midst of paradise, revealing through knowledge the way to life, [327] and when those who were first formed did not use this [knowledge] properly, they were, through the fraud of the Serpent, stripped naked. [328] For neither can life exist without knowledge, nor is knowledge secure without life. Wherefore both were planted close together. The Apostle, perceiving the force [of this conjunction], and blaming that knowledge which, without true doctrine, is admitted to influence life, [329] declares, "Knowledge puffeth up, but love edifieth." For he who thinks he knows anything without true knowledge, and such as is witnessed to by life, knows nothing, but is deceived by the Serpent, as not [330] loving life. But he who combines knowledge with fear, and seeks after life, plants in hope, looking for fruit. Let your heart be your wisdom; and let your life be true knowledge[331] inwardly received. Bearing this tree and displaying its fruit, thou shalt always gather[332] in those things which are desired by God, which the Serpent cannot reach, and to which deception does not approach; nor is Eve then corrupted, [333] but is trusted as a virgin; and salvation is manifested, and the Apostles are filled with understanding, and the Passover [334] of the Lord advances, and the choirs [335] are gathered together, and are arranged in proper order, and the Word rejoices in teaching the saints,--by whom the Father is glorified: to whom be glory for ever. Amen.[336]

Footnotes:

263. ἀποστόλων γενόμενος μαθητής. Cap. xi.

264. Literally, "trusting in what God, etc., they look down."

265. Or, "life."

266. Some read, "that you by hearing may be edified."

267. Or, "purified."

268. Literally, "which is deceiving."

269. Literally, "of what substance, or of what form."

270. Some make this and the following clauses affirmative instead of interrogative.

271. The text is here corrupt. Several attempts at emendation have been made, but without any marked success.

272. Some read, "Who of you would tolerate these things?" etc.

273. The text is here uncertain, and the sense obscure. The meaning seems to be, that by sprinkling their gods with blood, etc., they tended to prove that these were not possessed of sense.

274. The text here is very doubtful. We have followed that adopted by most critics.

275. Otto, resting on ms. authority, omits the negative, but the sense seems to require its insertion.

276. Literally, "lessening."

277. Comp. Gal. iv. 10.

278. This seems to refer to the practice of Jews in fixing the beginning of the day, and consequently of the Sabbath, from the rising of the stars. They used to say, that when three stars of moderate magnitude appeared, it was night; when two, it was twilight; and when only one, that day had not yet departed. It thus came to pass (according to their night-day (νυχθήμερον) reckoning), that whosoever engaged in work on the evening of Friday, the beginning of the Sabbath, after three stars of moderate size were visible, was held to have sinned, and had to present a trespass-offering; and so on, according to the fanciful rule described.

279. Otto supplies the lacuna which here occurs in the mss. so as to read καταδιαιρεῖν.

280. The great festivals of the Jews are here referred to on the one hand, and the day of atonement on the other.

281. Literally, "paradoxical."

282. Literally, "cast away foetuses."

283. Otto omits "bed," which is an emendation, and gives the second "common" the sense of unclean.

284. Comp. 2 Cor. x. 3.

285. Comp. Phil. iii. 20.

286. Comp. 2 Cor. vi. 9.

287. Comp. 2 Cor. vi. 10.

288. Comp. 2 Cor. iv. 12.

289. John xvii. 11, 14, 16.

290. Comp. 1 Pet. ii. 11.

291. Literally, "keeps together."

292. Literally, "keeps together."

293. Literally, "incorruption."

294. Or, "though punished, increase in

number daily."
295. Literally, "mysteries."
296. Literally, "elements."
297. The word "sun," though omitted in the mss., should manifestly be inserted.
298. Literally, "has received to observe."
299. Literally, "one of men."
300. "God" here refers to the person sent.
301. Comp. Mal. iii. 2. The Old Testament is frequently in mind, if not expressly quoted by Mathetes. A considerable gap here occurs in the mss.
302. Literally, "these things are the marvels and error."
303. Or, "known Him."
304. Comp. Matt. xix. 17.
305. Literally, "in a mystery."
306. Literally, "all things."
307. The sense is here very obscure. We have followed the text of Otto, who fills up the lacuna in the ms. as above. Others have, "to see, and to handle Him."
308. Literally, "economically."
309. Otto refers for a like contrast between these two times to Rom. iii. 21-26, Rom. v. 20 and Gal. iv. 4. Comp. Acts xvii. 30.
310. The reading and sense are doubtful.
311. Both the text and rendering are here somewhat doubtful, but the sense will in any case be much the same.
312. Many variations here occur in the way in which the lacuna of the mss. is to be supplied. They do not, however, greatly affect the meaning.
313. In the ms. "saying" is here inserted, as if the words had been regarded as a quotation from Isa. liii. 11.
314. See Bossuet, who quotes it as from Justin Martyr (Tom. iii. p. 171). Sermon on Circumcision.

315. That is, before Christ appeared.
316. Comp. Matt. vi. 25, etc. Mathetes, in a single sentence, expounds a most practical text with comprehensive views.
317. Thus Otto supplies the lacuna; others conjecture somewhat different supplements.
318. So Böhl. Sylburgius and Otto read, "in the earth."
319. Some render, "nor do I rashly seek to persuade others."
320. Some propose to read, "and becoming a friend to the Word."
321. It has been proposed to connect this with the preceding sentence, and read, "have known the mysteries of the Father, viz., for what purpose He sent the Word."
322. Comp. 1 Tim. iii. 16.
323. Or, "esteemed."
324. Or, "given."
325. Literally, "bringing forth."
326. That is, in Paradise.
327. Literally "revealing life."
328. Or, "deprived of it."
329. Literally, "knowledge without the truth of a command exercised to life." See 1 Cor. viii. 1.
330. The ms. is here defective. Some read, "on account of the love of life."
331. Or, "true word," or "reason."
332. Or, "reap."
333. The meaning seems to be, that if the tree of true knowledge and life be planted within you, you shall continue free from blemishes and sins.
334. This looks like a reference to the Apocalypse, Rev. v. 9., Rev. xix. 7., Rev. xx. 5.
335. Here Bishop Wordsworth would read κλῆροι, cites 1 Pet. v. 3, and refers to Suicer (Lexicon) in voce κλῆρος.
336. Note the Clement-like doxology.

Polycarp

Introductory Note to the Epistle of Polycarp to the Philippians

[a.d. 65-100-155.] The Epistle of Polycarp is usually made a sort of preface to those of Ignatius, for reasons which will be obvious to the reader. Yet he was born later, and lived to a much later period. They seem to have been friends from the days of their common pupilage under St. John; and there is nothing improbable in the conjecture of Usher, that he was the "angel of the church in Smyrna," to whom the Master says, "Be thou faithful unto death, and I will give thee a crown of life." His pupil Irenæus gives us one of the very few portraits of an apostolic man which are to be found in antiquity, in a few sentences which are a picture: "I could describe the very place in which the blessed Polycarp sat and taught; his going out and coming in; the whole tenor of his life; his personal appearance; how he would speak of the conversations he had held with John and with others who had seen the Lord. How did he make mention of their words and of whatever he had heard from them respecting the Lord." Thus he unconsciously tantalizes our reverent curiosity. Alas! that such conversations were not written for our learning. But there is a wise Providence in what is withheld, as well as in the inestimable treasures we have received.

Irenæus will tell us more concerning him, his visit to Rome, his rebuke of Marcion, and incidental anecdotes, all which are instructive. The expression which he applied to Marcion is found in this Epistle. Other facts of interest are found in the Martyrdom, which follows in these pages. His death, in extreme old age under the first of the Antonines, has been variously dated; but we may accept the date we have given, as rendered probable by that of the Paschal question, which he so lovingly settled with Anicetus, Bishop of Rome.

The Epistle to the Philippians is the more interesting as denoting the state of that beloved church, the firstborn of European churches, and so greatly endeared to St. Paul. It abounds in practical wisdom, and is rich in Scripture and Scriptural allusions. It reflects the spirit of St. John, alike in its lamb-like and its aquiline features: he is as loving as the beloved disciple himself when he speaks of Christ and his church, but "the son of thunder" is echoed in his rebukes of threatened corruptions in faith and morals. Nothing can be more clear than his view of the doctrines of grace; but he writes like the disciple of St. John, though in perfect harmony with St. Paul's hymn-like eulogy of Christian love.

The following is the original Introductory Notice:--

The authenticity of the following Epistle can on no fair grounds be questioned. It is abundantly established by external testimony, and is also supported by the internal evidence. Irenæus says (Adv. Hær., iii. 3): "There is extant an Epistle of Polycarp written to the Philippians, most satisfactory, from which those that have a mind to do so may learn the character of his faith," etc. This passage is embodied by Eusebius in his Ecclesiastical History (iv. 14); and in another place the same writer refers to the Epistle before us as an undoubted production of Polycarp (Hist. Eccl., iii. 36). Other ancient testimonies might easily be added, but are superfluous, inasmuch as there is a general consent among scholars at the present day that we have in this letter an authentic production of the renowned Bishop of Smyrna.

Of Polycarp's life little is known, but that little is highly interesting. Irenæus was his disciple, and tells us that "Polycarp was instructed by the apostles, and was brought into contact with many who had seen Christ" (Adv. Hær., iii. 3; Euseb. Hist. Eccl., iv. 14). There is also a very graphic account given of Polycarp by Irenæus in his Epistle to Florinus, to which the reader is referred. It has been preserved by Eusebius (Hist. Eccl., v. 20).

The Epistle before us is not perfect in any of the Greek mss. which contain it. But the chapters wanting in Greek are contained in an ancient Latin version. While there is no ground for supposing, as some have done, that the whole Epistle is spurious, there seems considerable force in the arguments by which many others have sought to prove chap. xiii. to be an interpolation.

The date of the Epistle cannot be satisfactorily determined. It depends on the conclusion we reach as to some points, very difficult and obscure, connected with that account of the martyrdom of Polycarp which has come down to us. We shall not, however, probably be far wrong if we fix it about the middle of the second century.

The Epistle of Polycarp to the Philippians [337]

Polycarp, and the presbyters [338] with him, to the Church of God sojourning at Philippi: Mercy to you, and peace from God Almighty, and from the Lord Jesus Christ, our Saviour, be multiplied.

Chapter I - Praise of the Philippians

I have greatly rejoiced with you in our Lord Jesus Christ, because ye have followed the example [339] of true love [as displayed by God], and have accompanied, as became you, those who were bound in chains, the fitting ornaments of saints, and which are indeed the diadems of the true elect of God and our Lord; and because the strong root of your faith, spoken of in days [340] long gone by, endureth even until now, and bringeth forth fruit to our Lord Jesus Christ, who for our sins suffered even unto death, [but] "whom God raised from the dead, having loosed the bands of the grave." [341] "In whom, though now ye see Him not, ye believe, and believing, rejoice with joy unspeakable and full of glory;" [342] into which joy many desire to enter, knowing that "by grace ye are saved, not of works," [343] but by the will of God through Jesus Christ.

Chapter II - An exhortation to virtue

"Wherefore, girding up your loins," [344] "serve the Lord in fear" [345] and truth, as those who have forsaken the vain, empty talk and error of the multitude, and "believed in Him who raised up our Lord Jesus Christ from the dead, and gave Him glory," [346] and a throne at His right hand. To Him all things [347] in heaven and on earth are subject. Him every spirit serves. He comes as the Judge of the living and the dead. [348] His blood will God require of those who do not believe in Him. [349] But He who raised Him up from the dead will raise [350] up us also, if we do His will, and walk in His commandments, and love what He loved, keeping ourselves from all unrighteousness, covetousness, love of money, evil speaking, false witness; "not rendering evil for evil, or railing for railing," [351] or blow for blow, or cursing for cursing, but being mindful of what the Lord said in His teaching: "Judge not, that ye be not judged;" [352] forgive, and it shall be forgiven unto you; [353] be merciful, that ye may obtain mercy; [354] with what measure ye mete, it shall be measured to you again;" [355] and once more, "Blessed are the poor, and those that are persecuted for righteousness' sake, for theirs is the kingdom of God." [356]

Chapter III - Expressions of personal unworthiness

These things, brethren, I write to you concerning righteousness, not because I take anything upon myself, but because ye have invited me to do so. For neither I, nor any other such one, can come up to the wisdom [357] of the blessed and glorified Paul. He, when among you, accurately and stedfastly taught the word of truth in the presence of those who were then alive. And when absent from you, he wrote you a letter, [358] which, if you carefully study, you will find to be the means of building you up in that faith which has been given you, and which, being followed by hope, and preceded by love towards God, and Christ, and our neighbour, "is the mother of us all." [359] For if any one be inwardly possessed of these graces, he hath fulfilled the command of righteousness, since he that hath love is far from all sin.

Chapter IV - Various exhortations

"But the love of money is the root of all evils." [360] Knowing, therefore, that "as we brought nothing into the world, so we can carry nothing out," [361] let us arm ourselves with the armour of righteousness; [362] and let us teach, first of all, ourselves to walk in the commandments of the Lord. Next, [teach] your wives [to walk] in the faith given to them, and in love and purity tenderly loving their own husbands in all truth, and loving all [others] equally in all chastity; and to train up their children in the knowledge and fear of God. Teach the widows to be discreet as respects the faith of the Lord, praying continually [363] for all, being far from all slandering, evil-speaking, false-witnessing, love of money, and every kind of evil; knowing that they are the altar [364] of God, that He clearly perceives all things, and that nothing is hid from Him, neither reasonings, nor reflections, nor any one of the secret things of the heart.

Chapter V - The duties of deacons, youths, and virgins

Knowing, then, that "God is not mocked," [365] we ought to walk worthy of His commandment and glory. In like manner should the deacons be blameless before the face of His righteousness, as being the servants of God and Christ, [366] and not of men. They must not be slanderers, double-tongued, [367] or lovers of money, but temperate in all things, compassionate, industrious, walking according to the truth of the Lord, who was the servant [368] of all. If we please Him in this present world, we shall receive also the future world, according as He has promised to us that He will raise us again from the dead, and that if we live [369] worthily of Him, "we shall also reign together with Him," [370] provided only we believe. In like manner, let the young men also be blameless in all things, being especially careful to preserve purity, and keeping themselves in, as with a bridle, from every kind of evil. For it is well that they should be cut off from [371] the lusts that are in the world, since "every lust warreth against the spirit;" [372] and "neither fornicators, nor effeminate, nor abusers of themselves with mankind, shall inherit the kingdom of God," [373] nor those who do things inconsistent and unbecoming. Wherefore, it is needful to abstain from all these things, being subject to the presbyters and deacons, as unto God and Christ. The virgins also must walk in a blameless and pure conscience.

Chapter VI - The duties of presbyters and others

And let the presbyters be compassionate and merciful to all, bringing back those that wander, visiting all the sick, and not neglecting the widow, the orphan, or the poor, but always "providing for that which is becoming in the sight of God and man;" [374] abstaining from all wrath, respect of persons, and unjust judgment; keeping far off from all covetousness, not quickly crediting [an evil report] against any one, not severe in judgment, as knowing that we are all under a debt of sin. If then we entreat the Lord to forgive us, we ought also ourselves to forgive; [375] for we are before the eyes of our Lord and God, and "we must all appear at the judgment-seat of Christ, and must every one give an account of himself." [376] Let us then serve Him in fear, and with all reverence, even as He Himself has commanded us, and as the apostles who preached the Gospel unto us, and the prophets who proclaimed beforehand the coming of the Lord [have alike taught us]. Let us be zealous in the pursuit of that which is good, keeping ourselves from causes of offence, from false brethren, and from those who in hypocrisy bear the name of the Lord, and draw away vain men into error.

Chapter VII - Avoid the Docetæ, and persevere in fasting and prayer

"For whosoever does not confess that Jesus Christ has come in the flesh, is antichrist;" [377] and whosoever does not confess the testimony of the cross, [378] is of the devil; and whosoever perverts the oracles of the Lord to his own lusts, and says that there is neither a resurrection nor a judgment, he is the first-born of Satan. [379] Wherefore, forsaking the vanity of many, and their false doctrines, let us return to the word which has been handed down to us from [380] the beginning; "watching unto prayer," [381] and persevering in fasting; beseeching in our supplications the all-seeing God "not to lead us into temptation," [382] as the Lord has said: "The spirit truly is willing, but the flesh is weak."[383]

Chapter VIII - Persevere in hope and patience

Let us then continually persevere in our hope, and the earnest of our righteousness, which is Jesus Christ, "who bore our sins in His own body on the tree," [384] "who did no sin, neither was guile found in His mouth," [385] but endured all things for us, that we might live in Him. [386] Let us then be imitators of His patience; and if we suffer [387] for His name's sake, let us glorify Him. [388] For He has set us this example [389] in Himself, and we have believed that such is the case.

Chapter IX - Patience inculcated

I exhort you all, therefore, to yield obedience to the word of righteousness, and to exercise all patience, such as ye have seen [set] before your eyes, not only in the case of the blessed Ignatius, and Zosimus, and Rufus, but also in others among yourselves, and in Paul himself, and the rest of the apostles. [This do] in the assurance that all these have not run [390] in vain, but in faith and righteousness, and that they are [now] in their due place in the presence of the Lord, with whom also they suffered. For they loved not this present world, but Him who died for us, and for our sakes was raised again by God from the dead.

Chapter X - Exhortation to the practice of virtue [391]

Stand fast, therefore, in these things, and follow the example of the Lord, being firm and unchangeable in the faith, loving the brotherhood, [392] and being attached to one another, joined together in the truth, exhibiting the meekness of the Lord in your intercourse with one another, and despising no one. When you can do good, defer it not, because "alms delivers from death." [393] Be all of you subject one to another [394] "having your conduct blameless among the Gentiles," [395] that ye may both receive praise for your good works, and the Lord may not be blasphemed through you. But woe to him by whom the name of the Lord is blasphemed! [396] Teach, therefore, sobriety to all, and manifest it also in your own conduct.

Chapter XI - Expression of grief on account of Valens

I am greatly grieved for Valens, who was once a presbyter among you, because he so little understands the place that was given him [in the Church]. I exhort you, therefore, that ye abstain from covetousness, [397] and that ye be chaste and truthful. "Abstain from every form of evil." [398] For if a man cannot govern himself in such matters, how shall he enjoin them on others? If a man does not keep himself from covetousness, [399] he shall be defiled by idolatry, and shall be judged as one of the heathen. But who of us are ignorant of the judgment of the Lord? "Do we not know that the saints shall judge the world?" [400] as Paul teaches. But I have neither seen nor heard of any such thing among you, in the midst of whom the blessed Paul laboured, and who are commended [401] in the beginning of his Epistle. For he boasts of you in all those Churches which alone then knew the Lord; but we [of Smyrna] had not yet known Him. I am deeply grieved, therefore, brethren, for him (Valens) and his wife; to whom may the Lord grant true repentance! And be ye then moderate in regard to this matter, and "do not count such as enemies," [402] but call them back as suffering and straying members, that ye may save your whole body. For by so acting ye shall edify yourselves. [403]

Chapter XII - Exhortation to various graces

For I trust that ye are well versed in the Sacred Scriptures, and that nothing is hid from you; but to me this privilege is not yet granted. [404] It is declared then in these Scriptures, "Be ye angry, and sin not," [405] and, "Let not the sun go down upon your wrath." [406] Happy is he who remembers[407] this, which I believe to be the case with you. But may the God and Father of our Lord Jesus Christ, and Jesus Christ Himself, who is the Son of God, and our everlasting High Priest, build you up in faith and truth, and in all meekness, gentleness, patience, long-suffering, forbearance, and purity; and may He bestow on you a lot and portion among His saints, and on us with you, and on all that are under heaven, who shall believe in our Lord Jesus Christ, and in His Father, who "raised Him from the dead." [408] Pray for all the saints. Pray also for kings, [409] and potentates, and princes, and for those that persecute and hate you, [410] and for the enemies of the cross, that your fruit may be manifest to all, and that ye may be perfect in Him.

Chapter XIII - Concerning the transmission of epistles

Both you and Ignatius [411] wrote to me, that if any one went [from this] into Syria, he should carry your letter [412] with him; which request I will attend to if I find a fitting opportunity, either personally, or through some other acting for me, that your desire may be fulfilled. The Epistles of Ignatius written by him [413] to us, and all the rest [of his Epistles] which we have by us, we have sent to you, as you requested. They are subjoined to this Epistle, and by them ye may be greatly profited; for they treat of faith and patience, and all things that tend to edification in our Lord. Any[414] more certain information you may have obtained respecting both Ignatius himself, and those that were [415] with him, have the goodness to make known [416] to us.

Chapter XIV - Conclusion

These things I have written to you by Crescens, whom up to the present [417] time I have recommended unto you, and do now recommend. For he has acted blamelessly among us, and I believe also among you. Moreover, ye will hold his sister in esteem when she comes to you. Be ye safe in the Lord Jesus Christ. Grace be with you all. [418] Amen.

Footnotes:

337. The title of this Epistle in most of the mss. is, "The Epistle of St. Polycarp, Bishop of Smyrna, and holy martyr, to the Philippians."

338. Or, "Polycarp, and those who with him are presbyters."

339. Literally, "ye have received the patterns of true love."

340. Phil. i. 5.

341. Acts ii. 24. Literally, "having loosed the pains of Hades."

342. 1 Pet. i. 8.

343. Eph. ii. 8, 9.
344. Comp. 1 Pet. i. 13; Eph. vi. 14.
345. Ps. ii. 11.
346. 1 Pet. i. 21.
347. Comp. 1 Pet. iii. 22; Phil. ii. 10.
348. Comp. Acts xvii. 31.
349. Or, "who do not obey him."
350. Comp 1 Cor. vi. 14; 2 Cor. iv. 14; Rom. viii. 11.
351. 1 Pet. iii. 9.
352. Matt. vii. 1.
353. Matt. vi. 12, 14; Luke vi. 37.
354. Luke vi. 36.
355. Matt. vii. 2; Luke vi. 38.
356. Matt. v. 3, 10; Luke vi. 20.
357. Comp. 2 Pet. iii. 15.
358. The form is plural, but one Epistle is probably meant. So, even in English, "letters" may be classically used for a single letter, as we say "by these presents." But even we might speak of St. Paul as having written his Epistles to us; so the Epistles to Thessalonica and Corinth might more naturally still be referred to here.
359. Comp. Gal. iv. 26.
360. 1 Tim. vi. 10.
361. 1 Tim. vi. 7.
362. Comp. Eph. vi. 11.
363. Comp. 1 Thess. v. 17.
364. Some here read, "altars."
365. Gal. vi. 7.
366. Some read, "God in Christ."
367. Comp. 1 Tim. iii. 8.
368. Comp. Matt. xx. 28.
369. Πολιτευσώμεθα, referring to the whole conduct; comp. Phil. i. 27.
370. 2 Tim. ii. 12.
371. Some read, ἀνακύπτεσθαι, "to emerge from." So Chevallier, but not Wake nor Jacobson. See the note of latter, ad loc.
372. 1 Pet. ii. 11.
373. 1 Cor. vi. 9, 10.
374. Rom. xii. 17; 2 Cor. viii. 31.
375. Matt. vi. 12-14.
376. Rom. xiv. 10-12; 2 Cor. v. 10.
377. 1 John iv. 3.
378. Literally, "the martyrdom of the cross," which some render, "His suffering on the cross."
379. The original, perhaps, of Eusebius (Hist. iv. cap. 14). It became a common-place expression in the Church.
380. Comp. Jude 3.
381. 1 Pet. iv. 7.
382. Matt. vi. 13; Matt. xxvi. 41.
383. Matt. xxvi. 41; Mark xiv. 38.
384. 1 Pet. ii. 24.
385. 1 Pet. ii. 22.
386. Comp. 1 John iv. 9.
387. Comp. Acts v. 41; 1 Pet. iv. 16.
388. Some read, "we glorify Him."
389. Comp. 1 Pet. ii. 21.
390. Comp. Phil. ii. 16; Gal. ii. 2.
391. This and the two following chapters are preserved only in a Latin version. See Jacobson, ad loc.
392. Comp. 1 Pet. ii. 17.
393. Tobit iv. 10, Tobit xii. 9.
394. Comp. 1 Pet. v. 5.
395. 1 Pet. ii. 12.
396. Isa. lii. 5.
397. Some think that incontinence on the part of the Valens and his wife is referred to. For many reasons I am glad the translators have preferred the reading πλεονεξίας. The next word, chaste, sufficiently rebukes the example of Valens. For once I venture not to coincide with Jacobson's comment.
398. 1 Thess. v. 22.
399. Some think that incontinence on the part of the Valens and his wife is referred to. For many reasons I am glad the translators have preferred the reading πλεονεξίας. The next word, chaste, sufficiently rebukes the example of Valens. For once I venture not to coincide with Jacobson's comment.
400. 1 Cor. vi. 2.
401. Some read, "named;" comp. Phil. i. 5.
402. 2 Thess. iii. 15.
403. Comp. 1 Cor. xii. 26.
404. This passage is very obscure. Some render it as follows: "But at present it is not granted unto me to practise that which is written, Be ye angry," etc.
405. Ps. iv. 5.
406. Eph. iv. 26.
407. Some read, "believes."
408. Gal. i. 1.
409. Comp. 1 Tim. ii. 2.
410. Matt. v. 44.
411. Comp. Ep. of Ignatius to Polycarp, chap. viii.
412. Or, "letters."
413. Reference is here made to the two letters of Ignatius, one to Polycarp himself, and the other to the church at Smyrna.
414. Henceforth, to the end, we have only the Latin version.
415. The Latin version reads "are," which has been corrected as above.
416. Polycarp was aware of the death of Ignatius (chap. ix.), but was as yet apparently ignorant of the circumstances attending it. Who can fail to be touched by these affectionate yet entirely calm expressions as to his martyred friend and brother? Martyrdom was the habitual end of Christ's soldiers, and Polycarp expected his own; hence his restrained and temperate

words of interest.

417. Some read, "in this present Epistle."

418. Others read, "and in favour with all yours."

Introductory Note to the Epistle Concerning the Martyrdom of Polycarp

Internal evidence goes far to establish the credit which Eusebius lends to this specimen of the martyrologies, certainly not the earliest if we accept that of Ignatius as genuine. As an encyclical of one of "the seven churches" to another of the same Seven, and as bearing witness to their aggregation with others into the unity of "the Holy and Catholic Church," it is a very interesting witness, not only to an article of the creed, but to the original meaning and acceptance of the same. More than this, it is evidence of the strength of Christ perfected in human weakness; and thus it affords us an assurance of grace equal to our day in every time of need. When I see in it, however, an example of what a noble army of martyrs, women and children included, suffered in those days "for the testimony of Jesus," and in order to hand down the knowledge of the Gospel to these boastful ages of our own, I confess myself edified by what I read, chiefly because I am humbled and abashed in comparing what a Christian used to be, with what a Christian is, in our times, even at his best estate.

That this Epistle has been interpolated can hardly be doubted, when we compare it with the unvarnished specimen, in Eusebius. As for the "fragrant smell" that came from the fire, many kinds of wood emit the like in burning; and, apart from Oriental warmth of colouring, there seems nothing incredible in the narrative if we except "the dove" (chap. xvi.), which, however, is probably a corrupt reading, [419] as suggested by our translators. The blade was thrust into the martyr's left side; and this, opening the heart, caused the outpouring of a flood, and not a mere trickling. But, though Greek thus amended is a plausible conjecture, there seems to have been nothing of the kind in the copy quoted by Eusebius. On the other hand, note the truly catholic and scriptural testimony: "We love the martyrs, but the Son of God we worship: it is impossible for us to worship any other."

Bishop Jacobson assigns more than fifty pages to this martyrology, with a Latin version and abundant notes. To these I must refer the student, who may wish to see this attractive history in all the light of critical scholarship and, often, of admirable comment.

The following is the original Introductory Notice:--

The following letter purports to have been written by the Church at Smyrna to the Church at Philomelium, and through that Church to the whole Christian world, in order to give a succinct account of the circumstances attending the martyrdom of Polycarp. It is the earliest of all the Martyria, and has generally been accounted both the most interesting and authentic. Not a few, however, deem it interpolated in several passages, and some refer it to a much later date than the middle of the second century, to which it has been commonly ascribed. We cannot tell how much it may owe to the writers (chap. xxii.) who successively transcribed it. Great part of it has been engrossed by Eusebius in his Ecclesiastical History (iv. 15); and it is instructive to observe, that some of the most startling miraculous phenomena recorded in the text as it now stands, have no place in the narrative as given by that early historian of the Church. Much discussion has arisen respecting several particulars contained in this Martyrium; but into these disputes we do not enter, having it for our aim simply to present the reader with as faithful a translation as possible of this very interesting monument of Christian antiquity.

The Encyclical Epistle of the Church at Smyrna Concerning the Martyrdom of the Holy Polycarp

The Church of God which sojourns at Smyrna, to the Church of God sojourning in Philomelium, [420] and to all the congregations [421] of the Holy and Catholic Church in every place: Mercy, peace, and love from God the Father, and our Lord Jesus Christ, be multiplied.

Chapter I - Subject of which we write

We have written to you, brethren, as to what relates to the martyrs, and especially to the blessed Polycarp, who put an end to the persecution, having, as it were, set a seal upon it by his martyrdom. For almost all the events that happened previously [to this one], took place that the Lord might show us from above a martyrdom becoming the Gospel. For he waited to be delivered up, even as the Lord had done, that we also might become his followers, while we look not merely at what concerns ourselves but have regard also to our neighbours. For it is the part of a true and well-founded love, not only to wish one's self to be saved, but also all the brethren.

Chapter II - The wonderful constancy of the martyrs

All the martyrdoms, then, were blessed and noble which took place according to the will of God. For it becomes us who profess [422] greater piety than others, to ascribe the authority over all things to God. And truly, [423] who can fail to admire their nobleness of mind, and their patience, with that love towards their Lord which they displayed?--who, when they were so torn with scourges, that the frame of their bodies, even to the very inward veins and arteries, was laid open, still patiently endured, while even those that stood by pitied and bewailed them. But they reached such a pitch of magnanimity, that not one of them let a sigh or a groan escape them; thus proving to us all that those holy martyrs of Christ, at the very time when they suffered such torments, were absent from the body, or rather, that the Lord then stood by them, and communed with them. And, looking to the grace of Christ, they despised all the torments of this world, redeeming themselves from eternal punishment by [the suffering of] a single hour. For this reason the fire of their savage executioners appeared cool to them. For they kept before their view escape from that fire which is eternal and never shall be quenched, and looked forward with the eyes of their heart to those good things which are laid up for such as endure; things "which ear hath not heard, nor eye seen, neither have entered into the heart of man," [424] but were revealed by the Lord to them, inasmuch as they were no longer men, but had already become angels. And, in like manner, those who were condemned to the wild beasts endured dreadful tortures, being stretched out upon beds full of spikes, and subjected to various other kinds of torments, in order that, if it were possible, the tyrant might, by their lingering tortures, lead them to a denial [of Christ].

Chapter III - The constancy of Germanicus. The death of Polycarp is demanded

For the devil did indeed invent many things against them; but thanks be to God, he could not prevail over all. For the most noble Germanicus strengthened the timidity of others by his own patience, and fought heroically [425] with the wild beasts. For, when the proconsul sought to persuade him, and urged him [426] to take pity upon his age, he attracted the wild beast towards himself, and provoked it, being desirous to escape all the more quickly from an unrighteous and impious world. But upon this the whole multitude, marvelling at the nobility of mind displayed by the devout and godly race of Christians, [427] cried out, "Away with the Atheists; let Polycarp be sought out!"

Chapter IV - Quintus the apostate

Now one named Quintus, a Phrygian, who was but lately come from Phrygia, when he saw the wild beasts, became afraid. This was the man who forced himself and some others to come forward voluntarily [for trial]. Him the proconsul, after many entreaties, persuaded to swear and to offer sacrifice. Wherefore, brethren, we do not commend those who give themselves up [to suffering], seeing the Gospel does not teach so to do. [428]

Chapter V - The departure and vision of Polycarp

But the most admirable Polycarp, when he first heard [that he was sought for], was in no measure disturbed, but resolved to continue in the city. However, in deference to the wish of many, he was persuaded to leave it. He departed, therefore, to a country house not far distant from the city. There he stayed with a few [friends], engaged in nothing else night and day than praying for all men, and for the Churches throughout the world, according to his usual custom. And while he was praying, a vision presented itself to him three days before he was taken; and, behold, the pillow under his head seemed to him on fire. Upon this, turning to those that were with him, he said to them prophetically, "I must be burnt alive."

Chapter VI - Polycarp is betrayed by a servant

And when those who sought for him were at hand, he departed to another dwelling, whither his pursuers immediately came after him. And when they found him not, they seized upon two youths [that were there], one of whom, being subjected to torture, confessed. It was thus impossible that he should continue hid, since those that betrayed him were of his own household. The Irenarch [429] then (whose office is the same as that of the Cleronomus [430]), by name Herod, hastened to bring him into the stadium. [This all happened] that he might fulfil his special lot, being made a partaker of Christ, and that they who betrayed him might undergo the punishment of Judas himself.

Chapter VII - Polycarp is found by his pursuers

His pursuers then, along with horsemen, and taking the youth with them, went forth at supper-time on the day of the preparation [431] with their usual weapons, as if going out against a robber. [432] And being come about evening [to the place where he was], they found him lying down in the upper room of [433] a certain little house, from which he might have escaped into another place; but he refused, saying, "The will of God [434] be done." [435] So when he heard that they were come, he went down and spake with them. And as those that were present marvelled at his age and constancy, some of them said. "Was so much effort [436] made to capture such a venerable man?" [437] Immediately then, in that very hour, he ordered that something to eat and drink should be set before them, as much indeed as they cared for, while he besought them to allow him an hour to pray without disturbance. And on their giving him leave, he stood and prayed, being full of the grace of God, so that he could not cease [438] for two full hours, to the astonishment of them that heard him, insomuch that many began to repent that they had come forth against so godly and venerable an old man.

Chapter VIII - Polycarp is brought into the city

Now, as soon as he had ceased praying, having made mention of all that had at any time come in contact with him, both small and great, illustrious and obscure, as well as the whole Catholic Church throughout the world, the time of his departure having arrived, they set him upon an ass, and conducted him into the city, the day being that of the great Sabbath. And the Irenarch Herod, accompanied by his father Nicetes (both riding in a chariot [439]), met him, and taking him up into the chariot, they seated themselves beside him, and endeavoured to persuade him, saying, "What harm is there in saying, Lord Cæsar, [440] and in sacrificing, with the other ceremonies observed on such occasions, and so make sure of safety?" But he at first gave them no answer; and when they continued to urge him, he said, "I shall not do as you advise me." So they, having no hope of persuading him, began to speak bitter [441] words unto him, and cast him with violence out of the chariot, [442] insomuch that, in getting down from the carriage, he dislocated his leg [443] [by the fall]. But without being disturbed, [444] and as if suffering nothing, he went eagerly forward with all haste, and was conducted to the stadium, where the tumult was so great, that there was no possibility of being heard.

Chapter IX - Polycarp refuses to revile Christ

Now, as Polycarp was entering into the stadium, there came to him a voice from heaven, saying, "Be strong, and show thyself a man, O Polycarp!" No one saw who it was that spoke to him; but those of our brethren who were present heard the voice. And as he was brought forward, the tumult became great when they heard that Polycarp was taken. And when he came near, the proconsul asked him whether he was Polycarp. On his confessing that he was, [the proconsul] sought to persuade him to deny [Christ], saying, "Have respect to thy old age," and other similar things, according to their custom, [such as], "Swear by the fortune of Cæsar; repent, and say, Away with the Atheists." But Polycarp, gazing with a stern countenance on all the multitude of the wicked heathen then in the stadium, and waving his hand towards them, while with groans he looked up to heaven, said, "Away with the Atheists." [445] Then, the proconsul urging him, and saying, "Swear, and I will set thee at liberty, reproach Christ;" Polycarp declared, "Eighty and six years have I served Him, and He never did me any injury: how then can I blaspheme my King and my Saviour?"

Chapter X - Polycarp confesses himself a Christian

And when the proconsul yet again pressed him, and said, "Swear by the fortune of Cæsar," he answered, "Since thou art vainly urgent that, as thou sayest, I should swear by the fortune of Cæsar, and pretendest not to know who and what I am, hear me declare with boldness, I am a Christian. And if you wish to learn what the doctrines [446] of Christianity are, appoint me a day, and thou shalt hear them." The proconsul replied, "Persuade the people." But Polycarp said, "To thee I have thought it right to offer an account [of my faith]; for we are taught to give all due honour (which entails no injury upon ourselves) to the powers and authorities which are ordained of God. [447] But as for these, I do not deem them worthy of receiving any account from me." [448]

Chapter XI - No threats have any effect on Polycarp

The proconsul then said to him, "I have wild beasts at hand; to these will I cast thee, except thou repent." But he answered, "Call them then, for we are not accustomed to repent of what is good in order to adopt that which is evil; [449] and it is well for me to be changed from what is evil to what is righteous." [450] But again the proconsul said to him, "I will cause thee to be consumed by fire, seeing thou despisest the wild beasts, if thou wilt not repent." But Polycarp said, "Thou threatenest me with fire which burneth for an hour, and after a little is extinguished, but art ignorant of the fire of the coming judgment and of eternal punishment, reserved for the ungodly. But why tarriest thou? Bring forth what thou wilt."

Chapter XII - Polycarp is sentenced to be burned

While he spoke these and many other like things, he was filled with confidence and joy, and his countenance was full of grace, so that not merely did it not fall as if troubled by the things said to him, but, on the contrary, the proconsul was astonished, and sent his herald to proclaim in the midst of the stadium thrice, "Polycarp has confessed that he is a Christian." This proclamation having been made by the herald, the whole multitude both of the heathen and Jews, who dwelt at Smyrna, cried out with uncontrollable fury, and in a loud voice, "This is the teacher of Asia, [451] the father of the Christians, and the overthrower of our gods, he who has been teaching many not to sacrifice, or to worship the gods." Speaking thus, they cried out, and besought Philip the Asiarch [452] to let loose a lion upon Polycarp. But Philip answered that it was not lawful for him to do so, seeing the shows [453] of wild beasts were already finished. Then it seemed good to them to cry out with one consent, that Polycarp should be burnt alive. For thus it behooved the vision which was revealed to him in regard to his pillow to be fulfilled, when, seeing it on fire as he was praying, he turned about and said prophetically to the faithful that were with him, "I must be burnt alive."

Chapter XIII - The funeral pile is erected

This, then, was carried into effect with greater speed than it was spoken, the multitudes immediately gathering together wood and fagots out of the shops and baths; the Jews especially, according to custom, eagerly assisting them in it. And when the funeral pile was ready, Polycarp, laying aside all his garments, and loosing his girdle, sought also to take off his sandals,--a thing he was not accustomed to do, inasmuch as every one of the faithful was always eager who should first touch his skin. For, on account of his holy life, [454] he was, even before his martyrdom, adorned [455] with every kind of good. Immediately then they surrounded him with those substances which had been prepared for the funeral pile. But when they were about also to fix him with nails, he said, "Leave me as I am; for He that giveth me strength to endure the fire, will also enable me, without your securing me by nails, to remain without moving in the pile."

Chapter XIV - The prayer of Polycarp

They did not nail him then, but simply bound him. And he, placing his hands behind him, and being bound like a distinguished ram [taken] out of a great flock for sacrifice, and prepared to be an acceptable burnt-offering unto God, looked up to heaven, and said, "O Lord God Almighty, the Father of thy beloved and blessed Son Jesus Christ, by whom we have received the knowledge of Thee, the God of angels and powers, and of every creature, and of the whole race of the righteous who live before thee, I give Thee thanks that Thou hast counted me worthy of this day and this hour, that I should have a part in the number of Thy martyrs, in the cup [456] of thy Christ, to the resurrection of eternal life, both of soul and body, through the incorruption [imparted] by the Holy Ghost. Among whom may I be accepted this day before Thee as a fat [457] and acceptable sacrifice, according as Thou, the ever-truthful [458] God, hast foreordained, hast revealed beforehand to me, and now hast fulfilled. Wherefore also I praise Thee for all things, I bless Thee, I glorify Thee, along with the everlasting and heavenly Jesus Christ, Thy beloved Son, with whom, to Thee, and the Holy Ghost, be glory both now and to all coming ages. Amen." [459]

Chapter XV - Polycarp is not injured by the fire

When he had pronounced this amen, and so finished his prayer, those who were appointed for the purpose kindled the fire. And as the flame blazed forth in great fury, [460] we, to whom it was given to witness it, beheld a great miracle, and have been preserved that we might report to others what then took place. For the fire, shaping itself into the form of an arch, like the sail of a ship when filled with the wind, encompassed as by a circle the body of the martyr. And he appeared within not like flesh which is burnt, but as bread that is baked, or as gold and silver glowing in a furnace. Moreover, we perceived such a sweet odour [coming from the pile], as if frankincense or some such precious spices had been smoking [461] there.

Chapter XVI - Polycarp is pierced by a dagger

At length, when those wicked men perceived that his body could not be consumed by the fire, they commanded an executioner to go near and pierce him through with a dagger. And on his doing this, there came forth a dove, [462] and a great quantity of blood, so that the fire was extinguished; and all the people wondered that there should be such a difference between the unbelievers and the elect, of whom this most admirable Polycarp was one, having in our own times been an apostolic and prophetic teacher, and bishop of the Catholic Church which is in Smyrna. For every word that went out of his mouth either has been or shall yet be accomplished.

Chapter XVII - The Christians are refused Polycarp's body

But when the adversary of the race of the righteous, the envious, malicious, and wicked one, perceived the impressive [463] nature of his martyrdom, and [considered] the blameless life he had led from the beginning, and how he was now crowned with the wreath of immortality, having beyond dispute received his reward, he did his utmost that not the least memorial of him should be taken away by us, although many desired to do this, and to become possessors [464] of his holy flesh. For this end he suggested it to Nicetes, the father of Herod and brother of Alce, to go and entreat the governor not to give up his body to be buried, "lest," said he, "forsaking Him that was crucified, they begin to worship this one." This he said at the suggestion and urgent persuasion of the Jews, who also watched us, as we sought to take him out of the fire, being ignorant of this, that it is neither possible for us ever to forsake Christ, who suffered for the salvation of such as shall be saved throughout the whole world (the blameless one for sinners [465]), nor to worship any other. For Him indeed, as being the Son of God, we adore; but the martyrs, as disciples and followers of the Lord, we worthily love on account of their extraordinary [466] affection towards their own King and Master, of whom may we also be made companions [467] and fellow-disciples!

Chapter XVIII - The body of Polycarp is burned

The centurion then, seeing the strife excited by the Jews, placed the body [468] in the midst of the fire, and consumed it. Accordingly, we afterwards took up his bones, as being more precious than the most exquisite jewels, and more purified [469] than gold, and deposited them in a fitting place, whither, being gathered together, as opportunity is allowed us, with joy and rejoicing, the Lord shall grant us to celebrate the anniversary [470] of his martyrdom, both in memory of those who have already finished their course, [471] and for the exercising and preparation of those yet to walk in their steps.

Chapter XIX - Praise of the martyr Polycarp

This, then, is the account of the blessed Polycarp, who, being the twelfth that was martyred in Smyrna (reckoning those also of Philadelphia), yet occupies a place of his own [472] in the memory of all men, insomuch that he is everywhere spoken of by the heathen themselves. He was not merely an illustrious teacher, but also a pre-eminent martyr, whose martyrdom all desire to imitate, as having been altogether consistent with the Gospel of Christ. For, having through patience overcome the unjust governor, and thus acquired the crown of immortality, he now, with the apostles and all the righteous [in heaven], rejoicingly glorifies God, even the Father, and blesses our Lord Jesus Christ, the Saviour of our souls, the Governor of our bodies, and the Shepherd of the Catholic Church throughout the world. [473]

Chapter XX - This epistle is to be transmitted to the brethren

Since, then, ye requested that we would at large make you acquainted with what really took place, we have for the present sent you this summary account through our brother Marcus. When, therefore, ye have yourselves read this Epistle, [474] be pleased to send it to the brethren at a greater distance, that they also may glorify the Lord, who makes such choice of His own servants. To Him who is able to bring us all by His grace and goodness [475] into his everlasting kingdom, through His only-begotten Son Jesus Christ, to Him be glory, and honour, and power, and majesty, for ever. Amen. Salute all the saints. They that are with us salute you, and Evarestus, who wrote this Epistle, with all his house.

Chapter XXI - The date of the martyrdom

Now, the blessed Polycarp suffered martyrdom on the second day of the month Xanthicus just begun, [476] the seventh day before the Kalends of May, on the great Sabbath, at the eighth hour. [477] He was taken by Herod, Philip the Trallian being high priest, [478] Statius Quadratus being proconsul, but Jesus Christ being King for ever, to whom be glory, honour, majesty, and an everlasting throne, from generation to generation. Amen.

Chapter XXII - Salutation

We wish you, brethren, all happiness, while you walk according to the doctrine of the Gospel of Jesus Christ; with whom be glory to God the Father and the Holy Spirit, for the salvation of His holy elect, after whose example [479] the blessed Polycarp suffered, following in whose steps may we too be found in the kingdom of Jesus Christ!

These things [480] Caius transcribed from the copy of Irenæus (who was a disciple of Polycarp), having himself been intimate with Irenæus. And I Socrates transcribed them at Corinth from the copy of Caius. Grace be with you all.

And I again, Pionius, wrote them from the previously written copy, having carefully searched into them, and the blessed Polycarp having manifested them to me through a revelation, even as I shall show in what follows. I have collected these things, when they had almost faded away through the lapse of time, that the Lord Jesus Christ may also gather me along with His elect into His heavenly kingdom, to whom, with the Father and the Holy Spirit, be glory for ever and ever. Amen.

Footnotes:

419. See an ingenious conjecture in Bishop Wordsworth's Hippolytus and the Church of Rome, p. 318, C.
420. Some read, "Philadelphia," but on inferior authority. Philomelium was a city of Phrygia.
421. The word in the original is παροικίαις, from which the English "parishes" is derived.
422. Literally, "who are more pious."
423. The account now returns to the illustration of the statement made in the first sentence.
424. 1 Cor. ii. 9.
425. Or, "illustriously."
426. Or, "said to him."
427. Literally, "the nobleness of the God-loving and God-fearing race of Christians."
428. Comp. Matt. x. 23.
429. It was the duty of the Irenarch to apprehend all seditious troublers of the public peace.
430. Some think that those magistrates bore this name that were elected by lot.
431. That is, on Friday.
432. Comp. Matt. xxvi. 55.
433. Or, "in."
434. Some read "the Lord"
435. Comp. Matt. vi. 10; Acts xxi. 14.
436. Or, "diligence."
437. Jacobson reads, "and marvelling that they had used so great diligence to capture," etc.
438. Or, "be silent."
439. Jacobson deems these words an interpolation.
440. Or, "Cæsar is Lord," all the mss. having κύριος instead of κύριε, as usually printed.
441. Or, "terrible."
442. Or, "cast him down" simply, the following words being, as above, an interpolation.
443. Or, "sprained his ankle."
444. Or, "not turning back."
445. Referring the words to the heathen, and not to the Christians, as was desired.
446. Or, "an account of Christianity."
447. Comp. Rom. xiii. 1-7; Tit. iii. 1.
448. Or, "of my making any defence to them."
449. Literally, "repentance from things better to things worse is a change impossible to us."
450. That is, to leave this world for a better.
451. Some read, "ungodliness," but the above seems preferable.
452. The Asiarchs were those who superintended all arrangements connected with the games in the several provinces.
453. Literally, "the baiting of dogs."
454. Literally, "good behaviour."
455. Some think this implies that Polycarp's skin was believed to possess a miraculous efficacy.
456. Comp. Matt. xx. 22, Matt. xxvi. 39; Mark x. 38.
457. Literally, "in a fat," etc., or, "in a rich".
458. Literally, "the not false and true God."
459. Eusebius (Hist. Eccl., iv. 15) has preserved a great portion of this Martyrium, but in a text considerably differing from that we have followed. Here, instead of "and," he has "in the Holy Ghost."
460. Literally, "a great flame shining forth."
461. Literally, "breathing."
462. Eusebius omits all mention of the dove, and many have thought the text to be here corrupt. It has been proposed to read ἐπ' ἀριστερᾷ, "on the left hand side," instead of περιστερά, "a dove."
463. Literally, "greatness."
464. The Greek, literally translated, is, "and to have fellowship with his holy flesh."
465. This clause is omitted by Eusebius: it was probably interpolated by some transcriber, who had in his mind 1

Pet. iii. 18.

466. Literally, "unsurpassable."
467. Literally, "fellow-partakers."
468. Or, "him."
469. Or, "more tried."
470. Literally, "the birth-day."
471. Literally, "been athletes."
472. Literally, "is alone remembered."
473. Several additions are here made. One ms. has, "and the all-holy and life-giving Spirit;" while the old Latin version reads, "and the Holy Spirit, by whom we know all things."
474. Literally, "having learned these things."
475. Literally, "gift."
476. The translation is here very doubtful. Wake renders the words μηνὸς ἰσταμένου, "of the present month."
477. Great obscurity hangs over the chronology here indicated. According to Usher, the Smyrnæans began the month Xanthicus on the 25th of March. But the seventh day before the Kalends of May is the 25th of April. Some, therefore, read Ἀπριλλίων instead of Μαίον. The great Sabbath is that before the passover. The "eighth hour" may correspond either to our 8 a.m. or 2 p.m.
478. Called before (chap. xii.) Asiarch.
479. Literally, "according as."
480. What follows is, of course, no part of the original Epistle.

Ignatius

Introductory Note to the Epistles of Ignatius

[a.d. 30-107.] The seductive myth which represents this Father as the little child whom the Lord placed in the midst of his apostles (St. Matt. xviii. 2) indicates at least the period when he may be supposed to have been born. That he and Polycarp were fellow-disciples under St. John, is a tradition by no means inconsistent with anything in the Epistles of either. His subsequent history is sufficiently indicated in the Epistles which follow.

Had not the plan of this series been so exclusively that of a mere revised reprint, the writings of Ignatius themselves would have made me diffident as to the undertaking. It seems impossible for any one to write upon the subject of these precious remains, without provoking controversy. This publication is designed as an Eirenicon, and hence "few words are best," from one who might be supposed incapable of an unbiased opinion on most of the points which have been raised in connection with these Epistles. I must content myself therefore, by referring the studious reader to the originals as edited by Bishop Jacobson, with a Latin version and copious annotations. That revered and learned divine honoured me with his friendship; and his precious edition has been my frequent study, with theological students, almost ever since it appeared in 1840. It is by no means superannuated by the vigorous Ignatian literature which has since sprung up, and to which reference will be made elsewhere. But I am content to leave the whole matter, without comment, to the minds of Christians of whatever school and to their independent conclusions. It is a great thing to present them in a single volume with the shorter and longer Epistles duly compared, and with the Curetonian version besides. One luxury only I may claim, to relieve the drudging task-work of a mere reviser. Surely I may point out some of the proverbial wisdom of this great disciple, which has often stirred my soul, as with the trumpet heard by St. John in Patmos. In him, indeed, the lions encountered a lion, one truly begotten of "the Lion of the tribe of Judah." Take, then, as a specimen, these thrilling injunctions from his letter to Polycarp, to whom he bequeathed his own spirit, and in whom he well knew the Church would recognize a sort of survival of St. John himself. If the reader has any true perception of the rhythm and force of the Greek language, let him learn by heart the originals of the following aphorisms:--

1. Find time to pray without ceasing.
2. Every wound is not healed with the same remedy.
3. The times demand thee, as pilots the haven.
4. The crown is immortality. [481]
5. Stand like a beaten anvil. [482]
6. It is the part of a good athlete to be bruised and to prevail.
7. Consider the times: look for Him who is above time.
8. Slight not the menservants and the handmaids.
9. Let your stewardship define your work. 10. A Christian is not his own master, but waits upon God.

Ignatius so delighted in his name Theophorus (sufficiently expounded in his own words to Trajan or his official representative), that it is worth noting how deeply the early Christians felt and believed in (2 Cor. vi. 16) the indwelling Spirit.

Ignatius has been censured for his language to the Romans, in which he seems to crave martyrdom. But he was already condemned, in law a dead man, and felt himself at liberty to glory in his tribulations. Is it more than modern Christians often too lightly sing? --

"Let cares like a wild deluge come,
And storms of sorrow fall," etc.

So the holy martyr adds, "Only let me attain unto Jesus Christ."

The Epistle to the Romans is utterly inconsistent with any conception on his part, that Rome was the see and residence of a bishop holding any other than fraternal relations with himself. It is very noteworthy that it is devoid of expressions, elsewhere made emphatic, [483] which would have been much insisted upon had they been found herein. Think what use would have been made of it, had the words which he addresses to the Smyrnæans (chap. viii.) to strengthen their fidelity to

The Apostolic Fathers
Polycarp, been found in this letter to the Romans, especially as in this letter we first find the use of the phrase "Catholic Church" in patristic writings. He defines it as to be found "where Jesus Christ is," words which certainly do not limit it to communion with a professed successor of St. Peter.

The following is the original Introductory Notice:--

The epistles ascribed to Ignatius have given rise to more controversy than any other documents connected with the primitive Church. As is evident to every reader on the very first glance at these writings, they contain numerous statements which bear on points of ecclesiastical order that have long divided the Christian world; and a strong temptation has thus been felt to allow some amount of prepossession to enter into the discussion of their authenticity or spuriousness. At the same time, this question has furnished a noble field for the display of learning and acuteness, and has, in the various forms under which it has been debated, given rise to not a few works of the very highest ability and scholarship. We shall present such an outline of the controversy as may enable the reader to understand its position at the present day.

There are, in all, fifteen Epistles which bear the name of Ignatius. These are the following: One to the Virgin Mary, two to the Apostle John, one to Mary of Cassobelæ, one to the Tarsians, one to the Antiochians, one to Hero, a deacon of Antioch, one to the Philippians; one to the Ephesians, one to the Magnesians, one to the Trallians, one to the Romans, one to the Philadelphians, one to the Smyrnæans, and one to Polycarp. The first three exist only in Latin: all the rest are extant also in Greek.

It is now the universal opinion of critics, that the first eight of these professedly Ignatian letters are spurious. They bear in themselves indubitable proofs of being the production of a later age than that in which Ignatius lived. Neither Eusebius nor Jerome makes the least reference to them; and they are now by common consent set aside as forgeries, which were at various dates, and to serve special purposes, put forth under the name of the celebrated Bishop of Antioch.

But after the question has been thus simplified, it still remains sufficiently complex. Of the seven Epistles which are acknowledged by Eusebius (Hist. Eccl., iii. 36), we possess two Greek recensions, a shorter and a longer. It is plain that one or other of these exhibits a corrupt text, and scholars have for the most part agreed to accept the shorter form as representing the genuine letters of Ignatius. This was the opinion generally acquiesced in, from the time when critical editions of these Epistles began to be issued, down to our own day. Criticism, indeed, fluctuated a good deal as to which Epistles should be accepted and which rejected. Archp. Usher (1644), Isaac Vossius (1646), J. B. Cotelerius (1672), Dr. T. Smith (1709), and others, edited the writings ascribed to Ignatius in forms differing very considerably as to the order in which they were arranged, and the degree of authority assigned them, until at length, from about the beginning of the eighteenth century, the seven Greek Epistles, of which a translation is here given, came to be generally accepted in their shorter form as the genuine writings of Ignatius.

Before this date, however, there had not been wanting some who refused to acknowledge the authenticity of these Epistles in either of the recensions in which they were then known to exist. By far the most learned and elaborate work maintaining this position was that of Daillé (or Dallæus), published in 1666. This drew forth in reply the celebrated Vindiciæ of Bishop Pearson, which appeared in 1672. It was generally supposed that this latter work had established on an immoveable foundation the genuineness of the shorter form of the Ignatian Epistles; and, as we have stated above, this was the conclusion almost universally accepted down to our own day. The only considerable exception to this concurrence was presented by Whiston, who laboured to maintain in his Primitive Christianity Revived (1711) the superior claims of the longer recension of the Epistles, apparently influenced in doing so by the support which he thought they furnished to the kind of Arianism which he had adopted.

But although the shorter form of the Ignatian letters had been generally accepted in preference to the longer, there was still a pretty prevalent opinion among scholars, that even it could not be regarded as absolutely free from interpolations, or as of undoubted authenticity. Thus said Lardner, in his Credibility of the Gospel History (1743): "have carefully compared the two editions, and am very well satisfied, upon that comparison, that the larger are an interpolation of the smaller, and not the smaller an epitome or abridgment of the larger. ... But whether the smaller themselves are the genuine writings of Ignatius, Bishop of Antioch, is a question that has been much disputed, and has employed the pens of the ablest critics. And whatever positiveness some may have shown on either side, I must own I have found it a very difficult question."

This expression of uncertainty was repeated in substance by Jortin (1751), Mosheim (1755), Griesbach (1768), Rosenmüller (1795), Neander (1826), and many others; some going so far as to deny that we have any authentic remains of Ignatius at all, while others, though admitting the seven shorter letters as being probably his, yet strongly suspected that they were not free from interpolation. Upon the whole, however, the shorter recension was, until recently, accepted without much opposition, and chiefly in dependence on the work of Bishop Pearson above mentioned, as exhibiting the genuine form of the Epistles of Ignatius.

But a totally different aspect was given to the question by the discovery of a Syriac version of three of these Epistles among the mss. procured from the monastery of St. Mary Deipara, in the desert of Nitria, in Egypt. In the years 1838, 1839, and again in 1842, Archdeacon Tattam visited that monastery, and succeeded in obtaining for the English Government a vast number of ancient Syriac manuscripts. On these being deposited in the British Museum, the late Dr. Cureton, who then had charge of the Syriac department, discovered among them, first, the Epistle to Polycarp, and then again, the same Epistle, with those to the Ephesians and to the Romans, in two other volumes of manuscripts.

As the result of this discovery, Cureton published in 1845 a work, entitled, The Ancient Syriac Version of the Epistles of St. Ignatius to Polycarp, the Ephesian, and the Romans, etc., in which he argued that these Epistles represented more accurately than any formerly published what Ignatius had actually written. This, of course, opened up the controversy afresh. While some accepted the views of Cureton, others very strenuously opposed them. Among the former was the late Chev. Bunsen; among the latter, an anonymous writer in the English Review, and Dr. Hefele, in his third edition of the Apostolic Fathers. In reply to those who had controverted his arguments, Cureton published his Vindiciæ Ignatianæ in 1846, and his Corpus Ignatianum in 1849. He begins his introduction to the last-named work with the following sentences: "Exactly three centuries and a half intervened between the time when three Epistles in Latin, attributed to St. Ignatius, first issued from the press, and the publication in 1845 of three letters in Syriac bearing the name of the same apostolic writer. Very few years passed before the former were almost universally regarded as false and spurious; and it seems not improbable that scarcely a longer period will elapse before the latter be almost as generally acknowledged and received as the only true and genuine letters of the venerable Bishop of Antioch that have either come down to our times, or were ever known in the earliest ages of the Christian Church."

Had the somewhat sanguine hope thus expressed been realized, it would have been unnecessary for us to present to the English reader more than a translation of these three Syriac Epistles. But the Ignatian controversy is not yet settled. There are still those who hold that the balance of argument is in favour of the shorter Greek, as against these Syriac Epistles. They regard the latter as an epitome of the former, and think the harshness which, according to them, exists in the sequence of thoughts and sentences, clearly shows that this is the case. We have therefore given all the forms of the Ignatian letters which have the least claim on our attention. [484] The reader may judge, by comparison for himself, which of these is to be accepted as genuine, supposing him disposed to admit the claims of any one of them. We content ourselves with laying the materials for judgment before him, and with referring to the above-named works in which we find the whole subject discussed. As to the personal history of Ignatius, almost nothing is known. The principal source of information regarding him is found in the account of his martyrdom, to which the reader is referred. Polycarp alludes to him in his Epistle to the Philippians (chap. ix.), and also to his letters (chap. xiii.). Irenæus quotes a passage from his Epistle to the Romans (Adv. Hær., v. 28; Epist. ad Rom., chap. iv.), without, however, naming him. Origen twice refers to him, first in the preface to his Comm. on the Song of Solomon, where he quotes a passage from the Epistle of Ignatius to the Romans, and again in his sixth homily on St. Luke, where he quotes from the Epistle to the Ephesians, both times naming the author. It is unnecessary to give later references.

Supposing the letters of Ignatius and the account of his martyrdom to be authentic, we learn from them that he voluntarily presented himself before Trajan at Antioch, the seat of his bishopric, when that prince was on his first expedition against the Parthians and Armenians (a.d. 107); and on professing himself a Christian, was condemned to the wild beasts. After a long and dangerous voyage he came to Smyrna, of which Polycarp was bishop, and thence wrote his four Epistles to the Ephesians, the Magnesians, the Trallians, and the Romans. From Smyrna he came to Troas, and tarrying there a few days, he wrote to the Philadelphians, the Smyrnæans, and Polycarp. He then came on to Neapolis, and passed through the whole of Macedonia. Finding a ship at Dyrrachium in Epirus about to sail into Italy, he embarked, and crossing the Adriatic, was brought to Rome, where he perished on the 20th of December 107, or, as some think, who deny a twofold expedition of Trajan against the Parthians, on the same day of the year a.d. 116.

Footnotes:

481. Does not this seem a pointed allusion to Rev. ii. 10?

482. Στῆθι ὡς ἄκμων τυπτόμενος.

483. See To the Tralliaus, cap. 13. Much might have been made, had it been found here, out of the reference to Christ the

High Priest (Philadelphians, cap. 9).

484. The other Epistles, bearing the name of Ignatius, will be found in the Appendix; so that the English reader possesses in this volume a complete collection of the Ignatian letters.

The Epistle of Ignatius to the Ephesians Shorter and Longer Versions

Ignatius, who is also called Theophorus, to the Church which is at Ephesus, in Asia, deservedly most happy, being blessed in the greatness and fulness of God the Father, and predestinated before the beginning [485] of time, that it should be always for an enduring and unchangeable glory, being united [486] and elected through the true passion by the will of the Father, and Jesus Christ, our God: Abundant happiness through Jesus Christ, and His undefiled grace.

Ignatius, who is also called Theophorus, to the Church which is at Ephesus, in Asia, deservedly most happy, being blessed in the greatness and fulness of God the Father, and predestinated before the beginning [487] of time, that it should be always for an enduring and unchangeable glory, being united [488] and elected through the true passion by the will of God the Father, and of our Lord Jesus Christ our Saviour: Abundant happiness through Jesus Christ, and His undefiled joy. [489]

Chapter I - Praise of the Ephesians

I have become acquainted with your name, much-beloved in God, which ye have acquired by the habit of righteousness, according to the faith and love in Jesus Christ our Saviour. Being the followers [490] of God, and stirring up [491] yourselves by the blood of God, ye have perfectly accomplished the work which was beseeming to you. For, on hearing that I came bound from Syria for the common name and hope, trusting through your prayers to be permitted to fight with beasts at Rome, that so by martyrdom I may indeed become the disciple of Him "who gave Himself for us, an offering and sacrifice to God," [492] [ye hastened to see me [493]]. I received, therefore, [494] your whole multitude in the name of God, through Onesimus, a man of inexpressible love, [495] and your bishop in the flesh, whom I pray you by Jesus Christ to love, and that you would all seek to be like him. And blessed be He who has granted unto you, being worthy, to obtain such an excellent bishop.

I have become acquainted with your greatly-desired name in God, which ye have acquired by the habit of righteousness, according to the faith and love in Christ Jesus our Saviour. Being the followers [496] of the love of God towards man, and stirring up [497] yourselves by the blood of Christ, you have perfectly accomplished the work which was beseeming to you. For, on hearing that I came bound from Syria for the sake of Christ, our common hope, trusting through your prayers to be permitted to fight with beasts at Rome, that so by martyrdom I may indeed become the disciple of Him "who gave Himself for us, an offering and a sacrifice to God," [498] [ye hastened to see me[499]]. I have therefore received your whole multitude in the name of God, through Onesimus, a man of inexpressible love, [500] and who is your bishop, whom I pray you by Jesus Christ to love, and that you would all seek to be like him. Blessed be God, who has granted unto you, who are yourselves so excellent, to obtain such an excellent bishop.

Chapter II - Congratulations and entreaties

As to my fellow-servant Burrhus, your deacon in regard to God and blessed in all things, [501] I beg that he may continue longer, both for your honour and that of your bishop. And Crocus also, worthy both of God and you, whom I have received as the manifestation [502] of your love, hath in all things refreshed [503] me, as the Father of our Lord Jesus Christ shall also refresh [504] him; together with Onesimus, and Burrhus, and Euplus, and Fronto, by means of whom, I have, as to love, beheld all of you. May I always have joy of you, if indeed I be worthy of it. It is therefore befitting that you should in every way glorify Jesus Christ, who hath glorified you, that by a unanimous obedience "ye may be perfectly joined together in the same mind, and in the same judgment, and may all speak the same thing concerning the same thing," [505] and that, being subject to the bishop and the presbytery, ye may in all respects be sanctified.

As to our fellow-servant Burrhus, your deacon in regard to God and blessed in all things, I pray that he may continue blameless for the honour of the Church, and of your most blessed bishop. Crocus also, worthy both of God and you, whom we have received as the manifestation [506] of your love to us, hath in all things refreshed [507] me, and "hath not been ashamed of my chain," [508] as the Father of our Lord Jesus Christ will also refresh [509] him; together with Onesimus, and Burrhus, and

Euplus, and Fronto, by means of whom I have, as to love, beheld all of you. May I always have joy of you, if indeed I be worthy of it. It is therefore befitting that you should in every way glorify Jesus Christ, who hath glorified you, that by a unanimous obedience "ye may be perfectly joined together in the same mind and in the same judgment, and may all speak the same thing concerning the same thing," [510] and that, being subject to the bishop and the presbytery, ye may in all respects be sanctified.

Chapter III - Exhortations to unity

I do not issue orders to you, as if I were some great person. For though I am bound for the name [of Christ], I am not yet perfect in Jesus Christ. For now I begin to be a disciple, and I speak to you as fellow-disciples with me. For it was needful for me to have been stirred up by you in faith, exhortation, patience, and long-suffering. But inasmuch as love suffers me not to be silent in regard to you, I have therefore taken [511] upon me first to exhort you that ye would all run together in accordance with the will of God. For even Jesus Christ, our inseparable life, is the [manifested] will of the Father; as also bishops, settled everywhere to the utmost bounds [of the earth], are so by the will of Jesus Christ.

I do not issue orders to you, as if I were some great person. For though I am bound for His name, I am not yet perfect in Jesus Christ. For now I begin to be a disciple, and I speak to you as my fellow-servants. For it was needful for me to have been admonished by you in faith, exhortation, patience, and long-suffering. But inasmuch as love suffers me not to be silent in regard to you, I have therefore taken [512] upon me first to exhort you that ye would run together in accordance with the will of God. For even Jesus Christ does all things according to the will of the Father, as He Himself declares in a certain place, "I do always those things that please Him." [513] Wherefore it behoves us also to live according to the will of God in Christ, and to imitate Him as Paul did. For, says he, "Be ye followers of me, even as I also am of Christ." [514]

Chapter IV - The same continued

Wherefore it is fitting that ye should run together in accordance with the will of your bishop, which thing also ye do. For your justly renowned presbytery, worthy of God, is fitted as exactly to the bishop as the strings are to the harp. Therefore in your concord and harmonious love, Jesus Christ is sung. And do ye, man by man, become a choir, that being harmonious in love, and taking up the song of God in unison, ye may with one voice sing to the Father through Jesus Christ, so that He may both hear you, and perceive by your works that ye are indeed the members of His Son. It is profitable, therefore, that you should live in an unblameable unity, that thus ye may always enjoy communion with God.

Wherefore it is fitting that ye also should run together in accordance with the will of the bishop who by God's appointment [515] rules over you. Which thing ye indeed of yourselves do, being instructed by the Spirit. For your justly-renowned presbytery, being worthy of God, is fitted as exactly to the bishop as the strings are to the harp. Thus, being joined together in concord and harmonious love, of which Jesus Christ is the Captain and Guardian, do ye, man by man, become but one choir; so that, agreeing together in concord, and obtaining [516] a perfect unity with God, ye may indeed be one in harmonious feeling with God the Father, and His beloved Son Jesus Christ our Lord. For, says He, "Grant unto them, Holy Father, that as I and Thou are one, they also may be one in us." [517] It is therefore profitable that you, being joined together with God in an unblameable unity, should be the followers of the example of Christ, of whom also ye are members.

Chapter V - The praise of unity

For if I in this brief space of time, have enjoyed such fellowship with your bishop --I mean not of a mere human, but of a spiritual nature--how much more do I reckon you happy who are so joined to him as the Church is to Jesus Christ, and as Jesus Christ is to the Father, that so all things may agree in unity! Let no man deceive himself: if any one be not within the altar, he is deprived of the bread of God. For if the prayer of one or two possesses [518] such power, how much more that of the bishop and the whole Church! He, therefore, that does not assemble with the Church, has even [519] by this manifested his pride, and condemned himself. For it is written, "God resisteth the proud." [520] Let us be careful, then, not to set ourselves in opposition to the bishop, in order that we may be subject to God.

For if I, in this brief space of time, have enjoyed such fellowship with your bishop --I mean not of a mere human, but of a spiritual nature--how much more do I reckon you happy, who so depend [521] on him as the Church does on the Lord Jesus, and the Lord does on God and His Father, that so all things may agree in unity! Let no man deceive himself: if any one be not within the altar, he is deprived of the bread of God. For if the prayer of one or two possesses [522] such power that Christ stands in the midst of them, how much more will the prayer of the bishop and of the whole

Church, ascending up in harmony to God, prevail for the granting of all their petitions in Christ! He, therefore, that separates himself from such, and does not meet in the society where sacrifices [523] are offered, and with "the Church of the first-born whose names are written in heaven," is a wolf in sheep's clothing, [524] while he presents a mild outward appearance. Do ye, beloved, be careful to be subject to the bishop, and the presbyters and the deacons. For he that is subject to these is obedient to Christ, who has appointed them; but he that is disobedient to these is disobedient to Christ Jesus. And "he that obeyeth not [525] the Son shall not see life, but the wrath of God abideth on him." For he that yields not obedience to his superiors is self-confident, quarrelsome, and proud. But "God," says [the Scripture] "resisteth the proud, but giveth grace to the humble;" [526] and, "The proud have greatly transgressed." The Lord also says to the priests, "He that heareth you, heareth Me; and he that heareth Me, heareth the Father that sent Me. He that despiseth you, despiseth Me; and he that despiseth Me, despiseth Him that sent Me."

Chapter VI - Have respect to the bishop as to Christ Himself

Now the more any one sees the bishop keeping silence, [527] the more ought he to revere him. For we ought to receive every one whom the Master of the house sends to be over His household,[528] as we would do Him that sent him. It is manifest, therefore, that we should look upon the bishop even as we would upon the Lord Himself. And indeed Onesimus himself greatly commends your good order in God, that ye all live according to the truth, and that no sect [529] has any dwelling-place among you. Nor, indeed, do ye hearken to any one rather than to Jesus Christ speaking in truth.

The more, therefore, you see the bishop silent, the more do you reverence him. For we ought to receive every one whom the Master of the house sends to be over His household, [530] as we would do Him that sent him. It is manifest, therefore, that we should look upon the bishop even as we would look upon the Lord Himself, standing, as he does, before the Lord. For "it behoves the man who looks carefully about him, and is active in his business, to stand before kings, and not to stand before slothful men." [531] And indeed Onesimus himself greatly commends your good order in God, that ye all live according to the truth, and that no sect has any dwelling-place among you. Nor indeed do ye hearken to any one rather than to Jesus Christ, the true Shepherd and Teacher. And ye are, as Paul wrote to you, "one body and one spirit, because ye have also been called in one hope of the faith. [532] Since also "there is one Lord, one faith, one baptism, one God and Father of all, who is over all, and through all, and in all." [533] Such, then, are ye, having been taught by such instructors, Paul the Christ-bearer, and Timothy the most faithful.

Chapter VII - Beware of false teachers

For some are in the habit of carrying about the name [of Jesus Christ] in wicked guile, while yet they practise things unworthy of God, whom ye must flee as ye would wild beasts. For they are ravening dogs, who bite secretly, against whom ye must be on your guard, inasmuch as they are men who can scarcely be cured. There is one Physician who is possessed both of flesh and spirit; both made and not made; God existing in flesh; true life in death; both of Mary and of God; first possible and then impossible,-- [534] even Jesus Christ our Lord.

But some most worthless persons are in the habit of carrying about the name [of Jesus Christ] in wicked guile, while yet they practise things unworthy of God, and hold opinions contrary to the doctrine of Christ, to their own destruction, and that of those who give credit to them, whom you must avoid as ye would wild beasts. For "the righteous man who avoids them is saved for ever; but the destruction of the ungodly is sudden, and a subject of rejoicing." [535] For "they are dumb dogs, that cannot bark," [536] raving mad, and biting secretly, against whom ye must be on your guard, since they labour under an incurable disease. But our Physician is the only true God, the unbegotten and unapproachable, the Lord of all, the Father and Begetter of the only-begotten Son. We have also as a Physician the Lord our God, Jesus the Christ, the only-begotten Son and Word, before time began, [537] but who afterwards became also man, of Mary the virgin. For "the Word was made flesh." [538] Being incorporeal, He was in the body; being impassible, He was in a passible body; being immortal, He was in a mortal body; being life, He became subject to corruption, that He might free our souls from death and corruption, and heal them, and might restore them to health, when they were diseased with ungodliness and wicked lusts.

Chapter VIII - Renewed praise of the Ephesians

Let not then any one deceive you, as indeed ye are not deceived, inasmuch as ye are wholly devoted to God. For since there is no strife raging among you which might distress you, ye are certainly living in accordance with God's will. I am far inferior to you, and require to be sanctified by your Church of Ephesus, so renowned throughout the world. They that are carnal cannot do those things which are spiritual, nor they that are spiritual the things which are carnal; even as faith cannot do the works of unbelief, nor unbelief the works of faith. But even those things which ye do according to the flesh are spiritual; for ye do all things in Jesus Christ.

Let not then any one deceive you, as indeed ye are not deceived; for ye are wholly devoted to God. For when there is no evil desire within you, which might defile and torment you, then do ye live in accordance with the will of God, and are [the servants] of Christ. Cast ye out that which defiles [539] you, who are of the [540] most holy Church of the Ephesians, which is so famous and celebrated throughout the world. They that are carnal cannot do those things which are spiritual, nor they that are spiritual the things which are carnal; even as faith cannot do the works of unbelief, nor unbelief the works of faith. But ye, being full of the Holy Spirit, do nothing according to the flesh, but all things according to the Spirit. Ye are complete in Christ Jesus, "who is the Saviour of all men, specially of them that believe." [541]

Chapter IX - Ye have given no heed to false teachers

Nevertheless, I have heard of some who have passed on from this to you, having false doctrine, whom ye did not suffer to sow among you, but stopped your ears, that ye might not receive those things which were sown by them, as being stones [542] of the temple of the Father, prepared for the building of God the Father, and drawn up on high by the instrument of Jesus Christ, which is the cross, [543] making use of the Holy Spirit as a rope, while your faith was the means by which you ascended, and your love the way which led up to God. Ye, therefore, as well as all your fellow-travellers, are God-bearers, temple-bearers, Christ-bearers, bearers of holiness, adorned in all respects with the commandments of Jesus Christ, in whom also I exult that I have been thought worthy, by means of this Epistle, to converse and rejoice with you, because with respect to your Christian life [544] ye love nothing but God only.

Nevertheless, I have heard of some who have passed in among you, holding the wicked doctrine of the strange and evil spirit; to whom ye did not allow entrance to sow their tares, but stopped your ears that ye might not receive that error which was proclaimed by them, as being persuaded that that spirit which deceives the people does not speak the things of Christ, but his own, for he is a lying spirit. But the Holy Spirit does not speak His own things, but those of Christ, and that not from himself, but from the Lord; even as the Lord also announced to us the things that He received from the Father. For, says He, "the word which ye hear is not Mine, but the Father's, who sent Me." [545] And says He of the Holy Spirit, "He shall not speak of Himself, but whatsoever things He shall hear from Me." [546] And He says of Himself to the Father, "I have," says He, "glorified Thee upon the earth; I have finished the work which, Thou gavest Me; I have manifested Thy name to men." [547] And of the Holy Ghost, "He shall glorify Me, for He receives of Mine." [548] But the spirit of deceit preaches himself, and speaks his own things, for he seeks to please himself. He glorifies himself, for he is full of arrogance. He is lying, fraudulent, soothing, flattering, treacherous, rhapsodical, trifling, inharmonious, verbose, sordid, and timorous. From his power Jesus Christ will deliver you, who has founded you upon the rock, as being chosen stones, well fitted for the divine edifice of the Father, and who are raised up on high by Christ, who was crucified for you, making use of the Holy Spirit as a rope, and being borne up by faith, while exalted by love from earth to heaven, walking in company with those that are undefiled. For, says [the Scripture], "Blessed are the undefiled in the way, who walk in the law of the Lord." [549] Now the way is unerring, namely, Jesus Christ. For, says He, "I am the way and the life." [550] And this way leads to the Father. For "no man," says He, "cometh to the Father but by Me." [551] Blessed, then, are ye who are God-bearers, spirit-bearers, temple-bearers, bearers of holiness, adorned in all respects with the commandments of Jesus Christ, being "a royal priesthood, a holy nation, a peculiar people," [552] on whose account I rejoice exceedingly, and have had the privilege, by this Epistle, of conversing with "the saints which are at Ephesus, the faithful in Christ Jesus." [553] I rejoice, therefore, over you, that ye do not give heed to vanity, and love nothing according to the flesh, but according to God.

Chapter X - Exhortations to prayer, humility, etc.

And pray ye without ceasing in behalf of other men. For there is in them hope of repentance that they may attain to God. See, [554] then, that they be instructed by your works, if in no other way. Be ye meek in response to their wrath, humble in opposition to their boasting: to their blasphemies return [555] your prayers; in contrast to their error, be ye stedfast [556] in the faith; and for their cruelty, manifest your gentleness. While we take care not to imitate their conduct, let us be found their brethren in all true kindness; and let us seek to be followers of the Lord (who ever more unjustly treated, more destitute, more condemned?), that so no plant of the devil may be found in you, but ye may remain in all holiness and sobriety in Jesus Christ, both with respect to the flesh and spirit.

And pray ye without ceasing in behalf of other men; for there is hope of the repentance, that they may attain to God. For "cannot he that falls arise again, and he that goes astray return?" [557] Permit them, then, to be instructed by you. Be ye therefore the ministers of God, and the mouth of

Christ. For thus saith the Lord, "If ye take forth the precious from the vile, ye shall be as my mouth." [558] Be ye humble in response to their wrath; oppose to their blasphemies your earnest prayers; while they go astray, stand ye stedfast in the faith. Conquer ye their harsh temper by gentleness, their passion by meekness. For "blessed are the meek;" [559] and Moses was meek above all men; [560] and David was exceeding meek. [561] Wherefore Paul exhorts as follows: "The servant of the Lord must not strive, but be gentle towards all men, apt to teach, patient, in meekness instructing those that oppose themselves." [562] Do not seek to avenge yourselves on those that injure you, for says [the Scripture], "If I have returned evil to those who returned evil to me." [563] Let us make them brethren by our kindness. For say ye to those that hate you, Ye are our brethren, that the name of the Lord may be glorified. And let us imitate the Lord, "who, when He was reviled, reviled not again;" [564] when He was crucified, He answered not; "when He suffered, He threatened not;" [565] but prayed for His enemies, "Father, forgive them; they know not what they do." [566] If any one, the more he is injured, displays the more patience, blessed is he. If any one is defrauded, if any one is despised, for the name of the Lord, he truly is the servant of Christ. Take heed that no plant of the devil be found among you, for such a plant is bitter and salt. "Watch ye, and be ye sober," [567] in Christ Jesus.

Chapter XI - An exhortation to fear God, etc.

The last times are come upon us. Let us therefore be of a reverent spirit, and fear the long-suffering of God, that it tend not to our condemnation. For let us either stand in awe of the wrath to come, or show regard for the grace which is at present displayed-- one of two things. Only [in one way or another] let us be found in Christ Jesus unto the true life. Apart from Him, let nothing attract [568] you, for whom I bear about these bonds, these spiritual jewels, by which may I arise through your prayers, of which I entreat I may always be a partaker, that I may be found in the lot of the Christians of Ephesus, who have always been of the same mind with the apostles through the power of Jesus Christ.

The last times are come upon us. Let us therefore be of a reverent spirit, and fear the long suffering of God, lest we despise the riches of His goodness and forbearance. [569] For let us either fear the wrath to come, or let us love the present joy in the life that now is; and let our present and true joy be only this, to be found in Christ Jesus, that we may truly live. Do not at any time desire so much as even to breathe apart from Him. For He is my hope; He is my boast; He is my never-failing riches, on whose account I bear about with me these bonds from Syria to Rome, these spiritual jewels, in which may I be perfected through your prayers, and become a partaker of the sufferings of Christ, and have fellowship with Him in His death, His resurrection from the dead, and His everlasting life. [570] May I attain to this, so that I may be found in the lot of the Christians of Ephesus, who have always had intercourse with the apostles by the power of Jesus Christ, with Paul, and John, and Timothy the most faithful.

Chapter XII - Praise of the Ephesians

I know both who I am, and to whom I write. I am a condemned man, ye have been the objects of mercy; I am subject to danger, ye are established in safety. Ye are the persons through [571] whom those pass that are cut off for the sake of God. Ye are initiated into the mysteries of the Gospel with Paul, the holy, the martyred, the deservedly most happy, at whose feet [572] may I be found, when I shall attain to God; who in all his Epistles makes mention of you in Christ Jesus.

I know both who I am, and to whom I write. I am the very insignificant Ignatius, who have my lot with [573] those who are exposed to danger and condemnation. But ye have been the objects of mercy, and are established in Christ. I am one delivered over [to death], but the least of all those that have been cut off for the sake of Christ, "from the blood of righteous Abel" [574] to the blood of Ignatius. Ye are initiated into the mysteries of the Gospel with Paul, the holy, the martyred, inasmuch as he was "a chosen vessel;" [575] at whose feet may I be found, and at the feet of the rest of the saints, when I shall attain to Jesus Christ, who is always mindful of you in His prayers.

Chapter XIII - Exhortation to meet together frequently for the worship of God

Take heed, then, often to come together to give thanks to God, and show forth His praise. For when ye assemble frequently in the same place, the powers of Satan are destroyed, and the destruction at which he aims [576] is prevented by the unity of your faith. Nothing is more precious than peace, by which all war, both in heaven and earth, [577] is brought to an end.

Take heed, then, often to come together to give thanks to God, and show forth His praise. For when ye come frequently together in the same place, the powers of Satan are destroyed, and his "fiery darts" [578] urging to sin fall back ineffectual. For your concord and harmonious faith prove his destruction, and the torment of his assistants. Nothing is better than that peace which is according to Christ, by which all war, both of aërial and terrestrial spirits, is brought to an end. "For we wrestle not against blood and flesh, but against principalities and powers, and against the rulers of the darkness of this world, against spiritual wickedness in heavenly places." [579]

Chapter XIV - Exhortations to faith and love

None of these things is hid from you, if ye perfectly possess that faith and love towards Christ Jesus [580] which are the beginning and the end of life. For the beginning is faith, and the end is love.[581] Now these two, being inseparably connected together, [582] are of God, while all other things which are requisite for a holy life follow after them. No man [truly] making a profession of faith sinneth; [583] nor does he that possesses love hate any one. The tree is made manifest by its fruit; [584] so those that profess themselves to be Christians shall be recognised by their conduct. For there is not now a demand for mere profession, [585] but that a man be found continuing in the power of faith to the end.

Wherefore none of the devices of the devil shall be hidden from you, if, like Paul, ye perfectly possess that faith and love towards Christ [586] which are the beginning and the end of life. The beginning of life is faith, and the end is love. And these two being inseparably connected together, do perfect the man of God; while all other things which are requisite to a holy life follow after them. No man making a profession of faith ought to sin, nor one possessed of love to hate his brother. For He that said, "Thou shalt love the Lord thy God," [587] said also, "and thy neighbour as thyself." [588] Those that profess themselves to be Christ's are known not only by what they say, but by what they practise. "For the tree is known by its fruit." [589]

Chapter XV - Exhortation to confess Christ by silence as well as speech

It is better for a man to be silent and be [a Christian], than to talk and not to be one. It is good to teach, if he who speaks also acts. There is then one Teacher, who spake and it was done; while even those things which He did in silence are worthy of the Father. He who possesses the word of Jesus, is truly able to hear even His very silence, that he may be perfect, and may both act as he speaks, and be recognised by his silence. There is nothing which is hid from God, but our very secrets are near to Him. Let us therefore do all things as those who have Him dwelling in us, that we may be His temples, [590] and He may be in us as our God, which indeed He is, and will manifest Himself before our faces. Wherefore we justly love Him.

It is better for a man to be silent and be [a Christian], than to talk and not to be one. "The kingdom of God is not in word, but in power." [591] Men "believe with the heart, and confess with the mouth," the one "unto righteousness," the other "unto salvation." [592] It is good to teach, if he who speaks also acts. For he who shall both "do and teach, the same shall be great in the kingdom." [593] Our Lord and God, Jesus Christ, the Son of the living God, first did and then taught, as Luke testifies, "whose praise is in the Gospel through all the Churches." [594] There is nothing which is hid from the Lord, but our very secrets are near to Him. Let us therefore do all things as those who have Him dwelling in us, that we may be His temples, [595] and He may be in us as God. Let Christ speak in us, even as He did in Paul. Let the Holy Spirit teach us to speak the things of Christ in like manner as He did.

Chapter XVI - The fate of false teachers

Do not err, my brethren. [596] Those that corrupt families shall not inherit the kingdom of God.[597] If, then, those who do this as respects the flesh have suffered death, how much more shall this be the case with any one who corrupts by wicked doctrine the faith of God, for which Jesus Christ was crucified! Such an one becoming defiled [in this way], shall go away into everlasting fire, and so shall every one that hearkens unto him.

Do not err, my brethren. [598] Those that corrupt families shall not inherit the kingdom of God.[599] And if those that corrupt mere human families are condemned to death, how much more shall those suffer everlasting punishment who endeavour to corrupt the Church of Christ, for which the Lord Jesus, the only-begotten Son of God, endured the cross, and submitted to death! Whosoever, "being waxen fat," [600] and "become gross," sets at nought His doctrine, shall go into hell. In like manner, every one that has received from God the power of distinguishing, and yet follows an unskilful shepherd, and receives a false opinion for the truth, shall be punished. "What communion hath light with darkness? or Christ with Belial? Or what portion hath he that believeth with an infidel? or the temple of God with idols?" [601] And in like manner say I, what communion hath truth with falsehood? or righteousness with unrighteousness? or true doctrine with that which is false?

Chapter XVII - Beware of false doctrines

For this end did the Lord suffer the ointment to be poured upon His head, [602] that He might breathe immortality into His Church. Be not ye anointed with the bad odour of the doctrine of the prince of this world; let him not lead you away captive from the life which is set before you. And why are we not all prudent, since we have received the knowledge of God, which is Jesus Christ? Why do we foolishly perish, not recognising the gift which the Lord has of a truth sent to us?

For this end did the Lord suffer the ointment to be poured upon His head, [603] that His Church might breathe forth immortality. For saith [the Scripture], "Thy name is as ointment poured forth; therefore have the virgins loved Thee; they have drawn Thee; at the odour of Thine ointments we will run after Thee." [604] Let no one be anointed with the bad odour of the doctrine of [the prince of] this world; let not the holy Church of God be led captive by his subtlety, as was the first woman. [605] Why do we not, as gifted with reason, act wisely? When we had received from Christ, and had grafted in us the faculty of judging concerning God, why do we fall headlong into ignorance? and why, through a careless neglect of acknowledging the gift which we have received, do we foolishly perish?

Chapter XVIII - The glory of the cross

Let my spirit be counted as nothing [606] for the sake of the cross, which is a stumbling-block [607] to those that do not believe, but to us salvation and life eternal. "Where is the wise man? where the disputer?" [608] Where is the boasting of those who are styled prudent? For our God, Jesus Christ, was, according to the appointment [609] of God, conceived in the womb by Mary, of the seed of David, but by the Holy Ghost. He was born and baptized, that by His passion He might purify the water.

The cross of Christ is indeed a stumbling-block to those that do not believe, but to the believing it is salvation and life eternal. "Where is the wise man? where the disputer?" [610] Where is the boasting of those who are called mighty? For the Son of God, who was begotten before time began, [611] and established all things according to the will of the Father, He was conceived in the womb of Mary, according to the appointment of God, of the seed of David, and by the Holy Ghost. For says [the Scripture], "Behold, a virgin shall be with child, and shall bring forth a son, and He shall be called Immanuel." [612] He was born and was baptized by John, that He might ratify the institution committed to that prophet.

Chapter XIX - Three celebrated mysteries

Now the virginity of Mary was hidden from the prince of this world, as was also her offspring, and the death of the Lord; three mysteries of renown, [613] which were wrought in silence by [614] God. How, then, was He manifested to the world? [615] A star shone forth in heaven above all the other stars, the light of which was inexpressible, while its novelty struck men with astonishment. And all the rest of the stars, with the sun and moon, formed a chorus to this star, and its light was exceedingly great above them all. And there was agitation felt as to whence this new spectacle came, so unlike to everything else [in the heavens]. Hence every kind of magic was destroyed, and every bond of wickedness disappeared; ignorance was removed, and the old kingdom abolished, God Himself being manifested in human form for the renewal of eternal life. And now that took a beginning which had been prepared by God. Henceforth all things were in a state of tumult, because He meditated the abolition of death.

Now the virginity of Mary was hidden from the prince of this world, as was also her offspring, and the death of the Lord; three mysteries of renown, [616] which were wrought in silence, but have been revealed to us. A star shone forth in heaven above all that were before it, and its light was inexpressible, while its novelty struck men with astonishment. And all the rest of the stars, with the sun and moon, formed a chorus to this star. It far exceeded them all in brightness, and agitation was felt as to whence this new spectacle [proceeded]. Hence worldly wisdom became folly; conjuration was seen to be mere trifling; and magic became utterly ridiculous. Every law [617] of wickedness vanished away; the darkness of ignorance was dispersed; and tyrannical authority was destroyed, God being manifested as a man, and man displaying power as God. But neither was the former a mere imagination, [618] nor did the second imply a bare humanity; [619] but the one was absolutely true, [620] and the other an economical arrangement. [621] Now that received a beginning which was perfected by God. [622] Henceforth all things were in a state of tumult, because He meditated the abolition of death.

Chapter XX - Promise of another letter

If Jesus Christ shall graciously permit me through your prayers, and if it be His will, I shall, in a second little work which I will write to you, make further manifest to you [the nature of] the dispensation of which I have begun [to treat], with respect to the new man, Jesus Christ, in His faith and in His love, in His suffering and in His resurrection. Especially [will I do this [623]] if the Lord make known to me that ye come together man by man in common through grace, individually, [624] in one faith, and in Jesus Christ, who was of the seed of David according to the flesh, being both the Son of man and the Son of God, so that ye obey the bishop and the presbytery with an undivided mind, breaking one and the same bread, which is the medicine of immortality, and the antidote to prevent us from dying, but [which causes] that we should live for ever in Jesus Christ.

Chapter XX - Exhortations to stedfastness and unity

Stand fast, brethren, in the faith of Jesus Christ, and in His love, in His passion, and in His resurrection. Do ye all come together in common, and individually, [625] through grace, in one faith of God the Father, and of Jesus Christ His only-begotten Son, and "the first-born of every creature,"[626] but of the seed of David according to the flesh, being under the guidance of the Comforter, in obedience to the bishop and the presbytery with an undivided mind, breaking one and the same bread, which is the medicine of immortality, and the antidote which prevents us from dying, but a cleansing remedy driving away evil, [which causes] that we should live in God through Jesus Christ.

Chapter XXI - Conclusion

My soul be for yours and theirs [627] whom, for the honour of God, ye have sent to Smyrna; whence also I write to you, giving thanks unto the Lord, and loving Polycarp even as I do you. Remember me, as Jesus Christ also remembered you. Pray ye for the Church which is in Syria, whence I am led bound to Rome, being the last of the faithful who are there, even as I have been thought worthy to be chosen [628] to show forth the honour of God. Farewell in God the Father, and in Jesus Christ, our common hope.

My soul be for yours and theirs [629] whom, for the honour of God, ye have sent to Smyrna; whence also I write to you, giving thanks to the Lord, and loving Polycarp even as I do you. Remember me, as Jesus Christ also remembers you, who is blessed for evermore. Pray ye for the Church of Antioch which is in Syria, whence I am led bound to Rome, being the last of the faithful that are there, who [630] yet have been thought worthy to carry these chains to the honour of God. Fare ye well in God the Father, and the Lord Jesus Christ, our common hope, and in the Holy Ghost. Fare ye well. Amen. Grace [be with you]. [631]

Footnotes:

485. Literally, "before the ages."
486. These words may agree with "glory," but are better applied to the "Church."
487. Literally, "before the ages."
488. These words may agree with "glory," but are better applied to the "Church."
489. Some read, as in the shorter recension, "grace."
490. Literally, "imitators;" comp. Eph. v. 1.
491. Comp. in the Greek, 2 Tim. i. 6.
492. Eph. v. 2.
493. This is wanting in the Greek.
494. Literally, "since therefore," without any apodosis.
495. Or, "unspeakably beloved."
496. Literally, "imitators;" comp. Eph. v. 1.
497. Comp. in the Greek, 2 Tim. i. 6.
498. Eph. v. 2.
499. This is wanting in the Greek.
500. Or, "unspeakably beloved."
501. Or, "our most blessed deacon in all things pertaining to God."
502. Literally, "pattern."
503. Comp. 1 Cor. xvi. 18, etc.
504. Comp. 1 Cor. xvi. 18, etc.
505. 1 Cor. i. 10.
506. Literally, "pattern."
507. Comp. 1 Cor. xvi. 18, etc.
508. Comp. 2 Tim. i. 16.
509. Comp. 1 Cor. xvi. 18, etc.
510. 1 Cor. i. 10.
511. Comp. Philem. 8, 9.
512. Comp. Philem. 8, 9.
513. John viii. 29.
514. 1 Cor. xi. 1.
515. Literally, "according to God."
516. Literally, "receiving a union to God in oneness."
517. John xvii. 11, 12.
518. Matt. xviii. 19.
519. Or, "already."
520. Prov. iii. 34; Jas. iv. 6; 1 Pet. v. 5.
521. Some read, "mixed up with."
522. Matt. xviii. 19.

523. Literally, "in the assembly of sacrifices."
524. Matt. vii. 15.
525. Or, "believeth not" (John iii. 36).
526. Prov. iii. 34; Jas. iv. 6; 1 Pet. v. 5.
527. That is, "showing forbearance."
528. Comp. Matt. xxiv. 25.
529. Or, "heresy."
530. Comp. Matt. xxiv. 25.
531. Prov. xxii. 29, after LXX.
532. Eph. iv. 4.
533. Eph. iv. 5, 6.
534. This clause is wanting in the Greek, and has been supplied from the ancient Latin version.
535. Prov. x. 25, Prov. xi. 3.
536. Isa. lvi. 10
537. Or, "before the ages."
538. John i. 14.
539. It is difficult to translate περίψημα in this and similar passages; comp. 1 Cor. iv. 13.
540. Literally, "and the."
541. 1 Tim. iv. 10.
542. Comp. 1 Pet. ii. 5.
543. Comp. John xii. 32.
544. Literally, "according to the other life."
545. John xiv. 24.
546. John xvi. 13.
547. John xvii. 4, 6.
548. John xvi. 14.
549. Ps. cxix. 1.
550. John xiv. 6.
551. John xiv. 6.
552. 1 Pet. ii. 9.
553. Eph. i. 1.
554. Literally, "permit."
555. The verb is here omitted in the original.
556. Comp. Col. i. 23.
557. Jer. viii. 4.
558. Jer. xv. 19.
559. Matt. v. 4.
560. Num. xii. 3.
561. Ps. cxxxi. 2.
562. 2 Tim. ii. 24, 25.
563. Ps. vii. 4.
564. 1 Pet. ii. 23.
565. 1 Pet. ii. 23.
566. Luke xxiii. 34.
567. 1 Pet. iv. 7.
568. Literally, "let nothing become you."
569. Rom. ii. 4.
570. Phil. iii. 10.
571. Literally, "ye are the passage of."
572. Literally, "footsteps."
573. Literally, "am like to."
574. Matt. xxiii. 35.
575. Acts ix. 15.
576. Literally, "his destruction."
577. Literally, "of heavenly and earthly things."
578. Eph. vi. 16.
579. Eph. vi. 12.
580. 1 Tim. i. 14.
581. 1 Tim. i. 5.
582. Literally, "being in unity."
583. Comp. 1 John iii. 7.
584. Matt. xii. 33.
585. Literally, "there is not now the work of profession."
586. 1 Tim. i. 14.
587. Luke x. 27.
588. Luke x. 27.
589. Matt. xii. 33.
590. 1 Cor. vi. 19.
591. 1 Cor. iv. 20.
592. Rom. x. 10.
593. Matt. v. 19.
594. 2 Cor. viii. 18.
595. 1 Cor. vi. 19.
596. Comp. Jas. i. 16.
597. 1 Cor. vi. 9, 10.
598. Comp. Jas. i. 16.
599. 1 Cor. vi. 9, 10.
600. Deut. xxxii. 15.
601. 2 Cor. vi. 14-16.
602. Comp. John xii. 7.
603. Comp. John xii. 7.
604. Cant. i. 3, 4.
605. Literally, "before the ages."
606. Again, περίψημα, translated "offscouring," 1 Cor. iv. 13.
607. Comp. 1 Cor. i. 18.
608. 1 Cor. i. 20.
609. Or, "economy," or "dispensation." Comp. Col. i. 25; 1 Tim. i. 4.
610. 1 Cor. i. 20.
611. Literally, "before the ages."
612. Isa. vii. 14; Matt. i. 23.
613. Literally, "of noise."
614. Or, "in the silence of God"-- divine silence.
615. Literally, "to the ages."
616. Literally, "of noise."
617. Some read, "bond."
618. Literally, "opinion."
619. Literally, "bareness."
620. Literally, "truth."
621. Literally, "an economy."
622. Or, "that which was perfect received a beginning from God."
623. The punctuation and meaning are here doubtful.
624. Literally, "by name."
625. Literally, "by name."
626. Col. i. 15.

627. Some render, "May I, in my turn, be the means of refreshing you and those," etc.

628. Literally, "to be found for."

629. Some render, "May I, in my turn, be the means of refreshing you and those," etc.

630. Some read, "even as."

631. Some omit, "Grace be with you."

The Epistle of Ignatius to the Magnesians Shorter and Longer Versions

Ignatius, who is also called Theophorus, to the [Church] blessed in the grace of God the Father, in Jesus Christ our Saviour, in whom I salute the Church which is at Magnesia, near the Mæander, and wish it abundance of happiness in God the Father, and in Jesus Christ.

Ignatius, who is also called Theophorus, to the [Church] blessed in the grace of God the Father, in Jesus Christ our Saviour, in whom I salute the Church which is at Magnesia, near the Mæander, and wish it abundance of happiness in God the Father, and in Jesus Christ, our Lord, in whom may you have abundance of happiness.

Chapter I - Reason of writing the epistle

Having been informed of your godly [632] love, so well-ordered, I rejoiced greatly, and determined to commune with you in the faith of Jesus Christ. For as one who has been thought worthy of the most honourable of all names, [633] in those bonds which I bear about, I commend the Churches, in which I pray for a union both of the flesh and spirit of Jesus Christ, the constant source of our life, and of faith and love, to which nothing is to be preferred, but especially of Jesus and the Father, in whom, if we endure all the assaults of the prince of this world, and escape them, we shall enjoy God.

Having been informed of your godly [634] love, so well-ordered, I rejoiced greatly, and determined to commune with you in the faith of Jesus Christ. For as one who has been thought worthy of a divine and desirable name, in those bonds which I bear about, I commend the Churches, in which I pray for a union both of the flesh and spirit of Jesus Christ, "who is the Saviour of all men, but specially of them that believe;" [635] by whose blood ye were redeemed; by whom ye have known God, or rather have been known by Him; [636] in whom enduring, ye shall escape all the assaults of this world: for "He is faithful, who will not suffer you to be tempted above that which ye are able." [637]

Chapter II - I rejoice in your messengers

Since, then, I have had the privilege of seeing you, through Damas your most worthy bishop, and through your worthy presbyters Bassus and Apollonius, and through my fellow-servant the deacon Sotio, whose friendship may I ever enjoy, inasmuch as he is subject to the bishop as to the grace of God, and to the presbytery as to the law of Jesus Christ, [I now write [638] to you].

Since, then, I have had the privilege of seeing you, through Damas your most worthy [639] bishop, and through your worthy [640] presbyters Bassus and Apollonius, and through my fellow-servant the deacon Sotio, whose friendship may I ever enjoy, [641] inasmuch as he, by the grace of God, is subject to the bishop and presbytery, in the law of Jesus Christ, [I now write [642] to you].

Chapter III - Honour your youthful bishop

Now it becomes you also not to treat your bishop too familiarly on account of his youth, [643] but to yield him all reverence, having respect to [644] the power of God the Father, as I have known even holy presbyters do, not judging rashly, from the manifest youthful appearance [645] [of their bishop], but as being themselves prudent in God, submitting to him, or rather not to him, but to the Father of Jesus Christ, the bishop of us all. It is therefore fitting that you should, after no hypocritical fashion, obey [your bishop], in honour of Him who has willed us [so to do], since he that does not so deceives not [by such conduct] the bishop that is visible, but seeks to mock Him that is invisible. And all such conduct has reference not to man, [646] but to God, who knows all secrets.

Now it becomes you also not to despise the age of your bishop, but to yield him all reverence, according to the will of God the Father, as I have known even holy presbyters do, not having regard to the manifest youth [of their bishop], but to his knowledge in God; inasmuch as "not the ancient are [necessarily] wise, nor do the aged understand prudence; but there is a spirit in men." [647] For Daniel the wise, at twelve years of age, became possessed of the divine Spirit, and convicted the elders, who in vain carried their grey hairs, of being false accusers, and of lusting after the beauty of another man's wife. [648] Samuel also, when he was but a little child, reproved Eli, who was ninety years old, for giving honour to his sons rather than to God. [649] In like manner, Jeremiah also received this message from God, "Say not, I am a child." [650] Solomon too, and Josiah, [exemplified the same thing.] The former, being made king at twelve years of age, gave that terrible and difficult judgment in the case of the two women concerning their children. [651] The latter, coming to the throne when eight years old [652] cast down the altars and temples [of the idols], and burned down the groves, for they were dedicated to demons, and not to God. And he slew the false priests, as the corrupters and deceivers of men, and not the worshippers of the Deity. Wherefore youth is not to be despised when it is devoted to God. But he is to be despised who is of a wicked mind, although he be old, and full of wicked days. [653] Timothy the Christ-bearer was young, but hear what his teacher writes to him: "Let no man despise thy youth, but be thou an example of the believers in word and in conduct." [654] It is becoming, therefore, that ye also should be obedient to your bishop, and contradict him in nothing; for it is a fearful thing to contradict any such person. For no one does [by such conduct] deceive him that is visible, but does [in reality] seek to mock Him that is invisible, who, however, cannot be mocked by any one. And every such act has respect not to man, but to God. For God says to Samuel, "They have not mocked thee, but Me." [655] And Moses declares, "For their murmuring is not against us, but against the Lord God." [656] No one of those has, [in fact,] remained unpunished, who rose up against their superiors. For Dathan and Abiram did not speak against the law, but against Moses, [657] and were cast down alive into Hades. Korah also, [658] and the two hundred and fifty who conspired with him against Aaron, were destroyed by fire. Absalom, again, [659] who had slain his brother, became suspended on a tree, and had his evil-designing heart thrust through with darts. In like manner was Abeddadan [660] beheaded for the same reason. Uzziah,[661] when he presumed to oppose the priests and the priesthood, was smitten with leprosy. Saul also was dishonoured, [662] because he did not wait for Samuel the high priest. It behoves you, therefore, also to reverence your superiors.

Chapter IV - Some wickedly act independently of the bishop

It is fitting, then, not only to be called Christians, but to be so in reality: as some indeed give one the title of bishop, but do all things without him. Now such persons seem to me to be not possessed of a good conscience, seeing they are not stedfastly gathered together according to the commandment.

It is fitting, then, not only to be called Christians, but to be so in reality. For it is not the being called so, but the being really so, that renders a man blessed. To those who indeed talk of the bishop, but do all things without him, will He who is the true and first Bishop, and the only High Priest by nature, declare, "Why call ye Me Lord, and do not the things which I say?" [663] For such persons seem to me not possessed of a good conscience, but to be simply dissemblers and hypocrites.

Chapter V - Death is the fate of all such

Seeing, then, all things have an end, these two things are simultaneously set before us--death and life; and every one shall go unto his own place. For as there are two kinds of coins, the one of God, the other of the world, and each of these has its special character stamped upon it, [so is it also here.] [664] The unbelieving are of this world; but the believing have, in love, the character of God the Father by Jesus Christ, by whom, if we are not in readiness to die into His passion, [665] His life is not in us.

Seeing, then, all things have an end, and there is set before us life upon our observance [of God's precepts], but death as the result of disobedience, and every one, according to the choice he makes, shall go to his own place, let us flee from death, and make choice of life. For I remark, that two different characters are found among men--the one true coin, the other spurious. The truly devout man is the right kind of coin, stamped by God Himself. The ungodly man, again, is false coin, unlawful, spurious, counterfeit, wrought not by God, but by the devil. I do not mean to say that there are two different human natures, but that there is one humanity, sometimes belonging to God, and sometimes to the devil. If any one is truly religious, he is a man of God; but if he is irreligious, he is a man of the devil, made such, not by nature, but by his own choice. The unbelieving bear the image of the prince of wickedness. The believing possess the image of their Prince, God the Father, and Jesus Christ, through whom, if we are not in readiness to die for the truth into His passion, [666] His life is not in us.

Chapter VI - Preserve harmony

Since therefore I have, in the persons before mentioned, beheld the whole multitude of you in faith and love, I exhort you to study to do all things with a divine harmony, [667] while your bishop presides in the place of God, and your presbyters in the place of the assembly of the apostles, along with your deacons, who are most dear to me, and are entrusted with the ministry of Jesus Christ, who was with the Father before the beginning of time, [668] and in the end was revealed. Do ye all then, imitating the same divine conduct, [669] pay respect to one another, and let no one look upon his neighbour after the flesh, but do ye continually love each other in Jesus Christ. Let nothing exist among you that may divide you; but be ye united with your bishop, and those that preside over you, as a type and evidence of your immortality. [670]

Since therefore I have, in the persons before mentioned, beheld the whole multitude of you in faith and love, I exhort you to study to do all things with a divine harmony, [671] while your bishop presides in the place of God, and your presbyters in the place of the assembly of the apostles, along with your deacons, who are most dear to me, and are entrusted with the ministry of Jesus Christ. He, being begotten by the Father before the beginning of time, [672] was God the Word, the only-begotten Son, and remains the same for ever; for "of His kingdom there shall be no end," [673] says Daniel the prophet. Let us all therefore love one another in harmony, and let no one look upon his neighbour according to the flesh, but in Christ Jesus. Let nothing exist among you which may divide you; but be ye united with your bishop, being through him subject to God in Christ.

Chapter VII - Do nothing without the bishop and presbyters

As therefore the Lord did nothing without the Father, being united to Him, neither by Himself nor by the apostles, so neither do ye anything without the bishop and presbyters. Neither endeavour that anything appear reasonable and proper to yourselves apart; but being come together into the same place, let there be one prayer, one supplication, one mind, one hope, in love and in joy undefiled. There is one Jesus Christ, than whom nothing is more excellent. Do ye therefore all run together as into one temple of God, as to one altar, as to one Jesus Christ, who came forth from one Father, and is with and has gone to one.

As therefore the Lord does nothing without the Father, for says He, "I can of mine own self do nothing," [674] so do ye, neither presbyter, nor deacon, nor layman, do anything without the bishop. Nor let anything appear commendable to you which is destitute of his approval. [675] For every such thing is sinful, and opposed [to the will of] God. Do ye all come together into the same place for prayer. Let there be one common supplication, one mind, one hope, with faith unblameable in Christ Jesus, than which nothing is more excellent. Do ye all, as one man, run together into the temple of God, as unto one altar, to one Jesus Christ, the High Priest of the unbegotten God.

Chapter VIII - Caution against false doctrines

Be not deceived with strange doctrines, nor with old fables, which are unprofitable. For if we still live according to the Jewish law, we acknowledge that we have not received grace. For the divinest prophets lived according to Christ Jesus. On this account also they were persecuted, being inspired by His grace to fully convince the unbelieving that there is one God, who has manifested Himself by Jesus Christ His Son, who is His eternal Word, not proceeding forth from silence, [676] and who in all things pleased Him that sent Him.

Be not deceived with strange doctrines, "nor give heed to fables and endless genealogies," [677] and things in which the Jews make their boast. "Old things are passed away: behold, all things have become new." [678] For if we still live according to the Jewish law, and the circumcision of the flesh, we deny that we have received grace. For the divinest prophets lived according to Jesus Christ. On this account also they were persecuted, being inspired by grace to fully convince the unbelieving that there is one God, the Almighty, who has manifested Himself by Jesus Christ His Son, who is His Word, not spoken, but essential. For He is not the voice of an articulate utterance, but a substance begotten by divine power, who has in all things pleased Him that sent Him. [679]

Chapter IX - Let us live with Christ

If, therefore, those who were brought up in the ancient order of things [680] have come to the possession of a new [681] hope, no longer observing the Sabbath, but living in the observance [682] of the Lord's Day, on which also our life has sprung up again by Him and by His death--whom some deny, by which mystery we have obtained faith, [683] and therefore endure, that we may be found the disciples of Jesus Christ, our only Master--how shall we be able to live apart from Him, whose disciples the prophets themselves in the Spirit did wait for Him as their Teacher? And therefore He whom they rightly waited for, being come, raised them from the dead. [684]

If, then, those who were conversant with the ancient Scriptures came to newness of hope, expecting the coming of Christ, as the Lord teaches us when He says, "If ye had believed Moses, ye would have believed Me, for he wrote of Me;" [685] and again, "Your father Abraham rejoiced to see My day, and he saw it, and was glad; for before Abraham was, I am;" [686] how shall we be able to live without Him? The prophets were His servants, and foresaw Him by the Spirit, and waited for Him as their Teacher, and expected Him as their Lord and Saviour, saying, "He will come and save us." [687] Let us therefore no longer keep the Sabbath after the Jewish manner, and rejoice in days of idleness; for "he that does not work, let him not eat." [688] For say the [holy] oracles, "In the sweat of thy face shalt thou eat thy bread." [689] But let every one of you keep the Sabbath after a spiritual manner, rejoicing in meditation on the law, not in relaxation of the body, admiring the workmanship of God, and not eating things prepared the day before, nor using lukewarm drinks, and walking within a prescribed space, nor finding delight in dancing and plaudits which have no sense in them. [690] And after the observance of the Sabbath, let every friend of Christ keep the Lord's Day as a festival, the resurrection-day, the queen and chief of all the days [of the week]. Looking forward to this, the prophet declared, "To the end, for the eighth day," [691] on which our life both sprang up again, and the victory over death was obtained in Christ, whom the children of perdition, the enemies of the Saviour, deny, "whose god is their belly, who mind earthly things," [692] who are "lovers of pleasure, and not lovers of God, having a form of godliness, but denying the power thereof." [693] These make merchandise of Christ, corrupting His word, and giving up Jesus to sale: they are corrupters of women, and covetous of other men's possessions, swallowing up wealth [694] insatiably; from whom may ye be delivered by the mercy of God through our Lord Jesus Christ!

Chapter X - Beware of Judaizing

Let us not, therefore, be insensible to His kindness. For were He to reward us according to our works, we should cease to be. Therefore, having become His disciples, let us learn to live according to the principles of Christianity. [695] For whosoever is called by any other name besides this, is not of God. Lay aside, therefore, the evil, the old, the sour leaven, and be ye changed into the new leaven, which is Jesus Christ. Be ye salted in Him, lest any one among you should be corrupted, since by your savour ye shall be convicted. It is absurd to profess [696] Christ Jesus, and to Judaize. For Christianity did not embrace [697] Judaism, but Judaism Christianity, that so every tongue which believeth might be gathered together to God.

Let us not, therefore, be insensible to His kindness. For were He to reward us according to our works, we should cease to be. For "if Thou, Lord, shalt mark iniquities, O Lord, who shall stand?" [698] Let us therefore prove ourselves worthy of that name which we have received. For whosoever is called by any other name besides this, he is not of God; for he has not received the prophecy which speaks thus concerning us: "The people shall be called by a new name, which the Lord shall name them, and shall be a holy people." [699] This was first fulfilled in Syria; for "the disciples were called Christians at Antioch," [700] when Paul and Peter were laying the foundations of the Church. Lay aside, therefore, the evil, the old, the corrupt leaven, [701] and be ye changed into the new leaven of grace. Abide in Christ, that the stranger [702] may not have dominion over you. It is absurd to speak of Jesus Christ with the tongue, and to cherish in the mind a Judaism which has now come to an end. For where there is Christianity there cannot be Judaism. For Christ is one, in whom every nation that believes, and every tongue that confesses, is gathered unto God. And those that were of a stony heart have become the children of Abraham, the friend of God; [703] and in his seed all those have been blessed [704] who were ordained to eternal life [705] in Christ.

Chapter XI - I write these things to warn you

These things [I address to you], my beloved, not that I know any of you to be in such a state;[706] but, as less than any of you, I desire to guard you beforehand, that ye fall not upon the hooks of vain doctrine, but that ye attain to full assurance in regard to the birth, and passion, and resurrection which took place in the time of the government of Pontius Pilate, being truly and certainly accomplished by Jesus Christ, who is our hope, [707] from which may no one of you ever be turned aside.

These things [I address to you], my beloved, not that I know any of you to be in such a state;[708] but, as less than any of you, I desire to guard you beforehand, that ye fall not upon the hooks of vain doctrine, but that ye may rather attain to a full assurance in Christ, who was begotten by the Father before all ages, but was afterwards born of the Virgin Mary without any intercourse with man. He also lived a holy life, and healed every kind of sickness and disease among the people, and wrought signs and wonders for the benefit of men; and to those who had fallen into the error of polytheism He made known the one and only true God, His Father, and underwent the passion, and endured the cross at the hands of the Christ-killing Jews, under Pontius Pilate the governor and Herod the king. He also died, and rose again, and ascended into the heavens to Him that sent Him, and is sat down at His right hand, and shall come at the end of the world, with His Father's glory, to judge the living and the dead, and to render to every one according to his works. [709] He who knows these things with a full assurance, and believes them, is happy; even as ye are now the lovers of God and of Christ, in the full assurance of our hope, from which may no one of us [710] ever be turned aside!

Chapter XII - Ye are superior to me

May I enjoy you in all respects, if indeed I be worthy! For though I am bound, I am not worthy to be compared to any of you that are at liberty. I know that ye are not puffed up, for ye have Jesus Christ in yourselves. And all the more when I commend you, I know that ye cherish modesty [711] of spirit; as it is written, "The righteous man is his own accuser." [712]

May I enjoy you in all respects, if indeed I be worthy! For though I am bound, I am not worthy to be compared to one of you that are at liberty. I know that ye are not puffed up, for ye have Jesus in yourselves. And all the more when I commend you, I know that ye cherish modesty[713] of spirit; as it is written, "The righteous man is his own accuser;" [714] and again, "Declare thou first thine iniquities, that thou mayest be justified;" [715] and again, "When ye shall have done all things that are commanded you, say, We are unprofitable servants;" [716] "for that which is highly esteemed among men is abomination in the sight of God." [717] For says [the Scripture], "God be merciful to me a sinner." [718] Therefore those great ones, Abraham and Job, [719] styled themselves "dust and ashes" [720] before God. And David says, "Who am I before Thee, O Lord, that Thou hast glorified me hitherto?" [721] And Moses, who was "the meekest of all men," [722] saith to God, "I am of a feeble voice, and of a slow tongue." [723] Be ye therefore also of a humble spirit, that ye may be exalted; for "he that abaseth himself shall be exalted, and he that exalteth himself shall be abased." [724]

Chapter XIII - Be established in faith and unity

Study, therefore, to be established in the doctrines of the Lord and the apostles, that so all things, whatsoever ye do, may prosper both in the flesh and spirit; in faith and love; in the Son, and in the Father, and in the Spirit; in the beginning and in the end; with your most admirable bishop, and the well-compacted spiritual crown of your presbytery, and the deacons who are according to God. Be ye subject to the bishop, and to one another, as Jesus Christ to the Father, according to the flesh, and the apostles to Christ, and to the Father, and to the Spirit; that so there may be a union both fleshly and spiritual.

Study, therefore, to be established in the doctrines of the Lord and the apostles, that so all things, whatsoever ye do, may prosper, both in the flesh and spirit, in faith and love, with your most admirable bishop, and the well-compacted [725] spiritual crown of your presbytery, and the deacons who are according to God. Be ye subject to the bishop, and to one another, as Christ to the Father, that there may be a unity according to God among you.

Chapter XIV - Your prayers requested

Knowing as I do that ye are full of God, I have but briefly exhorted you. Be mindful of me in your prayers, that I may attain to God; and of the Church which is in Syria, whence I am not worthy to derive my name: for I stand in need of your united prayer in God, and your love, that the Church which is in Syria may be deemed worthy of being refreshed [726] by your Church.

Knowing as I do that ye are full of all good, I have but briefly exhorted you in the love of Jesus Christ. Be mindful of me in your prayers, that I may attain to God; and of the Church which is in Syria, of whom I am not worthy to be called bishop. For I stand in need of your united prayer in God, and of your love, that the Church which is in Syria may be deemed worthy, by your good order, of being edified [727] in Christ.

Chapter XV - Salutations

The Ephesians from Smyrna (whence I also write to you), who are here for the glory of God, as ye also are, who have in all things refreshed me, salute you, along with Polycarp, the bishop of the Smyrnæans. The rest of the Churches, in honour of Jesus Christ, also salute you. Fare ye well in the harmony of God, ye who have obtained the inseparable Spirit, who is Jesus Christ.

The Ephesians from Smyrna (whence I also write to you), who are here for the glory of God, as ye also are, who have in all things refreshed me, salute you, as does also Polycarp. The rest of the Churches, in honour of Jesus Christ, also salute you. Fare ye well in harmony, ye who have obtained the inseparable Spirit, in Christ Jesus, by the will of God.

Footnotes:

632. Literally, "according to God."
633. Literally, "of the most God-becoming name," referring either to the appellation "Theophorus," or to that of "martyr" or "confessor."
634. Literally, "according to God."
635. 1 Tim. iv. 10.
636. Comp. Gal. iv. 9.
637. 1 Cor. x. 13.
638. The apodosis is here wanting in the original, but must evidently be supplied in some such way as above.
639. Literally, "worthy of God."
640. Literally, "worthy of God."

The Apostolic Fathers

641. Literally, "whom may I enjoy."
642. The apodosis is here wanting in the original, but must evidently be supplied in some such way as above.
643. Literally, "to use the age of your bishop."
644. Literally, "according to."
645. Literally, "youthful condition."
646. Literally, "to flesh."
647. Job xxxii. 8, 9.
648. Susanna (Apoc.).
649. 1 Sam. iii. 1.
650. Jer. i. 7.
651. 1 Kings iii. 16.
652. 2 Kings xxii., xxiii.
653. Susanna 52 (Apoc.).
654. 1 Tim. iv. 12.
655. 1 Sam. viii. 7.
656. Ex. xvi. 8.
657. Num. xvi. 1.
658. Num. xvi. 31.
659. 2 Sam. xviii. 14.
660. Sheba is referred to under this name: see 2 Sam. xx. 22.
661. 2 Chron. xxvi. 20.
662. 1 Sam. xiii. 11.
663. Luke vi. 46.
664. The apodosis is wanting in the original, and some prefer finding it in the following sentence.
665. Or, "after the likeness of His passion."
666. Or, "after the likeness of His passion."
667. Literally, "in harmony of God."
668. Literally, "before the ages."
669. Literally, "receiving the like manners of God."
670. The meaning is here doubtful.
671. Literally, "in harmony of God."
672. Literally, "before the ages."
673. Dan. ii. 44, Dan. vii. 14, 27.
674. John v. 30.
675. Or, "contrary to his judgment."
676. Some have argued that the Gnostic Στγή, silence, is here referred to, and have consequently inferred that this epistle could not have been written by Ignatius.
677. 1 Tim. i. 4.
678. 2 Cor. v. 17.
679. Some read ὑποστήσαντι, "that gave Him His hypostasis, or substance."
680. Literally, "in old things."
681. Or, "newness of."
682. Or, "according to."
683. Literally, "we have received to believe."
684. Comp. Matt. xxvii. 52.
685. John v. 46.
686. John viii. 56, 58.
687. Isa. xxxv. 4.
688. 2 Thess. iii. 10.
689. Gen. iii. 19.
690. Reference is here made to well-known Jewish opinions and practices with respect to the Sabbath. The Talmud fixes 2000 cubits as the space lawful to be traversed. Philo (De Therap.) refers to the dancing, etc.
691. Ps. vi., Ps. xii. (inscrip.). N.B.-- The reference is to the title of these two psalms, as rendered by the LXX. Εἰς τὸ τέλος ὑπὲρ τῆς ὀγδόης.
692. Phil. iii. 18, 19.
693. 2 Tim. iii. 4.
694. Literally, "whirlpools of wealth."
695. Literally, "according to Christianity."
696. Some read, "to name."
697. Literally, "believe into," merge into.
698. Ps. cxxx. 3.
699. Isa. lxii. 2, 12.
700. Acts xi. 26.
701. 1 Cor. v. 7.
702. Or, "enemy."
703. Matt. iii. 9; Isa. xli. 8; Jas. ii. 23. Some read, "children of God, friends of Abraham."
704. Gen. xxviii. 14.
705. Acts xiii. 48.
706. i.e., addicted to the error of Judaizing.
707. 1 Tim. i. 1.
708. i.e., addicted to the error of Judaizing.
709. 2 Tim. iv. 1; Rom. ii. 6.
710. Some read, "of you."
711. Literally, "are reverent."
712. Prov. xviii. 17. (LXX).
713. Literally, "are reverent."
714. Prov. xviii. 17. (LXX).
715. Isa. xliii. 26.
716. Luke xvii. 10.
717. Luke xvi. 15.
718. Luke xviii. 13.
719. Some read, "Jacob."
720. Gen. xviii. 27; Job xxx. 19.
721. 1 Chron. xvii. 16.
722. Num. xii. 3.
723. Ex. iv. 10.
724. Luke xiv. 11.
725. Literally, "well-woven."
726. Literally, "of being sprinkled with dew."
727. Literally, "of being fed as by a shepherd."

The Epistle of Ignatius to the Trallians Shorter and Longer Versions

Ignatius, who is also called Theophorus, to the holy Church which is at Tralles, in Asia, beloved of God, the Father of Jesus Christ, elect, and worthy of God, possessing peace through the flesh, and blood, and passion of Jesus Christ, who is our hope, through our rising again to Him, [728] which also I salute in its fulness, [729] and in the apostolical character, [730] and wish abundance of happiness.

Ignatius, who is also called Theophorus, to the holy Church which is at Tralles, beloved by God the Father, and Jesus Christ, elect, and worthy of God, possessing peace through the flesh and Spirit of Jesus Christ, who is our hope, in His passion by the cross and death, and in His resurrection, which also I salute in its fulness, [731] and in the apostolical character, [732] and wish abundance of happiness.

Chapter I - Acknowledgment of their excellence

I know that ye possess an unblameable and sincere mind in patience, and that not only in present practice, [733] but according to inherent nature, as Polybius your bishop has shown me, who has come to Smyrna by the will of God and Jesus Christ, and so sympathized in the joy which I, who am bound in Christ Jesus, possess, that I beheld your whole multitude in him. Having therefore received through him the testimony of your good-will, according to God, I gloried to find you, as I knew you were, the followers of God.

I know that ye possess an unblameable and sincere mind in patience, and that not only for present use, [734] but as a permanent possession, as Polybius your bishop has shown me, who has come to Smyrna by the will of God the Father, and the Lord Jesus Christ, His Son, with the co-operation of the Spirit, and so sympathized in the joy which I, who am bound in Christ Jesus, possess, that I beheld your whole multitude in Him. Having therefore received through him the testimony of your good-will according to God, I gloried to find that you were the followers of Jesus Christ the Saviour.

Chapter II - Be subject to the bishop, etc.

For, since ye are subject to the bishop as to Jesus Christ, ye appear to me to live not after the manner of men, but according to Jesus Christ, who died for us, in order, by believing in His death, ye may escape from death. It is therefore necessary that, as ye indeed do, so without the bishop ye should do nothing, but should also be subject to the presbytery, as to the apostle of Jesus Christ, who is our hope, in whom, if we live, we shall [at last] be found. It is fitting also that the deacons, as being [the ministers] of the mysteries of Jesus Christ, should in every respect be pleasing to all.[735] For they are not ministers of meat and drink, but servants of the Church of God. They are bound, therefore, to avoid all grounds of accusation [against them], as they would do fire.

Be ye subject to the bishop as to the Lord, for "he watches for your souls, as one that shall give account to God." [736] Wherefore also, ye appear to me to live not after the manner of men, but according to Jesus Christ, who died for us, in order that, by believing in His death, ye may by baptism be made partakers of His resurrection. It is therefore necessary, whatsoever things ye do, to do nothing without the bishop. And be ye subject also to the presbytery, as to the apostles of Jesus Christ, who is our hope, in whom, if we live, we shall be found in Him. It behoves you also, in every way, to please the deacons, who are [ministers] of the mysteries of Christ Jesus; for they are not ministers of meat and drink, but servants of the Church of God. They are bound, therefore, to avoid all grounds of accusation [against them], as they would a burning fire. Let them, then, prove themselves to be such.

Chapter III - Honour the deacons, etc.

In like manner, let all reverence the deacons as an appointment [737] of Jesus Christ, and the bishop as Jesus Christ, who is the Son of the Father, and the presbyters as the sanhedrim of God, and assembly of the apostles. Apart from these, there is no Church. [738] Concerning all this, I am persuaded that ye are of the same opinion. For I have received the manifestation [739] of your love, and still have it with me, in your bishop, whose very appearance is highly instructive, [740] and his meekness of itself a power; whom I imagine even the ungodly must reverence, seeing they are [741] also pleased that I do not spare myself. But shall I, when permitted to write on this point, reach such a height of self-esteem, that though being a condemned [742] man, I should issue commands to you as if I were an apostle?

And do ye reverence them as Christ Jesus, of whose place they are the keepers, even as the bishop is the representative of the Father of all things, and the presbyters are the sanhedrim of God, and assembly [743] of the apostles of Christ. Apart from these there is no elect Church, no congregation of holy ones, no assembly of saints. I am persuaded that ye also are of this opinion. For I have received the manifestation [744] of your love, and still have it with me, in your bishop, whose very appearance is highly instructive, and his meekness of itself a power; whom I imagine even the ungodly must reverence. Loving you as I do, I avoid writing in any severer strain to you, that I may not seem harsh to any, or wanting [in tenderness]. I am indeed bound for the sake of Christ, but I am not yet worthy of Christ. But when I am perfected, perhaps I shall then become so. I do not issue orders like an apostle.

Chapter IV - I have need of humility

I have great knowledge in God, [745] but I restrain myself, lest I should perish through boasting. For now it is needful for me to be the more fearful; and not give heed to those that puff me up. For they that speak to me [in the way of commendation] scourge me. For I do indeed desire to suffer, but I know not if I be worthy to do so. For this longing, though it is not manifest to many, all the more vehemently assails me. [746] I therefore have need of meekness, by which the prince of this world is brought to nought.

But I measure myself, that I may not perish through boasting: but it is good to glory in the Lord. [747] And even though I were established [748] in things pertaining to God, yet then would it befit me to be the more fearful, and not give heed to those that vainly puff me up. For those that commend me scourge me. [I do indeed desire to suffer [749]], but I know not if I be worthy to do so. For the envy of the wicked one is not visible to many, but it wars against me. I therefore have need of meekness, by which the devil, the prince of this world, is brought to nought.

Chapter V - I will not teach you profound doctrines

Am I not able to write to you of heavenly things? But I fear to do so, lest I should inflict injury on you who are but babes [in Christ]. Pardon me in this respect, lest, as not being able to receive [such doctrines], ye should be strangled by them. For even I, though I am bound [for Christ], yet am not on that account able to understand heavenly things, and the places [750] of the angels, and their gatherings under their respective princes, things visible and invisible. Without reference to such abstruse subjects, I am still but a learner [in other respects [751]]; for many things are wanting to us, that we come not short of God.

For might [752] not I write to you things more full of mystery? But I fear to do so, lest I should inflict injury on you who are but babes [in Christ]. Pardon me in this respect, lest, as not being able to receive their weighty import, [753] ye should be strangled by them. For even I, though I am bound [for Christ], and am able to understand heavenly things, the angelic orders, and the different sorts[754] of angels and hosts, the distinctions between powers and dominions, and the diversities between thrones and authorities, the mightiness of the Æons, and the pre-eminence of the cherubim and seraphim, the sublimity of the spirit, the kingdom of the Lord, and above all, the incomparable majesty of Almighty God--though I am acquainted with these things, yet am I not therefore by any means perfect; nor am I such a disciple as Paul or Peter. For many things are yet wanting to me, that I may not fall short of God.

Chapter VI - Abstain from the poison of heretics

I therefore, yet not I, but the love of Jesus Christ, entreat you that ye use Christian nourishment only, and abstain from herbage of a different kind; I mean heresy. For those [755] [that are given to this] mix [756] up Jesus Christ with their own poison, speaking things which are unworthy of credit, like those who administer a deadly drug in sweet wine, which he who is ignorant of does greedily [757] take, with a fatal pleasure [758] leading to his own death.

I therefore, yet not I, out the love of Jesus Christ, "entreat you that ye all speak the same thing, and that there be no divisions among you; but that ye be perfectly joined together in the same mind, and in the same judgment." [759] For there are some vain talkers [760] and deceivers, not Christians, but Christ-betrayers, [761] bearing about the name of Christ in deceit, and "corrupting the word" [762] of the Gospel; while they intermix the poison of their deceit with their persuasive talk, [763] as if they mingled aconite with sweet wine, that so he who drinks, being deceived in his taste by the very great sweetness of the draught, may incautiously meet with his death. One of the ancients gives us this advice, "Let no man be called good who mixes good with evil." [764] For they speak of

Christ, not that they may preach Christ, but that they may reject Christ; and they speak [765] of the law, not that they may establish the law, but that they may proclaim things contrary to it. For they alienate Christ from the Father, and the law from Christ. They also calumniate His being born of the Virgin; they are ashamed of His cross; they deny His passion; and they do not believe His resurrection. They introduce God as a Being unknown; they suppose Christ to be unbegotten; and as to the Spirit, they do not admit that He exists. Some of them say that the Son is a mere man, and that the Father, Son, and Holy Spirit are but the same person, and that the creation is the work of God, not by Christ, but by some other strange power.

Chapter VII - The same continued

Be on your guard, therefore, against such persons. And this will be the case with you if you are not puffed up, and continue in intimate union with [766] Jesus Christ our God, and the bishop, and the enactments of the apostles. He that is within the altar is pure, but [767] he that is without is not pure; that is, he who does anything apart from the bishop, and presbytery, and deacons, [768] such a man is not pure in his conscience.

Be on your guard, therefore, against such persons, that ye admit not of a snare for your own souls. And act so that your life shall be without offence to all men, lest ye become as "a snare upon a watch-tower, and as a net which is spread out." [769] For "he that does not heal himself in his own works, is the brother of him that destroys himself." [770] If, therefore, ye also put away conceit, arrogance, disdain, and haughtiness, it will be your privilege to be inseparably united to God, for "He is nigh unto those that fear Him." [771] And says He, "Upon whom will I look, but upon him that is humble and quiet, and that trembles at my words?" [772] And do ye also reverence your bishop as Christ Himself, according as the blessed apostles have enjoined you. He that is within the altar is pure, wherefore also he is obedient to the bishop and presbyters: but he that is without is one that does anything apart from the bishop, the presbyters, and the deacons. Such a person is defiled in his conscience, and is worse than an infidel. For what is the bishop but one who beyond all others possesses all power and authority, so far as it is possible for a man to possess it, who according to his ability has been made an imitator of the Christ of God? [773] And what is the presbytery but a sacred assembly, the counsellors and assessors of the bishop? And what are the deacons but imitators of the angelic powers, [774] fulfilling a pure and blameless ministry unto him, as the holy Stephen did to the blessed James, Timothy and Linus to Paul, Anencletus and Clement to Peter? He, therefore, that will not yield obedience to such, must needs be one utterly without God, an impious man who despises Christ, and depreciates His appointments.

Chapter VIII - Be on your guard against the snares of the devil

Not that I know there is anything of this kind among you; but I put you on your guard, inasmuch as I love you greatly, and foresee the snares of the devil. Wherefore, clothing [775] yourselves with meekness, be ye renewed [776] in faith, that is the flesh of the Lord, and in love, that is the blood of Jesus Christ. Let no one of you cherish any grudge against his neighbour. Give no occasion to the Gentiles, lest by means of a few foolish men the whole multitude [of those that believe] in God be evil spoken of. For, "Woe to him by whose vanity my name is blasphemed among any." [777]

Now I write these things unto you, not that I know there are any such persons among you; nay, indeed I hope that God will never permit any such report to reach my ears, He "who spared not His Son for the sake of His holy Church." [778] But foreseeing the snares of the wicked one, I arm you beforehand by my admonitions, as my beloved and faithful children in Christ, furnishing you with the means of protection [779] against the deadly disease of unruly men, by which do ye flee from the disease [780] [referred to] by the good-will of Christ our Lord. Do ye therefore, clothing [781] yourselves with meekness, become the imitators of His sufferings, and of His love, wherewith [782] He loved us when He gave Himself a ransom [783] for us, that He might cleanse us by His blood from our old ungodliness, and bestow life on us when we were almost on the point of perishing through the depravity that was in us. Let no one of you, therefore, cherish any grudge against his neighbour. For says our Lord, "Forgive, and it shall be forgiven unto you." [784] Give no occasion to the Gentiles, lest "by means of a few foolish men the word and doctrine [of Christ] be blasphemed." [785] For says the prophet, as in the person of God, "Woe to him by whom my name is blasphemed among the Gentiles." [786]

Chapter IX - Reference to the history of Christ

Stop your ears, therefore, when any one speaks to you at variance with [787] Jesus Christ, who was descended from David, and was also of Mary; who was truly born, and did eat and drink. He was truly persecuted under Pontius Pilate; He was truly crucified, and [truly] died, in the sight of beings in heaven, and on earth, and under the earth. He was also truly raised from the dead, His

Father quickening Him, even as after the same manner His Father will so raise up us who believe in Him by Christ Jesus, apart from whom we do not possess the true life.

Stop your ears, therefore, when any one speaks to you at variance with [788] Jesus Christ, the Son of God, who was descended from David, and was also of Mary; who was truly begotten of God and of the Virgin, but not after the same manner. For indeed God and man are not the same. He truly assumed a body; for "the Word was made flesh," [789] and lived upon earth without sin. For says He, "Which of you convicteth me of sin?" [790] He did in reality both eat and drink. He was crucified and died under Pontius Pilate. He really, and not merely in appearance, was crucified, and died, in the sight of beings in heaven, and on earth, and under the earth. By those in heaven I mean such as are possessed of incorporeal natures; by those on earth, the Jews and Romans, and such persons as were present at that time when the Lord was crucified; and by those under the earth, the multitude that arose along with the Lord. For says the Scripture, "Many bodies of the saints that slept arose,"[791] their graves being opened. He descended, indeed, into Hades alone, but He arose accompanied by a multitude; and rent asunder that means [792] of separation which had existed from the beginning of the world, and cast down its partition-wall. He also rose again in three days, the Father raising Him up; and after spending forty days with the apostles, He was received up to the Father, and "sat down at His right hand, expecting till His enemies are placed under His feet." [793] On the day of the preparation, then, at the third hour, He received the sentence from Pilate, the Father permitting that to happen; at the sixth hour He was crucified; at the ninth hour He gave up the ghost; and before sunset He was buried. [794] During the Sabbath He continued under the earth in the tomb in which Joseph of Arimathæa had laid Him. At the dawning of the Lord's day He arose from the dead, according to what was spoken by Himself, "As Jonah was three days and three nights in the whale's belly, so shall the Son of man also be three days and three nights in the heart of the earth." [795] The day of the preparation, then, comprises the passion; the Sabbath embraces the burial; the Lord's Day contains the resurrection.

Chapter X - The reality of Christ's passion

But if, as some that are without God, that is, the unbelieving, say, that He only seemed to suffer (they themselves only seeming to exist), then why am I in bonds? Why do I long to be exposed to [796] the wild beasts? Do I therefore die in vain? [797] Am I not then guilty of falsehood [798] against [the cross of] the Lord?

But if, as some that are without God, that is, the unbelieving, say, He became man in appearance [only], that He did not in reality take unto Him a body, that He died in appearance [merely], and did not in very deed suffer, then for what reason am I now in bonds, and long to be exposed to [799] the wild beasts? In such a case, I die in vain, and am guilty of falsehood [800] against the cross of the Lord. Then also does the prophet in vain declare, "They shall look on Him whom they have pierced, and mourn over themselves as over one beloved." [801] These men, therefore, are not less unbelievers than were those that crucified Him. But as for me, I do not place my hopes in one who died for me in appearance, but in reality. For that which is false is quite abhorrent to the truth. Mary then did truly conceive a body which had God inhabiting it. And God the Word was truly born of the Virgin, having clothed Himself with a body of like passions with our own. He who forms all men in the womb, was Himself really in the womb, and made for Himself a body of the seed of the Virgin, but without any intercourse of man. He was carried in the womb, even as we are, for the usual period of time; and was really born, as we also are; and was in reality nourished with milk, and partook of common meat and drink, even as we do. And when He had lived among men for thirty years, He was baptized by John, really and not in appearance; and when He had preached the Gospel three years, and done signs and wonders, He who was Himself the Judge was judged by the Jews, falsely so called, and by Pilate the governor; was scourged, was smitten on the cheek, was spit upon; He wore a crown of thorns and a purple robe; He was condemned: He was crucified in reality, and not in appearance, not in imagination, not in deceit. He really died, and was buried, and rose from the dead, even as He prayed in a certain place, saying, "But do Thou, O Lord, raise me up again, and I shall recompense them." [802] And the Father, who always hears Him, [803] answered and said, "Arise, O God, and judge the earth; for Thou shalt receive all the heathen for Thine inheritance." [804] The Father, therefore, who raised Him up, will also raise us up through Him, apart from whom no one will attain to true life. For says He, "I am the life; he that believeth in me, even though he die, shall live: and every one that liveth and believeth in me, even though he die, shall live for ever." [805] Do ye therefore flee from these ungodly heresies; for they are the inventions of the devil, that serpent who was the author of evil, and who by means of the woman deceived Adam, the father of our race.

Chapter XI - Avoid the deadly errors of the Docetæ

Flee, therefore, those evil offshoots [of Satan], which produce death-bearing fruit, whereof if any one tastes, he instantly dies. For these men are not the planting of the Father. For if they were, they would appear as branches of the cross, and their fruit would be incorruptible. By it [806] He calls you through His passion, as being His members. The head, therefore, cannot be born by itself, without its members; God, who is [the Saviour] Himself, having promised their union. [807]

Do ye also avoid those wicked offshoots of his, [808] Simon his firstborn son, and Menander, and Basilides, and all his wicked mob of followers, [809] the worshippers of a man, whom also the prophet Jeremiah pronounces accursed. [810] Flee also the impure Nicolaitanes, falsely so called, [811] who are lovers of pleasure, and given to calumnious speeches. Avoid also the children of the evil one, Theodotus and Cleobulus, who produce death-bearing fruit, whereof if any one tastes, he instantly dies, and that not a mere temporary death, but one that shall endure for ever. These men are not the planting of the Father, but are an accursed brood. And says the Lord, "Let every plant which my heavenly Father has not planted be rooted up." [812] For if they had been branches of the Father, they would not have been "enemies of the cross of Christ," [813] but rather of those who "killed the Lord of glory." [814] But now, by denying the cross, and being ashamed of the passion, they cover the transgression of the Jews, those fighters against God, those murderers of the Lord; for it were too little to style them merely murderers of the prophets. But Christ invites you to [share in] His immortality, by His passion and resurrection, inasmuch as ye are His members.

Chapter XII - Continue in unity and love

I salute you from Smyrna, together with the Churches of God which are with me, who have refreshed me in all things, both in the flesh and in the spirit. My bonds, which I carry about with me for the sake of Jesus Christ (praying that I may attain to God), exhort you. Continue in harmony among yourselves, and in prayer with one another; for it becomes every one of you, and especially the presbyters, to refresh the bishop, to the honour of the Father, of Jesus Christ, and of the apostles. I entreat you in love to hear me, that I may not, by having written, be a testimony against you. And do ye also pray for me, who have need of your love, along with the mercy of God, that I may be worthy of the lot for which I am destined, and that I may not be found reprobate.

I salute you from Smyrna, together with the Churches of God which are with me, whose rulers have refreshed me in every respect, both in the flesh and in the spirit. My bonds, which I carry about with me for the sake of Jesus Christ (praying that I may attain to God), exhort you. Continue in harmony among yourselves, and in supplication; for it becomes every one of you, and especially the presbyters, to refresh the bishop, to the honour of the Father, and to the honour of Jesus Christ and of the apostles. I entreat you in love to hear me, that I may not, by having thus written, be a testimony against you. And do ye also pray for me, who have need of your love, along with the mercy of God, that I may be thought worthy to attain the lot for which I am now designed, and that I may not be found reprobate.

Chapter XIII - Conclusion

The love of the Smyrnæans and Ephesians salutes you. Remember in your prayers the Church which is in Syria, from which also I am not worthy to receive my appellation, being the last [815] of them. Fare ye well in Jesus Christ, while ye continue subject to the bishop, as to the command [of God], and in like manner to the presbytery. And do ye, every man, love one another with an undivided heart. Let my spirit be sanctified [816] by yours, not only now, but also when I shall attain to God. For I am as yet exposed to danger. But the Father is faithful in Jesus Christ to fulfil both mine and your petitions: in whom may ye be found unblameable.

The love of the Smyrnæans and Ephesians salutes you. Remember our Church which is in Syria, from which I am not worthy to receive my appellation, being the last [817] of those of that place. Fare ye well in the Lord Jesus Christ, while ye continue subject to the bishop, and in like manner to the presbyters and to the deacons. And do ye, every man, love one another with an undivided heart. My spirit salutes you, [818] not only now, but also when I shall have attained to God; for I am as yet exposed to danger. But the Father of Jesus Christ is faithful to fulfil both mine and your petitions: in whom may we be found without spot. May I have joy of you in the Lord.

Footnotes:

728. Some render, "in the resurrection which is by Him."

729. Either, "the whole members of the Church," or, "in the fulness of blessing."

730. Either, "as an apostle," or, "in the apostolic form."

731. Either, "the whole members of the Church," or, "in the fulness of blessing."

732. Either, "as an apostle," or, "in the apostolic form."

733. Literally, "not according to use, but according to nature."
734. Literally, "not for use, but for a possession."
735. It is doubtful whether this exhortation is addressed to the deacons or people; whether the former are urged in all respects to please the latter, or the latter in all points to be pleased with the former.
736. Heb. xiii. 17.
737. Literally, "commandment." The text, which is faulty in the ms., has been amended as above by Smith.
738. Literally, "no Church is called."
739. Or, "pattern."
740. Literally, "great instruction."
741. Some here follow a text similar to that of the longer recension.
742. Both the text and meaning are here very doubtful; some follow the reading of the longer recension.
743. Or, "conjunction."
744. Or, "pattern."
745. Literally, "I know many things in God."
746. A different turn altogether is given to this passage in the longer recension.
747. 1 Cor. i. 31.
748. Or, "confirmed."
749. Omitted in the ms.
750. Or, "stations."
751. Literally, "passing by this;" but both text and meaning are very doubtful.
752. ἐβουλόμην apparently by mistake for ἐδυνάμην.
753. Literally, "their force."
754. Or, "varieties of."
755. The ellipsis in the original is here very variously supplied.
756. Literally, "interweave."
757. Or, "sweetly."
758. The construction is here difficult and doubtful.
759. 1 Cor. i. 10.
760. Tit. i. 10.
761. Literally, "Christ-sellers."
762. 2 Cor. ii. 17.
763. Literally, "sweet address."
764. Apost. Constitutions, vi. 13.
765. Supplied from the old Latin version.
766. Literally, "unseparated from."
767. This clause is inserted from the ancient Latin version.
768. The text has "deacon."
769. ὅς. v. 1.
770. Prov. xviii. 9 (LXX).
771. Ps. lxxxv. 9.
772. Isa. lxvi. 2.
773. Some render, "being a resemblance according to the power of Christ."
774. Some read, "imitators of Christ, ministering to the bishop, as Christ to the Father."
775. Literally, "taking up."
776. Or, "renew yourselves."
777. Isa. lii. 5.
778. Rom. viii. 32.
779. Literally, "making you drink beforehand what will preserve you."
780. Or, "from which disease."
781. Literally, "taking up."
782. Comp. Eph. ii. 4.
783. Comp. 1 Tim. ii. 6.
784. Matt. vi. 14.
785. 1 Tim. vi. 1; Tit. ii. 5.
786. Isa. lii. 5.
787. Literally, "apart from."
788. Literally, "apart from."
789. John i. 14.
790. John viii. 46.
791. Matt. xxvii. 52.
792. Literally, "hedge," or "fence."
793. Heb. x. 12, 13.
794. Some read, "He was taken down from the cross, and laid in a new tomb."
795. Matt. xii. 40.
796. Literally, "to fight with."
797. Some read this and the following clause affirmatively, instead of interrogatively.
798. The meaning is, that is they spoke the truth concerning the phantasmal character of Christ's death, then Ignatius was guilty of a practical falsehood in suffering for what was false.
799. Literally, "to fight with."
800. The meaning is, that if they spoke the truth concerning the phantasmal character of Christ's death, then Ignatius was guilty of a practical falsehood in suffering for what was false.
801. Zech. xii. 10.
802. Ps. xli. 10.
803. Comp. John xi. 42.
804. Ps. lxxxii. 8.
805. John xi. 25, 26.
806. i.e., the cross.
807. Both text and meaning here are doubtful.
808. i.e., Satan's.
809. Literally, "loud, confused noise."
810. The Ebionites, who denied the divine nature of our Lord, are here referred to.
811. It seems to be here denied that Nicolas was the founder of this school of heretics.
812. Matt. xv. 13.
813. Phil. iii. 18.
814. 1 Cor. ii. 8.
815. i.e., the least.

816. The shorter recension reads ἁγνίζετε, and the longer also hesitates between this and ἀσπάζεται. With the former reading the meaning is very obscure: it has been corrected as above to ἁγνίζηται.

817. i.e., the least.

818. The shorter recension reads ἁγνίζετε, and the longer also hesitates between this and ἀσπάζεται. With the former reading the meaning is very obscure: it has been corrected as above to ἁγνίζηται.

The Epistle of Ignatius to the Romans Shorter and Longer Versions

Ignatius, who is also called Theophorus, to the Church which has obtained mercy, through the majesty of the Most High Father, and Jesus Christ, His only-begotten Son; the Church which is beloved and enlightened by the will of Him that willeth all things which are according to the love of Jesus Christ our God, which also presides in the place of the region of the Romans, worthy of God, worthy of honour, worthy of the highest happiness, worthy of praise, worthy of obtaining her every desire, worthy of being deemed holy, [819] and which presides over love, is named from Christ, and from the Father, which I also salute in the name of Jesus Christ, the Son of the Father: to those who are united, both according to the flesh and spirit, to every one of His commandments; who are filled inseparably with the grace of God, and are purified from every strange taint, [I wish] abundance of happiness unblameably, in Jesus Christ our God.

Ignatius, who is also called Theophorus, to the Church which has obtained mercy, through the majesty of the Most High God the Father, and of Jesus Christ, His only-begotten Son; the Church which is sanctified and enlightened by the will of God, who formed all things that are according to the faith and love of Jesus Christ, our God and Saviour; the Church which presides in the place of the region of the Romans, and which is worthy of God, worthy of honour, worthy of the highest happiness, worthy of praise, worthy of credit, [820] worthy of being deemed holy, [821] and which presides over love, is named from Christ, and from the Father, and is possessed of the Spirit, which I also salute in the name of Almighty God, and of Jesus Christ His Son: to those who are united, both according to the flesh and spirit, to every one of His commandments, who are filled inseparably with all the grace of God, and are purified from every strange taint, [I wish] abundance of happiness unblameably, in God, even the Father, and our Lord Jesus Christ.

Chapter I - As a prisoner, I hope to see you

Through prayer [822] to God I have obtained the privilege of seeing your most worthy faces, [823] and have even [824] been granted more than I requested; for I hope as a prisoner in Christ Jesus to salute you, if indeed it be the will of God that I be thought worthy of attaining unto the end. For the beginning has been well ordered, if I may obtain grace to cling to [825] my lot without hindrance unto the end. For I am afraid of your love, [826] lest it should do me an injury. For it is easy for you to accomplish what you please; but it is difficult for me to attain to God, if ye spare me.

Through prayer to God I have obtained the privilege of seeing your most worthy faces, [827] even as I earnestly begged might be granted me; for as a prisoner in Christ Jesus I hope to salute you, if indeed it be the will [of God] that I be thought worthy of attaining unto the end. For the beginning has been well ordered, if I may obtain grace to cling to [828] my lot without hindrance unto the end. For I am afraid of your love, [829] lest it should do me an injury. For it is easy for you to accomplish what you please; but it is difficult for me to attain to God, if ye do not spare me, [830] under the pretence of carnal affection.

Chapter II - Do not save me from martyrdom

For it is not my desire to act towards you as a man-pleaser, [831] but as pleasing God, even as also ye please Him. For neither shall I ever have such [another] opportunity of attaining to God; nor will ye, if ye shall now be silent, ever be entitled to [832] the honour of a better work. For if ye are silent concerning me, I shall become God's; but if you show your love to my flesh, I shall again have to run my race. Pray, then, do not seek to confer any greater favour upon me than that I be sacrificed to God while the altar is still prepared; that, being gathered together in love, ye may sing praise to the Father, through Christ Jesus, that God has deemed me, the bishop of Syria, worthy to be sent for [833] from the east unto the west. It is good to set from the world unto God, that I may rise again to Him.

For it is not my desire that ye should please men, but God, even as also ye do please Him. For neither shall I ever hereafter have such an opportunity of attaining to God; nor will ye, if ye shall now be silent, ever be entitled to [834] the honour of a better work. For if ye are silent concerning me, I shall become God's; but if ye show your love to my flesh, I shall again have to run my race. Pray, then, do not seek to confer any greater favour upon me than that I be sacrificed to God, while the altar is still prepared; that, being gathered together in love, ye may sing praise to the Father, through Christ Jesus, that God has deemed me, the bishop of Syria, worthy to be sent for [835] from the east unto the west, and to become a martyr [836] in behalf of His own precious [837] sufferings, so as to pass from the world to God, that I may rise again unto Him.

Chapter III - Pray rather that I may attain to martyrdom

Ye have never envied any one; ye have taught others. Now I desire that those things may be confirmed [by your conduct], which in your instructions ye enjoin [on others]. Only request in my behalf both inward and outward strength, that I may not only speak, but [truly] will; and that I may not merely be called a Christian, but really be found to be one. For if I be truly found [a Christian], I may also be called one, and be then deemed faithful, when I shall no longer appear to the world. Nothing visible is eternal. [838] "For the things which are seen are temporal, but the things which are not seen are eternal." [839] For our God, Jesus Christ, now that He is with [840] the Father, is all the more revealed [in His glory]. Christianity is not a thing [841] of silence only, but also of [manifest] greatness.

Ye have never envied any one; ye have taught others. Now I desire that those things may be confirmed [by your conduct], which in your instructions ye enjoin [on others]. Only request in my behalf both inward and outward strength, that I may not only speak, but [truly] will, so that I may not merely be called a Christian, but really found to be one. For if I be truly found [a Christian], I may also be called one, and be then deemed faithful, when I shall no longer appear to the world. Nothing visible is eternal. "For the things which are seen are temporal, but the things which are not seen are eternal." [842] The Christian is not the result [843] of persuasion, but of power. [844] When he is hated by the world, he is beloved of God. For says [the Scripture], "If ye were of this world, the world would love its own; but now ye are not of the world, but I have chosen you out of it: continue in fellowship with me." [845]

Chapter IV - Allow me to fall a prey to the wild beasts

I write to the Churches, and impress on them all, that I shall willingly die for God, unless ye hinder me. I beseech of you not to show an unseasonable good-will towards me. Suffer me to become food for the wild beasts, through whose instrumentality it will be granted me to attain to God. I am the wheat of God, and let me be ground by the teeth of the wild beasts, that I may be found the pure bread of Christ. Rather entice the wild beasts, that they may become my tomb, and may leave nothing of my body; so that when I have fallen asleep [in death], I may be no trouble to any one. Then shall I truly be a disciple of Christ, when the world shall not see so much as my body. Entreat Christ for me, that by these instruments [846] I may be found a sacrifice [to God]. I do not, as Peter and Paul, issue commandments unto you. They were apostles; I am but a condemned man: they were free, [847] while I am, even until now, a servant. But when I suffer, I shall be the freed-man of Jesus, and shall rise again emancipated in Him. And now, being a prisoner, I learn not to desire anything worldly or vain.

I write to all the Churches, and impress on them all, that I shall willingly die for God, unless ye hinder me. I beseech of you not to show an unseasonable good-will towards me. Suffer me to become food for the wild beasts, through whose instrumentality it will be granted me to attain to God. I am the wheat of God, and am ground by the teeth of the wild beasts, that I may be found the pure bread of God. Rather entice the wild beasts, that they may become my tomb, and may leave nothing of my body; so that when I have fallen asleep [in death], I may not be found troublesome to any one. Then shall I be a true disciple of Jesus Christ, when the world shall not see so much as my body. Entreat the Lord for me, that by these instruments [848] I may be found a sacrifice to God. I do not, as Peter and Paul, issue commandments unto you. They were apostles of Jesus Christ, but I am the very least [of believers]: they were free, [849] as the servants of God; while I am, even until now, a servant. But when I suffer, I shall be the freed-man of Jesus Christ, and shall rise again emancipated in Him. And now, being in bonds for Him, I learn not to desire anything worldly or vain.

Chapter V - I desire to die

From Syria even unto Rome I fight with beasts, [850] both by land and sea, both by night and day, being bound to ten leopards, I mean a band of soldiers, who, even when they receive benefits, [851] show themselves all the worse. But I am the more instructed by their injuries [to act as a disciple of Christ]; "yet am I not thereby justified." [852] May I enjoy the wild beasts that are prepared for me; and I pray they may be found eager to rush upon me, which also I will entice to devour me speedily, and not deal with me as with some, whom, out of fear, they have not touched. But if they be unwilling to assail me, I will compel them to do so. Pardon me [in this]: I know what is for my benefit. Now I begin to be a disciple. And let no one, of things visible or invisible, envy [853] me that I should attain to Jesus Christ. Let fire and the cross; let the crowds of wild beasts; let tearings, [854] breakings, and dislocations of bones; let cutting off of members; let shatterings of the whole body; and let all the dreadful [855] torments of the devil come upon me: only let me attain to Jesus Christ.

From Syria even unto Rome I fight with beasts, [856] both by land and sea, both by night and day, being bound to ten leopards, I mean a band of soldiers, who, even when they receive benefits,[857] show themselves all the worse. But I am the more instructed by their injuries [to act as a disciple of Christ]; "yet am I not thereby justified." [858] May I enjoy the wild beasts that are prepared for me; and I pray that they may be found eager to rush upon me, which also I will entice to devour me speedily, and not deal with me as with some, whom, out of fear, they have not touched. But if they be unwilling to assail me, I will compel them to do so. Pardon me [in this] I know what is for my benefit. Now I begin to be a disciple, and have [859] no desire after anything visible or invisible, that I may attain to Jesus Christ. Let fire and the cross; let the crowds of wild beasts; let breakings, tearings, and separations of bones; let cutting off of members; let bruising to pieces of the whole body; and let the very torment of the devil come upon me: only let me attain to Jesus Christ.

Chapter VI - By death I shall attain true life

All the pleasures of the world, and all the kingdoms of this earth, [860] shall profit me nothing. It is better for me to die in behalf of [861] Jesus Christ, than to reign over all the ends of the earth. "For what shall a man be profited, if he gain the whole world, but lose his own soul?" [862] Him I seek, who died for us: Him I desire, who rose again for our sake. This is the gain which is laid up for me. Pardon me, brethren: do not hinder me from living, do not wish to keep me in a state of death; [863] and while I desire to belong to God, do not ye give me over to the world. Suffer me to obtain pure light: when I have gone thither, I shall indeed be a man of God. Permit me to be an imitator of the passion of my God. If any one has Him within himself, let him consider what I desire, and let him have sympathy with me, as knowing how I am straitened.

All the ends of the world, and all the kingdoms of this earth, [864] shall profit me nothing. It is better for me to die for the sake of Jesus Christ, than to reign over all the ends of the earth. "For what is a man profited, if he gain the whole world, but lose his own soul?" I long after the Lord, the Son of the true God and Father, even Jesus Christ. Him I seek, who died for us and rose again. Pardon me, brethren: do not hinder me in attaining to life; for Jesus is the life of believers. Do not wish to keep me in a state of death, [865] for life without Christ is death. While I desire to belong to God, do not ye give me over to the world. Suffer me to obtain pure light: when I have gone thither, I shall indeed be a man of God. Permit me to be an imitator of the passion of Christ, my God. If any one has Him within himself, let him consider what I desire, and let him have sympathy with me, as knowing how I am straitened.

Chapter VII - Reason of desiring to die

The prince of this world would fain carry me away, and corrupt my disposition towards God. Let none of you, therefore, who are [in Rome] help him; rather be ye on my side, that is, on the side of God. Do not speak of Jesus Christ, and yet set your desires on the world. Let not envy find a dwelling-place among you; nor even should I, when present with you, exhort you to it, be ye persuaded to listen to me, but rather give credit to those things which I now write to you. For though I am alive while I write to you, yet I am eager to die. My love [866] has been crucified, and there is no fire in me desiring to be fed; [867] but there is within me a water that liveth and speaketh,[868] saying to me inwardly, Come to the Father. I have no delight in corruptible food, nor in the pleasures of this life. I desire the bread of God, the heavenly bread, the bread of life, which is the flesh of Jesus Christ, the Son of God, who became afterwards of the seed of David and Abraham; and I desire the drink of God, namely His blood, which is incorruptible love and eternal life.

The prince of this world would fain carry me away, and corrupt my disposition towards God. Let none of you, therefore, who are [in Rome] help him; rather be ye on my side, that is, on the side of God. Do not speak of Jesus Christ, and yet prefer this world to Him. Let not envy find a dwelling-place among you; nor even should I, when present with you, exhort you to it, be ye persuaded, but rather give credit to those things which I now write to you. For though I am alive while I write to you, yet I am eager to die for the sake of Christ. My love [869] has been crucified, and there is no fire in me that loves anything; but there is living water springing up in me, [870] and which says to me inwardly, Come to the Father. I have no delight in corruptible food, nor in the pleasures of this life. I desire the bread of God, the heavenly bread, the bread of life, which is the flesh of Jesus Christ, the Son of God, who became afterwards of the seed of David and Abraham; and I desire the drink, namely His blood, which is incorruptible love and eternal life.

Chapter VIII - Be ye favourable to me

I no longer wish to live after the manner of men, and my desire shall be fulfilled if ye consent. Be ye willing, then, that ye also may have your desires fulfilled. I entreat you in this brief letter; do ye give credit to me. Jesus Christ will reveal these things to you, [so that ye shall know] that I speak truly. He [871] is the mouth altogether free from falsehood, by which the Father has truly spoken. Pray ye for me, that I may attain [the object of my desire]. I have not written to you according to the flesh, but according to the will of God. If I shall suffer, ye have wished [well] to me; but if I am rejected, ye have hated me.

I no longer wish to live after the manner of men, and my desire shall be fulfilled if ye consent. "I am crucified with Christ: nevertheless I live; yet no longer I, since Christ liveth in me." [872] I entreat you in this brief letter: do not refuse me; believe me that I love Jesus, who was delivered [to death] for my sake. "What shall I render to the Lord for all His benefits towards me?" [873] Now God, even the Father, and the Lord Jesus Christ, shall reveal these things to you, [so that ye shall know] that I speak truly. And do ye pray along with me, that I may attain my aim in the Holy Spirit. I have not written to you according to the flesh, but according to the will of God. If I shall suffer, ye have loved me; but if I am rejected, ye have hated me.

Chapter IX - Pray for the church in Syria

Remember in your prayers the Church in Syria, which now has God for its shepherd, instead of me. Jesus Christ alone will oversee it, and your love [will also regard it]. But as for me, I am ashamed to be counted one of them; for indeed I am not worthy, as being the very last of them, and one born out of due time. [874] But I have obtained mercy to be somebody, if I shall attain to God. My spirit salutes you, and the love of the Churches that have received me in the name of Jesus Christ, and not as a mere passer-by. For even those Churches which were not [875] near to me in the way, I mean according to the flesh, [876] have gone before me, [877] city by city, [to meet me.]

Remember in your prayers the Church which is in Syria, which, instead of me, has now for its shepherd the Lord, who says, "I am the good Shepherd." And He alone will oversee it, as well as your love towards Him. But as for me, I am ashamed to be counted one of them; for I am not worthy, as being the very last of them, and one born out of due time. But I have obtained mercy to be somebody, if I shall attain to God. My spirit salutes you, and the love of the Churches which have received me in the name of Jesus Christ, and not as a mere passer-by. For even those Churches which were not near to me in the way, have brought me forward, city by city.

Chapter X - Conclusion

Now I write these things to you from Smyrna by the Ephesians, who are deservedly most happy. There is also with me, along with many others, Crocus, one dearly beloved by me. [878] As to those who have gone before me from Syria to Rome for the glory of God, I believe that you are acquainted with them; to whom, [then,] do ye make known that I am at hand. For they are all worthy, both of God and of you; and it is becoming that you should refresh them in all things. I have written these things unto you, on the day before the ninth of the Kalends of September (that [879] is, on the twenty-third day of August). Fare ye well to the end, in the patience of Jesus Christ. Amen.

Footnotes:

819. Or, "most holy."
820. Or as in the shorter recension.
821. Or, "most holy."
822. Some read, "since I have," leaving out the following "for," and finding the apodosis in "I hope to salute you."
823. Literally, "worthy of God."
824. Some read, "which I much desired to do."
825. Literally, "to receive."
826. He probably refers here, and in what follows, to the influence which their earnest prayers in his behalf might have with God.
827. Literally, "worthy of God."
828. Literally, "to receive."
829. He probably refers here, and in what follows, to the influence which their earnest prayers in his behalf might have with God.
830. Some read γε instead of me, and translate as in shorter recension.
831. Some translate as in longer recension, but there is in the one case ὑμῖν, and in the other ὑμᾶς.
832. Literally, "have to be inscribed to."
833. Literally, "to be found and sent for."
834. Literally, "have to be inscribed to."
835. Literally, "to be found and sent for."
836. The text is here in great

confusion.
837. Literally, "beautiful." Some read, "it is good," etc.
838. Some read, "good."
839. 2 Cor. iv. 18. This quotation is not found in the old Latin version of the shorter recension.
840. Or, "in."
841. Literally, "work."
842. 2 Cor. iv. 18. This quotation is not found in the old Latin version of the shorter recension.
843. Literally, "work."
844. The meaning is here doubtful.
845. John xv. 19.
846. i.e., by the teeth of the wild beasts.
847. "Free," probably from human infirmity.
848. i.e., by the teeth of the wild beasts.
849. "Free," probably from human infirmity.
850. Comp. 1 Cor. xv. 32, where the word is also used figuratively.
851. Probably the soldiers received gifts from the Christians, to treat Ignatius with kindness.
852. 1 Cor. iv. 4.
853. In the shorter recension there is ζηλώσῃ, and in the longer ζηλῶσαι; hence the variety of rendering, but the translation is by no means certain.
854. Some deem this and the following word spurious.
855. Literally, "evil."
856. Comp. 1 Cor. xv. 32, where the word is also used figuratively.
857. Probably the soldiers received gifts from the Christians, to treat Ignatius with kindness.

858. 1 Cor. iv. 4.
859. In the shorter recension there is ζηλώσῃ, and in the longer ζηλῶσαι; hence the variety of rendering, but the translation is by no means certain.
860. Literally, "this age."
861. Literally, "into."
862. Matt. xvi. 26. Some omit this quotation.
863. Literally, "to die."
864. Literally, "this age."
865. Literally, "to die."
866. Some understand by love in this passage, Christ Himself; others regard it as referring to the natural desires of the heart.
867. Literally, "desiring material."
868. The text and meaning are here doubtful. We have followed Hefele, who understands by the water the Holy Spirit, and refers to John vii. 38.
869. Some understand by love in this passage, Christ Himself; others regard it as referring to the natural desires of the heart.
870. Comp. John iv. 14.
871. Some refer this to Ignatius himself.
872. Gal. ii. 20.
873. Ps. cxvi. 12.
874. Comp. 1 Cor. xv. 8, 9.
875. Some refer this to the jurisdiction of Ignatius.
876. i.e., the outward road he had to travel.
877. Or, "have sent me forward;" comp. Tit. iii. 13.
878. Literally, "the name desired to me."
879. This clause is evidently an explanatory gloss which has crept into the text.

The Epistle of Ignatius to the Philadelphians Shorter and Longer Versions

Ignatius, who is also called Theophorus, to the Church of God the Father, and our Lord Jesus Christ, which is at Philadelphia, in Asia, which has obtained mercy, and is established in the harmony of God, and rejoiceth unceasingly [881] in the passion of our Lord, and is filled with all mercy through his resurrection; which I salute in the blood of Jesus Christ, who is our eternal and enduring joy, especially if [men] are in unity with the bishop, the presbyters, and the deacons, who have been appointed according to the mind of Jesus Christ, whom He has established in security, after His own will, and by His Holy Spirit.

Ignatius, who is also called Theophorus, to the Church of God the Father, and of the Lord Jesus Christ, which is at Philadelphia, which has obtained mercy through love, and is established in the harmony of God, and rejoiceth unceasingly, [882] in the passion of our Lord Jesus, and is filled with all mercy through His resurrection; which I salute in the blood of Jesus Christ, who is our eternal and enduring joy, especially to those who are in unity with the bishop, and the presbyters, and the deacons, who have been appointed by the will of God the Father, through the Lord Jesus Christ, who, according to His own will, has firmly established His Church upon a rock, by a spiritual building, not made with hands, against which the winds and the floods have beaten, yet have not been able to overthrow it: [883] yea, and may spiritual wickedness never be able to do so, but be thoroughly weakened by the power of Jesus Christ our Lord.

Chapter I - Praise of the bishop

Which bishop, [884] I know, obtained the ministry which pertains to the common [weal], not of himself, neither by men, [885] nor through vainglory, but by the love of God the Father, and the Lord Jesus Christ; at whose meekness I am struck with admiration, and who by his silence is able to accomplish more than those who vainly talk. For he is in harmony with the commandments [of God], even as the harp is with its strings. Wherefore my soul declares his mind towards God a happy one, knowing it to be virtuous and perfect, and that his stability as well as freedom from all anger is after the example of the infinite [886] meekness of the living God.

Having beheld your bishop, I know that he was not selected to undertake the ministry which pertains to the common [weal], either by himself or by men, [887] or out of vainglory, but by the love of Jesus Christ, and of God the Father, who raised Him from the dead; at whose meekness I am struck with admiration, and who by His silence is able to accomplish more than they who talk a great deal. For he is in harmony with the commandments and ordinances of the Lord, even as the strings are with the harp, and is no less blameless than was Zacharias the priest. [888] Wherefore my soul declares his mind towards God a happy one, knowing it to be virtuous and perfect, and that his stability as well as freedom from all anger is after the example of the infinite meekness of the living God.

Chapter II - Maintain union with the bishop

Wherefore, as children of light and truth, flee from division and wicked doctrines; but where the shepherd is, there do ye as sheep follow. For there are many wolves that appear worthy of credit, who, by means of a pernicious pleasure, carry captive [889] those that are running towards God; but in your unity they shall have no place.

Wherefore, as children of light and truth, avoid the dividing of your unity, and the wicked doctrine of the heretics, from whom "a defiling influence has gone forth into all the earth." [890] But where the shepherd is, there do ye as sheep follow. For there are many wolves in sheep's clothing, [891] who, by means of a pernicious pleasure, carry captive [892] those that are running towards God; but in your unity they shall have no place.

Chapter III - Avoid schismatics

Keep yourselves from those evil plants which Jesus Christ does not tend, because they are not the planting of the Father. Not that I have found any division among you, but exceeding purity. For as many as are of God and of Jesus Christ are also with the bishop. And as many as shall, in the exercise of repentance, return into the unity of the Church, these, too, shall belong to God, that they may live according to Jesus Christ. Do not err, my brethren. If any man follows him that makes a schism in the Church, he shall not inherit the kingdom of God. If any one walks according to a strange [893] opinion, he agrees not with the passion [of Christ.].

Keep yourselves, then, from those evil plants which Jesus Christ does not tend, but that wild beast, the destroyer of men, because they are not the planting of the Father, but the seed of the wicked one. Not that I have found any division among you do I write these things; but I arm you beforehand, as the children of God. For as many as are of Christ are also with the bishop; but as many as fall away from him, and embrace communion with the accursed, these shall be cut off along with them. For they are not Christ's husbandry, but the seed of the enemy, from whom may you ever be delivered by the prayers of the shepherd, that most faithful and gentle shepherd who presides over you. I therefore exhort you in the Lord to receive with all tenderness those that repent and return to the unity of the Church, that through your kindness and forbearance they may recover [894] themselves out of the snare of the devil, and becoming worthy of Jesus Christ, may obtain eternal salvation in the kingdom of Christ. Brethren, be not deceived. If any man follows him that separates from the truth, he shall not inherit the kingdom of God; and if any man does not stand aloof from the preacher of falsehood, he shall be condemned to hell. For it is obligatory neither to separate from the godly, nor to associate with the ungodly. If any one walks according to a strange[895] opinion, he is not of Christ, nor a partaker of His passion; but is a fox, [896] a destroyer of the vineyard of Christ. Have no fellowship [897] with such a man, lest ye perish along with him, even should he be thy father, thy son, thy brother, or a member of thy family. For says [the Scripture], "Thine eye shall not spare him." [898] You ought therefore to "hate those that hate God, and to waste away [with grief] on account of His enemies." [899] I do not mean that you should beat them or persecute them, as do the Gentiles "that know not the Lord and God;" [900] but that you should regard them as your enemies, and separate yourselves from them, while yet you admonish them, and exhort them to repentance, if it may be they will hear, if it may be they will submit themselves. For our God is a lover of mankind, and "will have all men to be saved, and to come to the knowledge of the truth." [901] Wherefore "He makes His sun to rise upon the evil and on the good, and sendeth rain on the just and on the unjust;" [902] of whose kindness the Lord, wishing us also to be imitators, says, "Be ye perfect, even as also your Father that is in heaven is perfect." [903]

Chapter IV - Have but one Eucharist, etc.

Take ye heed, then, to have but one Eucharist. For there is one flesh of our Lord Jesus Christ, and one cup to [show forth [904]] the unity of His blood; one altar; as there is one bishop, along with the presbytery and deacons, my fellow-servants: that so, whatsoever ye do, ye may do it according to [the will of] God.

I have confidence of you in the Lord, that ye will be of no other mind. Wherefore I write boldly to your love, which is worthy of God, and exhort you to have but one faith, and one [kind of] preaching, and one Eucharist. For there is one flesh of the Lord Jesus Christ; and His blood which was shed for us is one; one loaf also is broken to all [the communicants], and one cup is distributed among them all: there is but one altar for the whole Church, and one bishop, with the presbytery and deacons, my fellow-servants. Since, also, there is but one unbegotten Being, God, even the Father; and one only-begotten Son, God, the Word and man; and one Comforter, the Spirit of truth; and also one preaching, and one faith, and one baptism; [905] and one Church which the holy apostles established from one end of the earth to the other by the blood of Christ, and by their own sweat and toil; it behoves you also, therefore, as "a peculiar people, and a holy nation," [906] to perform all things with harmony in Christ. Wives, be ye subject to your husbands in the fear of God; [907] and ye virgins, to Christ in purity, not counting marriage an abomination, but desiring that which is better, not for the reproach of wedlock, but for the sake of meditating on the law. Children, obey your parents, and have an affection for them, as workers together with God for your birth [into the world]. Servants, be subject to your masters in God, that ye may be the freed-men of Christ. [908] Husbands, love your wives, as fellow-servants of God, as your own body, as the partners of your life, and your co-adjutors in the procreation of children. Virgins, have Christ alone before your eyes, and His Father in your prayers, being enlightened by the Spirit. May I have pleasure in your purity, as that of Elijah, or as of Joshua the son of Nun, as of Melchizedek, or as of Elisha, as of Jeremiah, or as of John the Baptist, as of the beloved disciple, as of Timothy, as of Titus, as of Evodius, as of Clement, who departed this life in [perfect] chastity, [909] Not, however, that I blame the other blessed [saints] because they entered into the married state, of which I have just spoken. [910] For I pray that, being found worthy of God, I may be found at their feet in the kingdom, as at the feet of Abraham, and Isaac, and Jacob; as of Joseph, and Isaiah, and the rest of the prophets; as of Peter, and Paul, and the rest of the apostles, that were married men. For they entered into these marriages not for the sake of appetite, but out of regard for the propagation of mankind. Fathers, "bring up your children in the nurture and admonition of the Lord;" [911] and teach them the holy

Scriptures, and also trades, that they may not indulge in idleness. Now [the Scripture] says, "A righteous father educates [his children] well; his heart shall rejoice in a wise son." [912] Masters, be gentle towards your servants, as holy Job has taught you; [913] for there is one nature, and one family of mankind. For "in Christ there is neither bond nor free." [914] Let governors be obedient to Cæsar; soldiers to those that command them; deacons to the presbyters, as to high-priests; the presbyters, and deacons, and the rest of the clergy, together with all the people, and the soldiers, and the governors, and Cæsar [himself], to the bishop; the bishop to Christ, even as Christ to the Father. And thus unity is preserved throughout. Let not the widows be wanderers about, nor fond of dainties, nor gadders from house to house; but let them be like Judith, noted for her seriousness; and like Anna, eminent for her sobriety. I do not ordain these things as an apostle: for "who am I, or what is my father's house," [915] that I should pretend to be equal in honour to them? But as your "fellow-soldier," [916] I hold the position of one who [simply] admonishes you.

Chapter V - Pray for me

My brethren, I am greatly enlarged in loving you; and rejoicing exceedingly [over you], I seek to secure your safety. Yet it is not I, but Jesus Christ, for whose sake being bound I fear the more, inasmuch as I am not yet perfect. But your prayer to God shall make me perfect, that I may attain to that portion which through mercy has been allotted me, while I flee to the Gospel as to the flesh of Jesus, and to the apostles as to the presbytery of the Church. And let us also love the prophets, because they too have proclaimed the Gospel, [917] and placed their hope in Him, [918] and waited for Him; in whom also believing, they were saved, through union to Jesus Christ, being holy men, worthy of love and admiration, having had witness borne to them by Jesus Christ, and being reckoned along with [us] in the Gospel of the common hope.

My brethren, I am greatly enlarged in loving you; and rejoicing exceedingly [over you], I seek to secure your safety. Yet it is not I, but the Lord Jesus through me; for whose sake being bound, I fear the more, for I am not yet perfect. But your prayer to God shall make me perfect, that I may attain that to which I have been called, while I flee to the Gospel as to the flesh of Jesus Christ, and to the apostles as the presbytery of the Church. I do also love the prophets as those who announced Christ, and as being partakers of the same Spirit with the apostles. For as the false prophets and the false apostles drew [to themselves] one and the same wicked, deceitful, and seducing [919] spirit; so also did the prophets and the apostles receive from God, through Jesus Christ, one and the same Holy Spirit, who is good, and sovereign, [920] and true, and the Author of [saving] knowledge. [921] For there is one God of the Old and New Testament, "one Mediator between God and men," for the creation of both intelligent and sensitive beings, and in order to exercise a beneficial and suitable providence [over them]. There is also one Comforter, who displayed [922] His power in Moses, and the prophets, and apostles. All the saints, therefore, were saved by Christ, hoping in Him, and waiting for Him; and they obtained through Him salvation, being holy ones, worthy of love and admiration, having testimony borne to them by Jesus Christ, in the Gospel of our common hope.

Chapter VI - Do not accept Judaism

But if any one preach the Jewish law [923] unto you, listen not to him. For it is better to hearken to Christian doctrine from a man who has been circumcised, than to Judaism from one uncircumcised. But if either of such persons do not speak concerning Jesus Christ, they are in my judgment but as monuments and sepulchres of the dead, upon which are written only the names of men. Flee therefore the wicked devices and snares of the prince of this world, lest at any time being conquered [924] by his artifices, [925] ye grow weak in your love. But be ye all joined together [926] with an undivided heart. And I thank my God that I have a good conscience in respect to you, and that no one has it in his power to boast, either privately or publicly, that I have burdened [927] any one either in much or in little. And I wish for all among whom I have spoken, that they may not possess that for a testimony against them.

If any one preaches the one God of the law and the prophets, but denies Christ to be the Son of God, he is a liar, even as also is his father the devil, [928] and is a Jew falsely so called, being possessed of [929] mere carnal circumcision. If any one confesses Christ Jesus the Lord, but denies the God of the law and of the prophets, saying that the Father of Christ is not the Maker of heaven and earth, he has not continued in the truth any more than his father the devil, [930] and is a disciple of Simon Magus, not of the Holy Spirit. If any one says there is one God, and also confesses Christ Jesus, but thinks the Lord to be a mere man, and not the only-begotten [931] God, and Wisdom, and the Word of God, and deems Him to consist merely of a soul and body, such an one is a serpent, that preaches deceit and error for the destruction of men. And such a man is poor in understanding, even as by name he is an Ebionite. [932] If any one confesses the truths mentioned, [933] but calls lawful wedlock, and the procreation of children, destruction and pollution, or deems certain kinds of food abominable, such an one has the apostate dragon dwelling within him. If any one confesses the

Father, and the Son, and the Holy Ghost, and praises the creation, but calls the incarnation merely an appearance, and is ashamed of the passion, such an one has denied the faith, not less than the Jews who killed Christ. If any one confesses these things, and that God the Word did dwell in a human body, being within it as the Word, even as the soul also is in the body, because it was God that inhabited it, and not a human soul, but affirms that unlawful unions are a good thing, and places the highest happiness [934] in pleasure, as does the man who is falsely called a Nicolaitan, this person can neither be a lover of God, nor a lover of Christ, but is a corrupter of his own flesh, and therefore void of the Holy Spirit, and a stranger to Christ. All such persons are but monuments and sepulchres of the dead, upon which are written only the names of dead men. Flee, therefore, the wicked devices and snares of the spirit which now worketh in the children of this world, [935] lest at any time being overcome, [936] ye grow weak in your love. But be ye all joined together [937] with an undivided heart and a willing mind, "being of one accord and of one judgment," [938] being always of the same opinion about the same things, both when you are at ease and in danger, both in sorrow and in joy. I thank God, through Jesus Christ, that I have a good conscience in respect to you, and that no one has it in his power to boast, either privately or publicly, that I have burdened any one either in much or in little. And I wish for all among whom I have spoken, that they may not possess that for a testimony against them.

Chapter VII - I have exhorted you to unity

For though some would have deceived me according to the flesh, yet the Spirit, as being from God, is not deceived. For it knows both whence it comes and whither it goes, [939] and detects the secrets [of the heart]. For, when I was among you, I cried, I spoke with a loud voice: Give heed to the bishop, and to the presbytery and deacons. Now, some suspected me of having spoken thus, as knowing beforehand the division caused by some among you. [940] But He is my witness, for whose sake I am in bonds, that I got no intelligence from any man. [941] But the Spirit proclaimed these words: Do nothing without the bishop; keep your bodies [942] as the temples of God; [943] love unity; avoid divisions; be the followers of Jesus Christ, even as He is of His Father.

For though some would have deceived me according to the flesh, yet my spirit is not deceived; for I have received it from God. For it knows both whence it comes and whither it goes, and detects the secrets [of the heart]. For when I was among you, I cried, I spoke with a loud voice--the word is not mine, but God's--Give heed to the bishop, and to the presbytery and deacons. But if ye suspect that I spake thus, as having learned beforehand the division caused by some among you, He is my witness, for whose sake I am in bonds, that I learned nothing of it from the mouth of any man. But the Spirit made an announcement to me, saying as follows: Do nothing without the bishop; keep your bodies [944] as the temples of God; love unity; avoid divisions; be ye followers of Paul, and of the rest of the apostles, even as they also were of Christ.

Chapter VIII - The same continued

I therefore did what belonged to me, as a man devoted to [945] unity. For where there is division and wrath, God doth not dwell. To all them that repent, the Lord grants forgiveness, if they turn in penitence to the unity of God, and to communion with the bishop. [946] I trust [as to you] in the grace of Jesus Christ, who shall free you from every bond. And I exhort you to do nothing out of strife, but according to the doctrine of Christ. When I heard some saying, If I do not find it in the ancient[947] Scriptures, I will not believe the Gospel; on my saying to them, It is written, they answered me, That remains to be proved. But to me Jesus Christ is in the place of all that is ancient: His cross, and death, and resurrection, and the faith [948] which is by Him, are undefiled monuments of antiquity; by which I desire, through your prayers, to be justified.

I therefore did what belonged to me, as a man devoted to unity; adding this also, that where there is diversity of judgment, and wrath, and hatred, God does not dwell. To all them that repent, God grants forgiveness, if they with one consent return to the unity of Christ, and communion with the bishop. [949] I trust to the grace of Jesus Christ, that He will free you from every bond of wickedness. [950] I therefore exhort you that ye do nothing out of strife, [951] but according to the doctrine of Christ. For I have heard some saying, If I do not find the Gospel in the archives, I will not believe it. To such persons I say that my archives are Jesus Christ, to disobey whom is manifest destruction. My authentic archives are His cross, and death, and resurrection, and the faith which bears on these things, by which I desire, through your prayers, to be justified. He who disbelieves the Gospel disbelieves everything along with it. For the archives ought not to be preferred to the Spirit. [952] "It is hard to kick against the pricks;" [953] it is hard to disbelieve Christ; it is hard to reject the preaching of the apostles.

Chapter IX - The Old Testament is good: the New Testament is better

The priests [954] indeed are good, but the High Priest is better; to whom the holy of holies has been committed, and who alone has been trusted with the secrets of God. He is the door of the Father, by which enter in Abraham, and Isaac, and Jacob, and the prophets, and the apostles, and the Church. All these have for their object the attaining to the unity of God. But the Gospel possesses something transcendent [above the former dispensation], viz., the appearance of our Lord Jesus Christ, His passion and resurrection. For the beloved prophets announced Him, [955] but the Gospel is the perfection of immortality. [956] All these things are good together, if ye believe in love.

The priests [957] indeed, and the ministers of the word, are good; but the High Priest is better, to whom the holy of holies has been committed, and who alone has been entrusted with the secrets of God. The ministering powers of God are good. The Comforter is holy, and the Word is holy, the Son of the Father, by whom He made all things, and exercises a providence over them all. This is the Way [958] which leads to the Father, the Rock, [959] the Defence, [960] the Key, the Shepherd, [961] the Sacrifice, the Door [962] of knowledge, through which have entered Abraham, and Isaac, and Jacob, Moses and all the company of the prophets, and these pillars of the world, the apostles, and the spouse of Christ, on whose account He poured out His own blood, as her marriage portion, that He might redeem her. All these things tend towards the unity of the one and only true God. But the Gospel possesses something transcendent [above the former dispensation], viz. the appearing of our Saviour Jesus Christ, His passion, and the resurrection itself. For those things which the prophets announced, saying, "Until He come for whom it is reserved, and He shall be the expectation of the Gentiles," [963] have been fulfilled in the Gospel, [our Lord saying,] "Go ye and teach all nations, baptizing them in the name of the Father, and of the Son, and of the Holy Ghost." [964] All then are good together, the law, the prophets, the apostles, the whole company [of others] that have believed through them: only if we love one another.

Chapter X - Congratulate the inhabitants of Antioch on the close of the persecution

Since, according to your prayers, and the compassion which ye feel in Christ Jesus, it is reported to me that the Church which is at Antioch in Syria possesses peace, it will become you, as a Church of God, to elect a deacon to act as the ambassador of God [for you] to [the brethren there], that he may rejoice along with them when they are met together, and glorify the name [of God]. Blessed is he in Jesus Christ, who shall be deemed worthy of such a ministry; and ye too shall be glorified. And if ye are willing, it is not beyond your power to do this, for the sake [965] of God; as also the nearest Churches have sent, in some cases bishops, and in others presbyters and deacons.

Since, according to your prayers, and the compassion which ye feel in Christ Jesus, it is reported to me that the Church which is at Antioch in Syria possesses peace, it will become you, as a Church of God, to elect a bishop to act as the ambassador of God [for you] to [the brethren] there, that it may be granted them to meet together, and to glorify the name of God. Blessed is he in Christ Jesus, who shall be deemed worthy of such a ministry; and if ye be zealous [in this matter], ye shall receive glory in Christ. And if ye are willing, it is not altogether beyond your power to do this, for the sake of [966] God; as also the nearest Churches have sent, in some cases bishops, and in others presbyters and deacons.

Chapter XI - Thanks and salutation

Now, as to Philo the deacon, of Cilicia, a man of reputation, who still ministers to me in the word of God, along with Rheus Agathopus, an elect man, who has followed me from Syria, not regarding [967] his life,--these bear witness in your behalf; and I myself give thanks to God for you, that ye have received them, even as the Lord you. But may those that dishonoured them be forgiven through the grace of Jesus Christ! The love of the brethren at Troas salutes you; whence also I write to you by Burrhus, who was sent along with me by the Ephesians and Smyrnæans, to show their respect. [968] May the Lord Jesus Christ honour them, in whom they hope, in flesh, and soul, and faith, and love, and concord! Fare ye well in Christ Jesus, our common hope.

Now, as to Philo the deacon, a man of Cilicia, of high reputation, who still ministers to me in the word of God, along with Gaius and Agathopus, an elect man, who has followed me from Syria, not regarding [969] his life,--these also bear testimony in your behalf. And I myself give thanks to God for you, because ye have received them: and the Lord will also receive you. But may those that dishonoured them be forgiven through the grace of Jesus Christ, "who wisheth not the death of the sinner, but his repentance." [970] The love of the brethren at Troas salutes you; whence also I write to you by Burrhus, [971] who was sent along with me by the Ephesians and Smyrnæans, to show their respect: [972] whom the Lord Jesus Christ will requite, in whom they hope, in flesh, and soul, and spirit, and faith, and love, and concord. Fare ye well in the Lord Jesus Christ, our common hope, in

The Apostolic Fathers
the Holy Ghost.

Footnotes:

881. Or, "inseparably."
882. Or, "inseparably."
883. Comp. Matt. vii. 25.
884. The bishop previously referred to.
885. Comp. Gal. i. 1.
886. Literally, "all."
887. Comp. Gal. i. 1.
888. Luke i. 6.
889. Comp. 2 Tim. iii. 6.
890. Jer. xxiii. 15.
891. Comp. Matt. vii. 15.
892. Comp. 2 Tim. iii. 6.
893. i.e., heretical.
894. 2 Tim. ii. 26.
895. i.e., heretical.
896. Comp. Cant. ii. 15.
897. Comp. 1 Cor. v. 11.
898. Deut. xiii. 6, 18.
899. Ps. cxix. 21.
900. 1 Thess. iv. 5.
901. 1 Tim. ii. 4.
902. Matt. v. 45.
903. Matt. v. 48.
904. Literally, "into."
905. Eph. iv. 5.
906. Tit. ii. 14; 1 Pet. ii. 9
907. Eph. v. 22.
908. 1 Cor. vii. 22.
909. There was a prevalent opinion among the ancient Christian writers, that all these holy men lived a life of chaste. celibacy.
910. Or, "it is not because, etc., that I have mentioned these."
911. Eph. vi. 4.
912. Prov. xxiii. 24.
913. Job xxxi. 13, 15.
914. Gal. iii. 28.
915. 1 Sam. xviii. 18; 2 Sam. vii. 18.
916. Phil. ii. 25.
917. Literally, "have proclaimed in reference to the Gospel."
918. In Christ.
919. Literally, "people-deceiving."
920. Comp. Ps. li. 12 (LXX.).
921. Literally, "teaching."
922. Or, "wrought."
923. Literally, "Judaism."
924. Literally, "oppressed."
925. Or, "will."
926. Some render, "come together into the same place."
927. Apparently by attempting to impose the yoke of Judaism.
928. Comp. John viii 44.
929. Literally, "beneath."
930. Comp. John viii 44.
931. Comp. the reading sanctioned by the ancient authorities, John i. 18.
932. From a Hebrew word meaning "poor."
933. Or, "these things."
934. Literally, "the end of happiness."
935. Comp. Eph. ii. 2.
936. Literally, "oppressed."
937. Some render, "come together into the same place."
938. Phil. ii. 2.
939. John iii. 8.
940. Some translate, "as foreseeing the division to arise among you."
941. Literally, "did not know from human flesh."
942. Literally, "your flesh."
943. Comp. 1 Cor. iii. 16, 1 Cor. vi. 19.
944. Literally, "your flesh."
945. Literally, "prepared for."
946. Literally, "to the assembly of the bishop."
947. The meaning here is very doubtful. Some read ἐν τοῖς ἀρχαίοις, as translated above; others prefer ἐν τοῖς ἀρχείοις, as in the longer recension.
948. i.e., the system of Christian doctrine.
949. Literally, "to the assembly of the bishop."
950. Comp. Isa. lviii. 6.
951. Phil. ii. 3.
952. Or, "the archives of the Spirit are not exposed to all."
953. Acts xxvi. 14.
954. i.e., the Jewish priests.
955. Literally, "proclaimed as to him."
956. The meaning is doubtful. Comp. 2 Tim. i. 10.
957. i.e., the Jewish priests.
958. John xiv. 6.
959. 1 Cor. x. 4.
960. Literally, "the hedge."
961. John x. 11.
962. John x. 9.
963. Gen. xlix. 10.
964. Matt. xxviii. 19.
965. Literally, "for the name of."
966. Literally, "for the name of."
967. Literally, "bidding farewell to."
968. Or, "for the sake of honour."
969. Literally, "bidding farewell to."
970. Comp. Ezek. xviii. 23, 32, Ezek. xxxiii. 11; 2 Pet. iii. 9.
971. The ms. has "Burgus."
972. Or, "for the sake of honour."

The Epistle of Ignatius to the Smyrnæans Shorter and Longer Versions

Ignatius, who is also called Theophorus, to the Church of God the Father, and of the beloved Jesus Christ, which has through mercy obtained every kind of gift, which is filled with faith and love, and is deficient in no gift, most worthy of God, and adorned with holiness: [973] the Church which is at Smyrna, in Asia, wishes abundance of happiness, through the immaculate Spirit and word of God.

Ignatius, who is also called Theophorus, to the Church of God the most high Father, and His beloved Son Jesus Christ, which has through mercy obtained every kind of gift, which is filled with faith and love, and is deficient in no gift, most worthy of God, and adorned with holiness: [974] the Church which is at Smyrna, in Asia, wishes abundance of happiness, through the immaculate Spirit and word of God.

Chapter I - Thanks to God for your faith

I Glorify God, even Jesus Christ, who has given you such wisdom. For I have observed that ye are perfected in an immoveable faith, as if ye were nailed to the cross of our Lord Jesus Christ, both in the flesh and in the spirit, and are established in love through the blood of Christ, being fully persuaded with respect to our Lord, that He was truly of the seed of David according to the flesh, [975] and the Son of God according to the will and power [976] of God, that He was truly born of a virgin, was baptized by John, in order that all righteousness might be fulfilled [977] by Him; and was truly, under Pontius Pilate and Herod the tetrarch, nailed [to the cross] for us in His flesh. Of this fruit [978] we are by His divinely-blessed passion, that He might set up a standard [979] for all ages, through His resurrection, to all His holy and faithful [followers], whether among Jews or Gentiles, in the one body of His Church.

I Glorify the God and Father of our Lord Jesus Christ, who by Him has given you such wisdom. For I have observed that ye are perfected in an immoveable faith, as if ye were nailed to the cross of our Lord Jesus Christ, both in the flesh and in the spirit, and are established in love through the blood of Christ, being fully persuaded, in very truth, with respect to our Lord Jesus Christ, that He was the Son of God, "the first-born of every creature," [980] God the Word, the only-begotten Son, and was of the seed of David according to the flesh, [981] by the Virgin Mary; was baptized by John, that all righteousness might be fulfilled [982] by Him; that He lived a life of holiness without sin, and was truly, under Pontius Pilate and Herod the tetrarch, nailed [to the cross] for us in His flesh. From whom we also derive our being, [983] from His divinely-blessed passion, that He might set up a standard for the ages, through His resurrection, to all His holy and faithful [followers], whether among Jews or Gentiles, in the one body of His Church.

Chapter II - Christ's true passion

Now, He suffered all these things for our sakes, that we might be saved. And He suffered truly, even as also He truly raised up Himself, not, as certain unbelievers maintain, that He only seemed to suffer, as they themselves only seem to be [Christians]. And as they believe, so shall it happen unto them, when they shall be divested of their bodies, and be mere evil spirits. [984]

Now, He suffered all these things for us; and He suffered them really, and not in appearance only, even as also He truly rose again. But not, as some of the unbelievers, who are ashamed of the formation of man, and the cross, and death itself, affirm, that in appearance only, and not in truth, He took a body of the Virgin, and suffered only in appearance, forgetting, as they do, Him who said, "The Word was made flesh;" [985] and again, "Destroy this temple, and in three days I will raise it up;" [986] and once more, "If I be lifted up from the earth, I will draw all men unto Me." [987] The Word therefore did dwell in flesh, for "Wisdom built herself an house." [988] The Word raised up again His own temple on the third day, when it had been destroyed by the Jews fighting against Christ. The Word, when His flesh was lifted up, after the manner of the brazen serpent in the wilderness, drew all men to Himself for their eternal salvation. [989]

Chapter III - Christ was possessed of a body after His resurrection

For I know that after His resurrection also He was still possessed of flesh, [990] and I believe that He is so now. When, for instance, He came to those who were with Peter, He said to them, "Lay hold, handle Me, and see that I am not an incorporeal spirit." [991] And immediately they touched Him, and believed, being convinced both by His flesh and spirit. For this cause also they despised death, and were found its conquerors. [992] And after his resurrection He did eat and drink with them, as being possessed of flesh, although spiritually He was united to the Father.

And I know that He was possessed of a body not only in His being born and crucified, but I also know that He was so after His resurrection, and believe that He is so now. When, for instance, He came to those who were with Peter, He said to them, "Lay hold, handle Me, and see that I am not an incorporeal spirit." [993] "For a spirit hath not flesh and bones, as ye see Me have." [994] And He says to Thomas, "Reach hither thy finger into the print of the nails, and reach hither thy hand, and thrust it into My side;" [995] and immediately they believed that He was Christ. Wherefore Thomas also says to Him, "My Lord, and my God." [996] And on this account also did they despise death, for it were too little to say, indignities and stripes. Nor was this all; but also after He had shown Himself to them, that He had risen indeed, and not in appearance only, He both ate and drank with them during forty entire days. And thus was He, with the flesh, received up in their sight unto Him that sent Him, being with that same flesh to come again, accompanied by glory and power. For, say the [holy] oracles, "This same Jesus, who is taken up from you into heaven, shall so come, in like manner as ye have seen Him go unto heaven." [997] But if they say that He will come at the end of the world without a body, how shall those "see Him that pierced Him," [998] and when they recognise Him, "mourn for themselves?" [999] For incorporeal beings have neither form nor figure, nor the aspect [1000] of an animal possessed of shape, because their nature is in itself simple.

Chapter IV - Beware of these heretics

I give you these instructions, beloved, assured that ye also hold the same opinions [as I do]. But I guard you beforehand from those beasts in the shape of men, whom you must not only not receive, but, if it be possible, not even meet with; only you must pray to God for them, if by any means they may be brought to repentance, which, however, will be very difficult. Yet Jesus Christ, who is our true life, has the power of [effecting] this. But if these things were done by our Lord only in appearance, then am I also only in appearance bound. And why have I also surrendered myself to death, to fire, to the sword, to the wild beasts? But, [in fact,] he who is near to the sword is near to God; he that is among the wild beasts is in company with God; provided only he be so in the name of Jesus Christ. I undergo all these things that I may suffer together with Him, [1001] He who became a perfect man inwardly strengthening me. [1002]

I give you these instructions, beloved, assured that ye also hold the same opinions [as I do]. But I guard you beforehand from these beasts in the shape of men, from whom you must not only turn away, but even flee from them. Only you must pray for them, if by any means they may be brought to repentance. For if the Lord were in the body in appearance only, and were crucified in appearance only, then am I also bound in appearance only. And why have I also surrendered myself to death, to fire, to the sword, to the wild beasts? But, [in fact,] I endure all things for Christ, not in appearance only, but in reality, that I may suffer together with Him, while He Himself inwardly strengthens me; for of myself I have no such ability.

Chapter V - Their dangerous errors

Some ignorantly [1003] deny Him, or rather have been denied by Him, being the advocates of death rather than of the truth. These persons neither have the prophets persuaded, nor the law of Moses, nor the Gospel even to this day, nor the sufferings we have individually endured. For they think also the same thing regarding us. [1004] For what does any one profit me, if he commends me, but blasphemes my Lord, not confessing that He was [truly] possessed of a body? [1005] But he who does not acknowledge this, has in fact altogether denied Him, being enveloped in death. [1006] I have not, however, thought good to write the names of such persons, inasmuch as they are unbelievers. Yea, far be it from me to make any mention of them, until they repent and return to [a true belief in] Christ's passion, which is our resurrection.

Some have ignorantly denied Him, and advocate falsehood rather than the truth. These persons neither have the prophecies persuaded, nor the law of Moses, nor the Gospel even to this day, nor the sufferings we have individually endured. For they think also the same thing regarding us. For what does it profit, if any one commends me, but blasphemes my Lord, not owning Him to be God incarnate? [1007] He that does not confess this, has in fact altogether denied Him, being enveloped in death. I have not, however, thought good to write the names of such persons, inasmuch as they are unbelievers; and far be it from me to make any mention of them, until they repent.

Chapter VI - Unbelievers in the blood of Christ shall be condemned

Let no man deceive himself. Both the things which are in heaven, and the glorious angels, [1008] and rulers, both visible and invisible, if they believe not in the blood of Christ, shall, in consequence, incur condemnation. [1009] "He that is able to receive it, let him receive it." [1010] Let not [high] place puff any one up: for that which is worth all is [1011] faith and love, to which nothing is to be preferred. But consider those who are of a different opinion with respect to the grace of Christ which has come unto us, how opposed they are to the will of God. They have no regard for love; no care for the widow, or the orphan, or the oppressed; of the bond, or of the free; of the hungry, or of the thirsty.

Let no man deceive himself. Unless he believes that Christ Jesus has lived in the flesh, and shall confess His cross and passion, and the blood which He shed for the salvation of the world, he shall not obtain eternal life, whether he be a king, or a priest, or a ruler, or a private person, a master or a servant, a man or a woman. "He that is able to receive it, let him receive it." [1012] Let no man's place, or dignity, or riches, puff him up; and let no man's low condition or poverty abase him. For the chief points are faith towards God, hope towards Christ, the enjoyment of those good things for which we look, and love towards God and our neighbour. For, "Thou shall love the Lord thy God with all thy heart, and thy neighbour as thyself." [1013] And the Lord says, "This is life eternal, to know the only true God, and Jesus Christ whom He has sent." [1014] And again, "A new commandment give I unto you, that ye love one another. On these two commandments hang all the law and the prophets." [1015] Do ye, therefore, notice those who preach other doctrines, how they affirm that the Father of Christ cannot be known, and how they exhibit enmity and deceit in their dealings with one another. They have no regard for love; they despise the good things we expect hereafter; they regard present things as if they were durable; they ridicule him that is in affliction; they laugh at him that is in bonds.

Chapter VII - Let us stand aloof from such heretics

They abstain from the Eucharist and from prayer, [1016] because they confess not the Eucharist to be the flesh of our Saviour Jesus Christ, which suffered for our sins, and which the Father, of His goodness, raised up again. Those, therefore, who speak against this gift of God, incur death [1017] in the midst of their disputes. But it were better for them to treat it with respect, [1018] that they also might rise again. It is fitting, therefore, that ye should keep aloof from such persons, and not to speak of [1019] them either in private or in public, but to give heed to the prophets, and above all, to the Gospel, in which the passion [of Christ] has been revealed to us, and the resurrection has been fully proved. [1020] But avoid all divisions, as the beginning of evils.

They are ashamed of the cross; they mock at the passion; they make a jest of the resurrection. They are the offspring of that spirit who is the author of all evil, who led Adam, [1021] by means of his wife, to transgress the commandment, who slew Abel by the hands of Cain, who fought against Job, who was the accuser of Joshua [1022] the son of Josedech, who sought to "sift the faith" [1023] of the apostles, who stirred up the multitude of the Jews against the Lord, who also now "worketh in the children of disobedience; [1024] from whom the Lord Jesus Christ will deliver us, who prayed that the faith of the apostles might not fail, [1025] not because He was not able of Himself to preserve it, but because He rejoiced in the pre-eminence of the Father. It is fitting, therefore, that we should keep aloof from such persons, and neither in private nor in public to talk with [1026] them; but to give heed to the law, and the prophets, and to those who have preached to you the word of salvation. But flee from all abominable heresies, and those that cause schisms, as the beginning of evils.

Chapter VIII - Let nothing be done without the bishop

See that ye all follow the bishop, even as Jesus Christ does the Father, and the presbytery as ye would the apostles; and reverence the deacons, as being the institution [1027] of God. Let no man do anything connected with the Church without the bishop. Let that be deemed a proper [1028] Eucharist, which is [administered] either by the bishop, or by one to whom he has entrusted it. Wherever the bishop shall appear, there let the multitude [of the people] also be; even as, wherever Jesus Christ is, there is the Catholic Church. It is not lawful without the bishop either to baptize or to celebrate a love-feast; but whatsoever he shall approve of, that is also pleasing to God, so that everything that is done may be secure and valid. [1029]

See that ye all follow the bishop, even as Christ Jesus does the Father, and the presbytery as ye would the apostles. Do ye also reverence the deacons, as those that carry out [through their office] the appointment of God. Let no man do anything connected with the Church without the bishop. Let that be deemed a proper [1030] Eucharist, which is [administered] either by the bishop, or by one to whom he has entrusted it. Wherever the bishop shall appear, there let the multitude [of the people] also be; even as where Christ is, there does all the heavenly host stand by, waiting upon Him as the Chief Captain of the Lord's might, and the Governor of every intelligent nature. It is not lawful without the bishop either to baptize, or to offer, or to present sacrifice, or to celebrate a love-feast. [1031] But that which seems good to him, is also well-pleasing to God, that everything ye do may be secure and valid.

Chapter IX - Honour the bishop

Moreover, [1032] it is in accordance with reason that we should return to soberness [of conduct], and, while yet we have opportunity, exercise repentance towards God. It is well to reverence [1033] both God and the bishop. He who honours the bishop has been honoured by God; he who does anything without the knowledge of the bishop, does [in reality] serve the devil. Let all things, then, abound to you through grace, for ye are worthy. Ye have refreshed me in all things, and Jesus Christ [shall refresh] you. Ye have loved me when absent as well as when present. May God recompense you, for whose sake, while ye endure all things, ye shall attain unto Him.

Moreover, it is in accordance with reason that we should return to soberness [of conduct], and, while yet we have opportunity, exercise repentance towards God. For "in Hades there is no one who can confess his sins." [1034] For "behold the man, and his work is before him." [1035] And [the Scripture saith], "My son, honour thou God and the king." [1036] And say I, Honour thou God indeed, as the Author and Lord of all things, but the bishop as the high-priest, who bears the image of God--of God, inasmuch as he is a ruler, and of Christ, in his capacity of a priest. After Him, we must also honour the king. For there is no one superior to God, or even like to Him, among all the beings that exist. Nor is there any one in the Church greater than the bishop, who ministers as a priest to God for the salvation of the whole world. Nor, again, is there any one among rulers to be compared with the king, who secures peace and good order to those over whom he rules. He who honours the bishop shall be honoured by God, even as he that dishonours him shall be punished by God. For if he that rises up against kings is justly held worthy of punishment, inasmuch as he dissolves public order, of how much sorer punishment, suppose ye, shall he be thought worthy, [1037] who presumes to do anything without the bishop, thus both destroying the [Church's] unity, and throwing its order into confusion? For the priesthood is the very highest point of all good things among men, against which whosoever is mad enough to strive, dishonours not man, but God, and Christ Jesus, the First-born, and the only High Priest, by nature, of the Father. Let all things therefore be done by you with good order in Christ. Let the laity be subject to the deacons; the deacons to the presbyters; the presbyters to the bishop; the bishop to Christ, even as He is to the Father. As ye, brethren, have refreshed me, so will Jesus Christ refresh you. Ye have loved me when absent, as well as when present. God will recompense you, for whose sake ye have shown such kindness towards His prisoner. For even if I am not worthy of it, yet your zeal [to help me] is an admirable [1038] thing. For "he who honours a prophet in the name of a prophet, shall receive a prophet's reward." [1039] It is manifest also, that he who honours a prisoner of Jesus Christ shall receive the reward of the martyrs.

Chapter X - Acknowledgment of their kindness

Ye have done well in receiving Philo and Rheus Agathopus as servants [1040] of Christ our God, who have followed me for the sake of God, and who give thanks to the Lord in your behalf, because ye have in every way refreshed them. None of these things shall be lost to you. May my spirit be for you, [1041] and my bonds, which ye have not despised or been ashamed of; nor shall Jesus Christ, our perfect hope, be ashamed of you.

Ye have done well in receiving Philo, and Gaius, and Agathopus, who, being the servants [1042] of Christ, have followed me for the sake of God, and who greatly bless the Lord in your behalf, because ye have in every way refreshed them. None of those things which ye have done to them shall be passed by without being reckoned unto you. "The Lord grant" to you "that ye may find mercy of the Lord in that day!" [1043] May my spirit be for you, [1044] and my bonds, which ye have not despised or been ashamed of. Wherefore, neither shall Jesus Christ, our perfect hope, be ashamed of you.

Chapter XI - Request to them to send a messenger to Antioch

Your prayer has reached to the Church which is at Antioch in Syria. Coming from that place bound with chains, most acceptable to God, [1045] I salute all; I who am not worthy to be styled from thence, inasmuch as I am the least of them. Nevertheless, according to the will of God, I have been thought worthy [of this honour], not that I have any sense [1046] [of having deserved it], but by the grace of God, which I wish may be perfectly given to me, that through your prayers I may attain to God. In order, therefore, that your work may be complete both on earth and in heaven, it is fitting that, for the honour of God, your Church should elect some worthy delegate; [1047] so that he, journeying into Syria, may congratulate them that they are [now] at peace, and are restored to [1048] their proper greatness, and that their proper constitution [1049] has been re-established among them. It seems then to me a becoming thing, that you should send some one of your number with an epistle, so that, in company with them, he may rejoice [1050] over the tranquillity which, according to the will of God, they have obtained, and because that, through your prayers, they have now reached the harbour. As persons who are perfect, ye should also aim at [1051] those things which are perfect. For when ye are desirous to do well, God is also ready to assist you.

Your prayers have reached to the Church of Antioch, and it is at peace. Coming from that place bound, I salute all; I who am not worthy to be styled from thence, inasmuch as I am the least of them. Nevertheless, according to the will of God, I have been thought worthy [of this honour], not that I have any sense [1052] [of having deserved it], but by the grace of God, which I wish may be perfectly given to me, that through your prayers I may attain to God. In order, therefore, that your work may be complete both on earth and in heaven, it is fitting that, for the honour of God, your Church should elect some worthy delegate; [1053] so that he, journeying into Syria, may congratulate them that they are [now] at peace, and are restored to their proper greatness, and that their proper constitution [1054] has been re-established among them. What appears to me proper to be done is this, that you should send some one of your number with an epistle, so that, in company with them, he may rejoice over the tranquillity which, according to the will of God, they have obtained, and because that, through your prayers, I have secured Christ as a safe harbour. As persons who are perfect, ye should also aim at [1055] those things which are perfect. For when ye are desirous to do well, God is also ready to assist you.

Chapter XII - Salutations

The love of the brethren at Troas salutes you; whence also I write to you by Burrhus, whom ye sent with me, together with the Ephesians, your brethren, and who has in all things refreshed me. And I would that all may imitate him, as being a pattern of a minister [1056] of God. Grace will reward him in all things. I salute your most worthy [1057] bishop, and your very venerable [1058] presbytery, and your deacons, my fellow-servants, and all of you individually, as well as generally, in the name of Jesus Christ, and in His flesh and blood, in His passion and resurrection, both corporeal and spiritual, in union with God and you. [1059] Grace, mercy, peace, and patience, be with you for evermore!

The love of your brethren at Troas salutes you; whence also I write to you by Burgus, whom ye sent with me, together with the Ephesians, your brethren, and who has in all things refreshed me. And I would that all may imitate him, as being a pattern of a minister of God. The grace of the Lord will reward him in all things. I salute your most worthy bishop Polycarp, and your venerable presbytery, and your Christ-bearing deacons, my fellow-servants, and all of you individually, as well as generally, in the name of Christ Jesus, and in His flesh and blood, in His passion and resurrection, both corporeal and spiritual, in union with God and you. Grace, mercy, peace, and patience, be with you in Christ for evermore!

Chapter XIII - Conclusion

I salute the families of my brethren, with their wives and children, and the virgins who are called widows. [1060] Be ye strong, I pray, in the power of the Holy Ghost. Philo, who is with me, greets you. I salute the house of Tavias, and pray that it may be confirmed in faith and love, both corporeal and spiritual. I salute Alce, my well-beloved, [1061] and the incomparable Daphnus, and Eutecnus, and all by name. Fare ye well in the grace of God.

I salute the families of my brethren, with their wives and children, and those that are ever virgins, and the widows. Be ye strong, I pray, in the power of the Holy Ghost. Philo, my fellow-servant, who is with me, greets you. I salute the house of Tavias, and pray that it may be confirmed in faith and love, both corporeal and spiritual. I salute Alce, my well-beloved, [1062] and the incomparable Daphnus, and Eutecnus, and all by name. Fare ye well in the grace of God, and of our Lord Jesus Christ, being filled with the Holy Spirit, and divine and sacred wisdom.

Footnotes:

973. Literally, "holy-bearing."
974. Literally, "holy-bearing."
975. Rom. i. 3.
976. Theodoret, in quoting this passage, reads, "the Godhead and power."
977. Matt. iii. 15.
978. i.e., the cross, "fruit" being put for Christ on the tree.
979. Isa. v. 26, Isa. xlix. 22.
980. Col. i. 15.
981. Rom. i. 3.
982. Matt. iii. 15.
983. Literally, "we are."
984. Or, "seeing that they are phantasmal and diabolical," as some render, but the above is preferable.
985. John i. 14.
986. John ii. 19.

987. John xii. 32.
988. Prov. ix. 1.
989. Num. xxi. 9; John iii. 14.
990. Literally, "in the flesh."
991. Literally, "demon." According to Jerome, this quotation is from the Gospel of the Nazarenes. Comp. Luke xxiv. 39.
992. Literally, "above death."
993. Literally, "demon." According to Jerome, this quotation is from the Gospel of the Nazarenes. Comp. Luke xxiv. 39.
994. Luke xxiv. 39.
995. John xx. 27.
996. John xx. 28.
997. Acts i. 11.
998. Rev. i. 7.
999. Zech. xii. 10.
1000. Or, "mark."
1001. Comp. Rom. viii. 17.
1002. Comp. Phil. iv. 13.
1003. Or, "foolishly."
1004. i.e., As they imagine Christ to have suffered only in appearance, so they believe that we suffer in vain.
1005. Literally, "a flesh-bearer."
1006. Literally, "a death-bearer."
1007. Literally, "a flesh-bearer."
1008. Literally, "the glory of the angels."
1009. Literally, "judgment is to them."
1010. Matt. xix. 12.
1011. Literally, "the whole is."
1012. Matt. xix. 12.
1013. Deut. vi. 5.
1014. John xvii. 31.
1015. John xiii. 34; Matt. xxii. 40.
1016. Theodoret, in quoting this passage, reads προσφοράς, "offering."
1017. Literally, "die disputing."
1018. Literally, "to love." Some think there is a reference to the agapæ, or love-feasts.
1019. The reading is περί in the one case, and μετά in the other, though the latter meaning seems preferable. Most of the mss. of the longer recension read περί, as in the shorter.
1020. Literally, "perfected."
1021. Literally, "drove Adam out of."
1022. Zech. iii. 1.
1023. Luke xxii. 31.
1024. Eph. ii. 2.
1025. Luke xxii. 32.
1026. The reading is περί in the one case, and μετά in the other, though the latter meaning seems preferable. Most of the mss. of the longer recension read περί, as in the shorter.
1027. Or, "command."
1028. Or, "firm."
1029. Or, "firm."
1030. Or, "firm."
1031. Some refer the words to the Lord's Supper.
1032. Or, "finally."
1033. Literally, "to know."
1034. Ps. vi. 5.
1035. Isa. lxii. 11.
1036. Prov. xxiv. 21.
1037. Comp. Heb. x. 29.
1038. Or, "great."
1039. Matt. x. 41.
1040. Or, "deacons."
1041. Comp. Epistle of Ignatius to Ephesians, chap. xxi.; to Polycarp, chap. ii. vi.
1042. Or, "deacons."
1043. 2 Tim. i. 18.
1044. Comp. Epistle of Ignatius to Ephesians, chap. xxi.; to Polycarp, chap. ii. vi.
1045. Literally, "most becoming of God."
1046. Or, "from any conscience."
1047. Literally, "God-ambassador."
1048. Or, "having received."
1049. Literally, "body."
1050. Literally, "may glorify with him."
1051. Or, "think of."
1052. Or, "from any conscience."
1053. Literally, "God-ambassador."
1054. Literally, "body."
1055. Or, "think of."
1056. Or, "the ministry."
1057. Literally, "worthy of God."
1058. Literally, "most becoming of God."
1059. Literally, "in the union of God and of you."
1060. The deaconesses seem to have been called widows.
1061. Literally, "the name desired of me."
1062. Literally, "the name desired of me."

The Epistle of Ignatius to Polycarp Shorter and Longer Versions

Ignatius, who is also called Theophorus, to Polycarp, Bishop of the Church of the Smyrnæans, or rather, who has, as his own bishop, God the Father, and the Lord Jesus Christ: [wishes] abundance of happiness.

Ignatius, bishop of Antioch, and a witness for Jesus Christ, to Polycarp, Bishop of the Church of the Smyrnæans, or rather, who has, as his own bishop, God the Father, and Jesus Christ: [wishes] abundance of happiness.

Chapter I - Commendation and exhortation

Having obtained good proof that thy mind is fixed in God as upon an immoveable rock, I loudly glorify [His name] that I have been thought worthy [to behold] thy blameless face, [1063] which may I ever enjoy in God! I entreat thee, by the grace with which thou art clothed, to press forward in thy course, and to exhort all that they may be saved. Maintain thy position with all care, both in the flesh and spirit. Have a regard to preserve unity, than which nothing is better. Bear with all, even as the Lord does with thee. Support [1064] all in love, as also thou doest. Give thyself to prayer without ceasing. [1065] Implore additional understanding to what thou already hast. Be watchful, possessing a sleepless spirit. Speak to every man separately, as God enables thee. [1066] Bear the infirmities of all, as being a perfect athlete [in the Christian life]. where the labour is great, the gain is all the more.

Having obtained good proof that thy mind is fixed in God as upon an immoveable rock, I loudly glorify [His name] that I have been thought worthy to behold thy blameless face, [1067] which may I ever enjoy in God! I entreat thee, by the grace with which thou art clothed, to press forward in thy course, and to exhort all that they may be saved. Maintain thy position with all care, both in the flesh and spirit. Have a regard to preserve unity, than which nothing is better. Bear with all even as the Lord does with thee. Support [1068] all in love, as also thou doest. Give thyself to prayer without ceasing. [1069] Implore additional understanding to what thou already hast. Be watchful, possessing a sleepless spirit. Speak to every man separately, as God enables thee. [1070] Bear the infirmities of all, as being a perfect athlete [in the Christian life], even as does the Lord of all. For says [the Scripture], "He Himself took our infirmities, and bare our sicknesses." [1071] Where the labour is great, the gain is all the more.

Chapter II - Exhortations

If thou lovest the good disciples, no thanks are due to thee on that account; but rather seek by meekness to subdue the more troublesome. Every kind of wound is not healed with the same plaster. Mitigate violent attacks [of disease] by gentle applications. [1072] Be in all things "wise as a serpent, and harmless as a dove." [1073] For this purpose thou art composed of both flesh and spirit, that thou mayest deal tenderly [1074] with those [evils] that present themselves visibly before thee. And as respects those that are not seen, [1075] pray that [God] would reveal them unto thee, in order that thou mayest be wanting in nothing, but mayest abound in every gift. The times call for thee, as pilots do for the winds, and as one tossed with tempest seeks for the haven, so that both thou [and those under thy care] may attain to God. Be sober as an athlete of God: the prize set before thee is immortality and eternal life, of which thou art also persuaded. In all things may my soul be for thine, [1076] and my bonds also, which thou hast loved.

If thou lovest the good disciples, no thanks are due to thee on that account; but rather seek by meekness to subdue the more troublesome. Every kind of wound is not healed with the same plaster. Mitigate violent attacks [of disease] by gentle applications. [1077] Be in all things "wise as a serpent, and harmless always as a dove." [1078] For this purpose thou art composed of both soul and body, art both fleshly and spiritual, that thou mayest correct those [evils] that present themselves visibly before thee; and as respects those that are not seen, mayest pray that these should be revealed to thee, so that thou mayest be wanting in nothing, but mayest abound in every gift. The times call upon thee to pray. For as the wind aids the pilot of a ship, and as havens are advantageous for safety to a tempest-tossed vessel, so is also prayer to thee, in order that thou mayest attain to God. Be sober as an athlete of God, whose will is immortality and eternal life; of which thou art also persuaded. In all things may my soul be for thine, [1079] and my bonds also, which thou hast loved.

Chapter III - Exhortations

Let not those who seem worthy of credit, but teach strange doctrines, [1080] fill thee with apprehension. Stand firm, as does an anvil which is beaten. It is the part of a noble [1081] athlete to be wounded, and yet to conquer. And especially, we ought to bear all things for the sake of God, that He also may bear with us. Be ever becoming more zealous than what thou art. Weigh carefully the times. Look for Him who is above all time, eternal and invisible, yet who became visible for our sakes; impalpable and impassible, yet who became passible on our account; and who in every kind of way suffered for our sakes.

Let not those who seem worthy of credit, but teach strange doctrines, [1082] fill thee with apprehension. Stand firm, as does an anvil which is beaten. It is the part of a noble [1083] athlete to be wounded, and yet to conquer. And especially we ought to bear all things for the sake of God, that He also may bear with us, and bring us into His kingdom. Add more and more to thy diligence; run thy race with increasing energy; weigh carefully the times. Whilst thou art here, be a conqueror; for here is the course, and there are the crowns. Look for Christ, the Son of God; who was before time, yet appeared in time; who was invisible by nature, yet visible in the flesh; who was impalpable, and could not be touched, as being without a body, but for our sakes became such, might be touched and handled in the body; who was impassible as God, but became passible for our sakes as man; and who in every kind of way suffered for our sakes.

Chapter IV - Exhortations

Let not widows be neglected. Be thou, after the Lord, their protector [1084] and friend. Let nothing be done without thy consent; neither do thou anything without the approval of God, which indeed thou dost not, inasmuch as thou art stedfast. Let your assembling together be of frequent [1085] occurrence: seek after all by name. [1086] Do not despise either male or female slaves, yet neither let them be puffed up with conceit, but rather let them submit themselves [1087] the more, for the glory of God, that they may obtain from God a better liberty. Let them not long to be set free [from slavery] at the public expense, that they be not found slaves to their own desires.

Let not the widows be neglected. Be thou, after the Lord, their protector and friend. Let nothing be done without thy consent; neither do thou anything without the approval of God, which indeed thou doest not. Be thou stedfast. Let your assembling together be of frequent [1088] occurrence: seek after all by name. [1089] Do not despise either male or female slaves, yet neither let them be puffed up with conceit, but rather let them submit themselves [1090] the more, for the glory of God, that they may obtain from God a better liberty. Let them not wish to be set free [from slavery] at the public expense, that they be not found slaves to their own desires.

Chapter V - The duties of husbands and wives

Flee evil arts; but all the more discourse in public regarding them. [1091] Speak to my sisters, that they love the Lord, and be satisfied with their husbands both in the flesh and spirit. In like manner also, exhort my brethren, in the name of Jesus Christ, that they love their wives, even as the Lord the Church. [1092] If any one can continue in a state of purity, [1093] to the honour of Him who is Lord of the flesh, [1094] let him so remain without boasting. If he begins to boast, he is undone; and if he reckon himself greater than the bishop, he is ruined. But it becomes both men and women who marry, to form their union with the approval of the bishop, that their marriage may be according to God, and not after their own lust. Let all things be done to the honour of God. [1095]

Flee evil arts; but all the more discourse in public regarding them. Speak to my sisters, that they love the Lord, and be satisfied with their husbands both in the flesh and spirit. In like manner also, exhort my brethren, in the name of Jesus Christ, that they love their wives, even as the Lord the Church. If any one can continue in a state of purity, [1096] to the honour of the flesh of the Lord, let him so remain without boasting. If he shall boast, he is undone; and if he seeks to be more prominent [1097] than the bishop, he is ruined. But it becomes both men and women who marry, to form their union with the approval of the bishop, that their marriage may be according to the Lord, and not after their own lust. Let all things be done to the honour of God. [1098]

Chapter VI - The duties of the Christian flock

Give ye [1099] heed to the bishop, that God also may give heed to you. My soul be for theirs [1100] that are submissive to the bishop, to the presbyters, and to the deacons, and may my portion be along with them in God! Labour together with one another; strive in company together; run together; suffer together; sleep together; and awake together, as the stewards, and associates, [1101] and servants of God. Please ye Him under whom ye fight, and from whom ye receive your wages. Let none of you be found a deserter. Let your baptism endure as your arms; your faith as your helmet; your love as your spear; your patience as a complete panoply. Let your works be the charge [1102] assigned to you, that ye may receive a worthy recompense. Be long-suffering, therefore, with one another, in meekness, as God is towards you. May I have joy of you for ever! [1103]

Give ye [1104] heed to the bishop, that God also may give heed to you. My soul be for theirs [1105] that are submissive to the bishop, to the presbytery, and to the deacons: may I have my portion with them from God! Labour together with one another; strive in company together; run together; suffer together; sleep together; and awake together, as the stewards, and associates, [1106] and servants of God. Please ye Him under whom ye fight, and from whom ye shall receive your wages. Let none of you be found a deserter. Let your baptism endure as your arms; your faith as your helmet; your love as your spear; your patience as a complete panoply. Let your works be the charge assigned to you, that you may obtain for them a most worthy [1107] recompense. Be long-suffering, therefore, with one another, in meekness, and God shall be so with you. May I have joy of you for ever! [1108]

Chapter VII - Request that Polycarp would send a messenger to Antioch

Seeing that the Church which is at Antioch in Syria is, as report has informed me, at peace, through your prayers, I also am the more encouraged, resting without anxiety in God, [1109] if indeed by means of suffering I may attain to God, so that, through your prayers, I may be found a disciple [of Christ]. [1110] It is fitting, O Polycarp, most blessed in God, to assemble a very solemn [1111] council, and to elect one whom you greatly love, and know to be a man of activity, who may be designated the messenger of God; [1112] and to bestow on him this honour that he may go into Syria, and glorify your ever active love to the praise of Christ. A Christian has not power over himself, but must always be ready for [1113] the service of God. Now, this work is both God's and yours, when ye shall have completed it to His glory. [1114] For I trust that, through grace, ye are prepared for every good work pertaining to God. Knowing, therefore, your energetic love of the truth, I have exhorted you by this brief Epistle.

Seeing that the Church which is at Antioch in Syria is, as report has informed me, at peace, through your prayers, I also am the more encouraged, resting without anxiety in God, [1115] if indeed by means of suffering I may attain to God, so that, through your prayers, I may be found a disciple [of Christ]. It is fitting, O Polycarp, most blessed in God, to assemble a very solemn [1116] council, and to elect one whom you greatly love, and know to be a man of activity, who may be designated the messenger of God; [1117] and to bestow on him the honour of going into Syria, so that, going into Syria, he may glorify your ever active love to the praise of God. A Christian has not power over himself, but must always be ready for [1118] the service of God. Now, this work is both God's and yours, when ye shall have completed it. For I trust that, through grace, ye are prepared for every good work pertaining to God. Knowing your energetic love of the truth, I have exhorted you by this brief Epistle.

Chapter VIII - Let other churches also send to Antioch

Inasmuch as I have not been able to write to all the Churches, because I must suddenly sail from Troas to Neapolis, as the will [1119] [of the emperor] enjoins, [I beg that] thou, as being acquainted with the purpose [1120] of God, wilt write to the adjacent Churches, that they also may act in like manner, such as are able to do so sending messengers, [1121] and the others transmitting letters through those persons who are sent by thee, that thou [1122] mayest be glorified by a work [1123] which shall be remembered for ever, as indeed thou art worthy to be. I salute all by name, and in particular the wife of Epitropus, with all her house and children. I salute Attalus, my beloved. I salute him who shall be deemed worthy to go [from you] into Syria. Grace shall be with him for ever, and with Polycarp that sends him. I pray for your happiness for ever in our God, Jesus Christ, by whom continue ye in the unity and under the protection of God, [1124] I salute Alce, my dearly beloved. [1125] Fare ye well in the Lord.

Inasmuch, therefore, as I have not been able to write to all Churches, because I must suddenly sail from Troas to Neapolis, as the will [1126] [of the emperor] enjoins, [I beg that] thou, as being acquainted with the purpose [1127] of God, wilt write to the adjacent Churches, that they also may act in like manner, such as are able to do so sending messenger, and the others transmitting letters through those persons who are sent by thee, that thou mayest be glorified by a work [1128] which shall be remembered for ever, as indeed thou art worthy to be. I salute all by name, and in particular the wife of Epitropus, with all her house and children. I salute Attalus, my beloved. I salute him who shall be deemed worthy to go [from you] into Syria. Grace shall be with him for ever, and with Polycarp that sends him. I pray for your happiness for ever in our God, Jesus Christ, by whom continue ye in the unity and under the protection of God. I salute Alce, my dearly beloved. [1129] Amen. Grace [be with you]. Fare ye well in the Lord.

Footnotes:

1063. i.e., to make personal acquaintance with one esteemed so highly.
1064. Or, "tolerate."
1065. Comp. 1 Thess. v. 17.
1066. Some read, "according to thy practice."
1067. i.e., to make personal acquaintance with one esteemed so highly.
1068. Or, "tolerate."
1069. Comp. 1 Thess. v. 17.
1070. Some read, "according to thy practice."
1071. Matt. viii. 17.
1072. Literally, "paroxysms by embrocations."
1073. Matt. x. 16.
1074. Literally, "flatter."
1075. Some refer this to the mysteries of God and others to things yet future.
1076. Comp. Epistle of Ignatius to the Ephesians, chap. xxi., etc.
1077. Literally, "paroxysms by embrocations."
1078. Matt. x. 16.
1079. Comp. Epistle of Ignatius to the Ephesians, chap. xxi., etc.
1080. Comp. 1 Tim. i. 3, 1 Tim. vi. 3.
1081. Literally, "great."
1082. Comp. 1 Tim. i. 3, 1 Tim. vi. 3.
1083. Literally, "great."
1084. The word in the original (φροντιστής) denotes one who thinks or cares for another.
1085. Some refer the words to more frequent meetings, and others to these meetings being more numerous; no comparison is necessarily implied.
1086. i.e., so as to bring them out to the public assembly.
1087. Or, "act the part of slaves."
1088. Some refer the words to more frequent meetings, and others to these meetings being more numerous; no comparison is necessarily implied.
1089. i.e., so as to bring them out to the public assembly.
1090. Or, "act the part of slaves."
1091. Some insert me, and render, "rather do not even speak of them."
1092. Eph. v. 25.
1093. i.e., in celibacy.
1094. Some render, "to the honour of the flesh of the Lord," as in the longer recension.
1095. Comp. 1 Cor. x. 31.
1096. i.e., in celibacy.
1097. Literally, "if he be known beyond the bishop."
1098. Comp. 1 Cor. x. 31.
1099. As this Epistle, though sent to the bishop, was meant to be read to the people, Ignatius here directly addresses them.
1100. Comp. chap. ii. etc.
1101. Or, "assessors."
1102. A military reference, simply implying the idea of faithful effort leading to future reward.
1103. Comp. Ignatius' Epistle to the Ephesians, chap. ii.
1104. As this Epistle, though sent to the bishop, was meant to be read to the people, Ignatius here directly addresses them.
1105. Comp. chap. ii. etc.
1106. Or, "assessors."
1107. Literally, "worthy of God."
1108. Comp. Ignatius' Epistle to the Ephesians, chap. ii.
1109. Literally, "in freedom from care of God."
1110. Some read, "in the resurrection."
1111. Literally, "most befitting God."
1112. Literally, "God-runner."
1113. Literally, "at leisure for."
1114. Literally, "to Him."
1115. Literally, "in freedom from care of God."
1116. Literally, "most befitting God."
1117. Literally, "God-runner."
1118. Literally, "at leisure for."
1119. Some suppose the reference to be to the soldiers, or perhaps to God Himself.
1120. Or, "as possessed of the judgment."
1121. Literally, "men on foot."
1122. Some have the plural "ye" here.
1123. Literally, "an eternal work."
1124. Some propose to read, "and of the bishop."
1125. Literally, "name desired by me."
1126. Some suppose the reference to be to the soldiers, or perhaps to God Himself.
1127. Or, "as possessed of the judgment."
1128. Literally, "an eternal work."
1129. Literally, "name desired by me."

Introductory Note to the Syriac Version of the Ignatian Epistles

When the Syriac version of the Ignatian Epistles was introduced to the English world in 1845, by Mr. Cureton, the greatest satisfaction was expressed by many, who thought the inveterate controversy about to be settled. Lord Russell made the learned divine a canon of Westminster Abbey, and the critical Chevalier Bunsen [1130] committed himself as its patron. To the credit of the learned, in general, the work was gratefully received, and studied with scientific conscientiousness by Lightfoot and others. The literature of this period is valuable; and the result is decisive as to the Curetonian versions at least, which are fragmentary and abridged, and yet they are a valuable contribution to the study of the whole case.

The following is the original Introductory Notice:--

Some account of the discovery of the Syriac version of the Ignatian Epistles has been already given. We have simply to add here a brief description of the mss. from which the Syriac text has been printed. That which is named a by Cureton, contains only the Epistle to Polycarp, and exhibits the text of that Epistle which, after him, we have followed. He fixes its age somewhere in the first half of the sixth century, or before the year 550. The second ms., which Cureton refers to as b, is assigned by him to the seventh or eighth century. It contains the three Epistles of Ignatius, and furnishes the text here followed in the Epistles to the Ephesians and Romans. The third ms., which Cureton quotes as g, has no date, but, as he tells us, "belonged to the collection acquired by Moses of Nisibis in a.d. 931, and was written apparently about three or four centuries earlier." It contains the three Epistles to Polycarp, the Ephesians, and the Romans. The text of all these mss. is in several passages manifestly corrupt, and the translators appear at times to have mistaken the meaning of the Greek original.

[N.B.--Bunsen is forced to allow the fact that the discovery of the lost work of Hippolytus "throws new light on an obscure point of the Ignatian controversy," i.e., the Σιγή in the Epistle to the Magnesians (cap. viii.); but his treatment of the matter is unworthy of a candid scholar.]

Footnotes:

1130. See the extraordinary passage and note in his Hippolytus, vol. i. p. 58, etc.

The Epistle of Ignatius to Polycarp [1131]

Ignatius, who is [also called] Theophorus, to Polycarp, bishop of Smyrna, or rather, who has as his own bishop God the Father, and our Lord Jesus Christ: [wishes] abundance of happiness.

Chapter I

Because thy mind is acceptable to me, inasmuch as it is established in God, as on a rock which is immoveable, I glorify God the more exceedingly that I have been counted worthy of [seeing] thy face, which I longed after in God. Now I beseech thee, by the grace with which thou art clothed, to add [speed] to thy course, and that thou ever pray for all men that they may be saved, and that thou demand [1132] things which are befitting, with all assiduity both of the flesh and spirit. Be studious of unity, than which nothing is more precious. Bear with all men, even as our Lord beareth with thee. Show patience [1133] with all men in love, as [indeed] thou doest. Be stedfast in prayer. Ask for more understanding than that which thou [already] hast. Be watchful, as possessing a spirit which sleepeth not. Speak with every man according to the will of God. Bear the infirmities of all men as a perfect athlete; for where the labour is great, the gain is also great.

Chapter II

If thou lovest the good disciples only, thou hast no grace; [but] rather subdue those that are evil by gentleness. All [sorts of] wounds are not healed by the same medicine. Mitigate [the pain of] cutting [1134] by tenderness. Be wise as the serpent in everything, and innocent, with respect to those things which are requisite, even as the dove. For this reason thou art [composed] of both flesh and spirit, that thou mayest entice [1135] those things which are visible before thy face, and mayest ask, as to those which are concealed from thee, that they [too] may be revealed to thee, in order that thou be deficient in nothing, and mayest abound in all gifts. The time demands, even as a pilot does a ship, and as one who stands exposed to the tempest does a haven, that thou shouldst be worthy of God. Be thou watchful as an athlete of God. That which is promised to us is life eternal, which cannot be corrupted, of which things thou art also persuaded. In everything I will be instead [1136] of thy soul, and my bonds which thou hast loved.

Chapter III

Let not those who seem to be somewhat, and teach strange doctrines, strike thee with apprehension; but stand thou in the truth, as an athlete [1137] who is smitten, for it is [the part] of a great athlete to be smitten, and [yet] conquer. More especially is it fitting that we should bear everything for the sake of God, that He also may bear us. Be [still] more diligent than thou yet art. Be discerning of the times. Look for Him that is above the times, Him who has no times, Him who is invisible, Him who for our sakes became visible, Him who is impalpable, Him who is impassible, Him who for our sakes suffered, Him who endured everything in every form for our sakes.

Chapter IV

Let not the widows be overlooked; on account of [1138] our Lord be thou their guardian, and let nothing be done without thy will; also do thou nothing without the will of God, as indeed thou doest not. Stand rightly. Let there be frequent [1139] assemblies: ask every man [to them] by his name. Despise not slaves, either male or female; but neither let them be contemptuous, but let them labour the more as for the glory of God, that they may be counted worthy of a more precious freedom, which is of God. Let them not desire to be set free out of the common [fund], lest they be found the slaves of lust.

Chapter V

Flee wicked arts; but all the more discourse regarding them. Speak to my sisters, that they love in our Lord, and that their husbands be sufficient for them in the flesh and spirit. Then, again, charge my brethren in the name of our Lord Jesus Christ, that they love their wives, as our Lord His Church. If any man is able in power to continue in purity, [1140] to the honour of the flesh of our Lord, let him continue so without boasting; if he boasts, he is undone; if he become known apart from the bishop, he has destroyed himself. [1141] It is becoming, therefore, to men and women who marry, that they marry with the counsel of the bishop, that the marriage may be in our Lord, and not in lust. Let everything, therefore, be [done] for the honour of God.

Chapter VI

Look ye to the bishop, that God also may look upon you. I will be instead of the souls of those who are subject to the bishop, and the presbyters, and the deacons; with them may I have a portion in the presence of God! Labour together with one another, act as athletes [1142] together, run together, suffer together, sleep together, rise together. As stewards of God, and of His household, [1143] and His servants, please Him and serve Him, that ye may receive from Him the wages [promised]. Let none of you be rebellious. Let your baptism be to you as armour, and faith as a spear, and love as a helmet, and patience as a panoply. Let your treasures be your good works, that ye may receive the gift of God, as is just. Let your spirit be long-suffering towards each other with meekness, even as God [is] toward you. As for me, I rejoice in you at all times.

Chapter VII

The Christian has not power over himself, but is [ever] ready to be subject to God. [1144]

Chapter VIII

I salute him who is reckoned worthy to go to Antioch in my stead, as I commanded thee. [1145]

Footnotes:

1131. The inscription varies in each of the three Syriac mss., being in the first, "The Epistle of my lord Ignatius, the bishop;" in the second, "The Epistle of Ignatius;" and in the third, "The Epistle of Ignatius, bishop of Antioch."

1132. For "vindicate thy place" in the Greek.

1133. Literally, "draw out thy spirit."

1134. Cureton observes, as one alternative here, that "the Syrian translator seems to have read παράξυσμα for παροξυσμούς."

1135. Or, "flatter," probably meaning to "deal gently with."

1136. Thus the Syriac renders ἀντίψυχον in the Greek.

1137. The Greek has ἄκμων, "an anvil."

1138. The Greek has μετά, "after."

1139. Or, "constant," "regular."

1140. i.e., "in celibacy."

1141. Or, "corrupted himself."

1142. Literally, "make the contest."

1143. Literally, "sons of His house."

1144. These are the only parts of chaps. vii. and viii. in the Greek that are represented in the Syriac.

1145. These are the only parts of chaps. vii. and viii. in the Greek that are represented in the Syriac.

The Second Epistle of Ignatius to the Ephesians[1146]

Ignatius, who is [also called] Theophorus, to the Church which is blessed in the greatness of God the Father, and perfected; to her who was selected [1147] from eternity, that she might be at all times for glory, which abideth, and is unchangeable, and is perfected and chosen in the purpose of truth by the will of the Father of Jesus Christ our God; to her who is worthy of happiness; to her who is at Ephesus, in Jesus Christ, in joy which is unblameable: [wishes] abundance of happiness.

Chapter I

Inasmuch as your name, which is greatly beloved, is acceptable to me in God, [your name] which ye have acquired by nature, through a right and just will, and also by the faith and love of Jesus Christ our Saviour, and ye are imitators of God, and are fervent in the blood of God, and have speedily completed a work congenial to you; [for] when ye heard that I was bound, [1148] so as to be able to do nothing for the sake of the common name and hope (and I hope, through your prayers, that I may be devoured by beasts at Rome, so that by means of this of which I have been accounted worthy, I may be endowed with strength to be a disciple of God), ye were diligent to come and see me. Seeing, then, that we have become acquainted with your multitude [1149] in the name of God, by Onesimus, who is your bishop, in love which is unutterable, whom I pray that ye love in Jesus Christ our Lord, and that all of you imitate his example, [1150] for blessed is He who has given you such a bishop, even as ye deserve [to have]. [1151]

Chapter III [1152]

But inasmuch as love does not permit me to be silent in regard to you, on this account I have been forward to entreat of you that ye would be diligent in the will of God.

Chapter VIII [1153]

For, so long as there is not implanted in you any one lust which is able to torment you, behold, ye live in God. I rejoice in you, and offer supplication [1154] on account of you, Ephesians, a Church which is renowned in all ages. For those who are carnal are not able to do spiritual things, nor those that are spiritual carnal things; in like manner as neither can faith [do] those things which are foreign to faith, nor want of faith [do] what belongs to faith. For those things which ye have done in the flesh, even these are spiritual, because ye have done everything in Jesus Christ.

Chapter IX

And ye are prepared for the building of God the Father, and ye are raised up on high by the instrument of Jesus Christ, which is the cross; and ye are drawn by the rope, which is the Holy Spirit; and your pulley is your faith, and your love is the way which leadeth up on high to God.

Chapter X

Pray for all men; for there is hope of repentance for them, that they may be counted worthy of God. By your works especially let them be instructed. Against their harsh words be ye conciliatory, by meekness of mind and gentleness. Against their blasphemies do ye give yourselves to prayer; and against their error be ye armed with faith. Against their fierceness be ye peaceful and quiet, and be ye not astounded by them. Let us, then, be imitators of our Lord in meekness, and strive who shall more especially be injured, and oppressed, and defrauded.

Chapter XIV [1155]

The work is not of promise, [1156] unless a man be found in the power of faith, even to the end.

Chapter XV

It is better that a man should be silent while he is something, than that he should be talking when he is not; that by those things which he speaks he should act, and by those things of which he is silent he should be known.

Chapter XVIII [1157]

My spirit bows in adoration to the cross, which is a stumbling-block to those who do not believe, but is to you for salvation and eternal life.

Chapter XIX

There was concealed from the ruler of this world the virginity of Mary and the birth of our Lord, and the three renowned mysteries [1158] which were done in the tranquillity of God from the star. And here, at the manifestation of the Son, magic began to be destroyed, and all bonds were loosed; and the ancient kingdom and the error of evil was destroyed. Henceforward all things were moved together, and the destruction of death was devised, and there was the commencement of that which was perfected in God. [1159]

Footnotes:

1146. Another inscription is, "Epistle the Second, which is to the Ephesians."

1147. Literally, "separated."

1148. Literally, "bound from actions."

1149. Cureton renders, "have received your abundance," probably referring the words to gifts sent by the Ephesians to Ignatius.

1150. Literally, "be in his image."

1151. There is no Apodosis, unless it be found in what follows.

1152. The following clause is the whole of chap. iii. in the Greek, which is represented in the Syriac.

1153. Chaps. iv. v. vi. vii. of the Greek are totally omitted in the Syriac.

1154. Thus Cureton renders the words, referring in confirmation to the Peshito version of Phil. i. 4, but the meaning is doubtful.

1155. Chaps. xi. xii. xiii. of the Greek are totally wanting in the Syriac, and only these few words of chaps. xiv. and xv. are represented.

1156. The meaning seems to be that mere profession, without continuous practice, is nothing.

1157. Chaps. xvi. and xvii. of the Greek are totally wanting in the Syriac.

1158. Literally, "the mysteries of the shout." The meaning is here confused and obscure. See the Greek.

1159. Chaps. xx. and xxi. of the Greek are altogether wanting in the Syriac. N.B.-- See spurious Epistle to Philippians, cap. 4, infra. This concealment from Satan of the mystery of the incarnation is the explanation, according to the Fathers, of his tempting the Messiah, and prompting His crucifixion. Also, Christ the more profoundly humbled himself, "ne subtilis ille diaboli oculus magnum hoc pietatis deprehenderet sacramentum" (St. Bernard, opp. ii. 1944). Bernard also uses this opinion very strikingly (opp. ii. 1953) in one of his sermons, supposing that Satan discovered the secret too late for his own purpose, and then prompted the outcry, Come down from the cross, to defeat the triumph of the second Adam. (Comp. St. Mark i. 24 and St. Luke iv. 34, where, after the first defeat of the tempter, this demon suspects the second Adam, and tries to extort the secret).

The Third Epistle of the Same St. Ignatius [1160]

Ignatius, who is [also called] Theophorus, to the Church which has received grace through the greatness of the Father Most High; to her who presideth in the place of the region of the Romans, who is worthy of God, and worthy of life, and happiness, and praise, and remembrance, and is worthy of prosperity, and presideth in love, and is perfected in the law of Christ unblameable: [wishes] abundance of peace.

Chapter I

From of old have I prayed to God, that I might be counted worthy to behold your faces which are worthy of God: now, therefore, being bound in Jesus Christ, I hope to meet you and salute you, if it be the will [of God] that I should be accounted worthy to the end. For the beginning is well arranged, if I be counted worthy to attain to the end, that I may receive my portion, without hindrance, through suffering. For I am in fear of your love, lest it should injure me. As to you, indeed, it is easy for you to do whatsoever ye wish; but as to me, it is difficult for me to be accounted worthy of God, if indeed ye spare me not.

Chapter II

For there is no other time such as this, that I should be accounted worthy of God; neither will ye, if ye be silent, [ever] be found in a better work than this. If ye let me alone, I shall be the word of God; but if ye love my flesh, again am I [only] to myself a voice. Ye cannot give me anything more precious than this, that I should be sacrificed to God, while the altar is ready; that ye may be in one concord in love, and may praise God the Father through Jesus Christ our Lord, because He has deemed a bishop worthy to be God's, having called him from the east to the west. It is good that I should set from the world in God, that I may rise in Him to life. [1161]

Chapter III

Ye have never envied any man. Ye have taught others. Only pray ye for strength to be given to me from within and from without, that I may not only speak, but also may be willing, and that I may not merely be called a Christian, but also may be found to be [one]; for if I am found to be [so], I may then also be called [so]. Then [indeed] shall I be faithful, when I am no longer seen in the world. For there is nothing visible that is good. The work is not [a matter [1162]] of persuasion; but Christianity is great when the world hateth it.

Chapter IV

I write to all the Churches, and declare to all men, that I willingly die for the sake of God, if so be that ye hinder me not. I entreat of you not to be [affected] towards me with a love which is unseasonable. Leave me to become [the prey of] the beasts, that by their means I may be accounted worthy of God. I am the wheat of God, and by the teeth of the beasts I shall be ground, [1163] that I may be found the pure bread of God. Provoke ye greatly [1164] the wild beasts, that they may be for me a grave, and may leave nothing of my body, in order that, when I have fallen asleep, I may not be a burden upon any one. Then shall I be in truth a disciple of Jesus Christ, when the world seeth not even my body. Entreat of our Lord in my behalf, that through these instruments I may be found a sacrifice to God. I do not, like Peter and Paul, issue orders unto you. They are [1165] apostles, but I am one condemned; they indeed are free, but I am a slave, even until now. But if I suffer, I shall be the freed-man of Jesus Christ, and I shall rise in Him from the dead, free. And now being in bonds, I learn to desire nothing.

Chapter V

From Syria, and even unto Rome, I am cast among wild beasts, by sea and by land, by night and by day, being bound between ten leopards, which are the band of soldiers, who, even when I do good to them, all the more do evil unto me. I, however, am the rather instructed by their injurious treatment; [1166] but not on this account am I justified to myself. I rejoice in the beasts which are prepared for me, and I pray that they may in haste be found for me; and I will provoke them speedily to devour me, and not be as those which are afraid of some other men, [1167] and will not approach them: even should they not be willing to approach me, I will go with violence against them. Know me from myself what is expedient for me. [1168] Let no one [1169] envy me of those things which are seen and which are not seen, that I should be accounted worthy of Jesus Christ. Fire, and the cross, and the beasts that are prepared, cutting off of the limbs, and scattering of the bones, and crushing of the whole body, harsh torments of the devil--let these come upon me, but [1170] only let me be accounted worthy of Jesus Christ.

Chapter VI

The pains of the birth stand over against me. [1171]

Chapter VII

And my love is crucified, and there is no fire in me for another love. I do not desire the food of corruption, neither the lusts of this world. I seek the bread of God, which is the flesh of Jesus Christ; and I seek His blood, a drink which is love incorruptible.

Chapter IX [1172]

My spirit saluteth you, and the love of the Churches which received me as the name of Jesus Christ; for those also who were near to [my] way in the flesh, preceded me in every city.

[1173] [Now therefore, being about to arrive shortly in Rome, I know many things in God; but I keep myself within measure, that I may not perish through boasting: for now it is needful for me to fear the more, and not pay regard to those who puff me up. For they who say such things to me scourge me; for I desire to suffer, but I do not know if I am worthy. For zeal is not visible to many, but with me it has war. I have need, therefore, of meekness, by which the prince of this world is destroyed. I am able to write to you of heavenly things, but I fear lest I should do you an injury. Know me from myself. For I am cautious lest ye should not be able to receive [such knowledge], and should be perplexed. For even I, not because I am in bonds, and am able to know heavenly things, and the places of angels, and the stations of the powers that are seen and that are not seen, am on this account a disciple; for I am far short of the perfection which is worthy of God.] Be ye perfectly strong [1174] in the patience of Jesus Christ our God.

Here end the three Epistles of Ignatius, bishop and martyr. [1175]

Footnotes:

1160. Another inscription is, "The Third Epistle."

1161. Literally, "in life."

1162. The meaning is probably similar to that expressed in chap. xiv. of the Epistle to the Ephesians.

1163. Literally, "I am ground."

1164. Literally, "with provoking, provoke."

1165. Literally, "they are who are."

1166. Literally, "by their injury."

1167. Literally, "and not as that which is afraid of some other men." So Cureton translates, but remarks that the passage is evidently corrupt. The reference plainly is to the fact that the beasts sometimes refused to attack their intended victims. See the case of Blandina, as reported by Eusebius (Hist. Eccl., v. 1.).

1168. Cureton renders interrogatively, "What is expedient for me?" and remarks that "the meaning of the Syriac appears to be, I crave your indulgence to leave the knowledge of what is expedient for me to my own conscience.' "

1169. Literally, "nothing."

1170. Literally, "and."

1171. The Latin version translates the Greek here, "He adds gain to me."

1172. Chap. viii. of the Greek is entirely omitted in the Syriac.

1173. The following passage is not found in this Epistle in the Greek recensions, but forms, in substance, chaps. iv. and v. of the Epistle to the Trallians. Diverse views are held by critics as to its proper place, according to the degree of authority they ascribe to the Syriac version. Cureton maintains that this passage has been transferred by the forger of the Epistle to the Trallians, "to give a fiar colour to the fabrication by introducing a part of the genuine writing of Ignatius; while Hefele asserts that it is bound by the "closest connection" to the preceding chapter in the Epistle to the Trallians.

1174. Or, as in the Greek, "Fare ye well, to the end."

1175. N.B.--The aphoristic genius of Ignatius seems to be felt by his Syrian abbreviator, who reduces whole chapters to mere maxims.

Introductory Note to the Spurious Epistles of Ignatius

To the following introductory note of the translators nothing need be prefixed, except a grateful acknowledgment of the value of their labours and of their good judgment in giving us even these spurious writings for purposes of comparison. They have thus placed the materials for a complete understanding of the whole subject, before students who have a mind to subject it to a thorough and candid examination.

The following is the original Introductory Notice:--

We formerly stated that eight out of the fifteen Epistles bearing the name of Ignatius are now universally admitted to be spurious. None of them are quoted or referred to by any ancient writer previous to the sixth century. The style, moreover, in which they are written, so different from that of the other Ignatian letters, and allusions which they contain to heresies and ecclesiastical arrangements of a much later date than that of their professed author, render it perfectly certain that they are not the authentic production of the illustrious bishop of Antioch.

We cannot tell when or by whom these Epistles were fabricated. They have been thought to betray the same hand as the longer and interpolated form of the seven Epistles which are generally regarded as genuine. And some have conceived that the writer who gave forth to the world the Apostolic Constitutions under the name of Clement, was probably the author of these letters falsely ascribed to Ignatius, as well as of the longer recension of the seven Epistles which are mentioned by Eusebius.

It was a considerable time before editors in modern times began to discriminate between the true and the false in the writings attributed to Ignatius. The letters first published under his name were those three which exist only in Latin. These came forth in 1495 at Paris, being appended to a life of Becket, Archbishop of Canterbury. Some three years later, eleven Epistles, comprising those mentioned by Eusebius, and four others, were published in Latin, and passed through four or five editions. In 1536, the whole of the professedly Ignatian letters were published at Cologne in a Latin version; and this collection also passed through several editions. It was not till 1557 that the Ignatian Epistles appeared for the first time in Greek at Dillingen. After this date many editions came forth, in which the probably genuine were still mixed up with the certainly spurious, the three Latin letters, only being rejected as destitute of authority. Vedelius of Geneva first made the distinction which is now universally accepted, in an edition of these Epistles which he published in 1623; and he was followed by Archbishop Usher and others, who entered more fully into that critical examination of these writings which has been continued down even to our own day.

The reader will have no difficulty in detecting the internal grounds on which these eight letters are set aside as spurious. The difference of style from the other Ignatian writings will strike him even in perusing the English version which we have given, while it is of course much more marked in the original. And other decisive proofs present themselves in every one of the Epistles. In that to the Tarsians there is found a plain allusion to the Sabellian heresy, which did not arise till after the middle of the third century. In the Epistle to the Antiochians there is an enumeration of various Church officers, who were certainly unknown at the period when Ignatius lived. The Epistle to Hero plainly alludes to Manichæan errors, and could not therefore have been written before the third century. There are equally decisive proofs of spuriousness to be found in the Epistle to the Philippians, such as the references it contains to the Patripassian heresy originated by Praxeas in the latter part of the second century, and the ecclesiastical feasts, etc., of which it makes mention. The letter to Maria Cassobolita is of a very peculiar style, utterly alien from that of the other Epistles ascribed to Ignatius. And it is sufficient simply to glance at the short Epistles to St. John and the Virgin Mary, in order to see that they carry the stamp of imposture on their front; and, indeed, no sooner were they published than by almost universal consent they were rejected.

But though the additional Ignatian letters here given are confessedly spurious, we have thought it not improper to present them to the English reader in an appendix to our first volume. [1176] We have done so, because they have been so closely connected with the name of the bishop of Antioch, and also because they are in themselves not destitute of interest. We have, moreover, the satisfaction of thus placing for the first time within the reach of one acquainted only with our language, all the materials that have entered into the protracted agitation of the famous Ignatian controversy.

Footnotes:

1176. [Spurious writings, if they can be traced to antiquity, are always useful. Sometimes they are evidence of facts, always of opinions, ideas and fancies of their date; and often they enable us to identify the origin of corruptions. Even interpolations prove what later partisans would be glad to find, if they could, in early writers. They bear unwilling testimony to the absence of genuine evidence in favour of their assumptions.]

The Epistle of Ignatius to the Tarsians

Ignatius, who is also called Theophorus, to the Church which is at Tarsus, saved in Christ, worthy of praise, worthy of remembrance, and worthy of love: Mercy and peace from God the Father, and the Lord Jesus Christ, be ever multiplied.

Chapter I - His own sufferings: exhortation to stedfastness

From Syria even unto Rome I fight with beasts: not that I am devoured by brute beasts, for these, as ye know, by the will of God, spared Daniel, but by beasts in the shape of men, in whom the merciless wild beast himself lies hid, and pricks and wounds me day by day. But none of these hardships "move me, neither count I my life dear unto myself," [1177] in such a way as to love it better than the Lord. Wherefore I am prepared for [encountering] fire, wild beasts, the sword, or the cross, so that only I may see Christ my Saviour and God, who died for me. I therefore, the prisoner of Christ, who am driven along by land and sea, exhort you: "stand fast in the faith," [1178] and be ye steadfast, "for the just shall live by faith;" [1179] be ye unwavering, for "the Lord causes those to dwell in a house who are of one and the same character." [1180]

Chapter II - Cautions against false doctrine

I have learned that certain of the ministers of Satan have wished to disturb you, some of them asserting that Jesus was born [only [1181]] in appearance, was crucified in appearance, and died in appearance; others that He is not the Son of the Creator, and others that He is Himself God over all. [1182] Others, again, hold that He is a mere man, and others that this flesh is not to rise again, so that our proper course is to live and partake of a life of pleasure, for that this is the chief good to beings who are in a little while to perish. A swarm of such evils has burst in upon us. [1183] But ye have not "given place by subjection to them, no, not for one hour." [1184] For ye are the fellow-citizens as well as the disciples of Paul, who "fully preached the Gospel from Jerusalem, and round about unto Illyricum," [1185] and bare about "the marks of Christ" in his flesh. [1186]

Chapter III - The true doctrine respecting Christ

Mindful of him, do ye by all means know that Jesus the Lord was truly born of Mary, being made of a woman; and was as truly crucified. For, says he, "God forbid that I should glory, save in the cross of the Lord Jesus." [1187] And He really suffered, and died, and rose again. For says [Paul], "If Christ should become passible, and should be the first to rise again from the dead." [1188] And again, "In that He died, He died unto sin once: but in that He liveth, He liveth unto God." [1189] Otherwise, what advantage would there be in [becoming subject to] bonds, if Christ has not died? what advantage in patience? what advantage in [enduring] stripes? And why such facts as the following: Peter was crucified; Paul and James were slain with the sword; John was banished to Patmos; Stephen was stoned to death by the Jews who killed the Lord? But, [in truth,] none of these sufferings were in vain; for the Lord was really crucified by the ungodly.

Chapter IV - Continuation

And [know ye, moreover], that He who was born of a woman was the Son of God, and He that was crucified was "the first-born of every creature," [1190] and God the Word, who also created all things. For says the apostle, "There is one God, the Father, of whom are all things; and one Lord Jesus Christ, by whom are all things." [1191] And again, "For there is one God, and one Mediator between God and man, the man Christ Jesus;" [1192] and, "By Him were all things created that are in heaven, and on earth, visible and invisible; and He is before all things, and by Him all things consist." [1193]

Chapter V - Refutation of the previously mentioned errors

And that He Himself is not God over all, and the Father, but His Son, He [shows when He] says, "I ascend unto my Father and your Father, and to my God and your God." [1194] And again, "When all things shall be subdued unto Him, then shall He also Himself be subject unto Him that put all things under Him, that God may be all in all." [1195] Wherefore it is one [Person] who put all things under, and who is all in all, and another [Person] to whom they were subdued, who also

Himself, along with all other things, becomes subject [to the former].

Chapter VI - Continuation

Nor is He a mere man, by whom and in whom all things were made; for "all things were made by Him." [1196] "When He made the heaven, I was present with Him; and I was there with Him, forming [the world along with Him], and He rejoiced in me daily." [1197] And how could a mere man be addressed in such words as these: "Sit Thou at My right hand?" [1198] And how, again, could such an one declare: "Before Abraham was, I am?" [1199] And, "Glorify Me with Thy glory which I had before the world was?" [1200] What man could ever say, "I came down from heaven, not to do Mine own will, but the will of Him that sent Me?" [1201] And of what man could it be said, "He was the true Light, which lighteth every man that cometh into the world: He was in the world, and the world was made by Him, and the world knew Him not. He came unto His own, and His own received Him not?" [1202] How could such a one be a mere man, receiving the beginning of His existence from Mary, and not rather God the Word, and the only-begotten Son? For "in the beginning was the Word, and the Word was with God, [1203] and the Word was God." [1204] And in another place, "The Lord created Me, the beginning of His ways, for His ways, for His works. Before the world did He found Me, and before all the hills did He beget Me." [1205]

Chapter VII - Continuation

And that our bodies are to rise again, He shows when He says, "Verily I say unto you, that the hour cometh, in the which all that are in the graves shall hear the voice of the Son of God; and they that hear shall live." [1206] And [says] the apostle, "For this corruptible must put on incorruption, and this mortal must put on immortality." [1207] And that we must live soberly and righteously, he [shows when he] says again, "Be not deceived: neither adulterers, nor effeminate persons, nor abusers of themselves with mankind, nor fornicators, nor revilers, nor drunkards, nor thieves, can inherit the kingdom of God." [1208] And again, "If the dead rise not, then is not Christ raised; our preaching therefore is vain, and your faith is also vain: ye are yet in your sins. Then they also that are fallen asleep in Christ have perished. If in this life only we have hope in Christ, we are of all men most miserable. If the dead rise not, let us eat and drink, for to-morrow we die." [1209] But if such be our condition and feelings, wherein shall we differ from asses and dogs, who have no care about the future, but think only of eating, and of indulging [1210] such appetites as follow after eating? For they are unacquainted with any intelligence moving within them.

Chapter VIII - Exhortations to holiness and good order

May I have joy of you in the Lord! Be ye sober. Lay aside, every one of you, all malice and beast-like fury, evil-speaking, calumny, filthy speaking, ribaldry, whispering, arrogance, drunkenness, lust, avarice, vainglory, envy, and everything akin to these. "But put ye on the Lord Jesus Christ, and make no provision for the flesh, to fulfil the lusts thereof." [1211] Ye presbyters, be subject to the bishop; ye deacons, to the presbyters; and ye, the people, to the presbyters and the deacons. Let my soul be for theirs who preserve this good order; and may the Lord be with them continually!

Chapter IX - Exhortations to the discharge of relative duties

Ye husbands, love your wives; and ye wives, your husbands. Ye children, reverence your parents. Ye parents, "bring up your children in the nurture and admonition of the Lord." [1212] Honour those [who continue] in virginity, as the priestesses of Christ; and the widows [that persevere] in gravity of behaviour, as the altar of God. Ye servants, wait upon your masters with [respectful] fear. Ye masters, issue orders to your servants with tenderness. Let no one among you be idle; for idleness is the mother of want. I do not enjoin these things as being a person of any consequence, although I am in bonds [for Christ]; but as a brother, I put you in mind of them. The Lord be with you!

Chapter X - Salutations

May I enjoy your prayers! Pray ye that I may attain to Jesus. I commend unto you the Church which is at Antioch. The Churches of Philippi, [1213] whence also I write to you, salute you. Philo, your deacon, to whom also I give thanks as one who has zealously ministered to me in all things, salutes you. Agathopus, the deacon from Syria, who follows me in Christ, salutes you. "Salute ye one another with a holy kiss." [1214] I salute you all, both male and female, who are in Christ. Fare ye well in body, and soul, and in one Spirit; and do not ye forget me. The Lord be with you!

Footnotes:

1177. Acts xx. 24.
1178. 1 Cor. xvi. 13.
1179. Hab. ii. 4; Gal. iii. 11.
1180. Ps. lxviii. 7 (after the LXX).
1181. Some omit this.
1182. That is, as appears afterwards from chap. v., so as to have no personality distinct from the Father.
1183. The translation is here somewhat doubtful.
1184. Gal. ii. 5.
1185. Rom. xv. 19.
1186. Gal. vi. 17.
1187. Gal. vi. 14.
1188. Acts xxvi. 23 (somewhat inaccurately rendered in English version).
1189. Rom. vi. 10.
1190. Col. i. 15.
1191. 1 Cor. viii. 6.
1192. 1 Tim. ii. 5.
1193. Col. i. 16, 17.
1194. John xx. 17.
1195. 1 Cor. xv. 28.
1196. John i. 3.
1197. Prov. viii. 27, 30.
1198. Ps. cx. 1.
1199. John viii. 58.
1200. John xvii. 5.
1201. John vi. 38.
1202. John i. 9, 10, 11.
1203. John i. 1.
1204. Some insert here John i. 3.
1205. Prov. viii. 22, 23, 25.
1206. John v. 25, 28.
1207. 1 Cor. xv. 53.
1208. 1 Cor. vi. 9.
1209. 1 Cor. xv. 13, 14, 17, 18, 19, 32.
1210. Literally, "coming also to the appetite of those things after eating." The text is doubtful.
1211. Rom. xiii. 14.
1212. Eph. vi. 4.
1213. Literally, "of the Philippians."
1214. 1 Pet. v. 14.

The Epistle of Ignatius to the Antiochians

Ignatius, who is also called Theophorus, to the Church sojourning in Syria, which has obtained mercy from God, and been elected by Christ, and which first [1215] received the name Christ, [wishes] happiness in God the Father, and the Lord Jesus Christ.

Chapter I - Cautions against error

The Lord has rendered my bonds light and easy since I learnt that you are in peace, that you live in all harmony both of the flesh and spirit. "I therefore, the prisoner of the Lord, [1216] beseech you, that ye walk worthy of the vocation wherewith ye are called," [1217] guarding against those heresies of the wicked one which have broken in upon us, to the deceiving and destruction of those that accept of them; but that ye give heed to the doctrine of the apostles, and believe both the law and the prophets: that ye reject every Jewish and Gentile error, and neither introduce a multiplicity of gods, nor yet deny Christ under the pretence of [maintaining] the unity of God.

Chapter II - The true doctrine respecting God and Christ

For Moses, the faithful servant of God, when he said, "The Lord thy God is one Lord," [1218] and thus proclaimed that there was only one God, did yet forthwith confess also our Lord when he said, "The Lord rained upon Sodom and Gomorrah fire and brimstone from the Lord." [1219] And again, "And God [1220] said, Let Us make man after our image: and so God made man, after the image of God made He him." [1221] And further, "In the image of God made He man." [1222] And that [the Son of God] was to be made man, [Moses shows when] he says, "A prophet shall the Lord raise up unto you of your brethren, like unto me." [1223]

Chapter III - The same continued

The prophets also, when they speak as in the person of God, [saying,] "I am God, the first [of beings], and I am also the last, [1224] and besides Me there is no God," [1225] concerning the Father of the universe, do also speak of our Lord Jesus Christ. "A Son," they say, has been given to us, on whose shoulder the government is from above; and His name is called the Angel of great counsel, Wonderful, Counsellor, the strong and mighty God." [1226] And concerning His incarnation, "Behold, a virgin shall be with Child, and shall bring forth a Son; and they shall call his name Immanuel." [1227] And concerning the passion, "He was led as a sheep to the slaughter; and as a lamb before her shearers is dumb, I also was an innocent lamb led to be sacrificed." [1228]

Chapter IV - Continuation

The Evangelists, too, when they declared that the one Father was "the only true God," [1229] did not omit what concerned our Lord, but wrote: "In the beginning was the Word, and the Word was with God, and the Word was God. The same was in the beginning with God. All things were made by Him, and without Him was not anything made that was made." [1230] And concerning the incarnation: "The Word," says [the Scripture], "became flesh, and dwelt among us." [1231] And again: "The book of the generation of Jesus Christ, the son of David, the son of Abraham." [1232] And those very apostles, who said "that there is one God," [1233] said also that "there is one Mediator between God and men." [1234] Nor were they ashamed of the incarnation and the passion. For what says [one]? "The man Christ Jesus, who gave Himself" [1235] for the life and salvation of the world.

Chapter V - Denunciation of false teachers

Whosoever, therefore, declares that there is but one God, only so as to take away the divinity of Christ, is a devil, [1236] and an enemy of all righteousness. He also that confesseth Christ, yet not as the Son of the Maker of the world, but of some other unknown [1237] being, different from Him whom the law and the prophets have proclaimed, this man is an instrument of the devil. And he that rejects the incarnation, and is ashamed of the cross for which I am in bonds, this man is antichrist. [1238] Moreover, he who affirms Christ to be a mere man is accursed, according to the [declaration of the] prophet, [1239] since he puts not his trust in God, but in man. Wherefore also he is unfruitful, like the wild myrtle-tree.

Chapter VI - Renewed cautions

These things I write to you, thou new olive-tree of Christ, not that I am aware you hold any such opinions, but that I may put you on your guard, as a father does his children. Beware, therefore, of those that hasten to work mischief, those "enemies of the cross of Christ, whose end is destruction, whose glory is in their shame." [1240] Beware of those "dumb dogs," those trailing serpents, those scaly [1241] dragons, those asps, and basilisks, and scorpions. For these are subtle wolves, [1242] and apes that mimic the appearance of men.

Chapter VII - Exhortation to consistency of conduct

Ye have been the disciples of Paul and Peter; do not lose what was committed to your trust. Keep in remembrance Euodias, [1243] your deservedly-blessed pastor, into whose hands the government over you was first entrusted by the apostles. Let us not bring disgrace upon our Father. Let us prove ourselves His true-born children, and not bastards. Ye know after what manner I have acted among you. The things which, when present, I spoke to you, these same, when absent, I now write to you. "If any man love not the Lord Jesus Christ, let him be Anathema." [1244] Be ye followers of me. [1245] My soul be for yours, when I attain to Jesus. Remember my bonds. [1246]

Chapter VIII - Exhortations to the presbyters and others

Ye presbyters, "feed the flock which is among you," [1247] till God shall show who is to hold the rule over you. For "I am now ready to be offered," [1248] that I "may win Christ." [1249] Let the deacons know of what dignity they are, and let them study to be blameless, that they may be the followers of Christ. Let the people be subject to the presbyters and the deacons. Let the virgins know to whom they have consecrated themselves.

Chapter IX - Duties of husbands, wives, parents, and children

Let the husbands love their wives, remembering that, at the creation, one woman, and not many, was given to one man. Let the wives honour their husbands, as their own flesh; and let them not presume to address them by their names. [1250] Let them also be chaste, reckoning their husbands as their only partners, to whom indeed they have been united according to the will of God. Ye parents, impart a holy training to your children. Ye children, "honour your parents, that it may be well with you." [1251]

Chapter X - Duties of masters and servants

Ye masters, do not treat your servants with haughtiness, but imitate patient Job, who declares, "I did not despise [1252] the cause [1253] of my man-servant, or of my maid-servant, when they contended with me. For what in that case shall I do when the Lord makes an inquisition regarding me?" [1254] And you know what follows. Ye servants, do not provoke your masters to anger in anything, lest ye become the authors of incurable mischiefs to yourselves.

Chapter XI - Inculcation of various moral duties

Let no one addicted to idleness eat, [1255] lest he become a wanderer about, and a whoremonger. Let drunkenness, anger, envy, reviling, clamour, and blasphemy "be not so much as named among you." [1256] Let not the widows live a life of pleasure, lest they wax wanton against the word. [1257] Be subject to Cæsar in everything in which subjection implies no [spiritual] danger. Provoke not those that rule over you to wrath, that you may give no occasion against yourselves to those that seek for it. But as to the practice of magic, or the impure love of boys, or murder, it is superfluous to write to you, since such vices are forbidden to be committed even by the Gentiles. I do not issue commands on these points as if I were an apostle; but, as your fellow-servant, I put you in mind of them.

Chapter XII - Salutations

I salute the holy presbytery. I salute the sacred deacons, and that person most dear to me, [1258] whom may I behold, through the Holy Spirit, occupying my place when I shall attain to Christ. My soul be in place of his. I salute the sub-deacons, the readers, the singers, the doorkeepers, the labourers, [1259] the exorcists, the confessors. [1260] I salute the keepers of the holy gates, the deaconesses in Christ. I salute the virgins betrothed to Christ, of whom may I have joy in the Lord Jesus. [1261] I salute the people of the Lord, from the smallest to the greatest, and all my sisters in the Lord.

Chapter XIII - Salutations continued

I salute Cassian and his partner in life, and their very dear children. Polycarp, that most worthy bishop, who is also deeply interested in you, salutes you; and to him I have commended you in the Lord. The whole Church of the Smyrnæans, indeed, is mindful of you in their prayers in the Lord. Onesimus, the pastor of the Ephesians, salutes you. Damas, [1262] the bishop of Magnesia, salutes you. Polybius, bishop of the Trallians, salutes you. Philo and Agathopus, the deacons, my companions, salute you, "Salute one another with a holy kiss." [1263]

Chapter XIV - Conclusion

I write this letter to you from Philippi. May He who is alone unbegotten, keep you stedfast both in the spirit and in the flesh, through Him who was begotten before time [1264] began! And may I behold you in the kingdom of Christ! I salute him who is to bear rule over you in my stead: may I have joy of him in the Lord! Fare ye well in God, and in Christ, being enlightened by the Holy Spirit.

Footnotes:

1215. Comp. Acts xi. 26.
1216. Literally, "in the Lord."
1217. Eph. iv. 1.
1218. Deut. vi. 4; Mark xii. 29.
1219. Gen. xix. 24.
1220. The ms. has "Lord."
1221. Gen. i. 26, 27.
1222. Gen. v. 1, Gen. ix. 6.
1223. Deut. xviii. 15; Acts iii. 22, Acts vii. 37.
1224. Literally, "after these things."
1225. Isa. xliv. 6.
1226. Isa. ix. 6.
1227. Isa. vii. 14; Matt. i. 23.
1228. Isa. liii. 7; Jer. xi. 19.
1229. John xvii. 3.
1230. John i. 1.
1231. John i. 14.
1232. Matt. i. 1.
1233. 1 Cor. viii. 4, 6; Gal. iii. 20.
1234. Eph. iv. 5, 6; 1 Tim. ii. 5.
1235. 1 Tim. ii. 5.
1236. Comp. John vi. 70. Some read, "the son of the devil."
1237. Or, "that cannot be known."
1238. Comp. 1 John ii. 22, 1 John iv. 3; 2 John 7.
1239. Jer. xvii. 5.
1240. Phil. iii. 18, 19.
1241. The text is here doubtful.
1242. Literally, "fox-like thoes," lynxes being perhaps intended.
1243. Some think that this is the same person as the Euodias referred to by St. Paul, Phil. iv. 2; but, as appears from the Greek (ver. 3, αἵτινες), the two persons there mentioned were women.
1244. 1 Cor. xvi. 22.
1245. Comp. 1 Cor. iv. 16.
1246. Comp. Col. iv. 18.
1247. 1 Pet. v. 2.
1248. 2 Tim. iv. 6.
1249. Phil. iii. 8.
1250. Comp. 1 Pet. iii. 6.
1251. Eph. vi. 1, 3.
1252. Literally, "If I did despise."
1253. Or, "judgment."
1254. Job xxxi. 13, 14.
1255. Comp. 2 Thess. iii. 10.
1256. Eph. v. 3.
1257. 1 Tim. v. 6, 11.
1258. Literally, "the name desirable to me," referring to Hero the deacon.
1259. A class of persons connected with the Church, whose duty it was to bury the bodies of the martyrs and others.
1260. Such as voluntarily confessed Christ before Gentile rulers.
1261. Some insert here a clause referring to widows.
1262. Or, as some read, "Demas."
1263. 2 Cor. xiii. 12.
1264. Literally, "before ages."

The Epistle of Ignatius to Hero, a Deacon of Antioch

Ignatius, who is also called Theophorus, to Hero, the deacon of Christ, and the servant of God, a man honoured by God, and most dearly loved as well as esteemed, who carries Christ and the Spirit within him, and who is mine own son in faith and love: Grace, mercy, and peace from Almighty God, and from Christ Jesus our Lord, His only-begotten Son, "who gave Himself for our sins, that He might deliver us from the present evil world," [1265] and preserve us unto His heavenly kingdom.

Chapter I - Exhortations to earnestness and moderation

I Exhort thee in God, that thou add [speed] to thy course, and that thou vindicate thy dignity. Have a care to preserve concord with the saints. Bear [the burdens of] the weak, that "thou mayest fulfil the law of Christ." [1266] Devote [1267] thyself to fasting and prayer, but not beyond measure, lest thou destroy thyself [1268] thereby. Do not altogether abstain from wine and flesh, for these things are not to be viewed with abhorrence, since [the Scripture] saith, "Ye shall eat the good things of the earth." [1269] And again, "Ye shall eat flesh even as herbs." [1270] And again, "Wine maketh glad the heart of man, and oil exhilarates, and bread strengthens him." [1271] But all are to be used with moderation, as being the gifts of God. "For who shall eat or who shall drink without Him? For if anything be beautiful, it is His; and if anything be good, it is His." [1272] Give attention to reading, [1273] that thou mayest not only thyself know the laws, but mayest also explain them to others, as the earnest servant [1274] of God. "No man that warreth entangleth himself with the affairs of this life, that he may please him who hath chosen him to be a soldier; and if a man also strive for masteries, yet is he not crowned except he strive lawfully." [1275] I that am in bonds pray that my soul may be in place of yours.

Chapter II - Cautions against false teachers

Every one that teaches anything beyond what is commanded, though he be [deemed] worthy of credit, though he be in the habit of fasting, though he live in continence, though he work miracles, though he have the gift of prophecy, let him be in thy sight as a wolf in sheep's clothing,[1276] labouring for the destruction of the sheep. If any one denies the cross, and is ashamed of the passion, let him be to thee as the adversary himself. "Though he gives all his goods to feed the poor, though he remove mountains, though he give his body to be burned," [1277] let him be regarded by thee as abominable. If any one makes light of the law or the prophets, which Christ fulfilled at His coming, let him be to thee as antichrist. If any one says that the Lord is a mere man, he is a Jew, a murderer of Christ.

Chapter III - Exhortations as to ecclesiastical duties

"Honour widows that are widows indeed." [1278] Be the friend of orphans; for God is "the Father of the fatherless, and the Judge of the widows." [1279] Do nothing without the bishops; for they are priests, and thou a servant of the priests. They baptize, offer sacrifice, [1280] ordain, and lay on hands; but thou ministerest to them, as the holy Stephen did at Jerusalem to James and the presbyters. Do not neglect the sacred meetings [1281] [of the saints]; inquire after every one by name. "Let no man despise thy youth, but be thou an example to the believers, both in word and conduct." [1282]

Chapter IV - Servants and women are not to be despised

Be not ashamed of servants, for we possess the same nature in common with them. Do not hold women in abomination, for they have given thee birth, and brought thee up. It is fitting, therefore, to love those that were the authors of our birth (but only in the Lord), inasmuch as a man can produce no children without a woman. It is right, therefore, that we should honour those who have had a part in giving us birth. "Neither is the man without the woman, nor the woman without the man," [1283] except in the case of those who were first formed. For the body of Adam was made out of the four elements, and that of Eve out of the side of Adam. And, indeed, the altogether peculiar birth of the Lord was of a virgin alone. [This took place] not as if the lawful union [of man and wife] were abominable, but such a kind of birth was fitting to God. For it became the Creator not to make use of the ordinary method of generation, but of one that was singular and strange, as being the Creator.

Chapter V - Various relative duties

Flee from haughtiness, "for the Lord resisteth the proud." [1284] Abhor falsehood, for says [the Scripture], "Thou shalt destroy all them that speak lies." [1285] Guard against envy, for its author is the devil, and his successor Cain, who envied his brother, and out of envy committed murder. Exhort my sisters to love God, and be content with their own husbands only. In like manner, exhort my brethren also to be content with their own wives. Watch over the virgins, as the precious treasures of Christ. Be long-suffering, [1286] that thou mayest be great in wisdom. Do not neglect the poor, in so far as thou art prosperous. For "by alms and fidelity sins are purged away." [1287]

Chapter VI - Exhortations to purity and caution

Keep thyself pure as the habitation of God. Thou art the temple of Christ. Thou art the instrument of the Spirit. Thou knowest in what way I have brought thee up. Though I am the least of men, do thou seek to follow me, be thou an imitator of my conduct. I do not glory in the world, but in the Lord. I exhort Hero, my son; "but let him that glorieth, glory in the Lord." [1288] May I have joy of thee, my dear son, whose guardian may He be who is the only unbegotten God, and the Lord Jesus Christ! Do not believe all persons, do not place confidence in all; nor let any man get the better of thee by flattery. For many are the ministers of Satan; and "he that is hasty to believe is light of heart." [1289]

Chapter VII - Solemn charge to Hero, as future bishop of Antioch

Keep God in remembrance, and thou shalt never sin. Be not double-minded [1290] in thy prayers; for blessed is he who doubteth not. For I believe in the Father of the Lord Jesus Christ, and in His only-begotten Son, that God will show me, Hero, upon my throne. Add speed, therefore, [1291] to thy course. I charge thee before the God of the universe, and before Christ, and in the presence of the Holy Spirit, and of the ministering ranks [of angels], keep in safety that deposit which I and Christ have committed to thee, and do not judge thyself unworthy of those things which have been shown by God [to me] concerning thee. I hand over to thee the Church of Antioch. I have commended you to Polycarp in the Lord Jesus Christ.

Chapter VIII - Salutations

The bishops, Onesimus, Bitus, Damas, Polybius, and all they of Philippi (whence also I have written to thee), salute thee in Christ. Salute the presbytery worthy of God: salute my holy fellow-deacons, of whom may I have joy in Christ, both in the flesh and in the spirit. Salute the people of the Lord, from the smallest to the greatest, every one by name; whom I commit to thee as Moses did [the Israelites] to Joshua, who was their leader after him. And do not reckon this which I have said presumptuous on my part; for although we are not such as they were, yet we at least pray that we may be so, since indeed we are the children of Abraham. Be strong, therefore, O Hero, like a hero, and like a man. For from henceforth thou shalt lead [1292] in and out the people of the Lord that are in Antioch, and so "the congregation of the Lord shall not be as sheep which have no shepherd."[1293]

Chapter IX - Concluding salutations and instructions

Salute Cassian, my host, and his most serious-minded partner in life, and their very dear children, to whom may "God grant that they find mercy of the Lord in that day," [1294] on account of their ministrations to us, whom also I commend to thee in Christ. Salute by name all the faithful in Christ that are at Laodicea. Do not neglect those at Tarsus, but look after them steadily, confirming them in the Gospel. I salute in the Lord, Maris the bishop of Neapolis, near Anazarbus. Salute thou also Mary my daughter, distinguished both for gravity and erudition, as also "the Church which is in her house." [1295] May my soul be in place of hers: she is the very pattern of pious women. May the Father of Christ, by His only-begotten Son, preserve thee in good health, and of high repute in all things, to a very old age, for the benefit of the Church of God! Farewell in the Lord, and pray thou that I may be perfected.

Footnotes:

1265. Gal. i. 4.
1266. Gal. vi. 2.
1267. Literally, "having leisure for."
1268. Literally, "cast thyself down."
1269. Isa. i. 19.
1270. Gen. ix. 3.
1271. Ps. civ. 15.
1272. Eccl. ii. 25 (after LXX.); Zech. ix. 17.
1273. Comp. 1 Tim. iv. 13.
1274. Literally, "athlete."
1275. 2 Tim. ii. 4.
1276. Comp. Matt. vii. 15.
1277. 1 Cor. xiii. 2.
1278. 1 Tim. v. 3.
1279. Ps. lxviii. 5.
1280. The term ἱερουργέω, which we have translated as above, is one whose signification is disputed. It occurs once in the New Testament (Rom. xv. 16) where it is translated in our English version simply "ministering." Etymologically, it means "to act as a priest," and we have in our translation followed Hesychius (Cent. iv.), who explains it as meaning "to offer sacrifice." The whole passage in the Epistle to the Romans, where this word occurs may be compared (original Greek) with Mal. i. 11, Heb. v. 1, etc.
1281. Specifically, assemblies for the celebration of the Lord's Supper.
1282. 1 Tim. iv. 12.
1283. 1 Cor. xi. 11.
1284. Jas. iv. 6; 1 Pet. v. 5.
1285. Ps. v. 6.
1286. Prov. xiv. 29.
1287. Prov. xv. 27 (after LXX.: Prov. xvi. 6 in English version)
1288. 1 Cor. i. 31; 2 Cor. x. 17.
1289. Sirach xix. 4.
1290. Comp. Jas. i. 6, 8.
1291. Comp. Epistle to the Antiochians, chap. xii.
1292. Comp. Deut. xxxi. 7, 23.
1293. Num. xxvii. 17.
1294. 2 Tim. i. 18.
1295. Col. iv. 15.

The Epistle of Ignatius to the Philippians

Ignatius, who is also called Theophorus, to the Church of God which is at Philippi, which has obtained mercy in faith, and patience, and love unfeigned: Mercy and peace from God the Father, and the Lord Jesus Christ, "who is the Saviour of all men, specially of them that believe." [1296]

Chapter I - Reason for writing the epistle

Being mindful of your love and of your zeal in Christ, which ye have manifested towards us, we thought it fitting to write to you, who display such a godly and spiritual love to the brethren, [1297] to put you in remembrance of your Christian course, [1298] "that ye all speak the same thing, being of one mind, thinking the same thing, and walking by the same rule of faith," [1299] as Paul admonished you. For if there is one God of the universe, the Father of Christ, "of whom are all things;" [1300] and one Lord Jesus Christ, our [Lord], "by whom are all things;" [1301] and also one Holy Spirit, who wrought [1302] in Moses, and in the prophets and apostles; and also one baptism, which is administered that we should have fellowship with the death of the Lord; [1303] and also one elect Church; there ought likewise to be but one faith in respect to Christ. For "there is one Lord, one faith, one baptism; one God and Father of all, who is through all, and in all." [1304]

Chapter II - Unity of the three divine persons

There is then one God and Father, and not two or three; One who is; and there is no other besides Him, the only true [God]. For "the Lord thy God," saith [the Scripture], "is one Lord." [1305] And again, "Hath not one God created us? Have we not all one Father? [1306] And there is also one Son, God the Word. For "the only-begotten Son," saith [the Scripture], "who is in the bosom of the Father." [1307] And again, "One Lord Jesus Christ." [1308] And in another place, "What is His name, or what His Son's name, that we may know?" [1309] And there is also one Paraclete. [1310] For "there is also," saith [the Scripture], "one Spirit," [1311] since "we have been called in one hope of our calling."[1312] And again, "We have drunk of one Spirit," [1313] with what follows. And it is manifest that all these gifts [possessed by believers] "worketh one and the self-same Spirit." [1314] There are not then either three Fathers, [1315] or three Sons, or three Paracletes, but one Father, and one Son, and one Paraclete. Wherefore also the Lord, when He sent forth the apostles to make disciples of all nations, commanded them to "baptize in the name of the Father, and of the Son, and of the Holy Ghost," [1316] not unto one [person] having three names, nor into three [persons] who became incarnate, but into three possessed of equal honour.

Chapter III - Christ was truly born, and died

For there is but One that became incarnate, and that neither the Father nor the Paraclete, but the Son only, [who became so] not in appearance or imagination, but in reality. For "the Word became flesh." [1317] For "Wisdom builded for herself a house." [1318] And God the Word was born as man, with a body, of the Virgin, without any intercourse of man. For [it is written], "A virgin shall conceive in her womb, and bring forth a son." [1319] He was then truly born, truly grew up, truly ate and drank, was truly crucified, and died, and rose again. He who believes these things, as they really were, and as they really took place, is blessed. He who believeth them not is no less accursed than those who crucified the Lord. For the prince of this world rejoiceth when any one denies the cross, since he knows that the confession of the cross is his own destruction. For that is the trophy which has been raised up against his power, which when he sees, he shudders, and when he hears of, is afraid.

Chapter IV - The malignity and folly of Satan

And indeed, before the cross was erected, he (Satan) was eager that it should be so; and he "wrought" [for this end] "in the children of disobedience." [1320] He wrought in Judas, in the Pharisees, in the Sadducees, in the old, in the young, and in the priests. But when it was just about to be erected, he was troubled, and infused repentance into the traitor, and pointed him to a rope to hang himself with, and taught him [to die by] strangulation. He terrified also the silly woman, disturbing her by dreams; and he, who had tried every means to have the cross prepared, now endeavoured to put a stop to its erection; [1321] not that he was influenced by repentance on account of the greatness of his crime (for in that case he would not be utterly depraved), but because he perceived his own destruction [to be at hand]. For the cross of Christ was the beginning of his condemnation, the beginning of his death, the beginning of his destruction. Wherefore, also, he works in some that they should deny the cross, be ashamed of the passion, call the death an appearance, mutilate and explain away the birth of the Virgin, and calumniate the [human] nature[1322] itself as being abominable. He fights along with the Jews to a denial of the cross, and with the Gentiles to the calumniating of Mary, [1323] who are heretical in holding that Christ possessed a mere phantasmal body. [1324] For the leader of all wickedness assumes manifold [1325] forms, beguiler of men as he is, inconsistent, and even contradicting himself, projecting one course and then following another. For he is wise to do evil, but as to what good may be he is totally ignorant. And indeed he is full of ignorance, on account of his voluntary want of reason: for how can he be deemed anything else who does not perceive reason when it lies at his very feet?

Chapter V - Apostrophe to Satan

For if the Lord were a mere man, possessed of a soul and body only, why dost thou mutilate and explain away His being born with the common nature of humanity? Why dost thou call the passion a mere appearance, as if it were any strange thing happening to a [mere] man? And why dost thou reckon the death of a mortal to be simply an imaginary death? But if, [on the other hand,] He is both God and man, then why dost thou call it unlawful to style Him "the Lord of glory," [1326] who is by nature unchangeable? Why dost thou say that it is unlawful to declare of the Lawgiver who possesses a human soul, "The Word was made flesh," [1327] and was a perfect man, and not merely one dwelling in a man? But how came this magician into existence, who of old formed all nature that can be apprehended either by the senses or intellect, according to the will of the Father; and, when He became incarnate, healed every kind of disease and infirmity? [1328]

Chapter VI - Continuation

And how can He be but God, who raises up the dead, sends away the lame sound of limb, cleanses the lepers, restores sight to the blind, and either increases or transmutes existing substances, as the five loaves and the two fishes, and the water which became wine, and who puts to flight thy whole host by a mere word? And why dost thou abuse the nature of the Virgin, and style her members disgraceful, since thou didst of old display such in public processions, [1329] and didst order them to be exhibited naked, males in the sight of females, and females to stir up the unbridled lust of males? But now these are reckoned by thee disgraceful, and thou pretendest to be full of modesty, thou spirit of fornication, not knowing that then only anything becomes disgraceful when it is polluted by wickedness. But when sin is not present, none of the things that have been created are shameful, none of them evil, but all very good. But inasmuch as thou art blind, thou revilest these things.

Chapter VII - Continuation: inconsistency of Satan

And how, again, does Christ not at all appear to thee to be of the Virgin, but to be God over all, [1330] and the Almighty? Say, then, who sent Him? Who was Lord over Him? And whose will did He obey? And what laws did He fulfil, since He was subject neither to the will nor power of any one? And while you deny that Christ was born, [1331] you affirm that the unbegotten was begotten, and that He who had no beginning was nailed to the cross, by whose permission I am unable to say. But thy changeable tactics do not escape me, nor am I ignorant that thou art wont to walk with slanting and uncertain [1332] steps. And thou art ignorant who really was born, thou who pretendest to know everything.

Chapter VIII - Continuation: ignorance of Satan

For many things are unknown [1333] to thee; [such as the following]: the virginity of Mary; the wonderful birth; Who it was that became incarnate; the star which guided those who were in the east; the Magi who presented gifts; the salutation of the archangel to the Virgin; the marvellous conception of her that was betrothed; the announcement of the boy-forerunner respecting the son of the Virgin, and his leaping in the womb on account of what was foreseen; the songs of the angels over Him that was born; the glad tidings announced to the shepherds; the fear of Herod lest his kingdom should be taken from him; the command to slay the infants; the removal into Egypt, and the return from that country to the same region; the infant swaddling-bands; the human registration; the nourishing by means of milk; the name of father given to Him who did not beget; the manger because there was not room [elsewhere]; no human preparation [for the Child]; the gradual growth, human speech, hunger, thirst, journeyings, weariness; the offering of sacrifices, and then also circumcision, baptism; the voice of God over Him that was baptized, as to who He was and whence

[He had come]; the testimony of the Spirit and the Father from above; the voice of John the prophet when it signified the passion by the appellation of "the Lamb;" the performance of divers miracles, manifold healings; the rebuke of the Lord ruling both the sea and the winds; evil spirits expelled; thou thyself subjected to torture, and, when afflicted by the power of Him who had been manifested, not having it in thy power to do anything.

Chapter IX - Continuation: ignorance of Satan

Seeing these things, thou wast in utter perplexity. [1334] And thou wast ignorant that it was a virgin that should bring forth; but the angels' song of praise struck thee with astonishment, as well as the adoration of the Magi, and the appearance of the star. Thou didst revert to thy state of [wilful] ignorance, because all the circumstances seemed to thee trifling; [1335] for thou didst deem the swaddling-bands, the circumcision, and the nourishment by means of milk contemptible: [1336] these things appeared to thee unworthy of God. Again, thou didst behold a man who remained forty days and nights without tasting human food, along with ministering angels at whose presence thou didst shudder, when first of all thou hadst seen Him baptized as a common man, and knewest not the reason thereof. But after His [lengthened] fast thou didst again assume thy wonted audacity, and didst tempt Him when hungry, as if He had been an ordinary man, not knowing who He was. For thou saidst, "If thou be the Son of God, command that these stones be made bread." [1337] Now, this expression, "If thou be the Son," is an indication of ignorance. For if thou hadst possessed real knowledge, thou wouldst have understood that the Creator can with equal ease both create what does not exist, and change that which already has a being. And thou temptedst by means of hunger[1338] Him who nourisheth all that require food. And thou temptedst the very "Lord of glory,"[1339] forgetting in thy malevolence that "man shall not live by bread alone, but by every word that proceedeth out of the mouth of God." For if thou hadst known that He was the Son of God, thou wouldst also have understood that He who had kept his [1340] body from feeling any want for forty days and as many nights, could have also done the same for ever. Why, then, does He suffer hunger? In order to prove that He had assumed a body subject to the same feelings as those of ordinary men. By the first fact He showed that He was God, and by the second that He was also man.

Chapter X - Continuation: audacity of Satan

Darest thou, then, who didst fall "as lightning" [1341] from the very highest glory, to say to the Lord, "Cast thyself down from hence [1342] [to Him] to whom the things that are not are reckoned as if they were, [1343] and to provoke to a display of vainglory Him that was free from all ostentation? And didst thou pretend to read in Scripture concerning Him: "For He hath given His angels charge concerning Thee, and in their hands they shall bear Thee up, lest thou shouldest dash Thy foot against a stone?" [1344] At the same time thou didst pretend to be ignorant of the rest, furtively concealing what [the Scripture] predicted concerning thee and thy servants: "Thou shalt tread upon the adder and the basilisk; the lion and the dragon shall thou trample under foot." [1345]

Chapter XI - Continuation: audacity of Satan

If, therefore, thou art trodden down under the feet of the Lord, how dost thou tempt Him that cannot be tempted, forgetting that precept of the lawgiver, "Thou shall not tempt the Lord thy God?" [1346] Yea, thou even darest, most accursed one, to appropriate the works of God to thyself, and to declare that the dominion over these was delivered to thee. [1347] And thou dost set forth thine own fall as an example to the Lord, and dost promise to give Him what is really His own, if He would fall down and worship thee. [1348] And how didst thou not shudder, O thou spirit more wicked through thy malevolence than all other wicked spirits, to utter such words against the Lord? Through thine appetite [1349] wast thou overcome, and through thy vainglory wast thou brought to dishonour: through avarice and ambition dost thou [now] draw on [others] to ungodliness. Thou, O Belial, dragon, apostate, crooked serpent, rebel against God, outcast from Christ, alien from the Holy Spirit, exile from the ranks of the angels, reviler of the laws of God, enemy of all that is lawful, who didst rise up against the first-formed of men, and didst drive forth [from obedience to] the commandment [of God] those who had in no respect injured thee; thou who didst raise up against Abel the murderous Cain; thou who didst take arms against Job: dost thou say to the Lord, "If Thou wilt fall down and worship me?" Oh what audacity! Oh what madness! Thou runaway slave, thou incorrigible [1350] slave, dost thou rebel against the good Lord? Dost thou say to so great a Lord, the God of all that either the mind or the senses can perceive, "If Thou wilt fall down and worship me?"

Chapter XII - The meek reply of Christ

But the Lord is long-suffering, and does not reduce to nothing him who in his ignorance dares [to utter] such words, but meekly replies, "Get thee hence, Satan."[1351] He does not say, "Get thee behind Me," for it is not possible that he should be converted; but, "Begone, Satan," to the course which thou hast chosen. "Begone" to those things to which, through thy malevolence, thou hast been called. For I know Who I am, and by Whom I have been sent, and Whom it behoves Me to worship. For "thou shalt worship the Lord thy God, and Him only shalt thou serve."[1352] I know the one [God]; I am acquainted with the only [Lord] from whom thou hast become an apostate. I am not an enemy of God; I acknowledge His pre-eminence; I know the Father, who is the author of my generation.

Chapter XIII - Various exhortations and directions

These things, brethren, out of the affection which I entertain for you, I have felt compelled to write, exhorting you with a view to the glory of God, not as if I were a person of any consequence, but simply as a brother. Be ye subject to the bishop, to the presbyters, and to the deacons. Love one another in the Lord, as being the images of God. Take heed, ye husbands, that ye love your wives as your own members. Ye wives also, love your husbands, as being one with them in virtue of your union. If any one lives in chastity or continence, let him not be lifted up, lest he lose his reward. Do not lightly esteem the festivals. Despise not the period of forty days, for it comprises an imitation of the conduct of the Lord. After the week of the passion, do not neglect to fast on the fourth and sixth days, distributing at the same time of thine abundance to the poor. If any one fasts on the Lord's Day or on the Sabbath, except on the paschal Sabbath only, he is a murderer of Christ.

Chapter XIV - Farewells and cautions

Let your prayers be extended to the Church of Antioch, whence also I as a prisoner am being led to Rome. I salute the holy bishop Polycarp; I salute the holy bishop Vitalius, and the sacred presbytery, and my fellow-servants the deacons; in whose stead may my soul be found. Once more I bid farewell to the bishop, and to the presbyters in the Lord. If any one celebrates the passover along with the Jews, or receives the emblems of their feast, he is a partaker with those that killed the Lord and His apostles.

Chapter XV - Salutations. Conclusion

Philo and Agathopus the deacons salute you. I salute the company of virgins, and the order of widows; of whom may I have joy! I salute the people of the Lord, from the least unto the greatest. I have sent you this letter through Euphanius the reader, a man honoured of God, and very faithful, happening to meet with him at Rhegium, just as he was going on board ship. Remember my bonds[1353] that I may be made perfect in Christ. Fare ye well in the flesh, the soul, and the spirit, while ye think of things perfect, and turn yourselves away from the workers of iniquity, who corrupt the word of truth, and are strengthened inwardly by the grace of our Lord Jesus Christ.

Footnotes:

1296. 1 Tim. iv. 10.
1297. Literally, "to your brother-loving spiritual love according to God."
1298. Literally, "course in Christ."
1299. 1 Cor. i. 10; Phil. ii. 2, Phil. iii. 16.
1300. 1 Cor. viii. 6.
1301. 1 Cor. viii. 6.
1302. 1 Cor. xii. 11.
1303. Literally, "which is given unto the death of the Lord."
1304. Eph. iv. 5.
1305. Deut. vi. 4; Mark xii. 29.
1306. Mal. ii. 10.
1307. John i. 18.
1308. 1 Cor. viii. 6.
1309. Prov. xxx. 4.
1310. i.e., "Advocate" or "Comforter;" comp. John xiv. 16.
1311. Eph. iv. 4.
1312. 1 Cor. xii. 13.
1313. Eph. iv. 4.
1314. 1 Cor. xii. 11.
1315. Comp. Athanasian Creed.
1316. Matt. xxviii. 19.
1317. John i. 14.
1318. Prov. ix. 1.
1319. Isa. vii. 14.
1320. Eph. ii. 2.
1321. This is the idea worked out by St. Bernard. See my note (supra) suffixed to the Syriac Epistle to Ephesians.
1322. The various Gnostic sects are here referred to, who held that matter was essentially evil, and therefore denied the reality of our Lord's incarnation.
1323. The ms. has μαγείας, "of magic;" we have followed the emendation proposed by Faber.
1324. Literally, "heretical in respect to

phantasy."

1325. Literally, is "various," or "manifold."
1326. 1 Cor. ii. 8.
1327. John i. 14.
1328. Matt. iv. 23, Matt. ix. 35.
1329. Reference seems to be made to obscene heathen practices.
1330. i.e., so as to have no separate personality from the Father. Comp. Epistle to the Tarsians, chap. ii.
1331. Literally, "and taking away Christ from being born."
1332. Literally, "double."
1333. According to many of the Fathers, Satan was in great ignorance as to a multitude of points connected with Christ. See my note at end of the Syriac Epistle to Ephesians, supra.
1334. Literally, "thou wast dizzy in the head."
1335. Literally, "on account of the paltry things."
1336. Literally, "small."
1337. Matt. iv. 3.
1338. Or, "the belly."
1339. 1 Cor. ii. 8.
1340. Some insert, "corruptible."
1341. Luke x. 18.
1342. Matt. iv. 6.
1343. Comp. Rom. iv. 17.
1344. Matt. iv. 6.
1345. Ps. xci. 13.
1346. Deut. vi. 16.
1347. Luke iv. 6.
1348. Matt. iv. 9.
1349. Or, "belly."
1350. Or, "that always needs whipping."
1351. Matt. iv. 10.
1352. Matt. iv. 10; Deut. vi. 13.
1353. Comp. Col. iv. 18.

The Epistle of Maria the Proselyte to Ignatius

Mary of Cassobelæ to Ignatius [1354]

Maria, a proselyte of Jesus Christ, to Ignatius Theophorus, most blessed bishop of the apostolic Church which is at Antioch, beloved in God the Father, and Jesus: Happiness and safety. We all [1355] beg for thee joy and health in Him.

Chapter I - Occasion of the epistle

Since Christ has, to our wonder, [1356] been made known among us to be the Son of the living God, and to have become man in these last times by means of the Virgin Mary, [1357] of the seed of David and Abraham, according to the announcements previously made regarding Him and through Him by the company of the prophets, we therefore beseech and entreat that, by thy wisdom, Maris our friend, bishop of our native Neapolis, [1358] which is near Zarbus, [1359] and Eulogius, and Sobelus the presbyter, be sent to us, that we be not destitute of such as preside over the divine word as Moses also says, "Let the Lord God look out a man who shall guide this people, and the congregation of the Lord shall not be as sheep which have no shepherd." [1360]

Chapter II - Youth may be allied with piety and discretion

But as to those whom we have named being young men, do not, thou blessed one, have any apprehension. For I would have you know that they are wise about the flesh, and are insensible to its passions, they themselves glowing with all the glory of a hoary head through their own [1361] intrinsic merits, and though but recently called as young men to the priesthood. [1362] Now, call thou into exercise [1363] thy thoughts through the Spirit that God has given to thee by Christ, and thou wilt remember [1364] that Samuel, while yet a little child, was called a seer, and was reckoned in the company of the prophets, that he reproved the aged Eli for transgression, since he had honoured his infatuated sons above God the author of all things, and had allowed them to go unpunished, when they turned the office of the priesthood into ridicule, and acted violently towards thy people.

Chapter III - Examples of youthful devotedness

Moreover, the wise Daniel, while he was a young man, passed judgment on certain vigorous old men, [1365] showing them that they were abandoned wretches, and not [worthy to be reckoned] elders, and that, though Jews by extraction, they were Canaanites in practice. And Jeremiah, when on account of his youth he declined the office of a prophet entrusted to him by God, was addressed in these words: "Say not, I am a youth; for thou shalt go to all those to whom I send thee, and thou shalt speak according to all that I command thee; because I am with thee." [1366] And the wise Solomon, when only in the twelfth year of his age, [1367] had wisdom to decide the important question concerning the children of the two women, [1368] when it was unknown to whom these respectively belonged; so that the whole people were astonished at such wisdom in a child, and venerated him as being not a mere youth, but a full-grown man. And he solved the hard questions of the queen of the Ethiopians, which had profit in them as the streams of the Nile [have fertility], in such a manner that that woman, though herself so wise, was beyond measure astonished. [1369]

Chapter IV - The same subject continued

Josiah also, beloved of God, when as yet he could scarcely speak articulately, convicts those who were possessed of a wicked spirit as being false in their speech, and deceivers of the people. He also reveals the deceit of the demons, and openly exposes those that are no gods; yea, while yet an infant he slays their priests, and overturns their altars, and defiles the place where sacrifices were offered with dead bodies, and throws down the temples, and cuts down the groves, and breaks in pieces the pillars, and breaks open the tombs of the ungodly, that not a relic of the wicked might any longer exist. [1370] To such an extent did he display zeal in the cause of godliness, and prove himself a punisher of the ungodly, while he as yet faltered in speech like a child. David, too, who was at once a prophet and a king, and the root of our Saviour according to the flesh, while yet a youth is anointed by Samuel to be king. [1371] For he himself says in a certain place, "I was small among my brethren, and the youngest in the house of my father." [1372]

Chapter V - Expressions of respect for Ignatius

But time would fail me if I should endeavour to enumerate [1373] all those that pleased God in their youth, having been entrusted by God with either the prophetical, the priestly, or the kingly office. And those which have been mentioned may suffice, by way of bringing the subject to thy remembrance. But I entreat thee not to reckon me presumptuous or ostentatious [in writing as I have done]. For I have set forth these statements, not as instructing thee, but simply as suggesting the matter to the remembrance of my father in God. For I know my own place, [1374] and do not compare myself with such as you. I salute thy holy clergy, and thy Christ-loving people who are ruled under thy care as their pastor. All the faithful with us salute thee. Pray, blessed shepherd, that I may be in health as respects God.

Footnotes:

1354. Nothing can be said with certainty as to the place here referred to. Some have conceived that the ordinary reading, Maria Cassobolita, is incorrect, and that it should be changed to Maria Castabalitis, supposing the reference to be to Castabala, a well-known city of Cilicia. But this and other proposed emendations rest upon mere conjecture.

1355. Some propose to read, "always."

1356. Or, "wonderfully."

1357. The ms. has, "and."

1358. The ms. has Ἡμελάπης, which Vossius and others deem a mistake for ἡμεδαπῆς, as translated above.

1359. The same as Azarbus (comp. Epist. to Hero, chap. ix.).

1360. Num. xxvii. 16, 17.

1361. Literally, "in themselves."

1362. Literally, "in recent newness of priesthood."

1363. Literally, "call up."

1364. Literally, "know."

1365. The ancient Latin version translates ὠμογέροντας "cruel old men," which perhaps suits the reference better.

1366. Jer. i. 7.

1367. Comp. for similar statements to those here made, Epistle to the Magnesians (longer), chap. iii.

1368. Literally, "understood the great question of the ignorance of the women respecting their children."

1369. Literally, "out of herself."

1370. 2 Kings xxii., xxiii.

1371. 1 Sam. xvi.

1372. Ps. cl. 1 (in the Septuagint; not found at all in Hebrew).

1373. Literally, "to trace up."

1374. Literally, "measure" or "limits."

The Epistle of Ignatius to Mary at Neapolis, Near Zarbus

Ignatius, who is also called Theaphorus, to her who has obtained mercy through the grace of the most high God the Father, and Jesus Christ the Lord, who died for us, to Mary, my daughter, most faithful, worthy of God, and bearing Christ [in her heart], wishes abundance of happiness in God.

Chapter I - Acknowledgment of her excellence and wisdom

Sight indeed is better than writing, inasmuch as, being one [1375] of the company of the senses, it not only, by communicating proofs of friendship, honours him who receives them, but also, by those which it in turn receives, enriches the desire for better things. But the second harbour of refuge, as the phrase runs, is the practice of writing, which we have received, as a convenient haven, by thy faith, from so great a distance, seeing that by means of a letter we have learned the excellence that is in thee. For the souls of the good, O thou wisest [1376] of women! resemble fountains of the purest water; for they allure by their beauty passers-by to drink of them, even though these should not be thirsty. And thy intelligence invites us, as by a word of command, to participate in those divine draughts which gush forth so abundantly in thy soul.

Chapter II - His own condition

But I, O thou blessed woman, not being now so much my own master as in the power of others, am driven along by the varying wills of many adversaries, [1377] being in one sense in exile, in another in prison, and in a third in bonds. But I pay no regard to these things. Yea, by the injuries inflicted on me through them, I acquire all the more the character of a disciple, that I may attain to Jesus Christ. May I enjoy the torments which are prepared for me, seeing that "the sufferings of this present time are not worthy [to be compared] with the glory which shall be revealed in us." [1378]

Chapter III - He had complied with her request

I have gladly acted as requested in thy letter, [1379] having no doubt respecting those persons whom thou didst prove to be men of worth. For I am sure that thou barest testimony to them in the exercise of a godly judgment, [1380] and not through the influence of carnal favour. And thy numerous quotations of Scripture passages exceedingly delighted me, which, when I had read, I had no longer a single doubtful thought respecting the matter. For I did not hold that those things were simply to be glanced over by my eyes, of which I had received from thee such an incontrovertible demonstration. May I be in place of thy soul, because thou lovest Jesus, the Son of the living God. Wherefore also He Himself says to thee, "I love them that love Me; and those that seek Me shall find peace." [1381]

Chapter IV - Commendation and exhortation

Now it occurs to me to mention, that the report is true which I heard of thee whilst thou wast at Rome with the blessed father [1382] Linus, whom the deservedly-blessed Clement, a hearer of Peter and Paul, has now succeeded. And by this time thou hast added a hundred-fold to thy reputation; and may thou, O woman! still further increase it. I greatly desired to come unto you, that I might have rest with you; but "the way of man is not in himself." [1383] For the military guard [under which I am kept] hinders my purpose, and does not permit me to go further. Nor indeed, in the state I am now in, can I either do or suffer anything. Wherefore deeming the practice of writing the second resource of friends for their mutual encouragement, I salute thy sacred soul, beseeching of thee to add still further to thy vigour. For our present labour is but little, while the reward which is expected is great.

Chapter V - Salutations and good wishes

Avoid those that deny the passion of Christ, and His birth according to the flesh: and there are many at present who suffer under this disease. But it would be absurd to admonish thee on other points, seeing that thou art perfect in every good work and word, and able also to exhort others in Christ. Salute all that are like-minded with thyself, and who hold fast to their salvation in Christ. The presbyters and deacons, and above all the holy Hero, salute thee. Cassian my host salutes thee, as well as my sister, his wife, and their very dear children. May the Lord sanctify thee for evermore in the enjoyment both of bodily and spiritual health, and may I see thee in Christ obtaining the crown!

Footnotes:

1375. Literally, "a part."
1376. Literally, "all-wise."
1377. Literally, "by the many wills of the adversaries."
1378. Rom. viii. 18.
1379. Literally, "I have gladly fulfilled the things commanded by thee in the letter."
1380. Literally, "by a judgment of God."
1381. Prov. viii. 17 (loosely quoted from LXX.).
1382. The original is πάπα, common to primitive bishops.
1383. Jer. x. 23.

The Epistle of Ignatius to St. John the Apostle

Ignatius, and the brethren who are with him, to John the holy presbyter.

We are deeply grieved at thy delay in strengthening us by thy addresses and consolations. If thy absence be prolonged, it will disappoint many of us. Hasten then to come, for we believe that it is expedient. There are also many of our women here, who are desirous to see Mary [the mother] of Jesus, and wish day by day to run off from us to you, that they may meet with her, and touch those breasts of hers which nourished the Lord Jesus, and may inquire of her respecting some rather secret matters. But Salome also, [the daughter of Anna,] whom thou lovest, who stayed with her five months at Jerusalem, and some other well-known persons, relate that she is full of all graces and all virtues, after the manner of a virgin, fruitful in virtue and grace. And, as they report, she is cheerful in persecutions and afflictions, free from murmuring in the midst of penury and want, grateful to those that injure her, and rejoices when exposed to troubles: she sympathizes with the wretched and the afflicted as sharing in their afflictions, and is not slow to come to their assistance. Moreover, she shines forth gloriously as contending in the fight of faith against the pernicious conflicts of vicious [1384] principles or conduct. She is the lady of our new religion and repentance,[1385] and the handmaid among the faithful of all works of piety. She is indeed devoted to the humble, and she humbles herself more devotedly than the devoted, and is wonderfully magnified by all, while at the same time she suffers detraction from the Scribes and Pharisees. Besides these points, many relate to us numerous other things regarding her. We do not, however, go so far as to believe all in every particular; nor do we mention such to thee. But, as we are informed by those who are worthy of credit, there is in Mary the mother of Jesus an angelic purity of nature allied with the nature of humanity. [1386] And such reports as these have greatly excited our emotions, and urge us eagerly to desire a sight of this (if it be lawful so to speak) heavenly prodigy and most sacred marvel. But do thou in haste comply with this our desire; and fare thou well. Amen.

Footnotes:

1384. Literally, "of vices."

1385. Some mss. and editions seem with propriety to omit this word.

1386. Literally, "a nature of angelic purity is allied to human nature."

A Second Epistle of Ignatius to St. John

His friend [1387] Ignatius to John the holy presbyter

If thou wilt give me leave, I desire to go up to Jerusalem, and see the faithful [1388] saints who are there, especially Mary the mother, whom they report to be an object of admiration and of affection to all. For who would not rejoice to behold and to address her who bore the true God from her [1389] own womb, provided he is a friend of our faith and religion? And in like manner [I desire to see] the venerable James, who is surnamed Just, whom they relate to be very like Christ Jesus in appearance, [1390] in life, and in method of conduct, as if he were a twin-brother of the same womb. They say that, if I see him, I see also Jesus Himself, as to all the features and aspect of His body. Moreover, [I desire to see] the other saints, both male and female. Alas! why do I delay? Why am I kept back? Kind [1391] teacher, bid me hasten [to fulfil my wish], and fare thou well. Amen.

Footnotes:

1387. Literally, "his own."
1388. Some omit this word.
1389. Literally, "of herself." Some read, instead of "de se," "deorum," when the translation will be, "the true God of gods."
1390. Or, "face." Some omit the word.
1391. Or, "good."

The Epistle of Ignatius to the Virgin Mary

Her friend [1392] Ignatius to the Christ-bearing Mary.

Thou oughtest to have comforted and consoled me who am a neophyte, and a disciple of thy [beloved] John. For I have heard things wonderful to tell respecting thy [son] Jesus, and I am astonished by such a report. But I desire with my whole heart to obtain information concerning the things which I have heard from thee, who wast always intimate and allied with Him, and who wast acquainted with [all] His secrets. I have also written to thee at another time, and have asked thee concerning the same things. Fare thou well; and let the neophytes who are with me be comforted of thee, and by thee, and in thee. Amen.

Footnotes:

1392. Literally, "his own." [Mary is here called χριστοτόκος, and not θεοτόκος, which suggests a Nestorian forgery.]

Reply of the Blessed Virgin to this Letter

The lowly handmaid of Christ Jesus to Ignatius, her beloved fellow-disciple
The things which thou hast heard and learned from John concerning Jesus are true. Believe them, cling to them, and hold fast the profession of that Christianity which thou hast embraced, and conform thy habits and life to thy profession. Now I will come in company with John to visit thee, and those that are with thee. Stand fast in the faith, [1393] and show thyself a man; nor let the fierceness of persecution move thee, but let thy spirit be strong and rejoice in God thy Saviour. [1394] Amen.

Footnotes:
1393. 1 Cor. xvi. 13.

1394. Luke i. 47.

Introductory Note to the Martyrdom of Ignatius

The learned dissertation of Pearson, on the difficulties of reconciling the supposed year of the martyrdom with the history of Trajan, etc., is given entire in Jacobson (vol. ii. p. 524), against the decision of Usher for a.d. 107. Pearson accepts a.d. 116. Consult also the preface of Dr. Thomas Smith, [1395] in the same work (p. 518), on the text of the original and of the Latin versions, and on the credibility of the narrative. Our learned translators seem to think the text they have used, to be without interpolation. If the simple-minded faithful of those days, so near the age of miracles, appear to us, in some degree, enthusiasts, let us remember the vision of Col. Gardiner, accredited by Doddridge, Lord Lyttleton's vision (see Boswell, anno 1784, chap. xi.), accepted by Johnson and his contemporaries, and the interesting narrative of the pious Mr. Tennent of New Jersey, attested by so many excellent and intelligent persons, almost of our own times.

The following is the Introductory Notice of the translators:--

The following account of the martyrdom of Ignatius professes, in several passages, to have been written by those who accompanied him on his voyage to Rome, and were present on the occasion of his death (chaps. v. vi. vii.). And if the genuineness of this narrative, as well as of the Ignatian Epistles, be admitted, there can be little doubt that the persons in question were Philo and Agathopus, with Crocus perhaps, all of whom are mentioned by Ignatius (Epist. to Smyr., chap. x.; to Philad., chap. xi.; to Rom., chap. x.) as having attended him on that journey to Rome which resulted in his martyrdom. But doubts have been started, by Daillé and others, as to the date and authorship of this account. Some of these rest upon internal considerations, but the weightiest objection is found in the fact that no reference to this narrative is to be traced during the first six centuries of our era. [1396] This is certainly a very suspicious circumstance, and may well give rise to some hesitation in ascribing the authorship to the immediate companions and friends of Ignatius. On the other hand, however, this account of the death of Ignatius is in perfect harmony with the particulars recounted by Eusebius and Chrysostom regarding him. Its comparative simplicity, too, is greatly in its favour. It makes no reference to the legends which by and by connected themselves with the name of Ignatius. As is well known, he came in course of time to be identified with the child whom Christ (Matt. xviii. 2) set before His disciples as a pattern of humility. It was said that the Saviour took him up in His arms, and that hence Ignatius derived his name of Theophorus; [1397] that is, according to the explanation which this legend gives of the word, one carried by God. But in chap. ii. of the following narrative we find the term explained to mean, "one who has Christ in his breast;" and this simple explanation, with the entire silence preserved as to the marvels afterwards connected with the name of Ignatius, is certainly a strong argument in favour of the early date and probable genuineness of the account. Some critics, such as Usher and Grabe, have reckoned the latter part of the narrative spurious, while accepting the former; but there appears to be a unity about it which requires us either to accept it in toto, or to reject it altogether. [1398]

The Martyrdom of Ignatius

Chapter I - Desire of Ignatius for martyrdom

When Trajan, not long since, [1399] succeeded to the empire of the Romans, Ignatius, the disciple of John the apostle, a man in all respects of an apostolic character, governed the Church of the Antiochians with great care, having with difficulty escaped the former storms of the many persecutions under Domitian, inasmuch as, like a good pilot, by the helm of prayer and fasting, by the earnestness of his teaching, and by his [constant [1400]] spiritual labour, he resisted the flood that rolled against him, fearing [only] lest he should lose any of those who were deficient in courage, or apt to suffer from their simplicity. [1401] Wherefore he rejoiced over the tranquil state of the Church, when the persecution ceased for a little time, but was grieved as to himself, that he had not yet attained to a true love to Christ, nor reached the perfect rank of a disciple. For he inwardly reflected, that the confession which is made by martyrdom, would bring him into a yet more intimate relation to the Lord. Wherefore, continuing a few years longer with the Church, and, like a divine lamp, enlightening every one's understanding by his expositions of the [Holy [1402]] Scriptures, he [at length] attained the object of his desire.

Chapter II - Ignatius is condemned by Trajan

For Trajan, in the ninth [1403] year of his reign, being lifted up [with pride], after the victory he had gained over the Scythians and Dacians, and many other nations, and thinking that the religious body of the Christians were yet wanting to complete the subjugation of all things to himself, and [thereupon] threatening them with persecution unless they should agree to [1404] worship dæmons, as did all other nations, thus compelled [1405] all who were living godly lives either to sacrifice [to idols] or die. Wherefore the noble soldier of Christ [Ignatius], being in fear for the Church of the Antiochians, was, in accordance with his own desire, brought before Trajan, who was at that time staying at Antioch, but was in haste [to set forth] against Armenia and the Parthians. And when he was set before the emperor Trajan, [that prince] said unto him, "Who art thou, wicked wretch, [1406] who settest [1407] thyself to transgress our commands, and persuadest others to do the same, so that they should miserably perish?" Ignatius replied, "No one ought to call Theophorus [1408] wicked; for all evil spirits [1409] have departed from the servants of God. But if, because I am an enemy to these [spirits], you call me wicked in respect to them, I quite agree with you; for inasmuch as I have Christ the King of heaven [within me], I destroy all the devices of these [evil spirits]." Trajan answered, "And who is Theophorus?" Ignatius replied, "He who has Christ within his breast." Trajan said, "Do we not then seem to you to have the gods in our mind, whose assistance we enjoy in fighting against our enemies?" Ignatius answered, "Thou art in error when thou callest the dæmons of the nations gods. For there is but one God, who made heaven, and earth, and the sea, and all that are in them; and one Jesus Christ, the only-begotten Son of God, whose kingdom may I enjoy." Trajan said, "Do you mean Him who was crucified under Pontius Pilate?" Ignatius replied, "I mean Him who crucified my sin, with him who was the inventor of it, [1410] and who has condemned [and cast down] all the deceit and malice of the devil under the feet of those who carry Him in their heart." Trajan said, "Dost thou then carry within thee Him that was crucified?" Ignatius replied, "Truly so; for it is written, I will dwell in them, and walk in them.' " [1411] Then Trajan pronounced sentence as follows: "We command that Ignatius, who affirms that he carries about within him Him that was crucified, be bound by soldiers, and carried to the great [city] Rome, there to be devoured by the beasts, for the gratification of the people." When the holy martyr heard this sentence, he cried out with joy, "I thank thee, O Lord, that Thou hast vouchsafed to honour me with a perfect love towards Thee, and hast made me to be bound with iron chains, like [1412] Thy Apostle Paul." Having spoken thus, he then, with delight, clasped the chains about him; and when he had first prayed for the Church, and commended it with tears to the Lord, he was hurried away by the savage cruelty [1413] of the soldiers, like a distinguished ram [1414] the leader of a goodly flock, that he might be carried to Rome, there to furnish food to the bloodthirsty beasts.

Chapter III - Ignatius sails to Smyrna

Wherefore, with great alacrity and joy, through his desire to suffer, he came down from Antioch to Seleucia, from which place he set sail. And after a great deal of suffering he came to Smyrna, where he disembarked with great joy, and hastened to see the holy Polycarp, [formerly] his fellow-disciple, and [now] bishop of Smyrna. For they had both, in old times, been disciples of St. John the Apostle. Being then brought to him, and having communicated to him some spiritual gifts, and glorying in his bonds, he entreated of him to labour [1415] along with him for the fulfilment of his desire; earnestly indeed asking this of the whole Church (for the cities and Churches of Asia had welcomed [1416] the holy man through their bishops, and presbyters, and deacons, all hastening to meet him, if by any means they might receive from him some [1417] spiritual gift), but above all, the holy Polycarp, that, by means of the wild beasts, he soon disappearing from this world, might be manifested before the face of Christ.

Chapter IV - Ignatius writes to the churches

And these things he thus spake, and thus testified, extending his love to Christ so far as one who was about to [1418] secure heaven through his good confession, and the earnestness of those who joined their prayers to his in regard to his [approaching] conflict; and to give a recompense to the Churches, who came to meet him through their rulers, sending [1419] letters of thanksgiving to them, which dropped spiritual grace, along with prayer and exhortation. Wherefore, seeing all men so kindly affected towards him, and fearing lest the love of the brotherhood should hinder his zeal towards the Lord, [1420] while a fair door of suffering martyrdom was opened to him, he wrote to the Church of the Romans the Epistle which is here subjoined.

(See the Epistle as formerly given.)

Chapter V - Ignatius is brought to Rome

Having therefore, by means of this Epistle, settled, [1421] as he wished, those of the brethren at Rome who were unwilling [for his martyrdom]; and setting sail from Smyrna (for Christophorus was pressed by the soldiers to hasten to the public spectacles in the mighty [city] Rome, that, being given up to the wild beasts in the sight of the Roman people, he might attain to the crown for which he strove), he [next] landed at Troas. Then, going on from that place to Neapolis, he went [on foot] by Philippi through Macedonia, and on to that part of Epirus which is near Epidamnus; and finding a ship in one of the seaports, he sailed over the Adriatic Sea, and entering from it on the Tyrrhene, he passed by the various islands and cities, until, when Puteoli came in sight, he was eager there to disembark, having a desire to tread in the footsteps of the Apostle Paul. [1422] But a violent wind arising did not suffer him to do so, the ship being driven rapidly forwards; [1423] and, simply expressing his delight [1424] over the love of the brethren in that place, he sailed by. Wherefore, continuing to enjoy fair winds, we were reluctantly hurried on in one day and a night, mourning [as we did] over the coming departure from us of this righteous man. But to him this happened just as he wished, since he was in haste as soon as possible to leave this world, that he might attain to the Lord whom he loved. Sailing then into the Roman harbour, and the unhallowed sports being just about to close, the soldiers began to be annoyed at our slowness, but the bishop rejoicingly yielded to their urgency.

Chapter VI - Ignatius is devoured by the beasts at Rome

They pushed forth therefore from the place which is called Portus; [1425] and (the [1426] fame of all relating to the holy martyr being already spread abroad) we met the brethren full of fear and joy; rejoicing indeed because they were thought worthy to meet with Theophorus, but struck with fear because so eminent a man was being led to death. Now he enjoined some to keep silence who, in their fervent zeal, were saying [1427] that they would appease the people, so that they should not demand the destruction of this just one. He being immediately aware of this through the Spirit, [1428] and having saluted them all, and begged of them to show a true affection towards him, and having dwelt [on this point] at greater length than in his Epistle, [1429] and having persuaded them not to envy him hastening to the Lord, he then, after he had, with all the brethren kneeling [beside him], entreated the Son of God in behalf of the Churches, that a stop might be put to the persecution, and that mutual love might continue among the brethren, was led with all haste into the amphitheatre. Then, being immediately thrown in, according to the command of Cæsar given some time ago, the public spectacles being just about to close (for it was then a solemn day, as they deemed it, being that which is called the thirteenth [1430] in the Roman tongue, on which the people were wont to assemble in more than ordinary numbers [1431]), he was thus cast to the wild beasts close beside the temple, [1432] that so by them the desire of the holy martyr Ignatius should be fulfilled, according to that which is written, "The desire of the righteous is acceptable [1433] [to God]," to the effect that he might not be troublesome to any of the brethren by the gathering of his remains, even as he had in his Epistle expressed a wish beforehand that so his end might be. For only the harder portions of his holy remains were left, which were conveyed to Antioch and wrapped [1434] in linen, as an inestimable treasure left to the holy Church by the grace which was in the martyr.

Chapter VII - Ignatius appears in a vision after his death

Now these things took place on the thirteenth day before the Kalends of January, that is, on the twentieth of December, [1435] Sura and Senecio being then the consuls of the Romans for the second time. Having ourselves been eye-witnesses of these things, and having spent the whole night in tears within the house, and having entreated the Lord, with bended knees and much prayer, that He would give us weak men full assurance respecting the things which were done, [1436] it came to pass, on our falling into a brief slumber, that some of us saw the blessed Ignatius suddenly standing by us and embracing us, while others beheld him again praying for us, and others still saw him dropping with sweat, as if he had just come from his great labour, and standing by the Lord. When, therefore, we had with great joy witnessed these things, and had compared our several visions [1437] together, we sang praise to God, the giver of all good things, and expressed our sense of the happiness of the holy [martyr]; and now we have made known to you both the day and the time [when these things happened], that, assembling ourselves together according to the time of his martyrdom, we may have fellowship with the champion and noble martyr of Christ, who trod under foot the devil, and perfected the course which, out of love to Christ, he had desired, in Christ Jesus our Lord; by whom, and with whom, be glory and power to the Father, with the Holy Spirit, for evermore! Amen.

Footnotes:

1395. He published an edition of Ignatius, Oxford, 1709.

1396. A most remarkable statement. "References" may surely be traced, at least in Eusebius (iii. 36) and Irenæus (Adv. Hæres. v. 28), if not in Jerome, etc. But the sermon of St. Chrysostom (Opp. ii. 593) seems almost, in parts, a paraphrase.

1397. See on this matter Jacobson's note (vol ii. p. 262), and reference to Pearson (Vind. Ignat., part ii. cap. 12). The false accentuation (Θεόφορος) occurs in some copies to support the myth of the child Ignatius as the God-borne instead of the God-bearing; i.e., carried by Christ, instead of carrying the Spirit of Christ within.

1398. But see the note in Jacobson, vol. ii. p.557.

1399. The date of Trajan's accession was a.d. 98.

1400. The text here is somewhat doubtful.

1401. Literally, "any of the fainthearted and more guileless."

1402. This word is of doubtful authority.

1403. The numeral is uncertain. In the old Latin version we find "the fourth," which Grabe has corrected into the nineteenth. The choice lies between "ninth" and "nineteenth," i.e., a.d. 107 or a.d. 116.

1404. Literally, "would choose to submit to."

1405. Some read, "fear compelled."

1406. Literally, "evil-dæmon."

1407. Literally, "art zealous."

1408. Or, "one who carries God."

1409. Literally, "the dæmons."

1410. The Latin version reads, "Him who bore my sin, with its inventor, upon the cross."

1411. 2 Cor. vi. 16.

1412. Literally, "with."

1413. Or, "beast-like."

1414. Better, "like the noble leader," etc.; remitting κριὸς to the margin, as an ignoble word to English ears.

1415. It is doubtful if this clause should be referred to Polycarp.

1416. Or, "received."

1417. Literally, "a portion of."

1418. The Latin version has, "that he was to." But compare the martyr's Epistle to the Romans (cap. 5); "yet am I not thereby justified," --a double reference to St. Paul's doctrine, 1 Cor. iv. 4 and 1 Cor. xiii. 3. See also his quotation (Sept., Prov. xviii. 17). Epistle to Magnesians, cap 12.

1419. The punctuation and construction are here doubtful.

1420. Or, "should prevent him from hastening to the Lord."

1421. Or, "corrected."

1422. Comp. Acts xxviii. 13, 14.

1423. Literally, "the ship being driven onwards from the stern."

1424. Literally, "declaring happy."

1425. Of which we shall learn more when we come to Hippolytus. Trajan had just improved the work of Claudius at this haven, near Ostia.

1426. Literally, "for the."

1427. Literally, "boiling and saying."

1428. Or, "in spirit."

1429. i.e., in his Epistle to the Romans.

1430. The Saturnalia were then celebrated.

1431. Literally, "they came together zealously."

1432. The amphitheatre itself was sacred to several of the gods. But (παρὰ τῷ ναῷ) the original indicates the cella or shrine, in the centre of the amphitheatre where the image of Pluto was exhibited. A plain cross, until the late excavations, marked the very spot.

1433. Prov. x. 24.

1434. Or, "deposited."

1435. The Greeks celebrate this martyrdom, to this day, on the twentieth of December.

1436. To the effect, viz., that the martyrdom of Ignatius had been acceptable to God.

1437. Literally, "the visions of the dreams."

Barnabas

Introductory Note to the Epistle of Barnabas

[a.d. 100.] The writer of this Epistle is supposed to have been an Alexandrian Jew of the times of Trajan and Hadrian. He was a layman; but possibly he bore the name of "Barnabas," and so has been confounded with his holy and apostolic name-sire. It is more probable that the Epistle, being anonymous, was attributed to St. Barnabas, by those who supposed that apostle to be the author of the Epistle to the Hebrews, and who discovered similarities in the plan and purpose of the two works. It is with great reluctance that I yield to modern scholars, in dismissing the ingenious and temperate argument of Archbishop Wake [1438] for the apostolic origin of this treatise. The learned Lardner [1439] shares his convictions; and the very interesting and ingenious views of Jones [1440] never appeared to me satisfactory, weighed with preponderating arguments, on the other side.[1441]

The Maccabæan spirit of the Jews never burned more furiously than after the destruction of Jerusalem, and while it was kindling the conflagration that broke out under Barchochebas, and blazed so terribly in the insurrection against Hadrian.[1442] It is not credible that the Jewish Christians at Alexandria and elsewhere were able to emancipate themselves from their national spirit; and accordingly the old Judaizing, which St. Paul had anathematized and confuted, would assert itself again. If such was the occasion of this Epistle, as I venture to suppose, a higher character must be ascribed to it than could otherwise be claimed. This accounts, also, for the degree of favour with which it was accepted by the primitive faithful.

It is interesting as a specimen of their conflicts with a persistent Judaism which St. Paul had defeated and anathematized, but which was ever cropping out among believers originally of the Hebrews.[1443] Their own habits of allegorizing, and their Oriental tastes, must be borne in mind, if we are readily disgusted with our author's fancies and refinements. St. Paul himself pays a practical tribute to their modes of thought, in his Epistle to the Galatians iv. 24. This is the ad hominem form of rhetoric, familiar to all speakers, which laid even the apostle open to the slander of enemies (2 Cor. xii. 16),--that he was "crafty," and caught men with guile. It is interesting to note the more Occidental spirit of Cyprian, as compared with our author, when he also contends with Judaism. Doubtless we have in the pseudo-Barnabas something of that oeconomy which is always capable of abuse, and which was destined too soon to overleap the bounds of its moral limitations.

It is to be observed that this writer sometimes speaks as a Gentile, a fact which some have found it difficult to account for, on the supposition that he was a Hebrew, if not a Levite as well. But so, also, St. Paul sometimes speaks as a Roman, and sometimes as a Jew; and, owing to the mixed character of the early Church, he writes to the Romans iv. 1 as if they were all Israelites, and again to the same Church (Rom. xi. 13) as if they were all Gentiles. So this writer sometimes identifies himself with Jewish thought as a son of Abraham, and again speaks from the Christian position as if he were a Gentile, thus identifying himself with the catholicity of the Church.

But the subject thus opened is vast; and "the Epistle of Barnabas," so called, still awaits a critical editor, who at the same time shall be a competent expositor. Nobody can answer these requisitions, who is unable, for this purpose, to be a Christian of the days of Trajan.

But it will be observed that this version has great advantages over any of its predecessor, and is a valuable acquisition to the student. The learned translators have had before them the entire Greek text of the fourth century, disfigured it is true by corruptions, but still very precious, the rather as they have been able to compare it with the text of Hilgenfeld. Their editorial notes are sufficient for our own plan; and little has been left for me to do, according to the scheme of this publication, save to revise the "copy" for printing. I am glad to presume no further into such a labyrinth, concerning which the learned and careful Wake modestly professes, "I have endeavoured to attain to the sense of my author, and to make him as plain and easy as I was able. If in anything I have chanced to mistake him, I have only this to say for myself: that he must be better acquainted with the road than I pretend to be, who will undertake to travel so long a journey in the dark and never to miss his way."

The following is the original Introductory Notice:--

Nothing certain is known as to the author of the following Epistle. The writer's name is

Barnabas, but scarcely any scholars now ascribe it to the illustrious friend and companion of St. Paul. External and internal evidence here come into direct collision. The ancient writers who refer to this Epistle unanimously attribute it to Barnabas the Levite, of Cyprus, who held such an honourable place in the infant Church. Clement of Alexandria does so again and again (Strom., ii. 6, ii. 7, etc.). Origen describes it as "a Catholic Epistle" (Cont. Cels., i. 63), and seems to rank it among the Sacred Scriptures (Comm. in Rom., i. 24). Other statements have been quoted from the fathers, to show that they held this to be an authentic production of the apostolic Barnabas; and certainly no other name is ever hinted at in Christian antiquity as that of the writer. But notwithstanding this, the internal evidence is now generally regarded as conclusive against this opinion. On perusing the Epistle, the reader will be in circumstances to judge of this matter for himself. He will be led to consider whether the spirit and tone of the writing, as so decidedly opposed to all respect for Judaism--the numerous inaccuracies which it contains with respect to Mosaic enactments and observances--the absurd and trifling interpretations of Scripture which it suggests--and the many silly vaunts of superior knowledge in which its writer indulges--can possibly comport with its ascription to the fellow--labourer of St. Paul. When it is remembered that no one ascribes the Epistle to the apostolic Barnabas till the times of Clement of Alexandria, and that it is ranked by Eusebius among the "spurious" writings, which, however much known and read in the Church, were never regarded as authoritative, little doubt can remain that the external evidence is of itself weak, and should not make us hesitate for a moment in refusing to ascribe this writing to Barnabas the Apostle.

The date, object, and intended reader of the Epistle can only be doubtfully inferred from some statements which it contains. It was clearly written after the destruction of Jerusalem, since reference is made to that event (chap. xvi.), but how long after is matter of much dispute. The general opinion is, that its date is not later than the middle of the second century, and that it cannot be placed earlier than some twenty or thirty years before. In point of style, both as respects thought and expression, a very low place must be assigned it. We know nothing certain of the region in which the author lived, or where the first readers were to be found. The intention of the writer, as he himself states (chap. i), was "to perfect the knowledge" of those to whom he wrote. Hilgenfeld, who has devoted much attention to this Epistle, holds that "it was written at the close of the first century by a Gentile Christian of the school of Alexandria, with the view of winning back, or guarding from a Judaic form of Christianity, those Christians belonging to the same class as himself."

Until the recent discovery of the Codex Sinaiticus by Tischendorf, the first four and a half chapters were known only in an ancient Latin version. The whole Greek text is now happily recovered, though it is in many places very corrupt. We have compared its readings throughout, and noted the principal variations from the text represented in our version. We have also made frequent reference to the text adopted by Hilgenfeld in his recent edition of the Epistle (Lipsiæ, T. O. Weigel, 1886).

The Epistle of Barnabas [1444]

Chapter I - After the salutation, the writer declares that he would communicate to his brethren something of that which he had himself received

All hail, ye sons and daughters, in the name of our Lord [1445] Jesus Christ, who loved us in peace.

Seeing that the divine fruits [1446] of righteousness abound among you, I rejoice exceedingly and above measure in your happy and honoured spirits, because ye have with such effect received the engrafted [1447] spiritual gift. Wherefore also I inwardly rejoice the more, hoping to be saved, because I truly perceive in you the Spirit poured forth from the rich Lord [1448] of love. Your greatly desired appearance has thus filled me with astonishment over you. [1449] I am therefore persuaded of this, and fully convinced in my own mind, that since I began to speak among you I understand many things, because the Lord hath accompanied me in the way of righteousness. I am also on this account bound [1450] by the strictest obligation to love you above my own soul, because great are the faith and love dwelling in you, while you hope for the life which He has promised. [1451] Considering this, therefore, that if I should take the trouble to communicate to you some portion of what I have myself received, it will prove to me a sufficient reward that I minister to such spirits, I have hastened briefly to write unto you, in order that, along with your faith, ye might have perfect knowledge. The doctrines of the Lord, then, are three: [1452] the hope of life, the beginning and the completion of it. For the Lord hath made known to us by the prophets both the things which are past and present, giving us also the first-fruits of the knowledge [1453] of things to come, which things as we see accomplished, one by one, we ought with the greater richness of faith [1454] and elevation of spirit to draw near to Him with reverence. [1455] I then, not as your teacher, but as one of yourselves, will set forth a few things by which in present circumstances ye may be rendered the more joyful.

Chapter II - The Jewish sacrifices are now abolished

Since, therefore, the days are evil, and Satan [1456] possesses the power of this world, we ought to give heed to ourselves, and diligently inquire into the ordinances of the Lord. Fear and patience, then, are helpers of our faith; and long-suffering and continence are things which fight on our side. While these remain pure in what respects the Lord, Wisdom, Understanding, Science, and Knowledge rejoice along with them. [1457] For He hath revealed to us by all the prophets that He needs neither sacrifices, nor burnt-offerings, nor oblations, saying thus, "What is the multitude of your sacrifices unto Me, saith the Lord? I am full of burnt-offerings, and desire not the fat of lambs, and the blood of bulls and goats, not when ye come to appear before Me: for who hath required these things at your hands? Tread no more My courts, not though ye bring with you fine flour. Incense is a vain abomination unto Me, and your new moons and sabbaths I cannot endure." [1458] He has therefore abolished these things, that the new law of our Lord Jesus Christ, which is without the yoke of necessity, might have a human oblation. [1459] And again He says to them, "Did I command your fathers, when they went out from the land of Egypt, to offer unto Me burnt-offerings and sacrifices? But this rather I commanded them, Let no one of you cherish any evil in his heart against his neighbour, and love not an oath of falsehood." [1460] We ought therefore, being possessed of understanding, to perceive the gracious intention of our Father; for He speaks to us, desirous that we, not [1461] going astray like them, should ask how we may approach Him. To us, then, He declares, "A sacrifice [pleasing] to God is a broken spirit; a smell of sweet savour to the Lord is a heart that glorifieth Him that made it." [1462] We ought therefore, brethren, carefully to inquire concerning our salvation, lest the wicked one, having made his entrance by deceit, should hurl [1463] us forth from our [true] life.

Chapter III - The fasts of the Jews are not true fasts, nor acceptable to God

He says then to them again concerning these things, "Why do ye fast to Me as on this day, saith the Lord, that your voice should be heard with a cry? I have not chosen this fast, saith the Lord, that a man should humble his soul. Nor, though ye bend your neck like a ring, and put upon you sackcloth and ashes, will ye call it an acceptable fast." [1464] To us He saith, "Behold, this is the fast that I have chosen, saith the Lord, not that a man should humble his soul, but that he should loose every band of iniquity, untie the fastenings of harsh agreements, restore to liberty them that are bruised, tear in pieces every unjust engagement, feed the hungry with thy bread, clothe the naked when thou seest him, bring the homeless into thy house, not despise the humble if thou behold him, and not [turn away] from the members of thine own family. Then shall thy dawn break forth, and thy healing shall quickly spring up, and righteousness shall go forth before thee, and the glory of God shall encompass thee; and then thou shalt call, and God shall hear thee; whilst thou art yet speaking, He shall say, Behold, I am with thee; if thou take away from thee the chain [binding others], and the stretching forth of the hands [1465] [to swear falsely], and words of murmuring, and give cheerfully thy bread to the hungry, and show compassion to the soul that has been humbled."[1466] To this end, therefore, brethren, He is long-suffering, foreseeing how the people whom He has prepared shall with guilelessness believe in His Beloved. For He revealed all these things to us beforehand, that we should not rush forward as rash acceptors of their laws. [1467]

Chapter IV - Antichrist is at hand: let us therefore avoid Jewish errors

It therefore behoves us, who inquire much concerning events at hand, [1468] to search diligently into those things which are able to save us. Let us then utterly flee from all the works of iniquity, lest these should take hold of us; and let us hate the error of the present time, that we may set our love on the world to come: let us not give loose reins to our soul, that it should have power to run with sinners and the wicked, lest we become like them. The final stumbling-block (or source of danger) approaches, concerning which it is written, as Enoch [1469] says, "For for this end the Lord has cut short the times and the days, that His Beloved may hasten; and He will come to the inheritance." And the prophet also speaks thus: "Ten kingdoms shall reign upon the earth, and a little king shall rise up after them, who shall subdue under one three of the kings." [1470] In like manner Daniel says concerning the same, "And I beheld the fourth beast, wicked and powerful, and more savage than all the beasts of the earth, and how from it sprang up ten horns, and out of them a little budding horn, and how it subdued under one three of the great horns." [1471] Ye ought therefore to understand. And this also I further beg of you, as being one of you, and loving you both individually and collectively more than my own soul, to take heed now to yourselves, and not to be like some, adding largely to your sins, and saying, "The covenant is both theirs and ours." [1472] But they thus finally lost it, after Moses had already received it. For the Scripture saith, "And Moses was fasting in the mount forty days and forty nights, and received the covenant from the Lord, tables of stone written with the finger of the hand of the Lord;" [1473] but turning away to idols, they lost it. For the Lord speaks thus to Moses: "Moses go down quickly; for the people whom thou hast brought out of the land of Egypt have transgressed." [1474] And Moses understood [the meaning of God], and cast the two tables out of his hands; and their covenant was broken, in order that the covenant of the beloved Jesus might be sealed upon our heart, in the hope which flows from believing in Him. [1475] Now, being desirous to write many things to you, not as your teacher, but as becometh one who loves you, I have taken care not to fail to write to you from what I myself possess, with a view to your purification. [1476] We take earnest [1477] heed in these last days; for the whole [past] time of your faith will profit you nothing, unless now in this wicked time we also withstand coming sources of danger, as becometh the sons of God. That the Black One [1478] may find no means of entrance, let us flee from every vanity, let us utterly hate the works of the way of wickedness. Do not, by retiring apart, live a solitary life, as if you were already [fully] justified; but coming together in one place, make common inquiry concerning what tends to your general welfare. For the Scripture saith, "Woe to them who are wise to themselves, and prudent in their own sight!" [1479] Let us be spiritually-minded: let us be a perfect temple to God. As much as in us lies, let us meditate upon the fear of God, and let us keep His commandments, that we may rejoice in His ordinances. The Lord will judge the world without respect of persons. Each will receive as he has done: if he is righteous, his righteousness will precede him; if he is wicked, the reward of wickedness is before him. Take heed, lest resting at our ease, as those who are the called [of God], we should fall asleep in our sins, and the wicked prince, acquiring power over us, should thrust us away from the kingdom of the Lord. And all the more attend to this, my brethren, when ye reflect and behold, that after so great signs and wonders were wrought in Israel, they were thus [at length] abandoned. Let us beware lest we be found [fulfilling that saying], as it is written, "Many are called, but few are chosen." [1480]

Chapter V - The new covenant, founded on the sufferings of Christ, tends to our salvation, but to the Jews' destruction

For to this end the Lord endured to deliver up His flesh to corruption, that we might be sanctified through the remission of sins, which is effected by His blood of sprinkling. For it is written concerning Him, partly with reference to Israel, and partly to us; and [the Scripture] saith thus: "He was wounded for our transgressions, and bruised for our iniquities: with His stripes we are healed. He was brought as a sheep to the slaughter, and as a lamb which is dumb before its shearer." [1481] Therefore we ought to be deeply grateful to the Lord, because He has both made known to us things that are past, and hath given us wisdom concerning things present, and hath not left us without understanding in regard to things which are to come. Now, the Scripture saith, "Not unjustly are nets spread out for birds." [1482] This means that the man perishes justly, who, having a knowledge of the way of righteousness, rushes off into the way of darkness. And further, my brethren: if the Lord endured to suffer for our soul, He being Lord of all the world, to whom God said at the foundation of the world, "Let us make man after our image, and after our likeness," [1483] understand how it was that He endured to suffer at the hand of men. The prophets, having obtained grace from Him, prophesied concerning Him. And He (since it behoved Him to appear in flesh), that He might abolish death, and reveal the resurrection from the dead, endured [what and as He did], in order that He might fulfil the promise made unto the fathers, and by preparing a new people for Himself, might show, while He dwelt on earth, that He, when He has raised mankind, will also judge them. Moreover, teaching Israel, and doing so great miracles and signs, He preached [the truth] to him, and greatly loved him. But when He chose His own apostles who were to preach His Gospel, [He did so from among those] who were sinners above all sin, that He might show He came "not to call the righteous, but sinners to repentance." [1484] Then He manifested Himself to be the Son of God. For if He had not come in the flesh, how could men have been saved by beholding Him? [1485] Since looking upon the sun which is to cease to exist, and is the work of His hands, their eyes are not able to bear his rays. The Son of God therefore came in the flesh with this view, that He might bring to a head the sum of their sins who had persecuted His prophets [1486] to the death. For this purpose, then, He endured. For God saith, "The stroke of his flesh is from them;" [1487] and [1488] "when I shall smite the Shepherd, then the sheep of the flock shall be scattered." [1489] He himself willed thus to suffer, for it was necessary that He should suffer on the tree. For says he who prophesies regarding Him, "Spare my soul from the sword, [1490] fasten my flesh with nails; for the assemblies of the wicked have risen up against me." [1491] And again he says, "Behold, I have given my back to scourges, and my cheeks to strokes, and I have set my countenance as a firm rock." [1492]

Chapter VI - The sufferings of Christ, and the new covenant, were announced by the prophets

When, therefore, He has fulfilled the commandment, what saith He? "Who is he that will contend with Me? let him oppose Me: or who is he that will enter into judgment with Me? let him draw near to the servant of the Lord." [1493] "Woe unto you, for ye shall all wax old, like a garment, and the moth shall eat you up." [1494] And again the prophet says, "Since [1495] as a mighty stone He is laid for crushing, behold I cast down for the foundations of Zion a stone, precious, elect, a corner-stone, honourable." Next, what says He? "And he who shall trust [1496] in it shall live for ever." Is our hope, then, upon a stone? Far from it. But [the language is used] inasmuch as He laid his flesh [as a foundation] with power; for He says, "And He placed me as a firm rock." [1497] And the prophet says again, "The stone which the builders rejected, the same has become the head of the corner." [1498] And again he says, "This is the great and wonderful day which the Lord hath made." [1499] I write the more simply unto you, that ye may understand. I am the off-scouring of your love. [1500] What, then, again says the prophet? "The assembly of the wicked surrounded me; they encompassed me as bees do a honeycomb," [1501] and "upon my garment they cast lots." [1502] Since, therefore, He was about to be manifested and to suffer in the flesh, His suffering was foreshown. For the prophet speaks against Israel, "Woe to their soul, because they have counselled an evil counsel against themselves,[1503] saying, Let us bind the just one, because he is displeasing to us." [1504] And Moses also says to them, [1505] "Behold these things, saith the Lord God: Enter into the good land which the Lord swore [to give] to Abraham, and Isaac, and Jacob, and inherit ye it, a land flowing with milk and honey." [1506] What, then, says Knowledge? [1507] Learn: "Trust," she says, "in Him who is to be manifested to you in the flesh--that is, Jesus." For man is earth in a suffering state, for the formation of Adam was from the face of the earth. What, then, meaneth this: "into the good land, a land flowing with milk and honey?" Blessed be our Lord, who has placed in us wisdom and understanding of secret things. For the prophet says, "Who shall understand the parable of the Lord, except him who is wise and prudent, and who loves his Lord?" [1508] Since, therefore, having renewed us by the remission of our sins, He hath made us after another pattern, [it is His purpose] that we should possess the soul of children, inasmuch as He has created us anew by His Spirit. [1509] For the Scripture says concerning us, while He speaks to the Son, "Let Us make man after Our image, and after Our likeness; and let them have dominion over the beasts of the earth, and the fowls of heaven, and the fishes of the sea." [1510] And the Lord said, on beholding the fair creature [1511] man, "Increase, and multiply, and replenish the earth." [1512] These things [were spoken] to the Son. Again, I will show thee how, in respect to us, [1513] He has accomplished a second fashioning in these last days. The Lord says, "Behold, I will make [1514] the last like the first." [1515] In reference to this, then, the prophet proclaimed, "Enter ye into the land flowing with milk and honey, and have dominion over it." [1516] Behold, therefore, we have been refashioned, as again He says in another prophet, "Behold, saith the Lord, I will take away from these, that is, from those whom the Spirit of the Lord foresaw, their stony hearts, and I will put hearts of flesh within them," [1517] because He [1518] was to be manifested in flesh, and to sojourn among us. For, my brethren, the habitation of our heart is a holy temple to the Lord. [1519] For again saith the Lord, "And wherewith shall I appear before the Lord my God, and be glorified?" [1520] He says, [1521] "I will confess to thee in the Church in the midst [1522] of my brethren; and I will praise thee in the midst of the assembly of the saints." [1523] We, then, are they whom He has led into the good land. What, then, mean milk and honey? This, that as the infant is kept alive first by honey, and then by milk, so also we, being quickened and kept alive by the faith of the promise and by the word, shall live ruling over the earth. But He said above, [1524] "Let them increase, and rule over the fishes." [1525] Who then is able to govern the beasts, or the fishes, or the fowls of heaven? For we ought to perceive that to govern implies authority, so that one should command and rule. If, therefore, this does not exist at present, yet still He has promised it to us. When? When we ourselves also have been made perfect [so as] to become heirs of the covenant of the Lord. [1526]

Chapter VII - Fasting, and the goat sent away, were types of Christ

Understand, then, ye children of gladness, that the good Lord has foreshown all things to us, that we might know to whom we ought for everything to render thanksgiving and praise. If therefore the Son of God, who is Lord [of all things], and who will judge the living and the dead, suffered, that His stroke might give us life, let us believe that the Son of God could not have suffered except for our sakes. Moreover, when fixed to the cross, He had given Him to drink vinegar and gall. Hearken how the priests of the people [1527] gave previous indications of this. His commandment having been written, the Lord enjoined, that whosoever did not keep the fast should be put to death, because He also Himself was to offer in sacrifice for our sins the vessel of the Spirit, in order that the type established in Isaac when he was offered upon the altar might be fully accomplished. What, then, says He in the prophet? "And let them eat of the goat which is offered, with fasting, for all their sins." [1528] Attend carefully: "And let all the priests alone eat the inwards, unwashed with vinegar." Wherefore? Because to me, who am to offer my flesh for the sins of my new people, ye are to give gall with vinegar to drink: eat ye alone, while the people fast and mourn in sackcloth and ashes. [These things were done] that He might show that it was necessary for Him to suffer for them. [1529] How, [1530] then, ran the commandment? Give your attention. Take two goats of goodly aspect, and similar to each other, and offer them. And let the priest take one as a burnt-offering for sins. [1531] And what should they do with the other? "Accursed," says He, "is the one." Mark how the type of Jesus [1532] now comes out. "And all of you spit upon it, and pierce it, and encircle its head with scarlet wool, and thus let it be driven into the wilderness." And when all this has been done, he who bears the goat brings it into the desert, and takes the wool off from it, and places that upon a shrub which is called Rachia, [1533] of which also we are accustomed to eat the fruits [1534] when we find them in the field. Of this [1535] kind of shrub alone the fruits are sweet. Why then, again, is this? Give good heed. [You see] "one upon the altar, and the other accursed;" and why [do you behold] the one that is accursed crowned? Because they shall see Him then in that day having a scarlet robe about his body down to his feet; and they shall say, Is not this He whom we once despised, and pierced, and mocked, and crucified? Truly this is [1536] He who then declared Himself to be the Son of God. For how like is He to Him! [1537] With a view to this, [He required] the goats to be of goodly aspect, and similar, that, when they see Him then coming, they may be amazed by the likeness of the goat. Behold, then, [1538] the type of Jesus who was to suffer. But why is it that they place the wool in the midst of thorns? It is a type of Jesus set before the view of the Church. [They [1539] place the wool among thorns], that any one who wishes to bear it away may find it necessary to suffer much, because the thorn is formidable, and thus obtain it only as the result of suffering. Thus also, says He, "Those who wish to behold Me, and lay hold of My kingdom, must through tribulation and suffering obtain Me." [1540]

Chapter VIII - The red heifer a type of Christ

Now what do you suppose this to be a type of, that a command was given to Israel, that men of the greatest wickedness [1541] should offer a heifer, and slay and burn it, and, that then boys should take the ashes, and put these into vessels, and bind round a stick [1542] purple wool along with hyssop, and that thus the boys should sprinkle the people, one by one, in order that they might be purified from their sins? Consider how He speaks to you with simplicity. The calf [1543] is Jesus: the sinful men offering it are those who led Him to the slaughter. But now the men are no longer guilty, are no longer regarded as sinners. [1544] And the boys that sprinkle are those that have proclaimed to us the remission of sins and purification of heart. To these He gave authority to preach the Gospel, being twelve in number, corresponding to the twelve tribes [1545] of Israel. But why are there three boys that sprinkle? To correspond [1546] to Abraham, and Isaac, and Jacob, because these were great with God. And why was the wool [placed] upon the wood? Because by wood Jesus holds His kingdom, so that [through the cross] those believing on Him shall live for ever. But why was hyssop joined with the wool? Because in His kingdom the days will be evil and polluted in which we shall be saved, [and] because he who suffers in body is cured through the cleansing [1547] efficacy of hyssop. And on this account the things which stand thus are clear to us, but obscure to them because they did not hear the voice of the Lord.

Chapter IX - The spiritual meaning of circumcision

He speaks moreover concerning our ears, how He hath circumcised both them and our heart. The Lord saith in the prophet, "In the hearing of the ear they obeyed me." [1548] And again He saith, "By hearing, those shall hear who are afar off; they shall know what I have done." [1549] And, "Be ye circumcised in your hearts, saith the Lord." [1550] And again He says, "Hear, O Israel, for these things saith the Lord thy God." [1551] And once more the Spirit of the Lord proclaims, "Who is he that wishes to live for ever? By hearing let him hear the voice of my servant." [1552] And again He saith, "Hear, O heaven, and give ear, O earth, for God [1553] hath spoken." [1554] These are in proof. [1555] And again He saith, "Hear the word of the Lord, ye rulers of this people." [1556] And again He saith, "Hear, ye children, the voice of one crying in the wilderness." [1557] Therefore He hath circumcised our ears, that we might hear His word and believe, for the circumcision in which they trusted is abolished. [1558] For He declared that circumcision was not of the flesh, but they transgressed because an evil angel deluded them. [1559] He saith to them, "These things saith the Lord your God"--(here [1560] I find a new[1561] commandment)--"Sow not among thorns, but circumcise yourselves to the Lord." [1562] And why speaks He thus: "Circumcise the stubbornness of your heart, and harden not your neck?" [1563] And again: "Behold, saith the Lord, all the nations are uncircumcised [1564] in the flesh, but this people are uncircumcised in heart." [1565] But thou wilt say, "Yea, verily the people are circumcised for a seal." But so also is every Syrian and Arab, and all the priests of idols: are these then also within the bond of His covenant? [1566] Yea, the Egyptians also practise circumcision. Learn then, my children, concerning all things richly, [1567] that Abraham, the first who enjoined circumcision, looking forward in spirit to Jesus, practised that rite, having received the mysteries [1568] of the three letters. For [the Scripture] saith, "And Abraham circumcised ten, and eight, and three hundred men of his household." [1569] What, then, was the knowledge given to him in this? Learn the eighteen first, and then the three hundred. [1570] The ten and the eight are thus denoted--Ten by I, and Eight by E. [1571] You have [the initials of the, name of] Jesus. And because [1572] the cross was to express the grace [of our redemption] by the letter T, he says also, "Three Hundred." He signifies, therefore, Jesus by two letters, and the cross by one. He knows this, who has put within us the engrafted [1573] gift of His doctrine. No one has been admitted by me to a more excellent piece of knowledge [1574] than this, but I know that ye are worthy.

Chapter X - Spiritual significance of the precepts of Moses respecting different kinds of food

Now, wherefore did Moses say, "Thou shalt not eat the swine, nor the eagle, nor the hawk, nor the raven, nor any fish which is not possessed of scales?" [1575] He embraced three doctrines in his mind [in doing so]. Moreover, the Lord saith to them in Deuteronomy, "And I will establish my ordinances among this people." [1576] Is there then not a command of God [that] they should not eat [these things]? There is, but Moses spoke with a spiritual reference. [1577] For this reason he named the swine, as much as to say, "Thou shalt not join thyself to men who resemble swine." For when they live in pleasure, they forget their Lord; but when they come to want, they acknowledge the Lord. And [in like manner] the swine, when it has eaten, does not recognize its master; but when hungry it cries out, and on receiving food is quiet again. "Neither shalt thou eat," says he "the eagle, nor the hawk, nor the kite, nor the raven." "Thou shalt not join thyself," he means, "to such men as know not how to procure food for themselves by labour and sweat, but seize on that of others in their iniquity, and although wearing an aspect of simplicity, are on the watch to plunder others." [1578] So these birds, while they sit idle, inquire how they may devour the flesh of others, proving themselves pests [to all] by their wickedness. "And thou shalt not eat," he says, "the lamprey, or the polypus, or the cuttlefish." He means, "Thou shalt not join thyself or be like to such men as are ungodly to the end, and are condemned [1579] to death." In like manner as those fishes, above accursed, float in the deep, not swimming [on the surface] like the rest, but make their abode in the mud which lies at the bottom. Moreover, "Thou shall not," he says, "eat the hare." Wherefore? "Thou shall not be a corrupter of boys, nor like unto such." [1580] Because the hare multiplies, year by year, the places of its conception; for as many years as it lives so many [1581] it has. Moreover, "Thou shall not eat the hyena." He means, "Thou shall not be an adulterer, nor a corrupter, nor be like to them that are such." Wherefore? Because that animal annually changes its sex, and is at one time male, and at another female. Moreover, he has rightly detested the weasel. For he means, "Thou shalt not be like to those whom we hear of as committing wickedness with the mouth, [1582] on account of their uncleanness; nor shall thou be joined to those impure women who commit iniquity with the mouth. For this animal conceives by the mouth." Moses then issued [1583] three doctrines concerning meats with a spiritual significance; but they received them according to fleshly desire, as if he had merely spoken of [literal] meats. David, however, comprehends the knowledge of the three doctrines, and speaks in like manner: "Blessed is the man who hath not walked in the counsel of the ungodly," [1584] even as the fishes [referred to] go in darkness to the depths [of the sea]; "and hath not stood in the way of sinners," even as those who profess to fear the Lord, but go astray like swine; "and hath not sat in the seat of scorners," [1585] even as those birds that lie in wait for prey. Take a full and firm grasp of this spiritual [1586] knowledge. But Moses says still further, "Ye shall eat every animal that is cloven-footed and ruminant." What does he mean? [The ruminant animal denotes him] who, on receiving food, recognizes Him that nourishes him, and being satisfied by Him, [1587] is visibly made glad. Well spake [Moses], having respect to the commandment. What, then, does he mean? That we ought to join ourselves to those that fear the Lord, those who meditate in their heart on the commandment which they have received, those who both utter the judgments of the Lord and observe them, those who know that meditation is a work of gladness, and who ruminate [1588] upon the word of the Lord. But what means the cloven-footed? That the righteous man also walks in this world, yet looks forward to the holy state [1589] [to come]. Behold how well Moses legislated. But how was it possible for them to understand or comprehend these things? We then, rightly understanding his commandments, [1590] explain them as the Lord intended. For this purpose He circumcised our ears and our hearts, that we might understand these things.

Chapter XI - Baptism and the cross prefigured in the Old Testament

Let us further inquire whether the Lord took any care to foreshadow the water [of baptism] and the cross. Concerning the water, indeed, it is written, in reference to the Israelites, that they should not receive that baptism which leads to the remission of sins, but should procure [1591] another for themselves. The prophet therefore declares, "Be astonished, O heaven, and let the earth tremble[1592] at this, because this people hath committed two great evils: they have forsaken Me, a living fountain, and have hewn out for themselves broken cisterns. [1593] Is my holy hill Zion a desolate rock? For ye shall be as the fledglings of a bird, which fly away when the nest is removed." [1594] And again saith the prophet, "I will go before thee and make level the mountains, and will break the brazen gates, and bruise in pieces the iron bars; and I will give thee the secret,[1595] hidden, invisible treasures, that they may know that I am the Lord God." [1596] And "He shall dwell in a lofty cave of the strong rock." [1597] Furthermore, what saith He in reference to the Son? "His water is sure; [1598] ye shall see the King in His glory, and your soul shall meditate on the fear of the Lord."[1599] And again He saith in another prophet, "The man who doeth these things shall be like a tree planted by the courses of waters, which shall yield its fruit in due season; and his leaf shall not fade, and all that he doeth shall prosper. Not so are the ungodly, not so, but even as chaff, which the wind sweeps away from the face of the earth. Therefore the ungodly shall not stand in judgment, nor sinners in the counsel of the just; for the Lord knoweth the way of the righteous, but the way of the ungodly shall perish." [1600] Mark how He has described at once both the water and the cross. For these words imply, Blessed are they who, placing their trust in the cross, have gone down into the water; for, says He, they shall receive their reward in due time: then He declares, I will recompense them. But now He saith, [1601] "Their leaves shall not fade." This meaneth, that every word which proceedeth out of your mouth in faith and love shall tend to bring conversion and hope to many. Again, another prophet saith, "And the land of Jacob shall be extolled above every land." [1602] This meaneth the vessel of His Spirit, which He shall glorify. Further, what says He? "And there was a river flowing on the right, and from it arose beautiful trees; and whosoever shall eat of them shall live for ever." [1603] This meaneth, [1604] that we indeed descend into the water full of sins and defilement, but come up, bearing fruit in our heart, having the fear [of God] and trust in Jesus in our spirit. "And whosoever shall eat of these shall live for ever," This meaneth: Whosoever, He declares, shall hear thee speaking, and believe, shall live for ever.

Chapter XII - The cross of Christ frequently announced in the Old Testament

In like manner He points to the cross of Christ in another prophet, who saith, [1605] "And when shall these things be accomplished? And the Lord saith, When a tree shall be bent down, and again arise, and when blood shall flow out of wood." [1606] Here again you have an intimation concerning the cross, and Him who should be crucified. Yet again He speaks of this [1607] in Moses, when Israel was attacked by strangers. And that He might remind them, when assailed, that it was on account of their sins they were delivered to death, the Spirit speaks to the heart of Moses, that he should make a figure of the cross, [1608] and of Him about to suffer thereon; for unless they put their trust in Him, they shall be overcome for ever. Moses therefore placed one weapon above another in the midst of the hill, [1609] and standing upon it, so as to be higher than all the people, he stretched forth his hands,[1610] and thus again Israel acquired the mastery. But when again he let down his hands, they were again destroyed. For what reason? That they might know that they could not be saved unless they put their trust in Him. [1611] And in another prophet He declares, "All day long I have stretched forth My hands to an unbelieving people, and one that gainsays My righteous way." [1612] And again Moses makes a type of Jesus, [signifying] that it was necessary for Him to suffer, [and also] that He would be the author of life [1613] [to others], whom they believed to have destroyed on the cross [1614] when Israel was falling. For since transgression was committed by Eve through means of the serpent, [the Lord] brought it to pass that every [kind of] serpents bit them, and they died, [1615] that He might convince them, that on account of their transgression they were given over to the straits of death. Moreover Moses, when he commanded, "Ye shall not have any graven or molten [image] for your God," [1616] did so that he might reveal a type of Jesus. Moses then makes a brazen serpent, and places it upon a beam, [1617] and by proclamation assembles the people. When, therefore, they were come together, they besought Moses that he would offer sacrifice [1618] in their behalf, and pray for their recovery. And Moses spake unto them, saying, "When any one of you is bitten, let him come to the serpent placed on the pole; and let him hope and believe, that even though dead, it is able to give him life, and immediately he shall be restored." [1619] And they did so. Thou hast in this also [an indication of] the glory of Jesus; for in Him and to Him are all things. [1620] What, again, says Moses to Jesus (Joshua) the son of Nave, when he gave him [1621] this name, as being a prophet, with this view only, that all the people might hear that the Father would reveal all things concerning His Son Jesus to the son [1622] of Nave? This name then being given him when he sent him to spy out the land, he said, "Take a book into thy hands, and write what the Lord declares, that the Son of God will in the last days cut off from the roots all the house of Amalek." [1623] Behold again: Jesus who was manifested, both by type and in the flesh, [1624] is not the Son of man, but the Son of God. Since, therefore, they were to say that Christ was the son [1625] of David, fearing and understanding the error of the wicked, he saith, "The Lord said unto my Lord, Sit at My right hand, until I make Thine enemies Thy footstool." [1626] And again, thus saith Isaiah, "The Lord said to Christ, [1627] my Lord, whose right hand I have holden, [1628] that the nations should yield obedience before Him; and I will break in pieces the strength of kings." [1629] Behold how David calleth Him Lord and the Son of God.

Chapter XIII - Christians, and not Jews, the heirs of the covenant

But let us see if this people [1630] is the heir, or the former, and if the covenant belongs to us or to them. Hear ye now what the Scripture saith concerning the people. Isaac prayed for Rebecca his wife, because she was barren; and she conceived. [1631] Furthermore also, Rebecca went forth to inquire of the Lord; and the Lord said to her, "Two nations are in thy womb, and two peoples in thy belly; and the one people shall surpass the other, and the elder shall serve the younger." [1632] You ought to understand who was Isaac, who Rebecca, and concerning what persons He declared that this people should be greater than that. And in another prophecy Jacob speaks more clearly to his son Joseph, saying, "Behold, the Lord hath not deprived me of thy presence; bring thy sons to me, that I may bless them." [1633] And he brought Manasseh and Ephraim, desiring that Manasseh [1634] should be blessed, because he was the elder. With this view Joseph led him to the right hand of his father Jacob. But Jacob saw in spirit the type of the people to arise afterwards. And what says [the Scripture]? And Jacob changed the direction of his hands, and laid his right hand upon the head of Ephraim, the second and younger, and blessed him. And Joseph said to Jacob, "Transfer thy right hand to the head of Manasseh, [1635] for he is my first-born son." [1636] And Jacob said, "I know it, my son, I know it; but the elder shall serve the younger: yet he also shall be blessed." [1637] Ye see on whom he laid [1638] [his hands], that this people should be first, and heir of the covenant. If then, still further, the same thing was intimated through Abraham, we reach the perfection of our knowledge. What, then, says He to Abraham? "Because thou hast believed, [1639] it is imputed to thee for righteousness: behold, I have made thee the father of those nations who believe in the Lord while in [a state of] uncircumcision." [1640]

Chapter XIV - The Lord hath given us the testament which Moses received and broke

Yes [it is even so]; but let us inquire if the Lord has really given that testament which He swore to the fathers that He would give [1641] to the people. He did give it; but they were not worthy to receive it, on account of their sins. For the prophet declares, "And Moses was fasting forty days and forty nights on Mount Sinai, that he might receive the testament of the Lord for the people." [1642] And he received from the Lord [1643] two tables, written in the spirit by the finger of the hand of the Lord. And Moses having received them, carried them down to give to the people. And the Lord said to Moses, "Moses, Moses, go down quickly; for thy people hath sinned, whom thou didst bring out of the land of Egypt." [1644] And Moses understood that they had again [1645] made molten images; and he threw the tables out of his hands, and the tables of the testament of the Lord were broken. Moses then received it, but they proved themselves unworthy. Learn now how we have received it. Moses, as a servant, [1646] received it; but the Lord himself, having suffered in our behalf, hath given it to us, that we should be the people of inheritance. But He was manifested, in order that they might be perfected in their iniquities, and that we, being constituted heirs through Him, [1647] might receive the testament of the Lord Jesus, who was prepared for this end, that by His personal manifestation, redeeming our hearts (which were already wasted by death, and given over to the iniquity of error) from darkness, He might by His word enter into a covenant with us. For it is written how the Father, about to redeem [1648] us from darkness, commanded Him to prepare [1649] a holy people for Himself. The prophet therefore declares, "I, the Lord Thy God, have called Thee in righteousness, and will hold Thy hand, and will strengthen Thee; and I have given Thee for a covenant to the people, for a light to the nations, to open the eyes of the blind, and to bring forth from fetters them that are bound, and those that sit in darkness out of the prison-house." [1650] Ye perceive, [1651] then, whence we have been redeemed. And again, the prophet says, "Behold, I have appointed Thee as a light to the nations, that Thou mightest be for salvation even to the ends of the earth, saith the Lord God that redeemeth thee." [1652] And again, the prophet saith, "The Spirit of the Lord is upon me; because He hath anointed me to preach the Gospel to the humble: He hath sent me to heal the broken-hearted, to proclaim deliverance to the captives, and recovery of sight to the blind; to announce the acceptable year of the Lord, and the day of recompense; to comfort all that mourn."[1653]

Chapter XV - The false and the true Sabbath

Further, [1654] also, it is written concerning the Sabbath in the Decalogue which [the Lord] spoke, face to face, to Moses on Mount Sinai, "And sanctify ye the Sabbath of the Lord with clean hands and a pure heart." [1655] And He says in another place, "If my sons keep the Sabbath, then will I cause my mercy to rest upon them." [1656] The Sabbath is mentioned at the beginning of the creation [thus]: "And God made in six days the works of His hands, and made an end on the seventh day, and rested on it, and sanctified it." [1657] Attend, my children, to the meaning of this expression, "He finished in six days." This implieth that the Lord will finish all things in six thousand years, for a day is [1658] with Him a thousand years. And He Himself testifieth, [1659] saying, "Behold, to-day [1660] will be as a thousand years." [1661] Therefore, my children, in six days, that is, in six thousand years, all things will be finished. "And He rested on the seventh day." This meaneth: when His Son, coming [again], shall destroy the time of the wicked man, [1662] and judge the ungodly, and change the sun, and the moon, [1663] and the stars, then shall He truly rest on the seventh day. Moreover, He says, "Thou shalt sanctify it with pure hands and a pure heart." If, therefore, any one can now sanctify the day which God hath sanctified, except he is pure in heart in all things, [1664] we are deceived. [1665] Behold, therefore: [1666] certainly then one properly resting sanctifies it, when we ourselves, having received the promise, wickedness no longer existing, and all things having been made new by the Lord, shall be able to work righteousness. [1667] Then we shall be able to sanctify it, having been first sanctified ourselves. [1668] Further, He says to them, "Your new moons and your Sabbaths I cannot endure." [1669] Ye perceive how He speaks: Your present Sabbaths are not acceptable to Me, but that is which I have made, [namely this,] when, giving rest to all things, I shall make a beginning of the eighth day, that is, a beginning of another world. Wherefore, also, we keep the eighth day with joyfulness, the day also on which Jesus rose again from the dead. [1670] And [1671] when He had manifested Himself, He ascended into the heavens.

Chapter XVI - The spiritual temple of God

Moreover, I will also tell you concerning the temple, how the wretched [Jews], wandering in error, trusted not in God Himself, but in the temple, as being the house of God. For almost after the manner of the Gentiles they worshipped Him in the temple. [1672] But learn how the Lord speaks, when abolishing it: "Who hath meted out heaven with a span, and the earth with his palm? Have not I?" [1673] "Thus saith the Lord, Heaven is My throne, and the earth My footstool: what kind of house will ye build to Me, or what is the place of My rest?" [1674] Ye perceive that their hope is vain. Moreover, He again says, "Behold, they who have cast down this temple, even they shall build it up again." [1675] It has so happened. [1676] For through their going to war, it was destroyed by their enemies; and now they, as the servants of their enemies, shall rebuild it. Again, it was revealed that the city and the temple and the people of Israel were to be given up. For the Scripture saith, "And it shall come to pass in the last days, that the Lord will deliver up the sheep of His pasture, and their sheep-fold and tower, to destruction." [1677] And it so happened as the Lord had spoken. Let us inquire, then, if there still is a temple of God. There is--where He himself declared He would make and finish it. For it is written, "And it shall come to pass, when the week is completed, the temple of God shall be built in glory in the name of the Lord." [1678] I find, therefore, that a temple does exist. Learn, then, how it shall be built in the name of the Lord. Before we believed in God, the habitation of our heart was corrupt and weak, as being indeed like a temple made with hands. For it was full of idolatry, and was a habitation of demons, through our doing such things as were opposed to [the will of] God. But it shall be built, observe ye, in the name of the Lord, in order that the temple of the Lord may be built in glory. How? Learn [as follows]. Having received the forgiveness of sins, and placed our trust in the name of the Lord, we have become new creatures, formed again from the beginning. Wherefore in our habitation God truly dwells in us. How? His word of faith; His calling [1679] of promise; the wisdom of the statutes; the commands of the doctrine; He himself prophesying in us; He himself dwelling in us; opening to us who were enslaved by death the doors of the temple, that is, the mouth; and by giving us repentance introduced us into the incorruptible temple. [1680] He then, who wishes to be saved, looks not to man, [1681] but to Him who dwelleth in him, and speaketh in him, amazed at never having either heard him utter such words with his mouth, nor himself having ever desired to hear them. [1682] This is the spiritual temple built for the Lord.

Chapter XVII - Conclusion of the first part of the epistle

As far as was possible, and could be done with perspicuity, I cherish the hope that, according to my desire, I have omitted none [1683] of those things at present [demanding consideration], which bear upon your salvation. For if I should write to you about things future, [1684] ye would not understand, because such knowledge is hid in parables. These things then are so.

Chapter XVIII - Second part of the epistle. The two ways

But let us now pass to another sort of knowledge and doctrine. There are two ways of doctrine and authority, the one of light, and the other of darkness. But there is a great difference between these two ways. For over one are stationed the light-bringing angels of God, but over the other the angels [1685] of Satan. And He indeed (i.e., God) is Lord for ever and ever, but he (i.e., Satan) is prince of the time [1686] of iniquity.

Chapter XIX - The way of light

The way of light, then, is as follows. If any one desires to travel to the appointed place, he must be zealous in his works. The knowledge, therefore, which is given to us for the purpose of walking in this way, is the following. Thou shalt love Him that created thee: [1687] thou shalt glorify Him that redeemed thee from death. Thou shalt be simple in heart, and rich in spirit. Thou shalt not join thyself to those who walk in the way of death. Thou shalt hate doing what is unpleasing to God: thou shalt hate all hypocrisy. Thou shalt not forsake the commandments of the Lord. Thou shalt not exalt thyself, but shalt be of a lowly mind. [1688] Thou shalt not take glory to thyself. Thou shalt not take evil counsel against thy neighbour. Thou shalt not allow over-boldness to enter into thy soul. [1689] Thou shalt not commit fornication: thou shalt not commit adultery: thou shalt not be a corrupter of youth. Thou shalt not let the word of God issue from thy lips with any kind of impurity. [1690] Thou shalt not accept persons when thou reprovest any one for transgression. Thou shalt be meek: thou shalt be peaceable. Thou shalt tremble at the words which thou hearest. [1691] Thou shalt not be mindful of evil against thy brother. Thou shalt not be of doubtful mind [1692] as to whether a thing shall be or not. Thou shalt not take the name [1693] of the Lord in vain. Thou shalt love thy neighbour more than thine own soul. [1694] Thou shalt not slay the child by procuring abortion; nor, again, shalt thou destroy it after it is born. Thou shalt not withdraw thy hand from thy son, or from thy daughter, but from their infancy thou shalt teach them the fear of the Lord. [1695] Thou shalt not covet what is thy neighbour's, nor shalt thou be avaricious. Thou shalt not be joined in soul with the haughty, but thou shalt be reckoned with the righteous and lowly. Receive thou as good things the trials [1696] which come upon thee. [1697] Thou shalt not be of double mind or of double tongue, [1698] for a double tongue is a snare of death. Thou shalt be subject [1699] to the Lord, and to [other] masters as the image of God, with modesty and fear. Thou shalt not issue orders with bitterness to thy maidservant or thy man-servant, who trust in the same [God [1700]], lest thou shouldst not [1701] reverence that God who is above both; for He came to call men not according to their outward appearance, [1702] but according as the Spirit had prepared them. [1703] Thou shalt communicate in all things with thy neighbour; thou shalt not call [1704] things thine own; for if ye are partakers in common of things which are incorruptible, [1705] how much more [should you be] of those things which are corruptible! [1706] Thou shalt not be hasty with thy tongue, for the mouth is a snare of death. As far as possible, thou shalt be pure in thy soul. Do not be ready to stretch forth thy hands to take, whilst thou contractest them to give. Thou shalt love, as the apple of thine eye, every one that speaketh to thee the word of the Lord. Thou shalt remember the day of judgment, night and day. Thou shalt seek out every day the faces of the saints, [1707] either by word examining them, and going to exhort them, and meditating how to save a soul by the word, [1708] or by thy hands thou shalt labour for the redemption of thy sins. Thou shalt not hesitate to give, nor murmur when thou givest. "Give to every one that asketh thee," [1709] and thou shalt know who is the good Recompenser of the reward. Thou shalt preserve what thou hast received [in charge], neither adding to it nor taking from it. To the last thou shalt hate the wicked [1710] [one]. [1711] Thou shalt judge righteously. Thou shalt not make a schism, but thou shalt pacify those that contend by bringing them together. Thou shalt confess thy sins. Thou shalt not go to prayer with an evil conscience. This is the way of light. [1712]

Chapter XX - The way of darkness

But the way of darkness [1713] is crooked, and full of cursing; for it is the way of eternal [1714] death with punishment, in which way are the things that destroy the soul, viz., idolatry, over-confidence, the arrogance of power, hypocrisy, double-heartedness, adultery, murder, rapine, haughtiness, transgression, [1715] deceit, malice, self-sufficiency, poisoning, magic, avarice, [1716] want of the fear of God. [In this way, too,] are those who persecute the good, those who hate truth, those who love falsehood, those who know not the reward of righteousness, those who cleave not to that which is good, those who attend not with just judgment to the widow and orphan, those who watch not to the fear of God, [but incline] to wickedness, from whom meekness and patience are far off; persons who love vanity, follow after a reward, pity not the needy, labour not in aid of him who is overcome with toil; who are prone to evil-speaking, who know not Him that made them, who are murderers of children, destroyers of the workmanship of God; who turn away him that is in want, who oppress the afflicted, who are advocates of the rich, who are unjust judges of the poor, and who are in every respect transgressors.

Chapter XXI - Conclusion

It is well, therefore, [1717] that he who has learned the judgments of the Lord, as many as have been written, should walk in them. For he who keepeth these shall be glorified in the kingdom of God; but he who chooseth other things [1718] shall be destroyed with his works. On this account there will be a resurrection, [1719] on this account a retribution. I beseech you who are superiors, if you will receive any counsel of my good-will, have among yourselves those to whom you may show kindness: do not forsake them. For the day is at hand on which all things shall perish with the evil [one]. The Lord is near, and His reward. Again, and yet again, I beseech you: be good lawgivers [1720] to one another; continue faithful counsellors of one another; take away from among you all hypocrisy. And may God, who ruleth over all the world, give to you wisdom, intelligence, understanding, knowledge of His judgments, [1721] with patience. And be ye [1722] taught of God, inquiring diligently what the Lord asks from you; and do it that ye maybe safe in the day of judgment. [1723] And if you have any remembrance of what is good, be mindful of me, meditating on these things, in order that both my desire and watchfulness may result in some good. I beseech you, entreating this as a favour. While yet you are in this fair vessel, [1724] do not fail in any one of those things, [1725] but unceasingly seek after them, and fulfil every commandment; for these things are worthy. [1726] Wherefore I have been the more earnest to write to you, as my ability served, [1727] that I might cheer you. Farewell, ye children of love and peace. The Lord of glory and of all grace be with your spirit. Amen. [1728]

Footnotes:

1438. Discourse (p. 148) to his Genuine Epistles of the Apostolical Fathers. Philadelphia, 1846.

1439. Works, ii. 250, note; and iv. 128.

1440. On the Canon, vol. ii. p. 431.

1441. To those who may adhere to the older opinion, let me commend the eloquent and instructive chapter (xxiii.) in Farrar's Life of St. Paul.

1442. Hadrian's purpose to rebuild their city seems to be pointed out in chap. xvi.

1443. M. Renan may be read with pain, and yet with profit, in much that his Gallio-spirit suggests on this subject. Chap. v., St. Paul, Paris, 1884.

1444. The Codex Sinaiticus has simply "Epistle of Barnabas" for title; Dressel gives, "Epistle of Barnabas the Apostle," from the Vatican ms. of the Latin text.

1445. The Cod. Sin. has simply, "the Lord."

1446. Literally, "the judgments of God being great and rich towards you;" but, as Hefele remarks, δικαίωμα seems here to have the meaning of righteousness, as in Rom. v. 18.

1447. This appears to be the meaning of the Greek, and is confirmed by the ancient Latin version. Hilgenfeld, however, following Cod. Sin., reads "thus," instead of "because," and separates the clauses.

1448. The Latin reads, "spirit infused into you from the honourable fountain of God."

1449. This sentence is entirely omitted in the Latin.

1450. The Latin text is here quite different, and seems evidently corrupt. We have followed the Cod. Sin., as does Hilgenfeld.

1451. Literally, "in the hope of His life."

1452. The Greek is here totally unintelligible: it seems impossible either to punctuate or construe it. We may attempt to represent it as follows: "The doctrines of the Lord, then, are three: Life, Faith, and Hope, our beginning and end; and Righteousness, the beginning and the end of judgment; Love and Joy and the Testimony of gladness for works of righteousness." We have followed the ancient Latin text, which Hilgenfeld also adopts, though Weitzäcker and others prefer the Greek.

1453. Instead of "knowledge" (γνώσεως), Cod. Sin. has "taste" (γεύσεως).

1454. Literally, "we ought more richly and loftily to approach His fear."

1455. Instead of, "to Him with fear," the reading of Cod. Sin., the Latin has, "to His altar," which Hilgenfeld adopts.

1456. The Latin text is literally, "the adversary;" the Greek has, "and he that worketh possesseth power;" Hilgenfeld reads, "he that worketh against," the idea expressed above being intended.

1457. Or, "while these things continue, those which respect the Lord rejoice in purity along with them-- Wisdom," etc.

1458. Isa. i. 11-14, from the Sept., as is the case throughout. We have given the quotation as it stands in Cod. Sin.

1459. Thus in the Latin. The Greek reads, "might not have a man-made oblation." The Latin text seems preferable, implying that, instead of the outward sacrifices of the law, there is now required a dedication of man himself. Hilgenfeld follows the Greek.

1460. Jer. vii. 22; Zech. viii. 17.

1461. So the Greek. Hilgenfeld, with the Latin, omits "not."

1462. Ψ. li. 19. There is nothing in Scripture corresponding to the last clause.

1463. Literally, "sling us out."

1464. Isa. lviii. 4, 5.

1465. The original here is χειροτονίαν, from the LXX. Hefele remarks, that it may refer to the stretching forth of the hands, either to swear falsely, or to mock and insult one's neighbour.

1466. Isa. lviii. 6-10.

1467. The Greek is here unintelligible: the Latin has, "that we should not rush on, as if proselytes to their law."

1468. Or it might be rendered, "things present." Cotelerius reads, "de his instantibus."

1469. The Latin reads, "Daniel" instead of "Enoch;" comp. Dan. ix. 24-27.

1470. Dan. vii. 24, very loosely quoted.

1471. Dan. vii. 7, 8, also very inaccurately cited.

1472. We here follow the Latin text in preference to the Greek, which reads merely, "the covenant is ours." What follows seems to show the correctness of the Latin, as the author proceeds to deny that the Jews had any further interest in the promises.

1473. Ex. xxxi. 18, Ex. xxxiv. 28.

1474. Ex. xxxii. 7; Deut. ix. 12.

1475. Literally, "in hope of His faith."

1476. The Greek is here incorrect and unintelligible; and as the Latin omits the clause, our translation is merely conjectural. Hilgenfeld's text, if we give a somewhat peculiar meaning to ἐλλιπεῖν, may be translated: "but as it is becoming in one who loves you not to fail in giving you what we have, I, though the very offscouring of you, have been eager to write to you."

1477. So the Cod. Sin. Hilgenfeld reads, with the Latin, "let us take."

1478. The Latin here departs entirely from the Greek text, and quotes as a saying of "the Son of God" the following precept, nowhere to be found in the New Testament: "Let us resist all iniquity, and hold it in hatred." Hilgenfeld joins this clause to the former sentence.

1479. Isa. v. 21.

1480. An exact quotation from Matt. xx. 16 or Matt. xxii. 14. It is worthy of notice that this is the first example in the writings of the Fathers of a citation from any book of the New Testament, preceded by the authoritative formula, "it is written."

1481. Isa. liii. 5, 7.

1482. Prov. i. 17, from the LXX, which has mistaken the meaning.

1483. Gen. i. 26.

1484. Matt. ix. 13; Mark ii. 17; Luke v. 32.

1485. The Cod. Sin. reads, "neither would men have been saved by seeing Him."

1486. Cod. Sin. has, "their prophets," but the corrector has changed it as above.

1487. A very loose reference to Isa. liii. 8.

1488. Cod. Sin. omits "and," and reads, "when they smite their own shepherd, then the sheep of the pasture shall be scattered and fail."

1489. Zech. xiii. 7.

1490. Cod. Sin. inserts "and."

1491. These are inaccurate and confused quotations from Ψ. xxii. 16, 20, and Ψ. cxix. 120.

1492. Isa. l. 6, 7.

1493. Isa. l. 8.

1494. Isa. l. 9.

1495. The Latin omits "since," but it is found in all the Greek mss.

1496. Cod. Sin. has "believe." Isa. viii. 14, Isa. xxviii. 16.

1497. Isa. l. 7.

1498. Ps. cxviii. 22.

1499. Ps. cxviii. 24.

1500. Comp. 1 Cor. iv. 13. The meaning is, "My love to you is so great, that I am ready to be or to do all things for you."

1501. Ps. xxii. 17, Ψ. cxviii. 12.

1502. Ps. xxii. 19.

1503. Isa. iii. 9.

1504. Wisdom ii. 12. This apocryphal book is thus quoted as Scripture, and intertwined with it.

1505. Cod. Sin. reads, "What says the other prophet Moses unto them?"

1506. Ex. xxxiii. 1; Lev. xx. 24.

1507. The original word is "Gnosis," the knowledge peculiar to advanced Christians, by which they understand the mysteries of Scripture.

1508. Not found in Scripture. Comp. Isa. xl. 13; Prov. i. 6. Hilgenfeld, however, changes the usual punctuation, which places a colon after prophet, and reads, "For the prophet speaketh the parable of the Lord. Who shall understand," etc.

1509. The Greek is here very elliptical and obscure: "His Spirit" is inserted above, from the Latin.

1510. Gen. i. 26.

1511. Cod. Sin. has "our fair

formation."

1512. Gen. i. 28.
1513. Cod. Sin. inserts, "the Lord says."
1514. Cod. Sin. has "I make."
1515. Not in Scripture, but comp. Matt. xx. 16, and 2 Cor. v. 17.
1516. Ex. xxxiii. 3.
1517. Ezek. xi. 19, Ezek. xxxvi. 26.
1518. Cod. Sin. inserts "Himself;" comp. John i. 14.
1519. Comp. Eph. ii. 21.
1520. Comp. Ψ. xlii. 2.
1521. Cod. Sin. omits "He says."
1522. Cod. Sin. omits "in the midst."
1523. Ps. xxii. 23; Heb. ii. 12.
1524. Cod. Sin. has "But we said above."
1525. Gen. i. 28.
1526. These are specimens of the "Gnosis," or faculty of bringing out the hidden spiritual meaning of Scripture referred to before. Many more such interpretations follow.
1527. Cod. Sin. reads "temple," which is adopted by Hilgenfeld.
1528. Not to be found in Scripture, as is the case also with what follows. Hefele remarks, that "certain false traditions respecting the Jewish rites seem to have prevailed among the Christians of the second century, of which Barnabas here adopts some, as do Justin (Dial. c. Try. 40) and Tertullian (adv. Jud. 14; adv. Marc. iii. 7)."
1529. Cod. Sin. has "by them."
1530. Cod. Sin. reads, "what commanded He?"
1531. Cod. Sin. reads, "one as a burnt-offering, and one for sins."
1532. Cod. Sin. reads, "type of God," but it has been corrected to "Jesus."
1533. In Cod. Sin. we find "Rachel." The orthography is doubtful, but there is little question that a kind of bramble-bush is intended.
1534. Thus the Latin interprets: others render "shoots."
1535. Cod. Sin. has "thus" instead of "this."
1536. Literally, "was."
1537. The text is here in great confusion, though the meaning is plain. Dressel reads, "For how are they alike, and why does He enjoin. that the goats should be good and alike?" The Cod. Sin. reads, "How is He like Him? For this that," etc.
1538. Cod. Sin. here inserts "the goat."
1539. Cod. Sin. reads, "for as he who .. so, says he," etc.
1540. Comp. Acts xiv. 22.
1541. Literally, "men in whom sins are perfect." Of this, and much more that follows, no mention is made in Scripture.
1542. Cod. Sin. has "upon sticks," and adds, "Behold again the type of the cross, both the scarlet wool and the hyssop,"-- adopted by Hilgenfeld.
1543. Cod. Sin. has, "the law is Christ Jesus," corrected to the above.
1544. The Greek text is, "then no longer sinful. men, no longer the glory of sinners," which Dressel defends and Hilgenfeld adopts, but which is surely corrupt.
1545. Literally, "in witness of the tribes."
1546. "In witness of."
1547. Thus the sense seems to require, and thus Dressel translates, though it is difficult to extract such a meaning from the Greek text.
1548. Ps. xviii. 44.
1549. Isa. xxxiii. 13.
1550. Jer. iv. 4.
1551. Jer. vii. 2.
1552. Ψ. xxxiv. 11-13. The first clause of this sentence is wanting in Cod. Sin.
1553. Cod. Sin. has "Lord."
1554. Isa. i. 2.
1555. In proof of the spiritual meaning of circumcision; but Hilgenfeld joins the words to the preceding sentence.
1556. Isa. i. 10.
1557. Cod. Sin. reads, "it is the voice," corrected, however, as above.
1558. Cod. Sin. has, "that we might hear the word, and not only believe," plainly a corrupt text.
1559. Cod. Sin., at first hand, has "slew them," but is corrected as above.
1560. The meaning is here very obscure, but the above rendering and punctuation seem preferable to any other.
1561. Cod. Sin., with several other mss., leaves out "new."
1562. Jer. iv. 3. Cod. Sin. has "God" instead of "Lord."
1563. Deut. x. 16.
1564. This contrast seems to be marked in the original. Cod. Sin. has, "Behold, receive again."
1565. Jer. ix. 25, 26.
1566. Dressel and Hilgenfeld read, "their covenant," as does Cod. Sin.; we have followed Hefele.
1567. Cod. Sin. has "children of love," omitting "richly," and inserting it before "looking forward."
1568. Literally, "doctrines."
1569. Not found in Scripture: but comp. Gen. xvii. 26, 27, Gen. xiv. 14.
1570. Cod. Sin. inserts, "and then

making a pause."

1571. This sentence is altogether omitted by inadvertence in Cod. Sin.

1572. Some mss. here read, "and further:" the above is the reading in Cod. Sin., and is also that of Hefele.

1573. This is rendered in the Latin, "the more profound gift," referring, as it does, to the Gnosis of the initiated. The same word is used in chap. i.

1574. Literally, "has learned a more germane (or genuine) word from me," being an idle vaunt on account of the ingenuity in interpreting Scripture he has just displayed.

1575. Cod. Sin. has "portion," corrected, however, as above. See Lev. xi. and Deut. xiv.

1576. Deut. iv. 1.

1577. Literally, "in spirit."

1578. Cod. Sin. inserts, "and gaze about for some way of escape on account of their greediness, even as these birds alone do not procure food for themselves (by labour), but sitting idle, seek to devour the flesh of others." The text as above seems preferable: Hilgenfeld, however, follows the Greek.

1579. Cod. Sin. has, "condemned already."

1580. Dressel has a note upon this passage, in which he refers the words we have rendered, "corrupters of boys," to those who by their dissolute lives waste their fortunes, and so entail destruction on their children; but this does not appear satisfactory. Comp. Clem. Alex. Pædag. ii. 10.

1581. We have left τρύπας untranslated. Cavities, i.e., of conception.

1582. Cod. Sin. has, "with the body through uncleanness," and so again in the last clause.

1583. Cod. Sin. inserts, "having received."

1584. Ψ. i. 1.

1585. Literally, "of the pestilent."

1586. Cod. Sin. reads, "perfectly," instead of "perfect," as do most mss.; but, according to Dressel, we should read, "have a perfect knowledge concerning the food." Hilgenfeld follows the Greek.

1587. Or, "resting upon Him."

1588. Cod. Sin. here has the singular, "one who ruminates."

1589. Literally, "holy age."

1590. Cod. Sin. inserts again, "rightly."

1591. Literally, "should build."

1592. Cod. Sin. has, "confine still more," corrected to "tremble still more."

1593. Cod. Sin. has, "have dug a pit of death." See Jer. ii. 12, 13.

1594. Comp. Isa. xvi. 1, 2.

1595. Literally, "dark." Cod. Sin. has, "of darkness."

1596. Isa. xlv. 2, 3.

1597. Isa. xxxiii. 16. Cod. Sin. has, "thou shalt dwell."

1598. Cod. Sin. entirely omits the question given above, and joins "the water is sure" to the former sentence.

1599. Isa. xxxiii. 16-18.

1600. Ps. i. 3-6.

1601. Cod. Sin. has, "what meaneth?"

1602. Zeph. iii. 19.

1603. Ezek. xlvii. 12.

1604. Omitted in Cod. Sin.

1605. Cod. Sin. refers this to God, and not to the prophet.

1606. From some unknown apocryphal book. Hilgenfeld compares Hab. ii. 11.

1607. Cod. Sin. reads, "He speaks to Moses."

1608. Cod. Sin. omits "and."

1609. Cod. Sin. reads πυγμῆς, which must here be translated "heap" or "mass." According to Hilgenfeld, however, πυγμή is here equivalent to πυγμαχία, "a fight." The meaning would then be, that "Moses piled weapon upon weapon in the midst of the battle," instead of "hill" (πήγης), as above.

1610. Thus standing in the form of a cross.

1611. Or, as some read, "in the cross."

1612. Isa. lxv. 2.

1613. Cod. Sin. has, "and He shall make him alive."

1614. Literally, "the sign."

1615. Comp. Num. xxi. 6-9; John iii. 14-18.

1616. Deut. xxvii. 15. Cod. Sin. reads, "molten or graven."

1617. Instead of ἐν δοκῷ, "on a beam," Cod. Sin. with other mss. has ἐνδόξως, "manifestly," which is adopted by Hilgenfeld.

1618. Cod. Sin. simply reads, "offer supplication."

1619. Num. xxi. 9.

1620. Comp. Col. i. 16.

1621. Cod. Sin. has the imperative, "Put on him;" but it is connected as above.

1622. Cod. Sin. closes the sentence with Jesus, and inserts, "Moses said therefore to Jesus."

1623. Ex. xvii. 14.

1624. Comp. 1 Tim. iii. 16.

1625. That is, merely human: a reference is supposed to be the Ebionites.

1626. Ps. cx. 1; Matt. xxii. 43-45.

1627. Cod. Sin. corrects "to Cyrus," as LXX.

1628. Cod. Sin. has, "he has taken

hold."

1629. Isa. xlv. 1.
1630. That is, "Christians."
1631. Gen. xxv. 21.
1632. Gen. xxv. 23.
1633. Gen. xlviii. 11, 9.
1634. Cod. Sin. reads each time "Ephraim," by a manifest mistake, instead of Manasseh.
1635. Cod. Sin. reads each time "Ephraim," by a manifest mistake, instead of Manasseh.
1636. Gen. xlviii. 18.
1637. Gen. xlviii. 19.
1638. Or, "of whom he willed."
1639. Cod. Sin. has, "when alone believing," and is followed by Hilgenfeld to this effect: "What, then, says He to Abraham, when, alone believing, he was placed in righteousness? Behold," etc.
1640. Gen. xv. 6, Gen. xvii. 5; comp. Rom. iv. 3.
1641. Cod. Sin. absurdly repeats "to give."
1642. Ex. xxiv. 18.
1643. Ex. xxxi. 18.
1644. Ex. xxxii. 7; Deut. ix. 12.
1645. Cod. Sin. reads, "for themselves."
1646. Comp. Heb. iii. 5.
1647. Cod. Sin. and other mss. read, "through Him who inherited."
1648. Cod. Sin. refers this to Christ.
1649. Cod. Sin. reads, "be prepared." Hilgenfeld follows Cod. Sin. so far, and reads, "For it is written how the Father commanded Him who was to redeem us from darkness (αὐτῷ--λυτρωσάμενος) to prepare a holy people for Himself."
1650. Isa. xlii. 6, 7.
1651. Cod. Sin. has, "we know."
1652. Isa. xlix. 6. The text of Cod. Sin., and of the other mss., is here in great confusion: we have followed that given by Hefele.
1653. Isa. lxi. 1, 2.
1654. Cod. Sin. reads "because," but this is corrected to "moreover."
1655. Ex. xx. 8; Deut. v. 12.
1656. Jer. xvii. 24, 25.
1657. Gen. ii. 2. The Hebrew text is here followed, the Septuagint reading "sixth" instead of "seventh."
1658. Cod. Sin. reads "signifies."
1659. Cod. Sin. adds, "to me."
1660. Cod. Sin. reads, "The day of the Lord shall be as a thousand years."
1661. Ps. xc. 4; 2 Pet. iii. 8.
1662. Cod. Sin. seems properly to omit "of the wicked man."
1663. Cod. Sin. places stars before moon.
1664. Cod. Sin. reads "again," but is corrected as above.
1665. The meaning is, "If the Sabbaths of the Jews were the true Sabbath, we should have been deceived by God, who demands pure hands and a pure heart."--Hefele.
1666. Cod. Sin. has, "But if not." Hilgenfeld's text of this confused passage reads as follows: "Who then can sanctify the day which God has sanctified, except the man who is of a pure heart? We are deceived (or mistaken) in all things. Behold, therefore," etc.
1667. Cod. Sin. reads, "resting aright, we shall sanctify it, having been justified, and received the promise, iniquity no longer existing, but all things having been made new by the Lord."
1668. Cod. Sin. reads, "Shall we not then?"
1669. Isa. i. 13.
1670. "Barnabas here bears testimony to the observance of the Lord's Day in early times."--Hefele.
1671. We here follow the punctuation of Dressel: Hefele places only a comma between the clauses, and inclines to think that the writer implies that the ascension of Christ took place on the first day of the week.
1672. That is, "they worshipped the temple instead of Him."
1673. Isa. xl. 12.
1674. Isa. lxvi. 1.
1675. Comp. Isa. xlix. 17 (Sept.).
1676. Cod. Sin. omits this.
1677. Comp. Isa. v., Jer. xxv.; but the words do not occur in Scripture.
1678. Dan. ix. 24-27; Hag. ii. 10.
1679. Cod. Sin. reads, "the calling."
1680. Cod. Sin. gives the clauses of this sentence separately, each occupying a line.
1681. That is, the man who is engaged in preaching the Gospel.
1682. Such is the punctuation adopted by Hefele, Dressel, and Hilgenfeld.
1683. Cod. Sin. reads, "my soul hopes that it has not omitted anything."
1684. Cod. Sin., "about things present or future." Hilgenfeld's text of this passage is as follows: "My mind and soul hopes that, according to my desire, I have omitted none of the things that pertain to salvation. For if I should write to you about things present or future," etc. Hefele gives the text as above, and understands the meaning to be, "points bearing on the present argument."
1685. Comp. 2 Cor. xii. 7.
1686. Cod. Sin. reads, "of the present

time of iniquity."

1687. Cod. Sin. inserts, "Thou shalt fear Him that formed thee."

1688. Cod. Sin. adds, "in all things."

1689. Literally, "shalt not give insolence to thy soul."

1690. "That is, while proclaiming the Gospel, thou shalt not in any way be of corrupt morals."--Hefele.

1691. Isa. lxvi. 2. All the preceding clauses are given in Cod. Sin. in distinct lines.

1692. Comp. Jas. i. 8.

1693. Cod. Sin. has "thy name," but this is corrected as above.

1694. Cod. Sin. corrects to, "as thine own soul."

1695. Cod. Sin. has, "of God."

1696. "Difficulties," or "troubles."

1697. Cod. Sin. adds, "knowing that without God nothing happens."

1698. Cod. Sin. has, "talkative," and omits the following clause.

1699. Cod. Sin. has, "Thou shalt be subject (ὑποταγήσῃ-- untouched by the corrector) to masters as a type of God."

1700. Inserted in Cod. Sin.

1701. Cod. Sin. has, "they should not."

1702. Comp. Eph. vi. 9.

1703. Comp. Rom. viii. 29, 30.

1704. Cod. Sin. has, "and not call."

1705. Cod. Sin. has, "in that which is incorruptible."

1706. Cod. Sin. has, "in things that are subject to death," but is corrected as above.

1707. Or, "the persons of the saints." Cod. Sin. omits this clause, but it is added by the corrector.

1708. The text is here confused in all the editions; we have followed that of Dressel. Cod. Sin. is defective. Hilgenfeld's text reads, "Thou shalt seek out every day the faces of the saints, either labouring by word and going to exhort them, and meditating to save a soul by the word, or by thy hands thou shalt labour for the redemption of thy sins"--almost identical with that given above.

1709. Cod. Sin. omits this quotation from Matt. v. 42 or Luke vi. 30, but it is added by a corrector.

1710. Cod. Sin. has, "hate evil."

1711. Cod. Sin. inserts "and."

1712. Cod. Sin. omits this clause: it is inserted by a corrector.

1713. Literally, "of the Black One."

1714. Cod. Sin. joins "eternal" with way, instead of death.

1715. Cod. Sin. reads "transgressions."

1716. Cod. Sin. omits "magic, avarice."

1717. Cod. Sin. omits "therefore."

1718. The things condemned in the previous chapter.

1719. Cod. Sin. has "resurrections," but is corrected as above.

1720. Cod. Sin. has, "lawgivers of good things."

1721. Cod. Sin. omits the preposition.

1722. Cod. Sin. omits this.

1723. Cod. Sin. reads, "that ye may be found in the day of judgment," which Hilgenfeld adopts.

1724. Literally, "While yet the good vessel is with you," i.e., as long as you are in the body.

1725. Cod. Sin. reads, "fail not in any one of yourselves," which is adopted by Hilgenfeld.

1726. Corrected in Cod. Sin. to, "it is worthy."

1727. Cod. Sin. omits this clause, but it is inserted by the corrector.

1728. Cod. Sin. omits "Amen," and adds at the close, "Epistle of Barnabas."

Papias

Introductory Note to the Fragments of Papias

[a.d. 70-155.] It seems unjust to the holy man of whose comparatively large contributions to early Christian literature such mere relics have been preserved, to set them forth in these versions, unaccompanied by the copious annotations of Dr. Routh. If even such crumbs from his table are not by any means without a practical value, with reference to the Canon and other matters, we may well credit the testimony (though disputed) of Eusebius, that he was a learned man, and well versed in the Holy Scripture. [1729] All who name poor Papias are sure to do so with the apologetic qualification of that historian, that he was of slender capacity. Nobody who attributes to him the millenarian fancies, of which he was but a narrator, as if these were the characteristics rather than the blemishes of his works, can fail to accept this estimate of our author. But more may be said when we come to the great name of Irenæus, who seems to make himself responsible for them. [1730]

Papias has the credit of association with Polycarp, in the friendship of St. John himself, and of "others who had seen the Lord." He is said to have been bishop of Hierapolis, in Phrygia, and to have died about the same time that Polycarp suffered; but even this is questioned. So little do we know of one whose lost books, could they be recovered, might reverse the received judgment, and establish his claim to the disputed tribute which makes him, like Apollos, "an eloquent man, and mighty in the Scriptures."

The following is the original Introductory Notice:--

The principal information in regard to Papias is given in the extracts made among the fragments from the works of Irenæus and Eusebius. He was bishop of the Church in Hierapolis, a city of Phrygia, in the first half of the second century. Later writers affirm that he suffered martyrdom about a.d. 163; some saying that Rome, others that Pergamus, was the scene of his death. He was a hearer of the Apostle John, and was on terms of intimate intercourse with many who had known the Lord and His apostles. From these he gathered the floating traditions in regard to the sayings of our Lord, and wove them into a production divided into five books. This work does not seem to have been confined to an exposition of the sayings of Christ, but to have contained much historical information.

Eusebius [1731] speaks of Papias as a man most learned in all things, and well acquainted with the Scriptures. In another passage [1732] he describes him as of small capacity. The fragments of Papias are translated from the text given in Routh's Reliquiæ Sacræ, vol. i. [1733]

Fragments of Papias

I. From the exposition of the oracles of the Lord [1734]

[The writings of Papias in common circulation are five in number, and these are called an Exposition of the Oracles of the Lord. Irenæus makes mention of these as the only works written by him, in the following words: "Now testimony is borne to these things in writing by Papias, an ancient man, who was a hearer of John, and a friend of Polycarp, in the fourth of his books; for five books were composed by him." Thus wrote Irenæus. Moreover, Papias himself, in the introduction to his books, makes it manifest that he was not himself a hearer and eye-witness of the holy apostles; but he tells us that he received the truths of our religion [1735] from those who were acquainted with them [the apostles] in the following words:]

But I shall not be unwilling to put down, along with my interpretations, [1736] whatsoever instructions I received with care at any time from the elders, and stored up with care in my memory, assuring you at the same time of their truth. For I did not, like the multitude, take pleasure in those who spoke much, but in those who taught the truth; nor in those who related strange commandments, [1737] but in those who rehearsed the commandments given by the Lord to faith, [1738] and proceeding from truth itself. If, then, any one who had attended on the elders came, I asked minutely after their sayings,--what Andrew or Peter said, or what was said by Philip, or by Thomas, or by James, or by John, or by Matthew, or by any other of the Lord's disciples: which things [1739]

Aristion and the presbyter John, the disciples of the Lord, say. For I imagined that what was to be got from books was not so profitable to me as what came from the living and abiding voice.

II [1740]

[The early Christians] called those who practised a godly guilelessness, [1741] children, [as is stated by Papias in the first book of the Lord's Expositions, and by Clemens Alexandrinus in his Pædagogue.]

III [1742]

Judas walked about in this world a sad [1743] example of impiety; for his body having swollen to such an extent that he could not pass where a chariot could pass easily, he was crushed by the chariot, so that his bowels gushed out. [1744]

IV [1745]

As the elders who saw John the disciple of the Lord remembered that they had heard from him how the Lord taught in regard to those times, and said]: "The days will come in which vines shall grow, having each ten thousand branches, and in each branch ten thousand twigs, and in each true twig ten thousand shoots, and in every one of the shoots ten thousand clusters, and on every one of the clusters ten thousand grapes, and every grape when pressed will give five-and-twenty metretes of wine. And when any one of the saints shall lay hold of a cluster, another shall cry out, I am a better cluster, take me; bless the Lord through me.' In like manner, [He said] that a grain of wheat would produce ten thousand ears, and that every ear would have ten thousand grains, and every grain would yield ten pounds of clear, pure, fine flour; and that apples, and seeds, and grass would produce in similar proportions; and that all animals, feeding then only on the productions of the earth, would become peaceable and harmonious, and be in perfect subjection to man." [1746] [Testimony is borne to these things in writing by Papias, an ancient man, who was a hearer of John and a friend of Polycarp, in the fourth of his books; for five books were composed by him. And he added, saying, "Now these things are credible to believers. And Judas the traitor," says he, "not believing, and asking, How shall such growths be accomplished by the Lord?' the Lord said, They shall see who shall come to them.' These, then, are the times mentioned by the prophet Isaiah: And the wolf shall lie down with the lamb,' etc. (Isa. xi. 6 ff.).")

V [1747]

As the presbyters say, then [1748] those who are deemed worthy of an abode in heaven shall go there, others shall enjoy the delights of Paradise, and others shall possess the splendour of the city;[1749] for everywhere the Saviour will be seen, according as they shall be worthy who see Him. But that there is this distinction between the habitation of those who produce an hundred-fold, and that of those who produce sixty-fold, and that of those who produce thirty-fold; for the first will be taken up into the heavens, the second class will dwell in Paradise, and the last will inhabit the city; and that on this account the Lord said, "In my Father's house are many mansions:" [1750] for all things belong to God, who supplies all with a suitable dwelling-place, even as His word says, that a share is given to all by the Father, [1751] according as each one is or shall be worthy. And this is the couch[1752] in which they shall recline who feast, being invited to the wedding. The presbyters, the disciples of the apostles, say that this is the gradation and arrangement of those who are saved, and that they advance through steps of this nature; and, moreover, they ascend through the Spirit to the Son, and through the Son to the Father; and that in due time the Son will yield up His work to the Father, even as it is said by the apostle, "For He must reign till He hath put all enemies under His feet. The last enemy that shall be destroyed is death." [1753] For in the times of the kingdom the just man who is on the earth shall forget to die. "But when He saith all things are put under Him, it is manifest that He is excepted which did put all things under Him. And when all things shall be subdued unto Him, then shall the Son also Himself be subject unto Him that put all things under Him, that God may be all in all." [1754]

VI [1755]

[Papias, who is now mentioned by us, affirms that he received the sayings of the apostles from those who accompanied them, and he moreover asserts that he heard in person Aristion and the presbyter John. [1756] Accordingly he mentions them frequently by name, and in his writings gives their traditions. Our notice of these circumstances may not be without its use. It may also be worth while to add to the statements of Papias already given, other passages of his in which he relates some miraculous deeds, stating that he acquired the knowledge of them from tradition. The residence of the Apostle Philip with his daughters in Hierapolis has been mentioned above. We must now point out how Papias, who lived at the same time, relates that he had received a wonderful narrative from the daughters of Philip. For he relates that a dead man was raised to life in his day. [1757] He also mentions another miracle relating to Justus, surnamed Barsabas, how he swallowed a deadly poison, and received no harm, on account of the grace of the Lord. The same person, moreover, has set down other things as coming to him from unwritten tradition, amongst these some strange parables and instructions of the Saviour, and some other things of a more fabulous nature. [1758] Amongst these he says that there will be a millennium after the resurrection from the dead, when the personal reign of Christ will be established on this earth. He moreover hands down, in his own writing, other narratives given by the previously mentioned Aristion of the Lord's sayings, and the traditions of the presbyter John. For information on these points, we can merely refer our readers to the books themselves; but now, to the extracts already made, we shall add, as being a matter of primary importance, a tradition regarding Mark who wrote the Gospel, which he [Papias] has given in the following words]: And the presbyter said this. Mark having become the interpreter of Peter, wrote down accurately whatsoever he remembered. It was not, however, in exact order that he related the sayings or deeds of Christ. For he neither heard the Lord nor accompanied Him. But afterwards, as I said, he accompanied Peter, who accommodated his instructions to the necessities [of his hearers], but with no intention of giving a regular narrative of the Lord's sayings. Wherefore Mark made no mistake in thus writing some things as he remembered them. For of one thing he took especial care, not to omit anything he had heard, and not to put anything fictitious into the statements. [This is what is related by Papias regarding Mark; but with regard to Matthew he has made the following statements]: Matthew put together the oracles [of the Lord] in the Hebrew language, and each one interpreted them as best he could. [The same person uses proofs from the First Epistle of John, and from the Epistle of Peter in like manner. And he also gives another story of a woman [1759] who was accused of many sins before the Lord, which is to be found in the Gospel according to the Hebrews.]

VII [1760]

Papias thus speaks, word for word: To some of them [angels] He gave dominion over the arrangement of the world, and He commissioned them to exercise their dominion well. And he says, immediately after this: but it happened that their arrangement came to nothing. [1761]

VIII [1762]

With regard to the inspiration of the book (Revelation), we deem it superfluous to add another word; for the blessed Gregory Theologus and Cyril, and even men of still older date, Papias, Irenæus, Methodius, and Hippolytus, bore entirely satisfactory testimony to it.

IX [1763]

Taking occasion from Papias of Hierapolis, the illustrious, a disciple of the apostle who leaned on the bosom of Christ, and Clemens, and Pantænus the priest of [the Church] of the Alexandrians, and the wise Ammonius, the ancient and first expositors, who agreed with each other, who understood the work of the six days as referring to Christ and the whole Church.

X [1764]

(1.) Mary the mother of the Lord; (2.) Mary the wife of Cleophas or Alphæus, who was the mother of James the bishop and apostle, and of Simon and Thaddeus, and of one Joseph; (3.) Mary Salome, wife of Zebedee, mother of John the evangelist and James; (4.) Mary Magdalene. These four are found in the Gospel. James and Judas and Joseph were sons of an aunt (2) of the Lord's. James also and John were sons of another aunt (3) of the Lord's. Mary (2), mother of James the Less and Joseph, wife of Alphæus was the sister of Mary the mother of the Lord, whom John names of Cleophas, either from her father or from the family of the clan, or for some other reason. Mary Salome (3) is called Salome either from her husband or her village. Some affirm that she is the same as Mary of Cleophas, because she had two husbands.

Footnotes:

1729. See Lardner, ii. p. 119.
1730. Against Heresies, book v. chap. xxxiii. See the prudent note of Canon Robertson (History of the Christ. Church, vol. i. p. 116).
1731. Hist. Eccl., iii. 39.
1732. Ibid.
1733. Where the fragments with learned annotations and elucidations fill forty-four pages.
1734. This fragment is found in Eusebius, Hist. Eccl. iii. 39.
1735. Literally, "the things of faith."
1736. Papias states that he will give an

exact account of what the elders said; and that, in addition to this, he will accompany this account with an explanation of the meaning and import of the statements.

1737. Literally, "commandments belonging to others," and therefore strange and novel to the followers of Christ.

1738. Given to faith has been variously understood. Either not stated in direct language, but like parables given in figures, so that only the faithful could understand; or entrusted to faith, that is, to those who were possessed of faith, the faithful.

1739. Which things: this is usually translated, "what Aristion and John say;" and the translation is admissible. But the words more naturally mean, that John and Aristion, even at the time of his writing, were telling him some of the sayings of the Lord.

1740. This fragment is found in the Scholia of Maximus on the works of Dionysius the Areopagite.

1741. Literally, "a guilelessness according to God."

1742. This fragment is found in OEcumenius.

1743. Literally, "great."

1744. Literally, "were emptied out." Theophylact, after quoting this passage, adds other particulars, as if they were derived from Papias. But see Routh, i. pp. 26, 27. He says that Judas's eyes were so swollen that they could not be seen, even by the optical instruments of physicians; and that the rest of his body was covered with runnings and worms. He further states, that he died in a solitary spot, which was left desolate until his time; and no one could pass the place without stopping up his nose with his hands.

1745. From Irenæus, Hær., v. 32. Hearsay at second-hand, and handed about among many, amounts to nothing as evidence. Note the reports of sermons, also, as they appear in our daily Journals. Whose reputation can survive if such be credited?.

1746. See Grabe, apud Routh, 1. 29.

1747. This fragment is found in Irenæus, Hær., v. 36; but it is a mere guess that the saying of the presbyters is taken from the work of Papias.

1748. In the future state.

1749. The new Jerusalem on earth.

1750. John xiv. 2.

1751. Commentators suppose that the reference here is to Matt. xx. 23.

1752. Matt. xxii. 10.

1753. 1 Cor. xv. 25, 26.

1754. 1 Cor. xv. 27, 28.

1755. From Eusebius, Hist. Eccl., iii. 39.

1756. A certain presbyter, of whom see Apost. Constitutions, vii. 46, where he is said to have been ordained by St. John, the Evangelist.

1757. "In his day" may mean "in the days of Papias," or "in the days of Philip." As the narrative came from the daughters of Philip, it is more likely that Philip's days are meant.

1758. Again, note the reduplicated hearsay. Not even Irenæus, much less Eusebius, should be accepted, otherwise than as retailing vague reports.

1759. Rufinus supposes this story to be the same as that now found in the textus receptus of Gospel of John viii. 1-11,--the woman taken in adultery.

1760. This extract is made from Andreas Cæsariensis, Bishop of Cæsarea in Cappodocia, circiter, A.D. 500.

1761. That is, that government of the world's affairs was a failure. An ancient writer takes τάξις to mean the arraying of the evil angels in battle against God.

1762. This also is taken from Andreas Cæsariensis. See Lardner, vol. v. 77.

1763. This fragment, or rather reference, is taken from Anastasius Sinaita. Routh gives, as another fragment, the repetition of the same statement by Anastasius.

1764. This fragment was found by Grabe in a ms. of the Bodleian Library, with the inscription on the margin, "Papia." Westcott states that it forms part of a dictionary written by "a mediæval Papias. He seems to have added the words, "Maria is called Illuminatrix, or Star of the Sea," etc, a middle-age device. The dictionary exists in ms. both at Oxford and Cambridge."

Justin Martyr

Introductory Note to the Writings of Justin Martyr

[a.d. 110-165.] Justin was a Gentile, but born in Samaria, near Jacob's well. He must have been well educated: he had travelled extensively, and he seems to have been a person enjoying at least a competence. After trying all other systems, his elevated tastes and refined perceptions made him a disciple of Socrates and Plato. So he climbed towards Christ. As he himself narrates the story of his conversion, it need not be anticipated here. What Plato was feeling after, he found in Jesus of Nazareth. The conversion of such a man marks a new era in the gospel history. The sub-apostolic age begins with the first Christian author,--the founder of theological literature. It introduced to mankind, as the mother of true philosophy, the despised teaching of those Galileans to whom their Master had said, "Ye are the light of the world."

And this is the epoch which forced this great truth upon the attention of contemplative minds. It was more than a hundred years since the angels had sung "Good-will to men;" and that song had now been heard for successive generations, breaking forth from the lips of sufferers on the cross, among lions, and amid blazing faggots. Here was a nobler Stoicism that needed interpretation. Not only choice spirits, despising the herd and boasting of a loftier intellectual sphere, were its professors; but thousands of men, women, and children, withdrawing themselves not at all from the ordinary and humble lot of the people, were inspired by it to live and die heroically and sublimely, --exhibiting a superiority to revenge and hate entirely unaccountable, praying for their enemies, and seeking to glorify their God by love to their fellow-men.

And in spite of Gallios and Neros alike, the gospel was dispelling the gross darkness. Of this, Pliny's letter to Trajan is decisive evidence. Even in Seneca we detect reflections of the daybreak. Plutarch writes as never a Gentile could have written until now. Plato is practically surpassed by him in his thoughts upon the "delays [1765] of the Divine Justice." Hadrian's address to his soul, in his dying moments, is a tribute to the new ideas which had been sown in the popular mind. And now the Antonines, impelled by something in the age, came forward to reign as "philosophers." At this moment, Justin Martyr confronts them like a Daniel. The "little stone" smites the imperial image in the face, not yet "in the toes." He tells the professional philosophers on a throne how false and hollow is all wisdom that is not meant for all humanity, and that is not capable of leavening the masses. He exposes the impotency of even Socratic philosophy: he shows, in contrast, the force that works in the words of Jesus; he points out their regenerating power. It is the mission of Justin to be a star in the West, leading its Wise Men to the cradle of Bethlehem.

The writings of Justin are deficient in charms of style; and, for us, there is something the reverse of attractive in the forms of thought which he had learned from the philosophers. [1766] If Plato had left us nothing but the Timæus, a Renan would doubtless have reproached him as of feeble intellectual power. So a dancing-master might criticise the movements of an athlete, or the writhings of St. Sebastian shot with arrows. The practical wisdom of Justin using the rhetoric of his times, and discomfiting false philosophy with its own weapons, is not appreciated by the fastidious Parisian. But the manly and heroic pleadings of the man, for a despised people with whom he had boldly identified himself; the intrepidity with which he defends them before despots, whose mere caprice might punish him with death; above all, the undaunted spirit with which he exposes the shame and absurdity of their inveterate superstition and reproaches the memory of Hadrian whom Antoninus had deified, as he had deified Antinous of loathsome history,--these are characteristics which every instinct of the unvitiated soul delights to honour. Justin cannot be refuted by a sneer.

He wore his philosopher's gown after his conversion, as a token that he had attained the only true philosophy. And seeing, that, after the conflicts and tests of ages, it is the only philosophy that lasts and lives and triumphs, its discoverer deserves the homage of mankind. Of the philosophic gown we shall hear again when we come to Tertullian. [1767]

The residue of Justin's history may be found in The Martyrdom and other pages soon to follow, as well as in the following Introductory Note of the able translators, Messrs. Dods and

Reith:--

Justin Martyr was born in Flavia Neapolis, a city of Samaria, the modern Nablous. The date of his birth is uncertain, but may be fixed about a.d. 114. His father and grandfather were probably of Roman origin. Before his conversion to Christianity he studied in the schools of the philosophers, searching after some knowledge which should satisfy the cravings of his soul. At last he became acquainted with Christianity, being at once impressed with the extraordinary fearlessness which the Christians displayed in the presence of death, and with the grandeur, stability, and truth of the teachings of the Old Testament. From this time he acted as an evangelist, taking every opportunity to proclaim the gospel as the only safe and certain philosophy, the only way to salvation. It is probable that he travelled much. We know that he was some time in Ephesus, and he must have lived for a considerable period in Rome. Probably he settled in Rome as a Christian teacher. While he was there, the philosophers, especially the Cynics, plotted against him, and he sealed his testimony to the truth by martyrdom.

The principal facts of Justin's life are gathered from his own writings. There is little clue to dates. It is agreed on all hands that he lived in the reign of Antoninus Pius, and the testimony of Eusebius and most credible historians renders it nearly certain that he suffered martyrdom in the reign of Marcus Aurelius. The Chronicon Paschale gives as the date 165 a.d.

The writings of Justin Martyr are among the most important that have come down to us from the second century. He was not the first that wrote an Apology in behalf of the Christians, but his Apologies are the earliest extant. They are characterized by intense Christian fervour, and they give us an insight into the relations existing between heathens and Christians in those days. His other principal writing, the Dialogue with Trypho, is the first elaborate exposition of the reasons for regarding Christ as the Messiah of the Old Testament, and the first systematic attempt to exhibit the false position of the Jews in regard to Christianity.

Many of Justin's writings have perished. Those works which have come to us bearing his name have been divided into three classes.

The first class embraces those which are unquestionably genuine, viz. the two Apologies, and the Dialogue with Trypho. Some critics have urged objections against Justin's authorship of the Dialogue; but the objections are regarded now as possessing no weight.

The second class consists of those works which are regarded by some critics as Justin's, and by others as not his. They are: 1. An Address to the Greeks; 2. A Hortatory Address to the Greeks; 3. On the Sole Government of God; 4. An Epistle to Diognetus; 5. Fragments from a work on the Resurrection; 6. And other Fragments. Whatever difficulty there may be in settling the authorship of these treatises, there is but one opinion as to their earliness. The latest of them, in all probability, was not written later than the third century.

The third class consists of those that are unquestionably not the works of Justin. These are: 1. An Exposition of the True Faith; 2. Replies to the Orthodox; 3. Christian Questions to Gentiles; 4. Gentile Questions to Christians; 5. Epistle to Zenas and Serenus; and 6. A Refutation of certain Doctrines of Aristotle. There is no clue to the date of the two last. There can be no doubt that the others were written after the Council of Nicæa, though, immediately after the Reformation, Calvin and others appealed to the first as a genuine writing of Justin's.

There is a curious question connected with the Apologies of Justin which have come down to us. Eusebius mentions two Apologies,--one written in the reign of Antoninus Pius, the other in the reign of Marcus Aurelius. Critics have disputed much whether we have these two Apologies in those now extant. Some have maintained, that what is now called the Second Apology was the preface of the first, and that the second is lost. Others have tried to show, that the so-called Second Apology is the continuation of the first, and that the second is lost. Others have supposed that the two Apologies which we have are Justin's two Apologies, but that Eusebius was wrong in affirming that the second was addressed to Marcus Aurelius; and others maintain, that we have in our two Apologies the two Apologies mentioned by Eusebius, and that our first is his first, and our second his second.

Footnotes:

1765. See Amyot's translation, and a more modern one by De Maistre (OEuvres, vol. ii. Paris, 1833). An edition of The Delays (the original, with notes by Professor Hackett) has appeared in America (Andover, circ., 1842), and is praised by Tayler Lewis.

1766. He quotes Plato's reference, e.g., to the X.; but the Orientals delighted in such conceits. Compare the Hebrew critics on the h (in Gen. i. 4), on which see Nordheimer, Gram., vol. i. p. 7, New York,

1838.
* 1767. It survives in the pulpits of Christendom--Greek, Latin, Anglican, Lutheran, etc.--to this day, in slightly different forms.

The First Apology of Justin

Chapter I - Address

To the Emperor Titus Ælius Adrianus Antoninus Pius Augustus Cæsar, and to his son Verissimus the Philosopher, and to Lucius the Philosopher, the natural son of Cæsar, and the adopted son of Pius, a lover of learning, and to the sacred Senate, with the whole People of the Romans, I, Justin, the son of Priscus and grandson of Bacchius, natives of Flavia Neapolis in Palestine, present this address and petition in behalf of those of all nations who are unjustly hated and wantonly abused, myself being one of them.

Chapter II - Justice demanded

Reason directs those who are truly pious and philosophical to honour and love only what is true, declining to follow traditional opinions, [1768] if these be worthless. For not only does sound reason direct us to refuse the guidance of those who did or taught anything wrong, but it is incumbent on the lover of truth, by all means, and if death be threatened, even before his own life, to choose to do and say what is right. Do you, then, since ye are called pious and philosophers, guardians of justice and lovers of learning, give good heed, and hearken to my address; and if ye are indeed such, it will be manifested. For we have come, not to flatter you by this writing, nor please you by our address, but to beg that you pass judgment, after an accurate and searching investigation, not flattered by prejudice or by a desire of pleasing superstitious men, nor induced by irrational impulse or evil rumours which have long been prevalent, to give a decision which will prove to be against yourselves. For as for us, we reckon that no evil can be done us, unless we be convicted as evil-doers or be proved to be wicked men; and you, you can kill, but not hurt us.

Chapter III - Claim of judicial investigation

But lest any one think that this is an unreasonable and reckless utterance, we demand that the charges against the Christians be investigated, and that, if these be substantiated, they be punished as they deserve; [or rather, indeed, we ourselves will punish them.] [1769] But if no one can convict us of anything, true reason forbids you, for the sake of a wicked rumour, to wrong blameless men, and indeed rather yourselves, who think fit to direct affairs, not by judgment, but by passion. And every sober-minded person will declare this to be the only fair and equitable adjustment, namely, that the subjects render an unexceptional account of their own life and doctrine; and that, on the other hand, the rulers should give their decision in obedience, not to violence and tyranny, but to piety and philosophy. For thus would both rulers and ruled reap benefit. For even one of the ancients somewhere said, "Unless both rulers and ruled philosophize, it is impossible to make states blessed." [1770] It is our task, therefore, to afford to all an opportunity of inspecting our life and teachings, lest, on account of those who are accustomed to be ignorant of our affairs, we should incur the penalty due to them for mental blindness; [1771] and it is your business, when you hear us, to be found, as reason demands, good judges. For if, when ye have learned the truth, you do not what is just, you will be before God without excuse.

Chapter IV - Christians unjustly condemned for their mere name

By the mere application of a name, nothing is decided, either good or evil, apart from the actions implied in the name; and indeed, so far at least as one may judge from the name we are accused of, we are most excellent people. [1772] But as we do not think it just to beg to be acquitted on account of the name, if we be convicted as evil-doers, so, on the other hand, if we be found to have committed no offence, either in the matter of thus naming ourselves, or of our conduct as citizens, it is your part very earnestly to guard against incurring just punishment, by unjustly punishing those who are not convicted. For from a name neither praise nor punishment could reasonably spring, unless something excellent or base in action be proved. And those among yourselves who are accused you do not punish before they are convicted; but in our case you receive the name as proof against us, and this although, so far as the name goes, you ought rather to punish our accusers. For we are accused of being Christians, and to hate what is excellent (Chrestian) is unjust. Again, if any of the accused deny the name, and say that he is not a Christian, you acquit him, as having no evidence against him as a wrong-doer; but if any one acknowledge that he is a Christian, you punish him on account of this acknowledgment. Justice requires that you inquire into the life both of him who confesses and of him who denies, that by his deeds it may be apparent what kind of man each is. For as some who have been taught by the Master, Christ, not to deny Him, give encouragement to others when they are put to the question, so in all probability do those who lead wicked lives give occasion to those who, without consideration, take upon them to accuse all the Christians of impiety and wickedness. And this also is not right. For of philosophy, too, some assume the name and the garb who do nothing worthy of their profession; and you are well aware, that those of the ancients whose opinions and teachings were quite diverse, are yet all called by the one name of philosophers. And of these some taught atheism; and the poets who have flourished among you raise a laugh out of the uncleanness of Jupiter with his own children. And those who now adopt such instruction are not restrained by you; but, on the contrary, you bestow prizes and honours upon those who euphoniously insult the gods.

Chapter V - Christians charged with atheism

Why, then, should this be? In our case, who pledge ourselves to do no wickedness, nor to hold these atheistic opinions, you do not examine the charges made against us; but, yielding to unreasoning passion, and to the instigation of evil demons, you punish us without consideration or judgment. For the truth shall be spoken; since of old these evil demons, effecting apparitions of themselves, both defiled women and corrupted boys, and showed such fearful sights to men, that those who did not use their reason in judging of the actions that were done, were struck with terror; and being carried away by fear, and not knowing that these were demons, they called them gods, and gave to each the name which each of the demons chose for himself. [1773] And when Socrates endeavoured, by true reason and examination, to bring these things to light, and deliver men from the demons, then the demons themselves, by means of men who rejoiced in iniquity, compassed his death, as an atheist and a profane person, on the charge that "he was introducing new divinities;" and in our case they display a similar activity. For not only among the Greeks did reason (Λόγος) prevail to condemn these things through Socrates, but also among the Barbarians were they condemned by Reason (or the Word, the Λόγος) Himself, who took shape, and became man, and was called Jesus Christ; and in obedience to Him, we not only deny that they who did such things as these are gods, [1774] but assert that they are wicked and impious demons, [1775] whose actions will not bear comparison with those even of men desirous of virtue.

Chapter VI - Charge of atheism refuted

Hence are we called atheists. And we confess that we are atheists, so far as gods of this sort are concerned, but not with respect to the most true God, the Father of righteousness and temperance and the other virtues, who is free from all impurity. But both Him, and the Son (who came forth from Him and taught us these things, and the host of the other good angels who follow and are made like to Him), [1776] and the prophetic Spirit, we worship and adore, knowing them in reason and truth, and declaring without grudging to every one who wishes to learn, as we have been taught.

Chapter VII - Each Christian must be tried by his own life

But some one will say, Some have ere now been arrested and convicted as evil-doers. For you condemn many, many a time, after inquiring into the life of each of the accused severally, but not on account of those of whom we have been speaking. [1777] And this we acknowledge, that as among the Greeks those who teach such theories as please themselves are all called by the one name "Philosopher," though their doctrines be diverse, so also among the Barbarians this name on which accusations are accumulated is the common property of those who are and those who seem wise. For all are called Christians. Wherefore we demand that the deeds of all those who are accused to you be judged, in order that each one who is convicted may be punished as an evil-doer, and not as a Christian; and if it is clear that any one is blameless, that he may be acquitted, since by the mere fact of his being a Christian he does no wrong. [1778] For we will not require that you punish our accusers; [1779] they being sufficiently punished by their present wickedness and ignorance of what is right.

Chapter VIII - Christians confess their faith in God

And reckon ye that it is for your sakes we have been saying these things; for it is in our power, when we are examined, to deny that we are Christians; but we would not live by telling a lie. For, impelled by the desire of the eternal and pure life, we seek the abode that is with God, the Father and Creator of all, and hasten to confess our faith, persuaded and convinced as we are that they who have proved to God [1780] by their works that they followed Him, and loved to abide with Him where there is no sin to cause disturbance, can obtain these things. This, then, to speak shortly, is what we expect and have learned from Christ, and teach. And Plato, in like manner, used to say that Rhadamanthus and Minos would punish the wicked who came before them; and we say that the same thing will be done, but at the hand of Christ, and upon the wicked in the same bodies united again to their spirits which are now to undergo everlasting punishment; and not only, as Plato said, for a period of a thousand years. And if any one say that this is incredible or impossible, this error of ours is one which concerns ourselves only, and no other person, so long as you cannot convict us of doing any harm.

Chapter IX - Folly of idol worship

And neither do we honour with many sacrifices and garlands of flowers such deities as men have formed and set in shrines and called gods; since we see that these are soulless and dead, and have not the form of God (for we do not consider that God has such a form as some say that they imitate to His honour), but have the names and forms of those wicked demons which have appeared. For why need we tell you who already know, into what forms the craftsmen, [1781] carving and cutting, casting and hammering, fashion the materials? And often out of vessels of dishonour, by merely changing the form, and making an image of the requisite shape, they make what they call a god; which we consider not only senseless, but to be even insulting to God, who, having ineffable glory and form, thus gets His name attached to things that are corruptible, and require constant service. And that the artificers of these are both intemperate, and, not to enter into particulars, are practised in every vice, you very well know; even their own girls who work along with them they corrupt. What infatuation! that dissolute men should be said to fashion and make gods for your worship, and that you should appoint such men the guardians of the temples where they are enshrined; not recognising that it is unlawful even to think or say that men are the guardians of gods.

Chapter X - How God is to be served

But we have received by tradition that God does not need the material offerings which men can give, seeing, indeed, that He Himself is the provider of all things. And we have been taught, and are convinced, and do believe, that He accepts those only who imitate the excellences which reside in Him, temperance, and justice, and philanthropy, and as many virtues as are peculiar to a God who is called by no proper name. And we have been taught that He in the beginning did of His goodness, for man's sake, create all things out of unformed matter; and if men by their works show themselves worthy of this His design, they are deemed worthy, and so we have received--of reigning in company with Him, being delivered from corruption and suffering. For as in the beginning He created us when we were not, so do we consider that, in like manner, those who choose what is pleasing to Him are, on account of their choice, deemed worthy of incorruption and of fellowship with Him. For the coming into being at first was not in our own power; and in order that we may follow those things which please Him, choosing them by means of the rational faculties He has Himself endowed us with, He both persuades us and leads us to faith. And we think it for the advantage of all men that they are not restrained from learning these things, but are even urged thereto. For the restraint which human laws could not effect, the Word, inasmuch as He is divine, would have effected, had not the wicked demons, taking as their ally the lust of wickedness which is in every man, and which draws variously to all manner of vice, scattered many false and profane accusations, none of which attach to us.

Chapter XI - What kingdom Christians look for

And when you hear that we look for a kingdom, you suppose, without making any inquiry, that we speak of a human kingdom; whereas we speak of that which is with God, as appears also from the confession of their faith made by those who are charged with being Christians, though they know that death is the punishment awarded to him who so confesses. For if we looked for a human kingdom, we should also deny our Christ, that we might not be slain; and we should strive to escape detection, that we might obtain what we expect. But since our thoughts are not fixed on the present, we are not concerned when men cut us off; since also death is a debt which must at all events be paid.

Chapter XII - Christians live as under God's eye

And more than all other men are we your helpers and allies in promoting peace, seeing that we hold this view, that it is alike impossible for the wicked, the covetous, the conspirator, and for the virtuous, to escape the notice of God, and that each man goes to everlasting punishment or salvation according to the value of his actions. For if all men knew this, no one would choose wickedness even for a little, knowing that he goes to the everlasting punishment of fire; but would by all means restrain himself, and adorn himself with virtue, that he might obtain the good gifts of God, and escape the punishments. For those who, on account of the laws and punishments you impose, endeavour to escape detection when they offend (and they offend, too, under the impression that it is quite possible to escape your detection, since you are but men), those persons, if they learned and were convinced that nothing, whether actually done or only intended, can escape the knowledge of God, would by all means live decently on account of the penalties threatened, as even you yourselves will admit. But you seem to fear lest all men become righteous, and you no longer have any to punish. Such would be the concern of public executioners, but not of good princes. But, as we before said, we are persuaded that these things are prompted by evil spirits, who demand sacrifices and service even from those who live unreasonably; but as for you, we presume that you who aim at [a reputation for] piety and philosophy will do nothing unreasonable. But if you also, like the foolish, prefer custom to truth, do what you have power to do. But just so much power have rulers who esteem opinion more than truth, as robbers have in a desert. And that you will not succeed is declared by the Word, than whom, after God who begat Him, we know there is no ruler more kingly and just. For as all shrink from succeeding to the poverty or sufferings or obscurity of their fathers, so whatever the Word forbids us to choose, the sensible man will not choose. That all these things should come to pass, I say, our Teacher foretold, He who is both Son and Apostle of God the Father of all and the Ruler, Jesus Christ; from whom also we have the name of Christians. Whence we become more assured of all the things He taught us, since whatever He beforehand foretold should come to pass, is seen in fact coming to pass; and this is the work of God, to tell of a thing before it happens, and as it was foretold so to show it happening. It were possible to pause here and add no more, reckoning that we demand what is just and true; but because we are well aware that it is not easy suddenly to change a mind possessed by ignorance, we intend to add a few things, for the sake of persuading those who love the truth, knowing that it is not impossible to put ignorance to flight by presenting the truth.

Chapter XIII - Christians serve God rationally

What sober-minded man, then, will not acknowledge that we are not atheists, worshipping as we do the Maker of this universe, and declaring, as we have been taught, that He has no need of streams of blood and libations and incense; whom we praise to the utmost of our power by the exercise of prayer and thanksgiving for all things wherewith we are supplied, as we have been taught that the only honour that is worthy of Him is not to consume by fire what He has brought into being for our sustenance, but to use it for ourselves and those who need, and with gratitude to Him to offer thanks by invocations and hymns [1782] for our creation, and for all the means of health, and for the various qualities of the different kinds of things, and for the changes of the seasons; and to present before Him petitions for our existing again in incorruption through faith in Him. Our teacher of these things is Jesus Christ, who also was born for this purpose, and was crucified under Pontius Pilate, procurator of Judæa, in the times of Tiberius Cæsar; and that we reasonably worship Him, having learned that He is the Son of the true God Himself, and holding Him in the second place, and the prophetic Spirit in the third, we will prove. For they proclaim our madness to consist in this, that we give to a crucified man a place second to the unchangeable and eternal God, the Creator of all; for they do not discern the mystery that is herein, to which, as we make it plain to you, we pray you to give heed.

Chapter XIV - The demons misrepresent Christian doctrine

For we forewarn you to be on your guard, lest those demons whom we have been accusing should deceive you, and quite divert you from reading and understanding what we say. For they strive to hold you their slaves and servants; and sometimes by appearances in dreams, and sometimes by magical impositions, they subdue all who make no strong opposing effort for their own salvation. And thus do we also, since our persuasion by the Word, stand aloof from them (i.e., the demons), and follow the only unbegotten God through His Son --we who formerly delighted in fornication, but now embrace chastity alone; we who formerly used magical arts, dedicate ourselves to the good and unbegotten God; we who valued above all things the acquisition of wealth and possessions, now bring what we have into a common stock, and communicate to every one in need; we who hated and destroyed one another, and on account of their different manners would not live[1783] with men of a different tribe, now, since the coming of Christ, live familiarly with them, and pray for our enemies, and endeavour to persuade those who hate us unjustly to live conformably to the good precepts of Christ, to the end that they may become partakers with us of the same joyful hope of a reward from God the ruler of all. But lest we should seem to be reasoning sophistically, we consider it right, before giving you the promised [1784] explanation, to cite a few precepts given by Christ Himself. And be it yours, as powerful rulers, to inquire whether we have been taught and do teach these things truly. Brief and concise utterances fell from Him, for He was no sophist, but His word was the power of God.

Chapter XV - What Christ himself taught

Concerning chastity, He uttered such sentiments as these: [1785] "Whosoever looketh upon a woman to lust after her, hath committed adultery with her already in his heart before God." And, "If thy right eye offend thee, cut it out; for it is better for thee to enter into the kingdom of heaven with one eye, than, having two eyes, to be cast into everlasting fire." And, "Whosoever shall marry her that is divorced from another husband, committeth adultery." [1786] And, "There are some who have been made eunuchs of men, and some who were born eunuchs, and some who have made themselves eunuchs for the kingdom of heaven's sake; but all cannot receive this saying." [1787] So that all who, by human law, are twice married, [1788] are in the eye of our Master sinners, and those who look upon a woman to lust after her. For not only he who in act commits adultery is rejected by Him, but also he who desires to commit adultery: since not only our works, but also our thoughts, are open before God. And many, both men and women, who have been Christ's disciples from childhood, remain pure at the age of sixty or seventy years; and I boast that I could produce such from every race of men. For what shall I say, too, of the countless multitude of those who have reformed intemperate habits, and learned these things? For Christ called not the just nor the chaste to repentance, but the ungodly, and the licentious, and the unjust; His words being, "I came not to call the righteous, but sinners to repentance." [1789] For the heavenly Father desires rather the repentance than the punishment of the sinner. And of our love to all, He taught thus: "If ye love them that love you, what new thing do ye? for even fornicators do this. But I say unto you, Pray for your enemies, and love them that hate you, and bless them that curse you, and pray for them that despitefully use you." [1790] And that we should communicate to the needy, and do nothing for glory, He said, "Give to him that asketh, and from him that would borrow turn not away; for if ye lend to them of whom ye hope to receive, what new thing do ye? even the publicans do this. Lay not up for yourselves treasure upon earth, where moth and rust doth corrupt, and where robbers break through; but lay up for yourselves treasure in heaven, where neither moth nor rust doth corrupt. For what is a man profited, if he shall gain the whole world, and lose his own soul? or what shall a man give in exchange for it? Lay up treasure, therefore, in heaven, where neither moth nor rust doth corrupt."[1791] And, "Be ye kind and merciful, as your Father also is kind and merciful, and maketh His sun to rise on sinners, and the righteous, and the wicked. Take no thought what ye shall eat, or what ye shall put on: are ye not better than the birds and the beasts? And God feedeth them. Take no thought, therefore, what ye shall eat, or what ye shall put on; for your heavenly Father knoweth that ye have need of these things. But seek ye the kingdom of heaven, and all these things shall be added unto you. For where his treasure is, there also is the mind of a man." [1792] And, "Do not these things to be seen of men; otherwise ye have no reward from your Father which is in heaven." [1793]

Chapter XVI - Concerning patience and swearing

And concerning our being patient of injuries, and ready to serve all, and free from anger, this is what He said: "To him that smiteth thee on the one cheek, offer also the other; and him that taketh away thy cloak or coat, forbid not. And whosoever shall be angry, is in danger of the fire. And every one that compelleth thee to go with him a mile, follow him two. And let your good works shine before men, that they, seeing them, may glorify your Father which is in heaven." [1794] For we ought not to strive; neither has He desired us to be imitators of wicked men, but He has exhorted us to lead all men, by patience and gentleness, from shame and the love of evil. And this indeed is proved in the case of many wó ὥνce were of your way of thinking, but have changed their violent and tyrannical disposition, being overcome either by the constancy which they have witnessed in their neighbours' lives, [1795] or by the extraordinary forbearance they have observed in their fellow-travellers when defrauded, or by the honesty of those with whom they have transacted business.

And with regard to our not swearing at all, and always speaking the truth, He enjoined as follows: "Swear not at all; but let your yea be yea, and your nay, nay; for whatsoever is more than these cometh of evil." [1796] And that we ought to worship God alone, He thus persuaded us: "The greatest commandment is, Thou shalt worship the Lord thy God, and Him only shalt thou serve, with all thy heart, and with all thy strength, the Lord God that made thee." [1797] And when a certain man came to Him and said, "Good Master," He answered and said, "There is none good but God only, who made all things." [1798] And let those who are not found living as He taught, be understood to be no Christians, even though they profess with the lip the precepts of Christ; for not those who make profession, but those who do the works, shall be saved, according to His word: "Not every one who saith to Me, Lord, Lord, shall enter into the kingdom of heaven, but he that doeth the will of My Father which is in heaven. For whosoever heareth Me, and doeth My sayings, heareth Him that sent Me. And many will say unto Me, Lord, Lord, have we not eaten and drunk in Thy name, and done wonders? And then will I say unto them, Depart from Me, ye workers of iniquity. Then shall there be wailing and gnashing of teeth, when the righteous shall shine as the sun, and the wicked are sent into everlasting fire. For many shall come in My name, clothed outwardly in sheep's clothing, but inwardly being ravening wolves. By their works ye shall know them. And every tree that bringeth not forth good fruit, is hewn down and cast into the fire." [1799] And as to those who are not living pursuant to these His teachings, and are Christians only in name, we demand that all such be punished by you.

Chapter XVII - Christ taught civil obedience

And everywhere we, more readily than all men, endeavour to pay to those appointed by you the taxes both ordinary and extraordinary, [1800] as we have been taught by Him; for at that time some came to Him and asked Him, if one ought to pay tribute to Cæsar; and He answered, "Tell Me, whose image does the coin bear?" And they said, "Cæsar's." And again He answered them, "Render therefore to Cæsar the things that are Cæsar's, and to God the things that are God's." [1801] Whence to God alone we render worship, but in other things we gladly serve you, acknowledging you as kings and rulers of men, and praying that with your kingly power you be found to possess also sound judgment. But if you pay no regard to our prayers and frank explanations, we shall suffer no loss, since we believe (or rather, indeed, are persuaded) that every man will suffer punishment in eternal fire according to the merit of his deed, and will render account according to the power he has received from God, as Christ intimated when He said, "To whom God has given more, of him shall more be required." [1802]

Chapter XVIII - Proof of immortality and the resurrection

For reflect upon the end of each of the preceding kings, how they died the death common to all, which, if it issued in insensibility, would be a godsend [1803] to all the wicked. But since sensation remains to all who have ever lived, and eternal punishment is laid up (i.e., for the wicked), see that ye neglect not to be convinced, and to hold as your belief, that these things are true. For let even necromancy, and the divinations you practise by immaculate children, [1804] and the evoking of departed human souls, [1805] and those who are called among the magi, Dream-senders and Assistant-spirits (Familiars), [1806] and all that is done by those who are skilled in such matters --let these persuade you that even after death souls are in a state of sensation; and those who are seized and cast about by the spirits of the dead, whom all call dæmoniacs or madmen; [1807] and what you repute as oracles, both of Amphilochus, Dodana, Pytho, and as many other such as exist; and the opinions of your authors, Empedocles and Pythagoras, Plato and Socrates, and the pit of Homer, [1808] and the descent of Ulysses to inspect these things, and all that has been uttered of a like kind. Such favour as you grant to these, grant also to us, who not less but more firmly than they believe in God; since we expect to receive again our own bodies, though they be dead and cast into the earth, for we maintain that with God nothing is impossible.

Chapter XIX - The resurrection possible

And to any thoughtful person would anything appear more incredible, than, if we were not in the body, and some one were to say that it was possible that from a small drop of human seed bones and sinews and flesh be formed into a shape such as we see? For let this now be said hypothetically: if you yourselves were not such as you now are, and born of such parents [and causes], and one were to show you human seed and a picture of a man, and were to say with confidence that from such a substance such a being could be produced, would you believe before you saw the actual production? No one will dare to deny [that such a statement would surpass belief]. In the same way, then, you are now incredulous because you have never seen a dead man rise again. But as at first you would not have believed it possible that such persons could be produced from the small drop, and yet now you see them thus produced, so also judge ye that it is not impossible that the bodies of men, after they have been dissolved, and like seeds resolved into earth, should in God's appointed time rise again and put on incorruption. For what power worthy of God those imagine who say, that each thing returns to that from which it was produced, and that beyond this not even God Himself can do anything, we are unable to conceive; but this we see clearly, that they would not have believed it possible that they could have become such and produced from such materials, as they now see both themselves and the whole world to be. And that it is better to believe even what is impossible to our own nature and to men, than to be unbelieving like the rest of the world, we have learned; for we know that our Master Jesus Christ said, that "what is impossible with men is possible with God," [1809] and, "Fear not them that kill you, and after that can do no more; but fear Him who after death is able to cast both soul and body into hell." [1810] And hell is a place where those are to be punished who have lived wickedly, and who do not believe that those things which God has taught us by Christ will come to pass.

Chapter XX - Heathen analogies to Christian doctrine

And the Sibyl [1811] and Hystaspes said that there should be a dissolution by God of things corruptible. And the philosophers called Stoics teach that even God Himself shall be resolved into fire, and they say that the world is to be formed anew by this revolution; but we understand that God, the Creator of all things, is superior to the things that are to be changed. If, therefore, on some points we teach the same things as the poets and philosophers whom you honour, and on other points are fuller and more divine in our teaching, and if we alone afford proof of what we assert, why are we unjustly hated more than all others? For while we say that all things have been produced and arranged into a world by God, we shall seem to utter the doctrine of Plato; and while we say that there will be a burning up of all, we shall seem to utter the doctrine of the Stoics: and while we affirm that the souls of the wicked, being endowed with sensation even after death, are punished, and that those of the good being delivered from punishment spend a blessed existence, we shall seem to say the same things as the poets and philosophers; and while we maintain that men ought not to worship the works of their hands, we say the very things which have been said by the comic poet Menander, and other similar writers, for they have declared that the workman is greater than the work.

Chapter XXI - Analogies to the history of Christ

And when we say also that the Word, who is the first-birth [1812] of God, was produced without sexual union, and that He, Jesus Christ, our Teacher, was crucified and died, and rose again, and ascended into heaven, we propound nothing different from what you believe regarding those whom you esteem sons of Jupiter. For you know how many sons your esteemed writers ascribed to Jupiter: Mercury, the interpreting word and teacher of all; Æsculapius, who, though he was a great physician, was struck by a thunderbolt, and so ascended to heaven; and Bacchus too, after he had been torn limb from limb; and Hercules, when he had committed himself to the flames to escape his toils; and the sons of Leda, and Dioscuri; and Perseus, son of Danae; and Bellerophon, who, though sprung from mortals, rose to heaven on the horse Pegasus. For what shall I say of Ariadne, and those who, like her, have been declared to be set among the stars? And what of the emperors who die among yourselves, whom you deem worthy of deification, and in whose behalf you produce some one who swears he has seen the burning Cæsar rise to heaven from the funeral pyre? And what kind of deeds are recorded of each of these reputed sons of Jupiter, it is needless to tell to those who already know. This only shall be said, that they are written for the advantage and encouragement [1813] of youthful scholars; for all reckon it an honourable thing to imitate the gods. But far be such a thought concerning the gods from every well-conditioned soul, as to believe that Jupiter himself, the governor and creator of all things, was both a parricide and the son of a parricide, and that being overcome by the love of base and shameful pleasures, he came in to Ganymede and those many women whom he had violated and that his sons did like actions. But, as we said above, wicked devils perpetrated these things. And we have learned that those only are deified who have lived near to God in holiness and virtue; and we believe that those who live wickedly and do not repent are punished in everlasting fire.

Chapter XXII - Analogies to the sonship of Christ

Moreover, the Son of God called Jesus, even if only a man by ordinary generation, yet, on account of His wisdom, is worthy to be called the Son of God; for all writers call God the Father of men and gods. And if we assert that the Word of God was born of God in a peculiar manner, different from ordinary generation, let this, as said above, be no extraordinary thing to you, who say that Mercury is the angelic word of God. But if any one objects that He was crucified, in this also He is on a par with those reputed sons of Jupiter of yours, who suffered as we have now enumerated. For their sufferings at death are recorded to have been not all alike, but diverse; so that not even by the peculiarity of His sufferings does He seem to be inferior to them; but, on the contrary, as we promised in the preceding part of this discourse, we will now prove Him superior-- or rather have already proved Him to be so--for the superior is revealed by His actions. And if we even affirm that He was born of a virgin, accept this in common with what you accept of Perseus. And in that we say that He made whole the lame, the paralytic, and those born blind, we seem to say what is very similar to the deeds said to have been done by Æsculapius.

Chapter XXIII - The argument

And that this may now become evident to you--(firstly [1814]) that whatever we assert in conformity with what has been taught us by Christ, and by the prophets who preceded Him, are alone true, and are older than all the writers who have existed; that we claim to be acknowledged, not because we say the same things as these writers said, but because we say true things: and (secondly) that Jesus Christ is the only proper Son who has been begotten by God, being His Word and first-begotten, and power; and, becoming man according to His will, He taught us these things for the conversion and restoration of the human race: and (thirdly) that before He became a man among men, some, influenced by the demons before mentioned, related beforehand, through the instrumentality of the poets, those circumstances as having really happened, which, having fictitiously devised, they narrated, in the same manner as they have caused to be fabricated the scandalous reports against us of infamous and impious actions, [1815] of which there is neither witness nor proof--we shall bring forward the following proof.

Chapter XXIV - Varieties of heathen worship

In the first place [we furnish proof], because, though we say things similar to what the Greeks say, we only are hated on account of the name of Christ, and though we do no wrong, are put to death as sinners; other men in other places worshipping trees and rivers, and mice and cats and crocodiles, and many irrational animals. Nor are the same animals esteemed by all; but in one place one is worshipped, and another in another, so that all are profane in the judgment of one another, on account of their not worshipping the same objects. And this is the sole accusation you bring against us, that we do not reverence the same gods as you do, nor offer to the dead libations and the savour of fat, and crowns for their statues, [1816] and sacrifices. For you very well know that the same animals are with some esteemed gods, with others wild beasts, and with others sacrificial victims.

Chapter XXV - False Gods abandoned by Christians

And, secondly, because we--who, out of every race of men, used to worship Bacchus the son of Semele, and Apollo the son of Latona (who in their loves with men did such things as it is shameful even to mention), and Proserpine and Venus (who were maddened with love of Adonis, and whose mysteries also you celebrate), or Æsculapius, or some one or other of those who are called gods--have now, through Jesus Christ, learned to despise these, though we be threatened with death for it, and have dedicated ourselves to the unbegotten and impossible God; of whom we are persuaded that never was he goaded by lust of Antiope, or such other women, or of Ganymede, nor was rescued by that hundred-handed giant whose aid was obtained through Thetis, nor was anxious on this account [1817] that her son Achilles should destroy many of the Greeks because of his concubine Briseis. Those who believe these things we pity, and those who invented them we know to be devils.

Chapter XXVI - Magicians not trusted by Christians

And, thirdly, because after Christ's ascension into heaven the devils put forward certain men who said that they themselves were gods; and they were not only not persecuted by you, but even deemed worthy of honours. There was a Samaritan, Simon, a native of the village called Gitto, who in the reign of Claudius Cæsar, and in your royal city of Rome, did mighty acts of magic, by virtue of the art of the devils operating in him. He was considered a god, and as a god was honoured by you with a statue, which statue was erected on the river Tiber, between the two bridges, and bore this inscription, in the language of Rome:--"Simoni Deo Sancto," [1818] "To Simon the holy God." And almost all the Samaritans, and a few even of other nations, worship him, and acknowledge him as the first god; and a woman, Helena, who went about with him at that time, and had formerly been a prostitute, they say is the first idea generated by him. And a man, Menander, also a Samaritan, of the town Capparetæa, a disciple of Simon, and inspired by devils, we know to have deceived many while he was in Antioch by his magical art. He persuaded those who adhered to him that they should never die, and even now there are some living who hold this opinion of his. And there is Marcion, a man of Pontus, who is even at this day alive, and teaching his disciples to believe in some other god greater than the Creator. And he, by the aid of the devils, has caused many of every nation to speak blasphemies, and to deny that God is the maker of this universe, and to assert that some other being, greater than He, has done greater works. All who take their opinions from these men, are, as we before said, [1819] called Christians; just as also those who do not agree with the philosophers in their doctrines, have yet in common with them the name of philosophers given to them. And whether they perpetrate those fabulous and shameful deeds [1820] --the upsetting of the lamp, and promiscuous intercourse, and eating human flesh--we know not; but we do know that they are neither persecuted nor put to death by you, at least on account of their opinions. But I have a treatise against all the heresies that have existed already composed, which, if you wish to read it, I will give you.

Chapter XXVII - Guilt of exposing children

But as for us, we have been taught that to expose newly-born children is the part of wicked men; and this we have been taught lest we should do any one an injury, and lest we should sin against God, first, because we see that almost all so exposed (not only the girls, but also the males) are brought up to prostitution. And as the ancients are said to have reared herds of oxen, or goats, or sheep, or grazing horses, so now we see you rear children only for this shameful use; and for this pollution a multitude of females and hermaphrodites, and those who commit unmentionable iniquities, are found in every nation. And you receive the hire of these, and duty and taxes from them, whom you ought to exterminate from your realm. And any one who uses such persons, besides the godless and infamous and impure intercourse, may possibly be having intercourse with his own child, or relative, or brother. And there are some who prostitute even their own children and wives, and some are openly mutilated for the purpose of sodomy; and they refer these mysteries to the mother of the gods, and along with each of those whom you esteem gods there is painted a serpent, [1821] a great symbol and mystery. Indeed, the things [1822] which you do openly and with applause, as if the divine light were overturned and extinguished, these you lay to our charge; which, in truth, does no harm to us who shrink from doing any such things, but only to those who do them and bear false witness against us.

Chapter XXVIII - God's care for men

For among us the prince of the wicked spirits is called the serpent, and Satan, and the devil, as you can learn by looking into our writings. And that he would be sent into the fire with his host, and the men who follow him, and would be punished for an endless duration, Christ foretold. For the reason why God has delayed to do this, is His regard for the human race. For He foreknows that some are to be saved by repentance, some even that are perhaps not yet born. [1823] In the beginning He made the human race with the power of thought and of choosing the truth and doing right, so that all men are without excuse before God; for they have been born rational and contemplative. And if any one disbelieves that God cares for these things, [1824] he will thereby either insinuate that God does not exist, or he will assert that though He exists He delights in vice, or exists like a stone, and that neither virtue nor vice are anything, but only in the opinion of men these things are reckoned good or evil. And this is the greatest profanity and wickedness.

Chapter XXIX - Continence of Christians

And again [we fear to expose children], lest some of them be not picked up, but die, and we become murderers. But whether we marry, it is only that we may bring up children; or whether we decline marriage, we live continently. And that you may understand that promiscuous intercourse is not one of our mysteries, one of our number a short time ago presented to Felix the governor in Alexandria a petition, craving that permission might be given to a surgeon to make him an eunuch. For the surgeons there said that they were forbidden to do this without the permission of the governor. And when Felix absolutely refused to sign such a permission, the youth remained single, and was satisfied with his own approving conscience, and the approval of those who thought as he did. And it is not out of place, we think, to mention here Antinous, who was alive but lately, and whom all were prompt, through fear, to worship as a god, though they knew both who he was and what was his origin. [1825]

Chapter XXX - Was Christ not a magician?

But lest any one should meet us with the question, What should prevent that He whom we call Christ, being a man born of men, performed what we call His mighty works by magical art, and by this appeared to be the Son of God? we will now offer proof, not trusting mere assertions, but being of necessity persuaded by those who prophesied [of Him] before these things came to pass, for with our own eyes we behold things that have happened and are happening just as they were predicted; and this will, we think appear even to you the strongest and truest evidence.

Chapter XXXI - Of the Hebrew prophets

There were, then, among the Jews certain men who were prophets of God, through whom the prophetic Spirit published beforehand things that were to come to pass, ere ever they happened. And their prophecies, as they were spoken and when they were uttered, the kings who happened to be reigning among the Jews at the several times carefully preserved in their possession, when they had been arranged in books by the prophets themselves in their own Hebrew language. And when

Ptolemy king of Egypt formed a library, and endeavoured to collect the writings of all men, he heard also of these prophets, and sent to Herod, who was at that time king of the Jews, [1826] requesting that the books of the prophets be sent to him. And Herod the king did indeed send them, written, as they were, in the foresaid Hebrew language. And when their contents were found to be unintelligible to the Egyptians, he again sent and requested that men be commissioned to translate them into the Greek language. And when this was done, the books remained with the Egyptians, where they are until now. They are also in the possession of all Jews throughout the world; but they, though they read, do not understand what is said, but count us foes and enemies; and, like yourselves, they kill and punish us whenever they have the power, as you can well believe. For in the Jewish war which lately raged, Barchochebas, the leader of the revolt of the Jews, gave orders that Christians alone should be led to cruel punishments, unless they would deny Jesus Christ and utter blasphemy. In these books, then, of the prophets we found Jesus our Christ foretold as coming, born of a virgin, growing up to man's estate, and healing every disease and every sickness, and raising the dead, and being hated, and unrecognised, and crucified, and dying, and rising again, and ascending into heaven, and being, and being called, the Son of God. We find it also predicted that certain persons should be sent by Him into every nation to publish these things, and that rather among the Gentiles [than among the Jews] men should believe on Him. And He was predicted before He appeared, first 5000 years before, and again 3000, then 2000, then 1000, and yet again 800; for in the succession of generations prophets after prophets arose.

Chapter XXXII - Christ predicted by Moses

Moses then, who was the first of the prophets, spoke in these very words: "The sceptre shall not depart from Judah, nor a lawgiver from between his feet, until He come for whom it is reserved; and He shall be the desire of the nations, binding His foal to the vine, washing His robe in the blood of the grape." [1827] It is yours to make accurate inquiry, and ascertain up to whose time the Jews had a lawgiver and king of their own. Up to the time of Jesus Christ, who taught us, and interpreted the prophecies which were not yet understood, [they had a lawgiver] as was foretold by the holy and divine Spirit of prophecy through Moses, "that a ruler would not fail the Jews until He should come for whom the kingdom was reserved" (for Judah was the forefather of the Jews, from whom also they have their name of Jews); and after He (i.e., Christ) appeared, you began to rule the Jews, and gained possession of all their territory. And the prophecy, "He shall be the expectation of the nations," signified that there would be some of all nations who should look for Him to come again. And this indeed you can see for yourselves, and be convinced of by fact. For of all races of men there are some who look for Him who was crucified in Judæa, and after whose crucifixion the land was straightway surrendered to you as spoil of war. And the prophecy, "binding His foal to the vine, and washing His robe in the blood of the grape," was a significant symbol of the things that were to happen to Christ, and of what He was to do. For the foal of an ass stood bound to a vine at the entrance of a village, and He ordered His acquaintances to bring it to Him then; and when it was brought, He mounted and sat upon it, and entered Jerusalem, where was the vast temple of the Jews which was afterwards destroyed by you. And after this He was crucified, that the rest of the prophecy might be fulfilled. For this "washing His robe in the blood of the grape" was predictive of the passion He was to endure, cleansing by His blood those who believe on Him. For what is called by the Divine Spirit through the prophet "His robe," are those men who believe in Him in whom abideth the seed [1828] of God, the Word. And what is spoken of as "the blood of the grape," signifies that He who should appear would have blood, though not of the seed of man, but of the power of God. And the first power after God the Father and Lord of all is the Word, who is also the Son; and of Him we will, in what follows, relate how He took flesh and became man. For as man did not make the blood of the vine, but God, so it was hereby intimated that the blood should not be of human seed, but of divine power, as we have said above. And Isaiah, another prophet, foretelling the same things in other words, spoke thus: "A star shall rise out of Jacob, and a flower shall spring from the root of Jesse; and His arm shall the nations trust." [1829] And a star of light has arisen, and a flower has sprung from the root of Jesse--this Christ. For by the power of God He was conceived by a virgin of the seed of Jacob, who was the father of Judah, who, as we have shown, was the father of the Jews; and Jesse was His forefather according to the oracle, and He was the son of Jacob and Judah according to lineal descent.

Chapter XXXIII - Manner of Christ's birth predicted

And hear again how Isaiah in express words foretold that He should be born of a virgin; for he spoke thus: "Behold, a virgin shall conceive, and bring forth a son, and they shall say for His name, God with us.'" [1830] For things which were incredible and seemed impossible with men, these God predicted by the Spirit of prophecy as about to come to pass, in order that, when they came to pass, there might be no unbelief, but faith, because of their prediction. But lest some, not understanding the prophecy now cited, should charge us with the very things we have been laying to the charge of the poets who say that Jupiter went in to women through lust, let us try to explain the words. This, then, "Behold, a virgin shall conceive," signifies that a virgin should conceive without intercourse. For if she had had intercourse with any one whatever, she was no longer a virgin; but the power of God having come upon the virgin, overshadowed her, and caused her while yet a virgin to conceive. And the angel of God who was sent to the same virgin at that time brought her good news, saying, "Behold, thou shalt conceive of the Holy Ghost, and shalt bear a Son, and He shall be called the Son of the Highest, and thou shalt call His name Jesus; for He shall save His people from their sins," [1831] --as they who have recorded all that concerns our Saviour Jesus Christ have taught, whom we believed, since by Isaiah also, whom we have now adduced, the Spirit of prophecy declared that He should be born as we intimated before. It is wrong, therefore, to understand the Spirit and the power of God as anything else than the Word, who is also the first-born of God, as the foresaid prophet Moses declared; and it was this which, when it came upon the virgin and overshadowed her, caused her to conceive, not by intercourse, but by power. And the name Jesus in the Hebrew language means Σωτήρ (Saviour) in the Greek tongue. Wherefore, too, the angel said to the virgin, "Thou shalt call His name Jesus, for He shall save His people from their sins." And that the prophets are inspired [1832] by no other than the Divine Word, even you, as I fancy, will grant.

Chapter XXXIV - Place of Christ's birth foretold

And hear what part of earth He was to be born in, as another prophet, Micah, foretold. He spoke thus: "And thou, Bethlehem, the land of Judah, art not the least among the princes of Judah; for out of thee shall come forth a Governor, who shall feed My people." [1833] Now there is a village in the land of the Jews, thirty-five stadia from Jerusalem, in which Jesus Christ was born, as you can ascertain also from the registers of the taxing made under Cyrenius, your first procurator in Judæa.

Chapter XXXV - Other fulfilled prophecies

And how Christ after He was born was to escape the notice of other men until He grew to man's estate, which also came to pass, hear what was foretold regarding this. There are the following predictions: [1834] --"Unto us a child is born, and unto us a young man is given, and the government shall be upon His shoulders;" [1835] which is significant of the power of the cross, for to it, when He was crucified, He applied His shoulders, as shall be more clearly made out in the ensuing discourse. And again the same prophet Isaiah, being inspired by the prophetic Spirit, said, "I have spread out my hands to a disobedient and gainsaying people, to those who walk in a way that is not good. They now ask of me judgment, and dare to draw near to God." [1836] And again in other words, through another prophet, He says, "They pierced My hands and My feet, and for My vesture they cast lots." [1837] And indeed David, the king and prophet, who uttered these things, suffered none of them; but Jesus Christ stretched forth His hands, being crucified by the Jews speaking against Him, and denying that He was the Christ. And as the prophet spoke, they tormented Him, and set Him on the judgment-seat, and said, Judge us. And the expression, "They pierced my hands and my feet," was used in reference to the nails of the cross which were fixed in His hands and feet. And after He was crucified they cast lots upon His vesture, and they that crucified Him parted it among them. And that these things did happen, you can ascertain from the Acts of Pontius Pilate. [1838] And we will cite the prophetic utterances of another prophet, Zephaniah,[1839] to the effect that He was foretold expressly as to sit upon the foal of an ass and to enter Jerusalem. The words are these: "Rejoice greatly, O daughter of Zion; shout, O daughter of Jerusalem: behold, thy King cometh unto thee; lowly, and riding upon an ass, and upon a colt the foal of an ass." [1840]

Chapter XXXVI - Different modes of prophecy

But when you hear the utterances of the prophets spoken as it were personally, you must not suppose that they are spoken by the inspired themselves, but by the Divine Word who moves them. For sometimes He declares things that are to come to pass, in the manner of one who foretells the future; sometimes He speaks as from the person of God the Lord and Father of all; sometimes as from the person of Christ; sometimes as from the person of the people answering the Lord or His Father, just as you can see even in your own writers, one man being the writer of the whole, but introducing the persons who converse. And this the Jews who possessed the books of the prophets did not understand, and therefore did not recognise Christ even when He came, but even hate us who say that He has come, and who prove that, as was predicted, He was crucified by them.

Chapter XXXVII - Utterances of the Father

And that this too may be clear to you, there were spoken from the person of the Father through Isaiah the prophet, the following words: "The ox knoweth his owner, and the ass his master's crib; but Israel doth not know, and My people hath not understood. Woe, sinful nation, a people full of sins, a wicked seed, children that are transgressors, ye have forsaken the Lord." [1841] And again elsewhere, when the same prophet speaks in like manner from the person of the Father, "What is the house that ye will build for Me? saith the Lord. The heaven is My throne, and the earth is My footstool." [1842] And again, in another place, "Your new moons and your sabbaths My soul hateth; and the great day of the fast and of ceasing from labour I cannot away with; nor, if ye come to be seen of Me, will I hear you: your hands are full of blood; and if ye bring fine flour, incense, it is abomination unto Me: the fat of lambs and the blood of bulls I do not desire. For who hath required this at your hands? But loose every bond of wickedness, tear asunder the tight knots of violent contracts, cover the houseless and naked, deal thy bread to the hungry." [1843] What kind of things are taught through the prophets from [the person of] God, you can now perceive.

Chapter XXXVIII - Utterances of the Son

And when the Spirit of prophecy speaks from the person of Christ, the utterances are of this sort: "I have spread out My hands to a disobedient and gainsaying people, to those who walk in a way that is not good." [1844] And again: "I gave My back to the scourges, and My cheeks to the buffetings; I turned not away My face from the shame of spittings; and the Lord was My helper: therefore was I not confounded: but I set My face as a firm rock; and I knew that I should not be ashamed, for He is near that justifieth Me." [1845] And again, when He says, "They cast lots upon My vesture, and pierced My hands and My feet. And I lay down and slept, and rose again, because the Lord sustained Me." [1846] And again, when He says, "They spake with their lips, they wagged the head, saying, Let Him deliver Himself." [1847] And that all these things happened to Christ at the hands of the Jews, you can ascertain. For when He was crucified, they did shoot out the lip, and wagged their heads, saying, "Let Him who raised the dead save Himself." [1848]

Chapter XXXIX - Direct predictions by the Spirit

And when the Spirit of prophecy speaks as predicting things that are to come to pass, He speaks in this way: "For out of Zion shall go forth the law, and the word of the Lord from Jerusalem. And He shall judge among the nations, and shall rebuke many people; and they shall beat their swords into ploughshares, and their spears into pruning-hooks: nation shall not lift up sword against nation, neither shall they learn war any more." [1849] And that it did so come to pass, we can convince you. For from Jerusalem there went out into the world, men, twelve in number, and these illiterate, of no ability in speaking: but by the power of God they proclaimed to every race of men that they were sent by Christ to teach to all the word of God; and we who formerly used to murder one another do not only now refrain from making war upon our enemies, but also, that we may not lie nor deceive our examiners, willingly die confessing Christ. For that saying, "The tongue has sworn, but the mind is unsworn," [1850] might be imitated by us in this matter. But if the soldiers enrolled by you, and who have taken the military oath, prefer their allegiance to their own life, and parents, and country, and all kindred, though you can offer them nothing incorruptible, it were verily ridiculous if we, who earnestly long for incorruption, should not endure all things, in order to obtain what we desire from Him who is able to grant it.

Chapter XL - Christ's advent foretold

And hear how it was foretold concerning those who published His doctrine and proclaimed His appearance, the above-mentioned prophet and king speaking thus by the Spirit of prophecy "Day unto day uttereth speech, and night unto night showeth knowledge. There is no speech nor language where their voice is not heard. Their voice has gone out into all the earth, and their words to the ends of the world. In the sun hath He set His tabernacle, and he as a bridegroom going out of his chamber shall rejoice as a giant to run his course." [1851] And we have thought it right and relevant to mention some other prophetic utterances of David besides these; from which you may learn how the Spirit of prophecy exhorts men to live, and how He foretold the conspiracy which was formed against Christ by Herod the king of the Jews, and the Jews themselves, and Pilate, who was your governor among them, with his soldiers; and how He should be believed on by men of every race; and how God calls Him His Son, and has declared that He will subdue all His enemies under Him; and how the devils, as much as they can, strive to escape the power of God the Father and Lord of all, and the power of Christ Himself; and how God calls all to repentance before the day of judgment comes. These things were uttered thus: "Blessed is the man who hath not walked in the counsel of the ungodly, nor stood in the way of sinners, nor sat in the seat of the scornful: but his delight is in the law of the Lord; and in His law will he meditate day and night. And he shall be like a tree planted by the rivers of waters, which shall give his fruit in his season; and his leaf shall not wither, and whatsoever he doeth shall prosper. The ungodly are not so, but are like the chaff which the wind driveth away from the face of the earth. Therefore the ungodly shall not stand in the judgment, nor sinners in the council of the righteous. For the Lord knoweth the way of the righteous; but the way of the ungodly shall perish. Why do the heathen rage, and the people imagine new things? The kings of the earth set themselves, and the rulers take counsel together, against the Lord, and against His Anointed, saying, Let us break their bands asunder, and cast their yoke from us. He that dwelleth in the heavens shall laugh at them, and the Lord shall have them in derision. Then shall He speak to them in His wrath, and vex them in His sore displeasure. Yet have I been set by Him a King on Zion His holy hill, declaring the decree of the Lord. The Lord said to Me, Thou art My Son; this day have I begotten Thee. Ask of Me, and I shall give Thee the heathen for Thine inheritance, and the uttermost parts of the earth as Thy possession. Thou shall herd them with a rod of iron; as the vessels of a potter shalt Thou dash them in pieces. Be wise now, therefore, O ye kings; be instructed, all ye judges of the earth. Serve the Lord with fear, and rejoice with trembling. Embrace instruction, lest at any time the Lord be angry, and ye perish from the right way, when His wrath has been suddenly kindled. Blessed are all they that put their trust in Him."[1852]

Chapter XLI - The crucifixion predicted

And again, in another prophecy, the Spirit of prophecy, through the same David, intimated that Christ, after He had been crucified, should reign, and spoke as follows: "Sing to the Lord, all the earth, and day by day declare His salvation. For great is the Lord, and greatly to be praised, to be feared above all the gods. For all the gods of the nations are idols of devils; but God made the heavens. Glory and praise are before His face, strength and glorying are in the habitation of His holiness. Give Glory to the Lord, the Father everlasting. Receive grace, and enter His presence, and worship in His holy courts. Let all the earth fear before His face; let it be established, and not shaken. Let them rejoice among the nations. The Lord hath reigned from the tree." [1853]

Chapter XLII - Prophecy using the past tense

But when the Spirit of prophecy speaks of things that are about to come to pass as if they had already taken place, --as may be observed even in the passages already cited by me, --that this circumstance may afford no excuse to readers [for misinterpreting them], we will make even this also quite plain. The things which He absolutely knows will take place, He predicts as if already they had taken place. And that the utterances must be thus received, you will perceive, if you give your attention to them. The words cited above, David uttered 1500 [1854] years before Christ became a man and was crucified; and no one of those who lived before Him, nor yet of His contemporaries, afforded joy to the Gentiles by being crucified. But our Jesus Christ, being crucified and dead, rose again, and having ascended to heaven, reigned; and by those things which were published in His name among all nations by the apostles, there is joy afforded to those who expect the immortality promised by Him.

Chapter XLIII - Responsibility asserted

But lest some suppose, from what has been said by us, that we say that whatever happens, happens by a fatal necessity, because it is foretold as known beforehand, this too we explain. We have learned from the prophets, and we hold it to be true, that punishments, and chastisements, and good rewards, are rendered according to the merit of each man's actions. Since if it be not so, but all things happen by fate, neither is anything at all in our own power. For if it be fated that this man, e.g., be good, and this other evil, neither is the former meritorious nor the latter to be blamed. And again, unless the human race have the power of avoiding evil and choosing good by free choice, they are not accountable for their actions, of whatever kind they be. But that it is by free choice they both walk uprightly and stumble, we thus demonstrate. We see the same man making a transition to opposite things. Now, if it had been fated that he were to be either good or bad, he could never have been capable of both the opposites, nor of so many transitions. But not even would some be good and others bad, since we thus make fate the cause of evil, and exhibit her as acting in opposition to herself; or that which has been already stated would seem to be true, that neither virtue nor vice is anything, but that things are only reckoned good or evil by opinion; which, as the true word shows, is the greatest impiety and wickedness. But this we assert is inevitable fate, that they who choose the good have worthy rewards, and they who choose the opposite have their merited awards. For not like other things, as trees and quadrupeds, which cannot act by choice, did God make man: for neither would he be worthy of reward or praise did he not of himself choose the good, but were created for this end; [1855] nor, if he were evil, would he be worthy of punishment, not being evil of himself, but being able to be nothing else than what he was made.

Chapter XLIV - Not nullified by prophecy

And the holy Spirit of prophecy taught us this, telling us by Moses that God spoke thus to the man first created: "Behold, before thy face are good and evil: choose the good." [1856] And again, by the other prophet Isaiah, that the following utterance was made as if from God the Father and Lord of all: "Wash you, make you clean; put away evils from your souls; learn to do well; judge the orphan, and plead for the widow: and come and let us reason together, saith the Lord: And if your sins be as scarlet, I will make them white as wool; and if they be red like as crimson, I will make them white as snow. And if ye be willing and obey Me, ye shall eat the good of the land; but if ye do not obey Me, the sword shall devour you: for the mouth of the Lord hath spoken it." [1857] And that expression, "The sword shall devour you," does not mean that the disobedient shall be slain by the sword, but the sword of God is fire, of which they who choose to do wickedly become the fuel. Wherefore He says, "The sword shall devour you: for the mouth of the Lord hath spoken it." And if He had spoken concerning a sword that cuts and at once despatches, He would not have said, shall devour. And so, too, Plato, when he says, "The blame is his who chooses, and God is blameless,"[1858] took this from the prophet Moses and uttered it. For Moses is more ancient than all the Greek writers. And whatever both philosophers and poets have said concerning the immortality of the soul, or punishments after death, or contemplation of things heavenly, or doctrines of the like kind, they have received such suggestions from the prophets as have enabled them to understand and interpret these things. And hence there seem to be seeds of truth among all men; but they are charged with not accurately understanding [the truth] when they assert contradictories. So that what we say about future events being foretold, we do not say it as if they came about by a fatal necessity; but God foreknowing all that shall be done by all men, and it being His decree that the future actions of men shall all be recompensed according to their several value, He foretells by the Spirit of prophecy that He will bestow meet rewards according to the merit of the actions done, always urging the human race to effort and recollection, showing that He cares and provides for men. But by the agency of the devils death has been decreed against those who read the books of Hystaspes, or of the Sibyl, [1859] or of the prophets, that through fear they may prevent men who read them from receiving the knowledge of the good, and may retain them in slavery to themselves; which, however, they could not always effect. For not only do we fearlessly read them, but, as you see, bring them for your inspection, knowing that their contents will be pleasing to all. And if we persuade even a few, our gain will be very great; for, as good husbandmen, we shall receive the reward from the Master.

Chapter XLV - Christ's session in heaven foretold

And that God the Father of all would bring Christ to heaven after He had raised Him from the dead, and would keep Him there [1860] until He has subdued His enemies the devils, and until the number of those who are foreknown by Him as good and virtuous is complete, on whose account He has still delayed the consummation--hear what was said by the prophet David. These are his words: "The Lord said unto My Lord, Sit Thou at My right hand, until I make Thine enemies Thy footstool. The Lord shall send to Thee the rod of power out of Jerusalem; and rule Thou in the midst of Thine enemies. With Thee is the government in the day of Thy power, in the beauties of Thy saints: from the womb of morning [1861] have I begotten Thee." [1862] That which he says, "He shall send to Thee the rod of power out of Jerusalem," is predictive of the mighty word, which His apostles, going forth from Jerusalem, preached everywhere; and though death is decreed against those who teach or at all confess the name of Christ, we everywhere both embrace and teach it. And if you also read these words in a hostile spirit, ye can do no more, as I said before, than kill us; which indeed does no harm to us, but to you and all who unjustly hate us, and do not repent, brings eternal punishment by fire.

Chapter XLVI - The Word in the world before Christ

But lest some should, without reason, and for the perversion of what we teach, maintain that we say that Christ was born one hundred and fifty years ago under Cyrenius, and subsequently, in the time of Pontius Pilate, taught what we say He taught; and should cry out against us as though all men who were born before Him were irresponsible--let let us anticipate and solve the difficulty. We have been taught that Christ is the first-born of God, and we have declared above that He is the Word of whom every race of men were partakers; and those who lived reasonably [1863] are Christians, even though they have been thought atheists; as, among the Greeks, Socrates and Heraclitus, and men like them; and among the barbarians, Abraham, and Ananias, and Azarias, and Mishael, and Elias, and many others whose actions and names we now decline to recount, because we know it would be tedious. So that even they who lived before Christ, and lived without reason, were wicked and hostile to Christ, and slew those who lived reasonably. But who, through the power of the Word, according to the will of God the Father and Lord of all, He was born of a virgin

The Apostolic Fathers

as a man, and was named Jesus, and was crucified, and died, and rose again, and ascended into heaven, an intelligent man will be able to comprehend from what has been already so largely said. And we, since the proof of this subject is less needful now, will pass for the present to the proof of those things which are urgent.

Chapter XLVII - Desolation of Judæa foretold

That the land of the Jews, then, was to be laid waste, hear what was said by the Spirit of prophecy. And the words were spoken as if from the person of the people wondering at what had happened. They are these: "Sion is a wilderness, Jerusalem a desolation. The house of our sanctuary has become a curse, and the glory which our fathers blessed is burned up with fire, and all its glorious things are laid waste: and Thou refrainest Thyself at these things, and hast held Thy peace, and hast humbled us very sore." [1864] And ye are convinced that Jerusalem has been laid waste, as was predicted. And concerning its desolation, and that no one should be permitted to inhabit it, there was the following prophecy by Isaiah: "Their land is desolate, their enemies consume it before them, and none of them shall dwell therein." [1865] And that it is guarded by you lest any one dwell in it, and that death is decreed against a Jew apprehended entering it, you know very well. [1866]

Chapter XLVIII - Christ's work and death foretold

And that it was predicted that our Christ should heal all diseases and raise the dead, hear what was said. There are these words: "At His coming the lame shall leap as an hart, and the tongue of the stammerer shall be clear speaking: the blind shall see, and the lepers shall be cleansed; and the dead shall rise, and walk about." [1867] And that He did those things, you can learn from the Acts of Pontius Pilate. And how it was predicted by the Spirit of prophecy that He and those who hoped in Him should be slain, hear what was said by Isaiah. These are the words: "Behold now the righteous perisheth, and no man layeth it to heart; and just men are taken away, and no man considereth. From the presence of wickedness is the righteous man taken, and his burial shall be in peace: he is taken from our midst." [1868]

Chapter XLIX - His rejection by the Jews foretold

And again, how it was said by the same Isaiah, that the Gentile nations who were not looking for Him should worship Him, but the Jews who always expected Him should not recognise Him when He came. And the words are spoken as from the person of Christ; and they are these "I was manifest to them that asked not for Me; I was found of them that sought Me not: I said, Behold Me, to a nation that called not on My name. I spread out My hands to a disobedient and gainsaying people, to those who walked in a way that is not good, but follow after their own sins; a people that provoketh Me to anger to My face." [1869] For the Jews having the prophecies, and being always in expectation of the Christ to come, did not recognise Him; and not only so, but even treated Him shamefully. But the Gentiles, who had never heard anything about Christ, until the apostles set out from Jerusalem and preached concerning Him, and gave them the prophecies, were filled with joy and faith, and cast away their idols, and dedicated themselves to the Unbegotten God through Christ. And that it was foreknown that these infamous things should be uttered against those who confessed Christ, and that those who slandered Him, and said that it was well to preserve the ancient customs, should be miserable, hear what was briefly said by Isaiah; it is this: "Woe unto them that call sweet bitter, and bitter sweet." [1870]

Chapter L - His humiliation predicted

But that, having become man for our sakes, He endured to suffer and to be dishonoured, and that He shall come again with glory, hear the prophecies which relate to this; they are these: "Because they delivered His soul unto death, and He was numbered with the transgressors, He has borne the sin of many, and shall make intercession for the transgressors. For, behold, My Servant shall deal prudently, and shall be exalted, and shall be greatly extolled. As many were astonished at Thee, so marred shall Thy form be before men, and so hidden from them Thy glory; so shall many nations wonder, and the kings shall shut their mouths at Him. For they to whom it was not told concerning Him, and they who have not heard, shall understand. O Lord, who hath believed our report? and to whom is the arm of the Lord revealed? We have declared before Him as a child, as a root in a dry ground. He had no form, nor glory; and we saw Him, and there was no form nor comeliness: but His form was dishonoured and marred more than the sons of men. A man under the stroke, and knowing how to bear infirmity, because His face was turned away: He was despised, and of no reputation. It is He who bears our sins, and is afflicted for us; yet we did esteem Him smitten, stricken, and afflicted. But He was wounded for our transgressions, He was bruised for our iniquities, the chastisement of peace was upon Him, by His stripes we are healed. All we, like sheep, have gone astray; every man has wandered in his own way. And He delivered Him for our sins; and He opened not His mouth for all His affliction. He was brought as a sheep to the slaughter, and as a lamb before his shearer is dumb, so He openeth not His mouth. In His humiliation, His judgment was taken away." [1871] Accordingly, after He was crucified, even all His acquaintances forsook Him, having denied Him; and afterwards, when He had risen from the dead and appeared to them, and had taught them to read the prophecies in which all these things were foretold as coming to pass, and when they had seen Him ascending into heaven, and had believed, and had received power sent thence by Him upon them, and went to every race of men, they taught these things, and were called apostles.

Chapter LI - The majesty of Christ

And that the Spirit of prophecy might signify to us that He who suffers these things has an ineffable origin, and rules His enemies, He spake thus: "His generation who shall declare? because His life is cut off from the earth: for their transgressions He comes to death. And I will give the wicked for His burial, and the rich for His death; because He did no violence, neither was any deceit in His mouth. And the Lord is pleased to cleanse Him from the stripe. If He be given for sin, your soul shall see His seed prolonged in days. And the Lord is pleased to deliver His soul from grief, to show Him light, and to form Him with knowledge, to justify the righteous who richly serveth many. And He shall bear our iniquities. Therefore He shall inherit many, and He shall divide the spoil of the strong; because His soul was delivered to death: and He was numbered with the transgressors; and He bare the sins of many, and He was delivered up for their transgressions."[1872] Hear, too, how He was to ascend into heaven according to prophecy. It was thus spoken: "Lift up the gates of heaven; be ye opened, that the King of glory may come in. Who is this King of glory? The Lord, strong and mighty." [1873] And how also He should come again out of heaven with glory, hear what was spoken in reference to this by the prophet Jeremiah. [1874] His words are: "Behold, as the Son of man He cometh in the clouds of heaven, and His angels with Him."[1875]

Chapter LII - Certain fulfilment of prophecy

Since, then, we prove that all things which have already happened had been predicted by the prophets before they came to pass, we must necessarily believe also that those things which are in like manner predicted, but are yet to come to pass, shall certainly happen. For as the things which have already taken place came to pass when foretold, and even though unknown, so shall the things that remain, even though they be unknown and disbelieved, yet come to pass. For the prophets have proclaimed two advents of His: the one, that which is already past, when He came as a dishonoured and suffering Man; but the second, when, according to prophecy, He shall come from heaven with glory, accompanied by His angelic host, when also He shall raise the bodies of all men who have lived, and shall clothe those of the worthy with immortality, and shall send those of the wicked, endued with eternal sensibility, into everlasting fire with the wicked devils. And that these things also have been foretold as yet to be, we will prove. By Ezekiel the prophet it was said: "Joint shall be joined to joint, and bone to bone, and flesh shall grow again; and every knee shall bow to the Lord, and every tongue shall confess Him." [1876] And in what kind of sensation and punishment the wicked are to be, hear from what was said in like manner with reference to this; it is as follows: "Their worm shall not rest, and their fire shall not be quenched;" [1877] and then shall they repent, when it profits them not. And what the people of the Jews shall say and do, when they see Him coming in glory, has been thus predicted by Zechariah the prophet: "I will command the four winds to gather the scattered children; I will command the north wind to bring them, and the south wind, that it keep not back. And then in Jerusalem there shall be great lamentation, not the lamentation of mouths or of lips, but the lamentation of the heart; and they shall rend not their garments, but their hearts. Tribe by tribe they shall mourn, and then they shall look on Him whom they have pierced; and they shall say, Why, O Lord, hast Thou made us to err from Thy way? The glory which our fathers blessed, has for us been turned into shame." [1878]

Chapter LIII - Summary of the prophecies

Though we could bring forward many other prophecies, we forbear, judging these sufficient for the persuasion of those who have ears to hear and understand; and considering also that those persons are able to see that we do not make mere assertions without being able to produce proof, like those fables that are told of the so-called sons of Jupiter. For with what reason should we believe of a crucified man that He is the first-born of the unbegotten God, and Himself will pass judgment on the whole human race, unless we had found testimonies concerning Him published before He came and was born as man, and unless we saw that things had happened accordingly--the devastation of the land of the Jews, and men of every race persuaded by His teaching through the apostles, and rejecting their old habits, in which, being deceived, they had their conversation; yea, seeing ourselves too, and knowing that the Christians from among the Gentiles are both more numerous and more true than those from among the Jews and Samaritans? For all the other human races are called Gentiles by the Spirit of prophecy; but the Jewish and Samaritan races are called the tribe of Israel, and the house of Jacob. And the prophecy in which it was predicted that there should be more believers from the Gentiles than from the Jews and Samaritans, we will produce: it ran thus: "Rejoice, O barren, thou that dost not bear; break forth and shout, thou that dost not travail, because many more are the children of the desolate than of her that hath an husband." [1879] For all the Gentiles were "desolate" of the true God, serving the works of their hands; but the Jews and Samaritans, having the word of God delivered to them by the prophets, and always expecting the Christ, did not recognise Him when He came, except some few, of whom the Spirit of prophecy by Isaiah had predicted that they should be saved. He spoke as from their person: "Except the Lord had left us a seed, we should have been as Sodom and Gomorrah." [1880] For Sodom and Gomorrah are related by Moses to have been cities of ungodly men, which God burned with fire and brimstone, and overthrew, no one of their inhabitants being saved except a certain stranger, a Chaldæan by birth, whose name was Lot; with whom also his daughters were rescued. And those who care may yet see their whole country desolate and burned, and remaining barren. And to show how those from among the Gentiles were foretold as more true and more believing, we will cite what was said by Isaiah [1881] the prophet; for he spoke as follows "Israel is uncircumcised in heart, but the Gentiles are uncircumcised in the flesh." So many things therefore, as these, when they are seen with the eye, are enough to produce conviction and belief in those who embrace the truth, and are not bigoted in their opinions, nor are governed by their passions.

Chapter LIV - Origin of heathen mythology

But those who hand down the myths which the poets have made, adduce no proof to the youths who learn them; and we proceed to demonstrate that they have been uttered by the influence of the wicked demons, to deceive and lead astray the human race. For having heard it proclaimed through the prophets that the Christ was to come, and that the ungodly among men were to be punished by fire, they put forward many to be called sons of Jupiter, under the impression that they would be able to produce in men the idea that the things which were said with regard to Christ were mere marvellous tales, like the things which were said by the poets. And these things were said both among the Greeks and among all nations where they [the demons] heard the prophets foretelling that Christ would specially be believed in; but that in hearing what was said by the prophets they did not accurately understand it, but imitated what was said of our Christ, like men who are in error, we will make plain. The prophet Moses, then, was, as we have already said, older than all writers; and by him, as we have also said before, it was thus predicted: "There shall not fail a prince from Judah, nor a lawgiver from between his feet, until He come for whom it is reserved; and He shall be the desire of the Gentiles, binding His foal to the vine, washing His robe in the blood of the grape." [1882] The devils, accordingly, when they heard these prophetic words, said that Bacchus was the son of Jupiter, and gave out that he was the discoverer of the vine, and they number wine [1883] [or, the ass] among his mysteries; and they taught that, having been torn in pieces, he ascended into heaven. And because in the prophecy of Moses it had not been expressly intimated whether He who was to come was the Son of God, and whether He would, riding on the foal, remain on earth or ascend into heaven, and because the name of "foal" could mean either the foal of an ass or the foal of a horse, they, not knowing whether He who was foretold would bring the foal of an ass or of a horse as the sign of His coming, nor whether He was the Son of God, as we said above, or of man, gave out that Bellerophon, a man born of man, himself ascended to heaven on his horse Pegasus. And when they heard it said by the other prophet Isaiah, that He should be born of a virgin, and by His own means ascend into heaven, they pretended that Perseus was spoken of. And when they knew what was said, as has been cited above, in the prophecies written aforetime, "Strong as a giant to run his course," [1884] they said that Hercules was strong, and had journeyed over the whole earth. And when, again, they learned that it had been foretold that He should heal every sickness, and raise the dead, they produced Æsculapius.

Chapter LV - Symbols of the cross

But in no instance, not even in any of those called sons of Jupiter, did they imitate the being crucified; for it was not understood by them, all the things said of it having been put symbolically. And this, as the prophet foretold, is the greatest symbol of His power and role; as is also proved by the things which fall under our observation. For consider all the things in the world, whether without this form they could be administered or have any community. For the sea is not traversed except that trophy which is called a sail abide safe in the ship; and the earth is not ploughed without it: diggers and mechanics do not their work, except with tools which have this shape. And the human form differs from that of the irrational animals in nothing else than in its being erect and having the hands extended, and having on the face extending from the forehead what is called the nose, through which there is respiration for the living creature; and this shows no other form than that of the cross. And so it was said by the prophet, "The breath before our face is the Lord Christ."[1885] And the power of this form is shown by your own symbols on what are called "vexilla" [banners] and trophies, with which all your state possessions are made, using these as the insignia of your power and government, even though you do so unwittingly. [1886] And with this form you consecrate the images of your emperors when they die, and you name them gods by inscriptions. Since, therefore, we have urged you both by reason and by an evident form, and to the utmost of our ability, we know that now we are blameless even though you disbelieve; for our part is done and finished.

Chapter LVI - The demons still mislead men

But the evil spirits were not satisfied with saying, before Christ's appearance, that those who were said to be sons of Jupiter were born of him; but after He had appeared, and been born among men, and when they learned how He had been foretold by the prophets, and knew that He should be believed on and looked for by every nation, they again, as was said above, put forward other men, the Samaritans Simon and Menander, who did many mighty works by magic, and deceived many, and still keep them deceived. For even among yourselves, as we said before, [1887] Simon was in the royal city Rome in the reign of Claudius Cæsar, and so greatly astonished the sacred senate and people of the Romans, that he was considered a god, and honoured, like the others whom you honour as gods, with a statue. Wherefore we pray that the sacred senate and your people may, along with yourselves, be arbiters of this our memorial, in order that if any one be entangled by that man's doctrines, he may learn the truth, and so be able to escape error; and as for the statue, if you please, destroy it.

Chapter LVII - And cause persecution

Nor can the devils persuade men that there will be no conflagration for the punishment of the wicked; as they were unable to effect that Christ should be hidden after He came. But this only can they effect, that they who live irrationally, and were brought up licentiously in wicked customs, and are prejudiced in their own opinions, should kill and hate us; whom we not only do not hate, but, as is proved, pity and endeavour to lead to repentance. For we do not fear death, since it is acknowledged we must surely die; and there is nothing new, but all things continue the same in this administration of things; and if satiety overtakes those who enjoy even one year of these things, they ought to give heed to our doctrines, that they may live eternally free both from suffering and from want. But if they believe that there is nothing after death, but declare that those who die pass into insensibility, then they become our benefactors when they set us free from sufferings and necessities of this life, and prove themselves to be wicked, and inhuman, and bigoted. For they kill us with no intention of delivering us, but cut us off that we may be deprived of life and pleasure.

Chapter LVIII - And raise up heretics

And, as we said before, the devils put forward Marcion of Pontus, who is even now teaching men to deny that God is the maker of all things in heaven and on earth, and that the Christ predicted by the prophets is His Son, and preaches another god besides the Creator of all, and likewise another son. And this man many have believed, as if he alone knew the truth, and laugh at us, though they have no proof of what they say, but are carried away irrationally as lambs by a wolf, and become the prey of atheistical doctrines, and of devils. For they who are called devils attempt nothing else than to seduce men from God who made them, and from Christ His first-begotten; and those who are unable to raise themselves above the earth they have riveted, and do now rivet, to things earthly, and to the works of their own hands; but those who devote themselves to the contemplation of things divine, they secretly beat back; and if they have not a wise sobermindedness, and a pure and passionless life, they drive them into godlessness.

Chapter LIX - Plato's obligation to Moses

And that you may learn that it was from our teachers--we mean the account given through the prophets-- that Plato borrowed his statement that God, having altered matter which was shapeless, made the world, hear the very words spoken through Moses, who, as above shown, was the first prophet, and of greater antiquity than the Greek writers; and through whom the Spirit of prophecy, signifying how and from what materials God at first formed the world, spake thus: "In the beginning God created the heaven and the earth. And the earth was invisible and unfurnished, and darkness was upon the face of the deep; and the Spirit of God moved over the waters. And God said, Let there be light; and it was so." So that both Plato and they who agree with him, and we ourselves, have learned, and you also can be convinced, that by the word of God the whole world was made out of the substance spoken of before by Moses. And that which the poets call Erebus, we know was spoken of formerly by Moses. [1888]

Chapter LX - Plato's doctrine of the cross

And the physiological discussion [1889] concerning the Son of God in the Timæus of Plato, where he says, "He placed him crosswise [1890] in the universe," he borrowed in like manner from Moses; for in the writings of Moses it is related how at that time, when the Israelites went out of Egypt and were in the wilderness, they fell in with poisonous beasts, both vipers and asps, and every kind of serpent, which slew the people; and that Moses, by the inspiration and influence of God, took brass, and made it into the figure of a cross, and set it in the holy tabernacle, and said to the people, "If ye look to this figure, and believe, ye shall be saved thereby." [1891] And when this was done, it is recorded that the serpents died, and it is handed down that the people thus escaped death. Which things Plato reading, and not accurately understanding, and not apprehending that it was the figure of the cross, but taking it to be a placing crosswise, he said that the power next to the first God was placed crosswise in the universe. And as to his speaking of a third, he did this because he read, as we said above, that which was spoken by Moses, "that the Spirit of God moved over the waters." For he gives the second place to the Λόγος which is with God, who he said was placed crosswise in the universe; and the third place to the Spirit who was said to be borne upon the water, saying, "And the third around the third." [1892] And hear how the Spirit of prophecy signified through Moses that there should be a conflagration. He spoke thus: "Everlasting fire shall descend, and shall devour to the pit beneath." [1893] It is not, then, that we hold the same opinions as others, but that all speak in imitation of ours. Among us these things can be heard and learned from persons who do not even know the forms of the letters, who are uneducated and barbarous in speech, though wise and believing in mind; some, indeed, even maimed and deprived of eyesight; so that you may understand that these things are not the effect of human wisdom, but are uttered by the power of God.

Chapter LXI - Christian baptism

I will also relate the manner in which we dedicated ourselves to God when we had been made new through Christ; lest, if we omit this, we seem to be unfair in the explanation we are making. As many as are persuaded and believe that what we teach and say is true, and undertake to be able to live accordingly, are instructed to pray and to entreat God with fasting, for the remission of their sins that are past, we praying and fasting with them. Then they are brought by us where there is water, and are regenerated in the same manner in which we were ourselves regenerated. For, in the name of God, the Father and Lord of the universe, and of our Saviour Jesus Christ, and of the Holy Spirit, they then receive the washing with water. For Christ also said, "Except ye be born again, ye shall not enter into the kingdom of heaven." [1894] Now, that it is impossible for those who have once been born to enter into their mothers' wombs, is manifest to all. And how those who have sinned and repent shall escape their sins, is declared by Esaias the prophet, as I wrote above; [1895] he thus speaks: "Wash you, make you clean; put away the evil of your doings from your souls; learn to do well; judge the fatherless, and plead for the widow: and come and let us reason together, saith the Lord. And though your sins be as scarlet, I will make them white like wool; and though they be as crimson, I will make them white as snow. But if ye refuse and rebel, the sword shall devour you: for the mouth of the Lord hath spoken it." [1896]

And for this [rite] we have learned from the apostles this reason. Since at our birth we were born without our own knowledge or choice, by our parents coming together, and were brought up in bad habits and wicked training; in order that we may not remain the children of necessity and of ignorance, but may become the children of choice and knowledge, and may obtain in the water the remission of sins formerly committed, there is pronounced over him who chooses to be born again, and has repented of his sins, the name of God the Father and Lord of the universe; he who leads to the laver the person that is to be washed calling him by this name alone. For no one can utter the name of the ineffable God; and if any one dare to say that there is a name, he raves with a hopeless madness. And this washing is called illumination, because they who learn these things are illuminated in their understandings. And in the name of Jesus Christ, who was crucified under Pontius Pilate, and in the name of the Holy Ghost, who through the prophets foretold all things about Jesus, he who is illuminated is washed.

Chapter LXII - Its imitation by demons

And the devils, indeed, having heard this washing published by the prophet, instigated those who enter their temples, and are about to approach them with libations and burnt-offerings, also to sprinkle themselves; and they cause them also to wash themselves entirely, as they depart [from the sacrifice], before they enter into the shrines in which their images are set. And the command, too, given by the priests to those who enter and worship in the temples, that they take off their shoes, the devils, learning what happened to the above-mentioned prophet Moses, have given in imitation of these things. For at that juncture, when Moses was ordered to go down into Egypt and lead out the people of the Israelites who were there, and while he was tending the flocks of his maternal uncle[1897] in the land of Arabia, our Christ conversed with him under the appearance of fire from a bush, and said, "Put off thy shoes, and draw near and hear." And he, when he had put off his shoes and drawn near, heard that he was to go down into Egypt and lead out the people of the Israelites there; and he received mighty power from Christ, who spoke to him in the appearance of fire, and went down and led out the people, having done great and marvellous things; which, if you desire to know, you will learn them accurately from his writings.

Chapter LXIII - How God appeared to Moses

And all the Jews even now teach that the nameless God spake to Moses; whence the Spirit of prophecy, accusing them by Isaiah the prophet mentioned above, said "The ox knoweth his owner, and the ass his master's crib; but Israel doth not know Me, and My people do not understand." [1898] And Jesus the Christ, because the Jews knew not what the Father was, and what the Son, in like manner accused them; and Himself said, "No one knoweth the Father, but the Son; nor the Son, but the Father, and they to whom the Son revealeth Him." [1899] Now the Word of God is His Son, as we have before said. And He is called Angel and Apostle; for He declares whatever we ought to know, and is sent forth to declare whatever is revealed; as our Lord Himself says, "He that heareth Me, heareth Him that sent Me." [1900] From the writings of Moses also this will be manifest; for thus it is written in them, "And the Angel of God spake to Moses, in a flame of fire out of the bush, and said, I am that I am, the God of Abraham, the God of Isaac, the God of Jacob, the God of thy fathers; go down into Egypt, and bring forth My people." [1901] And if you wish to learn what follows, you can do so from the same writings; for it is impossible to relate the whole here. But so much is written for the sake of proving that Jesus the Christ is the Son of God and His Apostle, being of old the Word, and appearing sometimes in the form of fire, and sometimes in the likeness of angels; but now, by the will of God, having become man for the human race, He endured all the sufferings which the devils instigated the senseless Jews to inflict upon Him; who, though they have it expressly affirmed in the writings of Moses, "And the angel of God spake to Moses in a flame of fire in a bush, and said, I am that I am, the God of Abraham, and the God of Isaac, and the God of Jacob," yet maintain that He who said this was the Father and Creator of the universe. Whence also the Spirit of prophecy rebukes them, and says, "Israel doth not know Me, my people have not understood Me." [1902] And again, Jesus, as we have already shown, while He was with them, said, "No one knoweth the Father, but the Son; nor the Son but the Father, and those to whom the Son will reveal Him." [1903] The Jews, accordingly, being throughout of opinion that it was the Father of the universe who spake to Moses, though He who spake to him was indeed the Son of God, who is called both Angel and Apostle, are justly charged, both by the Spirit of prophecy and by Christ Himself, with knowing neither the Father nor the Son. For they who affirm that the Son is the Father, are proved neither to have become acquainted with the Father, nor to know that the Father of the universe has a Son; who also, being the first-begotten Word of God, is even God. And of old He appeared in the shape of fire and in the likeness of an angel to Moses and to the other prophets; but now in the times of your reign, [1904] having, as we before said, become Man by a virgin, according to the counsel of the Father, for the salvation of those who believe on Him, He endured both to be set at nought and to suffer, that by dying and rising again He might conquer death. And that which was said out of the bush to Moses, "I am that I am, the God of Abraham, the God of Isaac, and the God of Jacob, and the God of your fathers," [1905] this signified that they, even though dead, are yet in existence, and are men belonging to Christ Himself. For they were the first of all men to busy themselves in the search after God; Abraham being the father of Isaac, and Isaac of Jacob, as Moses wrote.

Chapter LXIV - Further misrepresentations of the truth

From what has been already said, you can understand how the devils, in imitation of what was said by Moses, asserted that Proserpine was the daughter of Jupiter, and instigated the people to set up an image of her under the name of Kore [Cora, i.e., the maiden or daughter] at the spring-heads. For, as we wrote above, [1906] Moses said, "In the beginning God made the heaven and the earth. And the earth was without form and unfurnished: and the Spirit of God moved upon the face of the waters." In imitation, therefore, of what is here said of the Spirit of God moving on the waters, they said that Proserpine [or Cora] was the daughter of Jupiter.[1907] And in like manner also they craftily feigned that Minerva was the daughter of Jupiter, not by sexual union, but, knowing that God conceived and made the world by the Word, they say that Minerva is the first conception [ἔννοια]; which we consider to be very absurd, bringing forward the form of the conception in a female shape. And in like manner the actions of those others who are called sons of Jupiter sufficiently condemn them.

Chapter LXV - Administration of the sacraments

But we, after we have thus washed him who has been convinced and has assented to our teaching, bring him to the place where those who are called brethren are assembled, in order that we may offer hearty prayers in common for ourselves and for the baptized [illuminated] person, and for all others in every place, that we may be counted worthy, now that we have learned the truth, by our works also to be found good citizens and keepers of the commandments, so that we may be saved with an everlasting salvation. Having ended the prayers, we salute one another with a kiss.[1908] There is then brought to the president of the brethren [1909] bread and a cup of wine mixed with water; and he taking them, gives praise and glory to the Father of the universe, through the name of the Son and of the Holy Ghost, and offers thanks at considerable length for our being counted worthy to receive these things at His hands. And when he has concluded the prayers and thanksgivings, all the people present express their assent by saying Amen. This word Amen answers in the Hebrew language to γένοιτο [so be it]. And when the president has given thanks, and all the people have expressed their assent, those who are called by us deacons give to each of those present to partake of the bread and wine mixed with water over which the thanksgiving was pronounced, and to those who are absent they carry away a portion.

Chapter LXVI - Of the Eucharist

And this food is called among us Εὐχαριστία [1910] [the Eucharist], of which no one is allowed to partake but the man who believes that the things which we teach are true, and who has been washed with the washing that is for the remission of sins, and unto regeneration, and who is so living as Christ has enjoined. For not as common bread and common drink do we receive these; but in like manner as Jesus Christ our Saviour, having been made flesh by the Word of God, had both flesh and blood for our salvation, so likewise have we been taught that the food which is blessed by the prayer of His word, and from which our blood and flesh by transmutation are nourished, is the flesh and blood of that Jesus who was made flesh.[1911] For the apostles, in the memoirs composed by them, which are called Gospels, have thus delivered unto us what was enjoined upon them; that Jesus took bread, and when He had given thanks, said, "This do ye in remembrance of Me,[1912] this is My body;" and that, after the same manner, having taken the cup and given thanks, He said, "This is My blood;" and gave it to them alone. Which the wicked devils have imitated in the mysteries of Mithras, commanding the same thing to be done. For, that bread and a cup of water are placed with certain incantations in the mystic rites of one who is being initiated, you either know or can learn.

Chapter LXVII - Weekly worship of the Christians

And we afterwards continually remind each other of these things. And the wealthy among us help the needy; and we always keep together; and for all things wherewith we are supplied, we bless the Maker of all through His Son Jesus Christ, and through the Holy Ghost. And on the day called Sunday,[1913] all who live in cities or in the country gather together to one place, and the memoirs of the apostles or the writings of the prophets are read, as long as time permits; then, when the reader has ceased, the president verbally instructs, and exhorts to the imitation of these good things. Then we all rise together and pray, and, as we before said, when our prayer is ended, bread and wine and water are brought, and the president in like manner offers prayers and thanksgivings, according to his ability,[1914] and the people assent, saying Amen; and there is a distribution to each, and a participation of that over which thanks have been given,[1915] and to those who are absent a portion is sent by the deacons. And they who are well to do, and willing, give what each thinks fit; and what is collected is deposited with the president, who succours the orphans and widows and those who, through sickness or any other cause, are in want, and those who are in bonds and the strangers sojourning among us, and in a word takes care of all who are in need. But Sunday is the day on which we all hold our common assembly, because it is the first day on which God, having wrought a change in the darkness and matter, made the world; and Jesus Christ our Saviour on the same day rose from the dead. For He was crucified on the day before that of Saturn (Saturday); and on the day after that of Saturn, which is the day of the Sun, having appeared to His apostles and disciples, He taught them these things, which we have submitted to you also for your consideration.

Chapter LXVIII - Conclusion

And if these things seem to you to be reasonable and true, honour them; but if they seem nonsensical, despise them as nonsense, and do not decree death against those who have done no wrong, as you would against enemies. For we forewarn you, that you shall not escape the coming judgment of God, if you continue in your injustice; and we ourselves will invite you to do that which is pleasing to God. And though from the letter of the greatest and most illustrious Emperor Adrian, your father, we could demand that you order judgment to be given as we have desired, yet we have made this appeal and explanation, not on the ground of Adrian's decision, but because we know that what we ask is just. And we have subjoined the copy of Adrian's epistle, that you may know that we are speaking truly about this. And the following is the copy:--

Epistle of Adrian [1916] in behalf of the Christians

I have received the letter addressed to me by your predecessor Serenius Granianus, a most illustrious man; and this communication I am unwilling to pass over in silence, lest innocent persons be disturbed, and occasion be given to the informers for practising villany. Accordingly, if the inhabitants of your province will so far sustain this petition of theirs as to accuse the Christians in some court of law, I do not prohibit them from doing so. But I will not suffer them to make use of mere entreaties and outcries. For it is far more just, if any one desires to make an accusation, that you give judgment upon it. If, therefore, any one makes the accusation, and furnishes proof that the said men do anything contrary to the laws, you shall adjudge punishments in proportion to the offences. And this, by Hercules, you shall give special heed to, that if any man shall, through mere calumny, bring an accusation against any of these persons, you shall award to him more severe punishments in proportion to his wickedness.

Epistle of Antoninus to the common assembly of Asia [1917]

The Emperor Cæsar Titus Ælius Adrianus Antoninus Augustus Pius, Supreme Pontiff, in the fifteenth year of his tribuneship, Consul for the third time, Father of the fatherland, to the Common Assembly of Asia, greeting: I should have thought that the gods themselves would see to it that such offenders should not escape. For if they had the power, they themselves would much rather punish those who refuse to worship them; but it is you who bring trouble on these persons, and accuse as the opinion of atheists that which they hold, and lay to their charge certain other things which we are unable to prove. But it would be advantageous to them that they should be thought to die for that of which they are accused, and they conquer you by being lavish of their lives rather than yield that obedience which you require of them. And regarding the earthquakes which have already happened and are now occurring, it is not seemly that you remind us of them, losing heart whenever they occur, and thus set your conduct in contrast with that of these men; for they have much greater confidence towards God than you yourselves have. And you, indeed, seem at such times to ignore the gods, and you neglect the temples, and make no recognition of the worship of God. And hence you are jealous of those who do serve Him, and persecute them to the death. Concerning such persons, some others also of the governors of provinces wrote to my most divine father; to whom he replied that they should not at all disturb such persons, unless they were found to be attempting anything against the Roman government. And to myself many have sent intimations regarding such persons, to whom I also replied in pursuance of my father's judgment. But if any one has a matter to bring against any person of this class, merely as such a person, [1918] let the accused be acquitted of the charge, even though he should be found to be such a one; but let the accuser be amenable to justice.

Epistle of Marcus Aurelius to the senate, in which he testifies that the Christians were the cause of his victory [1919]

The Emperor Cæsar Marcus Aurelius Antoninus, Germanicus, Parthicus, Sarmaticus, to the People of Rome, and to the sacred Senate greeting: I explained to you my grand design, and what advantages I gained on the confines of Germany, with much labour and suffering, in consequence of the circumstance that I was surrounded by the enemy; I myself being shut up in Carnuntum by seventy-four cohorts, nine miles off. And the enemy being at hand, the scouts pointed out to us, and our general Pompeianus showed us that there was close on us a mass of a mixed multitude of 977,000 men, which indeed we saw; and I was shut up by this vast host, having with me only a battalion composed of the first, tenth, double and marine legions. Having then examined my own position, and my host, with respect to the vast mass of barbarians and of the enemy, I quickly betook myself to prayer to the gods of my country. But being disregarded by them, I summoned those who among us go by the name of Christians. And having made inquiry, I discovered a great number and vast host of them, and raged against them, which was by no means becoming; for afterwards I learned their power. Wherefore they began the battle, not by preparing weapons, nor arms, nor bugles; for such preparation is hateful to them, on account of the God they bear about in their conscience. Therefore it is probable that those whom we suppose to be atheists, have God as their ruling power entrenched in their conscience. For having cast themselves on the ground, they prayed not only for me, but also for the whole army as it stood, that they might be delivered from the present thirst and famine. For during five days we had got no water, because there was none; for we were in the heart of Germany, and in the enemy's territory. And simultaneously with their casting themselves on the ground, and praying to God (a God of whom I am ignorant), water poured from heaven, upon us most refreshingly cool, but upon the enemies of Rome a withering [1920] hail. And immediately we recognised the presence of God following on the prayer-a God unconquerable and indestructible. Founding upon this, then, let us pardon such as are Christians, lest they pray for and obtain such a weapon against ourselves. And I counsel that no such person be accused on the ground of his being a Christian. But if any one be found laying to the charge of a Christian that he is a Christian, I desire that it be made manifest that he who is accused as a Christian, and acknowledges that he is one, is accused of nothing else than only this, that he is a Christian; but that he who arraigns him be burned alive. And I further desire, that he who is entrusted with the government of the province shall not compel the Christian, who confesses and certifies such a matter, to retract; neither shall he commit him. And I desire that these things be confirmed by a decree of the Senate. And I command this my edict to be published in the Forum of Trajan, in order that it may be read. The prefect Vitrasius Pollio will see that it be transmitted to all the provinces round about, and that no one who wishes to make use of or to possess it be hindered from obtaining a copy from the document I now publish. [1921]

Footnotes:

1768. Literally, "the opinions of the ancients."

1769. Thirlby regarded the clause in brackets as an interpolation. There is considerable variety of opinion as to the exact meaning of the words amongst those who regard them as genuine.

1770. Plat. Rep., v. 18.

1771. That is to say, if the Christians refused or neglected to make their real opinions and practices known, they would share the guilt of those whom they thus kept in darkness.

1772. Justin avails himself here of the similarity in sound of the words Χριστὸς (Christ) and χρηστὸς (good, worthy, excellent). The play upon these words is kept up throughout this paragraph, and cannot be always represented to the English reader. But Justin was merely quoting and using, ad hominem, the popular blunder of which Suetonius (Life of Claudius, cap. 25) gives us an example, "impulsore Chresto." It will be observed again in others of these Fathers.

1773. 1 Cor. x. 20. Milton's admirable economy in working this truth into his great poem (i. 378) affords a sublime exposition of the mind of the Fathers on the origin of mythologies.

1774. The word δαίμων means in Greek a god, but the Christians used the word to signify an evil spirit. Justin uses the same word here for god and demon. The connection which Justin and other Christian writers supposed to exist between evil spirits and the gods of the heathens will be apparent from Justin's own statements. The word διάβολος, devil, is not applied to these demons. There is but one devil, but many demons.

1775. The word δαίμων means in Greek a god, but the Christians used the word to signify an evil spirit. Justin uses the same word here for god and demon. The connection which Justin and other Christian writers supposed to exist between evil spirits and the gods of the heathens will be apparent from Justin's own statements. The word διάβολος, devil, is not applied to these demons. There is but one devil, but many demons.

1776. This is the literal and obvious translation of Justin's words. But from c. 13, 16, and 61, it is evident that he did not desire to inculcate the worship of angels. We are therefore driven to adopt another translation of this passage, even though it be somewhat harsh. Two such translations have been proposed: the first connecting "us" and "the host of the other good angels" as the common object of the verb "taught;"

the second connecting "these things" with "the host of," etc., and making these two together the subject taught. In the first case the translation would stand, "taught these things to us and to the host," etc.; in the second case the translation would be, "taught us about these things, and about the host of the others who follow Him, viz. the good angels." I have ventured to insert parenthetic marks in the text, an obvious and simple resource to suggest the manifest intent of the author. Grabe's note in loc. gives another and very ingenious exegesis, but the simplest is best.

1777. i.e., according to Otto, "not on account of the sincere Christians of whom we have been speaking." According to Trollope, "not on account of (or at the instigation of) the demons before mentioned."

1778. Or, "as a Christian who has done no wrong."

1779. Compare the Rescript of Adrian appended to this Apology.

1780. Literally, "persuaded God."

1781. Isa. xliv. 9-20; Jer. x. 3.

1782. πομπὰς καὶ ὕμνους. "Grabe, and it should seem correctly, understands πομπὰς to be solemn prayers. ... He also remarks, that the ὕμνοι were either psalms of David, or some of those psalms and songs made by the primitive Christians, which are mentioned in Eusebius, H. E., v. 28." --Trollope.

1783. Literally, "would not use the same hearth or fire."

1784. See the end of chap. xii.

1785. The reader will notice that Justin quotes from memory, so that there are some slight discrepancies between the words of Jesus as here cited, and the same sayings as recorded in our Gospels.

1786. Matt. v. 28, 29, 32.

1787. Matt. xix. 12.

1788. διγαμίας ποιούμενοι, lit. contracting a double marriage. Of double marriages there are three kinds: the first, marriage with a second wife while the first is still alive and recognised as a lawful wife, or bigamy; the second, marriage with a second wife after divorce from the first, and third, marriage with a second wife after the death of the first. It is thought that Justin here refers to the second case.

1789. Matt. ix. 13.

1790. Matt. v. 46, 44; Luke vi. 28.

1791. Luke vi. 30, 34; Matt. vi. 19, Matt. xvi. 26, Matt. vi. 20.

1792. Luke vi. 36; Matt. v. 45, Matt. vi. 25, 26, 33, 21.

1793. Matt. vi. 1.

1794. Luke vi. 29; Matt. vi. 22, 41, 16.

1795. i.e., Christian neighbours.

1796. Matt. v. 34, 27.

1797. Mark xii. 30.

1798. Matt. xix. 6, 17.

1799. Matt. vii. 21, etc.; Luke xiii. 26; Matt. xiii. 42, Matt. vii. 15, 16, 19.

1800. φόρους καὶ εἰσφοράς. The former is the annual tribute; the latter, any occasional assessment. See Otto's Note, and Thucyd. iii. 19.

1801. Matt. xxii. 17, 19, 20, 21.

1802. Luke xii. 48.

1803. ἕρμαιον, a piece of unlooked-for luck, Hermes being the reputed giver of such gifts: vid. Liddell and Scott's Lex.; see also the Scholiast, quoted by Stallbaum in Plato's Phæd., p. 107, on a passage singularly analogous to this.

1804. Boys and girls, or even children prematurely taken from the womb, were slaughtered, and their entrails inspected, in the belief that the souls of the victims (being still conscious, as Justin is arguing) would reveal things hidden and future. Instances are abundantly cited by Otto and Trollope.

1805. This form of spirit-rapping was familiar to the ancients, and Justin again (Dial. c. Tryph., c. 105) uses the invocation of Samuel by the witch of Endor as a proof of the immortality of the soul.

1806. Valesius (on Euseb. H. E., iv. 7) states that the magi had two kinds of familiars: the first, who were sent to inspire men with dreams which might give them intimations of things future; and the second, who were sent to watch over men, and protect them from diseases and misfortunes. The first, he says, they called (as here) ὀνειροπομπούς, and the second παρέδρους.

1807. Justin is not the only author in ancient or recent times who has classed dæmoniacs and maniacs together; neither does he stand alone among the ancients in the opinion that dæmoniacs were possessed by the spirits of departed men. References will be found in Trollope's note. See this matter more fully illustrated in Kaye's Justin Martyr, pp. 105-111.

1808. See the Odyssey, book xi. line 25, where Ulysses is described as digging a pit or trench with his sword, and pouring libations, in order to collect around him the souls of the dead.

1809. Matt. xix. 26.

1810. Matt. x. 28.

1811. The Sibylline Oracles are now generally regarded as heathen fragments largely interpolated by unscrupulous men during the early ages of the Church. For an interesting account of these somewhat perplexing documents, see Burton's

The Apostolic Fathers
Lectures on the Ecclesiastical History of the First Three Centuries, Lect. xvii. The prophecies of Hystaspes were also commonly appealed to as genuine by the early Christians. See (on the Sibyls and Justin M.) Casaubon, Exercitationes, pp. 65 and 80. This work is a most learned and diversified thesaurus, in the form of strictures on Card. Baronius. Geneva, 1663.

1812. i.e., first-born.

1813. διαφοράν καὶ προτροπήν. The irony here is so obvious as to make the proposed reading (διαφθοράν καὶ παρατροπήν, corruption and depravation) unnecessary. Otto prefers the reading adopted above. Trollope, on the other hand, inclines to the latter reading, mainly on the score of the former expressions being unusual. See his very sensible note in loc.

1814. The Benedictine editor, Maranus, Otto, and Trollope, here note that Justin in this chapter promises to make good three distinct positions: 1st, That Christian doctrines alone are true, and are to be received, not on account of their resemblance to the sentiments of poets and philosophers, but on their own account; 2d, that Jesus Christ is the incarnate Son of God, and our teacher; 3d, that before His incarnation, the demons, having some knowledge of what He would accomplish, enabled the heathen poets and priestis in some points to anticipate, though in a distorted form, the facts of the incarnation. The first he establishes in chap. xxiv-xxix.; the second in chap. xxx.-liii.; and the third in chap. liv. et sq.

1815. We have here followed the reading and rendering of Trollope. But see reading of Langus, and Grabe's note, in the edition already cited, 1. 46.

1816. ἐν γραφαῖς στεφάνους. The only conjecture which seems at all probable is that of the Benedictine editor followed here. Grabe after Salmasius reads ἐν ῥαφαῖς and quotes Martial, Sutilis aptetur rosa crinibus. Translate, "patch-work garlands.".

1817. i.e., on account of the assistance gained for him by Thetis, and in return for it.

1818. It is very generally supposed that Justin was mistaken in understanding this to have been a statue erected to Simon Magus. This supposition rests on the fact that in the year 1574, there was dug up in the island of the Tiber a fragment of marble, with the inscription "Semoni Sanco Deo," etc., being probably the base of a statue erected to the Sabine deity Semo Sancus. This inscription Justin is supposed to have mistaken for the one he gives above. This has always seemed to us very slight evidence on which to reject so precise a statement as Justin here makes; a statement which he would scarcely have hazarded in an apology addressed to Rome, where every person had the means of ascertaining its accuracy. If, as is supposed, he made a mistake, it must have been at once exposed, and other writers would not have so frequently repeated the story as they have done. See Burton's Bampton Lectures, p. 374. See Note in Grabe (1. 51), and also mine, at the end.

1819. See chap. vii.

1820. Which were commonly charged against the Christians.

1821. Thirlby remarks that the serpent was the symbol specially of eternity, of power, and of wisdom, and that there was scarcely any divine attribute to which the heathen did not find some likeness in this animal. See also Hardwick's Christ and other Masters, vol. ii. 146 (2d ed.).

1822. Note how he retaliates upon the calumny (cap. xxvi.) of the "upsetting of the lamp.".

1823. Literally, "For He foreknows some about to be saved by repentance, and some not yet perhaps born."

1824. Those things which concern the salvation of man; so Trollope and the other interpreters, except Otto, who reads τούτων masculine, and understands it of the men first spoken of. See Plato (De Legibus, opp. ix. p. 98, Bipont., 1786), and the valuable edition of Book X. by Professor Tayler Lewis (p. 52. etc.). New York, 1845.

1825. For a sufficient account of the infamous history here alluded to and the extravagant grief of Hadrian, and the servility of the people, see Smith's Dictionary of Biography: "Antinous." Note, "all were prompt, through fear," etc. Thus we may measure the defiant intrepidity of this stinging sarcasm addressed to the "philosophers," with whose sounding titles this Apology begins.

1826. Some attribute this blunder in chronology to Justin, others to his transcribers: it was Eleazar the high priest to whom Ptolemy applied.

1827. Gen. xlix. 10.

1828. Grabe would here read, not σπέρμα, but πνεῦμα, the spirit; but the Benedictine, Otto, and Trollope all think that no change should be made.

1829. Isa. xi. 1.

1830. Isa. vii. 14.

1831. Luke i. 32; Matt. i. 21.

1832. θεοφοροῦνται, lit. are borne by a god--a word used of those who were supposed to be wholly under the influence of a deity.

1833. Mic. v. 2.

1834. These predictions have so little reference to the point Justin intends to make out, that some editors have supposed that a passage has here been lost. Others think the irrelevancy an insufficient ground for such a supposition. See below, cap. xl.

1835. Isa. ix. 6.

1836. Isa. lxv. 2, Isa. lviii. 2.

1837. Ps. xxii. 16.

1838. ἄκτων. These Acts of Pontius Pilate, or regular accounts of his procedure sent by Pilate to the Emperor Tiberius, are supposed to have been destroyed at an early period, possibly in consequence of the unanswerable appeals which the Christians constantly made to them. There exists a forgery in imitation of these Acts. See Trollope.

1839. The reader will notice that these are not the words of Zephaniah, but of Zechariah (ix. 9), to whom also Justin himself refers them in the Dial. Tryph., c. 53. Might be corrected in the text, therefore, as a clerical slip of the pen.

1840. Zech. ix. 9.

1841. Isa. i. 3. This quotation varies only in one word from that of the LXX.

1842. Isa. lxvi. 1.

1843. Isa. i. 14, Isa. lviii. 6.

1844. Isa. lxv. 2.

1845. Isa. l. 6.

1846. Ps. xxii. 18, Ψ. iii. 5.

1847. Ps. xxii. 7.

1848. Comp. Matt. xxvii. 39.

1849. Isa. ii. 3.

1850. Eurip., Hipp., 608.

1851. Ps. xix. 2, etc. Note how J. excuses himself for the apparent irrelevancy of some of his citations (cap. xxxv., note), though quite in the manner of Plato himself. These Scriptures were of novel interest, and was stimulating his readers to study the Septuagint.

1852. Ps. i., Ps. ii.

1853. Ps. xcvi. 1, etc. This last clause, which is not extant in our copies, either of the LXX, or of the Hebrew, Justin charged the Jews with erasing. See Dial. Tryph., c. 73. Concerning the eighteen Jewish alterations, see Pearson on the Creed, art. iv. p. 335. Ed. London, 1824.

1854. A chronological error, whether of the copyist or of Justin himself cannot be known.

1855. Or, "but were made so." The words are, ἀλλὰ τοῦτο γενόμενος and the meaning of Justin is sufficiently clear.

1856. Deut. xxx. 15, 19.

1857. Isa. i. 16, etc.

1858. Plato, Rep. x. On this remarkable passage refer to Biog. Note above. See, also, brilliant note of the sophist De Maistre, OEuvres, ii. p. 105. Ed. Paris, 1853.

1859. On the Orphica and Sibyllina, see Bull, Works, vol. vi. pp. 291-298.

1860. So, Thirlby, Otto, and Trollope seem all to understand the word κατέχειν; yet it seems worth considering whether Justin has not borrowed both the sense and the word from 2 Thess. ii. 6, 7.

1861. Or, "before the morning star."

1862. Ps. cx. 1, etc.

1863. μετὰ λόγου, "with reason," or "the Word." This remarkable passage on the salvability and accountability of the heathen is noteworthy. See, on St. Matt. xxv. 32, Morsels of Criticism by the eccentric but thoughtful Ed. King, p. 341. London, 1788.

1864. Isa. lxiv. 10-12.

1865. Isa. i. 7.

1866. Ad hominem, referring to the cruel decree of Hadrian, which the philosophic Antonines did not annul.

1867. Isa. xxxv. 6.

1868. Isa. lvii. 1.

1869. Isa. lxv. 1-3.

1870. Isa. v. 20.

1871. Isa. lii. 13-15, Isa. liii. 1-8.

1872. Isa. liii. 8-12.

1873. Ps. xxiv. 7.

1874. This prophecy occurs not in Jeremiah, but in Dan. vii. 13.

1875. Dan. vii. 13.

1876. Ezek. xxxvii. 7, 8; Isa. xlv. 24.

1877. Isa. lxvi. 24.

1878. Zech. xii. 3-14; Isa. lxiii. 17, Isa. lxiv. 11.

1879. Isa. liv. 1.

1880. Isa. i. 9.

1881. The following words are found, not in Isaiah, but in Jer. ix. 26.

1882. Gen. xlix. 10.

1883. In the ms. the reading is οἶνον (wine); but as Justin's argument seems to require ὄνον (an ass), Sylburg inserted this latter word in his edition; and this reading is approved by Grabe and Thirlby, and adopted by Otto and Trollope. It may be added, that ἀναγράφουσι is much more suitable to ὄνον than to οἶνον.

1884. Ps. xix. 5.

1885. From Lam. iv. 20 (Sept.).

1886. The Orientals delight in such refinements, but the "scandal of the cross" led the early Christians thus to retort upon the heathen; and the Labarum may have been the fruit of this very suggestion.

1887. See cap. xxvi. above, and note p. 187, below.

1888. Comp. Deut. xxxii. 22.

1889. Literally, "that which is treated physiologically."

1890. He impressed him as a χιασμα, i.e., in the form of the letter ch upon the universe. Plato is speaking of the soul of the universe. Timæus, Opp., vol. ix. p. 314. And see note of Langus (p. 37) on p. 113 of Grabe. Here crops out the Platonic philosopher speaking after the fashion of his contemporaries, perhaps to conciliate his sovereign. See Professor Jowett's Introduction to the Timæus, which will aid the students.

1891. Num. xxi. 8.
1892. Τὰ δὲ τρίτα περὶ τὸν τρίτον.
1893. Deut. xxxii. 22.
1894. John iii. 5.
1895. Chap. xliv.
1896. Isa. i. 16-20.
1897. Thirlby conjectures that Justin here confused in his mind the histories of Moses and Jacob.
1898. Isa. i. 3.
1899. Matt. xi. 27.
1900. Luke x. 16.
1901. Ex. iii. 6.
1902. Isa. i. 3.
1903. Matt. xi. 27.
1904. Rather, "of your empire.".
1905. Ex. iii. 6.
1906. Chap. lix.
1907. And therefore caused her to preside over the waters, as above.
1908. The kiss of charity, the kiss of peace, or "the peace" (ἡ εἰπήνη), was enjoined by the Apostle Paul in his Epistles to the Corinthians, Thessalonians, and Romans, and thence passed into a common Christian usage. It was continued in the Western Church, under regulations to prevent its abuse, until the thirteenth century. Stanley remarks (Corinthians, i. 414), "It is still continued in the worship of the Coptic Church."
1909. τῷ προεστῶτι τῶν ἀδελφῶν. This expression may quite legitimately be translated, "to that one of the brethren who was presiding."
1910. Literally, thanksgiving. See Matt. xxvi. 27.
1911. This passage is claimed alike by Calvinists, Lutherans, and Romanists; and, indeed, the language is so inexact, that each party may plausibly maintain that their own opinion is advocated by it. But the same might be said of the words of our Lord himself; and, if such widely separated Christians can all adopt this passage, who can be sorry?. The expression, "the prayer of His word," or of the word we have from Him, seems to signify the prayer pronounced over the elements, in imitation of our Lord's thanksgiving before breaking the bread. I must dissent from the opinion that the language is "inexact:" he expresses himself naturally as one who believes it is bread, but yet not "common bread." So Gelasius, Bishop of Rome (a.d. 490), "By the sacraments we are made partakers of the divine nature, and yet the substance and nature of bread and wine do not cease to be in them," etc. (See original in Bingham's Antiquities, book xv. cap. 5. See Chryost., Epist. ad. Cæsarium, tom. iii. p. 753. Ed. Migne.) Those desirous to pursue this inquiry will find the Patristic authorities in Historia Transubstantionis Papalis, etc., Edidit F. Meyrick, Oxford, 1858. The famous tractate of Ratranin (a.d. 840) was published at Oxford, 1838, with the homily of Ælfric (a.d. 960) in a cheap edition.

1912. Luke xxii. 19.
1913. τῇ τοῦ Ἡλίου λεγομένη ἡμέρα.
1914. ὅση δύναμις αὐτῷ,--a phrase over which there has been much contention, but which seems to admit of no other meaning than that given above. No need of any "contention." Langus renders, Pro virili suâ, and Grabe illustrates by reference to Apost. Const., lib. viii. cap. 12. Our own learned translators render the same phrase (cap. xiii., above) "to the utmost of our power." Some say this favours extemporary prayers, and others object. Oh! what matter either way? We all sing hymns, "according to our ability.".
1915. Or, of the eucharistic elements.
1916. Addressed to Minucius Fundanus. Generally credited as genuine.
1917. Regarded as spurious.
1918. That is, if any one accuses a Christian merely on the ground of his being a Christian.
1919. Spurious, no doubt; but the literature of the subject is very rich. See text and notes, Milman's Gibbon, vol. ii. 46.
1920. Literally, "fiery."
1921. Note I. (See capp. xxvi. and lvi.) In 1851 I recognised this stone in the Vatican, and read it with emotion. I copied it, as follows: "Semoni Sanco Deo Fidio Sacrvm Sex. Pompeius. S. P. F. Col. Mussianvs. Quinquennalis Decur Bidentalis Donum Dedit." The explanation is possibly this: Simon Magus was actually recognised as the God Semo, just as Barnabas and Paul were supposed to be Zeus and Hermes (Acts xiv. 12.), and were offered divine honours accordingly. Or the Samaritans may so have informed Justin on their understanding of this inscription, and with pride in the success of their countryman (Acts viii. 10.), whom they had recognised "as the great power of God." See Orelli (No. 1860), Insc., vol. i. 337. Note II. (The Thundering Legion.) The bas-relief on the column of

Antonine, in Rome, is a very striking complement of the story, but an answer to prayer is not a miracle. I simply transcribe from the American Translation of Alzog's Universal Church History the references there given to the Legio Fulminatrix:

"Tertull., Apol., cap. 5; Ad Scap., cap. 4; Euseb., v. 5; Greg. Nyss. Or., II in Martyr.; Oros., vii. 15; Dio. Cass. Epit.: Xiphilin., lib. lxxi. cap. 8; Jul. Capitol, in Marc. Antonin., cap. 24.".

The Second Apology of Justin for the Christians Addressed to the Roman Senate

Chapter I - Introduction

Romans, the things which have recently [1922] happened in your city under Urbicus, [1923] and the things which are likewise being everywhere unreasonably done by the governors, have compelled me to frame this composition for your sakes, who are men of like passions, and brethren, though ye know it not, and though ye be unwilling to acknowledge it on account of your glorying in what you esteem dignities. [1924] For everywhere, whoever is corrected by father, or neighbour, or child, or friend, or brother, or husband, or wife, for a fault, for being hard to move, for loving pleasure and being hard to urge to what is right (except those who have been persuaded that the unjust and intemperate shall be punished in eternal fire, but that the virtuous and those who lived like Christ shall dwell with God in a state that is free from suffering,--we mean, those who have become Christians), and the evil demons, who hate us, and who keep such men as these subject to themselves, and serving them in the capacity of judges, incite them, as rulers actuated by evil spirits, to put us to death. But that the cause of all that has taken place under Urbicus may become quite plain to you, I will relate what has been done.

Chapter II - Urbicus condemns the Christians to death

A certain woman lived with an intemperate [1925] husband; she herself, too, having formerly been intemperate. But when she came to the knowledge of the teachings of Christ she became sober-minded, and endeavoured to persuade her husband likewise to be temperate, citing the teaching of Christ, and assuring him that there shall be punishment in eternal fire inflicted upon those who do not live temperately and conformably to right reason. But he, continuing in the same excesses, alienated his wife from him by his actions. For she, considering it wicked to live any longer as a wife with a husband who sought in every way means of indulging in pleasure contrary to the law of nature, and in violation of what is right, wished to be divorced from him. And when she was overpersuaded by her friends, who advised her still to continue with him, in the idea that some time or other her husband might give hope of amendment, she did violence to her own feeling and remained with him. But when her husband had gone into Alexandria, and was reported to be conducting himself worse than ever, she--that she might not, by continuing in matrimonial connection with him, and by sharing his table and his bed, become a partaker also in his wickednesses and impieties--gave him what you call a bill of divorce, [1926] and was separated from him. But this noble husband of hers,--while he ought to have been rejoicing that those actions which formerly she unhesitatingly committed with the servants and hirelings, when she delighted in drunkenness and every vice, she had now given up, and desired that he too should give up the same,--when she had gone from him without his desire, brought an accusation against her, affirming that she was a Christian. And she presented a paper to thee, the Emperor, [1927] requesting that first she be permitted to arrange her affairs, and afterwards to make her defence against the accusation, when her affairs were set in order. And this you granted. And her quondam husband, since he was now no longer able to prosecute her, directed his assaults against a man, Ptolemæus, whom Urbicus punished, and who had been her teacher in the Christian doctrines. And this he did in the following way. He persuaded a centurion --who had cast Ptolemæus into prison, and who was friendly to himself--to take Ptolemæus and interrogate him on this sole point: whether he were a Christian? And Ptolemæus, being a lover of truth, and not of a deceitful or false disposition, when he confessed himself to be a Christian, was bound by the centurion, and for a long time punished in the prison. And, at last, when the man [1928] came to Urbicus, he was asked this one question only: whether he was a Christian? And again, being conscious of his duty, and the nobility of it through the teaching of Christ, he confessed his discipleship in the divine virtue. For he who denies anything either denies it because he condemns the thing itself, or he shrinks from confession because he is conscious of his own unworthiness or alienation from it, neither of which cases is that of the true Christian. And when Urbicus ordered him to be led away to punishment, one Lucius, who was also himself a Christian, seeing the unreasonable judgment that had thus been given, said to Urbicus: "What is the ground of this judgment? Why have you punished this man, not as an adulterer, nor fornicator, nor murderer, nor thief, nor robber, nor convicted of any crime at all, but who has only confessed that he is called by the name of Christian? This judgment of yours, O Urbicus, does not become the Emperor Pius, nor the philosopher, the son of Cæsar, nor the sacred senate." [1929] And he said nothing else in answer to Lucius than this: "You also seem to me to be such an one." And when Lucius answered, "Most certainly I am," he again ordered him also to be led away. And he professed his thanks, knowing that he was delivered from such wicked rulers, and was going to the Father and King of the heavens. And still a third having come forward, was condemned to be punished.

Chapter III - Justin accuses Crescens of ignorant prejudice against the Christians

I too, therefore, expect to be plotted against and fixed to the stake, by some of those I have named, or perhaps by Crescens, that lover of bravado and boasting; [1930] for the man is not worthy of the name of philosopher who publicly bears witness against us in matters which he does not understand, saying that the Christians are atheists and impious, and doing so to win favour with the deluded mob, and to please them. For if he assails us without having read the teachings of Christ, he is thoroughly depraved, and far worse than the illiterate, who often refrain from discussing or bearing false witness about matters they do not understand. Or, if he has read them and does not understand the majesty that is in them, or, understanding it, acts thus that he may not be suspected of being such [a Christian], he is far more base and thoroughly depraved, being conquered by illiberal and unreasonable opinion and fear. For I would have you to know that I proposed to him certain questions on this subject, and interrogated him, and found most convincingly that he, in truth, knows nothing. And to prove that I speak the truth, I am ready, if these disputations have not been reported to you, to conduct them again in your presence. And this would be an act worthy of a prince. But if my questions and his answers have been made known to you, you are already aware that he is acquainted with none of our matters; or, if he is acquainted with them, but, through fear of those who might hear him, does not dare to speak out, like Socrates, he proves himself, as I said before, no philosopher, but an opinionative man; [1931] at least he does not regard that Socratic and most admirable saying: "But a man must in no wise be honoured before the truth." [1932] But it is impossible for a Cynic, who makes indifference his end, to know any good but indifference.

Chapter IV - Why the Christians do not kill themselves

But lest some one say to us, "Go then all of you and kill yourselves, and pass even now to God, and do not trouble us," I will tell you why we do not so, but why, when examined, we fearlessly confess. We have been taught that God did not make the world aimlessly, but for the sake of the human race; and we have before stated that He takes pleasure in those who imitate His properties, and is displeased with those that embrace what is worthless either in word or deed. If, then, we all kill ourselves, we shall become the cause, as far as in us lies, why no one should be born, or instructed in the divine doctrines, or even why the human race should not exist; and we shall, if we so act, be ourselves acting in opposition to the will of God. But when we are examined, we make no denial, because we are not conscious of any evil, but count it impious not to speak the truth in all things, which also we know is pleasing to God, and because we are also now very desirous to deliver you from an unjust prejudice.

Chapter V - How the angels transgressed

But if this idea take possession of some one, that if we acknowledge God as our helper, we should not, as we say, be oppressed and persecuted by the wicked; this, too, I will solve. God, when He had made the whole world, and subjected things earthly to man, and arranged the heavenly elements for the increase of fruits and rotation of the seasons, and appointed this divine law--for these things also He evidently made for man--committed the care of men and of all things under heaven to angels whom He appointed over them. But the angels transgressed this appointment, and were captivated by love of women, and begat children who are those that are called demons; and besides, they afterwards subdued the human race to themselves, partly by magical writings, and partly by fears and the punishments they occasioned, and partly by teaching them to offer sacrifices, and incense, and libations, of which things they stood in need after they were enslaved by lustful passions; and among men they sowed murders, wars, adulteries, intemperate deeds, and all wickedness. Whence also the poets and mythologists, not knowing that it was the angels and those demons who had been begotten by them that did these things to men, and women, and cities, and nations, which they related, ascribed them to god himself, and to those who were accounted to be his very offspring, and to the offspring of those who were called his brothers, Neptune and Pluto, and to the children again of these their offspring. For whatever name each of the angels had given to himself and his children, by that name they called them.

Chapter VI - Names of God and of Christ, their meaning and power

But to the Father of all, who is unbegotten, there is no name given. For by whatever name He be called, He has as His elder the person who gives Him the name. But these words, Father, and God, and Creator, and Lord, and Master, are not names, but appellations derived from His good deeds and functions. And His Son, who alone is properly called Son, the Word, who also was with Him and was begotten before the works, when at first He created and arranged all things by Him, is called Christ, in reference to His being anointed and God's ordering all things through Him; this name itself also containing an unknown significance; as also the appellation "God" is not a name, but an opinion implanted in the nature of men of a thing that can hardly be explained. But "Jesus," His name as man and Saviour, has also significance. For He was made man also, as we before said, having been conceived according to the will of God the Father, for the sake of believing men, and for the destruction of the demons. And now you can learn this from what is under your own observation. For numberless demoniacs throughout the whole world, and in your city, many of our Christian men exorcising them in the name of Jesus Christ, who was crucified under Pontius Pilate, have healed and do heal, rendering helpless and driving the possessing devils out of the men, though they could not be cured by all the other exorcists, and those who used incantations and drugs.

Chapter VII - The world preserved for the sake of Christians. Man's responsibility

Wherefore God delays causing the confusion and destruction of the whole world, by which the wicked angels and demons and men shall cease to exist, because of the seed of the Christians, who know that they are the cause of preservation in nature. [1933] Since, if it were not so, it would not have been possible for you to do these things, and to be impelled by evil spirits; but the fire of judgment would descend and utterly dissolve all things, even as formerly the flood left no one but him only with his family who is by us called Noah, and by you Deucalion, from whom again such vast numbers have sprung, some of them evil and others good. For so we say that there will be the conflagration, but not as the Stoics, according to their doctrine of all things being changed into one another, which seems most degrading. But neither do we affirm that it is by fate that men do what they do, or suffer what they suffer, but that each man by free choice acts rightly or sins; and that it is by the influence of the wicked demons that earnest men, such as Socrates and the like, suffer persecution and are in bonds, while Sardanapalus, Epicurus, and the like, seem to be blessed in abundance and glory. The Stoics, not observing this, maintained that all things take place according to the necessity of fate. But since God in the beginning made the race of angels and men with free-will, they will justly suffer in eternal fire the punishment of whatever sins they have committed. And this is the nature of all that is made, to be capable of vice and virtue. For neither would any of them be praiseworthy unless there were power to turn to both [virtue and vice]. And this also is shown by those men everywhere who have made laws and philosophized according to right reason, by their prescribing to do some things and refrain from others. Even the Stoic philosophers, in their doctrine of morals, steadily honour the same things, so that it is evident that they are not very felicitous in what they say about principles and incorporeal things. For if they say that human actions come to pass by fate, they will maintain either that God is nothing else than the things which are ever turning, and altering, and dissolving into the same things, and will appear to have had a comprehension only of things that are destructible, and to have looked on God Himself as emerging both in part and in whole in every wickedness; [1934] or that neither vice nor virtue is anything; which is contrary to every sound idea, reason, and sense.

Chapter VIII - All have been hated in whom the Word has dwelt

And those of the Stoic school--since, so far as their moral teaching went, they were admirable, as were also the poets in some particulars, on account of the seed of reason [the Λόγος] implanted in every race of men--were, we know, hated and put to death,--Heraclitus for instance, and, among those of our own time, Musonius and others. For, as we intimated, the devils have always effected, that all those who anyhow live a reasonable and earnest life, and shun vice, be hated. And it is nothing wonderful; if the devils are proved to cause those to be much worse hated who live not according to a part only of the word diffused [among men], but by the knowledge and contemplation of the whole Word, which is Christ. And they, having been shut up in eternal fire, shall suffer their just punishment and penalty. For if they are even now overthrown by men through the name of Jesus Christ, this is an intimation of the punishment in eternal fire which is to be inflicted on themselves and those who serve them. For thus did both all the prophets foretell, and our own teacher Jesus teach. [1935]

Chapter IX - Eternal punishment not a mere threat

And that no one may say what is said by those who are deemed philosophers, that our assertions that the wicked are punished in eternal fire are big words and bugbears, and that we wish men to live virtuously through fear, and not because such a life is good and pleasant; I will briefly reply to this, that if this be not so, God does not exist; or, if He exists, He cares not for men, and neither virtue nor vice is anything, and, as we said before, lawgivers unjustly punish those who transgress good commandments. But since these are not unjust, and their Father teaches them by the word to do the same things as Himself, they who agree with them are not unjust. And if one object that the laws of men are diverse, and say that with some, one thing is considered good, another evil, while with others what seemed bad to the former is esteemed good, and what seemed good is esteemed bad, let him listen to what we say to this. We know that the wicked angels appointed laws conformable to their own wickedness, in which the men who are like them delight; and the right Reason, [1936] when He came, proved that not all opinions nor all doctrines are good, but that some are evil, while others are good. Wherefore, I will declare the same and similar things to such men as these, and, if need be, they shall be spoken of more at large. But at present I return to the subject.

Chapter X - Christ compared with Socrates

Our doctrines, then, appear to be greater than all human teaching; because Christ, who appeared for our sakes, became the whole rational being, both body, and reason, and soul. For whatever either lawgivers or philosophers uttered well, they elaborated by finding and contemplating some part of the Word. But since they did not know the whole of the Word, which is Christ, they often contradicted themselves. And those who by human birth were more ancient than Christ, when they attempted to consider and prove things by reason, were brought before the tribunals as impious persons and busybodies. And Socrates, who was more zealous in this direction than all of them, was accused of the very same crimes as ourselves. For they said that he was introducing new divinities, and did not consider those to be gods whom the state recognised. But he cast out from the state both Homer [1937] and the rest of the poets, and taught men to reject the wicked demons and those who did the things which the poets related; and he exhorted them to become acquainted with the God who was to them unknown, by means of the investigation of reason, saying, "That it is neither easy to find the Father and Maker of all, nor, having found Him, is it safe to declare Him to all." [1938] But these things our Christ did through His own power. For no one trusted in Socrates so as to die for this doctrine, but in Christ, who was partially known even by Socrates (for He was and is the Word who is in every man, and who foretold the things that were to come to pass both through the prophets and in His own person when He was made of like passions, and taught these things), not only philosophers and scholars believed, but also artisans and people entirely uneducated, despising both glory, and fear, and death; since He is a power of the ineffable Father, not the mere instrument of human reason. [1939]

Chapter XI - How Christians view death

But neither should we be put to death, nor would wicked men and devils be more powerful than we, were not death a debt due by every man that is born. Wherefore we give thanks when we pay this debt. And we judge it right and opportune to tell here, for the sake of Crescens and those who rave as he does, what is related by Xenophon. Hercules, says Xenophon, coming to a place where three ways met, found Virtue and Vice, who appeared to him in the form of women: Vice, in a luxurious dress, and with a seductive expression rendered blooming by such ornaments, and her eyes of a quickly melting tenderness, [1940] said to Hercules that if he would follow her, she would always enable him to pass his life in pleasure and adorned with the most graceful ornaments, such as were then upon her own person; and Virtue, who was of squalid look and dress, said, But if you obey me, you shall adorn yourself not with ornament nor beauty that passes away and perishes, but with everlasting and precious graces. And we are persuaded that every one who flees those things that seem to be good, and follows hard after what are reckoned difficult and strange, enters into blessedness. For Vice, when by imitation of what is incorruptible (for what is really incorruptible she neither has nor can produce) she has thrown around her own actions, as a disguise, the properties of virtue, and qualities which are really excellent, leads captive earthly-minded men, attaching to Virtue her own evil properties. But those who understood the excellences which belong to that which is real, are also uncorrupt in virtue. And this every sensible person ought to think both of Christians and of the athletes, and of those who did what the poets relate of the so-called gods, concluding as much from our contempt of death, even when it could be escaped. [1941]

Chapter XII - Christians proved innocent by their contempt of death

For I myself, too, when I was delighting in the doctrines of Plato, and heard the Christians slandered, and saw them fearless of death, and of all other things which are counted fearful, perceived that it was impossible that they could be living in wickedness and pleasure. For what sensual or intemperate man, or who that counts it good to feast on human flesh, [1942] could welcome death that he might be deprived of his enjoyments, and would not rather continue always the present life, and attempt to escape the observation of the rulers; and much less would he denounce himself when the consequence would be death? This also the wicked demons have now caused to be done by evil men. For having put some to death on account of the accusations falsely brought against us, they also dragged to the torture our domestics, either children or weak women, and by dreadful torments forced them to admit those fabulous actions which they themselves openly perpetrate; about which we are the less concerned, because none of these actions are really ours, and we have the unbegotten and ineffable God as witness both of our thoughts and deeds. For why did we not even publicly profess that these were the things which we esteemed good, and prove that these are the divine philosophy, saying that the mysteries of Saturn are performed when we slay a man, and that when we drink our fill of blood, as it is said we do, we are doing what you do before that idol you honour, and on which you sprinkle the blood not only of irrational animals, but also of men, making a libation of the blood of the slain by the hand of the most illustrious and noble man among you? And imitating Jupiter and the other gods in sodomy and shameless intercourse with woman, might we not bring as our apology the writings of Epicurus and the poets? But because we persuade men to avoid such instruction, and all who practise them and imitate such examples, as now in this discourse we have striven to persuade you, we are assailed in every kind of way. But we are not concerned, since we know that God is a just observer of all. But would that even now some one would mount a lofty rostrum, and shout with a loud voice; [1943] "Be ashamed, be ashamed, ye who charge the guiltless with those deeds which yourselves openly commit, and ascribe things which apply to yourselves and to your gods to those who have not even the slightest sympathy with them. Be ye converted; become wise."

Chapter XIII - How the Word has been in all men

For I myself, when I discovered the wicked disguise which the evil spirits had thrown around the divine doctrines of the Christians, to turn aside others from joining them, laughed both at those who framed these falsehoods, and at the disguise itself, and at popular opinion; and I confess that I both boast and with all my strength strive to be found a Christian; not because the teachings of Plato are different from those of Christ, but because they are not in all respects similar, as neither are those of the others, Stoics, and poets, and historians. For each man spoke well in proportion to the share he had of the spermatic word, [1944] seeing what was related to it. But they who contradict themselves on the more important points appear not to have possessed the heavenly [1945] wisdom, and the knowledge which cannot be spoken against. Whatever things were rightly said among all men, are the property of us Christians. For next to God, we worship and love the Word who is from the unbegotten and ineffable God, since also He became man for our sakes, that becoming a partaker of our sufferings, He might also bring us healing. For all the writers were able to see realities darkly through the sowing of the implanted word that was in them. For the seed and imitation imparted according to capacity is one thing, and quite another is the thing itself, of which there is the participation and imitation according to the grace which is from Him.

Chapter XIV - Justin prays that this appeal be published

And we therefore pray you to publish this little book, appending what you think right, that our opinions may be known to others, and that these persons may have a fair chance of being freed from erroneous notions and ignorance of good, who by their own fault are become subject to punishment; that so these things may be published to men, because it is in the nature of man to know good and evil; and by their condemning us, whom they do not understand, for actions which they say are wicked, and by delighting in the gods who did such things, and even now require similar actions from men, and by inflicting on us death or bonds or some other such punishment, as if we were guilty of these things, they condemn themselves, so that there is no need of other judges.

Chapter XV - Conclusion

And I despised the wicked and deceitful doctrine of Simon [1946] of my own nation. And if you give this book your authority, we will expose him before all, that, if possible, they may be converted. For this end alone did we compose this treatise. And our doctrines are not shameful, according to a sober judgment, but are indeed more lofty than all human philosophy: and if not so, they are at least unlike the doctrines of the Sotadists, and Philænidians, and Dancers, and

Epicureans, and such other teachings of the poets, which all are allowed to acquaint themselves with both as acted and as written. And henceforth we shall be silent, having done as much as we could, and having added the prayer that all men everywhere may be counted worthy of the truth. And would that you also, in a manner becoming piety and philosophy, [1947] would for your own sakes judge justly!

Footnotes:

1922. Literally, "both yesterday and the day before."

1923. See Grabe's note on the conjecture of Valesius that this prefect was Lollius Urbicus, the historian (vol. i. p. 1. and notes, p. 1).

1924. He has addressed them as "Romans," because in this they gloried together,--emperor, senate, soldiers, and citizens.

1925. ἀκολασταίνοντι, which word includes unchastity, as well as the other forms of intemperance. As we say, dissolute.

1926. ῥεπούδιον, i.e., "repudium," a bill of repudiation.

1927. Rather, "to thee, autocrat:" a very bold apostrophe, like that of Huss to the Emperor Sigismund, which crimsoned his forehead with a blush of shame.

1928. i e., Ptolemæus.

1929. On this passage, see Donaldson's Critical History, etc., vol. ii. p. 79.

1930. Words resembling "philosopher" in sound, viz. φιλοψόφου καὶ φιλοκόμπου. This passage is found elsewhere. See note, cap. viii., in the text preferred by Grabe.

1931. φιλόδοξος, which may mean a lover of vainglory.

1932. See Plato, Rep., p. 595.

1933. This is Dr. Donaldson's rendering of a clause on which the editors differ both as to reading and rendering.

1934. Literally, "becoming (γινόμενον) both through the parts and through the whole in every wickedness."

1935. Here, in Grabe's text, comes in the passage about Crescens.

1936. These words can be taken of the Λόγος as well as of the right reason diffused among men by Him.

1937. Plato, Rep., x. c. i. p. 595.

1938. Plat., Timæus, p. 28, C. (but "possible," and not "safe," is the word used by Plato).

1939. Certainly the author of this chapter, and others like it, cannot be accused of a feeble rhetoric.

1940. Another reading is πρὸς τὰς ὄψεις, referring to the eyes of the beholder; and which may be rendered, "speedily fascinating to the sight."

1941. Καὶ φευκτοῦ θανάτου may also be rendered, "even of death which men flee from."

1942. Alluding to the common accusation against the Christians.

1943. Literally, "with a tragic voice,"--the loud voice in which the Greek tragedies were recited through the mask persona.

1944. The word disseminated among men. St. Jas. i. 21.

1945. Literally, dimly seen at a distance.

1946. Simon Magus appears to be one with whom Justin is perfectly familiar, and hence we are not to conclude rashly that he blundered as to the divine honours rendered to him as the Sabine God.

1947. Another apostrophe, and a home thrust for "Pius the philosopher" and the emperor.

Dialogue of Justin, Philosopher and Martyr, with Trypho, a Jew

Chapter I - Introduction

While I was going about one morning in the walks of the Xystus, [1948] a certain man, with others in his company, having met me, and said, "Hail, O philosopher!" And immediately after saying this, he turned round and walked along with me; his friends likewise followed him. And I in turn having addressed him, said, "What is there important?"

And he replied, "I was instructed," says he "by Corinthus the Socratic in Argos, that I ought not to despise or treat with indifference those who array themselves in this dress [1949] but to show them all kindness, and to associate with them, as perhaps some advantage would spring from the intercourse either to some such man or to myself. It is good, moreover, for both, if either the one or the other be benefited. On this account, therefore, whenever I see any one in such costume, I gladly approach him, and now, for the same reason, have I willingly accosted you; and these accompany me, in the expectation of hearing for themselves something profitable from you."

"But who are you, most excellent man?" So I replied to him in jest. [1950]

Then he told me frankly both his name and his family. "Trypho," says he, "I am called; and I am a Hebrew of the circumcision, [1951] and having escaped from the war [1952] lately carried on there I am spending my days in Greece, and chiefly at Corinth."

"And in what," said I, "would you be profited by philosophy so much as by your own lawgiver and the prophets?"

"Why not?" he replied. "Do not the philosophers turn every discourse on God? and do not questions continually arise to them about His unity and providence? Is not this truly the duty of philosophy, to investigate the Deity?"

"Assuredly," said I, "so we too have believed. But the most [1953] have not taken thought of this, whether there be one or more gods, and whether they have a regard for each one of us or no, as if this knowledge contributed nothing to our happiness; nay, they moreover attempt to persuade us that God takes care of the universe with its genera and species, but not of me and you, and each individually, since otherwise we would surely not need to pray to Him night and day. But it is not difficult to understand the upshot of this; for fearlessness and license in speaking result to such as maintain these opinions, doing and saying whatever they choose, neither dreading punishment nor hoping for any benefit from God. For how could they? They affirm that the same things shall always happen; and, further, that I and you shall again live in like manner, having become neither better men nor worse. But there are some others, [1954] who, having supposed the soul to be immortal and immaterial, believe that though they have committed evil they will not suffer punishment (for that which is immaterial is insensible), and that the soul, in consequence of its immortality, needs nothing from God."

And he, smiling gently, said, "Tell us your opinion of these matters, and what idea you entertain respecting God, and what your philosophy is."

Chapter II - Justin describes his studies in philosophy

"I will tell you," said I, "what seems to me; for philosophy is, in fact, the greatest possession, and most honourable before God, [1955] to whom it leads us and alone commends us; and these are truly holy men who have bestowed attention on philosophy. What philosophy is, however, and the reason why it has been sent down to men, have escaped the observation of most; for there would be neither Platonists, nor Stoics, nor Peripatetics, nor Theoretics, [1956] nor Pythagoreans, this knowledge being one. [1957] I wish to tell you why it has become many-headed. It has happened that those who first handled it [i.e., philosophy], and who were therefore esteemed illustrious men, were succeeded by those who made no investigations concerning truth, but only admired the perseverance and self-discipline of the former, as well as the novelty of the doctrines; and each thought that to be true which he learned from his teacher: then, moreover, those latter persons handed down to their successors such things, and others similar to them; and this system was called by the name of him who was styled the father of the doctrine. Being at first desirous of personally conversing with one of these men, I surrendered myself to a certain Stoic; and having spent a considerable time with him, when I had not acquired any further knowledge of God (for he did not know himself, and said such instruction was unnecessary), I left him and betook myself to another, who was called a Peripatetic, and as he fancied, shrewd. And this man, after having entertained me for the first few days, requested me to settle the fee, in order that our intercourse might not be unprofitable. Him, too, for this reason I abandoned, believing him to be no philosopher at all. But when my soul was eagerly desirous to hear the peculiar and choice philosophy, I came to a Pythagorean, very celebrated--a man who thought much of his own wisdom. And then, when I had an interview with him, willing to become his hearer and disciple, he said, What then? Are you acquainted with music, astronomy, and geometry? Do you expect to perceive any of those things which conduce to a happy life, if you have not been first informed on those points which wean the soul from sensible objects, and render it fitted for objects which appertain to the mind, so that it can contemplate that which is honourable in its essence and that which is good in its essence?' Having commended many of these branches of learning, and telling me that they were necessary, he dismissed me when I confessed to him my ignorance. Accordingly I took it rather impatiently, as was to be expected when I failed in my hope, the more so because I deemed the man had some knowledge; but reflecting again on the space of time during which I would have to linger over those branches of learning, I was not able to endure longer procrastination. In my helpless condition it occurred to me to have a meeting with the Platonists, for their fame was great. I thereupon spent as much of my time as possible with one who had lately settled in our city, [1958] --a sagacious man, holding a high position among the Platonists,-- and I progressed, and made the greatest improvements daily. And the perception of immaterial things quite overpowered me, and the contemplation of ideas furnished my mind with wings, [1959] so that in a little while I supposed that I had become wise; and such was my stupidity, I expected forthwith to look upon God, for this is the end of Plato's philosophy.

Chapter III - Justin narrates the manner of his conversion

"And while I was thus disposed, when I wished at one period to be filled with great quietness, and to shun the path of men, I used to go into a certain field not far from the sea. And when I was near that spot one day, which having reached I purposed to be by myself, a certain old man, by no means contemptible in appearance, exhibiting meek and venerable manners, followed me at a little distance. And when I turned round to him, having halted, I fixed my eyes rather keenly on him.

"And he said, Do you know me?'

"I replied in the negative.

" Why, then,' said he to me, do you so look at me?'

" I am astonished,' I said, because you have chanced to be in my company in the same place; for I had not expected to see any man here.'

"And he says to me, I am concerned about some of my household. These are gone away from me; and therefore have I come to make personal search for them, if, perhaps, they shall make their appearance somewhere. But why are you here?' said he to me.

" I delight,' said I, in such walks, where my attention is not distracted, for converse with myself is uninterrupted; and such places are most fit for philology.' [1960]

" Are you, then, a philologian,' [1961] said he, but no lover of deeds or of truth? and do you not aim at being a practical man so much as being a sophist?'

" What greater work,' said I, could one accomplish than this, to show the reason which governs all, and having laid hold of it, and being mounted upon it, to look down on the errors of others, and their pursuits? But without philosophy and right reason, prudence would not be present to any man. Wherefore it is necessary for every man to philosophize, and to esteem this the greatest and most honourable work; but other things only of second-rate or third-rate importance, though, indeed, if they be made to depend on philosophy, they are of moderate value, and worthy of acceptance; but deprived of it, and not accompanying it, they are vulgar and coarse to those who pursue them.'

" Does philosophy, then, make happiness?' said he, interrupting.

" Assuredly,' I said, and it alone.'

" What, then, is philosophy?' he says; and what is happiness? Pray tell me, unless something hinders you from saying.'

" Philosophy, then,' said I, is the knowledge of that which really exists, and a clear perception of the truth; and happiness is the reward of such knowledge and wisdom.'

" But what do you call God?' said he.

" That which always maintains the same nature, and in the same manner, and is the cause of all other things --that, indeed, is God.' So I answered him; and he listened to me with pleasure, and thus again interrogated me:--

" Is not knowledge a term common to different matters? For in arts of all kinds, he who knows any one of them is called a skilful man in the art of generalship, or of ruling, or of healing equally. But in divine and human affairs it is not so. Is there a knowledge which affords understanding of human and divine things, and then a thorough acquaintance with the divinity and the righteousness of them?'

" Assuredly,' I replied.

" What, then? Is it in the same way we know man and God, as we know music, and arithmetic, and astronomy, or any other similar branch?'

" By no means,' I replied.

" You have not answered me correctly, then,' he said; for some [branches of knowledge] come to us by learning, or by some employment, while of others we have knowledge by sight. Now, if one were to tell you that there exists in India an animal with a nature unlike all others, but of such and such a kind, multiform and various, you would not know it before you saw it; but neither would you be competent to give any account of it, unless you should hear from one who had seen it.'

" Certainly not,' I said.

" How then,' he said, should the philosophers judge correctly about God, or speak any truth, when they have no knowledge of Him, having neither seen Him at any time, nor heard Him?'

" But, father,' said I, the Deity cannot be seen merely by the eyes, as other living beings can, but is discernible to the mind alone, as Plato says; and I believe him.'

Chapter IV - The soul of itself cannot see God

" Is there then,' says he, such and so great power in our mind? Or can a man not perceive by sense sooner? Will the mind of man see God at any time, if it is uninstructed by the Holy Spirit?'

" Plato indeed says,' replied I, that the mind's eye is of such a nature, and has been given for this end, that we may see that very Being when the mind is pure itself, who is the cause of all discerned by the mind, having no colour, no form, no greatness--nothing, indeed, which the bodily eye looks upon; but It is something of this sort, he goes on to say, that is beyond all essence, unutterable and inexplicable, but alone honourable and good, coming suddenly into souls well-dispositioned, on account of their affinity to and desire of seeing Him.'

" What affinity, then,' replied he, is there between us and God? Is the soul also divine and immortal, and a part of that very regal mind? And even as that sees God, so also is it attainable by us to conceive of the Deity in our mind, and thence to become happy?'

" Assuredly,' I said.

" And do all the souls of all living beings comprehend Him?' he asked; or are the souls of men of one kind and the souls of horses and of asses of another kind?'

" No; but the souls which are in all are similar,' I answered.

" Then,' says he, shall both horses and asses see, or have they seen at some time or other, God?'

" No,' I said; for the majority of men will not, saving such as shall live justly, purified by righteousness, and by every other virtue.'

" It is not, therefore,' said he, on account of his affinity, that a man sees God, nor because he has a mind, but because he is temperate and righteous?'

" Yes,' said I; and because he has that whereby he perceives God.'

" What then? Do goats or sheep injure any one?'

" No one in any respect,' I said.

" Therefore these animals will see [God] according to your account,' says he.

" No; for their body being of such a nature, is an obstacle to them.'

"He rejoined, If these animals could assume speech, be well assured that they would with greater reason ridicule our body; but let us now dismiss this subject, and let it be conceded to you as you say. Tell me, however, this: Does the soul see [God] so long as it is in the body, or after it has been removed from it?'

" So long as it is in the form of a man, it is possible for it,' I continue, to attain to this by means of the mind; but especially when it has been set free from the body, and being apart by itself, it gets possession of that which it was wont continually and wholly to love.'

" Does it remember this, then [the sight of God], when it is again in the man?'

" It does not appear to me so,' I said.

" What, then, is the advantage to those who have seen [God]? or what has he who has seen more than he who has not seen, unless he remember this fact, that he has seen?'

" I cannot tell,' I answered.

" And what do those suffer who are judged to be unworthy of this spectacle?' said he.

" They are imprisoned in the bodies of certain wild beasts, and this is their punishment.'

" Do they know, then, that it is for this reason they are in such forms, and that they have committed some sin?'

" I do not think so.'

" Then these reap no advantage from their punishment, as it seems: moreover, I would say that they are not punished unless they are conscious of the punishment.'

" No indeed.'

" Therefore souls neither see God nor transmigrate into other bodies; for they would know that so they are punished, and they would be afraid to commit even the most trivial sin afterwards. But that they can perceive that God exists, and that righteousness and piety are honourable, I also quite agree with you,' said he.

" You are right,' I replied.

Chapter V - The soul is not in its own nature immortal

" These philosophers know nothing, then, about these things; for they cannot tell what a soul is.'

" It does not appear so.'

" Nor ought it to be called immortal; for if it is immortal, it is plainly unbegotten.'

" It is both unbegotten and immortal, according to some who are styled Platonists.'

" Do you say that the world is also unbegotten?'

" Some say so. I do not, however, agree with them.'

" You are right; for what reason has one for supposing that a body so solid, possessing resistance, composite, changeable, decaying, and renewed every day, has not arisen from some cause? But if the world is begotten, souls also are necessarily begotten; and perhaps at one time they were not in existence, for they were made on account of men and other living creatures, if you will say that they have been begotten wholly apart, and not along with their respective bodies.'

" This seems to be correct.'

" They are not, then, immortal?'

" No; since the world has appeared to us to be begotten.'

" But I do not say, indeed, that all souls die; for that were truly a piece of good fortune to the evil. What then? The souls of the pious remain in a better place, while those of the unjust and wicked are in a worse, waiting for the time of judgment. Thus some which have appeared worthy of God never die; but others are punished so long as God wills them to exist and to be punished.'

" Is what you say, then, of a like nature with that which Plato in Timæus hints about the world, when he says that it is indeed subject to decay, inasmuch as it has been created, but that it will neither be dissolved nor meet with the fate of death on account of the will of God? Does it seem to you the very same can be said of the soul, and generally of all things? For those things which exist after [1962] God, or shall at any time exist, [1963] these have the nature of decay, and are such as may be blotted out and cease to exist; for God alone is unbegotten and incorruptible, and therefore He is God, but all other things after Him are created and corruptible. For this reason souls both die and are punished: since, if they were unbegotten, they would neither sin, nor be filled with folly, nor be cowardly, and again ferocious; nor would they willingly transform into swine, and serpents, and dogs; and it would not indeed be just to compel them, if they be unbegotten. For that which is unbegotten is similar to, equal to, and the same with that which is unbegotten; and neither in power nor in honour should the one be preferred to the other, and hence there are not many things which are unbegotten: for if there were some difference between them, you would not discover the cause of the difference, though you searched for it; but after letting the mind ever wander to infinity, you would at length, wearied out, take your stand on one Unbegotten, and say that this is the Cause of all. Did such escape the observation of Plato and Pythagoras, those wise men,' I said, who have been as a wall and fortress of philosophy to us?'

Chapter VI - These things were unknown to Plato and other philosophers

" It makes no matter to me,' said he, whether Plato or Pythagoras, or, in short, any other man held such opinions. For the truth is so; and you would perceive it from this. The soul assuredly is or has life. If, then, it is life, it would cause something else, and not itself, to live, even as motion would move something else than itself. Now, that the soul lives, no one would deny. But if it lives, it lives not as being life, but as the partaker of life; but that which partakes of anything, is different from that of which it does partake. Now the soul partakes of life, since God wills it to live. Thus, then, it will not even partake [of life] when God does not will it to live. For to live is not its attribute, as it is God's; but as a man does not live always, and the soul is not for ever conjoined with the body, since, whenever this harmony must be broken up, the soul leaves the body, and the man exists no longer; even so, whenever the soul must cease to exist, the spirit of life is removed from it, and there is no more soul, but it goes back to the place from whence it was taken.'

Chapter VII - The knowledge of truth to be sought from the prophets alone

" Should any one, then, employ a teacher?' I say, or whence may any one be helped, if not even in them there is truth?'

" There existed, long before this time, certain men more ancient than all those who are esteemed philosophers, both righteous and beloved by God, who spoke by the Divine Spirit, and foretold events which would take place, and which are now taking place. They are called prophets. These alone both saw and announced the truth to men, neither reverencing nor fearing any man, not influenced by a desire for glory, but speaking those things alone which they saw and which they heard, being filled with the Holy Spirit. Their writings are still extant, and he who has read them is very much helped in his knowledge of the beginning and end of things, and of those matters which the philosopher ought to know, provided he has believed them. For they did not use demonstration in their treatises, seeing that they were witnesses to the truth above all demonstration, and worthy of belief; and those events which have happened, and those which are happening, compel you to assent to the utterances made by them, although, indeed, they were entitled to credit on account of the miracles which they performed, since they both glorified the Creator, the God and Father of all things, and proclaimed His Son, the Christ [sent] by Him: which, indeed, the false prophets, who are filled with the lying unclean spirit, neither have done nor do, but venture to work certain wonderful deeds for the purpose of astonishing men, and glorify the spirits and demons of error. But pray that, above all things, the gates of light may be opened to you; for these things cannot be perceived or understood by all, but only by the man to whom God and His Christ have imparted wisdom.'

Chapter VIII - Justin by his colloquy is kindled with love to Christ

"When he had spoken these and many other things, which there is no time for mentioning at present, he went away, bidding me attend to them; and I have not seen him since. But straightway a flame was kindled in my soul; and a love of the prophets, and of those men who are friends of Christ, possessed me; and whilst revolving his words in my mind, I found this philosophy alone to be safe and profitable. Thus, and for this reason, I am a philosopher. Moreover, I would wish that all, making a resolution similar to my own, do not keep themselves away from the words of the Saviour. For they possess a terrible power in themselves, and are sufficient to inspire those who turn aside from the path of rectitude with awe; while the sweetest rest is afforded those who make a diligent practice of them. If, then, you have any concern for yourself, and if you are eagerly looking for salvation, and if you believe in God, you may--since you are not indifferent to the matter [1964] -- become acquainted with the Christ of God, and, after being initiated, [1965] live a happy life."

When I had said this, my beloved friends [1966] those who were with Trypho laughed; but he, smiling, says, "I approve of your other remarks, and admire the eagerness with which you study divine things; but it were better for you still to abide in the philosophy of Plato, or of some other man, cultivating endurance, self-control, and moderation, rather than be deceived by false words, and follow the opinions of men of no reputation. For if you remain in that mode of philosophy, and live blamelessly, a hope of a better destiny were left to you; but when you have forsaken God, and reposed confidence in man, what safety still awaits you? If, then, you are willing to listen to me (for I have already considered you a friend), first be circumcised, then observe what ordinances have been enacted with respect to the Sabbath, and the feasts, and the new moons of God; and, in a word, do all things which have been written in the law: and then perhaps you shall obtain mercy from God. But Christ --if He has indeed been born, and exists anywhere--is unknown, and does not even know Himself, and has no power until Elias come to anoint Him, and make Him manifest to all. And you, having accepted a groundless report, invent a Christ for yourselves, and for his sake are inconsiderately perishing."

Chapter IX - The Christians have not believed groundless stories

"I excuse and forgive you, my friend," I said. "For you know not what you say, but have been persuaded by teachers who do not understand the Scriptures; and you speak, like a diviner, whatever comes into your mind. But if you are willing to listen to an account of Him, how we have not been deceived, and shall not cease to confess Him,--although men's reproaches be heaped upon us, although the most terrible tyrant compel us to deny Him,--I shall prove to you as you stand here that we have not believed empty fables, or words without any foundation but words filled with the Spirit of God, and big with power, and flourishing with grace."

Then again those who were in his company laughed, and shouted in an unseemly manner. Then I rose up and was about to leave; but he, taking hold of my garment, said I should not accomplish that [1967] until I had performed what I promised. "Let not, then, your companions be so tumultuous, or behave so disgracefully," I said. "But if they wish, let them listen in silence; or, if some better occupation prevent them, let them go away; while we, having retired to some spot, and resting there, may finish the discourse." It seemed good to Trypho that we should do so; and accordingly, having agreed upon it, we retired to the middle space of the Xystus. Two of his friends, when they had ridiculed and made game of our zeal, went off. And when we were come to that place, where there are stone seats on both sides, those with Trypho, having seated themselves on the one side, conversed with each other, some one of them having thrown in a remark about the war waged in Judæa.

Chapter X - Trypho blames the Christians for this alone--the non-observance of the law

And when they ceased, I again addressed them thus:--

"Is there any other matter, my friends, in which we are blamed, than this, that we live not after the law, and are not circumcised in the flesh as your forefathers were, and do not observe sabbaths as you do? Are our lives and customs also slandered among you? And I ask this: have you also believed concerning us, that we eat men; and that after the feast, having extinguished the lights, we engage in promiscuous concubinage? Or do you condemn us in this alone, that we adhere to such tenets, and believe in an opinion, untrue, as you think?"

"This is what we are amazed at," said Trypho, "but those things about which the multitude speak are not worthy of belief; for they are most repugnant to human nature. Moreover, I am aware that your precepts in the so-called Gospel are so wonderful and so great, that I suspect no one can keep them; for I have carefully read them. But this is what we are most at a loss about: that you, professing to be pious, and supposing yourselves better than others, are not in any particular separated from them, and do not alter your mode of living from the nations, in that you observe no festivals or sabbaths, and do not have the rite of circumcision; and further, resting your hopes on a man that was crucified, you yet expect to obtain some good thing from God, while you do not obey His commandments. Have you not read, that that soul shall be cut off from his people who shall not have been circumcised on the eighth day? And this has been ordained for strangers and for slaves equally. But you, despising this covenant rashly, reject the consequent duties, and attempt to persuade yourselves that you know God, when, however, you perform none of those things which they do who fear God. If, therefore, you can defend yourself on these points, and make it manifest in what way you hope for anything whatsoever, even though you do not observe the law, this we would very gladly hear from you, and we shall make other similar investigations."

Chapter XI - The law abrogated; the New Testament promised and given by God

"There will be no other God, O Trypho, nor was there from eternity any other existing" (I thus addressed him), "but He who made and disposed all this universe. Nor do we think that there is one God for us, another for you, but that He alone is God who led your fathers out from Egypt with a strong hand and a high arm. Nor have we trusted in any other (for there is no other), but in Him in whom you also have trusted, the God of Abraham, and of Isaac, and of Jacob. But we do not trust through Moses or through the law; for then we would do the same as yourselves. But now [1968] --(for I have read that there shall be a final law, and a covenant, the chiefest of all, which it is now incumbent on all men to observe, as many as are seeking after the inheritance of God. For the law promulgated on Horeb is now old, and belongs to yourselves alone; but this is for all universally. Now, law placed against law has abrogated that which is before it, and a covenant which comes after in like manner has put an end to the previous one; and an eternal and final law--namely, Christ --has been given to us, and the covenant is trustworthy, after which there shall be no law, no commandment, no ordinance. Have you not read this which Isaiah says: Hearken unto Me, hearken unto Me, my people; and, ye kings, give ear unto Me: for a law shall go forth from Me, and My judgment shall be for a light to the nations. My righteousness approaches swiftly, and My salvation shall go forth, and nations shall trust in Mine arm?' [1969] And by Jeremiah, concerning this same new covenant, He thus speaks: Behold, the days come, saith the Lord, that I will make a new covenant with the house of Israel and with the house of Judah; not according to the covenant which I made with their fathers, in the day that I took them by the hand, to bring them out of the land of Egypt' [1970]). If, therefore, God proclaimed a new covenant which was to be instituted, and this for a light of the nations, we see and are persuaded that men approach God, leaving their idols and other unrighteousness, through the name of Him who was crucified, Jesus Christ, and abide by their confession even unto death, and maintain piety. Moreover, by the works and by the attendant miracles, it is possible for all to understand that He is the new law, and the new covenant, and the expectation of those who out of every people wait for the good things of God. For the true spiritual Israel, and descendants of Judah, Jacob, Isaac, and Abraham (who in uncircumcision was approved of and blessed by God on account of his faith, and called the father of many nations), are we who have been led to God through this crucified Christ, as shall be demonstrated while we proceed.

Chapter XII - The Jews violate the eternal law, and interpret ill that of Moses

I also adduced another passage in which Isaiah exclaims: " Hear My words, and your soul shall live; and I will make an everlasting covenant with you, even the sure mercies of David. Behold, I have given Him for a witness to the people: nations which know not Thee shall call on Thee; peoples who know not Thee shall escape to Thee, because of thy God, the Holy One of Israel; for He has glorified Thee.' [1971] This same law you have despised, and His new holy covenant you have slighted; and now you neither receive it, nor repent of your evil deeds. For your ears are closed, your eyes are blinded, and the heart is hardened,' Jeremiah [1972] has cried; yet not even then do you listen. The Lawgiver is present, yet you do not see Him; to the poor the Gospel is preached, the blind see, yet you do not understand. You have now need of a second circumcision, though you glory greatly in the flesh. The new law requires you to keep perpetual sabbath, and you, because you are idle for one day, suppose you are pious, not discerning why this has been commanded you: and if you eat unleavened bread, you say the will of God has been fulfilled. The Lord our God does not take pleasure in such observances: if there is any perjured person or a thief among you, let him cease to be so; if any adulterer, let him repent; then he has kept the sweet and true sabbaths of God. If any one has impure hands, let him wash and be pure.

Chapter XIII - Isaiah teaches that sins are forgiven through Christ's blood

"For Isaiah did not send you to a bath, there to wash away murder and other sins, which not even all the water of the sea were sufficient to purge; but, as might have been expected, this was that saving bath of the olden time which followed [1973] those who repented, and who no longer were purified by the blood of goats and of sheep, or by the ashes of an heifer, or by the offerings of fine flour, but by faith through the blood of Christ, and through His death, who died for this very reason, as Isaiah himself said, when he spake thus: The Lord shall make bare His holy arm in the eyes of all the nations, and all the nations and the ends of the earth shall see the salvation of God. Depart ye, depart ye, depart ye, [1974] go ye out from thence, and touch no unclean thing; go ye out of the midst of her, be ye clean that bear the vessels of the Lord, for [1975] ye go not with haste. For the Lord shall go before you; and the Lord, the God of Israel, shall gather you together. Behold, my servant shall deal prudently; and He shall be exalted, and be greatly glorified. As many were astonished at Thee, so Thy form and Thy glory shall be marred more than men. So shall many nations be astonished at Him, and the kings shall shut their mouths; for that which had not been told them concerning Him shall they see, and that which they had not heard shall they consider. Lord, who hath believed our report? and to whom is the arm of the Lord revealed? We have announced Him as a child before Him, as a root in a dry ground. He hath no form or comeliness, and when we saw Him He had no form or beauty; but His form is dishonoured, and fails more than the sons of men. He is a man in affliction, and acquainted with bearing sickness, because His face has been turned away; He was despised, and we esteemed Him not. He bears our sins, and is distressed for us; and we esteemed Him to be in toil and in affliction, and in evil treatment. But He was wounded for our transgressions, He was bruised for our iniquities; the chastisement of our peace was upon Him. With His stripes we are healed. All we, like sheep, have gone astray. Every man has turned to his own way; and the Lord laid on Him our iniquities, and by reason of His oppression He opens not His mouth. He was brought as a sheep to the slaughter; and as a lamb before her shearer is dumb, so He openeth not His mouth. In His humiliation His judgment was taken away. And who shall declare His generation? For His life is taken from the earth. Because of the transgressions of my people He came unto death. And I will give the wicked for His grave, and the rich for His death, because He committed no iniquity, and deceit was not found in His mouth. And the Lord wills to purify Him from affliction. If he has been given for sin, your soul shall see a long-lived seed. And the Lord wills to take His soul away from trouble, to show Him light, and to form Him in understanding, to justify the righteous One who serves many well. And He shall bear our sins; therefore He shall inherit many, and shall divide the spoil of the strong, because His soul was delivered to death; and He was numbered with the transgressors, and He bare the sins of many, and was delivered for their transgression. Sing, O barren, who bearest not; break forth and cry aloud, thou who dost not travail in pain: for more are the children of the desolate than the children of the married wife. For the Lord said, Enlarge the place of thy tent and of thy curtains; fix them, spare not, lengthen thy cords, and strengthen thy stakes: stretch forth to thy right and thy left; and thy seed shall inherit the Gentiles, and thou shalt make the desolate cities to be inherited. Fear not because thou art ashamed, neither be thou confounded because thou hast been reproached; for thou shalt forget everlasting shame, and shalt not remember the reproach of thy widowhood, because the Lord has made a name for Himself, and He who has redeemed thee shall be called through the whole earth the God of Israel. The Lord has called thee as [1976] a woman forsaken and grieved in spirit, as [1977] a woman hated from her youth.' [1978]

Chapter XIV - Righteousness is not placed in Jewish rites, but in the conversion of the heart given in baptism by Christ

"By reason, therefore, of this laver of repentance and knowledge of God, which has been ordained on account of the transgression of God's people, as Isaiah cries, we have believed, and testify that that very baptism which he announced is alone able to purify those who have repented; and this is the water of life. But the cisterns which you have dug for yourselves are broken and profitless to you. For what is the use of that baptism which cleanses the flesh and body alone? Baptize the soul from wrath and from covetousness, from envy, and from hatred; and, lo! the body is pure. For this is the symbolic significance of unleavened bread, that you do not commit the old deeds of wicked leaven. But you have understood all things in a carnal sense, and you suppose it to be piety if you do such things, while your souls are filled with deceit, and, in short, with every wickedness. Accordingly, also, after the seven days of eating unleavened bread, God commanded them to mingle new leaven, that is, the performance of other works, and not the imitation of the old and evil works. And because this is what this new Lawgiver demands of you, I shall again refer to the words which have been quoted by me, and to others also which have been passed over. They are related by Isaiah to the following effect: Hearken to me, and your soul shall live; and I will make with you an everlasting covenant, even the sure mercies of David. Behold, I have given Him for a witness to the people, a leader and commander to the nations. Nations which know not Thee shall call on Thee; and peoples who know not Thee shall escape unto Thee, because of Thy God, the Holy One of Israel, for He has glorified Thee. Seek ye God; and when you find Him, call on Him, so long as He may be nigh you. Let the wicked forsake his ways, and the unrighteous man his thoughts; and let him return unto the Lord, and he will obtain mercy, because He will abundantly pardon your sins. For my thoughts are not as your thoughts, neither are my ways as your ways; but as far removed as the heavens are from the earth, so far is my way removed from your way, and your thoughts from my thoughts. For as the snow or the rain descends from heaven, and shall not return till it waters the earth, and makes it bring forth and bud, and gives seed to the sower and bread for food, so shall My word be that goeth forth out of My mouth: it shall not return until it shall have accomplished all that I desired, and I shall make My commandments prosperous. For ye shall go out with joy, and be taught with gladness. For the mountains and the hills shall leap while they expect you, and all the trees of the fields shall applaud with their branches: and instead of the thorn shall come up the cypress, and instead of the brier shall come up the myrtle. And the Lord shall be for a name, and for an everlasting sign, and He shall not fail!' [1979] Of these and such like words written by the prophets, O Trypho," said I, "some have reference to the first advent of Christ, in which He is preached as inglorious, obscure, and of mortal appearance: but others had reference to His second advent, when He shall appear in glory and above the clouds; and your nation shall see and know Him whom they have pierced, as Hosea, one of the twelve prophets, and Daniel, foretold.

Chapter XV - In what the true fasting consists

"Learn, therefore, to keep the true fast of God, as Isaiah says, that you may please God. Isaiah has cried thus: Shout vehemently, and do not spare: lift up thy voice as with a trumpet, and show My people their transgressions, and the house of Jacob their sins. They seek Me from day to day, and desire to know My ways, as a nation that did righteousness, and forsook not the judgment of God. They ask of Me now righteous judgment, and desire to draw near to God, saying, Wherefore have we fasted, and Thou seest not? and afflicted our souls, and Thou hast not known? Because in the days of your fasting you find your own pleasure, and oppress all those who are subject to you. Behold, ye fast for strifes and debates, and smite the humble with your fists. Why do ye fast for Me, as to-day, so that your voice is heard aloud? This is not the fast which I have chosen, the day in which a man shall afflict his soul. And not even if you bend your neck like a ring, or clothe yourself in sackcloth and ashes, shall you call this a fast, and a day acceptable to the Lord. This is not the fast which I have chosen, saith the Lord; but loose every unrighteous bond, dissolve the terms of wrongous covenants, let the oppressed go free, and avoid every iniquitous contract. Deal thy bread to the hungry, and lead the homeless poor under thy dwelling; if thou seest the naked, clothe him; and do not hide thyself from thine own flesh. Then shall thy light break forth as the morning, and thy garments [1980] shall rise up quickly: and thy righteousness shall go before thee, and the glory of God shall envelope thee. Then shalt thou cry, and the Lord shall hear thee: while thou art speaking, He will say, Behold, I am here. And if thou take away from thee the yoke, and the stretching out of the hand, and the word of murmuring; and shalt give heartily thy bread to the hungry, and shalt satisfy the afflicted soul; then shall thy light arise in the darkness, and thy darkness shall be as the noon-day: and thy God shall be with thee continually, and thou shalt be satisfied according as thy soul desireth, and thy bones shall become fat, and shall be as a watered garden, and as a fountain of water, or as a land where water fails not.' [1981] Circumcise, therefore, the foreskin of your heart,' as the words of God in all these passages demand."

Chapter XVI - Circumcision given as a sign, that the Jews might be driven away for their evil deeds done to Christ and the Christians

"And God himself proclaimed by Moses, speaking thus: And circumcise the hardness of your hearts, and no longer stiffen the neck. For the Lord your God is both Lord of lords, and a great, mighty, and terrible God, who regardeth not persons, and taketh not rewards.' [1982] And in Leviticus: Because they have transgressed against Me, and despised Me, and because they have walked contrary to Me, I also walked contrary to them, and I shall cut them off in the land of their enemies. Then shall their uncircumcised heart be turned. [1983] For the circumcision according to the flesh, which is from Abraham, was given for a sign; that you may be separated from other nations, and from us; and that you alone may suffer that which you now justly suffer; and that your land may be desolate, and your cities burned with fire; and that strangers may eat your fruit in your presence, and not one of you may go up to Jerusalem.' [1984] For you are not recognised among the rest of men by any other mark than your fleshly circumcision. For none of you, I suppose, will venture to say that God neither did nor does foresee the events, which are future, nor foreordained his deserts for each one. Accordingly, these things have happened to you in fairness and justice, for you have slain the Just One, and His prophets before Him; and now you reject those who hope in Him, and in Him who sent Him--God the Almighty and Maker of all things --cursing in your synagogues those that believe on Christ. For you have not the power to lay hands upon us, on account of those who now have the mastery. But as often as you could, you did so. Wherefore God, by Isaiah, calls to you, saying, Behold how the righteous man perished, and no one regards it. For the righteous man is taken away from before iniquity. His grave shall be in peace, he is taken away from the midst. Draw near hither, ye lawless children, seed of the adulterers, and children of the whore. Against whom have you sported yourselves, and against whom have you opened the mouth, and against whom have you loosened the tongue?' [1985]

Chapter XVII - The Jews sent persons through the whole earth to spread calumnies on Christians

"For other nations have not inflicted on us and on Christ this wrong to such an extent as you have, who in very deed are the authors of the wicked prejudice against the Just One, and us who hold by Him. For after that you had crucified Him, the only blameless and righteous Man,-- through whose stripes those who approach the Father by Him are healed, --when you knew that He had risen from the dead and ascended to heaven, as the prophets foretold He would, you not only did not repent of the wickedness which you had committed, but at that time you selected and sent out from Jerusalem chosen men through all the land to tell that the godless heresy of the Christians had sprung up, and to publish those things which all they who knew us not speak against us. So that you are the cause not only of your own unrighteousness, but in fact of that of all other men. And Isaiah cries justly: By reason of you, My name is blasphemed among the Gentiles.' [1986] And: Woe unto their soul! because they have devised an evil device against themselves, saying, Let us bind the righteous, for he is distasteful to us. Therefore they shall eat the fruit of their doings. Woe unto the wicked! evil shall be rendered to him according to the works of his hands.' And again, in other words: [1987] Woe unto them that draw their iniquity as with a long cord, and their transgressions as with the harness of a heifer's yoke: who say, Let his speed come near; and let the counsel of the Holy One of Israel come, that we may know it. Woe unto them that call evil good, and good evil; that put light for darkness, and darkness for light; that put bitter for sweet, and sweet for bitter!' [1988] Accordingly, you displayed great zeal in publishing throughout all the land bitter and dark and unjust things against the only blameless and righteous Light sent by God.

For He appeared distasteful to you when He cried among you, It is written, My house is the house of prayer; but ye have made it a den of thieves!' [1989] He overthrew also the tables of the money-changers in the temple, and exclaimed, Woe unto you, Scribes and Pharisees, hypocrites! because ye pay tithe of mint and rue, but do not observe the love of God and justice. Ye whited sepulchres! appearing beautiful outward, but are within full of dead men's bones.' [1990] And to the Scribes, Woe unto you, Scribes! for ye have the keys, and ye do not enter in yourselves, and them that are entering in ye hinder; ye blind guides!'

Chapter XVIII - Christians would observe the law, if they did not know why it was instituted

"For since you have read, O Trypho, as you yourself admitted, the doctrines taught by our Saviour, I do not think that I have done foolishly in adding some short utterances of His to the prophetic statements. Wash therefore, and be now clean, and put away iniquity from your souls, as God bids you be washed in this laver, and be circumcised with the true circumcision. For we too would observe the fleshly circumcision, and the Sabbaths, and in short all the feasts, if we did not know for what reason they were enjoined you,--namely, on account of your transgressions and the hardness of your hearts. For if we patiently endure all things contrived against us by wicked men and demons, so that even amid cruelties unutterable, death and torments, we pray for mercy to those who inflict such things upon us, and do not wish to give the least retort to any one, even as the new Lawgiver commanded us: how is it, Trypho, that we would not observe those rites which do not harm us, --I speak of fleshly circumcision, and Sabbaths, and feasts?

Chapter XIX - Circumcision unknown before Abraham. The law was given by Moses on account of the hardness of their hearts

"It is this about which we are at a loss, and with reason, because, while you endure such things, you do not observe all the other customs which we are now discussing."

"This circumcision is not, however, necessary for all men, but for you alone, in order that, as I have already said, you may suffer these things which you now justly suffer. Nor do we receive that useless baptism of cisterns, for it has nothing to do with this baptism of life. Wherefore also God has announced that you have forsaken Him, the living fountain, and digged for yourselves broken cisterns which can hold no water. Even you, who are the circumcised according to the flesh, have need of our circumcision; but we, having the latter, do not require the former. For if it were necessary, as you suppose, God would not have made Adam uncircumcised; would not have had respect to the gifts of Abel when, being uncircumcised, he offered sacrifice, and would not have been pleased with the uncircumcision of Enoch, who was not found, because God had translated him. Lot, being uncircumcised, was saved from Sodom, the angels themselves and the Lord sending him out. Noah was the beginning of our race; yet, uncircumcised, along with his children he went into the ark. Melchizedek, the priest of the Most High, was uncircumcised; to whom also Abraham the first who received circumcision after the flesh, gave tithes, and he blessed him: after whose order God declared, by the mouth of David, that He would establish the everlasting priest. Therefore to you alone this circumcision was necessary, in order that the people may be no people, and the nation no nation; as also Hosea, [1991] one of the twelve prophets, declares. Moreover, all those righteous men already mentioned, though they kept no Sabbaths, [1992] were pleasing to God; and after them Abraham with all his descendants until Moses, under whom your nation appeared unrighteous and ungrateful to God, making a calf in the wilderness: wherefore God, accommodating Himself to that nation, enjoined them also to offer sacrifices, as if to His name, in order that you might not serve idols. Which precept, however, you have not observed; nay, you sacrificed your children to demons. And you were commanded to keep Sabbaths, that you might retain the memorial of God. For His word makes this announcement, saying, That ye may know that I am God who redeemed you.' [1993]

Chapter XX - Why choice of meats was prescribed

"Moreover, you were commanded to abstain from certain kinds of food, in order that you might keep God before your eyes while you ate and drank, seeing that you were prone and very ready to depart from His knowledge, as Moses also affirms: The people ate and drank, and rose up to play.' [1994] And again: Jacob ate, and was satisfied, and waxed fat; and he who was beloved kicked: he waxed fat, he grew thick, he was enlarged, and he forsook God who had made him.' [1995] For it was told you by Moses in the book of Genesis, that God granted to Noah, being a just man, to eat of every animal, but not of flesh with the blood, which is dead." [1996] And as he was ready to say, "as the green herbs," I anticipated him: "Why do you not receive this statement, as the green herbs,' in the sense in which it was given by God, to wit, that just as God has granted the herbs for sustenance to man, even so has He given the animals for the diet of flesh? But, you say, a distinction was laid down thereafter to Noah, because we do not eat certain herbs. As you interpret it, the thing is incredible. And first I shall not occupy myself with this, though able to say and to hold that every vegetable is food, and fit to be eaten. But although we discriminate between green herbs, not eating all, we refrain from eating some, not because they are common or unclean, but because they are bitter, or deadly, or thorny. But we lay hands on and take of all herbs which are sweet, very nourishing and good, whether they are marine or land plants. Thus also God by the mouth of Moses commanded you to abstain from unclean and improper [1997] and violent animals:

when, moreover, though you were eating manna in the desert, and were seeing all those wondrous acts wrought for you by God, you made and worshipped the golden calf.[1998] Hence he cries continually, and justly, They are foolish children, in whom is no faith.'[1999]

Chapter XXI - Sabbaths were instituted on account of the people's sins, and not for a work of righteousness

"Moreover, that God enjoined you to keep the Sabbath, and impose on you other precepts for a sign, as I have already said, on account of your unrighteousness, and that of your fathers,--as He declares that for the sake of the nations, lest His name be profaned among them, therefore He permitted some of you to remain alive,--these words of His can prove to you: they are narrated by Ezekiel thus: I am the Lord your God; walk in My statutes, and keep My judgments, and take no part in the customs of Egypt; and hallow My Sabbaths; and they shall be a sign between Me and you, that ye may know that I am the Lord your God. Notwithstanding ye rebelled against Me, and your children walked not in My statutes, neither kept My judgments to do them: which if a man do, he shall live in them. But they polluted My Sabbaths. And I said that I would pour out My fury upon them in the wilderness, to accomplish My anger upon them; yet I did it not; that My name might not be altogether profaned in the sight of the heathen. I led them out before their eyes, and I lifted up Mine hand unto them in the wilderness, that I would scatter them among the heathen, and disperse them through the countries; because they had not executed My judgments, but had despised My statutes, and polluted My Sabbaths, and their eyes were after the devices of their fathers. Wherefore I gave them also statutes which were not good, and judgments whereby they shall not live. And I shall pollute them in their own gifts, that I may destroy all that openeth the womb, when I pass through them.'[2000]

Chapter XXII - So also were sacrifices and oblations

"And that you may learn that it was for the sins of your own nation, and for their idolatries and not because there was any necessity for such sacrifices, that they were likewise enjoined, listen to the manner in which He speaks of these by Amos, one of the twelve, saying: Woe unto you that desire the day of the Lord! to what end is this day of the Lord for you? It is darkness and not light, as when a man flees from the face of a lion, and a bear meets him; and he goes into his house, and leans his hands against the wall, and the serpent bites him. Shall not the day of the Lord be darkness and not light, even very dark, and no brightness in it? I have hated, I have despised your feast-days, and I will not smell in your solemn assemblies: wherefore, though ye offer Me your burnt-offerings and sacrifices, I will not accept them; neither will I regard the peace-offerings of your presence. Take thou away from Me the multitude of thy songs and psalms; I will not hear thine instruments. But let judgment be rolled down as water, and righteousness as an impassable torrent. Have ye offered unto Me victims and sacrifices in the wilderness, O house of Israel? saith the Lord. And have ye taken up the tabernacle of Moloch, and the star of your god Raphan, the figures which ye made for yourselves? And I will carry you away beyond Damascus, saith the Lord, whose name is the Almighty God. Woe to them that are at ease in Zion, and trust in the mountain of Samaria: those who are named among the chiefs have plucked away the first-fruits of the nations: the house of Israel have entered for themselves. Pass all of you unto Calneh, and see; and from thence go ye unto Hamath the great, and go down thence to Gath of the strangers, the noblest of all these kingdoms, if their boundaries are greater than your boundaries. Ye who come to the evil day, who are approaching, and who hold to false Sabbaths; who lie on beds of ivory, and are at ease upon their couches; who eat the lambs out of the flock, and the sucking calves out of the midst of the herd; who applaud at the sound of the musical instruments; they reckon them as stable, and not as fleeting, who drink wine in bowls, and anoint themselves with the chief ointments, but they are not grieved for the affliction of Joseph. Wherefore now they shall be captives, among the first of the nobles who are carried away; and the house of evil-doers shall be removed, and the neighing of horses shall be taken away from Ephraim.'[2001] And again by Jeremiah: Collect your flesh, and sacrifices, and eat: for concerning neither sacrifices nor libations did I command your fathers in the day in which I took them by the hand to lead them out of Egypt.'[2002] And again by David, in the forty-ninth Psalm, He thus said: The God of gods, the Lord hath spoken, and called the earth, from the rising of the sun unto the going down thereof. Out of Zion is the perfection of His beauty. God, even our God, shall come openly, and shall not keep silence. Fire shall burn before Him, and it shall be very tempestuous round about Him. He shall call to the heavens above, and to the earth, that He may judge His people. Assemble to Him His saints; those that have made a covenant with Him by sacrifices. And the heavens shall declare His righteousness, for God is judge. Hear, O My people, and I will speak to thee; O Israel, and I will testify to thee, I am God, even thy God. I will not reprove thee for thy sacrifices; thy burnt-offerings are continually before me. I will take no bullocks out of thy house, nor he-goats out of thy folds: for all the beasts of the field are Mine, the herds and the oxen on the mountains. I know all the fowls of the heavens, and the beauty of the field is Mine. If I were hungry, I would not tell thee; for the world is Mine, and the fulness thereof. Will I eat the flesh of bulls, or drink the blood of goats? Offer unto God the sacrifice of praise, and pay thy vows unto the Most High, and call upon Me in the day of trouble, and I will deliver thee, and thou shalt glorify Me. But unto the wicked God saith, What hast thou to do to declare My statutes, and to take My covenant into thy mouth? But thou hast hated instruction, and cast My words behind thee. When thou sawest a thief, thou consentedst with him; and hast been partaker with the adulterer. Thy mouth has framed evil, and thy tongue has enfolded deceit. Thou sittest and speakest against thy brother; thou slanderest thine own mother's son. These things hast thou done, and I kept silence; thou thoughtest that I would be like thyself in wickedness. I will reprove thee, and set thy sins in order before thine eyes. Now consider this, ye that forget God, lest He tear you in pieces, and there be none to deliver. The sacrifice of praise shall glorify Me; and there is the way in which I shall show him My salvation.' [2003] Accordingly He neither takes sacrifices from you nor commanded them at first to be offered because they are needful to Him, but because of your sins. For indeed the temple, which is called the temple in Jerusalem, He admitted to be His house or court, not as though He needed it, but in order that you, in this view of it, giving yourselves to Him, might not worship idols. And that this is so, Isaiah says: What house have ye built Me? saith the Lord. Heaven is My throne, and earth is My footstool.' [2004]

Chapter XXIII - The opinion of the Jews regarding the law does an injury to God

"But if we do not admit this, we shall be liable to fall into foolish opinions, as if it were not the same God who existed in the times of Enoch and all the rest, who neither were circumcised after the flesh, nor observed Sabbaths, nor any other rites, seeing that Moses enjoined such observances; or that God has not wished each race of mankind continually to perform the same righteous actions: to admit which, seems to be ridiculous and absurd. Therefore we must confess that He, who is ever the same, has commanded these and such like institutions on account of sinful men, and we must declare Him to be benevolent, foreknowing, needing nothing, righteous and good. But if this be not so, tell me, sir, what you think of those matters which we are investigating." And when no one responded: "Wherefore, Trypho, I will proclaim to you, and to those who wish to become proselytes, the divine message which I heard from that man. [2005] Do you see that the elements are not idle, and keep no Sabbaths? Remain as you were born. For if there was no need of circumcision before Abraham, or of the observance of Sabbaths, of feasts and sacrifices, before Moses; no more need is there of them now, after that, according to the will of God, Jesus Christ the Son of God has been born without sin, of a virgin sprung from the stock of Abraham. For when Abraham himself was in uncircumcision, he was justified and blessed by reason of the faith which he reposed in God, as the Scripture tells. Moreover, the Scriptures and the facts themselves compel us to admit that He received circumcision for a sign, and not for righteousness. So that it was justly recorded concerning the people, that the soul which shall not be circumcised on the eighth day shall be cut off from his family. And, furthermore, the inability of the female sex to receive fleshly circumcision, proves that this circumcision has been given for a sign, and not for a work of righteousness. For God has given likewise to women the ability to observe all things which are righteous and virtuous; but we see that the bodily form of the male has been made different from the bodily form of the female; yet we know that neither of them is righteous or unrighteous merely for this cause, but [is considered righteous] by reason of piety and righteousness.

Chapter XXIV - The Christians' circumcision far more excellent

"Now, sirs," I said, "it is possible for us to show how the eighth day possessed a certain mysterious import, which the seventh day did not possess, and which was promulgated by God through these rites. But lest I appear now to diverge to other subjects, understand what I say: the blood of that circumcision is obsolete, and we trust in the blood of salvation; there is now another covenant, and another law has gone forth from Zion. Jesus Christ circumcises all who will--as was declared above --with knives of stone; [2006] that they may be a righteous nation, a people keeping faith, holding to the truth, and maintaining peace. Come then with me, all who fear God, who wish to see the good of Jerusalem. Come, let us go to the light of the Lord; for He has liberated His people, the house of Jacob. Come, all nations; let us gather ourselves together at Jerusalem, no longer plagued by war for the sins of her people. For I was manifest to them that sought Me not; I was found of them that asked not for Me;' [2007] He exclaims by Isaiah: I said, Behold Me, unto nations which were not called by My name. I have spread out My hands all the day unto a disobedient and gainsaying people, which walked in a way that was not good, but after their own sins. It is a people that provoketh Me to my face.' [2008]

Chapter XXV - The Jews boast in vain that they are sons of Abraham

"Those who justify themselves, and say they are sons of Abraham, shall be desirous even in a small degree to receive the inheritance along with you; [2009] as the Holy Spirit, by the mouth of Isaiah, cries, speaking thus while he personates them: Return from heaven, and behold from the habitation of Thy holiness and glory. Where is Thy zeal and strength? Where is the multitude of Thy mercy? for Thou hast sustained us, O Lord. For Thou art our Father, because Abraham is ignorant of us, and Israel has not recognised us. But Thou, O Lord, our Father, deliver us: from the beginning Thy name is upon us. O Lord, why hast Thou made us to err from Thy way? and hardened our hearts, so that we do not fear Thee? Return for Thy servants' sake, the tribes of Thine inheritance, that we may inherit for a little Thy holy mountain. We were as from the beginning, when Thou didst not bear rule over us, and when Thy name was not called upon us. If Thou wilt open the heavens, trembling shall seize the mountains before Thee: and they shall be melted, as wax melts before the fire; and fire shall consume the adversaries, and Thy name shall be manifest among the adversaries; the nations shall be put into disorder before Thy face. When Thou shalt do glorious things, trembling shall seize the mountains before Thee. From the beginning we have not heard, nor have our eyes seen a God besides Thee: and Thy works, [2010] the mercy which Thou shall show to those who repent. He shall meet those who do righteousness, and they shall remember Thy ways. Behold, Thou art wroth, and we were sinning. Therefore we have erred and become all unclean, and all our righteousness is as the rags of a woman set apart: and we have faded away like leaves by reason of our iniquities; thus the wind will take us away. And there is none that calleth upon Thy name, or remembers to take hold of Thee; for Thou hast turned away Thy face from us, and hast given us up on account of our sins. And now return, O Lord, for we are all Thy people. The city of Thy holiness has become desolate. Zion has become as a wilderness, Jerusalem a curse; the house, our holiness, and the glory which our fathers blessed, has been burned with fire; and all the glorious nations [2011] have fallen along with it. And in addition to these [misfortunes], O Lord, Thou hast refrained Thyself, and art silent, and hast humbled us very much.' " [2012]

And Trypho remarked, "What is this you say? that none of us shall inherit anything on the holy mountain of God?"

Chapter XXVI - No salvation to the Jews except through Christ

And I replied, "I do not say so; but those who have persecuted and do persecute Christ, if they do not repent, shall not inherit anything on the holy mountain. But the Gentiles, who have believed on Him, and have repented of the sins which they have committed, they shall receive the inheritance along with the patriarchs and the prophets, and the just men who are descended from Jacob, even although they neither keep the Sabbath, nor are circumcised, nor observe the feasts. Assuredly they shall receive the holy inheritance of God. For God speaks by Isaiah thus: I, the Lord God, have called Thee in righteousness, and will hold Thine hand, and will strengthen Thee; and I have given Thee for a covenant of the people, for a light of the Gentiles, to open the eyes of the blind, to bring out them that are bound from the chains, and those who sit in darkness from the prison-house.' [2013] And again: Lift up a standard [2014] for the people; for, lo, the Lord has made it heard unto the end of the earth. Say ye to the daughters of Zion, Behold, thy Saviour has come; having His reward, and His work before His face: and He shall call it a holy nation, redeemed by the Lord. And thou shalt be called a city sought out, and not forsaken. Who is this that cometh from Edom? in red garments from Bosor? This that is beautiful in apparel, going up with great strength? I speak righteousness, and the judgment of salvation. Why are Thy garments red, and Thine apparel as from the trodden wine-press? Thou art full of the trodden grape. I have trodden the wine-press all alone, and of the people there is no man with Me; and I have trampled them in fury, and crushed them to the ground, and spilled their blood on the earth. For the day of retribution has come upon them, and the year of redemption is present. And I looked, and there was none to help; and I considered, and none assisted: and My arm delivered; and My fury came on them, and I trampled them in My fury, and spilled their blood on the earth.' " [2015]

Chapter XXVII - Why God taught the same things by the prophets as by Moses

And Trypho said, "Why do you select and quote whatever you wish from the prophetic writings, but do not refer to those which expressly command the Sabbath to be observed? For Isaiah thus speaks: If thou shalt turn away thy foot from the Sabbaths, so as not to do thy pleasure on the holy day, and shalt call the Sabbaths the holy delights of thy God; if thou shalt not lift thy foot to work, and shalt not speak a word from thine own mouth; then thou shalt trust in the Lord, and He shall cause thee to go up to the good things of the land; and He shall feed thee with the inheritance of Jacob thy father: for the mouth of the Lord hath spoken it.' " [2016]

And I replied, "I have passed them by, my friends, not because such prophecies were contrary to me, but because you have understood, and do understand, that although God commands you by all the prophets to do the same things which He also commanded by Moses, it was on account of the hardness of your hearts, and your ingratitude towards Him, that He continually proclaims them, in order that, even in this way, if you repented, you might please Him, and neither sacrifice your children to demons, nor be partakers with thieves, nor lovers of gifts, nor hunters after revenge, nor fail in doing judgment for orphans, nor be inattentive to the justice due to the widow, nor have your hands full of blood. For the daughters of Zion have walked with a high neck, both sporting by winking with their eyes, and sweeping along their dresses. [2017] For they are all gone aside,' He exclaims, they are all become useless. There is none that understands, there is not so much as one. With their tongues they have practised deceit, their throat is an open sepulchre, the poison of asps is under their lips, destruction and misery are in their paths, and the way of peace they have not known.' [2018] So that, as in the beginning, these things were enjoined you because of your wickedness, in like manner because of your stedfastness in it, or rather your increased proneness to it, by means of the same precepts He calls you to a remembrance or knowledge of it. But you are a people hard-hearted and without understanding, both blind and lame, children in whom is no faith, as He Himself says, honouring Him only with your lips, far from Him in your hearts, teaching doctrines that are your own and not His. For, tell me, did God wish the priests to sin when they offer the sacrifices on the Sabbaths? or those to sin, who are circumcised and do circumcise on the Sabbaths; since He commands that on the eighth day--even though it happen to be a Sabbath-- those who are born shall be always circumcised? or could not the infants be operated upon one day previous or one day subsequent to the Sabbath, if He knew that it is a sinful act upon the Sabbaths? Or why did He not teach those--who are called righteous and pleasing to Him, who lived before Moses and Abraham, who were not circumcised in their foreskin, and observed no Sabbaths--to keep these institutions?"

Chapter XXVIII - True righteousness is obtained by Christ

And Trypho replied, "We heard you adducing this consideration a little ago, and we have given it attention: for, to tell the truth, it is worthy of attention; and that answer which pleases most --namely, that so it seemed good to Him--does not satisfy me. For this is ever the shift to which those have recourse who are unable to answer the question."

Then I said, "Since I bring from the Scriptures and the facts themselves both the proofs and the inculcation of them, do not delay or hesitate to put faith in me, although I am an uncircumcised man; so short a time is left you in which to become proselytes. If Christ's coming shall have anticipated you, in vain you will repent, in vain you will weep; for He will not hear you. Break up your fallow ground,' Jeremiah has cried to the people, and sow not among thorns. Circumcise yourselves to the Lord, and circumcise the foreskin of your heart.' [2019] Do not sow, therefore, among thorns, and in untilled ground, whence you can have no fruit. Know Christ; and behold the fallow ground, good, good and fat, is in your hearts. For, behold, the days come, saith the Lord, that I will visit all them that are circumcised in their foreskins; Egypt, and Judah, [2020] and Edom, and the sons of Moab. For all the nations are uncircumcised, and all the house of Israel are uncircumcised in their hearts.' [2021] Do you see how that God does not mean this circumcision which is given for a sign? For it is of no use to the Egyptians, or the sons of Moab, or the sons of Edom. But though a man be a Scythian or a Persian, if he has the knowledge of God and of His Christ, and keeps the everlasting righteous decrees, he is circumcised with the good and useful circumcision, and is a friend of God, and God rejoices in his gifts and offerings. But I will lay before you, my friends, the very words of God, when He said to the people by Malachi, one of the twelve prophets, I have no pleasure in you, saith the Lord; and I shall not accept your sacrifices at your hands: for from the rising of the sun unto its setting My name shall be glorified among the Gentiles; and in every place a sacrifice is offered unto My name, even a pure sacrifice: for My name is honoured among the Gentiles, saith the Lord; but ye profane it.' [2022] And by David He said, A people whom I have not known, served Me; at the hearing of the ear they obeyed Me.'[2023]

Chapter XXIX - Christ is useless to those who observe the law

"Let us glorify God, all nations gathered together; for He has also visited us. Let us glorify Him by the King of glory, by the Lord of hosts. For He has been gracious towards the Gentiles also; and our sacrifices He esteems more grateful than yours. What need, then, have I of circumcision, who have been witnessed to by God? What need have I of that other baptism, who have been baptized with the Holy Ghost? I think that while I mention this, I would persuade even those who are possessed of scanty intelligence. For these words have neither been prepared by me, nor embellished by the art of man; but David sung them, Isaiah preached them, Zechariah proclaimed them, and Moses wrote them. Are you acquainted with them, Trypho? They are contained in your

Scriptures, or rather not yours, but ours. [2024] For we believe them; but you, though you read them, do not catch the spirit that is in them. Be not offended at, or reproach us with, the bodily uncircumcision with which God has created us; and think it not strange that we drink hot water on the Sabbaths, since God directs the government of the universe on this day equally as on all others; and the priests, as on other days, so on this, are ordered to offer sacrifices; and there are so many righteous men who have performed none of these legal ceremonies, and yet are witnessed to by God Himself.

Chapter XXX - Christians possess the true righteousness

"But impute it to your own wickedness, that God even can be accused by those who have no understanding, of not having always instructed all in the same righteous statutes. For such institutions seemed to be unreasonable and unworthy of God to many men, who had not received grace to know that your nation were called to conversion and repentance of spirit, [2025] while they were in a sinful condition and labouring under spiritual disease; and that the prophecy which was announced subsequent to the death of Moses is everlasting. And this is mentioned in the Psalm, my friends. [2026] And that we, who have been made wise by them, confess that the statutes of the Lord are sweeter than honey and the honey-comb, is manifest from the fact that, though threatened with death, we do not deny His name. Moreover, it is also manifest to all, that we who believe in Him pray to be kept by Him from strange, i.e., from wicked and deceitful, spirits; as the word of prophecy, personating one of those who believe in Him, figuratively declares. For we do continually beseech God by Jesus Christ to preserve us from the demons which are hostile to the worship of God, and whom we of old time served, in order that, after our conversion by Him to God, we may be blameless. For we call Him Helper and Redeemer, the power of whose name even the demons do fear; and at this day, when they are exorcised in the name of Jesus Christ, crucified under Pontius Pilate, governor of Judæa, they are overcome. And thus it is manifest to all, that His Father has given Him so great power, by virtue of which demons are subdued to His name, and to the dispensation of His suffering.

Chapter XXXI - If Christ's power be now so great, how much greater at the second advent!

"But if so great a power is shown to have followed and to be still following the dispensation of His suffering, how great shall that be which shall follow His glorious advent! For He shall come on the clouds as the Son of man, so Daniel foretold, and His angels shall come with Him. These are the words: I beheld till the thrones were set; and the Ancient of days did sit, whose garment was white as snow, and the hair of His head like the pure wool. His throne was like a fiery flame, His wheels as burning fire. A fiery stream issued and came forth from before Him. Thousand thousands ministered unto Him, and ten thousand times ten thousand stood before Him. The books were opened, and the judgment was set. I beheld then the voice of the great words which the horn speaks: and the beast was beat down, and his body destroyed, and given to the burning flame. And the rest of the beasts were taken away from their dominion, and a period of life was given to the beasts until a season and time. I saw in the vision of the night, and, behold, one like the Son of man coming with the clouds of heaven; and He came to the Ancient of days, and stood before Him. And they who stood by brought Him near; and there were given Him power and kingly honour, and all nations of the earth by their families, and all glory, serve Him. And His dominion is an everlasting dominion, which shall not be taken away; and His kingdom shall not be destroyed. And my spirit was chilled within my frame, and the visions of my head troubled me. I came near unto one of them that stood by, and inquired the precise meaning of all these things. In answer he speaks to me, and showed me the judgment of the matters: These great beasts are four kingdoms, which shall perish from the earth, and shall not receive dominion for ever, even for ever and ever. Then I wished to know exactly about the fourth beast, which destroyed all [the others] and was very terrible, its teeth of iron, and its nails of brass; which devoured, made waste, and stamped the residue with its feet: also about the ten horns upon its head, and of the one which came up, by means of which three of the former fell. And that horn had eyes, and a mouth speaking great things; and its countenance excelled the rest. And I beheld that horn waging war against the saints, and prevailing against them, until the Ancient of days came; and He gave judgment for the saints of the Most High. And the time came, and the saints of the Most High possessed the kingdom. And it was told me concerning the fourth beast: There shall be a fourth kingdom upon earth, which shall prevail over all these kingdoms, and shall devour the whole earth, and shall destroy and make it thoroughly waste. And the ten horns are ten kings that shall arise; and one shall arise after them; [2027] and he shall surpass the first in evil deeds, and he shall subdue three kings, and he shall speak words against the Most High, and shall overthrow the rest of the saints of the Most High, and shall expect to change the seasons and the times. And it shall be delivered into his hands for a time, and times, and half a time.

And the judgment sat, and they shall take away his dominion, to consume and to destroy it unto the end. And the kingdom, and the power, and the great places of the kingdoms under the heavens, were given to the holy people of the Most High, to reign in an everlasting kingdom: and all powers shall be subject to Him, and shall obey Him. Hitherto is the end of the matter. I, Daniel, was possessed with a very great astonishment, and my speech was changed in me; yet I kept the matter in my heart.' " [2028]

Chapter XXXII - Trypho objecting that Christ is described as glorious by Daniel, Justin distinguishes two advents

And when I had ceased, Trypho said, "These and such like Scriptures, sir, compel us to wait for Him who, as Son of man, receives from the Ancient of days the everlasting kingdom. But this so-called Christ of yours was dishonourable and inglorious, so much so that the last curse contained in the law of God fell on him, for he was crucified."

Then I replied to him, "If, sirs, it were not said by the Scriptures which I have already quoted, that His form was inglorious, and His generation not declared, and that for His death the rich would suffer death, and with His stripes we should be healed, and that He would be led away like a sheep; and if I had not explained that there would be two advents of His,--one in which He was pierced by you; a second, when you shall know Him whom you have pierced, and your tribes shall mourn, each tribe by itself, the women apart, and the men apart,--then I must have been speaking dubious and obscure things. But now, by means of the contents of those Scriptures esteemed holy and prophetic amongst you, I attempt to prove all [that I have adduced], in the hope that some one of you may be found to be of that remnant which has been left by the grace of the Lord of Σαβαώθ for the eternal salvation. In order, therefore, that the matter inquired into may be plainer to you, I will mention to you other words also spoken by the blessed David, from which you will perceive that the Lord is called the Christ by the Holy Spirit of prophecy; and that the Lord, the Father of all, has brought Him again from the earth, setting Him at His own right hand, until He makes His enemies His footstool; which indeed happens from the time that our Lord Jesus Christ ascended to heaven, after He rose again from the dead, the times now running on to their consummation; and he whom Daniel foretells would have dominion for a time, and times, and an half, is even already at the door, about to speak blasphemous and daring things against the Most High. But you, being ignorant of how long he will have dominion, hold another opinion. For you interpret the time' as being a hundred years. But if this is so, the man of sin must, at the shortest, reign three hundred and fifty years, in order that we may compute that which is said by the holy Daniel-- and times'--to be two times only. All this I have said to you in digression, in order that you at length may be persuaded of what has been declared against you by God, that you are foolish sons; and of this, Therefore, behold, I will proceed to take away this people, and shall take them away; and I will strip the wise of their wisdom, and will hide the understanding of their prudent men;' [2029] and may cease to deceive yourselves and those who hear you, and may learn of us, who have been taught wisdom by the grace of Christ. The words, then, which were spoken by David, are these: [2030] The Lord said unto My Lord, Sit Thou at My right hand, until I make Thine enemies Thy footstool. The Lord shall send the rod of Thy strength out of Sion: rule Thou also in the midst of Thine enemies. With Thee shall be, in the day, the chief of Thy power, in the beauties of Thy saints. From the womb, before the morning star, have I begotten Thee. The Lord hath sworn, and will not repent: Thou art a priest for ever after the order of Melchizedek. The Lord is at Thy right hand: He has crushed kings in the day of His wrath: He shall judge among the heathen, He shall fill [with] the dead bodies. [2031] He shall drink of the brook in the way; therefore shall He lift up the head.'

Chapter XXXIII - Ps. cx. is not spoken of Hezekiah. He proves that Christ was first humble, then shall be glorious

"And," I continued, "I am not ignorant that you venture to expound this psalm as if it referred to king Hezekiah; but that you are mistaken, I shall prove to you from these very words forthwith. The Lord hath sworn, and will not repent,' it is said; and, Thou art a priest forever, after the order of Melchizedek,' with what follows and precedes. Not even you will venture to object that Hezekiah was either a priest, or is the everlasting priest of God; but that this is spoken of our Jesus, these expressions show. But your ears are shut up, and your hearts are made dull. [2032] For by this statement, The Lord hath sworn, and will not repent: Thou art a priest for ever, after the order of Melchizedek,' with an oath God has shown Him (on account of your unbelief) to be the High Priest after the order of Melchizedek; i.e., as Melchizedek was described by Moses as the priest of the Most High, and he was a priest of those who were in uncircumcision, and blessed the circumcised Abraham who brought him tithes, so God has shown that His everlasting Priest, called also by the Holy Spirit Lord, would be Priest of those in uncircumcision. Those too in circumcision who approach Him, that is, believing Him and seeking blessings from Him, He will both receive and bless. And that He shall be first humble as a man, and then exalted, these words at the end of the Psalm show: He shall drink of the brook in the way,' and then, Therefore shall He lift up the head.'

Chapter XXXIV - Nor does Ps. lxxii. apply to Solomon, whose faults Christians shudder at

"Further, to persuade you that you have not understood anything of the Scriptures, I will remind you of another psalm, dictated to David by the Holy Spirit, which you say refers to Solomon, who was also your king. But it refers also to our Christ. But you deceive yourselves by the ambiguous forms of speech. For where it is said, The law of the Lord is perfect,' you do not understand it of the law which was to be after Moses, but of the law which was given by Moses, although God declared that He would establish a new law and a new covenant. And where it has been said, O God, give Thy judgment to the king,' since Solomon was king, you say that the Psalm refers to him, although the words of the Psalm expressly proclaim that reference is made to the everlasting King, i.e., to Christ. For Christ is King, and Priest, and God, and Lord, and angel, and man, and captain, and stone, and a Son born, and first made subject to suffering, then returning to heaven, and again coming with glory, and He is preached as having the everlasting kingdom: so I prove from all the Scriptures. But that you may perceive what I have said, I quote the words of the Psalm; they are these: O God, give Thy judgment to the king, and Thy righteousness unto the king's son, to judge Thy people with righteousness, and Thy poor with judgment. The mountains shall take up peace to the people, and the little hills righteousness. He shall judge the poor of the people, and shall save the children of the needy, and shall abase the slanderer. He shall co-endure with the sun, and before the moon unto all generations. He shall come down like rain upon the fleece, as drops falling on the earth. In His days shall righteousness flourish, and abundance of peace until the moon be taken away. And He shall have dominion from sea to sea, and from the rivers unto the ends of the earth. Ethiopians shall fall down before Him, and His enemies shall lick the dust. The kings of Tarshish and the isles shall offer gifts; the kings of Arabia and Seba shall offer gifts; and all the kings of the earth shall worship Him, and all the nations shall serve Him: for He has delivered the poor from the man of power, and the needy that hath no helper. He shall spare the poor and needy, and shall save the souls of the needy: He shall redeem their souls from usury and injustice, and His name shall be honourable before them. And He shall live, and to Him shall be given of the gold of Arabia, and they shall pray continually for Him: they shall bless Him all the day. And there shall be a foundation on the earth, it shall be exalted on the tops of the mountains: His fruit shall be on Lebanon, and they of the city shall flourish like grass of the earth. His name shalt be blessed for ever. His name shall endure before the sun; and all tribes of the earth shall be blessed in Him, all nations shall call Him blessed. Blessed be the Lord, the God of Israel, wó ὦνly doeth wondrous things; and blessed be His glorious name for ever, and for ever and ever; and the whole earth shall be filled with His glory. Amen, amen.' [2033] And at the close of this Psalm which I have quoted, it is written, The hymns of David the son of Jesse are ended.' [2034] Moreover, that Solomon was a renowned and great king, by whom the temple called that at Jerusalem was built, I know; but that none of those things mentioned in the Psalm happened to him, is evident. For neither did all kings worship him; nor did he reign to the ends of the earth; nor did his enemies, falling before him, lick the dust. Nay, also, I venture to repeat what is written in the book of Kings as committed by him, how through a woman's influence he worshipped the idols of Sidon, which those of the Gentiles who know God, the Maker of all things through Jesus the crucified, do not venture to do, but abide every torture and vengeance even to the extremity of death, rather than worship idols, or eat meat offered to idols."

Chapter XXXV - Heretics confirm the Catholics in the faith

And Trypho said, "I believe, however, that many of those who say that they confess Jesus, and are called Christians, eat meats offered to idols, and declare that they are by no means injured in consequence." And I replied, "The fact that there are such men confessing themselves to be Christians, and admitting the crucified Jesus to be both Lord and Christ, yet not teaching His doctrines, but those of the spirits of error, causes us who are disciples of the true and pure doctrine of Jesus Christ, to be more faithful and stedfast in the hope announced by Him. For what things He predicted would take place in His name, these we do see being actually accomplished in our sight. For he said, Many shall come in My name, clothed outwardly in sheep's clothing, but inwardly they are ravening wolves.' " [2035] And, There shall be schisms and heresies.' [2036] And, Beware of false prophets, who shall come to you clothed outwardly in sheep's clothing, but inwardly they are ravening wolves.' [2037] And, Many false Christs and false apostles shall arise, and shall deceive many of the faithful.' [2038] There are, therefore, and there were many, my friends, who, coming forward in the name of Jesus, taught both to speak and act impious and blasphemous things; and these are called by us after the name of the men from whom each doctrine and opinion had its origin. (For some in one way, others in another, teach to blaspheme the Maker of all things, and Christ, who was foretold by Him as coming, and the God of Abraham, and of Isaac, and of Jacob, with whom we have nothing in common, since we know them to be atheists, impious, unrighteous, and sinful, and confessors of Jesus in name only, instead of worshippers of Him. Yet they style themselves Christians, just as certain among the Gentiles inscribe the name of God upon the works of their own hands, and partake in nefarious and impious rites.) Some are called Marcians, and some Valentinians, and some Basilidians, and some Saturnilians, and others by other names; each called after the originator of the individual opinion, just as each one of those who consider themselves philosophers, as I said before, thinks he must bear the name of the philosophy which he follows, from the name of the father of the particular doctrine. So that, in consequence of these events, we know that Jesus foreknew what would happen after Him, as well as in consequence of many other events which He foretold would befall those who believed on and confessed Him, the Christ. For all that we suffer, even when killed by friends, He foretold would take place; so that it is manifest no word or act of His can be found fault with. Wherefore we pray for you and for all other men who hate us; in order that you, having repented along with us, may not blaspheme Him who, by His works, by the mighty deeds even now wrought through His name, by the words He taught, by the prophecies announced concerning Him, is the blameless, and in all things irreproachable, Christ Jesus; but, believing on Him, may be saved in His second glorious advent, and may not be condemned to fire by Him."

Chapter XXXVI - He proves that Christ is called Lord of Hosts

Then he replied, "Let these things be so as you say--namely, that it was foretold Christ would suffer, and be called a stone; and after His first appearance, in which it had been announced He would suffer, would come in glory, and be Judge finally of all, and eternal King and Priest. Now show if this man be He of whom these prophecies were made."

And I said, "As you wish, Trypho, I shall come to these proofs which you seek in the fitting place; but now you will permit me first to recount the prophecies, which I wish to do in order to prove that Christ is called both God and Lord of hosts, and Jacob, in parable by the Holy Spirit; and your interpreters, as God says, are foolish, since they say that reference is made to Solomon and not to Christ, when he bore the ark of testimony into the temple which he built. The Psalm of David is this: The earth is the Lord's, and the fulness thereof; the world, and all that dwell therein. He hath founded it upon the seas, and prepared it upon the floods. Who shall ascend into the hill of the Lord? or who shall stand in His holy place? He that is clean of hands and pure of heart: who has not received his soul in vain, and has not sworn guilefully to his neighbour: he shall receive blessing from the Lord, and mercy from God his Saviour. This is the generation of them that seek the Lord, that seek the face of the God of Jacob. [2039] Lift up your gates, ye rulers; and be ye lift up, ye everlasting doors; and the King of glory shall come in. Who is this King of glory? The Lord strong and mighty in battle. Lift up your gates, ye rulers; and be ye lift up, ye everlasting doors; and the King of glory shall come in. Who is this King of glory? The Lord of hosts, He is the King of glory.' [2040] Accordingly, it is shown that Solomon is not the Lord of hosts; but when our Christ rose from the dead and ascended to heaven, the rulers in heaven, under appointment of God, are commanded to open the gates of heaven, that He who is King of glory may enter in, and having ascended, may sit on the right hand of the Father until He make the enemies His footstool, as has been made manifest by another Psalm. For when the rulers of heaven saw Him of uncomely and dishonoured appearance, and inglorious, not recognising Him, they inquired, Who is this King of glory?' And the Holy Spirit, either from the person of His Father, or from His own person, answers them, The Lord of hosts, He is this King of glory.' For every one will confess that not one of those who presided over the gates of the temple at Jerusalem would venture to say concerning Solomon, though he was so glorious a king, or concerning the ark of testimony, Who is this King of glory?'

Chapter XXXVII - The same is proved from other Psalms

"Moreover, in the diapsalm of the forty-sixth Psalm, reference is thus made to Christ: God went up with a shout, the Lord with the sound of a trumpet. Sing ye to our God, sing ye: sing to our King, sing ye; for God is King of all the earth: sing with understanding. God has ruled over the nations. God sits upon His holy throne. The rulers of the nations were assembled along with the God of Abraham, for the strong ones of God are greatly exalted on the earth.' [2041] And in the ninety-eighth Psalm, the Holy Spirit reproaches you, and predicts Him whom you do not wish to be king to be King and Lord, both of Samuel, and of Aaron, and of Moses, and, in short, of all the others. And the words of the Psalm are these: The Lord has reigned, let the nations be angry: [it is] He who sits upon the cherubim, let the earth be shaken. The Lord is great in Zion, and He is high above all the nations. Let them confess Thy great name, for it is fearful and holy, and the honour of the King loves judgment. Thou hast prepared equity; judgment and righteousness hast Thou performed in Jacob. Exalt the Lord our God, and worship the footstool of His feet; for He is holy. Moses and Aaron among His priests, and Samuel among those who call upon His name. They called (says the Scripture) on the Lord, and He heard them. In the pillar of the cloud He spake to them; for [2042] they kept His testimonies, and the commandment which he gave them. O Lord our God, Thou heardest them: O God, Thou wert propitious to them, and [yet] taking vengeance on all their inventions. Exalt the Lord our God, and worship at His holy hill; for the Lord our God is holy.'" [2043]

Chapter XXXVIII - It is an annoyance to the Jew that Christ is said to be adored. Justin confirms it, however, from Ps. xlv

And Trypho said, "Sir, it were good for us if we obeyed our teachers, who laid down a law that we should have no intercourse with any of you, and that we should not have even any communication with you on these questions. For you utter many blasphemies, in that you seek to persuade us that this crucified man was with Moses and Aaron, and spoke to them in the pillar of the cloud; then that he became man, was crucified, and ascended up to heaven, and comes again to earth, and ought to be worshipped."

Then I answered, "I know that, as the word of God says, this great wisdom of God, the Maker of all things, and the Almighty, is hid from you. Wherefore, in sympathy with you, I am striving to the utmost that you may understand these matters which to you are paradoxical; but if not, that I myself may be innocent in the day of judgment. For you shall hear other words which appear still more paradoxical; but be not confounded, nay, rather remain still more zealous hearers and investigators, despising the tradition of your teachers, since they are convicted by the Holy Spirit of inability to perceive the truths taught by God, and of preferring to teach their own doctrines. Accordingly, in the forty-fourth [forty-fifth] Psalm, these words are in like manner referred to Christ: My heart hath brought forth a good matter; [2044] I tell my works to the King. My tongue is the pen of a ready writer. Fairer in beauty than the sons of men: grace is poured forth into Thy lips: therefore hath God blessed Thee for ever. Gird Thy sword upon Thy thigh, O mighty One. Press on in Thy fairness and in Thy beauty, and prosper and reign, because of truth, and of meekness, and of righteousness: and Thy right hand shall instruct Thee marvellously. Thine arrows are sharpened, O mighty One; the people shall fall under Thee; in the heart of the enemies of the King [the arrows are fixed]. Thy throne, O God, is for ever and ever: a sceptre of equity is the sceptre of Thy kingdom. Thou hast loved righteousness, and hast hated iniquity; therefore thy God [2045] hath anointed Thee with the oil of gladness above Thy fellows. [He hath anointed Thee] with myrrh, [2046] and oil, and cassia, from Thy garments; from the ivory palaces, whereby they made Thee glad. Kings' daughters are in Thy honour. The queen stood at Thy right hand, clad in garments [2047] embroidered with gold. Hearken, O daughter, and behold, and incline thine ear, and forget thy people and the house of thy father: and the King shall desire thy beauty; because He is thy Lord, they shall worship Him also. And the daughter of Tyre [shall be there] with gifts. The rich of the people shall entreat Thy face. All the glory of the King's daughter [is] within, clad in embroidered garments of needlework. The virgins that follow her shall be brought to the King; her neighbours shall be brought unto Thee: they shall be brought with joy and gladness: they shall be led into the King's shrine. Instead of thy fathers, thy sons have been born: Thou shalt appoint them rulers over all the earth. I shall remember Thy name in every generation: therefore the people shall confess Thee for ever, and for ever and ever.'

Chapter XXXIX - The Jews hate the Christians who believe this. How great the distinction is between both!

"Now it is not surprising," I continued, "that you hate us who hold these opinions, and convict you of a continual hardness of heart. [2048] For indeed Elijah, conversing with God concerning you, speaks thus: Lord, they have slain Thy prophets, and digged down Thine altars: and I am left alone, and they seek my life.' And He answers him: I have still seven thousand men who have not bowed the knee to Baal.' [2049] Therefore, just as God did not inflict His anger on account of those seven thousand men, even so He has now neither yet inflicted judgment, nor does inflict it, knowing that daily some [of you] are becoming disciples in the name of Christ, and quitting the path of error; who are also receiving gifts, each as he is worthy, illumined through the name of this Christ. For one receives the spirit of understanding, another of counsel, another of strength, another of healing, another of foreknowledge, another of teaching, and another of the fear of God."

To this Trypho said to me, "I wish you knew that you are beside yourself, talking these sentiments."

And I said to him, "Listen, O friend, [2050] for I am not mad or beside myself; but it was prophesied that, after the ascent of Christ to heaven, He would deliver [2051] us from error and give us gifts. The words are these: He ascended up on high; He led captivity captive; He gave gifts to men.'[2052] Accordingly, we who have received gifts from Christ, who has ascended up on high, prove from the words of prophecy that you, the wise in yourselves, and the men of understanding in your own eyes,' [2053] are foolish, and honour God and His Christ by lip only. But we, who are instructed in the whole truth, [2054] honour Them both in acts, and in knowledge, and in heart, even unto death. But you hesitate to confess that He is Christ, as the Scriptures and the events witnessed and done in His name prove, perhaps for this reason, lest you be persecuted by the rulers, who, under the influence of the wicked and deceitful spirit, the serpent, will not cease putting to death and persecuting those who confess the name of Christ until He come again, and destroy them all, and render to each his deserts."

And Trypho replied, "Now, then, render us the proof that this man who you say was crucified and ascended into heaven is the Christ of God. For you have sufficiently proved by means of the Scriptures previously quoted by you, that it is declared in the Scriptures that Christ must suffer, and come again with glory, and receive the eternal kingdom over all the nations, every kingdom being made subject to Him: now show us that this man is He."

And I replied, "It has been already proved, sirs, to those who have ears, even from the facts which have been conceded by you; but that you may not think me at a loss, and unable to give proof of what you ask, as I promised, I shall do so at a fitting place. At present, I resume the consideration of the subject which I was discussing."

Chapter XL - He returns to the Mosaic laws, and proves that they were figures of the things which pertain to Christ

"The mystery, then, of the lamb which God enjoined to be sacrificed as the passover, was a type of Christ; with whose blood, in proportion to their faith in Him, they anoint their houses, i.e., themselves, who believe on Him. For that the creation which God created--to wit, Adam--was a house for the spirit which proceeded from God, you all can understand. And that this injunction was temporary, I prove thus. God does not permit the lamb of the passover to be sacrificed in any other place than where His name was named; knowing that the days will come, after the suffering of Christ, when even the place in Jerusalem shall be given over to your enemies, and all the offerings, in short, shall cease; and that lamb which was commanded to be wholly roasted was a symbol of the suffering of the cross which Christ would undergo. For the lamb, [2055] which is roasted, is roasted and dressed up in the form of the cross. For one spit is transfixed right through from the lower parts up to the head, and one across the back, to which are attached the legs of the lamb. And the two goats which were ordered to be offered during the fast, of which one was sent away as the scape [goat], and the other sacrificed, were similarly declarative of the two appearances of Christ: the first, in which the elders of your people, and the priests, having laid hands on Him and put Him to death, sent Him away as the scape [goat]; and His second appearance, because in the same place in Jerusalem you shall recognise Him whom you have dishonoured, and who was an offering for all sinners willing to repent, and keeping the fast which Isaiah speaks of, loosening the terms [2056] of the violent contracts, and keeping the other precepts, likewise enumerated by him, and which I have quoted, [2057] which those believing in Jesus do. And further, you are aware that the offering of the two goats, which were enjoined to be sacrificed at the fast, was not permitted to take place similarly anywhere else, but only in Jerusalem.

Chapter XLI - The oblation of fine flour was a figure of the Eucharist

"And the offering of fine flour, sirs," I said, "which was prescribed to be presented on behalf of those purified from leprosy, was a type of the bread of the Eucharist, the celebration of which our Lord Jesus Christ prescribed, in remembrance of the suffering which He endured on behalf of those who are purified in soul from all iniquity, in order that we may at the same time thank God for having created the world, with all things therein, for the sake of man, and for delivering us from the evil in which we were, and for utterly overthrowing [2058] principalities and powers by Him who suffered according to His will. Hence God speaks by the mouth of Malachi, one of the twelve [prophets], as I said before, [2059] about the sacrifices at that time presented by you: I have no pleasure in you, saith the Lord; and I will not accept your sacrifices at your hands: for, from the rising of the sun unto the going down of the same, My name has been glorified among the Gentiles, and in every place incense is offered to My name, and a pure offering: for My name is great among the Gentiles, saith the Lord: but ye profane it.' [2060] [So] He then speaks of those Gentiles, namely us, who in every place offer sacrifices to Him, i.e., the bread of the Eucharist, and also the cup of the Eucharist, affirming both that we glorify His name, and that you profane [it]. The command of circumcision, again, bidding [them] always circumcise the children on the eighth day, was a type of the true circumcision, by which we are circumcised from deceit and iniquity through Him who rose from the dead on the first day after the Sabbath, [namely through] our Lord Jesus Christ. For the first day after the Sabbath, remaining the first [2061] of all the days, is called, however, the eighth, according to the number of all the days of the cycle, and [yet] remains the first.

Chapter XLII - The bells on the priest's robe were a figure of the apostles

"Moreover, the prescription that twelve bells [2062] be attached to the [robe] of the high priest, which hung down to the feet, was a symbol of the twelve apostles, who depend on the power of Christ, the eternal Priest; and through their voice it is that all the earth has been filled with the glory and grace of God and of His Christ. Wherefore David also says: Their sound has gone forth into all the earth, and their words to the ends of the world.' [2063] And Isaiah speaks as if he were personating the apostles, when they say to Christ that they believe not in their own report, but in the power of Him who sent them. And so he says: Lord, who hath believed our report? and to whom is the arm of the Lord revealed? We have preached before Him as if [He were] a child, as if a root in a dry ground.' [2064] (And what follows in order of the prophecy already quoted. [2065]) But when the passage speaks as from the lips of many, We have preached before Him,' and adds, as if a child,' it signifies that the wicked shall become subject to Him, and shall obey His command, and that all shall become as one child. Such a thing as you may witness in the body: although the members are enumerated as many, all are called one, and are a body. For, indeed, a commonwealth and a church,[2066] though many individuals in number, are in fact as one, called and addressed by one appellation. And in short, sirs," said I, "by enumerating all the other appointments of Moses, I can demonstrate that they were types, and symbols, and declarations of those things which would happen to Christ, of those who it was foreknown were to believe in Him, and of those things which would also be done by Christ Himself. But since what I have now enumerated appears to me to be sufficient, I revert again to the order of the discourse. [2067]

Chapter XLIII - He concludes that the law had an end in Christ, who was born of the Virgin

"As, then, circumcision began with Abraham, and the Sabbath and sacrifices and offerings and feasts with Moses, and it has been proved they were enjoined on account of the hardness of your people's heart, so it was necessary, in accordance with the Father's will, that they should have an end in Him who was born of a virgin, of the family of Abraham and tribe of Judah, and of David; in Christ the Son of God, who was proclaimed as about to come to all the world, to be the everlasting law and the everlasting covenant, even as the forementioned prophecies show. And we, who have approached God through Him, have received not carnal, but spiritual circumcision, which Enoch and those like him observed. And we have received it through baptism, since we were sinners, by God's mercy; and all men may equally obtain it. But since the mystery of His birth now demands our attention I shall speak of it. Isaiah then asserted in regard to the generation of Christ, that it could not be declared by man, in words already quoted: [2068] Who shall declare His generation? for His life is taken from the earth: for the transgressions of my people was He led [2069] to death.' [2070] The Spirit of prophecy thus affirmed that the generation of Him who was to die, that we sinful men might be healed by His stripes, was such as could not be declared. Furthermore, that the men who believe in Him may possess the knowledge of the manner in which He came into the world, [2071] the Spirit of prophecy by the same Isaiah foretold how it would happen thus: And the Lord spoke again to Ahaz, saying, Ask for thyself a sign from the Lord thy God, in the depth, or in the height. And Ahaz said, I will not ask, neither will I tempt the Lord. And Isaiah said, Hear then, O house of David; Is it a small thing for you to contend with men, and how do you contend with the Lord? Therefore the Lord Himself will give you a sign. Behold, the virgin shall conceive, and shall bear a son, and his name shall be called Immanuel. Butter and honey shall he eat, before he knows or prefers the evil, and chooses out the good; [2072] for before the child knows good or ill, he rejects evil [2073] by choosing out the good. For before the child knows how to call father or mother, he shall receive the power of Damascus and the spoil of Samaria in presence of the king of Assyria. And the land shall be forsaken, [2074] which thou shalt with difficulty endure in consequence of the presence of its two kings. [2075] But God shall bring on thee, and on thy people, and on the house of thy father, days which have not yet come upon thee since the day in which Ephraim took away from Judah the king of Assyria.' [2076] Now it is evident to all, that in the race of Abraham according to the flesh no one has been born of a virgin, or is said to have been born [of a virgin], save this our Christ. But since you and your teachers venture to affirm that in the prophecy of Isaiah it is not said, Behold, the virgin shall conceive,' but, Behold, the young woman shall conceive, and bear a son;' and [since] you explain the prophecy as if [it referred] to Hezekiah, who was your king, I shall endeavour to discuss shortly this point in opposition to you, and to show that reference is made to Him who is acknowledged by us as Christ.

Chapter XLIV - The Jews in vain promise themselves salvation, which cannot be obtained except through Christ

"For thus, so far as you are concerned, I shall be found in all respects innocent, if I strive earnestly to persuade you by bringing forward demonstrations. But if you remain hard-hearted, or weak in [forming] a resolution, on account of death, which is the lot of the Christians, and are unwilling to assent to the truth, you shall appear as the authors of your own [evils]. And you deceive yourselves while you fancy that, because you are the seed of Abraham after the flesh, therefore you shall fully inherit the good things announced to be bestowed by God through Christ. For no one, not even of them, [2077] has anything to look for, but only those who in mind are assimilated to the faith of Abraham, and who have recognised all the mysteries: for I say, [2078] that some injunctions were laid on you in reference to the worship of God and practice of righteousness; but some injunctions and acts were likewise mentioned in reference to the mystery of Christ, on account of [2079] the hardness of your people's hearts. And that this is so, God makes known in Ezekiel, [when] He said concerning it: If Noah and Jacob [2080] and Daniel should beg either sons or daughters, the request would not be granted them.' [2081] And in Isaiah, of the very same matter He spake thus: The Lord God said, they shall both go forth and look on the members [of the bodies] of the men that have transgressed. For their worm shall not die, and their fire shall not be quenched, and they shall be a gazing-stock to all flesh.' [2082] So that it becomes you to eradicate this hope from your souls, and hasten to know in what way forgiveness of sins, and a hope of inheriting the promised good things, shall be yours. But there is no other [way] than this, --to become acquainted with this Christ, to be washed in the fountain [2083] spoken of by Isaiah for the remission of sins; and for the rest, to live sinless lives."

Chapter XLV - Those who were righteous before and under the law shall be saved by Christ

And Trypho said, "If I seem to interrupt these matters, which you say must be investigated, yet the question which I mean to put is urgent. Suffer me first."

And I replied, "Ask whatever you please, as it occurs to you; and I shall endeavour, after questions and answers, to resume and complete the discourse."

Then he said, "Tell me, then, shall those who lived according to the law given by Moses, live in the same manner with Jacob, Enoch, and Noah, in the resurrection of the dead, or not?"

I replied to him, "When I quoted, sir, the words spoken by Ezekiel, that even if Noah and Daniel and Jacob were to beg sons and daughters, the request would not be granted them,' but that each one, that is to say, shall be saved by his own righteousness, I said also, that those who regulated their lives by the law of Moses would in like manner be saved. For what in the law of Moses is naturally good, and pious, and righteous, and has been prescribed to be done by those who obey it; [2084] and what was appointed to be performed by reason of the hardness of the people's hearts; was similarly recorded, and done also by those who were under the law. Since those who did that which is universally, naturally, and eternally good are pleasing to God, they shall be saved through this Christ in the resurrection equally with those righteous men who were before them, namely Noah, and Enoch, and Jacob, and whoever else there be, along with those who have known[2085] this Christ, Son of God, who was before the morning star and the moon, and submitted to become incarnate, and be born of this virgin of the family of David, in order that, by this dispensation, the serpent that sinned from the beginning, and the angels like him, may be destroyed, and that death may be contemned, and for ever quit, at the second coming of the Christ Himself, those who believe in Him and live acceptably,--and be no more: when some are sent to be punished unceasingly into judgment and condemnation of fire; but others shall exist in freedom from suffering, from corruption, and from grief, and in immortality."

Chapter XLVI - Trypho asks whether a man who keeps the law even now will be saved. Justin proves that it contributes nothing to righteousness

"But if some, even now, wish to live in the observance of the institutions given by Moses, and yet believe in this Jesus who was crucified, recognising Him to be the Christ of God, and that it is given to Him to be absolute Judge of all, and that His is the everlasting kingdom, can they also be saved?" he inquired of me.

And I replied, "Let us consider that also together, whether one may now observe all the Mosaic institutions."

And he answered, "No. For we know that, as you said, it is not possible either anywhere to sacrifice the lamb of the passover, or to offer the goats ordered for the fast; or, in short, [to present] all the other offerings."

And I said, "Tell [me] then yourself, I pray, some things which can be observed; for you will be persuaded that, though a man does not keep or has not performed the eternal [2086] decrees, he may assuredly be saved."

Then he replied, "To keep the Sabbath, to be circumcised, to observe months, and to be washed if you touch anything prohibited by Moses, or after sexual intercourse."

And I said, "Do you think that Abraham, Isaac, Jacob, Noah, and Job, and all the rest before or after them equally righteous, also Sarah the wife of Abraham, Rebekah the wife of Isaac, Rachel the wife of Jacob, and Leah, and all the rest of them, until the mother of Moses the faithful servant, who observed none of these [statutes], will be saved?"

And Trypho answered, "Were not Abraham and his descendants circumcised?"

And I said, "I know that Abraham and his descendants were circumcised. The reason why circumcision was given to them I stated at length in what has gone before; and if what has been said does not convince you, [2087] let us again search into the matter. But you are aware that, up to Moses, no one in fact who was righteous observed any of these rites at all of which we are talking, or received one commandment to observe, except that of circumcision, which began from Abraham."

And he replied, "We know it, and admit that they are saved."

Then I returned answer, "You perceive that God by Moses laid all such ordinances upon you on account of the hardness of your people's hearts, in order that, by the large number of them, you might keep God continually, and in every action, before your eyes, and never begin to act unjustly or impiously. For He enjoined you to place around you [a fringe] of purple dye, [2088] in order that you might not forget God; and He commanded you to wear a phylactery, [2089] certain characters, which indeed we consider holy, being engraved on very thin parchment; and by these means stirring you up [2090] to retain a constant remembrance of God: at the same time, however, convincing you, that in your hearts you have not even a faint remembrance of God's worship. Yet not even so were you dissuaded from idolatry: for in the times of Elijah, when [God] recounted the number of those who had not bowed the knee to Baal, He said the number was seven thousand; and in Isaiah He rebukes you for having sacrificed your children to idols. But we, because we refuse to sacrifice to those to whom we were of old accustomed to sacrifice, undergo extreme penalties, and rejoice in death,--believing that God will raise us up by His Christ, and will make us incorruptible, and undisturbed, and immortal; and we know that the ordinances imposed by reason of the hardness of your people's hearts, contribute nothing to the performance of righteousness and of piety."

Chapter XLVII - Justin communicates with Christians who observe the law. Not a few Catholics do otherwise

And Trypho again inquired, "But if some one, knowing that this is so, after he recognises that this man is Christ, and has believed in and obeys Him, wishes, however, to observe these [institutions], will he be saved?"

I said, "In my opinion, Trypho, such an one will be saved, if he does not strive in every way to persuade other men, --I mean those Gentiles who have been circumcised from error by Christ, to observe the same things as himself, telling them that they will not be saved unless they do so. This you did yourself at the commencement of the discourse, when you declared that I would not be saved unless I observe these institutions."

Then he replied, "Why then have you said, In my opinion, such an one will be saved,' unless there are some [2091] who affirm that such will not be saved?"

"There are such people, Trypho," I answered; "and these do not venture to have any intercourse with or to extend hospitality to such persons; but I do not agree with them. But if some, through weak-mindedness, wish to observe such institutions as were given by Moses, from which they expect some virtue, but which we believe were appointed by reason of the hardness of the people's hearts, along with their hope in this Christ, and [wish to perform] the eternal and natural acts of righteousness and piety, yet choose to live with the Christians and the faithful, as I said before, not inducing them either to be circumcised like themselves, or to keep the Sabbath, or to observe any other such ceremonies, then I hold that we ought to join ourselves to such, and associate with them in all things as kinsmen and brethren. But if, Trypho," I continued, "some of your race, who say they believe in this Christ, compel those Gentiles who believe in this Christ to live in all respects according to the law given by Moses, or choose not to associate so intimately with them, I in like manner do not approve of them. But I believe that even those, who have been persuaded by them to observe the legal dispensation along with their confession of God in Christ, shall probably be saved. And I hold, further, that such as have confessed and known this man to be Christ, yet who have gone back from some cause to the legal dispensation, and have denied that this man is Christ, and have repented not before death, shall by no means be saved. Further, I hold that those of the seed of Abraham who live according to the law, and do not believe in this Christ before death, shall likewise not be saved, and especially those who have anathematized and do anathematize this very Christ in the synagogues, and everything by which they might obtain salvation and escape the vengeance of fire. ²⁰⁹² For the goodness and the loving-kindness of God, and His boundless riches, hold righteous and sinless the man who, as Ezekiel ²⁰⁹³ tells, repents of sins; and reckons sinful, unrighteous, and impious the man who falls away from piety and righteousness to unrighteousness and ungodliness. Wherefore also our Lord Jesus Christ said, In whatsoever things I shall take you, in these I shall judge you.' " ²⁰⁹⁴

Chapter XLVIII - Before the divinity of Christ is proved, he [Trypho] demands that it be settled that He is Christ

And Trypho said, "We have heard what you think of these matters. Resume the discourse where you left off, and bring it to an end. For some of it appears to me to be paradoxical, and wholly incapable of proof. For when you say that this Christ existed as God before the ages, then that He submitted to be born and become man, yet that He is not man of man, this [assertion] appears to me to be not merely paradoxical, but also foolish."

And I replied to this, "I know that the statement does appear to be paradoxical, especially to those of your race, who are ever unwilling to understand or to perform the [requirements] of God, but [ready to perform] those of your teachers, as God Himself declares. ²⁰⁹⁵ Now assuredly, Trypho,"I continued,"[the proof] that this man ²⁰⁹⁶ is the Christ of God does not fail, though I be unable to prove that He existed formerly as Son of the Maker of all things, being God, and was born a man by the Virgin. But since I have certainly proved that this man is the Christ of God, whoever He be, even if I do not prove that He pre-existed, and submitted to be born a man of like passions with us, having a body, according to the Father's will; in this last matter alone is it just to say that I have erred, and not to deny that He is the Christ, though it should appear that He was born man of men, and [nothing more] is proved [than this], that He has become Christ by election. For there are some, my friends," I said, "of our race, ²⁰⁹⁷ who admit that He is Christ, while holding Him to be man of men; with whom I do not agree, nor would I, ²⁰⁹⁸ even though most of those who have [now] the same opinions as myself should say so; since we were enjoined by Christ Himself to put no faith in human doctrines, ²⁰⁹⁹ but in those proclaimed by the blessed prophets and taught by Himself."

Chapter XLIX - To those who object that Elijah has not yet come, he replies that he is the precursor of the first advent

And Trypho said, "Those who affirm him to have been a man, and to have been anointed by election, and then to have become Christ, appear to me to speak more plausibly than you who hold those opinions which you express. For we all expect that Christ will be a man [born] of men, and that Elijah when he comes will anoint him. But if this man appear to be Christ, he must certainly be known as man [born] of men; but from the circumstance that Elijah has not yet come, I infer that this man is not He [the Christ]."

Then I inquired of him, "Does not Scripture, in the book of Zechariah, ²¹⁰⁰ say that Elijah shall come before the great and terrible day of the Lord?"

And he answered, "Certainly."

"If therefore Scripture compels you to admit that two advents of Christ were predicted to take place,--one in which He would appear suffering, and dishonoured, and without comeliness; but the other in which He would come glorious and Judge of all, as has been made manifest in many of the fore-cited passages,--shall we not suppose that the word of God has proclaimed that Elijah shall be the precursor of the great and terrible day, that is, of His second advent?"

"Certainly," he answered.

"And, accordingly, our Lord in His teaching," I continued, "proclaimed that this very thing would take place, saying that Elijah would also come. And we know that this shall take place when our Lord Jesus Christ shall come in glory from heaven; whose first manifestation the Spirit of God who was in Elijah preceded as herald in [the person of] John, a prophet among your nation; after whom no other prophet appeared among you. He cried, as he sat by the river Jordan: I baptize you with water to repentance; but He that is stronger than I shall come, whose shoes I am not worthy to bear: He shall baptize you with the Holy Ghost and with fire: whose fan is in His hand, and He will thoroughly purge His floor, and will gather the wheat into the barn; but the chaff He will burn up with unquenchable fire.' ²¹⁰¹ And this very prophet your king Herod had shut up in prison; and when his birthday was celebrated, and the niece ²¹⁰² of the same Herod by her dancing had pleased him, he told her to ask whatever she pleased. Then the mother of the maiden instigated her to ask the head of John, who was in prison; and having asked it, [Herod] sent and ordered the head of John to be brought in on a charger. Wherefore also our Christ said, [when He was] on earth, to those who were affirming that Elijah must come before Christ: Elijah shall come, and restore all things; but I say unto you, that Elijah has already come, and they knew him not, but have done to him whatsoever they chose.' [2103] And it is written, Then the disciples understood that He spake to them about John the Baptist.' "

And Trypho said, "This statement also seems to me paradoxical; namely, that the prophetic Spirit of God, who was in Elijah, was also in John."

To this I replied, "Do you not think that the same thing happened in the case of Joshua the son of Nave (Nun), who succeeded to the command of the people after Moses, when Moses was commanded to lay his hands on Joshua, and God said to him, I will take of the spirit which is in thee, and put it on him?' " [2104]

And he said, "Certainly."

"As therefore," I say, "while Moses was still among men, God took of the spirit which was in Moses and put it on Joshua, even so God was able to cause [the spirit] of Elijah to come upon John; in order that, as Christ at His first coming appeared inglorious, even so the first coming of the spirit, which remained always pure in Elijah [2105] like that of Christ, might be perceived to be inglorious. For the Lord said He would wage war against Amalek with concealed hand; and you will not deny that Amalek fell. But if it is said that only in the glorious advent of Christ war will be waged with Amalek, how great will the fulfilment [2106] of Scripture be which says, God will wage war against Amalek with concealed hand!' You can perceive that the concealed power of God was in Christ the crucified, before whom demons, and all the principalities and powers of the earth, tremble."

Chapter L - It is proved from Isaiah that John is the precursor of Christ

And Trypho said, "You seem to me to have come out of a great conflict with many persons about all the points we have been searching into, and therefore quite ready to return answers to all questions put to you. Answer me then, first, how you can show that there is another God besides the Maker of all things; and then you will show, [further], that He submitted to be born of the Virgin."

I replied, "Give me permission first of all to quote certain passages from the prophecy of Isaiah, which refer to the office of forerunner discharged by John the Baptist and prophet before this our Lord Jesus Christ."

"I grant it," said he.

Then I said, "Isaiah thus foretold John's forerunning: And Hezekiah said to Isaiah, Good is the word of the Lord which He spake: Let there be peace and righteousness in my days.' [2107] And, Encourage the people; ye priests, speak to the heart of Jerusalem, and encourage her, because her humiliation is accomplished. Her sin is annulled; for she has received of the Lord's hand double for her sins. A voice of one crying in the wilderness, Prepare the ways of the Lord; make straight the paths of our God. Every valley shall be filled up, and every mountain and hill shall be brought low: and the crooked shall be made straight, and the rough way shall be plain ways; and the glory of the Lord shall be seen, and all flesh shall see the salvation of God: for the Lord hath spoken it. A voice of one saying, Cry; and I said, What shall I cry? All flesh is grass, and all the glory of man as the flower of grass. The grass has withered, and the flower of it has fallen away; but the word of the Lord endureth for ever. Thou that bringest good tidings to Zion, go up to the high mountain; thou that bringest good tidings to Jerusalem, lift up thy voice with strength. Lift ye up, be not afraid; tell the cities of Judah, Behold your God! Behold, the Lord comes with strength, and [His] arm comes with authority. Behold, His reward is with Him, and His work before Him. As a shepherd He will tend His flock, and will gather the lambs with [His] arm, and cheer on her that is with young. Who has measured the water with [his] hand, and the heaven with a span, and all the earth with [his] fist? Who has weighed the mountains, and [put] the valleys into a balance? Who has known the mind of the Lord? And who has been His counsellor, and who shall advise Him? Or with whom did He take counsel, and he instructed Him? Or who showed Him judgment? Or who made Him to know the way of understanding? All the nations are reckoned as a drop of a bucket, and as a turning of a balance, and shall be reckoned as spittle. But Lebanon is not sufficient to burn, nor the beasts sufficient for a burnt-offering; and all the nations are considered nothing, and for nothing.' " [2108]

Chapter LI - It is proved that this prophecy has been fulfilled

And when I ceased, Trypho said, "All the words of the prophecy you repeat, sir, are ambiguous, and have no force in proving what you wish to prove." Then I answered, "If the prophets had not ceased, so that there were no more in your nation, Trypho, after this John, it is evident that what I say in reference to Jesus Christ might be regarded perhaps as ambiguous. But if John came first calling on men to repent, and Christ, while [John] still sat by the river Jordan, having come, put an end to his prophesying and baptizing, and preached also Himself, saying that the kingdom of heaven is at hand, and that He must suffer many things from the Scribes and Pharisees, and be crucified, and on the third day rise again, and would appear again in Jerusalem, and would again eat and drink with His disciples; and foretold that in the interval between His [first and second] advent, as I previously said, [2109] priests and false prophets would arise in His name, which things do actually appear; then how can they be ambiguous, when you may be persuaded by the facts? Moreover, He referred to the fact that there would be no longer in your nation any prophet, and to the fact that men recognised how that the New Testament, which God formerly announced [His intention of] promulgating, was then present, i.e., Christ Himself; and in the following terms: The law and the prophets were until John the Baptist; from that time the kingdom of heaven suffereth violence, and the violent take it by force. And if you can [2110] receive it, he is Elijah, who was to come. He that hath ears to hear, let him hear.' [2111]

Chapter LII - Jacob predicted two advents of Christ

"And it was prophesied by Jacob the patriarch [2112] that there would be two advents of Christ, and that in the first He would suffer, and that after He came there would be neither prophet nor king in your nation (I proceeded), and that the nations who believed in the suffering Christ would look for His future appearance. And for this reason the Holy Spirit had uttered these truths in a parable, and obscurely; for," I added, "it is said, Judah, thy brethren have praised thee: thy hands [shall be] on the neck of thine enemies; the sons of thy father shall worship thee. Judah is a lion's whelp; from the germ, my son, thou art sprung up. Reclining, he lay down like a lion, and like [a lion's] whelp: who shall raise him up? A ruler shall not depart from Judah, or a leader from his thighs, until that which is laid up in store for him shall come; and he shall be the desire of nations, binding his foal to the vine, and the foal of his ass to the tendril of the vine. He shall wash his garments in wine, and his vesture in the blood of the grape. His eyes shall be bright with [2113] wine, and his teeth white like milk.' [2114] Moreover, that in your nation there never failed either prophet or ruler, from the time when they began until the time when this Jesus Christ appeared and suffered, you will not venture shamelessly to assert, nor can you prove it. For though you affirm that Herod, after [2115] whose [reign] He suffered, was an Ashkelonite, nevertheless you admit that there was a high priest in your nation; so that you then had one who presented offerings according to the law of Moses, and observed the other legal ceremonies; also [you had] prophets in succession until John, (even then, too, when your nation was carried captive to Babylon, when your land was ravaged by war, and the sacred vessels carried off); there never failed to be a prophet among you, who was lord, and leader, and ruler of your nation. For the Spirit which was in the prophets anointed your kings, and established them. But after the manifestation and death of our Jesus Christ in your nation, there was and is nowhere any prophet: nay, further, you ceased to exist under your own king, your land was laid waste, and forsaken like a lodge in a vineyard; and the statement of Scripture, in the mouth of Jacob, And He shall be the desire of nations,' meant symbolically His two advents, and that the nations would believe in Him; which facts you may now at length discern. For those out of all the nations who are pious and righteous through the faith of Christ, look for His future appearance.

Chapter LIII - Jacob predicted that Christ would ride on an ass, and Zechariah confirms it

"And that expression, binding his foal to the vine, and the ass's foal to the vine tendril,' was a declaring beforehand both of the works wrought by Him at His first advent, and also of that belief in Him which the nations would repose. For they were like an unharnessed foal, which was not bearing a yoke on its neck, until this Christ came, and sent His disciples to instruct them; and they bore the yoke of His word, and yielded the neck to endure all [hardships], for the sake of the good things promised by Himself, and expected by them. And truly our Lord Jesus Christ, when He intended to go into Jerusalem, requested His disciples to bring Him a certain ass, along with its foal, which was bound in an entrance of a village called Bethphage; and having seated Himself on it, He entered into Jerusalem. And as this was done by Him in the manner in which it was prophesied in precise terms that it would be done by the Christ, and as the fulfilment was recognised, it became a clear proof that He was the Christ. And though all this happened and is proved from Scripture, you are still hard-hearted. Nay, it was prophesied by Zechariah, one of the twelve [prophets], that such would take place, in the following words: Rejoice greatly, daughter of Zion; shout, and declare, daughter of Jerusalem; behold, thy King shall come to thee, righteous, bringing salvation, meek, and lowly, riding on an ass, and the foal of an ass.' [2116] Now, that the Spirit of prophecy, as well as the patriarch Jacob, mentioned both an ass and its foal, which would be used by Him; and, further, that He, as I previously said, requested His disciples to bring both beasts; [this fact] was a prediction that you of the synagogue, along with the Gentiles, would believe in Him. For as the unharnessed colt was a symbol of the Gentiles even so the harnessed ass was a symbol of your nation. For you possess the law which was imposed [upon you] by the prophets. Moreover, the prophet Zechariah foretold that this same Christ would be smitten, and His disciples scattered: which also took place. For after His crucifixion, the disciples that accompanied Him were dispersed, until He rose from the dead, and persuaded them that so it had been prophesied concerning Him, that He would suffer; and being thus persuaded, they went into all the world, and taught these truths. Hence also we are strong in His faith and doctrine, since we have [this our] persuasion both from the prophets, and from those who throughout the world are seen to be worshippers of God in the name of that crucified One. The following is said, too, by Zechariah: O sword, rise up against My Shepherd, and against the man of My people, saith the Lord of hosts. Smite the Shepherd, and His flock shall be scattered.' [2117]

Chapter LIV - What the blood of the grape signifies

"And that expression which was committed to writing [2118] by Moses, and prophesied by the patriarch Jacob, namely, He shall wash His garments with wine, and His vesture with the blood of the grape,' signified that He would wash those that believe in Him with His own blood. For the Holy Spirit called those who receive remission of sins through Him, His garments; amongst whom He is always present in power, but will be manifestly present at His second coming. That the Scripture mentions the blood of the grape has been evidently designed, because Christ derives blood not from the seed of man, but from the power of God. For as God, and not man, has produced the blood of the vine, so also [the Scripture] has predicted that the blood of Christ would be not of the seed of man, but of the power of God. But this prophecy, sirs, which I repeated, proves that Christ is not man of men, begotten in the ordinary course of humanity."

Chapter LV - Trypho asks that Christ be proved God, but without metaphor. Justin promises to do so

And Trypho answered, "We shall remember this your exposition, if you strengthen [your solution of] this difficulty by other arguments: but now resume the discourse, and show us that the Spirit of prophecy admits another God besides the Maker of all things, taking care not to speak of the sun and moon, which, it is written, [2119] God has given to the nations to worship as gods; and oftentimes the prophets, employing [2120] this manner of speech, say that thy God is a God of gods, and a Lord of lords,' adding frequently, the great and strong and terrible [God].' For such expressions are used, not as if they really were gods, but because the Scripture is teaching us that the true God, who made all things, is Lord alone of those who are reputed gods and lords. And in order that the Holy Spirit may convince [us] of this, He said by the holy David, The gods of the nations, reputed gods, are idols of demons, and not gods;' [2121] and He denounces a curse on those who worship them."

And I replied, "I would not bring forward these proofs, Trypho, by which I am aware those who worship these [idols] and such like are condemned, but such [proofs] as no one could find any objection to. They will appear strange to you, although you read them every day; so that even from this fact we [2122] understand that, because of your wickedness, God has withheld from you the ability to discern the wisdom of His Scriptures; yet [there are] some exceptions, to whom, according to the grace of His long-suffering, as Isaiah said, He has left a seed of [2123] salvation, lest your race be utterly destroyed, like Sodom and Gomorrah. Pay attention, therefore, to what I shall record out of the holy Scriptures, which [2124] do not need to be expounded, but only listened to.

Chapter LVI - God who appeared to Moses is distinguished from God the Father

"Moses, then, the blessed and faithful servant of God, declares that He who appeared to Abraham under the oak in Mamre is God, sent with the two angels in His company to judge Sodom by Another who remains ever in the supercelestial places, invisible to all men, holding personal intercourse with none, whom we believe to be Maker and Father of all things; for he speaks thus: God appeared to him under the oak in Mamre, as he sat at his tent-door at noontide. And lifting up his eyes, he saw, and behold, three men stood before him; and when he saw them, he ran to meet them from the door of his tent; and he bowed himself toward the ground, and said;' " [2125] (and so on;) [2126] " Abraham gat up early in the morning to the place where he stood before the Lord: and he looked toward Sodom and Gomorrah, and toward the adjacent country, and beheld, and, lo, a flame went up from the earth, like the smoke of a furnace.' " And when I had made an end of quoting these words, I asked them if they had understood them.

And they said they had understood them, but that the passages adduced brought forward no proof that there is any other God or Lord, or that the Holy Spirit says so, besides the Maker of all things.

Then I replied, "I shall attempt to persuade you, since you have understood the Scriptures, [of the truth] of what I say, that there is, and that there is said to be, another God and Lord subject to [2127] the Maker of all things; who is also called an Angel, because He announces to men whatsoever the Maker of all things--above whom there is no other God--wishes to announce to them." And quoting once more the previous passage, I asked Trypho, "Do you think that God appeared to Abraham under the oak in Mamre, as the Scripture asserts?"

He said, "Assuredly."

"Was He one of those three," I said, "whom Abraham saw, and whom the Holy Spirit of prophecy describes as men?"

He said, "No; but God appeared to him, before the vision of the three. Then those three whom the Scripture calls men, were angels; two of them sent to destroy Sodom, and one to announce the joyful tidings to Sarah, that she would bear a son; for which cause he was sent, and having accomplished his errand, went away." [2128]

"How then," said I, "does the one of the three, who was in the tent, and who said, I shall return to thee hereafter, and Sarah shall have a son,' [2129] appear to have returned when Sarah had begotten a son, and to be there declared, by the prophetic word, God? But that you may clearly discern what I say, listen to the words expressly employed by Moses; they are these: And Sarah saw the son of Hagar the Egyptian bond-woman, whom she bore to Abraham, sporting with Isaac her son, and said to Abraham, Cast out this bond-woman and her son; for the son of this bond-woman shall not share the inheritance of my son Isaac. And the matter seemed very grievous in Abraham's sight, because of his son. But God said to Abraham, Let it not be grievous in thy sight because of the son, and because of the bond-woman. In all that Sarah hath said unto thee, hearken to her voice; for in Isaac shall thy seed be called.' [2130] Have you perceived, then, that He who said under the oak that He would return, since He knew it would be necessary to advise Abraham to do what Sarah wished him, came back as it is written; and is God, as the words declare, when they so speak: God said to Abraham, Let it not be grievous in thy sight because of the son, and because of the bond-woman?' " I inquired. And Trypho said, "Certainly; but you have not proved from this that there is another God besides Him who appeared to Abraham, and who also appeared to the other patriarchs and prophets. You have proved, however, that we were wrong in believing that the three who were in the tent with Abraham were all angels."

I replied again, "If I could not have proved to you from the Scriptures that one of those three is God, and is called Angel, [2131] because, as I already said, He brings messages to those to whom God the Maker of all things wishes [messages to be brought], then in regard to Him who appeared to Abraham on earth in human form in like manner as the two angels who came with Him, and who was God even before the creation of the world, it were reasonable for you to entertain the same belief as is entertained by the whole of your nation."

"Assuredly," he said, "for up to this moment this has been our belief."

Then I replied, "Reverting to the Scriptures, I shall endeavour to persuade you, that He who is said to have appeared to Abraham, and to Jacob, and to Moses, and who is called God, is distinct from Him who made all things,--numerically, I mean, not [distinct] in will. For I affirm that He has never at any time done [2132] anything which He who made the world--above whom there is no other God--has not wished Him both to do and to engage Himself with."

And Trypho said, "Prove now that this is the case, that we also may agree with you. For we do not understand you to affirm that He has done or said anything contrary to the will of the Maker of all things."

Then I said, "The Scripture just quoted by me will make this plain to you. It is thus: The sun was risen on the earth, and Lot entered into Segor (Zoar); and the Lord rained on Sodom sulphur and fire from the Lord out of heaven, and overthrew these cities and all the neighbourhood.' " [2133]

Then the fourth of those who had remained with Trypho said, "It [2134] must therefore necessarily be said that one of the two angels who went to Sodom, and is named by Moses in the Scripture Lord, is different from Him who also is God, and appeared to Abraham." [2135]

"It is not on this ground solely," I said, "that it must be admitted absolutely that some other one is called Lord by the Holy Spirit besides Him who is considered Maker of all things; not solely [for what is said] by Moses, but also [for what is said] by David. For there is written by him: The Lord says to my Lord, Sit on My right hand, until I make Thine enemies Thy footstool,' [2136] as I have already quoted. And again, in other words: Thy throne, O God, is for ever and ever. A sceptre of equity is the sceptre of Thy kingdom: Thou hast loved righteousness and hated iniquity: therefore God, even Thy God, hath anointed Thee with the oil of gladness above Thy fellows.' [2137] If, therefore, you assert that the Holy Spirit calls some other one God and Lord, besides the Father of all things and His Christ, answer me; for I undertake to prove to you from Scriptures themselves, that He whom the Scripture calls Lord is not one of the two angels that went to Sodom, but He who was with them, and is called God, that appeared to Abraham."

And Trypho said, "Prove this; for, as you see, the day advances, and we are not prepared for such perilous replies; since never yet have we heard any man investigating, or searching into, or proving these matters; nor would we have tolerated your conversation, had you not referred everything to the Scriptures: [2138] for you are very zealous in adducing proofs from them; and you are of opinion that there is no God above the Maker of all things."

Then I replied, "You are aware, then, that the Scripture says, And the Lord said to Abraham, Why did Sarah laugh, saying, Shall I truly conceive? for I am old. Is anything impossible with God? At the time appointed shall I return to thee according to the time of life, and Sarah shall have a son.'[2139] And after a little interval: And the men rose up from thence, and looked towards Sodom and Gomorrah; and Abraham went with them, to bring them on the way. And the Lord said, I will not conceal from Abraham, my servant, what I do.'[2140] And again, after a little, it thus says: The Lord said, The cry of Sodom and Gomorrah is great,[2141] and their sins are very grievous. I will go down now, and see whether they have done altogether according to their cry which has come unto me; and if not, that I may know. And the men turned away thence, and went to Sodom. But Abraham was standing before the Lord; and Abraham drew near, and said, Wilt Thou destroy the righteous with the wicked?' "[2142] (and so on,[2143] for I do not think fit to write over again the same words, having written them all before, but shall of necessity give those by which I established the proof to Trypho and his companions. Then I proceeded to what follows, in which these words are recorded:) " And the Lord went His way as soon as He had left communing with Abraham; and [Abraham] went to his place. And there came two angels to Sodom at even. And Lot sat in the gate of Sodom;'[2144] and what follows until, But the men put forth their hands, and pulled Lot into the house to them, and shut to the door of the house;'[2145] and what follows till, And the angels laid hold on his hand, and on the hand of his wife, and on the hands of his daughters, the Lord being merciful to him. And it came to pass, when they had brought them forth abroad, that they said, Save, save thy life. Look not behind thee, nor stay in all the neighbourhood; escape to the mountain, lest thou be taken along with [them]. And Lot said to them, I beseech [Thee], O Lord, since Thy servant hath found grace in Thy sight, and Thou hast magnified Thy righteousness, which Thou showest towards me in saving my life; but I cannot escape to the mountain, lest evil overtake me, and I die. Behold, this city is near to flee unto, and it is small: there I shall be safe, since it is small; and any soul shall live. And He said to him, Behold, I have accepted thee [2146] also in this matter, so as not to destroy the city for which thou hast spoken. Make haste to save thyself there; for I shall not do anything till thou be come thither. Therefore he called the name of the city Segor (Zoar). The sun was risen upon the earth; and Lot entered into Segor (Zoar). And the Lord rained on Sodom and Gomorrah sulphur and fire from the Lord out of heaven; and He overthrew these cities, and all the neighbourhood.'"[2147] And after another pause I added: "And now have you not perceived, my friends, that one of the three, who is both God and Lord, and ministers to Him who is in the heavens, is Lord of the two angels? For when [the angels] proceeded to Sodom, He remained behind, and communed with Abraham in the words recorded by Moses; and when He departed after the conversation, Abraham went back to his place. And when he came [to Sodom], the two angels no longer conversed with Lot, but Himself, as the Scripture makes evident; and He is the Lord who received commission from the Lord who [remains] in the heavens, i.e., the Maker of all things, to inflict upon Sodom and Gomorrah the [judgments] which the Scripture describes in these terms: The Lord rained down upon Sodom and Gomorrah sulphur and fire from the Lord out of heaven.' "

Chapter LVII - The Jew objects, why is He said to have eaten, if He be God? Answer of Justin

Then Trypho said when I was silent, "That Scripture compels us to admit this, is manifest; but there is a matter about which we are deservedly at a loss --namely, about what was said to the effect that [the Lord] ate what was prepared and placed before him by Abraham; and you would admit this."

I answered, "It is written that they ate; and if we believe [2148] that it is said the three ate, and not the two alone--who were really angels, and are nourished in the heavens, as is evident to us, even though they are not nourished by food similar to that which mortals use--(for, concerning the sustenance of manna which supported your fathers in the desert, Scripture speaks thus, that they ate angels' food): [if we believe that three ate], then I would say that the Scripture which affirms they ate bears the same meaning as when we would say about fire that it has devoured all things; yet it is not certainly understood that they ate, masticating with teeth and jaws. So that not even here should we be at a loss about anything, if we are acquainted even slightly with figurative modes of expression, and able to rise above them."

And Trypho said, "It is possible that [the question] about the mode of eating may be thus explained: [the mode, that is to say,] in which it is written, they took and ate what had been prepared by Abraham: so that you may now proceed to explain to us how this God who appeared to Abraham, and is minister to God the Maker of all things, being born of the Virgin, became man, of like passions with all, as you said previously."

Then I replied, "Permit me first, Trypho, to collect some other proofs on this head, so that you, by the large number of them, may be persuaded of [the truth of] it, and thereafter I shall explain what you ask."

And he said, "Do as seems good to you; for I shall be thoroughly pleased."

Chapter LVIII - The same is proved from the visions which appeared to Jacob

Then I continued, "I purpose to quote to you Scriptures, not that I am anxious to make merely an artful display of words; for I possess no such faculty, but God's grace alone has been granted to me to the understanding of His Scriptures, of which grace I exhort all to become partakers freely and bounteously, in order that they may not, through want of it, [2149] incur condemnation in the judgment which God the Maker of all things shall hold through my Lord Jesus Christ."

And Trypho said, "What you do is worthy of the worship of God; but you appear to me to feign ignorance when you say that you do not possess a store of artful words."

I again replied, "Be it so, since you think so; yet I am persuaded that I speak the truth. [2150] But give me your attention, that I may now rather adduce the remaining proofs."

"Proceed," said he.

And I continued: "It is again written by Moses, my brethren, that He who is called God and appeared to the patriarchs is called both Angel and Lord, in order that from this you may understand Him to be minister to the Father of all things, as you have already admitted, and may remain firm, persuaded by additional arguments. The word of God, therefore, [recorded] by Moses, when referring to Jacob the grandson of Abraham, speaks thus: And it came to pass, when the sheep conceived, that I saw them with my eyes in the dream: And, behold, the he-goats and the rams which leaped upon the sheep and she-goats were spotted with white, and speckled and sprinkled with a dun colour. And the Angel of God said to me in the dream, Jacob, Jacob. And I said, What is it, Lord? And He said, Lift up thine eyes, and see that the he-goats and rams leaping on the sheep and she-goats are spotted with white, speckled, and sprinkled with a dun colour. For I have seen what Laban doeth unto thee. I am the God who appeared to thee in Bethel, [2151] where thou anointedst a pillar and vowedst a vow unto Me. Now therefore arise, and get thee out of this land, and depart to the land of thy birth, and I shall be with thee.' [2152] And again, in other words, speaking of the same Jacob, it thus says: And having risen up that night, he took the two wives, and the two women-servants, and his eleven children, and passed over the ford Jabbok; and he took them and went over the brook, and sent over all his belongings. But Jacob was left behind alone, and an Angel [2153] wrestled with him until morning. And He saw that He is not prevailing against him, and He touched the broad part of his thigh; and the broad part of Jacob's thigh grew stiff while he wrestled with Him. And He said, Let Me go, for the day breaketh. But he said, I will not let Thee go, except Thou bless me. And He said to him, What is thy name? And he said, Jacob. And He said, Thy name shall be called no more Jacob, but Israel shall be thy name; for thou hast prevailed with God, and with men shalt be powerful. And Jacob asked Him, and said, Tell me Thy name. But he said, Why dost thou ask after My name? And He blessed him there. And Jacob called the name of that place Peniel, [2154] for I saw God face to face, and my soul rejoiced.' [2155] And again, in other terms, referring to the same Jacob, it says the following: And Jacob came to Luz, in the land of Canaan, which is Bethel, he and all the people that were with him. And there he built an altar, and called the name of that place Bethel; for there God appeared to him when he fled from the face of his brother Esau. And Deborah, Rebekah's nurse, died, and was buried beneath Bethel under an oak: and Jacob called the name of it The Oak of Sorrow. And God appeared again to Jacob in Luz, when he came out from Mesopotamia in Syria, and He blessed him. And God said to him, Thy name shall be no more called Jacob, but Israel shall be thy name.' [2156] He is called God, and He is and shall be God." And when all had agreed on these grounds, I continued: "Moreover, I consider it necessary to repeat to you the words which narrate how He who is both Angel and God and Lord, and who appeared as a man to Abraham, and who wrestled in human form with Jacob, was seen by him when he fled from his brother Esau. They are as follows: And Jacob went out from the well of the oath, [2157] and went toward Charran. [2158] And he lighted on a spot, and slept there, for the sun was set; and he gathered of the stones of the place, and put them under his head. And he slept in that place; and he dreamed, and, behold, a ladder was set up on the earth, whose top reached to heaven; and the angels of God ascended and descended upon it. And the Lord stood [2159] above it, and He said, I am the Lord, the God of Abraham thy father, and of Isaac; be not afraid: the land whereon thou liest, to thee will I give it, and to thy seed; and thy seed shall be as the dust of the earth, and shall be extended to the west, and south, and north, and east: and in thee, and in thy seed, shall all families of the earth be blessed. And, behold, I am with thee, keeping thee in every way wherein thou goest, and will bring thee again into this land; for I will not leave thee, until I have done all that I have spoken to thee of. And Jacob awaked out of his sleep, and said, Surely the Lord is in this place, and I knew it not. And he was afraid, and said, How dreadful is this place! this is none other than the house of God, and this is the gate of heaven. And Jacob rose up in the morning, and took the stone which he had placed under his head, and he set it up for a pillar, and poured oil upon the top of it; and Jacob called the name of the place The House of God, and the name of the city formerly was Ulammaus.' " [2160]

Chapter LIX - God distinct from the Father conversed with Moses

When I had spoken these words, I continued: "Permit me, further, to show you from the book of Exodus how this same One, who is both Angel, and God, and Lord, and man, and who appeared in human form to Abraham and Isaac, [2161] appeared in a flame of fire from the bush, and conversed with Moses." And after they said they would listen cheerfully, patiently, and eagerly, I went on: "These words are in the book which bears the title of Exodus: And after many days the king of Egypt died, and the children of Israel groaned by reason of the works;' [2162] and so on until, Go and gather the elders of Israel, and thou shalt say unto them, The Lord God of your fathers, the God of Abraham, the God of Isaac, and the God of Jacob, hath appeared to me, saying, I am surely beholding you, and the things which have befallen you in Egypt.' " [2163] In addition to these words, I went on: "Have you perceived, sirs, that this very God whom Moses speaks of as an Angel that talked to him in the flame of fire, declares to Moses that He is the God of Abraham, of Isaac, and of Jacob?"

Chapter LX - Opinions of the Jews with regard to Him who appeared in the bush

Then Trypho said, "We do not perceive this from the passage quoted by you, but [only this], that it was an angel who appeared in the flame of fire, but God who conversed with Moses; so that there were really two persons in company with each other, an angel and God, that appeared in that vision."

I again replied, "Even if this were so, my friends, that an angel and God were together in the vision seen by Moses, yet, as has already been proved to you by the passages previously quoted, it will not be the Creator of all things that is the God that said to Moses that He was the God of Abraham, and the God of Isaac, and the God of Jacob, but it will be He who has been proved to you to have appeared to Abraham, ministering to the will of the Maker of all things, and likewise carrying into execution His counsel in the judgment of Sodom; so that, even though it be as you say, that there were two--an angel and God--he who has but the smallest intelligence will not venture to assert that the Maker and Father of all things, having left all supercelestial matters, was visible on a little portion of the earth."

And Trypho said, "Since it has been previously proved that He who is called God and Lord, and appeared to Abraham, received from the Lord, who is in the heavens, that which He inflicted on the land of Sodom, even although an angel had accompanied the God who appeared to Moses, we shall perceive that the God who communed with Moses from the bush was not the Maker of all things, but He who has been shown to have manifested Himself to Abraham and to Isaac and to Jacob; who also is called and is perceived to be the Angel of God the Maker of all things, because He publishes to men the commands of the Father and Maker of all things."

And I replied, "Now assuredly, Trypho, I shall show that, in the vision of Moses, this same One alone who is called an Angel, and who is God, appeared to and communed with Moses. For the Scripture says thus: The Angel of the Lord appeared to him in a flame of fire from the bush; and he sees that the bush burns with fire, but the bush was not consumed. And Moses said, I will turn aside and see this great sight, for the bush is not burnt. And when the Lord saw that he is turning aside to behold, the Lord called to him out of the bush.' [2164] In the same manner, therefore, in which the Scripture calls Him who appeared to Jacob in the dream an Angel, then [says] that the same Angel who appeared in the dream spoke to him, [2165] saying, I am the God that appeared to thee when thou didst flee from the face of Esau thy brother;' and [again] says that, in the judgment which befell Sodom in the days of Abraham, the Lord had inflicted the punishment [2166] of the Lord who [dwells] in the heavens;--even so here, the Scripture, in announcing that the Angel of the Lord appeared to Moses, and in afterwards declaring him to be Lord and God, speaks of the same One, whom it declares by the many testimonies already quoted to be minister to God, who is above the world, above whom there is no other [God]."

Chapter LXI - Wisdom is begotten of the Father, as fire from fire

"I shall give you another testimony, my friends," said I, "from the Scriptures, that God begat before all creatures a Beginning, [2167] [who was] a certain rational power [proceeding] from Himself, who is called by the Holy Spirit, now the Glory of the Lord, now the Son, again Wisdom, again an Angel, then God, and then Lord and Λόγος; and on another occasion He calls Himself Captain, when He appeared in human form to Joshua the son of Nave (Nun). For He can be called by all those names, since He ministers to the Father's will, and since He was begotten of the Father by an act of will; [2168] just as we see [2169] happening among ourselves: for when we give out some word, we beget the word; yet not by abscission, so as to lessen the word [2170] [which remains] in us, when we give it out: and just as we see also happening in the case of a fire, which is not lessened when it has kindled [another], but remains the same; and that which has been kindled by it likewise appears to exist by itself, not diminishing that from which it was kindled. The Word of Wisdom, who is Himself this God begotten of the Father of all things, and Word, and Wisdom, and Power, and the Glory of the Begetter, will bear evidence to me, when He speaks by Solomon the following: If I shall declare to you what happens daily, I shall call to mind events from everlasting, and review them. The Lord made me the beginning of His ways for His works. From everlasting He established me in the beginning, before He had made the earth, and before He had made the deeps, before the springs of the waters had issued forth, before the mountains had been established. Before all the hills He begets me. God made the country, and the desert, and the highest inhabited places under the sky. When He made ready the heavens, I was along with Him, and when He set up His throne on the winds: when He made the high clouds strong, and the springs of the deep safe, when He made the foundations of the earth, I was with Him arranging. I was that in which He rejoiced; daily and at all times I delighted in His countenance, because He delighted in the finishing of the habitable world, and delighted in the sons of men. Now, therefore, O son, hear me. Blessed is the man who shall listen to me, and the mortal who shall keep my ways, watching [2171] daily at my doors, observing the posts of my ingoings. For my outgoings are the outgoings of life, and [my] will has been prepared by the Lord. But they who sin against me, trespass against their own souls; and they who hate me love death.' [2172]

Chapter LXII - The words "Let Us make man" agree with the testimony of Proverbs

"And the same sentiment was expressed, my friends, by the word of God [written] by Moses, when it indicated to us, with regard to Him whom it has pointed out, [2173] that God speaks in the creation of man with the very same design, in the following words: Let Us make man after our image and likeness. And let them have dominion over the fish of the sea, and over the fowl of the heaven, and over the cattle, and over all the earth, and over all the creeping things that creep on the earth. And God created man: after the image of God did He create him; male and female created He them. And God blessed them, and said, Increase and multiply, and fill the earth, and have power over it.' [2174] And that you may not change the [force of the] words just quoted, and repeat what your teachers assert,--either that God said to Himself, Let Us make,' just as we, when about to do something, oftentimes say to ourselves, Let us make;' or that God spoke to the elements, to wit, the earth and other similar substances of which we believe man was formed, Let Us make,'--I shall quote again the words narrated by Moses himself, from which we can indisputably learn that [God] conversed with some one who was numerically distinct from Himself, and also a rational Being. These are the words: And God said, Behold, Adam has become as one of us, to know good and evil.' [2175] In saying, therefore, as one of us,' [Moses] has declared that [there is a certain] number of persons associated with one another, and that they are at least two. For I would not say that the dogma of that heresy [2176] which is said to be among you [2177] is true, or that the teachers of it can prove that [God] spoke to angels, or that the human frame was the workmanship of angels. But this Offspring, which was truly brought forth from the Father, was with the Father before all the creatures, and the Father communed with Him; even as the Scripture by Solomon has made clear, that He whom Solomon calls Wisdom, was begotten as a Beginning before all His creatures and as Offspring by God, who has also declared this same thing in the revelation made by Joshua the son of Nave (Nun). Listen, therefore, to the following from the book of Joshua, that what I say may become manifest to you; it is this: And it came to pass, when Joshua was near Jericho, he lifted up his eyes, and sees a man standing over against him. And Joshua approached to Him, and said, Art thou for us, or for our adversaries? And He said to him, I am Captain of the Lord's host: now have I come. And Joshua fell on his face on the ground, and said to Him, Lord, what commandest Thou Thy servant? And the Lord's Captain says to Joshua, Loose the shoes off thy feet; for the place whereon thou standest is holy ground. And Jericho was shut up and fortified, and no one went out of it. And the Lord said to Joshua, Behold, I give into thine hand Jericho, and its king, [and] its mighty men.' " [2178]

Chapter LXIII - It is proved that this God was incarnate

And Trypho said, "This point has been proved to me forcibly, and by many arguments, my friend. It remains, then, to prove that He submitted to become man by the Virgin, according to the will of His Father; and to be crucified, and to die. Prove also clearly, that after this He rose again and ascended to heaven."

I answered, "This, too, has been already demonstrated by me in the previously quoted words of the prophecies, my friends; which, by recalling and expounding for your sakes, I shall endeavour to lead you to agree with me also about this matter. The passage, then, which Isaiah records, Who shall declare His generation? for His life is taken away from the earth,'[2179] --does it not appear to you to refer to One who, not having descent from men, was said to be delivered over to death by God for the transgressions of the people?--of whose blood, Moses (as I mentioned before), when speaking in parable, said, that He would wash His garments in the blood of the grape; since His blood did not spring from the seed of man, but from the will of God. And then, what is said by David, In the splendours of Thy holiness have I begotten Thee from the womb, before the morning star.[2180] The Lord hath sworn, and will not repent, Thou art a priest for ever, after the order of Melchizedek,'[2181] --does this not declare to you [2182] that [He was] from of old,[2183] and that the God and Father of all things intended Him to be begotten by a human womb? And speaking in other words, which also have been already quoted, [he says]: Thy throne, O God, is for ever and ever: a sceptre of rectitude is the sceptre of Thy kingdom. Thou hast loved righteousness, and hast hated iniquity: therefore God, even thy God, hath anointed Thee with the oil of gladness above Thy fellows. [He hath anointed Thee] with myrrh, and oil, and cassia from Thy garments, from the ivory palaces, whereby they made Thee glad. Kings' daughters are in Thy honour. The queen stood at Thy right hand, clad in garments embroidered with gold.[2184] Hearken, O daughter, and behold, and incline thine ear, and forget thy people and the house of thy father; and the King shall desire thy beauty: because he is thy Lord, and thou shalt worship Him.'[2185] Therefore these words testify explicitly that He is witnessed to by Him who established these things,[2186] as deserving to be worshipped, as God and as Christ. Moreover, that the word of God speaks to those who believe in Him as being one soul, and one synagogue, and one church, as to a daughter; that it thus addresses the church which has sprung from His name and partakes of His name (for we are all called Christians), is distinctly proclaimed in like manner in the following words, which teach us also to forget [our] old ancestral customs, when they speak thus:[2187] Hearken, O daughter, and behold, and incline thine ear; forget thy people and the house of thy father, and the King shall desire thy beauty: because He is thy Lord, and thou shalt worship Him.' "

Chapter LXIV - Justin adduces other proofs to the Jew, who denies that he needs this Christ

Here Trypho said, "Let Him be recognised as Lord and Christ and God, as the Scriptures declare, by you of the Gentiles, who have from His name been all called Christians; but we who are servants of God that made this same [Christ], do not require to confess or worship Him."

To this I replied, "If I were to be quarrelsome and light-minded like you, Trypho, I would no longer continue to converse with you, since you are prepared not to understand what has been said, but only to return some captious answer;[2188] but now, since I fear the judgment of God, I do not state an untimely opinion concerning any one of your nation, as to whether or not some of them may be saved by the grace of the Lord of Σαβαώθ. Therefore, although you act wrongfully, I shall continue to reply to any proposition you shall bring forward, and to any contradiction which you make; and, in fact, I do the very same to all men of every nation, who wish to examine along with me, or make inquiry at me, regarding this subject. Accordingly, if you had bestowed attention on the Scriptures previously quoted by me, you would already have understood, that those who are saved of your own nation are saved through this [2189] [man], and partake of His lot; and you would not certainly have asked me about this matter. I shall again repeat the words of David previously quoted by me, and beg of you to comprehend them, and not to act wrongfully, and stir each other up to give merely some contradiction. The words which David speaks, then, are these: The Lord has reigned; let the nations be angry: [it is] He who sits upon the cherubim; let the earth be shaken. The Lord is great in Zion; and He is high above all the nations. Let them confess Thy great name, for it is fearful and holy; and the honour of the king loves judgment. Thou hast prepared equity; judgment and righteousness hast Thou performed in Jacob. Exalt the Lord our God, and worship the footstool of His feet; for He is holy. Moses and Aaron among His priests, and Samuel among them that call upon His name; they called on the Lord, and He heard them. In the pillar of the cloud He spake to them; for they kept His testimonies and His commandments which He gave them.'[2190] And from the other words of David, also previously quoted, which you foolishly affirm refer to Solomon, [because] inscribed for Solomon, it can be proved that they do not refer to Solomon, and that this [Christ] existed before the sun, and that those of your nation who are saved shall be saved through Him. [The words] are these: O God, give Thy judgment to the king, and Thy righteousness unto the king's son. He shall judge [2191] Thy people with righteousness, and Thy poor with judgment. The mountains shall take up peace to the people, and the little hills righteousness. He shall judge the poor of the people, and shall save the children of the needy, and shall abase the slanderer: and He shall co-endure with the sun, and before the moon unto all generations;' and so on until, His name endureth before the sun, and all tribes of the earth shalt be blessed in Him. All nations shall call Him blessed. Blessed be the Lord, the God of Israel, wó ὤνly doeth wondrous things: and blessed be His glorious name for ever and ever: and the whole earth shall be filled with His glory. Amen, Amen.' [2192] And you remember from other words also spoken by David, and which I have mentioned before, how it is declared that He would come forth from the highest heavens, and again return to the same places, in order that you may recognise Him as God coming forth from above, and man living among men; and [how it is declared] that He will again appear, and they who pierced Him shall see Him, and shall bewail Him. [The words] are these: The heavens declare the glory of God, and the firmament showeth His handiwork. Day unto day uttereth speech, and night unto night showeth knowledge: They are not speeches or words whose voices are heard. Their sound has gone out through all the earth, and their words to the ends of the world. In the sun has he set his habitation; and he, like a bridegroom going forth from his chamber, will rejoice as a giant to run his race: from the highest heaven is his going forth, and he returns to the highest heaven, and there is not one who shall be hidden from his heat.' " [2193]

Chapter LXV - The Jew objects that God does not give His glory to another. Justin explains the passage

And Trypho said, "Being shaken [2194] by so many Scriptures, I know not what to say about the Scripture which Isaiah writes, in which God says that He gives not His glory to another, speaking thus I am the Lord God; this is my name; my glory will I not give to another, nor my virtues.' " [2195]

And I answered, "If you spoke these words, Trypho, and then kept silence in simplicity and with no ill intent, neither repeating what goes before nor adding what comes after, you must be forgiven; but if [you have done so] because you imagined that you could throw doubt on the passage, in order that I might say the Scriptures contradicted each other, you have erred. But I shall not venture to suppose or to say such a thing; and if a Scripture which appears to be of such a kind be brought forward, and if there be a pretext [for saying] that it is contrary [to some other], since I am entirely convinced that no Scripture contradicts another, I shall admit rather that I do not understand what is recorded, and shall strive to persuade those who imagine that the Scriptures are contradictory, to be rather of the same opinion as myself. With what intent, then, you have brought forward the difficulty, God knows. But I shall remind you of what the passage says, in order that you may recognise even from this very [place] that God gives glory to His Christ alone. And I shall take up some short passages, sirs, those which are in connection with what has been said by Trypho, and those which are also joined on in consecutive order. For I will not repeat those of another section, but those which are joined together in one. Do you also give me your attention. [The words] are these: Thus saith the Lord, the God that created the heavens, and made [2196] them fast, that established the earth, and that which is in it; and gave breath to the people upon it, and spirit to them who walk therein: I the Lord God have called Thee in righteousness, and will hold Thine hand, and will strengthen Thee; and I have given Thee for a covenant of the people, for a light of the Gentiles, to open the eyes of the blind, to bring out them that are bound from the chains, and those who sit in darkness from the prison-house. I am the Lord God; this is my name: my glory will I not give to another, nor my virtues to graven images. Behold, the former things are come to pass; new things which I announce, and before they are announced they are made manifest to you. Sing unto the Lord a new song: His sovereignty [is] from the end of the earth. [Sing], ye who descend into the sea, and continually sail [2197] [on it]; ye islands, and inhabitants thereof. Rejoice, O wilderness, and the villages thereof, and the houses; and the inhabitants of Cedar shall rejoice, and the inhabitants of the rock shall cry aloud from the top of the mountains: they shall give glory to God; they shall publish His virtues among the islands. The Lord God of hosts shall go forth, He shall destroy war utterly, He shall stir up zeal, and He shall cry aloud to the enemies with strength.'"[2198] And when I repeated this, I said to them, "Have you perceived, my friends, that God says He will give Him whom He has established as a light of the Gentiles, glory, and to no other; and not, as Trypho said, that God was retaining the glory to Himself?"

Then Trypho answered, "We have perceived this also; pass on therefore to the remainder of the discourse."

Chapter LXVI - He proves from Isaiah that God was born from a virgin

And I, resuming the discourse where I had left off [2199] at a previous stage, when proving that He was born of a virgin, and that His birth of a virgin had been predicted by Isaiah, quoted again the same prophecy. It is as follows And the Lord spoke again to Ahaz, saying, Ask for thyself a sign from the Lord thy God, in the depth or in the height. And Ahaz said I will not ask, neither will I tempt the Lord. And Isaiah said, Hear then, O house of David; Is it no small thing for you to contend with men? And how do you contend with the Lord? Therefore the Lord Himself will give you a sign; Behold, the virgin shall conceive, and shall bear a son, and they shall call his name Immanuel. Butter and honey shall he eat; before he knows or prefers the evil he will choose out the good. For before the child knows ill or good, he rejects evil by choosing out the good. For before the child knows how to call father or mother, he shall receive the power of Damascus, and the spoil of Samaria, in presence of the king of Assyria. And the land shall be forsaken, which [2200] thou shalt with difficulty endure in consequence of the presence of its two kings. But God shall bring on thee, and on thy people, and on the house of thy father, days which have not yet come upon thee since the day in which Ephraim took away from Judah the king of Assyria.' " [2201] And I continued: "Now it is evident to all, that in the race of Abraham according to the flesh no one has been born of a virgin, or is said to have been born [of a virgin], save this our Christ."

Chapter LXVII - Trypho compares Jesus with Perseus; and would prefer [to say] that He was elected [to be Christ] on account of observance of the law. Justin speaks of the law as formerly

And Trypho answered, "The Scripture has not, Behold, the virgin shall conceive, and bear a son,' but, Behold, the young woman shall conceive, and bear a son,' and so on, as you quoted. But the whole prophecy refers to Hezekiah, and it is proved that it was fulfilled in him, according to the terms of this prophecy. Moreover, in the fables of those who are called Greeks, it is written that Perseus was begotten of Danae, who was a virgin; he who was called among them Zeus having descended on her in the form of a golden shower. And you ought to feel ashamed when you make assertions similar to theirs, and rather [should] say that this Jesus was born man of men. And if you prove from the Scriptures that He is the Christ, and that on account of having led a life conformed to the law, and perfect, He deserved the honour of being elected to be Christ, [it is well]; but do not venture to tell monstrous phenomena, lest you be convicted of talking foolishly like the Greeks."

Then I said to this, "Trypho, I wish to persuade you, and all men in short, of this, that even though you talk worse things in ridicule and in jest, you will not move me from my fixed design; but I shall always adduce from the words which you think can be brought forward [by you] as proof [of your own views], the demonstration of what I have stated along with the testimony of the Scriptures. You are not, however, acting fairly or truthfully in attempting to undo those things in which there has been constantly agreement between us; namely, that certain commands were instituted by Moses on account of the hardness of your people's hearts. For you said that, by reason of His living conformably to law, He was elected and became Christ, if indeed He were proved to be so."

And Trypho said, "You admitted [2202] to us that He was both circumcised, and observed the other legal ceremonies ordained by Moses."

And I replied, "I have admitted it, and do admit it: yet I have admitted that He endured all these not as if He were justified by them, but completing the dispensation which His Father, the Maker of all things, and Lord and God, wished Him [to complete]. For I admit that He endured crucifixion and death, and the incarnation, and the suffering of as many afflictions as your nation put upon Him. But since again you dissent from that to which you but lately assented, Trypho, answer me: Are those righteous patriarchs who lived before Moses, who observed none of those [ordinances] which, the Scripture shows, received the commencement of [their] institution from Moses, saved, [and have they attained to] the inheritance of the blessed?"

And Trypho said, "The Scriptures compel me to admit it."

"Likewise I again ask you," said I, "did God enjoin your fathers to present the offerings and sacrifices because He had need of them, or because of the hardness of their hearts and tendency to idolatry?"

"The latter," said he, "the Scriptures in like manner compel us to admit."

"Likewise," said I, "did not the Scriptures predict that God promised to dispense a new covenant besides that which [was dispensed] in the mountain Horeb?"

This, too, he replied, had been predicted.

Then I said again, "Was not the old covenant laid on your fathers with fear and trembling, so that they could not give ear to God?"

He admitted it.

"What then?" said I: "God promised that there would be another covenant, not like that old one, and said that it would be laid on them without fear, and trembling, and lightnings, and that it would be such as to show what kind of commands and deeds God knows to be eternal and suited to every nation, and what commandments He has given, suiting them to the hardness of your people's hearts, as He exclaims also by the prophets."

"To this also," said he, "those who are lovers of truth and not lovers of strife must assuredly assent."

Then I replied, "I know not how you speak of persons very fond of strife, [since] you yourself oftentimes were plainly acting in this very manner, frequently contradicting what you had agreed to."

Chapter LXVIII - He complains of the obstinacy of Trypho; he answers his objection; he convicts the Jews of bad faith

And Trypho said, "You endeavour to prove an incredible and well-nigh impossible thing; [namely], that God endured to be born and become man."

"If I undertook," said I, "to prove this by doctrines or arguments of man, you should not bear with me. But if I quote frequently Scriptures, and so many of them, referring to this point, and ask you to comprehend them, you are hard-hearted in the recognition of the mind and will of God. But if you wish to remain for ever so, I would not be injured at all; and for ever retaining the same [opinions] which I had before I met with you, I shall leave you."

And Trypho said, "Look, my friend, you made yourself master of these [truths] with much labour and toil. [2203] And we accordingly must diligently scrutinize all that we meet with, in order to give our assent to those things which the Scriptures compel us [to believe]."

Then I said to this, "I do not ask you not to strive earnestly by all means, in making an investigation of the matters inquired into; but [I ask you], when you have nothing to say, not to contradict those things which you said you had admitted."

And Trypho said, "So we shall endeavour to do."

I continued again: "In addition to the questions I have just now put to you, I wish to put more: for by means of these questions I shall strive to bring the discourse to a speedy termination."

And Trypho said, "Ask the questions."

Then I said, "Do you think that any other one is said to be worthy of worship and called Lord and God in the Scriptures, except the Maker of all, and Christ, who by so many Scriptures was proved to you to have become man?"

And Trypho replied, "How can we admit this, when we have instituted so great an inquiry as to whether there is any other than the Father alone?"

Then I again said, "I must ask you this also, that I may know whether or not you are of a different opinion from that which you admitted some time ago." [2204]

He replied, "It is not, sir."

Then again I, "Since you certainly admit these things, and since Scripture says, Who shall declare His generation?' ought you not now to suppose that He is not the seed of a human race?"

And Trypho said, "How then does the Word say to David, that out of his loins God shall take to Himself a Son, and shall establish His kingdom, and shall set Him on the throne of His glory?"

And I said, "Trypho, if the prophecy which Isaiah uttered, Behold, the virgin shall conceive,' is said not to the house of David, but to another house of the twelve tribes, perhaps the matter would have some difficulty; but since this prophecy refers to the house of David, Isaiah has explained how that which was spoken by God to David in mystery would take place. But perhaps you are not aware of this, my friends, that there were many sayings written obscurely, or parabolically, or mysteriously, and symbolical actions, which the prophets who lived after the persons who said or did them expounded."

"Assuredly," said Trypho.

"If therefore, I shall show that this prophecy of Isaiah refers to our Christ, and not to Hezekiah, as you say, shall I not in this matter, too, compel you not to believe your teachers, who venture to assert that the explanation which your seventy elders that were with Ptolemy the king of the Egyptians gave, is untrue in certain respects? For some statements in the Scriptures, which appear explicitly to convict them of a foolish and vain opinion, these they venture to assert have not been so written. But other statements, which they fancy they can distort and harmonize with human actions, [2205] these, they say, refer not to this Jesus Christ of ours, but to him of whom they are pleased to explain them. Thus, for instance, they have taught you that this Scripture which we are now discussing refers to Hezekiah, in which, as I promised, I shall show they are wrong. And since they are compelled, they agree that some Scriptures which we mention to them, and which expressly prove that Christ was to suffer, to be worshipped, and [to be called] God, and which I have already recited to you, do refer indeed to Christ, but they venture to assert that this man is not Christ. But they admit that He will come to suffer, and to reign, and to be worshipped, and to be God; [2206] and this opinion I shall in like manner show to be ridiculous and silly. But since I am pressed to answer first to what was said by you in jest, I shall make answer to it, and shall afterwards give replies to what follows.

Chapter LXIX - The devil, since he emulates the truth, has invented fables about Bacchus, Hercules, and Æsculapius

"Be well assured, then, Trypho," I continued, "that I am established in the knowledge of and faith in the Scriptures by those counterfeits which he who is called the devil is said to have performed among the Greeks; just as some were wrought by the Magi in Egypt, and others by the false prophets in Elijah's days. For when they tell that Bacchus, son of Jupiter, was begotten by [Jupiter's] intercourse with Semele, and that he was the discoverer of the vine; and when they relate, that being torn in pieces, and having died, he rose again, and ascended to heaven; and when they introduce wine [2207] into his mysteries, do I not perceive that [the devil] has imitated the prophecy announced by the patriarch Jacob, and recorded by Moses? And when they tell that Hercules was strong, and travelled over all the world, and was begotten by Jove of Alcmene, and ascended to heaven when he died, do I not perceive that the Scripture which speaks of Christ, strong as a giant to run his race,' [2208] has been in like manner imitated? And when he [the devil] brings forward Æsculapius as the raiser of the dead and healer of all diseases, may I not say that in this matter likewise he has imitated the prophecies about Christ? But since I have not quoted to you such Scripture as tells that Christ will do these things, I must necessarily remind you of one such: from which you can understand, how that to those destitute of a knowledge of God, I mean the Gentiles, who, having eyes, saw not, and having a heart, understood not,' worshipping the images of wood, [how even to them] Scripture prophesied that they would renounce these [vanities], and hope in this Christ. It is thus written: Rejoice, thirsty wilderness: let the wilderness be glad, and blossom as the lily: the deserts of the Jordan shall both blossom and be glad: and the glory of Lebanon was given to it, and the honour of Carmel. And my people shall see the exaltation of the Lord, and the glory of God. Be strong, ye careless hands and enfeebled knees. Be comforted, ye faint in soul: be strong, fear not. Behold, our God gives, and will give, retributive judgment. He shall come and save us. Then the eyes of the blind shall be opened, and the ears of the deaf shall hear. Then the lame shall leap as an hart, and the tongue of the stammerers shall be distinct: for water has broken forth in the wilderness, and a valley in the thirsty land; and the parched ground shall become pools, and a spring of water shall [rise up] in the thirsty land.' [2209] The spring of living water which gushed forth from God in the land destitute of the knowledge of God, namely the land of the Gentiles, was this Christ, who also appeared in your nation, and healed those who were maimed, and deaf, and lame in body from their birth, causing them to leap, to hear, and to see, by His word. And having raised the dead, and causing them to live, by His deeds He compelled the men who lived at that time to recognise Him. But though they saw such works, they asserted it was magical art. For they dared to call Him a magician, and a deceiver of the people. Yet He wrought such works, and persuaded those who were [destined to] believe on Him; for even if any one be labouring under a defect of body, yet be an observer of the doctrines delivered by Him, He shall raise him up at His second advent perfectly sound, after He has made him immortal, and incorruptible, and free from grief.

Chapter LXX - So also the mysteries of Mithras are distorted from the prophecies of Daniel and Isaiah

"And when those who record the mysteries of Mithras say that he was begotten of a rock, and call the place where those who believe in him are initiated a cave, do I not perceive here that the utterance of Daniel, that a stone without hands was cut out of a great mountain, has been imitated by them, and that they have attempted likewise to imitate the whole of Isaiah's [2210] words? [2211] For they [2212] contrived that the words of righteousness be quoted also by them. [2213] But I must repeat to you the words of Isaiah referred to, in order that from them you may know that these things are so. They are these: Hear, ye that are far off, what I have done; those that are near shall know my might. The sinners in Zion are removed; trembling shall seize the impious. Who shall announce to you the everlasting place? The man who walks in righteousness, speaks in the right way, hates sin and unrighteousness, and keeps his hands pure from bribes, stops the ears from hearing the unjust judgment of blood closes the eyes from seeing unrighteousness: he shall dwell in the lofty cave of the strong rock. Bread shall be given to him, and his water [shall be] sure. Ye shall see the King with glory, and your eyes shall look far off. Your soul shall pursue diligently the fear of the Lord. Where is the scribe? where are the counsellors? where is he that numbers those who are nourished,--the small and great people? with whom they did not take counsel, nor knew the depth of the voices, so that they heard not. The people who are become depreciated, and there is no understanding in him who hears.' [2214] Now it is evident, that in this prophecy [allusion is made] to the bread which our Christ gave us to eat, [2215] in remembrance of His being made flesh for the sake of His believers, for whom also He suffered; and to the cup which He gave us to drink, [2216] in remembrance of His own blood, with giving of thanks. And this prophecy proves that we shall behold this very King with glory; and the very terms of the prophecy declare loudly, that the people foreknown to believe in Him were foreknown to pursue diligently the fear of the Lord. Moreover, these Scriptures are equally explicit in saying, that those who are reputed to know the writings of the Scriptures, and who hear the prophecies, have no understanding. And when I hear, Trypho," said I, "that Perseus was begotten of a virgin, I understand that the deceiving serpent counterfeited also this.

Chapter LXXI - The Jews reject the interpretation of the LXX., from which, moreover, they have taken away some passages

"But I am far from putting reliance in your teachers, who refuse to admit that the interpretation made by the seventy elders who were with Ptolemy [king] of the Egyptians is a correct one; and they attempt to frame another. And I wish you to observe, that they have altogether taken away many Scriptures from the translations effected by those seventy elders who were with Ptolemy, and by which this very man who was crucified is proved to have been set forth expressly as God, and man, and as being crucified, and as dying; but since I am aware that this is denied by all of your nation, I do not address myself to these points, but I proceed ^{2217} to carry on my discussions by means of those passages which are still admitted by you. For you assent to those which I have brought before your attention, except that you contradict the statement, Behold, the virgin shall conceive,' and say it ought to be read, Behold, the young woman shall conceive.' And I promised to prove that the prophecy referred, not, as you were taught, to Hezekiah, but to this Christ of mine: and now I shall go to the proof."

Here Trypho remarked, "We ask you first of all to tell us some of the Scriptures which you allege have been completely cancelled."

Chapter LXXII - Passages have been removed by the Jews from Esdras and Jeremiah

And I said, "I shall do as you please. From the statements, then, which Esdras made in reference to the law of the passover, they have taken away the following: And Esdras said to the people, This passover is our Saviour and our refuge. And if you have understood, and your heart has taken it in, that we shall humble Him on a standard, and ^{2218} thereafter hope in Him, then this place shall not be forsaken for ever, says the God of hosts. But if you will not believe Him, and will not listen to His declaration, you shall be a laughing-stock to the nations.' ^{2219} And from the sayings of Jeremiah they have cut out the following: I [was] like a lamb that is brought to the slaughter: they devised a device against me, saying, Come, let us lay on wood on His bread, and let us blot Him out from the land of the living; and His name shall no more be remembered.' ^{2220} And since this passage from the sayings of Jeremiah is still written in some copies [of the Scriptures] in the synagogues of the Jews (for it is only a short time since they were cut out), and since from these words it is demonstrated that the Jews deliberated about the Christ Himself, to crucify and put Him to death, He Himself is both declared to be led as a sheep to the slaughter, as was predicted by Isaiah, and is here represented as a harmless lamb; but being in a difficulty about them, they give themselves over to blasphemy. And again, from the sayings of the same Jeremiah these have been cut out: The Lord God remembered His dead people of Israel who lay in the graves; and He descended to preach to them His own salvation.' ^{2221}

Chapter LXXIII - [The words] "From the wood" have been cut out of Ps. xcvi

"And from the ninety-fifth (ninety-sixth) Psalm they have taken away this short saying of the words of David: From the wood.' ^{2222} For when the passage said, Tell ye among the nations, the Lord hath reigned from the wood,' they have left, Tell ye among the nations, the Lord hath reigned.' Now no one of your people has ever been said to have reigned as God and Lord among the nations, with the exception of Him only who was crucified, of whom also the Holy Spirit affirms in the same Psalm that He was raised again, and freed from [the grave], declaring that there is none like Him among the gods of the nations: for they are idols of demons. But I shall repeat the whole Psalm to you, that you may perceive what has been said. It is thus: Sing unto the Lord a new song; sing unto the Lord, all the earth. Sing unto the Lord, and bless His name; show forth His salvation from day to day. Declare His glory among the nations, His wonders among all people. For the Lord is great, and greatly to be praised: He is to be feared above all the gods. For all the gods of the nations are demons but the Lord made the heavens. Confession and beauty are in His presence; holiness and magnificence are in His sanctuary. Bring to the Lord, O ye countries of the nations, bring to the Lord glory and honour, bring to the Lord glory in His name. Take sacrifices, and go into His courts; worship the Lord in His holy temple. Let the whole earth be moved before Him: tell ye among the nations, the Lord hath reigned. ^{2223} For He hath established the world, which shall not be moved; He shall judge the nations with equity. Let the heavens rejoice, and the earth be glad; let the sea and its fulness shake. Let the fields and all therein be joyful. Let all the trees of the wood be glad before the Lord: for He comes, for He comes to judge the earth. He shall judge the world with righteousness, and the people with His truth.' "

Here Trypho remarked, "Whether [or not] the rulers of the people have erased any portion of the Scriptures, as you affirm, God knows; but it seems incredible."

"Assuredly," said I, "it does seem incredible. For it is more horrible than the calf which they made, when satisfied with manna on the earth; or than the sacrifice of children to demons; or than the slaying of the prophets. But," said I, "you appear to me not to have heard the Scriptures which I said they had stolen away. For such as have been quoted are more than enough to prove the points in dispute, besides those which are retained by us, [2224] and shall yet be brought forward."

Chapter LXXIV - The beginning of Ps. xcvi. is attributed to the Father [by Trypho]. But [it refers] to Christ by these words: "Tell ye among the nations that the Lord," etc.

Then Trypho said, "We know that you quoted these because we asked you. But it does not appear to me that this Psalm which you quoted last from the words of David refers to any other than the Father and Maker of the heavens and earth. You, however, asserted that it referred to Him who suffered, whom you also are eagerly endeavouring to prove to be Christ."

And I answered, "Attend to me, I beseech you, while I speak of the statement which the Holy Spirit gave utterance to in this Psalm; and you shall know that I speak not sinfully, and that we [2225] are not really bewitched; for so you shall be enabled of yourselves to understand many other statements made by the Holy Spirit. Sing unto the Lord a new song; sing unto the Lord, all the earth: sing unto the Lord, and bless His name; show forth His salvation from day to day, His wonderful works among all people.' He bids the inhabitants of all the earth, who have known the mystery of this salvation, i.e., the suffering of Christ, by which He saved them, sing and give praises to God the Father of all things, and recognise that He is to be praised and feared, and that He is the Maker of heaven and earth, who effected this salvation in behalf of the human race, who also was crucified and was dead, and who was deemed worthy by Him (God) to reign over all the earth. As [is clearly seen [2226]] also by the land into which [He said] He would bring [your fathers]; [for He thus speaks]: [2227] This people [shall go a whoring after other gods], and shall forsake Me, and shall break my covenant which I made with them in that day; and I will forsake them, and will turn away My face from them; and they shall be devoured, [2228] and many evils and afflictions shall find them out; and they shall say in that day, Because the Lord my God is not amongst us, these misfortunes have found us out. And I shall certainly turn away My face from them in that day, on account of all the evils which they have committed, in that they have turned to other gods.' [2229]

Chapter LXXV - It is proved that Jesus was the name of God in the book of Exodus

"Moreover, in the book of Exodus we have also perceived that the name of God Himself which, He says, was not revealed to Abraham or to Jacob, was Jesus, and was declared mysteriously through Moses. Thus it is written: And the Lord spake to Moses, Say to this people, Behold, I send My angel before thy face, to keep thee in the way, to bring thee into the land which I have prepared for thee. Give heed to Him, and obey Him; do not disobey Him. For He will not draw back from you; for My name is in Him.' [2230] Now understand that He who led your fathers into the land is called by this name Jesus, and first called Auses [2231] (Oshea). For if you shall understand this, you shall likewise perceive that the name of Him who said to Moses, for My name is in Him,' was Jesus. For, indeed, He was also called Israel, and Jacob's name was changed to this also. Now Isaiah shows that those prophets who are sent to publish tidings from God are called His angels and apostles. For Isaiah says in a certain place, Send me.' [2232] And that the prophet whose name was changed, Jesus [Joshua], was strong and great, is manifest to all. If, then, we know that God revealed Himself in so many forms to Abraham, and to Jacob, and to Moses, how are we at a loss, and do not believe that, according to the will of the Father of all things, it was possible for Him to be born man of the Virgin, especially after we have such [2233] Scriptures, from which it can be plainly perceived that He became so according to the will of the Father?"

Chapter LXXVI - From other passages the same majesty and government of Christ are proved

"For when Daniel speaks of one like unto the Son of man' who received the everlasting kingdom, does he not hint at this very thing? For he declares that, in saying like unto the Son of man,' He appeared, and was man, but not of human seed. And the same thing he proclaimed in mystery when he speaks of this stone which was cut out without hands. For the expression it was cut out without hands' signified that it is not a work of man, but [a work] of the will of the Father and God of all things, who brought Him forth. And when Isaiah says, Who shall declare His generation?' he meant that His descent could not be declared. Now no one who is a man of men has a descent that cannot be declared. And when Moses says that He will wash His garments in the blood of the grape, does not this signify what I have now often told you is an obscure prediction, namely, that He had blood, but not from men; just as not man, but God, has begotten the blood of the vine? And when Isaiah calls Him the Angel of mighty counsel, [2234] did he not foretell Him to be the Teacher of those truths which He did teach when He came [to earth]? For He alone taught openly those mighty counsels which the Father designed both for all those who have been and shall be well-pleasing to Him, and also for those who have rebelled against His will, whether men or angels, when He said: They shall come from the east [and from the west [2235]], and shall sit down with Abraham, and Isaac, and Jacob, in the kingdom of heaven: but the children of the kingdom shall be cast out into outer darkness.' [2236] And, Many shall say to Me in that day, Lord, Lord, have we not eaten, and drunk, and prophesied, and cast out demons in Thy name? And I will say to them, Depart from Me.' [2237] Again, in other words, by which He shall condemn those who are unworthy of salvation, He said, Depart into outer darkness, which the Father has prepared for Satan and his, angels.' [2238] And again, in other words, He said, I give unto you power to tread on serpents, and on scorpions, and on scolopendras, and on all the might of the enemy.' [2239] And now we, who believe on our Lord Jesus, who was crucified under Pontius Pilate, when we exorcise all demons and evil spirits, have them subjected to us. For if the prophets declared obscurely that Christ would suffer, and thereafter be Lord of all, yet that [declaration] could not be understood by any man until He Himself persuaded the apostles that such statements were expressly related in the Scriptures. For He exclaimed before His crucifixion: The Son of man must suffer many things, and be rejected by the Scribes and Pharisees, and be crucified, and on the third day rise again.' [2240] And David predicted that He would be born from the womb before sun and moon, [2241] according to the Father's will, and made Him known, being Christ, as God strong and to be worshipped."

Chapter LXXVII - He returns to explain the prophecy of Isaiah

Then Trypho said, "I admit that such and so great arguments are sufficient to persuade one; but I wish [you] to know that I ask you for the proof which you have frequently proposed to give me. Proceed then to make this plain to us, that we may see how you prove that that [passage] refers to this Christ of yours. For we assert that the prophecy relates to Hezekiah." And I replied, "I shall do as you wish. But show me yourselves first of all how it is said of Hezekiah, that before he knew how to call father or mother, he received the power of Damascus and the spoils of Samaria in the presence of the king of Assyria. For it will not be conceded to you, as you wish to explain it, that Hezekiah waged war with the inhabitants of Damascus and Samaria in presence of the king of Assyria. For before the child knows how to call father or mother,' the prophetic word said, He shall take the power of Damascus and spoils of Samaria in presence of the king of Assyria.' For if the Spirit of prophecy had not made the statement with an addition, Before the child knows how to call father or mother, he shall take the power of Damascus and spoils of Samaria,' but had only said, And shall bear a son, and he shall take the power of Damascus and spoils of Samaria,' then you might say that God foretold that he would take these things, since He foreknew it. But now the prophecy has stated it with this addition: Before the child knows how to call father or mother, he shall take the power of Damascus and spoils of Samaria.' And you cannot prove that such a thing ever happened to any one among the Jews. But we are able to prove that it happened in the case of our Christ. For at the time of His birth, Magi who came from Arabia worshipped Him, coming first to Herod, who then was sovereign in your land, and whom the Scripture calls king of Assyria on account of his ungodly and sinful character. For you know," continued I, "that the Holy Spirit oftentimes announces such events by parables and similitudes; just as He did towards all the people in Jerusalem, frequently saying to them, Thy father is an Amorite, and thy mother a Hittite.' [2242]

Chapter LXXVIII - He proves that this prophecy harmonizes with Christ alone, from what is afterwards written

"Now this king Herod, at the time when the Magi came to him from Arabia, and said they knew from a star which appeared in the heavens that a King had been born in your country, and that they had come to worship Him, learned from the elders of your people that it was thus written regarding Bethlehem in the prophet: And thou, Bethlehem, in the land of Judah, art by no means least among the princes of Judah; for out of thee shall go forth the leader who shall feed my people.'[2243] Accordingly the Magi from Arabia came to Bethlehem and worshipped the Child, and presented Him with gifts, gold and frankincense, and myrrh; but returned not to Herod, being warned in a revelation after worshipping the Child in Bethlehem. And Joseph, the spouse of Mary, who wished at first to put away his betrothed Mary, supposing her to be pregnant by intercourse with a man, i.e., from fornication, was commanded in a vision not to put away his wife; and the angel who appeared to him told him that what is in her womb is of the Holy Ghost. Then he was afraid, and did not put her away; but on the occasion of the first census which was taken in Judæa, under Cyrenius, he went up from Nazareth, where he lived, to Bethlehem, to which he belonged, to be enrolled; for his family was of the tribe of Judah, which then inhabited that region. Then along with Mary he is ordered to proceed into Egypt, and remain there with the Child until another revelation warn them to return into Judæa. But when the Child was born in Bethlehem, since Joseph could not find a lodging in that village, he took up his quarters in a certain cave near the village; and while they were there Mary brought forth the Christ and placed Him in a manger, and here the Magi who came from Arabia found Him. I have repeated to you," I continued, "what Isaiah foretold about the sign which foreshadowed the cave; but for the sake of those who have come with us to-day, I shall again remind you of the passage." Then I repeated the passage from Isaiah which I have already written, adding that, by means of those words, those who presided over the mysteries of Mithras were stirred up by the devil to say that in a place, called among them a cave, they were initiated by him. [2244] "So Herod, when the Magi from Arabia did not return to him, as he had asked them to do, but had departed by another way to their own country, according to the commands laid on them; and when Joseph, with Mary and the Child, had now gone into Egypt, as it was revealed to them to do; as he did not know the Child whom the Magi had gone to worship, ordered simply the whole of the children then in Bethlehem to be massacred. And Jeremiah prophesied that this would happen, speaking by the Holy Ghost thus: A voice was heard in Ramah, lamentation and much wailing, Rachel weeping for her children; and she would not be comforted, because they are not.' [2245] Therefore, on account of the voice which would be heard from Ramah, i.e., from Arabia (for there is in Arabia at this very time a place called Rama), wailing would come on the place where Rachel the wife of Jacob called Israel, the holy patriarch, has been buried, i.e., on Bethlehem; while the women weep for their own slaughtered children, and have no consolation by reason of what has happened to them. For that expression of Isaiah, He shall take the power of Damascus and spoils of Samaria,' foretold that the power of the evil demon that dwelt in Damascus should be overcome by Christ as soon as He was born; and this is proved to have happened. For the Magi, who were held in bondage [2246] for the commission of all evil deeds through the power of that demon, by coming to worship Christ, shows that they have revolted from that dominion which held them captive; and this [dominion] the Scripture has showed us to reside in Damascus. Moreover, that sinful and unjust power is termed well in parable, Samaria. [2247] And none of you can deny that Damascus was, and is, in the region of Arabia, although now it belongs to what is called Syrophoenicia. Hence it would be becoming for you, sirs, to learn what you have not perceived, from those who have received grace from God, namely, from us Christians; and not to strive in every way to maintain your own doctrines, dishonouring those of God. Therefore also this grace has been transferred to us, as Isaiah says, speaking to the following effect: This people draws near to Me, they honour Me with their lips, but their heart is far from Me; but in vain they worship Me, teaching the commands and doctrines of men. Therefore, behold, I will proceed [2248] to remove this people, and I shall remove them; and I shall take away the wisdom of their wise men, and bring to nothing the understanding of the prudent men.' " [2249]

Chapter LXXIX - He proves against Trypho that the wicked angels have revolted from God

On this, Trypho, who was somewhat angry, but respected the Scriptures, as was manifest from his countenance, said to me, "The utterances of God are holy, but your expositions are mere contrivances, as is plain from what has been explained by you; nay, even blasphemies, for you assert that angels sinned and revolted from God."

And I, wishing to get him to listen to me, answered in milder tones, thus: "I admire, sir, this piety of yours; and I pray that you may entertain the same disposition towards Him to whom angels are recorded to minister, as Daniel says; for [one] like the Son of man is led to the Ancient of days, and every kingdom is given to Him for ever and ever. But that you may know, sir," continued I, "that it is not our audacity which has induced us to adopt this exposition, which you reprehend, I shall give you evidence from Isaiah himself; for he affirms that evil angels have dwelt and do dwell in Tanis, in Egypt. These are [his] words: Woe to the rebellious children! Thus saith the Lord, You have taken counsel, but not through Me; and [made] agreements, but not through My Spirit, to add sins to sins; who have sinned [2250] in going down to Egypt (but they have not inquired at Me), that they may be assisted by Pharaoh, and be covered with the shadow of the Egyptians. For the shadow of Pharaoh shall be a disgrace to you, and a reproach to those who trust in the Egyptians; for the princes in Tanis [2251] are evil angels. In vain will they labour for a people which will not profit them by assistance, but [will be] for a disgrace and a reproach [to them].' [2252] And, further, Zechariah tells, as you yourself have related, that the devil stood on the right hand of Joshua the priest, to resist him; and [the Lord] said, The Lord, who has taken [2253] Jerusalem, rebuke thee.' [2254] And again, it is written in Job, [2255] as you said yourself, how that the angels came to stand before the Lord, and the devil came with them. And we have it recorded by Moses in the beginning of Genesis, that the serpent beguiled Eve, and was cursed. And we know that in Egypt there were magicians who emulated [2256] the mighty power displayed by God through the faithful servant Moses. And you are aware that David said, The gods of the nations are demons.' " [2257]

Chapter LXXX - The opinion of Justin with regard to the reign of a thousand years. Several Catholics reject it

And Trypho to this replied, "I remarked to you sir, that you are very anxious to be safe in all respects, since you cling to the Scriptures. But tell me, do you really admit that this place, Jerusalem, shall be rebuilt; and do you expect your people to be gathered together, and made joyful with Christ and the patriarchs, and the prophets, both the men of our nation, and other proselytes who joined them before your Christ came? or have you given way, and admitted this in order to have the appearance of worsting us in the controversies?"

Then I answered, "I am not so miserable a fellow, Trypho, as to say one thing and think another. I admitted to you formerly, [2258] that I and many others are of this opinion, and [believe] that such will take place, as you assuredly are aware; [2259] but, on the other hand, I signified to you that many who belong to the pure and pious faith, and are true Christians, think otherwise. Moreover, I pointed out to you that some who are called Christians, but are godless, impious heretics, teach doctrines that are in every way blasphemous, atheistical, and foolish. But that you may know that I do not say this before you alone, I shall draw up a statement, so far as I can, of all the arguments which have passed between us; in which I shall record myself as admitting the very same things which I admit to you. [2260] For I choose to follow not men or men's doctrines, but God and the doctrines [delivered] by Him. For if you have fallen in with some who are called Christians, but who do not admit this [truth], [2261] and venture to blaspheme the God of Abraham, and the God of Isaac, and the God of Jacob; who say there is no resurrection of the dead, and that their souls, when they die, are taken to heaven; do not imagine that they are Christians, even as one, if he would rightly consider it, would not admit that the Sadducees, or similar sects of Genistæ, Meristæ,[2262] Galilæans, Hellenists, [2263] Pharisees, Baptists, are Jews (do not hear me impatiently when I tell you what I think), but are [only] called Jews and children of Abraham, worshipping God with the lips, as God Himself declared, but the heart was far from Him. But I and others, who are right-minded Christians on all points, are assured that there will be a resurrection of the dead, and a thousand years [2264] in Jerusalem, which will then be built, adorned, and enlarged, [as] the prophets Ezekiel and Isaiah and others declare.

Chapter LXXXI - He endeavours to prove this opinion from Isaiah and the Apocalypse

"For Isaiah spake thus concerning this space of a thousand years: For there shall be the new heaven and the new earth, and the former shall not be remembered, or come into their heart; but they shall find joy and gladness in it, which things I create. For, Behold, I make Jerusalem a rejoicing, and My people a joy; and I shall rejoice over Jerusalem, and be glad over My people. And the voice of weeping shall be no more heard in her, or the voice of crying. And there shall be no more there a person of immature years, or an old man who shall not fulfil his days. [2265] For the young man shall be an hundred years old; [2266] but the sinner who dies an hundred years old, [2267] he shall be accursed. And they shall build houses, and shall themselves inhabit them; and they shall plant vines, and shall themselves eat the produce of them, and drink the wine. They shall not build, and others inhabit; they shall not plant, and others eat. For according to the days of the tree of life shall be the days of my people; the works of their toil shall abound. [2268] Mine elect shall not toil fruitlessly, or beget children to be cursed; for they shall be a seed righteous and blessed by the Lord, and their offspring with them. And it shall come to pass, that before they call I will hear; while they are still speaking, I shall say, What is it? Then shall the wolves and the lambs feed together, and the lion shall eat straw like the ox; but the serpent [shall eat] earth as bread. They shall not hurt or maltreat each other on the holy mountain, saith the Lord.' [2269] Now we have understood that the expression used among these words, According to the days of the tree [of life[2270]] shall be the days of my people; the works of their toil shall abound' obscurely predicts a thousand years. For as Adam was told that in the day he ate of the tree he would die, we know that he did not complete a thousand years. We have perceived, moreover, that the expression, The day of the Lord is as a thousand years,' [2271] is connected with this subject. And further, there was a certain man with us, whose name was John, one of the apostles of Christ, who prophesied, by a revelation that was made to him, that those who believed in our Christ would dwell [2272] a thousand years in Jerusalem; and that thereafter the general, and, in short, the eternal resurrection and judgment of all men would likewise take place. Just as our Lord also said, They shall neither marry nor be given in marriage, but shall be equal to the angels, the children of the God of the resurrection.' [2273]

Chapter LXXXII - *The prophetical gifts of the Jews were transferred to the Christians*

"For the prophetical gifts remain with us, even to the present time. And hence you ought to understand that [the gifts] formerly among your nation have been transferred to us. And just as there were false prophets contemporaneous with your holy prophets, so are there now many false teachers amongst us, of whom our Lord forewarned us to beware; so that in no respect are we deficient, since we know that He foreknew all that would happen to us after His resurrection from the dead and ascension to heaven. For He said we would be put to death, and hated for His name's sake; and that many false prophets and false Christs would appear in His name, and deceive many: and so has it come about. For many have taught godless, blasphemous, and unholy doctrines, forging them in His name; have taught, too, and even yet are teaching, those things which proceed from the unclean spirit of the devil, and which were put into their hearts. Therefore we are most anxious that you be persuaded not to be misled by such persons, since we know that every one who can speak the truth, and yet speaks it not, shall be judged by God, as God testified by Ezekiel, when He said, I have made thee a watchman to the house of Judah. If the sinner sin, and thou warn him not, he himself shall die in his sin; but his blood will I require at thine hand. But if thou warn him, thou shalt be innocent.' [2274] And on this account we are, through fear, very earnest in desiring to converse [with men] according to the Scriptures, but not from love of money, or of glory, or of pleasure. For no man can convict us of any of these [vices]. No more do we wish to live like the rulers of your people, whom God reproaches when He says, Your rulers are companions of thieves, lovers of bribes, followers of the rewards.' [2275] Now, if you know certain amongst us to be of this sort, do not for their sakes blaspheme the Scriptures and Christ, and do not assiduously strive to give falsified interpretations.

Chapter LXXXIII - *It is proved that the Psalm, "The Lord said to My Lord," etc., does not suit Hezekiah*

"For your teachers have ventured to refer the passage, The Lord says to my Lord, Sit at my right hand, till I make Thine enemies Thy footstool,' to Hezekiah; as if he were requested to sit on the right side of the temple, when the king of Assyria sent to him and threatened him; and he was told by Isaiah not to be afraid. Now we know and admit that what Isaiah said took place; that the king of Assyria desisted from waging war against Jerusalem in Hezekiah's days, and the angel of the Lord slew about 185,000 of the host of the Assyrians. But it is manifest that the Psalm does not refer to him. For thus it is written, The Lord says to my Lord, Sit at My right hand, till I make Thine enemies Thy footstool. He shall send forth a rod of power over [2276] Jerusalem, and it shall rule in the midst of Thine [2277] enemies. In the splendour of the saints before the morning star have I begotten Thee. The Lord hath sworn, and will not repent, Thou art a priest for ever after the order of Melchizedek.' Who does not admit, then, that Hezekiah is no priest for ever after the order of Melchizedek? And who does not know that he is not the redeemer of Jerusalem? And who does not know that he neither sent a rod of power into Jerusalem, nor ruled in the midst of his enemies; but that it was God who averted from him the enemies, after he mourned and was afflicted? But our Jesus, who has not yet come in glory, has sent into Jerusalem a rod of power, namely, the word of calling and repentance [meant] for all nations over which demons held sway, as David says, The gods of the nations are demons.' And His strong word has prevailed on many to forsake the demons whom they used to serve, and by means of it to believe in the Almighty God because the gods of the nations are demons. [2278] And we mentioned formerly that the statement, In the splendour of the saints before the morning star have I begotten Thee from the womb,' is made to Christ.

Chapter LXXXIV - That prophecy, "Behold, a virgin," etc., suits Christ alone

"Moreover, the prophecy, Behold, the virgin shall conceive, and bear a son,' was uttered respecting Him. For if He to whom Isaiah referred was not to be begotten of a virgin, of whom [2279] did the Holy Spirit declare, Behold, the Lord Himself shall give us a sign: behold, the virgin shall conceive, and bear a son?' For if He also were to be begotten of sexual intercourse, like all other first-born sons, why did God say that He would give a sign which is not common to all the first-born sons? But that which is truly a sign, and which was to be made trustworthy to mankind,--namely, that the first-begotten of all creation should become incarnate by the Virgin's womb, and be a child,--this he anticipated by the Spirit of prophecy, and predicted it, as I have repeated to you, in various ways; in order that, when the event should take place, it might be known as the operation of the power and will of the Maker of all things; just as Eve was made from one of Adam's ribs, and as all living beings were created in the beginning by the word of God. But you in these matters venture to pervert the expositions which your elders that were with Ptolemy king of Egypt gave forth, since you assert that the Scripture is not so as they have expounded it, but says, Behold, the young woman shall conceive,' as if great events were to be inferred if a woman should beget from sexual intercourse: which indeed all young women, with the exception of the barren, do; but even these, God, if He wills, is able to cause [to bear]. For Samuel's mother, who was barren, brought forth by the will of God; and so also the wife of the holy patriarch Abraham; and Elisabeth, who bore John the Baptist, and other such. So that you must not suppose that it is impossible for God to do anything He wills. And especially when it was predicted that this would take place, do not venture to pervert or misinterpret the prophecies, since you will injure yourselves alone, and will not harm God.

Chapter LXXXV - He proves that Christ is the Lord of Hosts from Ps. xxiv., and from his authority over demons

"Moreover, some of you venture to expound the prophecy which runs, Lift up your gates, ye rulers; and be ye lift up, ye everlasting doors, that the King of glory may enter,' [2280] as if it referred likewise to Hezekiah, and others of you [expound it] of Solomon; but neither to the latter nor to the former, nor, in short, to any of your kings, can it be proved to have reference, but to this our Christ alone, who appeared without comeliness, and inglorious, as Isaiah and David and all the Scriptures said; who is the Lord of hosts, by the will of the Father who conferred on Him [the dignity]; who also rose from the dead, and ascended to heaven, as the Psalm and the other Scriptures manifested when they announced Him to be Lord of hosts; and of this you may, if you will, easily be persuaded by the occurrences which take place before your eyes. For every demon, when exorcised in the name of this very Son of God --who is the First-born of every creature, who became man by the Virgin, who suffered, and was crucified under Pontius Pilate by your nation, who died, who rose from the dead, and ascended into heaven --is overcome and subdued. But though you exorcise any demon in the name of any of those who were amongst you--either kings, or righteous men, or prophets, or patriarchs--it will not be subject to you. But if any of you exorcise it in [the name of] the God of Abraham, and the God of Isaac, and the God of Jacob, it will perhaps be subject to you. Now assuredly your exorcists, I have said, [2281] make use of craft when they exorcise, even as the Gentiles do, and employ fumigations and incantations. [2282] But that they are angels and powers whom the word of prophecy by David [commands] to lift up the gates, that He who rose from the dead, Jesus Christ, the Lord of hosts, according to the will of the Father, might enter, the word of David has likewise showed; which I shall again recall to your attention for the sake of those who were not with us yesterday, for whose benefit, moreover, I sum up many things I said yesterday. And now, if I say this to you, although I have repeated it many times, I know that it is not absurd so to do. For it is a ridiculous thing to see the sun, and the moon, and the other stars, continually keeping the same course, and bringing round the different seasons; and to see the computer who may be asked how many are twice two, because he has frequently said that they are four, not ceasing to say again that they are four; and equally so other things, which are confidently admitted, to be continually mentioned and admitted in like manner; yet that he who founds his discourse on the prophetic Scriptures should leave them and abstain from constantly referring to the same Scriptures, because it is thought he can bring forth something better than Scripture. The passage, then, by which I proved that God reveals that there are both angels and hosts in heaven is this: Praise the Lord from the heavens: praise Him in the highest. Praise Him, all His angels: praise Him, all His hosts.' " [2283]

Then one of those who had come with them on the second day, whose name was Mnaseas, said, "We are greatly pleased that you undertake to repeat the same things on our account."

And I said, "Listen, my friends, to the Scripture which induces me to act thus. Jesus commanded [us] to love even [our] enemies, as was predicted by Isaiah in many passages, in which also is contained the mystery of our own regeneration, as well, in fact, as the regeneration of all who expect that Christ will appear in Jerusalem, and by their works endeavour earnestly to please Him. These are the words spoken by Isaiah: Hear the word of the Lord, ye that tremble at His word. Say, our brethren, to them that hate you and detest you, that the name of the Lord has been glorified. He has appeared to your joy, and they shall be ashamed. A voice of noise from the city, a voice from the temple, [2284] a voice of the Lord who rendereth recompense to the proud. Before she that travailed brought forth, and before the pains of labour came, she brought forth a male child. Who hath heard such a thing? and who hath seen such a thing? has the earth brought forth in one day? and has she produced a nation at once? for Zion has travailed and borne her children. But I have given such an expectation even to her that does not bring forth, said the Lord. Behold, I have made her that begetteth, and her that is barren, saith the Lord. Rejoice, O Jerusalem, and hold a joyous assembly, all ye that love her. Be glad, all ye that mourn for her, that ye may suck and be filled with the breast of her consolation, that having suck ye may be delighted with the entrance of His glory.' " [2285]

Chapter LXXXVI - There are various figures in the Old Testament of the wood of the cross by which Christ reigned

And when I had quoted this, I added, "Hear, then, how this Man, of whom the Scriptures declare that He will come again in glory after His crucifixion, was symbolized both by the tree of life, which was said to have been planted in paradise, and by those events which should happen to all the just. Moses was sent with a rod to effect the redemption of the people; and with this in his hands at the head of the people, he divided the sea. By this he saw the water gushing out of the rock; and when he cast a tree into the waters of Marah, which were bitter, he made them sweet. Jacob, by putting rods into the water-troughs, caused the sheep of his uncle to conceive, so that he should obtain their young. With his rod the same Jacob boasts that he had crossed the river. He said he had seen a ladder, and the Scripture has declared that God stood above it. But that this was not the Father, we have proved from the Scriptures. And Jacob, having poured oil on a stone in the same place, is testified to by the very God who appeared to him, that he had anointed a pillar to the God who appeared to him. And that the stone symbolically proclaimed Christ, we have also proved by many Scriptures; and that the unguent, whether it was of oil, or of stacte, [2286] or of any other compounded sweet balsams, had reference to Him, we have also proved, [2287] inasmuch as the word says: Therefore God, even Thy God, hath anointed Thee with the oil of gladness above Thy fellows.' [2288] For indeed all kings and anointed persons obtained from Him their share in the names of kings and anointed: just as He Himself received from the Father the titles of King, and Christ, and Priest, and Angel, and such like other titles which He bears or did bear. Aaron's rod, which blossomed, declared him to be the high priest. Isaiah prophesied that a rod would come forth from the root of Jesse, [and this was] Christ. And David says that the righteous man is like the tree that is planted by the channels of waters, which should yield its fruit in its season, and whose leaf should not fade.' [2289] Again, the righteous is said to flourish like the palm-tree. God appeared from a tree to Abraham, as it is written, near the oak in Mamre. The people found seventy willows and twelve springs after crossing the Jordan. [2290] David affirms that God comforted him with a rod and staff. Elisha, by casting a stick [2291] into the river Jordan, recovered the iron part of the axe with which the sons of the prophets had gone to cut down trees to build the house in which they wished to read and study the law and commandments of God; even as our Christ, by being crucified on the tree, and by purifying [us] with water, has redeemed us, though plunged in the direst offences which we have committed, and has made [us] a house of prayer and adoration. Moreover, it was a rod that pointed out Judah to be the father of Tamar's sons by a great mystery."

Chapter LXXXVII - Trypho maintains in objection these words: "And shall rest on Him," etc. They are explained by Justin

Hereupon Trypho, after I had spoken these words, said, "Do not now suppose that I am endeavouring, by asking what I do ask, to overturn the statements you have made; but I wish to receive information respecting those very points about which I now inquire. Tell me, then, how, when the Scripture asserts by Isaiah, There shall come forth a rod from the root of Jesse; and a flower shall grow up from the root of Jesse; and the Spirit of God shall rest upon Him, the spirit of wisdom and understanding, the spirit of counsel and might, the spirit of knowledge and piety: and the spirit of the fear of the Lord shall fill Him:' [2292] (now you admitted to me," continued he, "that this referred to Christ, and you maintain Him to be pre-existent God, and having become incarnate by God's will, to be born man by the Virgin:) how He can be demonstrated to have been pre-existent, who is filled with the powers of the Holy Ghost, which the Scripture by Isaiah enumerates, as if He were in lack of them?"

Then I replied, "You have inquired most discreetly and most prudently, for truly there does seem to be a difficulty; but listen to what I say, that you may perceive the reason of this also. The Scripture says that these enumerated powers of the Spirit have come on Him, not because He stood in need of them, but because they would rest in Him, i.e., would find their accomplishment in Him, so that there would be no more prophets in your nation after the ancient custom: and this fact you plainly perceive. For after Him no prophet has arisen among you. Now, that [you may know that] your prophets, each receiving some one or two powers from God, did and spoke the things which we have learned from the Scriptures, attend to the following remarks of mine. Solomon possessed the spirit of wisdom, Daniel that of understanding and counsel, Moses that of might and piety, Elijah that of fear, and Isaiah that of knowledge; and so with the others: each possessed one power, or one joined alternately with another; also Jeremiah, and the twelve [prophets], and David, and, in short, the rest who existed amongst you. Accordingly He [2293] rested, i.e., ceased, when He came, after whom, in the times of this dispensation wrought out by Him amongst men, [2294] it was requisite that such gifts should cease from you; and having received their rest in Him, should again, as had been predicted, become gifts which, from the grace of His Spirit's power, He imparts to those who believe in Him, according as He deems each man worthy thereof. I have already said, and do again say, that it had been prophesied that this would be done by Him after His ascension to heaven. It is accordingly said, [2295] He ascended on high, He led captivity captive, He gave gifts unto the sons of men.' And again, in another prophecy it is said: And it shall come to pass after this, I will pour out My Spirit on all flesh, and on My servants, and on My handmaids, and they shall prophesy.' [2296]

Chapter LXXXVIII - Christ has not received the Holy Spirit on account of poverty

"Now, it is possible to see amongst us women and men who possess gifts of the Spirit of God; so that it was prophesied that the powers enumerated by Isaiah would come upon Him, not because He needed power, but because these would not continue after Him. And let this be a proof to you, namely, what I told you was done by the Magi from Arabia, who as soon as the Child was born came to worship Him, for even at His birth He was in possession of His power; and as He grew up like all other men, by using the fitting means, He assigned its own [requirements] to each development, and was sustained by all kinds of nourishment, and waited for thirty years, more or less, until John appeared before Him as the herald of His approach, and preceded Him in the way of baptism, as I have already shown. And then, when Jesus had gone to the river Jordan, where John was baptizing, and when He had stepped into the water, a fire [2297] was kindled in the Jordan; and when He came out of the water, the Holy Ghost lighted on Him like a dove, [as] the apostles of this very Christ of ours wrote. Now, we know that he did not go to the river because He stood in need of baptism, or of the descent of the Spirit like a dove; even as He submitted to be born and to be crucified, not because He needed such things, but because of the human race, which from Adam had fallen under the power of death and the guile of the serpent, and each one of which had committed personal transgression. For God, wishing both angels and men, who were endowed with free-will, and at their own disposal, to do whatever He had strengthened each to do, made them so, that if they chose the things acceptable to Himself, He would keep them free from death and from punishment; but that if they did evil, He would punish each as He sees fit. For it was not His entrance into Jerusalem sitting on an ass, which we have showed was prophesied, that empowered Him to be Christ, but it furnished men with a proof that He is the Christ; just as it was necessary in the time of John that men have proof, that they might know who is Christ. For when John remained[2298] by the Jordan, and preached the baptism of repentance, wearing only a leathern girdle and a vesture made of camels' hair, eating nothing but locusts and wild honey, men supposed him to be Christ; but he cried to them, I am not the Christ, but the voice of one crying; for He that is stronger than I shall come, whose shoes I am not worthy to bear.' [2299] And when Jesus came to the Jordan, He was considered to be the son of Joseph the carpenter; and He appeared without comeliness, as the Scriptures declared; and He was deemed a carpenter (for He was in the habit of working as a carpenter when among men, making ploughs and yokes; by which He taught the symbols of righteousness and an active life); but then the Holy Ghost, and for man's sake, as I formerly stated, lighted on Him in the form of a dove, and there came at the same instant from the heavens a voice, which was uttered also by David when he spoke, personating Christ, what the Father would say to Him: Thou art My Son: this day have I begotten Thee;' [2300] [the Father] saying that His generation would take place for men, at the time when they would become acquainted with Him: Thou art My Son; this day have I begotten thee.' " [2301]

Chapter LXXXIX - The cross alone is offensive to Trypó ὦν account of the curse, yet it proves that Jesus is Christ

Then Trypho remarked, "Be assured that all our nation waits for Christ; and we admit that all the Scriptures which you have quoted refer to Him. Moreover, I do also admit that the name of Jesus, by which the the son of Nave (Nun) was called, has inclined me very strongly to adopt this view. But whether Christ should be so shamefully crucified, this we are in doubt about. For whosoever is crucified is said in the law to be accursed, so that I am exceedingly incredulous on this point. It is quite clear, indeed, that the Scriptures announce that Christ had to suffer; but we wish to learn if you can prove it to us whether it was by the suffering cursed in the law."

I replied to him, "If Christ was not to suffer, and the prophets had not foretold that He would be led to death on account of the sins of the people, and be dishonoured and scourged, and reckoned among the transgressors, and as a sheep be led to the slaughter, whose generation, the prophet says, no man can declare, then you would have good cause to wonder. But if these are to be characteristic of Him and mark Him out to all, how is it possible for us to do anything else than believe in Him most confidently? And will not as many as have understood the writings of the prophets, whenever they hear merely that He was crucified, say that this is He and no other?"

Chapter XC - The stretched-out hands of Moses signified beforehand the cross

"Bring us on, then," said [Trypho], "by the Scriptures, that we may also be persuaded by you; for we know that He should suffer and be led as a sheep. But prove to us whether He must be crucified and die so disgracefully and so dishonourably by the death cursed in the law. [2302] For we cannot bring ourselves even to think of this."

"You know," said I, "that what the prophets said and did they veiled by parables and types, as you admitted to us; so that it was not easy for all to understand the most [of what they said], since they concealed the truth by these means, that those who are eager to find out and learn it might do so with much labour."

They answered, "We admitted this."

"Listen, therefore," say I, "to what follows; for Moses first exhibited this seeming curse of Christ's by the signs which he made."

"Of what [signs] do you speak?" said he.

"When the people," replied I, "waged war with Amalek, and the son of Nave (Nun) by name Jesus (Joshua), led the fight, Moses himself prayed to God, stretching out both hands, and Hur with Aaron supported them during the whole day, so that they might not hang down when he got wearied. For if he gave up any part of this sign, which was an imitation of the cross, the people were beaten, as is recorded in the writings of Moses; but if he remained in this form, Amalek was proportionally defeated, and he who prevailed prevailed by the cross. For it was not because Moses so prayed that the people were stronger, but because, while one who bore the name of Jesus (Joshua) was in the forefront of the battle, he himself made the sign of the cross. For who of you knows not that the prayer of one who accompanies it with lamentation and tears, with the body prostrate, or with bended knees, propitiates God most of all? But in such a manner neither he nor any other one, while sitting on a stone, prayed. Nor even the stone symbolized Christ, as I have shown.

Chapter XCI - The cross was foretold in the blessings of Joseph, and in the serpent that was lifted up

"And God by Moses shows in another way the force of the mystery of the cross, when He said in the blessing wherewith Joseph was blessed, From the blessing of the Lord is his land; for the seasons of heaven, and for the dews, and for the deep springs from beneath, and for the seasonable fruits of the sun, [2303] and for the coming together of the months, and for the heights of the everlasting mountains, and for the heights of the hills, and for the ever-flowing rivers, and for the fruits of the fatness of the earth; and let the things accepted by Him who appeared in the bush come on the head and crown of Joseph. Let him be glorified among his brethren; [2304] his beauty is [like] the firstling of a bullock; his horns the horns of an unicorn: with these shall he push the nations from one end of the earth to another.' [2305] Now, no one could say or prove that the horns of an unicorn represent any other fact or figure than the type which portrays the cross. For the one beam is placed upright, from which the highest extremity is raised up into a horn, when the other beam is fitted on to it, and the ends appear on both sides as horns joined on to the one horn. And the part which is fixed in the centre, on which are suspended those who are crucified, also stands out like a horn; and it also looks like a horn conjoined and fixed with the other horns. And the expression, With these shall he push as with horns the nations from one end of the earth to another,' is indicative of what is now the fact among all the nations. For some out of all the nations, through the power of this mystery, having been so pushed, that is, pricked in their hearts, have turned from vain idols and demons to serve God. But the same figure is revealed for the destruction and condemnation of the unbelievers; even as Amalek was defeated and Israel victorious when the people came out of Egypt, by means of the type of the stretching out of Moses' hands, and the name of Jesus (Joshua), by which the son of Nave (Nun) was called. And it seems that the type and sign, which was erected to counteract the serpents which bit Israel, was intended for the salvation of those who believe that death was declared to come thereafter on the serpent through Him that would be crucified, but salvation to those who had been bitten by him and had betaken themselves to Him that sent His Son into the world to be crucified. [2306] For the Spirit of prophecy by Moses did not teach us to believe in the serpent, since it shows us that he was cursed by God from the beginning; and in Isaiah tells us that he shall be put to death as an enemy by the mighty sword, which is Christ.

Chapter XCII - Unless the scriptures be understood through God's great grace, God will not appear to have taught always the same righteousness

"Unless, therefore, a man by God's great grace receives the power to understand what has been said and done by the prophets, the appearance of being able to repeat the words or the deeds will not profit him, if he cannot explain the argument of them. And will they not assuredly appear contemptible to many, since they are related by those who understood them not? For if one should wish to ask you why, since Enoch, Noah with his sons, and all others in similar circumstances, who neither were circumcised nor kept the Sabbath, pleased God, God demanded by other leaders, and by the giving of the law after the lapse of so many generations, that those who lived between the times of Abraham and of Moses be justified by circumcision, and that those who lived after Moses be justified by circumcision and the other ordinances--to wit, the Sabbath, and sacrifices, and libations, [2307] and offerings; [God will be slandered] unless you show, as I have already said, that God who foreknew was aware that your nation would deserve expulsion from Jerusalem, and that none would be permitted to enter into it. (For [2308] you are not distinguished in any other way than by the fleshly circumcision, as I remarked previously. For Abraham was declared by God to be righteous, not on account of circumcision, but on account of faith. For before he was circumcised the following statement was made regarding him: Abraham believed God, and it was accounted unto him for righteousness.' [2309] And we, therefore, in the uncircumcision of our flesh, believing God through Christ, and having that circumcision which is of advantage to us who have acquired it --namely, that of the heart--we hope to appear righteous before and well-pleasing to God: since already we have received His testimony through the words of the prophets.) [And, further, God will be slandered unless you show] that you were commanded to observe the Sabbath, and to present offerings, and that the Lord submitted to have a place called by the name of God, in order that, as has been said, you might not become impious and godless by worshipping idols and forgetting God, as indeed you do always appear to have been. (Now, that God enjoined the ordinances of Sabbaths and offerings for these reasons, I have proved in what I previously remarked; but for the sake of those who came to-day, I wish to repeat nearly the whole.) For if this is not the case, God will be slandered, [2310] as having no foreknowledge, and as not teaching all men to know and to do the same acts of righteousness (for many generations of men appear to have existed before Moses); and the Scripture is not true which affirms that God is true and righteous, and all His ways are judgments, and there is no unrighteousness in him.' But since the Scripture is true, God is always willing that such even as you be neither foolish nor lovers of yourselves, in order that you may obtain the salvation of Christ, [2311] who pleased God, and received testimony from Him, as I have already said, by alleging proof from the holy words of prophecy.

Chapter XCIII - The same kind of righteousness is bestowed on all. Christ comprehends it in two precepts

"For [God] sets before every race of mankind that which is always and universally just, as well as all righteousness; and every race knows that adultery, and fornication, and homicide, [2312] and such like, are sinful; and though they all commit such practices, yet they do not escape from the knowledge that they act unrighteously whenever they so do, with the exception of those who are possessed with an unclean spirit, and who have been debased by education, by wicked customs, and by sinful institutions, and who have lost, or rather quenched and put under, their natural ideas. For we may see that such persons are unwilling to submit to the same things which they inflict upon others, and reproach each other with hostile consciences for the acts which they perpetrate. And hence I think that our Lord and Saviour Jesus Christ spoke well when He summed up all righteousness and piety in two commandments. They are these: Thou shalt love the Lord thy God with all thy heart, and with all thy strength, and thy neighbour as thyself.'[2313] For the man who loves God with all the heart, and with all the strength, being filled with a God-fearing mind, will reverence no other god; and since God wishes it, he would reverence that angel who is beloved by the same Lord and God. And the man who loves his neighbour as himself will wish for him the same good things that he wishes for himself, and no man will wish evil things for himself. Accordingly, he who loves his neighbour would pray and labour that his neighbour may be possessed of the same benefits as himself. Now nothing else is neighbour to man than that similarly-affectioned and reasonable being--man. Therefore, since all righteousness is divided into two branches, namely, in so far as it regards God and men, whoever, says the Scripture, loves the Lord God with all the heart, and all the strength, and his neighbour as himself, would be truly a righteous man. But you were never shown to be possessed of friendship or love either towards God, or towards the prophets, or towards yourselves, but, as is evident, you are ever found to be idolaters and murderers of righteous men, so that you laid hands even on Christ Himself; and to this very day you abide in your wickedness, execrating those who prove that this man who was crucified by you is the Christ. Nay, more than this, you suppose that He was crucified as hostile to and cursed by God, which supposition is the product of your most irrational mind. For though you have the means of understanding that this man is Christ from the signs given by Moses, yet you will not; but, in addition, fancying that we can have no arguments, you put whatever question comes into your minds, while you yourselves are at a loss for arguments whenever you meet with some firmly established Christian.

Chapter XCIV - In what sense he who hangs on a tree is cursed

"For tell me, was it not God who commanded by Moses that no image or likeness of anything which was in heaven above or which was on the earth should be made, and yet who caused the brazen serpent to be made by Moses in the wilderness, and set it up for a sign by which those bitten by serpents were saved? Yet is He free from unrighteousness. For by this, as I previously remarked, He proclaimed the mystery, by which He declared that He would break the power of the serpent which occasioned the transgression of Adam, and [would bring] to them that believe on Him [who was foreshadowed] by this sign, i.e., Him who was to be crucified, salvation from the fangs of the serpent, which are wicked deeds, idolatries, and other unrighteous acts. Unless the matter be so understood, give me a reason why Moses set up the brazen serpent for a sign, and bade those that were bitten gaze at it, and the wounded were healed; and this, too, when he had himself commanded that no likeness of anything whatsoever should be made."

On this, another of those who came on the second day said, "You have spoken truly: we cannot give a reason. For I have frequently interrogated the teachers about this matter, and none of them gave me a reason: therefore continue what you are speaking; for we are paying attention while you unfold the mystery, on account of which the doctrines of the prophets are falsely slandered."

Then I replied, "Just as God commanded the sign to be made by the brazen serpent, and yet He is blameless; even so, though a curse lies in the law against persons who are crucified, yet no curse lies on the Christ of God, by whom all that have committed things worthy of a curse are saved.[2314]

Chapter XCV - Christ took upon Himself the curse due to us

"For the whole human race will be found to be under a curse. For it is written in the law of Moses, Cursed is every one that continueth not in all things that are written in the book of the law to do them.'[2315] And no one has accurately done all, nor will you venture to deny this; but some more and some less than others have observed the ordinances enjoined. But if those who are under this law appear to be under a curse for not having observed all the requirements, how much more shall all the nations appear to be under a curse who practise idolatry, who seduce youths, and commit other crimes? If, then, the Father of all wished His Christ for the whole human family to take upon Him the curses of all, knowing that, after He had been crucified and was dead, He would raise Him up, why do you argue about Him, who submitted to suffer these things according to the Father's will, as if He were accursed, and do not rather bewail yourselves? For although His Father caused Him to suffer these things in behalf of the human family, yet you did not commit the deed as in obedience to the will of God. For you did not practise piety when you slew the prophets. And let none of you say: If His Father wished Him to suffer this, in order that by His stripes the human race might be healed, we have done no wrong. If, indeed, you repent of your sins, and recognise Him to be Christ, and observe His commandments, then you may assert this; for, as I have said before, remission of sins shall be yours. But if you curse Him and them that believe on Him, and, when you have the power, put them to death, how is it possible that requisition shall not be made of you, as of unrighteous and sinful men, altogether hard-hearted and without understanding, because you laid your hands on Him?

Chapter XCVI - That curse was a prediction of the things which the Jews would do

"For the statement in the law, Cursed is every one that hangeth on a tree,' [2316] confirms our hope which depends on the crucified Christ, not because He who has been crucified is cursed by God, but because God foretold that which would be done by you all, and by those like to you, who do not know [2317] that this is He who existed before all, who is the eternal Priest of God, and King, and Christ. And you clearly see that this has come to pass. For you curse in your synagogues all those who are called [2318] from Him Christians; and other nations effectively carry out the curse, putting to death those who simply confess themselves to be Christians; to all of whom we say, You are our brethren; rather recognise the truth of God. And while neither they nor you are persuaded by us, but strive earnestly to cause us to deny the name of Christ, we choose rather and submit to death, in the full assurance that all the good which God has promised through Christ He will reward us with. And in addition to all this we pray for you, that Christ may have mercy upon you. For He taught us to pray for our enemies also, saying, Love your enemies; be kind and merciful, as your heavenly Father is.' [2319] For we see that the Almighty God is kind and merciful, causing His sun to rise on the unthankful and on the righteous, and sending rain on the holy and on the wicked; all of whom He has taught us He will judge.

Chapter XCVII - Other predictions of the cross of Christ

"For it was not without design that the prophet Moses, when Hur and Aaron upheld his hands, remained in this form until evening. For indeed the Lord remained upon the tree almost until evening, and they buried Him at eventide; then on the third day He rose again. This was declared by David thus: With my voice I cried to the Lord, and He heard me out of His holy hill. I laid me down, and slept; I awaked, for the Lord sustained me.' [2320] And Isaiah likewise mentions concerning Him the manner in which He would die, thus: I have spread out My hands unto a people disobedient, and gainsaying, that walk in a way which is not good.' [2321] And that He would rise again, Isaiah himself said: His burial has been taken away from the midst, and I will give the rich for His death.' [2322] And again, in other words, David in the twenty-first [2323] Psalm thus refers to the suffering and to the cross in a parable of mystery: They pierced my hands and my feet; they counted all my bones. They considered and gazed on me; they parted my garments among themselves, and cast lots upon my vesture.' For when they crucified Him, driving in the nails, they pierced His hands and feet; and those who crucified Him parted His garments among themselves, each casting lots for what he chose to have, and receiving according to the decision of the lot. And this very Psalm you maintain does not refer to Christ; for you are in all respects blind, and do not understand that no one in your nation who has been called King or Christ has ever had his hands or feet pierced while alive, or has died in this mysterious fashion--to wit, by the cross--save this Jesus alone.

Chapter XCVIII - Predictions of Christ in Ps. xxii

"I shall repeat the whole Psalm, in order that you may hear His reverence to the Father, and how He refers all things to Him, and prays to be delivered by Him from this death; at the same time declaring in the Psalm who they are that rise up against Him, and showing that He has truly become man capable of suffering. It is as follows: O God, my God, attend to me: why hast Thou forsaken me? The words of my transgressions are far from my salvation. O my God, I will cry to Thee in the day-time, and Thou wilt not hear; and in the night-season, and it is not for want of understanding in me. But Thou, the Praise of Israel, inhabitest the holy place. Our fathers trusted in Thee; they trusted, and Thou didst deliver them. They cried unto Thee, and were delivered: they trusted in Thee, and were not confounded. But I am a worm, and no man; a reproach of men, and despised of the people. All they that see me laughed me to scorn; they spake with the lips, they shook the head: He trusted on the Lord: let Him deliver him, let Him save him, since he desires Him. For Thou art He that took me out of the womb; my hope from the breasts of my mother: I was cast upon Thee from the womb. Thou art my God from my mother's belly: be not far from me, for trouble is near; for there is none to help. Many calves have compassed me; fat bulls have beset me round. They opened their mouth upon me, as a ravening and roaring lion. All my bones are poured out and dispersed like water. My heart has become like wax melting in the midst of my belly. My strength is dried up like a potsherd; and my tongue has cleaved to my throat; and Thou hast brought me into the dust of death. For many dogs have surrounded me; the assembly of the wicked have beset me round. They pierced my hands and my feet, they did tell all my bones. They did look and stare upon me; they parted my garments among them, and cast lots upon my vesture. But do not Thou remove Thine assistance from me, O Lord: give heed to help me; deliver my soul from the sword, and my[2324] only-begotten from the hand of the dog. Save me from the lion's mouth, and my humility from the horns of the unicorns. I will declare Thy name to my brethren; in the midst of the Church will I praise Thee. Ye that fear the Lord, praise Him: all ye the seed of Jacob, glorify Him. Let all the seed of Israel fear Him.' "

Chapter XCIX - In the commencement of the Psalm are Christ's dying words

And when I had said these words, I continued: "Now I will demonstrate to you that the whole Psalm refers thus to Christ, by the words which I shall again explain. What is said at first--O God, my God, attend to me: why hast Thou forsaken me?'--announced from the beginning that which was to be said in the time of Christ. For when crucified, He spake: O God, my God, why hast Thou forsaken me?' And what follows: The words of my transgressions are far from my salvation. O my God, I will cry to Thee in the day-time, and Thou wilt not hear; and in the night-season, and it is not for want of understanding in me.' These, as well as the things which He was to do, were spoken. For on the day on which He was to be crucified, [2325] having taken three of His disciples to the hill called Olivet, situated opposite to the temple in Jerusalem, He prayed in these words: Father, if it be possible, let this cup pass from me.' [2326] And again He prayed: Not as I will, but as Thou wilt;' [2327] showing by this that He had become truly a suffering man. But lest any one should say, He did not know then that He had to suffer, He adds immediately in the Psalm: And it is not for want of understanding in me.' Even as there was no ignorance on God's part when He asked Adam where he was, or asked Cain where Abel was; but [it was done] to convince each what kind of man he was, and in order that through the record [of Scripture] we might have a knowledge of all: so likewise Christ declared that ignorance was not on His side, but on theirs, who thought that He was not the Christ, but fancied they would put Him to death, and that He, like some common mortal, would remain in Hades.

Chapter C - In what sense Christ is [called] Jacob, and Israel, and Son of Man

"Then what follows --But Thou, the praise of Israel, inhabitest the holy place'--declared that He is to do something worthy of praise and wonderment, being about to rise again from the dead on the third day after the crucifixion; and this He has obtained from the Father. For I have showed already that Christ is called both Jacob and Israel; and I have proved that it is not in the blessing of Joseph and Judah alone that what relates to Him was proclaimed mysteriously, but also in the Gospel it is written that He said: All things are delivered unto me by My Father;' and, No man knoweth the Father but the Son; nor the Son but the Father, and they to whom the Son will reveal Him.' [2328] Accordingly He revealed to us all that we have perceived by His grace out of the Scriptures, so that we know Him to be the first-begotten of God, and to be before all creatures; likewise to be the Son of the patriarchs, since He assumed flesh by the Virgin of their family, and submitted to become a man without comeliness, dishonoured, and subject to suffering. Hence, also, among His words He said, when He was discoursing about His future sufferings: The Son of man must suffer many things, and be rejected by the Pharisees and Scribes, and be crucified, and on the third day rise again.' [2329] He said then that He was the Son of man, either because of His birth by the Virgin, who was, as I said, of the family of David, [2330] and Jacob, and Isaac, and Abraham; or because Adam [2331] was the father both of Himself and of those who have been first enumerated from whom Mary derives her descent. For we know that the fathers of women are the fathers likewise of those children whom their daughters bear. For [Christ] called one of His disciples-- previously known by the name of Simon--Peter; since he recognised Him to be Christ the Son of God, by the revelation of His Father: and since we find it recorded in the memoirs of His apostles that He is the Son of God, and since we call Him the Son, we have understood that He proceeded before all creatures from the Father by His power and will (for He is addressed in the writings of the prophets in one way or another as Wisdom, and the Day, [2332] and the East, and a Sword, and a Stone, and a Rod, and Jacob, and Israel); and that He became man by the Virgin, in order that the disobedience which proceeded from the serpent might receive its destruction in the same manner in which it derived its origin. For Eve, who was a virgin and undefiled, having conceived the word of the serpent, brought forth disobedience and death. But the Virgin Mary received faith and joy, when the angel Gabriel announced the good tidings to her that the Spirit of the Lord would come upon her, and the power of the Highest would overshadow her: wherefore also the Holy Thing begotten of her is the Son of God; [2333] and she replied, Be it unto me according to thy word.' " [2334] And by her has He been born, to whom we have proved so many Scriptures refer, and by whom God destroys both the serpent and those angels and men who are like him; but works deliverance from death to those who repent of their wickedness and believe upon Him.

Chapter CI - Christ refers all things to the Father

"Then what follows of the Psalm is this, in which He says: Our fathers trusted in Thee; they trusted, and Thou didst deliver them. They cried unto Thee, and were not confounded. But I am a worm, and no man; a reproach of men, and despised of the people;' which show that He admits them to be His fathers, who trusted in God and were saved by Him, who also were the fathers of the Virgin, by whom He was born and became man; and He foretells that He shall be saved by the same God, but boasts not in accomplishing anything through His own will or might. For when on earth He acted in the very same manner, and answered to one who addressed Him as Good Master:' Why callest thou me good? One is good, my Father who is in heaven.' [2335] But when He says, I am a worm, and no man; a reproach of men, and despised of the people,' He prophesied the things which do exist, and which happen to Him. For we who believe on Him are everywhere a reproach, despised of the people;' for, rejected and dishonoured by your nation, He suffered those indignities which you planned against Him. And the following: All they that see me laughed me to scorn; they spake with the lips, they shook the head: He trusted in the Lord; let Him deliver him, since he desires Him;' this likewise He foretold should happen to Him. For they that saw Him crucified shook their heads each one of them, and distorted their lips, and twisting their noses to each other,[2336] they spake in mockery the words which are recorded in the memoirs of His apostles: He said he was the Son of God: let him come down; let God save him.'

Chapter CII - The prediction of the events which happened to Christ when He was born. Why God permitted it

"And what follows --My hope from the breasts of my mother. On Thee have I been cast from the womb; from my mother's belly Thou art my God: for there is no helper. Many calves have compassed me; fat bulls have beset me round. They opened their mouth upon me, as a ravening and a roaring lion. All my bones are poured out and dispersed like water. My heart has become like wax melting in the midst of my belly. My strength is become dry like a potsherd; and my tongue has cleaved to my throat' --foretold what would come to pass; for the statement, My hope from the breasts of my mother,' [is thus explained]. As soon as He was born in Bethlehem, as I previously remarked, king Herod, having learned from the Arabian Magi about Him, made a plot to put Him to death, and by God's command Joseph took Him with Mary and departed into Egypt. For the Father had decreed that He whom He had begotten should be put to death, but not before He had grown to manhood, and proclaimed the word which proceeded from Him. But if any of you say to us, Could not God rather have put Herod to death? I return answer by anticipation: Could not God have cut off in the beginning the serpent, so that he exist not, rather than have said, And I will put enmity between him and the woman, and between his seed and her seed?' [2337] Could He not have at once created a multitude of men? But yet, since He knew that it would be good, He created both angels and men free to do that which is righteous, and He appointed periods of time during which He knew it would be good for them to have the exercise of free-will; and because He likewise knew it would be good, He made general and particular judgments; each one's freedom of will, however, being guarded. Hence Scripture says the following, at the destruction of the tower, and division and alteration of tongues: And the Lord said, Behold, the people is one, and they have all one language; and this they have begun to do: and now nothing will be restrained from them of all which they have attempted to do.' [2338] And the statement, My strength is become dry like a potsherd, and my tongue has cleaved to my throat,' was also a prophecy of what would be done by Him according to the Father's will. For the power of His strong word, by which He always confuted the Pharisees and Scribes, and, in short, all your nation's teachers that questioned Him, had a cessation like a plentiful and strong spring, the waters of which have been turned off, when He kept silence, and chose to return no answer to any one in the presence of Pilate; as has been declared in the memoirs of His apostles, in order that what is recorded by Isaiah might have efficacious fruit, where it is written, The Lord gives me a tongue, that I may know when I ought to speak.' [2339] Again, when He said, Thou art my God; be not far from me,' He taught that all men ought to hope in God who created all things, and seek salvation and help from Him alone; and not suppose, as the rest of men do, that salvation can be obtained by birth, or wealth, or strength, or wisdom. And such have ever been your practices: at one time you made a calf, and always you have shown yourselves ungrateful, murderers of the righteous, and proud of your descent. For if the Son of God evidently states that He can be saved, [neither] [2340] because He is a son, nor because He is strong or wise, but that without God He cannot be saved, even though He be sinless, as Isaiah declares in words to the effect that even in regard to His very language He committed no sin (for He committed no iniquity or guile with His mouth), how do you or others who expect to be saved without this hope, suppose that you are not deceiving yourselves?

Chapter CIII - The Pharisees are the bulls: the roaring lion is Herod or the devil

"Then what is next said in the Psalm--For trouble is near, for there is none to help me. Many calves have compassed me; fat bulls have beset me round. They opened their mouth upon me as a ravening and roaring lion. All my bones are poured out and dispersed like water,'--was likewise a prediction of the events which happened to Him. For on that night when some of your nation, who had been sent by the Pharisees and Scribes, and teachers, [2341] came upon Him from the Mount [2342] of Olives, those whom Scripture called butting and prematurely destructive calves surrounded Him. And the expression, Fat bulls have beset me round,' He spoke beforehand of those who acted similarly to the calves, when He was led before your teachers. And the Scripture described them as bulls, since we know that bulls are authors of calves' existence. As therefore the bulls are the begetters of the calves, so your teachers were the cause why their children went out to the Mount of Olives to take Him and bring Him to them. And the expression, For there is none to help,' is also indicative of what took place. For there was not even a single man to assist Him as an innocent person. And the expression, They opened their mouth upon me like a roaring lion,' designates him who was then king of the Jews, and was called Herod, a successor of the Herod who, when Christ was born, slew all the infants in Bethlehem born about the same time, because he imagined that amongst them He would assuredly be of whom the Magi from Arabia had spoken; for he was ignorant of the will of Him that is stronger than all, how He had commanded Joseph and Mary to take the Child and depart into Egypt, and there to remain until a revelation should again be made to them to return into their own country. And there they did remain until Herod, who slew the infants in Bethlehem, was dead, and Archelaus had succeeded him. And he died before Christ came to the dispensation on the cross which was given Him by His Father. And when Herod succeeded Archelaus, having received the authority which had been allotted to him, Pilate sent to him by way of compliment Jesus bound; and God foreknowing that this would happen, had thus spoken: And they brought Him to the Assyrian, a present to the king.' [2343] Or He meant the devil by the lion roaring against Him: whom Moses calls the serpent, but in Job and Zechariah he is called the devil, and by Jesus is addressed as Satan, showing that a compounded name was acquired by him from the deeds which he performed. For Sata' in the Jewish and Syrian tongue means apostate; and Nas' is the word from which he is called by interpretation the serpent, i.e., according to the interpretation of the Hebrew term, from both of which there arises the single word Satanas. For this devil, when [Jesus] went up from the river Jordan, at the time when the voice spake to Him, Thou art my Son: this day have I begotten Thee,' [2344] is recorded in the memoirs of the apostles to have come to Him and tempted Him, even so far as to say to Him, Worship me;' and Christ answered him, Get thee behind me, Satan: thou shalt worship the Lord thy God, and Him only shalt thou serve.' [2345] For as he had deceived Adam, so he hoped [2346] that he might contrive some mischief against Christ also. Moreover, the statement, All my bones are poured out [2347] and dispersed like water; my heart has become like wax, melting in the midst of my belly,' was a prediction of that which happened to Him on that night when men came out against Him to the Mount of Olives to seize Him. For in the memoirs which I say were drawn up by His apostles and those who followed them, [it is recorded] that His sweat fell down like drops of blood while He was praying, and saying, If it be possible, let this cup pass:' [2348] His heart and also His bones trembling; His heart being like wax melting in His belly: [2349] in order that we may perceive that the Father wished His Son really [2350] to undergo such sufferings for our sakes, and may not say that He, being the Son of God, did not feel what was happening to Him and inflicted on Him. Further, the expression, My strength is dried up like a potsherd, and my tongue has cleaved to my throat,' was a prediction, as I previously remarked, of that silence, when He who convicted all your teachers of being unwise returned no answer at all.

Chapter CIV - Circumstances of Christ's death are predicted in this Psalm

"And the statement, Thou hast brought me into the dust of death; for many dogs have surrounded me: the assembly of the wicked have beset me round. They pierced my hands and my feet. They did tell all my bones. They did look and stare upon me. They parted my garments among them, and cast lots upon my vesture,'--was a prediction, as I said before, of the death to which the synagogue of the wicked would condemn Him, whom He calls both dogs and hunters, declaring that those who hunted Him were both gathered together and assiduously striving to condemn Him. And this is recorded to have happened in the memoirs of His apostles. And I have shown that, after His crucifixion, they who crucified Him parted His garments among them.

Chapter CV - The Psalm also predicts the crucifixion and the subject of the last prayers of Christ on Earth

"And what follows of the Psalm,--But Thou, Lord, do not remove Thine assistance from me; give heed to help me. Deliver my soul from the sword, and my [2351] only-begotten from the hand of the dog; save me from the lion's mouth, and my humility from the horns of the unicorns,'--was also information and prediction of the events which should befall Him. For I have already proved that He was the only-begotten of the Father of all things, being begotten in a peculiar manner Word and Power by Him, and having afterwards become man through the Virgin, as we have learned from the memoirs. Moreover, it is similarly foretold that He would die by crucifixion. For the passage, Deliver my soul from the sword, and my [2352] only-begotten from the hand of the dog; save me from the lion's mouth, and my humility from the horns of the unicorns,' is indicative of the suffering by which He should die, i.e., by crucifixion. For the horns of the unicorns,' I have already explained to you, are the figure of the cross only. And the prayer that His soul should be saved from the sword, and lion's mouth, and hand of the dog, was a prayer that no one should take possession of His soul: so that, when we arrive at the end of life, we may ask the same petition from God, who is able to turn away every shameless evil angel from taking our souls. And that the souls survive, I have shown [2353] to you from the fact that the soul of Samuel was called up by the witch, as Saul demanded. And it appears also, that all the souls of similar righteous men and prophets fell under the dominion of such powers, as is indeed to be inferred from the very facts in the case of that witch. Hence also God by His Son teaches [2354] us for whose sake these things seem to have been done, always to strive earnestly, and at death to pray that our souls may not fall into the hands of any such power. For when Christ was giving up His spirit on the cross, He said, Father, into Thy hands I commend my spirit,' [2355] as I have learned also from the memoirs. For He exhorted His disciples to surpass the pharisaic way of living, with the warning, that if they did not, they might be sure they could not be saved; and these words are recorded in the memoirs: Unless your righteousness exceed that of the Scribes and Pharisees, ye shall not enter into the kingdom of heaven.' [2356]

Chapter CVI - Christ's resurrection is foretold in the conclusion of the Psalm

"The remainder of the Psalm makes it manifest that He knew His Father would grant to Him all things which He asked, and would raise Him from the dead; and that He urged all who fear God to praise Him because He had compassion on all races of believing men, through the mystery of Him who was crucified; and that He stood in the midst of His brethren the apostles (who repented of their flight from Him when He was crucified, after He rose from the dead, and after they were persuaded by Himself that, before His passion He had mentioned to them that He must suffer these things, and that they were announced beforehand by the prophets), and when living with them sang praises to God, as is made evident in the memoirs of the apostles. The words are the following: I will declare Thy name to my brethren; in the midst of the Church will I praise Thee. Ye that fear the Lord, praise Him; all ye, the seed of Jacob, glorify Him. Let all the seed of Israel fear Him.' And when it is said that He changed the name of one of the apostles to Peter; and when it is written in the memoirs of Him that this so happened, as well as that He changed the names of other two brothers, the sons of Zebedee, to Boanerges, which means sons of thunder; this was an announcement of the fact that it was He by whom Jacob was called Israel, and Oshea called Jesus (Joshua), under whose name the people who survived of those that came from Egypt were conducted into the land promised to the patriarchs. And that He should arise like a star from the seed of Abraham, Moses showed beforehand when he thus said, A star shall arise from Jacob, and a leader from Israel;' [2357] and another Scripture says, Behold a man; the East is His name.' [2358] Accordingly, when a star rose in heaven at the time of His birth, as is recorded in the memoirs of His apostles, the Magi from Arabia, recognising the sign by this, came and worshipped Him.

Chapter CVII - The same is taught from the history of Jonah

"And that He would rise again on the third day after the crucifixion, it is written [2359] in the memoirs that some of your nation, questioning Him, said, Show us a sign;' and He replied to them, An evil and adulterous generation seeketh after a sign; and no sign shall be given them, save the sign of Jonah.' And since He spoke this obscurely, it was to be understood by the audience that after His crucifixion He should rise again on the third day. And He showed that your generation was more wicked and more adulterous than the city of Nineveh; for the latter, when Jonah preached to them, after he had been cast up on the third day from the belly of the great fish, that after three (in other versions, forty) [2360] days they should all perish, proclaimed a fast of all creatures, men and beasts, with sackcloth, and with earnest lamentation, with true repentance from the heart, and turning away from unrighteousness, in the belief that God is merciful and kind to all who turn from wickedness; so that the king of that city himself, with his nobles also, put on sackcloth and remained fasting and praying, and obtained their request that the city should not be overthrown. But when Jonah was grieved that on the (fortieth) third day, as he proclaimed, the city was not overthrown, by the dispensation of a gourd [2361] springing up from the earth for him, under which he sat and was shaded from the heat (now the gourd had sprung up suddenly, and Jonah had neither planted nor watered it, but it had come up all at once to afford him shade), and by the other dispensation of its withering away, for which Jonah grieved, [God] convicted him of being unjustly displeased because the city of Nineveh had not been overthrown, and said, Thou hast had pity on the gourd, for the which thou hast not laboured, neither madest it grow; which came up in a night, and perished in a night. And shall I not spare Nineveh, the great city, wherein dwell more than six score thousand persons that cannot discern between their right hand and their left hand; and also much cattle?' [2362]

Chapter CVIII - The resurrection of Christ did not convert the Jews. But through the whole world they have sent men to accuse Christ

"And though all the men of your nation knew the incidents in the life of Jonah, and though Christ said amongst you that He would give the sign of Jonah, exhorting you to repent of your wicked deeds at least after He rose again from the dead, and to mourn before God as did the Ninevites, in order that your nation and city might not be taken and destroyed, as they have been destroyed; yet you not only have not repented, after you learned that He rose from the dead, but, as I said before [2363] you have sent chosen and ordained men throughout all the world to proclaim that a godless and lawless heresy had sprung from one Jesus, a Galilæan deceiver, whom we crucified, but his disciples stole him by night from the tomb, where he was laid when unfastened from the cross, and now deceive men by asserting that he has risen from the dead and ascended to heaven. Moreover, you accuse Him of having taught those godless, lawless, and unholy doctrines which you mention to the condemnation of those who confess Him to be Christ, and a Teacher from and Son of God. Besides this, even when your city is captured, and your land ravaged, you do not repent, but dare to utter imprecations on Him and all who believe in Him. Yet we do not hate you or those who, by your means, have conceived such prejudices against us; but we pray that even now all of you may repent and obtain mercy from God, the compassionate and long-suffering Father of all.

Chapter CIX - The conversion of the Gentiles has been predicted by Micah

"But that the Gentiles would repent of the evil in which they led erring lives, when they heard the doctrine preached by His apostles from Jerusalem, and which they learned [2364] through them, suffer me to show you by quoting a short statement from the prophecy of Micah, one of the twelve [minor prophets]. This is as follows: And in the last days the mountain of the Lord shall be manifest, established on the top of the mountains; it shall be exalted above the hills, and people shall flow unto it. [2365] And many nations shall go, and say, Come, let us go up to the mountain of the Lord, and to the house of the God of Jacob; and they shall enlighten us in His way, and we shall walk in His paths: for out of Zion shall go forth the law, and the word of the Lord from Jerusalem. And He shall judge among many peoples, and shall rebuke strong nations afar off; and they shall beat their swords into ploughshares, and their spears into sickles: nation shall not lift up a sword against nation, neither shall they learn war any more. And each man shall sit under his vine and under his fig tree; and there shall be none to terrify: for the mouth of the Lord of hosts hath spoken it. For all people will walk in the name of their gods; but we will walk in the name of the Lord our God for ever. And it shall come to pass in that day, that I will assemble her that is afflicted, and gather her that is driven out, and whom I had plagued; and I shall make her that is afflicted a remnant, and her that is oppressed a strong nation. And the Lord shall reign over them in Mount Zion from henceforth, and even for ever.' " [2366]

Chapter CX - A portion of the prophecy already fulfilled in the Christians: the rest shall be fulfilled at the second advent

And when I had finished these words, I continued: "Now I am aware that your teachers, sirs, admit the whole of the words of this passage to refer to Christ; and I am likewise aware that they maintain He has not yet come; or if they say that He has come, they assert that it is not known who He is; but when He shall become manifest and glorious, then it shall be known who He is. And then, they say, the events mentioned in this passage shall happen, just as if there was no fruit as yet from the words of the prophecy. O unreasoning men! understanding not what has been proved by all these passages, that two advents of Christ have been announced: the one, in which He is set forth as suffering, inglorious, dishonoured, and crucified; but the other, in which He shall come from heaven with glory, when the man of apostasy, [2367] who speaks strange things against the Most High, shall venture to do unlawful deeds on the earth against us the Christians, who, having learned the true worship of God from the law, and the word which went forth from Jerusalem by means of the apostles of Jesus, have fled for safety to the God of Jacob and God of Israel; and we who were filled with war, and mutual slaughter, and every wickedness, have each through the whole earth changed our warlike weapons,-- our swords into ploughshares, and our spears into implements of tillage, --and we cultivate piety, righteousness, philanthropy, faith, and hope, which we have from the Father Himself through Him who was crucified; and sitting each under his vine, i.e., each man possessing his own married wife. For you are aware that the prophetic word says, And his wife shall be like a fruitful vine.' [2368] Now it is evident that no one can terrify or subdue us who have believed in Jesus over all the world. For it is plain that, though beheaded, and crucified, and thrown to wild beasts, and chains, and fire, and all other kinds of torture, we do not give up our confession; but the more such things happen, the more do others and in larger numbers become faithful, and worshippers of God through the name of Jesus. For just as if one should cut away the fruit-bearing parts of a vine, it grows up again, and yields other branches flourishing and fruitful; even so the same thing happens with us. For the vine planted by God and Christ the Saviour is His people. But the rest of the prophecy shall be fulfilled at His second coming. For the expression, He that is afflicted [and driven out],' i.e., from the world, [implies] that, so far as you and all other men have it in your power, each Christian has been driven out not only from his own property, but even from the whole world; for you permit no Christian to live. But you say that the same fate has befallen your own nation. Now, if you have been cast out after defeat in battle, you have suffered such treatment justly indeed, as all the Scriptures bear witness; but we, though we have done no such [evil acts] after we knew the truth of God, are testified to by God, that, together with the most righteous, and only spotless and sinless Christ, we are taken away out of the earth. For Isaiah cries, Behold how the righteous perishes, and no man lays it to heart; and righteous men are taken away, and no man considers it.' [2369]

Chapter CXI - The two advents were signified by the two goats. Other figures of the first advent, in which the Gentiles are freed by the blood of Christ

"And that it was declared by symbol, even in the time of Moses, that there would be two advents of this Christ, as I have mentioned previously, [is manifest] from the symbol of the goats presented for sacrifice during the fast. And again, by what Moses and Joshua did, the same thing was symbolically announced and told beforehand. For the one of them, stretching out his hands, remained till evening on the hill, his hands being supported; and this reveals a type of no other thing than of the cross: and the other, whose name was altered to Jesus (Joshua), led the fight, and Israel conquered. Now this took place in the case of both those holy men and prophets of God, that you may perceive how one of them could not bear up both the mysteries: I mean, the type of the cross and the type of the name. For this is, was, and shall be the strength of Him alone, whose name every power dreads, being very much tormented because they shall be destroyed by Him. Therefore our suffering and crucified Christ was not cursed by the law, but made it manifest that He alone would save those who do not depart from His faith. And the blood of the passover, sprinkled on each man's door-posts and lintel, delivered those who were saved in Egypt, when the first-born of the Egyptians were destroyed. For the passover was Christ, who was afterwards sacrificed, as also Isaiah said, He was led as a sheep to the slaughter.' [2370] And it is written, that on the day of the passover you seized Him, and that also during the passover you crucified Him. And as the blood of the passover saved those who were in Egypt, so also the blood of Christ will deliver from death those who have believed. Would God, then, have been deceived if this sign had not been above the doors? I do not say that; but I affirm that He announced beforehand the future salvation for the human race through the blood of Christ. For the sign of the scarlet thread, which the spies, sent to Jericho by Joshua, son of Nave (Nun), gave to Rahab the harlot, telling her to bind it to the window through which she let them down to escape from their enemies, also manifested the symbol of the blood of Christ, by which those who were at one time harlots and unrighteous persons out of all nations are saved, receiving remission of sins, and continuing no longer in sin.

Chapter CXII - The Jews expound these signs jejunely and feebly, and take up their attention only with insignificant matters

"But you, expounding these things in a low [and earthly] manner, impute much weakness to God, if you thus listen to them merely, and do not investigate the force of the words spoken. Since even Moses would in this way be considered a transgressor: for he enjoined that no likeness of anything in heaven, or on earth, or in the sea, be made; and then he himself made a brazen serpent and set it on a standard, and bade those who were bitten look at it: and they were saved when they

The Apostolic Fathers

looked at it. Will the serpent, then, which (I have already said) God had in the beginning cursed and cut off by the great sword, as Isaiah says, [2371] be understood as having preserved at that time the people? and shall we receive these things in the foolish acceptation of your teachers, and [regard] them not as signs? And shall we not rather refer the standard to the resemblance of the crucified Jesus, since also Moses by his outstretched hands, together with him who was named Jesus (Joshua), achieved a victory for your people? For in this way we shall cease to be at a loss about the things which the lawgiver did, when he, without forsaking God, persuaded the people to hope in a beast through which transgression and disobedience had their origin. And this was done and said by the blessed prophet with much intelligence and mystery; and there is nothing said or done by any one of the prophets, without exception, which one can justly reprehend, if he possess the knowledge which is in them. But if your teachers only expound to you why female camels are spoken of in this passage, and are not in that; or why so many measures of fine flour and so many measures of oil [are used] in the offerings; and do so in a low and sordid manner, while they never venture either to speak of or to expound the points which are great and worthy of investigation, or command you to give no audience to us while we expound them, and to come not into conversation with us; will they not deserve to hear what our Lord Jesus Christ said to them: Whited sepulchres, which appear beautiful outward, and within are full of dead men's bones; which pay tithe of mint, and swallow a camel: ye blind guides!' [2372] If, then, you will not despise the doctrines of those who exalt themselves and wish to be called Rabbi, Rabbi, and come with such earnestness and intelligence to the words of prophecy as to suffer the same inflictions from your own people which the prophets themselves did, you cannot receive any advantage whatsoever from the prophetic writings.

Chapter CXIII - Joshua was a figure of Christ

"What I mean is this. Jesus (Joshua), as I have now frequently remarked, who was called Oshea, when he was sent to spy out the land of Canaan, was named by Moses Jesus (Joshua). Why he did this you neither ask, nor are at a loss about it, nor make strict inquiries. Therefore Christ has escaped your notice; and though you read, you understand not; and even now, though you hear that Jesus is our Christ, you consider not that the name was bestowed on Him not purposelessly nor by chance. But you make a theological discussion as to why one a' was added to Abraham's first name; and as to why one r' was added to Sarah's name, you use similar high-sounding disputations. [2373] But why do you not similarly investigate the reason why the name of Oshea the son of Nave (Nun), which his father gave him, was changed to Jesus (Joshua)? But since not only was his name altered, but he was also appointed successor to Moses, being the only one of his contemporaries who came out from Egypt, he led the surviving people into the Holy Land; and as he, not Moses, led the people into the Holy Land, and as he distributed it by lot to those who entered along with him, so also Jesus the Christ will turn again the dispersion of the people, and will distribute the good land to each one, though not in the same manner. For the former gave them a temporary inheritance, seeing he was neither Christ who is God, nor the Son of God; but the latter, after the holy resurrection, [2374] shall give us the eternal possession. The former, after he had been named Jesus (Joshua), and after he had received strength from His Spirit, caused the sun to stand still. For I have proved that it was Jesus who appeared to and conversed with Moses, and Abraham, and all the other patriarchs without exception, ministering to the will of the Father; who also, I say, came to be born man by the Virgin Mary, and I lives for ever. For the latter is He after [2375] whom and by whom the Father will renew both the heaven and the earth; this is He who shall shine an eternal light in Jerusalem; this is he who is the king of Salem after the order of Melchizedek, and the eternal Priest of the Most High. The former is said to have circumcised the people a second time with knives of stone (which was a sign of this circumcision with which Jesus Christ Himself has circumcised us from the idols made of stone and of other materials), and to have collected together those who were circumcised from the uncircumcision, i.e., from the error of the world, in every place by the knives of stone, to wit, the words of our Lord Jesus. For I have shown that Christ was proclaimed by the prophets in parables a Stone and a Rock. Accordingly the knives of stone we shall take to mean His words, by means of which so many who were in error have been circumcised from uncircumcision with the circumcision of the heart, with which God by Jesus commanded those from that time to be circumcised who derived their circumcision from Abraham, saying that Jesus (Joshua) would circumcise a second time with knives of stone those who entered into that holy land.

Chapter CXIV - Some rules for discerning what is said about Christ. The circumcision of the Jews is very different from that which Christians receive

"For the Holy Spirit sometimes brought about that something, which was the type of the future, should be done clearly; sometimes He uttered words about what was to take place, as if it was then taking place, or had taken place. And unless those who read perceive this art, they will not be able to follow the words of the prophets as they ought. For example's sake, I shall repeat some prophetic passages, that you may understand what I say. When He speaks by Isaiah, He was led as a sheep to the slaughter, and like a lamb before the shearer,' [2376] He speaks as if the suffering had already taken place. And when He says again, I have stretched out my hands to a disobedient and gainsaying people;' [2377] and when He says, Lord, who hath believed our report?' [2378] --the words are spoken as if announcing events which had already come to pass. For I have shown that Christ is oftentimes called a Stone in parable, and in figurative speech Jacob and Israel. And again, when He says, I shall behold the heavens, the works of Thy fingers,' [2379] unless I understand His method of using words, [2380] I shall not understand intelligently, but just as your teachers suppose, fancying that the Father of all, the unbegotten God, has hands and feet, and fingers, and a soul, like a composite being; and they for this reason teach that it was the Father Himself who appeared to Abraham and to Jacob. Blessed therefore are we who have been circumcised the second time with knives of stone. For your first circumcision was and is performed by iron instruments, for you remain hard-hearted; but our circumcision, which is the second, having been instituted after yours, circumcises us from idolatry and from absolutely every kind of wickedness by sharp stones, i.e., by the words [preached] by the apostles of the corner-stone cut out without hands. And our hearts are thus circumcised from evil, so that we are happy to die for the name of the good Rock, which causes living water to burst forth for the hearts of those who by Him have loved the Father of all, and which gives those who are willing to drink of the water of life. But you do not comprehend me when I speak these things; for you have not understood what it has been prophesied that Christ would do, and you do not believe us who draw your attention to what has been written. For Jeremiah thus cries: Woe unto you! because you have forsaken the living fountain, and have digged for yourselves broken cisterns that can hold no water. Shall there be a wilderness where Mount Zion is, because I gave Jerusalem a bill of divorce in your sight?' [2381]

Chapter CXV - Prediction about the Christians in Zechariah. The malignant way which the Jews have in disputations

"But you ought to believe Zechariah when he shows in parable the mystery of Christ, and announces it obscurely. The following are his words: Rejoice, and be glad, O daughter of Zion: for, lo, I come, and I shall dwell in the midst of thee, saith the Lord. And many nations shall be added to the Lord in that day. And they shall be my people, and I will dwell in the midst of thee; and they shall know that the Lord of hosts hath sent me unto thee. And the Lord shall inherit Judah his portion in the holy land, and He shall choose Jerusalem again. Let all flesh fear before the Lord, for He is raised up out of His holy clouds. And He showed me Jesus (Joshua) the high priest standing before the angel [of the Lord [2382]]; and the devil stood at his right hand to resist him. And the Lord said to the devil, The Lord who hath chosen Jerusalem rebuke thee. Behold, is not this a brand plucked out of the fire?' " [2383]

As Trypho was about to reply and contradict me, I said, "Wait and hear what I say first: for I am not to give the explanation which you suppose, as if there had been no priest of the name of Joshua (Jesus) in the land of Babylon, where your nation were prisoners. But even if I did, I have shown that if there [2384] was a priest named Joshua (Jesus) in your nation, yet the prophet had not seen him in his revelation, just as he had not seen either the devil or the angel of the Lord by eyesight, and in his waking condition, but in a trance, at the time when the revelation was made to him. [2385] But I now say, that as [Scripture] said that the Son of Nave (Nun) by the name Jesus (Joshua) wrought powerful works and exploits which proclaimed beforehand what would be performed by our Lord; so I proceed now to show that the revelation made among your people in Babylon in the days of Jesus (Joshua) the priest, was an announcement of the things to be accomplished by our Priest, who is God, and Christ the Son of God the Father of all.

"Indeed, I wondered," continued I, "why a little ago you kept silence while I was speaking, and why you did not interrupt me when I said that the son of Nave (Nun) was the only one of contemporaries who came out of Egypt that entered the Holy Land along with the men described as younger than that generation. For you swarm and light on sores like flies. For though one should speak ten thousand words well, if there happen to be one little word displeasing to you, because not sufficiently intelligible or accurate, you make no account of the many good words, but lay hold of the little word, and are very zealous in setting it up as something impious and guilty; in order that, when you are judged with the very same judgment by God, you may have a much heavier account to render for your great audacities, whether evil actions, or bad interpretations which you obtain by falsifying the truth. For with what judgment you judge, it is righteous that you be judged withal.

Chapter CXVI - It is shown how this prophecy suits the Christians

"But to give you the account of the revelation of the holy Jesus Christ, I take up again my discourse, and I assert that even that revelation was made for us who believe on Christ the High Priest, namely this crucified One; and though we lived in fornication and all kinds of filthy conversation, we have by the grace of our Jesus, according to His Father's will, stripped ourselves of all those filthy wickednesses with which we were imbued. And though the devil is ever at hand to resist us, and anxious to seduce all to himself, yet the Angel of God, i.e., the Power of God sent to us through Jesus Christ, rebukes him, and he departs from us. And we are just as if drawn out from the fire, when purified from our former sins, and [rescued] from the affliction and the fiery trial by which the devil and all his coadjutors try us; out of which Jesus the Son of God has promised again to deliver us, [2386] and invest us with prepared garments, if we do His commandments; and has undertaken to provide an eternal kingdom [for us]. For just as that Jesus (Joshua), called by the prophet a priest, evidently had on filthy garments because he is said to have taken a harlot for a wife, [2387] and is called a brand plucked out of the fire, because he had received remission of sins when the devil that resisted him was rebuked; even so we, who through the name of Jesus have believed as one man in God the Maker of all, have been stripped, through the name of His first-begotten Son, of the filthy garments, i.e., of our sins; and being vehemently inflamed by the word of His calling, we are the true high priestly race of God, as even God Himself bears witness, saying that in every place among the Gentiles sacrifices are presented to Him well-pleasing and pure. Now God receives sacrifices from no one, except through His priests. [2388]

Chapter CXVII - Malachi's prophecy concerning the sacrifices of the Christians. It cannot be taken as referring to the prayers of Jews of the dispersion

"Accordingly, God, anticipating all the sacrifices which we offer through this name, and which Jesus the Christ enjoined us to offer, i.e., in the Eucharist of the bread and the cup, and which are presented by Christians in all places throughout the world, bears witness that they are well-pleasing to Him. But He utterly rejects those presented by you and by those priests of yours, saying, And I will not accept your sacrifices at your hands; for from the rising of the sun to its setting my name is glorified among the Gentiles (He says); but ye profane it.' [2389] Yet even now, in your love of contention, you assert that God does not accept the sacrifices of those who dwelt then in Jerusalem, and were called Israelites; but says that He is pleased with the prayers of the individuals of that nation then dispersed, and calls their prayers sacrifices. Now, that prayers and giving of thanks, when offered by worthy men, are the only perfect and well-pleasing sacrifices to God, I also admit. For such alone Christians have undertaken to offer, and in the remembrance effected by their solid and liquid food, whereby the suffering of the Son of God [2390] which He endured is brought to mind, whose name the high priests of your nation and your teachers have caused to be profaned and blasphemed over all the earth. But these filthy garments, which have been put by you on all who have become Christians by the name of Jesus, God shows shall be taken away from us, when He shall raise all men from the dead, and appoint some to be incorruptible, immortal, and free from sorrow in the everlasting and imperishable kingdom; but shall send others away to the everlasting punishment of fire. But as to you and your teachers deceiving yourselves when you interpret what the Scripture says as referring to those of your nation then in dispersion, and maintain that their prayers and sacrifices offered in every place are pure and well-pleasing, learn that you are speaking falsely, and trying by all means to cheat yourselves; for, first of all, not even now does your nation extend from the rising to the setting of the sun, but there are nations among which none of your race ever dwelt. For there is not one single race of men, whether barbarians, or Greeks, or whatever they may be called, nomads, or vagrants, or herdsmen living in tents, among whom prayers and giving of thanks are not offered through the name of the crucified Jesus. [2391] And then, [2392] as the Scriptures show, at the time when Malachi wrote this, your dispersion over all the earth, which now exists, had not taken place.

Chapter CXVIII - He exhorts to repentance before Christ comes; in whom Christians, since they believe, are far more religious than Jews

"So that you ought rather to desist from the love of strife, and repent before the great day of judgment come, wherein all those of your tribes who have pierced this Christ shall mourn, as I have shown has been declared by the Scriptures. And I have explained that the Lord sware, after the order of Melchizedek,' [2393] and what this prediction means; and the prophecy of Isaiah which says, His burial is taken away from the midst,' [2394] I have already said, referred to the future burying and rising again of Christ; and I have frequently remarked that this very Christ is the Judge of all the living and the dead. And Nathan likewise, speaking to David about Him, thus continued: I will be

His Father, and He shall be my Son; and my mercy shall I not take away from Him, as I did from them that went before Him; and I will establish Him in my house, and in His kingdom for ever.' [2395] And Ezekiel says, There shall be no other prince in the house but He.' [2396] For He is the chosen Priest and eternal King, the Christ, inasmuch as He is the Son of God; and do not suppose that Isaiah or the other prophets speak of sacrifices of blood or libations being presented at the altar on His second advent, but of true and spiritual praises and giving of thanks. And we have not in vain believed in Him, and have not been led astray by those who taught us such doctrines; but this has come to pass through the wonderful foreknowledge of God, in order that we, through the calling of the new and eternal covenant, that is, of Christ, might be found more intelligent and God-fearing than yourselves, who are considered to be lovers of God and men of understanding, but are not. Isaiah, filled with admiration of this, said: And kings shall shut their mouths: for those to whom no announcement has been made in regard to Him [2397] shall see; and those who heard not shall understand. Lord, who hath believed our report? and to whom is the arm of the Lord revealed?' [2398]

"And in repeating this, [2399] Trypho," I continued, "as far as is allowable, I endeavour to do so for the sake of those who came with you to-day, yet briefly and concisely."

Then he replied, "You do well; and though you repeat the same things at considerable length, be assured that I and my companions listen with pleasure."

Chapter CXIX - Christians are the holy people promised to Abraham. They have been called like Abraham

Then I said again, "Would you suppose, sirs, that we could ever have understood these matters in the Scriptures, if we had not received grace to discern by the will of Him whose pleasure it was? in order that the saying of Moses [2400] might come to pass, They provoked me with strange [gods], they provoked me to anger with their abominations. They sacrificed to demons whom they knew not; new gods that came newly up, whom their fathers knew not. Thou hast forsaken God that begat thee, and forgotten God that brought thee up. And the Lord saw, and was jealous, and was provoked to anger by reason of the rage of His sons and daughters: and He said, I will turn My face away from them, and I will show what shall come on them at the last; for it is a very froward generation, children in whom is no faith. They have moved Me to jealousy with that which is not God, they have provoked Me to anger with their idols; and I will move them to jealousy with that which is not a nation, I will provoke them to anger with a foolish people. For a fire is kindled from Mine anger, and it shall burn to Hades. It shall consume the earth and her increase, and set on fire the foundations of the mountains; I will heap mischief on them.' [2401] And after that Righteous One was put to death, we flourished as another people, and shot forth as new and prosperous corn; as the prophets said, And many nations shall betake themselves to the Lord in that day for a people: and they shall dwell in the midst of all the earth.' [2402] But we are not only a people, but also a holy people, as we have shown already. [2403] And they shall call them the holy people, redeemed by the Lord.' [2404] Therefore we are not a people to be despised, nor a barbarous race, nor such as the Carian and Phrygian nations; but God has even chosen us, and He has become manifest to those who asked not after Him. Behold, I am God,' He says, to the nation which called not on My name.' [2405] For this is that nation which God of old promised to Abraham, when He declared that He would make him a father of many nations; not meaning, however, the Arabians, or Egyptians, or Idumæans, since Ishmael became the father of a mighty nation, and so did Esau; and there is now a great multitude of Ammonites. Noah, moreover, was the father of Abraham, and in fact of all men; and others were the progenitors of others. What larger measure of grace, then, did Christ bestow on Abraham? This, namely, that He called him with His voice by the like calling, telling him to quit the land wherein he dwelt. And He has called all of us by that voice, and we have left already the way of living in which we used to spend our days, passing our time in evil after the fashions of the other inhabitants of the earth; and along with Abraham we shall inherit the holy land, when we shall receive the inheritance for an endless eternity, being children of Abraham through the like faith. For as he believed the voice of God, and it was imputed to him for righteousness, in like manner we, having believed God's voice spoken by the apostles of Christ, and promulgated to us by the prophets, have renounced even to death all the things of the world. Accordingly, He promises to him a nation of similar faith, God-fearing, righteous, and delighting the Father; but it is not you, in whom is no faith.'

Chapter CXX - Christians were promised to Isaac, Jacob, and Judah

"Observe, too, how the same promises are made to Isaac and to Jacob. For thus He speaks to Isaac: And in thy seed shall all the nations of the earth be blessed.' [2406] And to Jacob: And in thee and in thy seed shall all families of the earth be blessed.' [2407] He says that neither to Esau nor to Reuben, nor to any other; only to those of whom the Christ should arise, according to the dispensation, through the Virgin Mary. But if you would consider the blessing of Judah, you would perceive what I say. For the seed is divided from Jacob, and comes down through Judah, and Phares, and Jesse, and David. And this was a symbol of the fact that some of your nation would be found children of Abraham, and found, too, in the lot of Christ; but that others, who are indeed children of Abraham, would be like the sand on the sea-shore, barren and fruitless, much in quantity, and without number indeed, but bearing no fruit whatever, and only drinking the water of the sea. And a vast multitude in your nation are convicted of being of this kind, imbibing doctrines of bitterness and godlessness, but spurning the word of God. He speaks therefore in the passage relating to Judah: A prince shall not fail from Judah, nor a ruler from his thighs, till that which is laid up for him come; and He shall be the expectation of the nations.' [2408] And it is plain that this was spoken not of Judah, but of Christ. For all we out of all nations do expect not Judah, but Jesus, who led your fathers out of Egypt. For the prophecy referred even to the advent of Christ: Till He come for whom this is laid up, and He shall be the expectation of nations.' Jesus came, therefore, as we have shown at length, and is expected again to appear above the clouds; whose name you profane, and labour hard to get it profaned over all the earth. It were possible for me, sirs," I continued, "to contend against you about the reading which you so interpret, saying it is written, Till the things laid up for Him come;' though the Seventy have not so explained it, but thus, Till He comes for whom this is laid up.' But since what follows indicates that the reference is to Christ (for it is, and He shall be the expectation of nations'), I do not proceed to have a mere verbal controversy with you, as I have not attempted to establish proof about Christ from the passages of Scripture which are not admitted by you, [2409] which I quoted from the words of Jeremiah the prophet, and Esdras, and David; but from those which are even now admitted by you, which had your teachers comprehended, be well assured they would have deleted them, as they did those about the death of Isaiah, whom you sawed asunder with a wooden saw. And this was a mysterious type of Christ being about to cut your nation in two, and to raise those worthy of the honour to the everlasting kingdom along with the holy patriarchs and prophets; but He has said that He will send others to the condemnation of the unquenchable fire along with similar disobedient and impenitent men from all the nations. For they shall come,' He said, from the west and from the east, and shall sit down with Abraham, and Isaac, and Jacob in the kingdom of heaven; but the children of the kingdom shall be cast out into outer darkness.' [2410] And I have mentioned these things, taking nothing whatever into consideration, except the speaking of the truth, and refusing to be coerced by any one, even though I should be forthwith torn in pieces by you. For I gave no thought to any of my people, that is, the Samaritans, when I had a communication in writing with Cæsar, [2411] but stated that they were wrong in trusting to the magician Simon of their own nation, who, they say, is God above all power, and authority, and might."

Chapter CXXI - *From the fact that the Gentiles believe in Jesus, it is evident that He is Christ*

And as they kept silence, I went on: "[The Scripture], speaking by David about this Christ, my friends, said no longer that in His seed' the nations should be blessed, but in Him.' So it is here: His name shall rise up for ever above the sun; and in Him shall all nations be blessed.' [2412] But if all nations are blessed in Christ, and we of all nations believe in Him, then He is indeed the Christ, and we are those blessed by Him. God formerly gave the sun as an object of worship, [2413] as it is written, but no one ever was seen to endure death on account of his faith in the sun; but for the name of Jesus you may see men of every nation who have endured and do endure all sufferings, rather than deny Him. For the word of His truth and wisdom is more ardent and more light-giving than the rays of the sun, and sinks down into the depths of heart and mind. Hence also the Scripture said, His name shall rise up above the sun.' And again, Zechariah says, His name is the East.' [2414] And speaking of the same, he says that each tribe shall mourn.' [2415] But if He so shone forth and was so mighty in His first advent (which was without honour and comeliness, and very contemptible), that in no nation He is unknown, and everywhere men have repented of the old wickedness in each nation's way of living, so that even demons were subject to His name, and all powers and kingdoms feared His name more than they feared all the dead, shall He not on His glorious advent destroy by all means all those who hated Him, and who unrighteously departed from Him, but give rest to His own, rewarding them with all they have looked for? To us, therefore, it has been granted to hear, and to understand, and to be saved by this Christ, and to recognise all the [truths revealed] by the Father. Wherefore He said to Him: It is a great thing for Thee to be called my servant, to raise up the tribes of Jacob, and turn again the dispersed of Israel. I have appointed Thee for a light to the Gentiles, that Thou mayest be their salvation unto the end of the earth.' [2416]

Chapter CXXII - The Jews understand this of the proselytes without reason

"You think that these words refer to the stranger [2417] and the proselytes, but in fact they refer to us who have been illumined by Jesus. For Christ would have borne witness even to them; but now you are become twofold more the children of hell, as He said Himself. [2418] Therefore what was written by the prophets was spoken not of those persons, but of us, concerning whom the Scripture speaks: I will lead the blind by a way which they knew not; and they shall walk in paths which they have not known. And I am witness, saith the Lord God, and my servant whom I have chosen.' [2419] To whom, then, does Christ bear witness? Manifestly to those who have believed. But the proselytes not only do not believe, but twofold more than yourselves blaspheme His name, and wish to torture and put to death us who believe in Him; for in all points they strive to be like you. And again in other words He cries: I the Lord have called Thee in righteousness, and will hold Thine hand, and will strengthen Thee, and will give Thee for a covenant of the people, for a light of the Gentiles, to open the eyes of the blind, to bring out the prisoners from their bonds.' [2420] These words, indeed, sirs, refer also to Christ, and concern the enlightened nations; or will you say again, He speaks to them of the law and the proselytes?"

Then some of those who had come on the second day cried out as if they had been in a theatre, "But what? does He not refer to the law, and to those illumined by it? Now these are proselytes."

"No," I said, looking towards Trypho, "since, if the law were able to enlighten the nations and those who possess it, what need is there of a new covenant? But since God announced beforehand that He would send a new covenant, and an everlasting law and commandment, we will not understand this of the old law and its proselytes, but of Christ and His proselytes, namely us Gentiles, whom He has illumined, as He says somewhere: Thus saith the Lord, In an acceptable time have I heard Thee, and in a day of salvation have I helped Thee, and I have given Thee for a covenant of the people, to establish the earth, and to inherit the deserted.' [2421] What, then, is Christ's inheritance? Is it not the nations? What is the covenant of God? Is it not Christ? As He says in another place: Thou art my Son; this day have I begotten Thee. Ask of Me, and I shall give Thee the nations for Thine inheritance, and the uttermost parts of the earth for Thy possession.' [2422]

Chapter CXXIII - Ridiculous interpretations of the Jews. Christians are the true Israel

"As, therefore, all these latter prophecies refer to Christ and the nations, you should believe that the former refer to Him and them in like manner. For the proselytes have no need of a covenant, if, since there is one and the same law imposed on all that are circumcised, the Scripture speaks about them thus: And the stranger shall also be joined with them, and shall be joined to the house of Jacob;' [2423] and because the proselyte, who is circumcised that he may have access to the people, becomes like one of themselves, [2424] while we who have been deemed worthy to be called a people are yet Gentiles, because we have not been circumcised. Besides, it is ridiculous for you to imagine that the eyes of the proselytes are to be opened while your own are not, and that you be understood as blind and deaf while they are enlightened. And it will be still more ridiculous for you, if you say that the law has been given to the nations, but you have not known it. For you would have stood in awe of God's wrath, and would not have been lawless, wandering sons; being much afraid of hearing God always say, Children in whom is no faith. And who are blind, but my servants? and deaf, but they that rule over them? And the servants of God have been made blind. You see often, but have not observed; your ears have been opened, and you have not heard.' [2425] Is God's commendation of you honourable? and is God's testimony seemly for His servants? You are not ashamed though you often hear these words. You do not tremble at God's threats, for you are a people foolish and hard-hearted. Therefore, behold, I will proceed to remove this people,' saith the Lord; and I will remove them, and destroy the wisdom of the wise, and hide the understanding of the prudent.' [2426] Deservedly too: for you are neither wise nor prudent, but crafty and unscrupulous; wise only to do evil, but utterly incompetent to know the hidden counsel of God, or the faithful covenant of the Lord, or to find out the everlasting paths. Therefore, saith the Lord, I will raise up to Israel and to Judah the seed of men and the seed of beasts.' [2427] And by Isaiah He speaks thus concerning another Israel: In that day shall there be a third Israel among the Assyrians and the Egyptians, blessed in the land which the Lord of Σαβαώθ hath blessed, saying, blessed shall my people in Egypt and in Assyria be, and Israel mine inheritance.' [2428] Since then God blesses this people, and calls them Israel, and declares them to be His inheritance, how is it that you repent not of the deception you practise on yourselves, as if you alone were the Israel, and of execrating the people whom God has blessed? For when He speaks to Jerusalem and its environs, He thus added: And I will beget men upon you, even my people Israel; and they shall inherit you, and you shall be a possession for them; and you shall be no longer bereaved of them.' " [2429]

"What, then?" says Trypho; "are you Israel? and speaks He such things of you?"

"If, indeed," I replied to him, "we had not entered into a lengthy [2430] discussion on these topics, I might have doubted whether you ask this question in ignorance; but since we have brought the matter to a conclusion by demonstration and with your assent, I do not believe that you are ignorant of what I have just said, or desire again mere contention, but that you are urging me to exhibit the same proof to these men." And in compliance with the assent expressed in his eyes, I continued: "Again in Isaiah, if you have ears to hear it, God, speaking of Christ in parable, calls Him Jacob and Israel. He speaks thus: Jacob is my servant, I will uphold Him; Israel is mine elect, I will put my Spirit upon Him, and He shall bring forth judgment to the Gentiles. He shall not strive, nor cry, neither shall any one hear His voice in the street: a bruised reed He shall not break, and smoking flax He shall not quench; but He shall bring forth judgment to truth: He shall shine, [2431] and shall not be broken till He have set judgment on the earth. And in His name shall the Gentiles trust.' [2432] As therefore from the one man Jacob, who was surnamed Israel, all your nation has been called Jacob and Israel; so we from Christ, who begat us unto God, like Jacob, and Israel, and Judah, and Joseph, and David, are called and are the true sons of God, and keep the commandments of Christ."

Chapter CXXIV - Christians are the sons of God

And when I saw that they were perturbed because I said that we are the sons of God, I anticipated their questioning, and said, "Listen, sirs, how the Holy Ghost speaks of this people, saying that they are all sons of the Highest; and how this very Christ will be present in their assembly, rendering judgment to all men. The words are spoken by David, and are, according to your version of them, thus: God standeth in the congregation of gods; He judgeth among the gods. How long do ye judge unjustly, and accept the persons of the wicked? Judge for the orphan and the poor, and do justice to the humble and needy. Deliver the needy, and save the poor out of the hand of the wicked. They know not, neither have they understood; they walk on in darkness: all the foundations of the earth shall be shaken. I said, Ye are gods, and are all children of the Most High. But ye die like men, and fall like one of the princes. Arise, O God! judge the earth, for Thou shalt inherit all nations.' [2433] But in the version of the Seventy it is written, Behold, ye die like men, and fall like one of the princes,' [2434] in order to manifest the disobedience of men,--I mean of Adam and Eve,--and the fall of one of the princes, i.e., of him who was called the serpent, who fell with a great overthrow, because he deceived Eve. But as my discourse is not intended to touch on this point, but to prove to you that the Holy Ghost reproaches men because they were made like God, free from suffering and death, provided that they kept His commandments, and were deemed deserving of the name of His sons, and yet they, becoming like Adam and Eve, work out death for themselves; let the interpretation of the Psalm be held just as you wish, yet thereby it is demonstrated that all men are deemed worthy of becoming "gods," and of having power to become sons of the Highest; and shall be each by himself judged and condemned like Adam and Eve. Now I have proved at length that Christ is called God.

Chapter CXXV - He explains what force the word Israel has, and how it suits Christ

"I wish, sirs," I said, "to learn from you what is the force of the name Israel." And as they were silent, I continued: "I shall tell you what I know: for I do not think it right, when I know, not to speak; or, suspecting that you do know, and yet from envy or from voluntary ignorance deceive yourselves, [2435] to be continually solicitous; but I speak all things simply and candidly, as my Lord said: A sower went forth to sow the seed; and some fell by the wayside; and some among thorns, and some on stony ground, and some on good ground.' [2436] I must speak, then, in the hope of finding good ground somewhere; since that Lord of mine, as One strong and powerful, comes to demand back His own from all, and will not condemn His steward if He recognises that he, by the knowledge that the Lord is powerful and has come to demand His own, has given it to every bank, and has not digged for any cause whatsoever. Accordingly the name Israel signifies this, A man who overcomes power; for Isra is a man overcoming, and El is power. [2437] And that Christ would act so when He became man was foretold by the mystery of Jacob's wrestling with Him who appeared to him, in that He ministered to the will of the Father, yet nevertheless is God, in that He is the first-begotten of all creatures. For when He became man, as I previously remarked, the devil came to Him--i.e., that power which is called the serpent and Satan--tempting Him, and striving to effect His downfall by asking Him to worship him. But He destroyed and overthrew the devil, having proved him to be wicked, in that he asked to be worshipped as God, contrary to the Scripture; who is an apostate from the will of God. For He answers him, It is written, Thou shalt worship the Lord thy God, and Him only shall thou serve.' [2438] Then, overcome and convicted, the devil departed at that time. But since our Christ was to be numbed, i.e., by pain and experience of suffering, He made a previous intimation of this by touching Jacob's thigh, and causing it to shrink.

But Israel was His name from the beginning, to which He altered the name of the blessed Jacob when He blessed him with His own name, proclaiming thereby that all who through Him have fled for refuge to the Father, constitute the blessed Israel. But you, having understood none of this, and not being prepared to understand, since you are the children of Jacob after the fleshly seed, expect that you shall be assuredly saved. But that you deceive yourselves in such matters, I have proved by many words.

Chapter CXXVI - The various names of Christ according to both natures. It is shown that He is God, and appeared to the patriarchs

"But if you knew, Trypho," continued I, "who He is that is called at one time the Angel of great counsel, [2439] and a Man by Ezekiel, and like the Son of man by Daniel, and a Child by Isaiah, and Christ and God to be worshipped by David, and Christ and a Stone by many, and Wisdom by Solomon, and Joseph and Judah and a Star by Moses, and the East by Zechariah, and the Suffering One and Jacob and Israel by Isaiah again, and a Rod, and Flower, and Corner-Stone, and Son of God, you would not have blasphemed Him who has now come, and been born, and suffered, and ascended to heaven; who shall also come again, and then your twelve tribes shall mourn. For if you had understood what has been written by the prophets, you would not have denied that He was God, Son of the only, unbegotten, unutterable God. For Moses says somewhere in Exodus the following: The Lord spoke to Moses, and said to him, I am the Lord, and I appeared to Abraham, to Isaac, and to Jacob, being their God; and my name I revealed not to them, and I established my covenant with them.' [2440] And thus again he says, A man wrestled with Jacob,' [2441] and asserts it was God; narrating that Jacob said, I have seen God face to face, and my life is preserved.' And it is recorded that he called the place where He wrestled with him, appeared to and blessed him, the Face of God (Peniel). And Moses says that God appeared also to Abraham near the oak in Mamre, when he was sitting at the door of his tent at mid-day. Then he goes on to say: And he lifted up his eyes and looked, and, behold, three men stood before him; and when he saw them, he ran to meet them.' [2442] After a little, one of them promises a son to Abraham: Wherefore did Sarah laugh, saying, Shall I of a surety bear a child, and I am old? Is anything impossible with God? At the time appointed I will return, according to the time of life, and Sarah shall have a son. And they went away from Abraham.' [2443] Again he speaks of them thus: And the men rose up from thence, and looked toward Sodom.' [2444] Then to Abraham He who was and is again speaks: I will not hide from Abraham, my servant, what I intend to do.' " [2445] And what follows in the writings of Moses I quoted and explained; "from which I have demonstrated," I said, "that He who is described as God appeared to Abraham, to Isaac, and to Jacob, and the other patriarchs, was appointed under the authority of the Father and Lord, and ministers to His will." Then I went on to say what I had not said before: "And so, when the people desired to eat flesh, and Moses had lost faith in Him, who also there is called the Angel, and who promised that God would give them to satiety, He who is both God and the Angel, sent by the Father, is described as saying and doing these things. For thus the Scripture says: And the Lord said to Moses, Will the Lord's hand not be sufficient? thou shalt know now whether my word shall conceal thee or not.' [2446] And again, in other words, it thus says: But the Lord spake unto me, Thou shalt not go over this Jordan: the Lord thy God, who goeth before thy face, He shall cut off the nations.' [2447]

Chapter CXXVII - These passages of Scripture do not apply to the Father, but to the Word

"These and other such sayings are recorded by the lawgiver and by the prophets; and I suppose that I have stated sufficiently, that wherever [2448] God says, God went up from Abraham,' [2449] or, The Lord spake to Moses,' [2450] and The Lord came down to behold the tower which the sons of men had built,' [2451] or when God shut Noah into the ark,' [2452] you must not imagine that the unbegotten God Himself came down or went up from any place. For the ineffable Father and Lord of all neither has come to any place, nor walks, nor sleeps, nor rises up, but remains in His own place, wherever that is, quick to behold and quick to hear, having neither eyes nor ears, but being of indescribable might; and He sees all things, and knows all things, and none of us escapes His observation; and He is not moved or confined to a spot in the whole world, for He existed before the world was made. How, then, could He talk with any one, or be seen by any one, or appear on the smallest portion of the earth, when the people at Sinai were not able to look even on the glory of Him who was sent from Him; and Moses himself could not enter into the tabernacle which he had erected, when it was filled with the glory of God; and the priest could not endure to stand before the temple when Solomon conveyed the ark into the house in Jerusalem which he had built for it? Therefore neither Abraham, nor Isaac, nor Jacob, nor any other man, saw the Father and ineffable Lord of all, and also of Christ, but [saw] Him who was according to His will His Son, being God, and the Angel because He ministered to His will; whom also it pleased Him to be born man by the Virgin; who also was fire when He conversed with Moses from the bush. Since, unless we thus comprehend the Scriptures, it must follow that the Father and Lord of all had not been in heaven when what Moses wrote took place: And the Lord rained upon Sodom fire and brimstone from the Lord out of heaven;' [2453] and again, when it is thus said by David: Lift up your gates, ye rulers; and be ye lift up, ye everlasting gates; and the King of glory shall enter;' [2454] and again, when He says: The Lord says to my Lord, Sit at My right hand, till I make Thine enemies Thy footstool.' [2455]

Chapter CXXVIII - The Word is sent not as an inanimate power, but as a person begotten of the Father's substance

"And that Christ being Lord, and God the Son of God, and appearing formerly in power as Man, and Angel, and in the glory of fire as at the bush, so also was manifested at the judgment executed on Sodom, has been demonstrated fully by what has been said." Then I repeated once more all that I had previously quoted from Exodus, about the vision in the bush, and the naming of Joshua (Jesus), and continued: "And do not suppose, sirs, that I am speaking superfluously when I repeat these words frequently: but it is because I know that some wish to anticipate these remarks, and to say that the power sent from the Father of all which appeared to Moses, or to Abraham, or to Jacob, is called an Angel because He came to men (for by Him the commands of the Father have been proclaimed to men); is called Glory, because He appears in a vision sometimes that cannot be borne; is called a Man, and a human being, because He appears arrayed in such forms as the Father pleases; and they call Him the Word, because He carries tidings from the Father to men: but maintain that this power is indivisible and inseparable from the Father, just as they say that the light of the sun on earth is indivisible and inseparable from the sun in the heavens; as when it sinks, the light sinks along with it; so the Father, when He chooses, say they, causes His power to spring forth, and when He chooses, He makes it return to Himself. In this way, they teach, He made the angels. But it is proved that there are angels who always exist, and are never reduced to that form out of which they sprang. And that this power which the prophetic word calls God, as has been also amply demonstrated, and Angel, is not numbered [as different] in name only like the light of the sun, but is indeed something numerically distinct, I have discussed briefly in what has gone before; when I asserted that this power was begotten from the Father, by His power and will, but not by abscission, as if the essence of the Father were divided; as all other things partitioned and divided are not the same after as before they were divided: and, for the sake of example, I took the case of fires kindled from a fire, which we see to be distinct from it, and yet that from which many can be kindled is by no means made less, but remains the same.

Chapter CXXIX - That is confirmed from other passages of Scripture

"And now I shall again recite the words which I have spoken in proof of this point. When Scripture says, The Lord rained fire from the Lord out of heaven,' the prophetic word indicates that there were two in number: One upon the earth, who, it says, descended to behold the cry of Sodom; Another in heaven, who also is Lord of the Lord on earth, as He is Father and God; the cause of His power and of His being Lord and God. Again, when the Scripture records that God said in the beginning, Behold, Adam has become like one of Us,' [2456] this phrase, like one of Us,' is also indicative of number; and the words do not admit of a figurative meaning, as the sophists endeavour to affix on them, who are neither able nor to understand the truth. And it is written in the book of Wisdom: If I should tell you daily events, I would be mindful to enumerate them from the beginning. The Lord created me the beginning of His ways for His works. From everlasting He established me in the beginning, before He formed the earth, and before He made the depths, and before the springs of waters came forth, before the mountains were settled; He begets me before all the hills.' " [2457] When I repeated these words, I added: "You perceive, my hearers, if you bestow attention, that the Scripture has declared that this Offspring was begotten by the Father before all things created; and that which is begotten is numerically distinct from that which begets, any one will admit."

Chapter CXXX - He returns to the conversion of the Gentiles, and shows that it was foretold

And when all had given assent, I said: "I would now adduce some passages which I had not recounted before. They are recorded by the faithful servant Moses in parable, and are as follows: Rejoice, O ye heavens, with Him, and let all the angels of God worship Him;' " [2458] and I added what follows of the passage: " Rejoice, O ye nations, with His people, and let all the angels of God be strengthened in Him: for the blood of His sons He avenges, and will avenge, and will recompense His enemies with vengeance, and will recompense those that hate Him; and the Lord will purify the land of His people.' And by these words He declares that we, the nations, rejoice with His people, --to wit, Abraham, and Isaac, and Jacob, and the prophets, and, in short, all of that people who are well-pleasing to God, according to what has been already agreed on between us. But we will not receive it of all your nation; since we know from Isaiah [2459] that the members of those who have transgressed shall be consumed by the worm and unquenchable fire, remaining immortal; so that they become a spectacle to all flesh. But in addition to these, I wish, sirs," said I, "to add some other passages from the very words of Moses, from which you may understand that God has from of old dispersed all men according to their kindreds and tongues; and out of all kindreds has taken to Himself your kindred, a useless, disobedient, and faithless generation; and has shown that those who were selected out of every nation have obeyed His will through Christ,--whom He calls also Jacob, and names Israel, --and these, then, as I mentioned fully previously, must be Jacob and Israel. For when He says, Rejoice, O ye nations, with His people,' He allots the same inheritance to them, and does not call them by the same name; [2460] but when He says that they as Gentiles rejoice with His people, He calls them Gentiles to reproach you. For even as you provoked Him to anger by your idolatry, so also He has deemed those who were idolaters worthy of knowing His will, and of inheriting His inheritance.

Chapter CXXXI - How much more faithful to God the Gentiles are who are converted to Christ than the Jews

"But I shall quote the passage by which it is made known that God divided all the nations. It is as follows: Ask thy father, and he will show thee; thine elders, and they will tell thee; when the Most High divided the nations, as He dispersed the sons of Adam, He set the bounds of the nations according to the numbers of the children of Israel; and the Lord's portion became His people Jacob, and Israel was the lot of His inheritance.' " [2461] And having said this, I added: "The Seventy have translated it, He set the bounds of the nations according to the number of the angels of God.' But because my argument is again in nowise weakened by this, I have adopted your exposition. And you yourselves, if you will confess the truth, must acknowledge that we, who have been called by God through the despised and shameful mystery of the cross (for the confession of which, and obedience to which, and for our piety, punishments even to death have been inflicted on us by demons, and by the host of the devil, through the aid ministered to them by you), and endure all torments rather than deny Christ even by word, through whom we are called to the salvation prepared beforehand by the Father, are more faithful to God than you, who were redeemed from Egypt with a high hand and a visitation of great glory, when the sea was parted for you, and a passage left dry, in which [God] slew those who pursued you with a very great equipment, and splendid chariots, bringing back upon them the sea which had been made a way for your sakes; on whom also a pillar of light shone, in order that you, more than any other nation in the world, might possess a peculiar light, never-failing and never-setting; for whom He rained manna as nourishment, fit for the heavenly angels, in order that you might have no need to prepare your food; and the water at Marah was made sweet; and a sign of Him that was to be crucified was made, both in the matter of the serpents which bit you, as I already mentioned (God anticipating before the proper times these mysteries, in order to confer grace upon you, to whom you are always convicted of being thankless), as well as in the type of the extending of the hands of Moses, and of Oshea being named Jesus (Joshua); when you fought against Amalek: concerning which God enjoined that the incident be recorded, and the name of Jesus laid up in your understandings; saying that this is He who would blot out the memorial of Amalek from under heaven. Now it is clear that the memorial of Amalek remained after the son of Nave (Nun): but He makes it manifest through Jesus, who was crucified, of whom also those symbols were fore-announcements of all that would happen to Him, the demons would be destroyed, and would dread His name, and that all principalities and kingdoms would fear Him; and that they who believe in Him out of all nations would be shown as God-fearing and peaceful men; and the facts already quoted by me, Trypho, indicate this. Again, when you desired flesh, so vast a quantity of quails was given you, that they could not be told; for whom also water gushed from the rock; and a cloud followed you for a shade from heat, and covering from cold, declaring the manner and signification of another and new heaven; the latchets of your shoes did not break, and your shoes waxed not old, and your garments wore not away, but even those of the children grew along with them.

Chapter CXXXII - How great the power was of the name of Jesus in the Old Testament

"Yet after this you made a calf, and were very zealous in committing fornication with the daughters of strangers, and in serving idols. And again, when the land was given up to you with so great a display of power, that you witnessed [2462] the sun stand still in the heavens by the order of that man whose name was Jesus (Joshua), and not go down for thirty-six hours, as well as all the other miracles which were wrought for you as time served; [2463] and of these it seems good to me now to speak of another, for it conduces to your hereby knowing Jesus, whom we also know to have been Christ the Son of God, who was crucified, and rose again, and ascended to heaven, and will come again to judge all men, even up to Adam himself. You are aware, then," I continued, "that when the ark of the testimony was seized by the enemies of Ashdod, [2464] and a terrible and incurable malady had broken out among them, they resolved to place it on a cart to which they yoked cows that had recently calved, for the purpose of ascertaining by trial whether or not they had been plagued by God's power on account of the ark, and if God wished it to be taken back to the place from which it had been carried away. And when they had done this, the cows, led by no man, went not to the place whence the ark had been taken, but to the fields of a certain man whose name was Oshea, the same as his whose name was altered to Jesus (Joshua), as has been previously mentioned, who also led the people into the land and meted it out to them: and when the cows had come into these fields they remained there, showing to you thereby that they were guided by the name of power; [2465] just as formerly the people who survived of those that came out of Egypt, were guided into the land by him who had received the name Jesus (Joshua), who before was called Oshea.

Chapter CXXXIII - The hard-heartedness of the Jews, for whom the Christians pray

"Now, although these and all other such unexpected and marvellous works were wrought amongst and seen by you at different times, yet you are convicted by the prophets of having gone to such a length as offering your own children to demons; and besides all this, of having dared to do such things against Christ; and you still dare to do them: for all which may it be granted to you to obtain mercy and salvation from God and His Christ. For God, knowing before that you would do such things, pronounced this curse upon you by the prophet Isaiah: Woe unto their soul! they have devised evil counsel against themselves, saying, Let us bind the righteous man, for he is distasteful to us. Therefore they shall eat the fruit of their own doings. Woe to the wicked! evil, according to the works of his hands, shall befall him. O my people, your exactors glean you, and those who extort from you shall rule over you. O my people, they who call you blessed cause you to err, and disorder the way of your paths. But now the Lord shall assist His people to judgment, and He shall enter into judgment with the elders of the people and the princes thereof. But why have you burnt up my vineyard? and why is the spoil of the poor found in your houses? Why do you wrong my people, and put to shame the countenance of the humble?' [2466] Again, in other words, the same prophet spake to the same effect: Woe unto them that draw their iniquity as with a long cord, and their transgressions as with the harness of an heifer's yoke: who say, Let His speed come near, and let the counsel of the Holy One of Israel come, that we may know it. Woe unto them that call evil good, and good evil! that put light for darkness, and darkness for light! that put bitter for sweet, and sweet for bitter! Woe unto them that are wise in their own eyes, and prudent in their own sight! Woe unto those that are mighty among you, who drink wine, who are men of strength, who mingle strong drink! who justify the wicked for a reward, and take away justice from the righteous! Therefore, as the stubble shall be burnt by the coal of fire, and utterly consumed by the burning flame, their root shall be as wool, and their flower shall go up like dust. For they would not have the law of the Lord of Σαβαώθ, but despised [2467] the word of the Lord, the Holy One of Israel. And the Lord of Σαβαώθ was very angry, and laid His hands upon them, and smote them; and He was provoked against the mountains, and their carcases were in the midst like dung on the road. And for all this they have not repented, [2468] but their hand is still high.' [2469] For verily your hand is high to commit evil, because ye slew the Christ, and do not repent of it; but so far from that, ye hate and murder us who have believed through Him in the God and Father of all, as often as ye can; and ye curse Him without ceasing, as well as those who side with Him; while all of us pray for you, and for all men, as our Christ and Lord taught us to do, when He enjoined us to pray even for our enemies, and to love them that hate us, and to bless them that curse us.

Chapter CXXXIV - The marriages of Jacob are a figure of the Church

"If, then, the teaching of the prophets and of Himself moves you, it is better for you to follow God than your imprudent and blind masters, who even till this time permit each man to have four or five wives; and if any one see a beautiful woman and desire to have her, they quote the doings of Jacob [called] Israel, and of the other patriarchs, and maintain that it is not wrong to do such things; for they are miserably ignorant in this matter. For, as I before said, certain dispensations of weighty mysteries were accomplished in each act of this sort. For in the marriages of Jacob I shall mention what dispensation and prophecy were accomplished, in order that you may thereby know that your teachers never looked at the divine motive which prompted each act, but only at the grovelling and corrupting passions. Attend therefore to what I say. The marriages of Jacob were types of that which Christ was about to accomplish. For it was not lawful for Jacob to marry two sisters at once. And he serves Laban for [one of] the daughters; and being deceived in [the obtaining of] the younger, he again served seven years. Now Leah is your people and synagogue; but Rachel is our Church. And for these, and for the servants in both, Christ even now serves. For while Noah gave to the two sons the seed of the third as servants, now on the other hand Christ has come to restore both the free sons and the servants amongst them, conferring the same honour on all of them who keep His commandments; even as the children of the free women and the children of the bond women born to Jacob were all sons, and equal in dignity. And it was foretold what each should be according to rank and according to fore-knowledge. Jacob served Laban for speckled and many-spotted sheep; and Christ served, even to the slavery of the cross, for the various and many-formed races of mankind, acquiring them by the blood and mystery of the cross. Leah was weak-eyed; for the eyes of your souls are excessively weak. Rachel stole the gods of Laban, and has hid them to this day; and we have lost our paternal and material gods. Jacob was hated for all time by his brother; and we now, and our Lord Himself, are hated by you and by all men, though we are brothers by nature. Jacob was called Israel; and Israel has been demonstrated to be the Christ, who is, and is called, Jesus.

Chapter CXXXV - Christ is king of Israel, and Christians are the Israelitic race

"And when Scripture says, I am the Lord God, the Holy One of Israel, who have made known Israel your King,' [2470] will you not understand that truly Christ is the everlasting King? For you are aware that Jacob the son of Isaac was never a king. And therefore Scripture again, explaining to us, says what king is meant by Jacob and Israel: Jacob is my Servant, I will uphold Him; and Israel is mine Elect, my soul shall receive Him. I have given Him my Spirit; and He shall bring forth judgment to the Gentiles. He shall not cry, and His voice shall not be heard without. The bruised reed He shall not break, and the smoking flax He shall not quench, until He shall bring forth judgment to victory. He shall shine, and shall not be broken, until He set judgment on the earth. And in His name shall the Gentiles trust.' [2471] Then is it Jacob the patriarch in whom the Gentiles and yourselves shall trust? or is it not Christ? As, therefore, Christ is the Israel and the Jacob, even so we, who have been quarried out from the bowels of Christ, are the true Israelitic race. But let us attend rather to the very word: And I will bring forth,' He says, the seed out of Jacob, and out of Judah: and it shall inherit My holy mountain; and Mine Elect and My servants shall possess the inheritance, and shall dwell there; and there shall be folds of flocks in the thicket, and the valley of Achor shall be a resting-place of cattle for the people who have sought Me. But as for you, who forsake Me, and forget My holy mountain, and prepare a table for demons, and fill out drink for the demon, I shall give you to the sword. You shall all fall with a slaughter; for I called you, and you hearkened not, and did evil before me, and did choose that wherein I delighted not.' [2472] Such are the words of Scripture; understand, therefore, that the seed of Jacob now referred to is something else, and not, as may be supposed, spoken of your people. For it is not possible for the seed of Jacob to leave an entrance for the descendants of Jacob, or for [God] to have accepted the very same persons whom He had reproached with unfitness for the inheritance, and promise it to them again; but as there the prophet says, And now, O house of Jacob, come and let us walk in the light of the Lord; for He has sent away His people, the house of Jacob, because their land was full, as at the first, of soothsayers and divinations;' [2473] even so it is necessary for us here to observe that there are two seeds of Judah, and two races, as there are two houses of Jacob: the one begotten by blood and flesh, the other by faith and the Spirit.

The Apostolic Fathers

Chapter CXXXVI - The Jews, in rejecting Christ, rejected God who sent him

"For you see how He now addresses the people, saying a little before: As the grape shall be found in the cluster, and they will say, Destroy it not, for a blessing is in it; so will I do for My servant's sake: for His sake I will not destroy them all.' [2474] And thereafter He adds: And I shall bring forth the seed out of Jacob, and out of Judah.' It is plain then that if He thus be angry with them, and threaten to leave very few of them, He promises to bring forth certain others, who shall dwell in His mountain. But these are the persons whom He said He would sow and beget. For you neither suffer Him when He calls you, nor hear Him when He speaks to you, but have done evil in the presence of the Lord. But the highest pitch of your wickedness lies in this, that you hate the Righteous One, and slew Him; and so treat those who have received from Him all that they are and have, and who are pious, righteous, and humane. Therefore woe unto their soul,' says the Lord, [2475] for they have devised an evil counsel against themselves, saying, Let us take away the righteous, for he is distasteful to us.' For indeed you are not in the habit of sacrificing to Baal, as were your fathers, or of placing cakes in groves and on high places for the host of heaven: but you have not accepted God's Christ. For he who knows not Him, knows not the will of God; and he who insults and hates Him, insults and hates Him that sent Him. And whoever believes not in Him, believes not the declarations of the prophets, who preached and proclaimed Him to all.

Chapter CXXXVII - He exhorts the Jews to be converted

"Say no evil thing, my brothers, against Him that was crucified, and treat not scornfully the stripes wherewith all may be healed, even as we are healed. For it will be well if, persuaded by the Scriptures, you are circumcised from hard-heartedness: not that circumcision which you have from the tenets that are put into you; for that was given for a sign, and not for a work of righteousness, as the Scriptures compel you [to admit]. Assent, therefore, and pour no ridicule on the Son of God; obey not the Pharisaic teachers, and scoff not at the King of Israel, as the rulers of your synagogues teach you to do after your prayers: for if he that touches those who are not pleasing [2476] to God, is as one that touches the apple of God's eye, how much more so is he that touches His beloved! And that this is He, has been sufficiently demonstrated."

And as they kept silence, I continued: "My friends, I now refer to the Scriptures as the Seventy have interpreted them; for when I quoted them formerly as you possess them, I made proof of you [to ascertain] how you were disposed. [2477] For, mentioning the Scripture which says, Woe unto them! for they have devised evil counsel against themselves, saying' [2478] (as the Seventy have translated, I continued): Let us take away the righteous, for he is distasteful to us;' whereas at the commencement of the discussion I added what your version has: Let us bind the righteous, for he is distasteful to us.' But you had been busy about some other matter, and seem to have listened to the words without attending to them. But now, since the day is drawing to a close, for the sun is about to set, I shall add one remark to what I have said, and conclude. I have indeed made the very same remark already, but I think it would be right to bestow some consideration on it again.

Chapter CXXXVIII - Noah is a figure of Christ, who has regenerated us by water, and faith, and wood: [i.e., the cross.]

"You know, then, sirs," I said, "that God has said in Isaiah to Jerusalem: I saved thee in the deluge of Noah.' [2479] By this which God said was meant that the mystery of saved men appeared in the deluge. For righteous Noah, along with the other mortals at the deluge, i.e., with his own wife, his three sons and their wives, being eight in number, were a symbol of the eighth day, wherein Christ appeared when He rose from the dead, for ever the first in power. For Christ, being the first-born of every creature, became again the chief of another race regenerated by Himself through water, and faith, and wood, containing the mystery of the cross; even as Noah was saved by wood when he rode over the waters with his household. Accordingly, when the prophet says, I saved thee in the times of Noah,' as I have already remarked, he addresses the people who are equally faithful to God, and possess the same signs. For when Moses had the rod in his hands, he led your nation through the sea. And you believe that this was spoken to your nation only, or to the land. But the whole earth, as the Scripture says, was inundated, and the water rose in height fifteen cubits above all the mountains: so that it is evident this was not spoken to the land, but to the people who obeyed Him: for whom also He had before prepared a resting-place in Jerusalem, as was previously demonstrated by all the symbols of the deluge; I mean, that by water, faith, and wood, those who are afore-prepared, and who repent of the sins which they have committed, shall escape from the impending judgment of God.

Chapter CXXXIX - The blessings, and also the curse, pronounced by Noah were prophecies of the future

"For another mystery was accomplished and predicted in the days of Noah, of which you are not aware. It is this: in the blessings wherewith Noah blessed his two sons, and in the curse pronounced on his son's son. For the Spirit of prophecy would not curse the son that had been by God blessed along with [his brothers]. But since the punishment of the sin would cleave to the whole descent of the son that mocked at his father's nakedness, he made the curse originate with his son. [2480] Now, in what he said, he foretold that the descendants of Shem would keep in retention the property and dwellings of Canaan: and again that the descendants of Japheth would take possession of the property of which Shem's descendants had dispossessed Canaan's descendants; and spoil the descendants of Shem, even as they plundered the sons of Canaan. And listen to the way in which it has so come to pass. For you, who have derived your lineage from Shem, invaded the territory of the sons of Canaan by the will of God; and you possessed it. And it is manifest that the sons of Japheth, having invaded you in turn by the judgment of God, have taken your land from you, and have possessed it. Thus it is written: And Noah awoke from the wine, and knew what his younger son had done unto him; and he said, Cursed be Canaan, the servant; a servant shall he be unto his brethren. And he said, Blessed be the Lord God of Shem; and Canaan shall be his servant. May the Lord enlarge Japheth, and let him dwell in the houses of Shem; and let Canaan be his servant.' [2481] Accordingly, as two peoples were blessed,--those from Shem, and those from Japheth,--and as the offspring of Shem were decreed first to possess the dwellings of Canaan, and the offspring of Japheth were predicted as in turn receiving the same possessions, and to the two peoples there was the one people of Canaan handed over for servants; so Christ has come according to the power given Him from the Almighty Father, and summoning men to friendship, and blessing, and repentance, and dwelling together, has promised, as has already been proved, that there shall be a future possession for all the saints in this same land. And hence all men everywhere, whether bond or free, who believe in Christ, and recognise the truth in His own words and those of His prophets, know that they shall be with Him in that land, and inherit everlasting and incorruptible good.

Chapter CXL - In Christ all are free. The Jews hope for salvation in vain because they are sons of Abraham

"Hence also Jacob, as I remarked before, being himself a type of Christ, had married the two handmaids of his two free wives, and of them begat sons, for the purpose of indicating beforehand that Christ would receive even all those who amongst Japheth's race are descendants of Canaan, equally with the free, and would have the children fellow-heirs. And we are such; but you cannot comprehend this, because you cannot drink of the living fountain of God, but of broken cisterns which can hold no water, as the Scripture says. [2482] But they are cisterns broken, and holding no water, which your own teachers have digged, as the Scripture also expressly asserts, teaching for doctrines the commandments of men.' [2483] And besides, they beguile themselves and you, supposing that the everlasting kingdom will be assuredly given to those of the dispersion who are of Abraham, after the flesh, although they be sinners, and faithless, and disobedient towards God, which the Scriptures have proved is not the case. For if so, Isaiah would never have said this: And unless the Lord of Σαβαώθ had left us a seed, we would have been like Sodom and Gomorrah.' [2484] And Ezekiel: Even if Noah, and Jacob, and Daniel were to pray for sons or daughters, their request should not be granted.' [2485] But neither shall the father perish for the son, nor the son for the father; but every one for his own sin, and each shall be saved for his own righteousness.' [2486] And again Isaiah says: They shall look on the carcases [2487] of them that have transgressed: their worm shall not cease, and their fire shall not be quenched; and they shall be a spectacle to all flesh.' [2488] And our Lord, according to the will of Him that sent Him, who is the Father and Lord of all, would not have said, They shall come from the east, and from the west, and shall sit down with Abraham, and Isaac, and Jacob in the kingdom of heaven. But the children of the kingdom shall be cast out into outer darkness.' [2489] Furthermore, I have proved in what has preceded, [2490] that those who were foreknown to be unrighteous, whether men or angels, are not made wicked by God's fault, but each man by his own fault is what he will appear to be.

Chapter CXLI - Free-will in men and angels

"But that you may not have a pretext for saying that Christ must have been crucified, and that those who transgressed must have been among your nation, and that the matter could not have been otherwise, I said briefly by anticipation, that God, wishing men and angels to follow His will, resolved to create them free to do righteousness; possessing reason, that they may know by whom they are created, and through whom they, not existing formerly, do now exist; and with a law that they should be judged by Him, if they do anything contrary to right reason: and of ourselves we, men and angels, shall be convicted of having acted sinfully, unless we repent beforehand. But if the word of God foretells that some angels and men shall be certainly punished, it did so because it foreknew that they would be unchangeably [wicked], but not because God had created them so. So that if they repent, all who wish for it can obtain mercy from God: and the Scripture foretells that they shall be blessed, saying, Blessed is the man to whom the Lord imputeth not sin;' [2491] that is, having repented of his sins, that he may receive remission of them from God; and not as you deceive yourselves, and some others who resemble you in this, who say, that even though they be sinners, but know God, the Lord will not impute sin to them. We have as proof of this the one fall of David, which happened through his boasting, which was forgiven then when he so mourned and wept, as it is written. But if even to such a man no remission was granted before repentance, and only when this great king, and anointed one, and prophet, mourned and conducted himself so, how can the impure and utterly abandoned, if they weep not, and mourn not, and repent not, entertain the hope that the Lord will not impute to them sin? And this one fall of David, in the matter of Uriah's wife, proves, sirs," I said, "that the patriarchs had many wives, not to commit fornication, but that a certain dispensation and all mysteries might be accomplished by them; since, if it were allowable to take any wife, or as many wives as one chooses, and how he chooses, which the men of your nation do over all the earth, wherever they sojourn, or wherever they have been sent, taking women under the name of marriage, much more would David have been permitted to do this."

When I had said this, dearest Marcus Pompeius, I came to an end.

Chapter CXLII - The Jews return thanks, and leave Justin

Then Trypho, after a little delay, said, "You see that it was not intentionally that we came to discuss these points. And I confess that I have been particularly pleased with the conference; and I think that these are of quite the same opinion as myself. For we have found more than we expected, and more than it was possible to have expected. And if we could do this more frequently, we should be much helped in the searching of the Scriptures themselves. But since," he said, "you are on the eve of departure, and expect daily to set sail, do not hesitate to remember us as friends when you are gone."

"For my part," I replied, "if I had remained, I would have wished to do the same thing daily. But now, since I expect, with God's will and aid, to set sail, I exhort you to give all diligence in this very great struggle for your own salvation, and to be earnest in setting a higher value on the Christ of the Almighty God than on your own teachers."

After this they left me, wishing me safety in my voyage, and from every misfortune. And I, praying for them, said, "I can wish no better thing for you, sirs, than this, that, recognising in this way that intelligence is given to every man, you may be of the same opinion as ourselves, and believe that Jesus is the Christ of God." [2492]

Footnotes:

1948. This Xystus, on the authority of Euseb. (iv. 18), was at Ephesus. There, Philostratus mentions, Appolonius was wont to have disputations.--Otto.

1949. Euseb. (iv. 11): "Justin, in philosopher's garb, preached the word of God."

1950. In jest, no doubt, because quoting a line from Homer, Il., vi. 123. τίς δὲ σύ ἐσσι, φέριστε, καταθνητῶν ἀνθρώπων.

1951. i.e., "A Hebrew of the Hebrews" (Phil. iii. 5).

1952. The war instigated by Bar Cochba.

1953. The opinions of Stoics.--Otto.

1954. The Platonists.

1955. ho some omit, and put θεῷ of prev. cl. in this cl., reading so: "Philosophy is the greatest possession, and most honourable, and introduces us to God," etc.

1956. Maranus thinks that those who are different from the masters of practical philosophy are called Theoretics. I do not know whether they may be better designated Sceptics or Pyrrhonists.--Otto.

1957. Julian, Orat., vi., says: "Let no one divide our philosophy into many parts, or cut it into many parts, and especially let him not make many out of one: for as truth is one, so also is philosophy."

1958. Either Flavia Neapolis is indicated, or Ephesus.--Otto.

1959. Narrating his progress in the study of Platonic philosophy, he elegantly employs this trite phrase of Plato's.--Otto.

1960. Philology, used here to denote the exercise of reason.

1961. Philology, used here to denote the exercise of speech. The two-fold use of λόγος-- oratio and ratio--ought to be kept in view. The old man uses it in the former, Justin in the latter, sense.

1962. "Beside."

1963. Otto says: If the old man begins to speak here, then ἔχει must be read for ἔχειν. The received text makes it appear that Justin continues a quotation, or the substance of it, from Plato.

1964. According to one interpretation, this clause is applied to God: "If you believe in God, seeing He is not indifferent to the matter," etc. Maranus says that it means: A Jew who reads so much of Christ in the Old Testament, cannot be indifferent to the things which pertain to Him.

1965. Literally: having become perfect. Some refer the words to perfection of character; some initiation by baptism.

1966. Latin version, "beloved Pompeius."

1967. According to another reading, "I did not leave."

1968. Editors suppose that Justin inserts a long parenthesis here, from "for" to "Egypt." It is more natural to take this as an anacoluthon. Justin was going to say, "But now we trust through Christ," but feels that such a statement requires preliminary explanation.

1969. According to the LXX, Isa. li. 4, 5.

1970. Jer. xxxi. 31, 32.

1971. Isa. lv. 3 ff. according to LXX.

1972. Not in Jeremiah; some would insert, in place of Jeremiah, Isaiah or John. St. John xii. 40; Isa. vi. 10; where see full references in the English margin. But comp. Jer. vii. 24, 26, Jer. xi. 8, and Jer. xvii. 23.

1973. 1 Cor. x. 4. Otto reads: which he mentioned and which was for those who repented.

1974. Three times in Justin, not in LXX.

1975. Deviating slightly from LXX., omitting a clause.

1976. LXX. "not as," etc.

1977. LXX. "not as," etc.

1978. Isa. lii. 10 ff. following LXX. on to liv. 6.

1979. Isa. lv. 3 to end.

1980. ἱμάτια; some read ἰάματα, as in LXX., "thy health," the better reading probably.

1981. Isa. lviii. 1-12.

1982. Deut. x. 16 f.

1983. Lev. xxvi. 40, 41.

1984. See Apol., i. 47. The Jews By Hadrian's recent edict. were prohibited by law from entering Jerusalem on pain of death. And so Justin sees in circumcision their own punishment.

1985. Isa. lvii. 1-4.

1986. Isa. lii. 5.

1987. Isa. iii. 9 ff.

1988. Isa. v. 18, 20.

1989. Matt. xxi. 13.

1990. This and following quotation taken promiscuously from Matt. xxiii. and Luke xi.

1991. ὃς. i. and ὃς. ii.

1992. They did not Sabbatize; but Justin does not deny what is implied in many Scriptures, that they marked the week, and noted the seventh day. Gen. ii. 3, Gen. viii. 10, 12.

1993. Ezek. xx. 12.

1994. Ex. xxxii. 6.

1995. Deut. xxxii. 15.

1996. νεκριμαῖον, or "dieth of itself;" com. reading was ἐκριμαῖον, which was supposed to be derived from ἐκρίπτω, and to mean "which ought to be cast out:" the above was suggested by H. Stephanus.

1997. ἄδικος καὶ παράνομος.

1998. "The reasoning of St. Justin is not quite clear to interpreters. As we abstain from some herbs, not because they are forbidden by law, but because they are deadly; so the law of abstinence from improper and violent animals was imposed not on Noah, but on you as a yoke on account of your sins."--Maranus.

1999. Deut. xxxii. 6, 20.

2000. Ezek. xx. 19-26.

2001. Amos v. 18 to end, Amos vi. 1-7.

2002. Jer. vii. 21 f.

2003. Ps. l. (in E. V.).

2004. Isa. lxvi. 1.

2005. The man he met by the sea-shore.

2006. Josh. v. 2; Isa. xxvi. 2, 3.

2007. Isa. lxv. 1-3.

2008. Isa. lxv. 1-3.

2009. Other edd. have, "with us."

2010. Otto reads: "Thy works which Thou shalt do to those who wait for mercy."

2011. Some suppose the correct reading to be, "our glorious institutions manners, customs, or ordinances. have," etc., ἔθη for ἔθνη.

2012. Isa. lxiii. 15 to end, and Isa. lxiv.

2013. Isa. xlii. 6, 7.

2014. συσσεισμόν, "a shaking," is the original reading; but LXX has σύσσημον, a standard or signal, and this most edd. adopt.

2015. Isa. lxii. 10 to end, Isa. lxiii. 1-6.

2016. Isa. lviii. 13, 14.

2017. Isa. iii. 16.

2018. Various passages strung together; comp. Rom. iii. 10, and foll. verses.

2019. Jer. iv. 3.

2020. So in A.V., but supposed to be Idumæa.

2021. Jer. ix. 25 f.

2022. Mal. i. 10, etc.

2023. Ps. xviii. 43.

2024. This striking claim of the Old

Testament Scriptures is noteworthy.

2025. Or, "repentance of the Father;" πατρός for πνεύματος. Maranus explains the confusion on the ground of the similarity between the contractions for the words, πρς and πνς.

2026. Ps. xix.

2027. Literally, "And the ten horns, ten kings shall arise after them."

2028. Dan. vii. 9-28.

2029. Isa. xxix. 14.

2030. Ps. cx.

2031. πληρώσει πτώματα; Lat. version, implebit ruinas. Thirlby suggested that an omission has taken place in the mss. by the transcriber's fault.

2032. πεπήρωνται. Maranus thinks πεπώρωνται more probable, "hardened."

2033. Ps. lxxii.

2034. A striking passage in De Maistre (OEuvres, vol. vi. p. 275) is worthy of comparison.

2035. Matt. vii. 15.

2036. 1 Cor. xi. 19.

2037. Matt. vii. 15.

2038. Matt. xxiv. 11.

2039. Maranus remarks from Thirlby: "As Justin wrote a little before, and is called Jacob in parable,' it seems to convince us that Justin wrote, thy face, O Jacob.'" The meaning in this latter case becomes plain, if we observe that "O Israel" is equivalent to, and means, "O house of Jacob:" an apostrophe to the Church of the ancient people.

2040. Ps. xxiv.

2041. Ps. xlvii. 5-9. The diapsalm is here used for what follows the "Selah.".

2042. "For" wanting in both Codd.

2043. Ps. xcix.

2044. Hebrew and Greek, "a good word," i.e., the Λόγος.

2045. Or, "God, thy God."

2046. στακτή.

2047. Literally, "garments of gold, variegated."

2048. Literally, "of a hard-hearted opinion."

2049. 1 Kings xix. 14, 18.

2050. ὦ οὗτος. Or, Look you, listen!.

2051. Literally, "carry us captive."

2052. Ps. lxviii. 19.

2053. Isa. v. 21.

2054. Contrasting either Catholics with heretics, or Christians with Jews. Note this word Catholic, as here used in its legitimate primitive sense.

2055. Some think this particularly refers to the paschal lamb, others to any lamb which is roasted.

2056. Literally, "cords."

2057. Chap. xv.

2058. Literally, "overthrowing with a perfect overthrow."

2059. Chap. xxviii.

2060. Mal. i. 10-12.

2061. Or, "being the first."

2062. Ex. xxviii. 33 gives no definite number of bells. Otto presumes Justin to have confounded the bells and gems, which were twelve in number.

2063. Ps. xix. 4.

2064. Isa. liii. 1, 2.

2065. Chap. xiii.

2066. ἐκκλησία Lat. vers. has conventus.

2067. Literally, "to the discourse in order."

2068. Chap. xiii.

2069. Or, "was I led."

2070. Isa. liii. 8.

2071. Literally, "He was in the world, being born."

2072. See Chap. lxvi.

2073. Literally, "disobeys evil" (ἀπειθεῖ πονηρά). Conjectured: ἀπωθεῖ, and ἀπειθεῖ πονηρία.

2074. The mss. of Justin read, "shall be taken:" καταληφθήσεται. This is plainly a mistake for καταλειφθήσεται; but whether the mistake is Justin's or the transcribers', it would be difficult to say, as Thirlby remarks.

2075. The rendering of this doubtful: literally, "from the face of the two kings," and the words might go with "shall be forsaken."

2076. Isa. vii. 10-17 with Isa. viii. 4 inserted. The last clause may also be translated, "in which He took away from Judah Ephraim, even the king of Assyria."

2077. i.e., of Abraham's seed.

2078. Justin distinguishes between such essential acts as related to God's worship and the establishment of righteousness, and such ceremonial observances as had a mere temporary significance. The recognition of this distinction he alleges to be necessary to salvation: necessary in this sense, that justification must be placed not on the latter, but on the former; and without such recognition, a Jew would, as Justin says, rest his hopes on his noble descent from Abraham.

2079. More probably, "or on account of," etc.

2080. In Bible, "Job;" Maranus prefers "Jacob," and thinks the mention of his name very suitable to disprove the arrogant claims of Jacob's posterity.

2081. Ezek. xiv. 20.

2082. Isa. lxvi. 24.

2083. Some refer this to Christ's

baptism. See Cyprian, Adv. Jud. i. 24.-- Otto.

2084. It, i.e., the law, or "what in the law," etc.

2085. Those who live after Christ.

2086. "Eternal," i.e., as the Jew thinks.

2087. Literally, "put you out of countenance."

2088. Num. xv. 38.

2089. Deut. vi. 6.

2090. Literally, "importuning."

2091. "Or, Are there not some," etc.

2092. The text seems to be corrupt. Otto reads: "Do anathematize those who put their trust in this very Christ so as to obtain salvation," etc.

2093. Ezek. xxxiii. 11-20.

2094. Comp. St. John xii. 47, 48. Grabius thinks this taken from the apocryphal. Gospel according to the Hebrews. It is not in the New or Old Testament. Query. Is it not, rather, one of the traditional sayings preserved among early Christians?.

2095. Comp. Isa. xxix. 13.

2096. Or, "such a man."

2097. Some read, "of your race," referring to the Ebionites. Maranus believes the reference is to the Ebionites, and supports in a long note the reading "our," inasmuch as Justin would be more likely to associate these Ebionites with Christians than with Jews, even though they were heretics.

2098. Langus translates: "Nor would, indeed, many who are of the same opinion as myself say so."

2099. Note this emphatic testimony of primitive faith.

2100. Mal. iv. 5.

2101. Matt. iii. 11, 12.

2102. Literally, "cousin."

2103. Matt. xvii. 12.

2104. Num. xi. 17, spoken of the seventy elders. Justin confuses what is said here with Num. xxvii. 18 and Deut. xxxiv. 9.

2105. The meaning is, that no division of person took place. Elijah remained the same after as before his spirit was shed on John.

2106. Literally, "fruit."

2107. Isa. xxxix. 8.

2108. Isa. xl. 1-17.

2109. Chap. xxv.

2110. "Are willing."

2111. Matt. xi. 12-15.

2112. Gen. xlix. 5, 8, 9, 10, 11, 18, 24. These texts are frequently referred to by Justin.

2113. Or, "in comparison of."

2114. Gen. xlix. 8-12.

2115. ἀφ' οὗ; many translated "under whom," as if ἐφ' οὗ. This would be erroneous. Conjectured also ἔφυγε for ἔπαθεν.

2116. Zech. ix. 9.

2117. Zech. xiii. 7.

2118. Literally, "inquired into."

2119. Deut. iv. 19, an apparent i.e., evident. misinterpretation of the passage. But see St. John x. 33-36.

2120. Or, "misusing."

2121. Ps. xcvi. 5.

2122. Com. reading, "you;" evidently wrong.

2123. Literally, "for."

2124. Two constructions, "which" referring either to Scriptures as whole, or to what he records from them. Last more probable.

2125. Gen. xviii. 1, 2.

2126. Gen. xix. 27, 28; "and so on" inserted probably not by Justin, but by some copyist, as is evident from succeeding words.

2127. Some, "besides;" but probably as above.

2128. Or, "going away, departed."

2129. Gen. xviii. 10.

2130. Gen. xxi. 9-12.

2131. Or, "Messenger." The "Jehovah-angel" of the Pentateuch, passim. In the various passages in which Justin assigns the reason for Christ being called angel or messenger, Justin uses also the verb ἀγγέλλω, to convey messages, to announce. The similarity between ἄγγελος and ἀγγέλλω cannot be retained in English, and therefore the point of Justin's remarks is lost to the English reader.

2132. Some supply, "or said."

2133. Gen. xix. 23.

2134. Or, "We must of necessity think, that besides the one of the two angels who came down to Sodom, and whom the Scripture by Moses calls Lord, God Himself appeared to Abraham."

2135. This passage is rather confused: the translation is necessarily free, but, it is believed, correct. Justin's friend wishes to make out that two distinct individuals are called Lord or God in the narrative.

2136. Ps. cx. 1.

2137. Ps. xlv. 6, 7.

2138. Note again the fidelity of Justin to this principle, and the fact that in no other way could a Jew be persuaded to listen to a Christian. Acts xvii. 11.

2139. Gen. xviii. 13, 14.

2140. Gen. xviii. 16, 17.

2141. Literally, "is multiplied."

2142. Gen. xviii. 20-23.

2143. Comp. Note 2, p. 223.

2144. Gen. xviii. 33, Gen. xix. 1.
2145. Gen. xix. 10.
2146. Literally, "I have admired thy face."
2147. Gen. xix. 16-25.
2148. Literally, "hear."
2149. Literally, "for this sake." Note here and elsewhere the primitive rule as to the duty of all men to search the Scriptures.
2150. Or, "speak otherwise."
2151. Literally, "in the place of God."
2152. Gen. xxxi. 10-13.
2153. Some read, "a man."
2154. Literally, "the face of God."
2155. Gen. xxxii. 22-30.
2156. Gen. xxxv. 6-10.
2157. Or, "Beersheba."
2158. So, LXX. and N.T.; Heb. "Haran."
2159. Literally, "was set up."
2160. Gen. xxviii. 10-19. Οὐλαμλοὺζ. Sept. Luz Eng.
2161. Some conjecture "Jacob," others insert "Jacob" after "Isaac." Gen. xxii. The Jehovah-angel was seen no doubt by Isaac, as well as by his father.
2162. Ex. ii. 23.
2163. Ex. iii. 16.
2164. Ex. iii. 2-4.
2165. Gen. xxxv. 7.
2166. Literally, "judgment."
2167. Or, "in the beginning, before all creatures." Justin's reference to Josh. i. 13-15 deserves special consideration; for he supposes that the true Joshua (Jesus) was the substance, and the true "captain of salvation," of whom this one was but a shadow (Heb. iv. 8, margin), type, and pledge. See cap. lxii.
2168. The act of will or volition is on the part of the Father.
2169. Or, "Do we not see," etc.
2170. The word, λόγος translated "word," means both the thinking power or reason which produces ideas and the expression of these ideas. And Justin passes here from the one meaning to the other. When we utter a thought, the utterance of it does not diminish the power of thought in us, though in one sense the thought has gone away from us.
2171. The mss. of Justin read "sleeping," but this is regarded as the mistake of some careless transcriber.
2172. Prov. viii. 21 ff.
2173. Justin, since he is of opinion that the Word is the beginning of the universe, thinks that by these words, "in the beginning," Moses indicated the Word, like many other writers. Hence also he says in Ap. i. 23, that Moses declares the Word "to be begotten first by God." If this explanation does not satisfy, read, "with regard to Him whom I have pointed out" (Maranus).
2174. Gen. i. 26, 28.
2175. Gen. iii. 22.
2176. Heresy or sect.
2177. Or, "among us." Maranus pronounces against this latter reading for the following reasons: (1.) The Jews had their own heresies which supplied many things to the Christian heresies, especially to Menander and Saturninus. (2.) The sect which Justin here refutes was of opinion that God spoke to angels. But those angels, as Menander and Saturninus invented, "exhorted themselves, saying, Let us make," etc. (3.) The expression διδάσκαλοι suits the rabbins well. So Justin frequently calls them. (4.) Those teachers seem for no other cause to have put the words in the angels' mouths than to eradicate the testimony by which they proved divine persons.
2178. Josh. v. 13 ad fin., and Josh.vi. 1, 2.
2179. Isa. liii. 8.
2180. Note this beautiful rendering, Ψ. cx. 3.
2181. Ps. cx. 4.
2182. Or, "to us."
2183. ἄνωθεν; in Lat. vers. antiquitus, which Maranus prefers.
2184. Literally, "garments of gold, variegated."
2185. Ps. xlv. 6-11.
2186. The incarnation, etc.
2187. "Being so," literally.
2188. Literally, "but only sharpen yourselves to say something."
2189. Or, "this one.".
2190. Ps. xcix. 1-7.
2191. Or, "to judge," as in chap. xxxiv.
2192. Ps. lxxii. 1, etc.
2193. Ps. xix. 1-6.
2194. Literally, "importuned."
2195. Isa. xlii. 8.
2196. Literally, "fixed."
2197. Or, "ye islands which sail on it;" or without "continually."
2198. Isa. xlii. 5-13.
2199. Chap. xliii.
2200. ἦν, which is in chap. xliii., is here omitted, but ought to be inserted without doubt.
2201. Isa. vii. 10-17, with Isa. viii. 4 inserted between vers. 16 and 17.
2202. We have not seen that Justin admitted this; but it is not to be supposed that the passage where he did admit it has been lost, as Perionius suspected; for sometimes Justin refers to passages at other places, which he did not relate in their own

place. --Maranus.

2203. Note the courteous admission of Trypho, and the consent of both parties to the duty of searching the Scriptures.

2204. τέως: Vulg. παρὰ Θεῷ, vitiose. --Otto.

2205. The text is corrupt, and various emendations have been proposed.

2206. Or, "and to be worshipped as God."

2207. Or, "an ass." The ass was sacred to Bacchus; and many fluctuate between οἶνον and ὄνον.

2208. Ps. xix. 5.

2209. Isa. xxxv. 1-7.

2210. The text here has ταῦτα ποιῆσαι ὁμοίως. Maranus suggests Ἠσαίου for ποιῆσαι; and so we have translated.

2211. Justin says that the priests of Mithras imitated all the words of Isaiah about to be quoted; and to prove it, is content with a single example, namely, the precepts of righteousness, which they were wont to relate to him, as in these words of Isaiah: "He who walks in righteousness," etc. Justin omitted many other passages, as easy and obvious. For since Mithras is the same as fire, it manifestly answers to the fire of which Isaiah speaks. And since Justin reminded them who are initiated, that they are said to be initiated by Mithras himself, it was not necessary to remind them that the words of Isaiah are imitated in this: "You shall see the King with glory." Bread and water are referred to by Isaiah: so also in these mysteries of Mithras, Justin testifies that bread and a cup of water are placed before them (Apol. i.).--Maranus.

2212. i.e., the devils.

2213. i.e., the priests of Mithras.

2214. Isa. xxxiii. 13-19.

2215. Literally, "to do," ποιεῖν. The horrible charge of banqueting on blood, etc., constantly repeated against Christians, was probably based on the Eucharist. See Kaye's Illustrations from Tatian, Athenagorus, and Theoph. Antioch., cap. ix. p. 153.

2216. Literally, "to do," ποιεῖν. The horrible charge of banqueting on blood, etc., constantly repeated against Christians, was probably based on the Eucharist. See Kaye's Illustrations from Tatian, Athenagorus, and Theoph. Antioch., cap. ix. p. 153.

2217. Or, "profess."

2218. Or, "even if we."

2219. It is not known where this passage comes from.

2220. Jer. xi. 19.

2221. This is wanting in our Scriptures: it is cited by Iren., iii. 20, under the name of Isaiah, and in iv. 22 under that of Jeremiah.--Maranus.

2222. These words were not taken away by the Jews, but added by some Christian.--Otto. A statement not proved.

2223. It is strange that "from the wood" is not added; but the audacity of the copyists in such matters is well known.--Maranus.

2224. Many think, "you."

2225. In text, "you." Maranus suggests, as far better, "we."

2226. Something is here wanting; the suggested reading of Maranus has been adopted. As to omissions between this chapter and the next, critics are not agreed. The Benedictine editors see no proofs of them.

2227. Deut. xxxi. 16-18.

2228. Literally, "for food."

2229. The first conference seems to have ended hereabout. It occupied two days. But the student must consult the learned note of Kaye (Justin Martyr, p. 20. Rivingtons, London. 1853).

2230. Ex. xxiii. 20, 21.

2231. Num. xiii. 16.

2232. Isa. vi. 8.

2233. Or, "so many."

2234. Isa. ix. 6, according to LXX.

2235. Not in all edd.

2236. Matt. viii. 11.

2237. Matt. vii. 22.

2238. Matt. xxv. 41.

2239. Luke x. 19. "And on scolopendras" (i.e. centipedes) not in the original.

2240. Luke ix. 22.

2241. Justin puts "sun and moon" instead of "Lucifer." Ψ. cx. 3, Sept, compounded with Prov. viii. 27. Maranus says, David did predict, not that Christ would be born of Mary before sun and moon, but that it would happen before sun and moon that He would be born of a virgin.

2242. Ezek. xvi. 3.

2243. Mic. v. 2.

2244. Text has, by "them;" but Maranus says the artifice lay in the priest's compelling the initiated to say that Mithras himself was the initiator in the cave.

2245. Jer. xxxi. 15.

2246. Literally, "spoiled."

2247. Justin thinks the "spoils of Samaria" denote spoils of Satan; Tertull. thinks that they are spoils of Christ.

2248. Literally, "add."

2249. Isa. xxix. 13, 14.

2250. LXX. "who walk," πορευόμενοι for πονηρευόμενοι.

2251. In E. V. "Zoan."

2252. Isa. xxx. 1-5.

2253. ἐκδεξάμενος; in chap. cxv. inf.

it is ἐκλεξάμενος.

2254. Zech. iii. 1.

2255. Job i. 6.

2256. Maranus suggests the insertion of ἐποίησαν or ἐπείρασαν before ἐξισοῦσθαι.

2257. Ps. xcvi. 5.

2258. Justin made no previous allusion to this point, so far as we know from the writing preserved.

2259. Or, "so as to believe thoroughly that such will take place" (after "opinion").

2260. A hint of the origin of this work. See Kaye's Note, p. 18.

2261. i.e., resurrection.

2262. Maranus says, Hieron. thinks the Genistæ were so called because they were sprung from Abraham (γένος) the Meristæ so called because they separated the Scriptures. Josephus bears testimony to the fact that the sects of the Jews differed in regard to fate and providence; the Pharisees submitting all things indeed to God, with the exception of human will; the Essenes making no exceptions, and submitting all to God. I believe therefore that the Genistæ were so called because they believed the world to be in general governed by God; the Meristæ, because they believed that a fate or providence belonged to each man.

2263. Otto says, the author and chief of this sect of Galilæans was Judas Galilæus, who, after the exile of king Archelaus, when the Romans wished to raise a tax in Judæa, excited his countrymen to the retaining of their former liberty.--The Hellenists, or rather Hellenæans. No one mentions this sect but Justin; perhaps Herodians or Hillelæans (from R. Hillel).

2264. We have translated the text of Justin as it stands. Commentators make the sense, "and that there will be a thousand years in Jerusalem," or "that the saints will live a thousand years in Jerusalem."

2265. Literally, "time."

2266. Literally, "the son of an hundred years."

2267. Literally, "the son of an hundred years."

2268. Or, as in margin of A. V., "they shall make the works of their toil continue long," so reading παλαιώσουσιν for πλεονάσουσιν: thus also LXX.

2269. Isa. lxv. 17 to end.

2270. These words are not found in the mss.

2271. Ps. xc. 4; 2 Pet. iii. 8.

2272. Literally, "make." A very noteworthy passage, as a primitive exposition of Rev. xx. 4-5. See Kaye, chap. v.

2273. Luke xx. 35f.

2274. Ezek. iii. 17, 18, 19.

2275. Isa. i. 23.

2276. ἐπί, but afterwards εἰς. Maranus thinks that ἐπί is the insertion of some copyist.

2277. Or better, "His." This quotation from Ψ. cx. is put very differently from the previous quotation of the same Psalm in chap. xxxii. Justin often quotes from memory. Kaye, cap. viii.

2278. This last clause is thought to be an interpolation.

2279. Or, "why was it."

2280. Ps. xxiv. 7.

2281. Chap. lxxvi.

2282. κατάδεσμοι, by some thought to be verses by which evil spirits, once expelled, were kept from returning. Plato (Rep.) speaks of incantations by which demons were summoned to the help of those who practised such rites; but Justin refers to them only as being expelled. Others regard them as drugs.

2283. Ps. cxlviii. 1, 2. Kaye's citations (chap. ix. p. 181) from Tatian, concerning angels and demons, are valuable aids to the understanding of Justin in his frequent references to this subject.

2284. In both mss. "people."

2285. Isa. lxvi. 5-11.

2286. Myrrh. Christ the (Anointed) Rock is also referred to by Jacob (Gen. xlix. 24).

2287. In chap. lxiii. probably, where the same Psalm is quoted.

2288. Ps. xlv. 7.

2289. Ps. i. 3.

2290. The Red Sea, not the Jordan. Ex. xv. 27.

2291. Literally, "a tree."

2292. Isa. xi. 1 ff.

2293. He, that is, the Spirit. The following "He" is Christ.

2294. Or, "wrought out amongst His people." So Otto.

2295. Literally, "He said accordingly." Ψ. lxviii. 18.

2296. Joel ii. 28 f.

2297. The Shechinah probably attended the descent of the Holy Spirit, and what follows in the note seems a gratuitous explanation. The Ebionite corruption of a truth need not be resorted to. See chap. cxxviii: The fire in the bush. Justin learned this either from tradition or from apocryphal books. Mention is made of a fire both in the Ebionite Gospel and in another publication called Pauli prædicatio, the readers and users of which denied that the rite of baptism had been duly performed, unless quam mox in aquam descenderunt, statim super aquam ignis appareat.

2298. Literally, "sat."
2299. Isa. i. 27.
2300. Ps. ii. 7.
2301. The repetition seems quite superfluous.
2302. This intense abhorrence of the cross made it worth while to show that these similitudes existed under the law. They were ad hominem appeals, and suited to Jewish modes of thought.
2303. There is a variety of reading here: either ἀβύσσου πηγῶν κάτωθεν καθαρῶν: or, ἀβύσσου πηγῶν κάτωθεν, καὶ καθ' ὥραν γεννημάτων, κ.τ.λ., which we prefer.
2304. The translation in the text is a rendering of the Septuagint. The mss. of Justin read: "Being glorified as the first-born among his brethren."
2305. Deut. xxxiii. 13-17.
2306. A clumsy exposition of St. John iii. 14.
2307. Or, "ashes," σποδῶν for σπονδῶν.
2308. We have adopted the parenthesis inserted by Maranus. Langus would insert before it, τί ἕξετε ἀποκρίνασθαι; "What will you have to answer?"
2309. Gen. xv. 6.
2310. We have supplied this phrase twice above.
2311. Literally, salvation along with Christ, that is, salvation by the aid of Christ.
2312. ἀνδρομανία is read in mss. for ἀνδροφονία.
2313. Matt. xxii. 37.
2314. Gal. iii. 13.
2315. Deut. xxvii. 26.
2316. Deut. xxi. 23.
2317. We read ἐπισταμένων for ἐπισταμένων. Otherwise to be translated: "God foretold that which you did not know," etc.
2318. λεγομένων for γενομένων.
2319. Luke vi. 35.
2320. Ps. iii. 4, 5.
2321. Isa. lxv. 2; comp. also Rom. x. 21.
2322. Isa. liii. 9.
2323. That is, Ps. xxii. 16-18.
2324. Probably should be "Thy."
2325. Jewish computation of the evening as part of the succeeding day.
2326. Matt. xxvi. 39.
2327. Ibid.
2328. Matt. xi. 27.
2329. Matt. xvi. 21.
2330. Note this testimony to Mary's descent from David.
2331. The text is, αὐτὸν τὸν Ἀβραὰμ πατέρα. Thirlby proposed αὐτὸν τὸν Ἀδάμ: Maranus changed this into αὐτοῦ τὸν Ἀδὰμ πατέρα.
2332. It is not easy, says Maranus, to say in what Scripture Christ is so called. Clearly he refers to the Dayspring (St. Luke i. 78) as the LXX. render many texts of the O.T. See Zech. iii. 8. Perhaps Justin had in his mind the passage, "This the day which the Lord hath made" (Ψ. cxviii. 24). Clem. Alex. teaches that Christ is here referred to.
2333. Luke i. 35. See Meyer in loc.
2334. Luke i. 38.
2335. Luke xviii. 18 f.
2336. The text is corrupt, and the meaning doubtful. Otto translates: naribus inter se certantes.
2337. Gen. iii. 15.
2338. Gen. xi. 6.
2339. Isa. l. 4.
2340. Not found in mss.
2341. καὶ τῶν διδασκάλων, adopted instead of κατὰ τὴν διδασκαλίαν, "according to their instructions."
2342. ἀπὸ τοῦ ὄρους. Justin seems to have supposed that the Jews came on Christ from some point of the hill while He was in the valley below. Ἐπὶ τοῦ ὄρους and ἐπὶ τὸ ὄρος have been suggested.
2343. ὃς. x. 6.
2344. Ps. ii. 7; Matt. iii. 17.
2345. Matt. iv. 9, 10.
2346. Literally, "said."
2347. Maranus says it is hardly to be doubted that Justin read, "I am poured out like water," etc.
2348. Luke xxii. 44, 42.
2349. Breast, rather. The (κοίλη) cavity of the nobler viscera.
2350. Justin refers to the opinion of the Docetes, that Christ suffered in appearance merely, and not in reality.
2351. See note on chap. xcviii.
2352. Ibid.
2353. This demonstration is not given. It could not be. The woman was herself frightened by the direct interposition of God. 1 Sam. xxviii. 12, 13.
2354. Sylburg proposed δικαίους γίνεσθαι for δι οὕς γίν, "to strive earnestly to become righteous, and at death to pray."
2355. Luke xxiii. 46.
2356. Matt. v. 20.
2357. Num. xxiv. 17.
2358. Or, "Dayspring.". Zech. vi. 12 (according to LXX.).
2359. Matt. xii. 38 f.
2360. In the LXX. only three days are recorded, though in the Hebrew and other versions forty. The parenthetic clause is probably the work of a transcriber.
2361. Read κικυῶνα for σικυῶνα.
2362. Jon. iv. 10 f.

The Apostolic Fathers

2363. Chap. xvii.
2364. Read μαθόντα for παθόντα.
2365. Literally, "people shall place a river in it."
2366. Mic. iv. 1 ff.
2367. 2 Thess. ii. 3; and see chap. xxxii.
2368. Ps. cxxviii. 3.
2369. Isa. lvii. 1.
2370. Isa. liii. 7.
2371. Isa. xxvii. 1.
2372. Matt. xxiii. 27, 23, 24. Note the examples he gives of the rabbinical expositions. He consents to their principle, but gives nobler analogies.
2373. According to the LXX., Σάρα was altered to Σάῤῥα, and Ἄβραμ to Ἀβραάμ.
2374. Or, "resurrection of the saints."
2375. Justin seems to mean that the renewal of heaven and earth dates from the incarnation of Christ. St. Matt. xix. 28.
2376. Isa. liii. 7.
2377. Isa. lxv. 2.
2378. Isa. liii. 1.
2379. Ps. viii. 3.
2380. Literally, "the operation of His words." Editors have changed τὸν λόγον into τὸν λόγον or τοῦ λόγου: but there is no need of change.
2381. Jer. ii. 13.
2382. Omitted by Justin in this place.
2383. Zech. ii. 10-13, Zech. iii. 1, 2.
2384. The reading suggested by Maranus, εἰ μὲν ἦν.
2385. Noteworthy as to prophetic vision.
2386. Maranus changed ἀποσπᾷ into ἀποσπᾶν, an emendation adopted in our translation. Otto retains the reading of the ms. "out of which Jesus the Son of God again snatches us. He promised that He would clothe us with," etc.
2387. Justin either confuses Joshua son of Josedech with Hosea the prophet, or he refers to the Jewish tradition that "filthy garments" signified either an illicit marriage, or sins of the people, or the squalor of captivity.
2388. Isa. lxvi. 21; Rom. xv. 15, 16, 17 (Greek); 1 Pet. ii. 9.
2389. Mal. i. 10-12.
2390. Or, "God of God."
2391. Note this testimony to the catholicity of the Church in the second century. And see Kaye (compare with Gibbon), cap. vi. 112.
2392. εἶτα δὲ for εἰδότες.
2393. Ps. cx. 4.
2394. Isa. liii. 8.
2395. 2 Sam. vii. 14f.
2396. Ezek. xliv. 3.
2397. The mss. read "them." Otto has changed it to "Him."
2398. Isa. lii. 15, Isa. liii. 1.
2399. Let this apology be noted.
2400. Literally, "in the time of Moses."
2401. Deut. xxxii. 16-23.
2402. Zech. ii. 11.
2403. See chap. cx.
2404. Isa. lxii. 12.
2405. Isa. lxv. 1.
2406. Gen. xxvi. 4.
2407. Gen. xxviii. 14.
2408. Gen. xlix. 10.
2409. Note this important point. He forbears to cite the New Testament.
2410. Matt. viii. 11 f.
2411. The Apology, i. chap. xxvi.; ii. chap. xv.
2412. Ps. lxxii. 17.
2413. So Justin concludes from Deut. iv. 19; comp. chap. lv. The explanation is not very difficult (see Rom. i. 28), but the language of Justin is unguarded.
2414. Zech. vi. 12.
2415. Zech. xii. 12.
2416. Isa. xlix. 6.
2417. Γηόρα or Γειόρα. Found in LXX., Ex. xii. 19 and Isa. xiv. 1.
2418. Matt. xxiii. 15.
2419. Isa. xlii. 16, Isa. xliii. 10.
2420. Isa. xlii. 6.
2421. Isa. xlix. 8.
2422. Ps. ii. 7 f.
2423. Isa. xiv. 1.
2424. Literally, "a native of the land."
2425. Deut. xxxii. 20; Isa. xlii. 19 f.
2426. Isa. xxix. 14.
2427. Jer. xxxi. 27.
2428. Isa. xix. 24 f.
2429. Ezek. xxxvi. 12.
2430. I cannot forbear to note this "Americanism" in the text.
2431. LXX. ἀναλάμψει, as above. The reading of the text is ἀναληψει.
2432. Isa. xlii. 1-4.
2433. Ps. lxxxii.
2434. In the text there is certainly no distinction given. But if we read ὡς ἄνθρωπος (כְּאָדָם), "as a man," in the first quotation we shall be able to follow Justin's argument.
2435. The reading here is ἐπίσταμαι αὐτός, which is generally abandoned for ἀπατᾶν ἑαυτούς.
2436. Matt. xiii. 3.
2437. On Justin's Hebrew, see Kaye, p. 19.
2438. Matt. iv. 10.
2439. By Isaiah. "Counsellor" in English version.
2440. Ex. vi. 2 ff.

2441. Gen. xxxii. 24, 30.
2442. Gen. xviii. 2.
2443. Gen. xviii. 13 f.
2444. Gen. xviii. 16.
2445. Gen. xviii. 17.
2446. Num. xi. 23.
2447. Deut. xxxi. 2 f.
2448. ὅταυ πον instead of ὅταν μου.
2449. Gen. xviii. 22.
2450. Ex. vi. 29.
2451. Gen. xi. 5.
2452. Gen. vii. 16.
2453. Gen. xix. 24.
2454. Ps. xxiv. 7.
2455. Ps. cx. 1.
2456. Gen. iii. 22.
2457. Prov. viii. 22 ff.
2458. Deut. xxxii. 43.
2459. Isa. lxvi. 24.
2460. The reading is, "and calls them by the same name." But the whole argument shows that the Jews and Gentiles are distinguished by name. But that Gentiles are also called (Israel) by the same name is the point here.
2461. Deut. xxxii. 7 ff.
2462. Another Americanism. Greek, θεάσασθαι.
2463. The anacoluthon is in the original.
2464. See 1 Sam. v.
2465. Or, "by the power of the name." 1 Sam. vi. 14. Joshua in English version.
2466. Isa. iii. 9-15.
2467. Literally, "provoked."
2468. Literally, "turned away."
2469. Isa. v. 18-25.
2470. Isa. xliii. 15.
2471. Isa. xlii. 1-4.
2472. Isa. lxv. 9-12.
2473. Isa. ii. 5 f.
2474. Isa. lxv. 8 f.
2475. Isa. iii. 9.

2476. Zech. ii. 8.
2477. Justin's varied quotations of the same text seem to have been of purpose. But consult Kaye's most useful note as to the text of the LXX., in answer to objections of Wetstein, p. 20. ff.
2478. Isa. iii. 9.
2479. Isa. liv. 9 comes nearer to these words than any other passage; but still the exact quotation is not in Isaiah, or in any other part of Scripture. It is quite probable that Isa. liv. 9 was thus misunderstood by the Jews, as Trypho seems to acquiesce.
2480. But Justin goes on to show that it was prophetic foresight only: the curse cleaves only to wicked descendants, the authors of idolatry. It was removed by Christ. St. Matt. xv. 22-28.
2481. Gen. ix. 24-27.
2482. Jer. ii. 13.
2483. Isa. xxix. 13.
2484. Isa. i. 9.
2485. Ezek. xiv. 18, 20.
2486. Ezek. xviii. 20.
2487. Literally, "limbs."
2488. Isa. lxvi. 24.
2489. Matt. viii. 11 f.
2490. Chap. lxxxviii, cii.
2491. Ps. xxxii. 2.
2492. The last sentence is very dubious. For παντὶ ἀνθρώπινον νοῦν read παντὶ ἀνθρώπῳ τὸν νοῦν. For ποιήσητε read πιστεύσητε. And lastly, for τὸ ἡμῶν read τὸν Ἰησοῦν. But there is no doubt about the touching beauty of this close; and truly Trypho seems "not far from the kingdom of God." Note the marvellous knowledge of the Old Testament Scriptures, which Justin had acquired, and which he could use in conversation. His quotations from the Psalms, memoriter, are more accurate than others. See Kaye, p. 141.

The Discourse to the Greeks
[Translated by the Rev. M. Dods, M.A.]

Chapter I - Justin justifies his departure from Greek customs

Do not suppose, ye Greeks, that my separation from your customs is unreasonable and unthinking; for I found in them nothing that is holy or acceptable to God. For the very compositions of your poets are monuments of madness and intemperance. For any one who becomes the scholar of your most eminent instructor, is more beset by difficulties than all men besides. For first they say that Agamemnon, abetting the extravagant lust of his brother, and his madness and unrestrained desire, readily gave even his daughter to be sacrificed, and troubled all Greece that he might rescue Helen, who had been ravished by the leprous [2493] shepherd. But when in the course of the war they took captives, Agamemnon was himself taken captive by Chryseis, and for Briseis' sake kindled a feud with the son of Thetis. And Pelides himself, who crossed the river, [2494] overthrew Troy, and subdued Hector, this your hero became the slave of Polyxena, and was conquered by a dead Amazon; and putting off the god-fabricated armour, and donning the hymeneal robe, he became a sacrifice of love in the temple of Apollo. And the Ithacan Ulysses made a virtue of a vice. [2495] And indeed his sailing past the Sirens [2496] gave evidence that he was destitute of worthy prudence, because he could not depend on his prudence for stopping his ears. Ajax, son of Telamon, who bore the shield of sevenfold ox-hide, went mad when he was defeated in the contest with Ulysses for the armour. Such things I have no desire to be instructed in. Of such virtue I am not covetous, that I should believe the myths of Homer. For the whole rhapsody, the beginning and end both of the Iliad and the Odyssey is--a woman.

Chapter II - The Greek theogony exposed

But since, next to Homer, Hesiod wrote his Works and Days, who will believe his drivelling theogony? For they say that Chronos, the son of Ouranos, [2497] in the beginning slew his father, and possessed himself of his rule; and that, being seized with a panic lest he should himself suffer in the same way, he preferred devouring his children; but that, by the craft of the Curetes, Jupiter was conveyed away and kept in secret, and afterwards bound his father with chains, and divided the empire; Jupiter receiving, as the story goes, the air, and Neptune the deep, and Pluto the portion of Hades. But Pluto ravished Proserpine; and Ceres sought her child wandering through the deserts. And this myth was celebrated in the Eleusinian fire. [2498] Again, Neptune ravished Melanippe when she was drawing water, besides abusing a host of Nereids not a few, whose names, were we to recount them, would cost us a multitude of words. And as for Jupiter, he was a various adulterer, with Antiope as a satyr, with Danaë as gold, and with Europa as a bull; with Leda, moreover, he assumed wings. For the love of Semele proved both his unchastity and the jealousy of Semele. And they say that he carried off the Phrygian Ganymede to be his cup-bearer. These, then, are the exploits of the sons of Saturn. And your illustrious son of Latona [Apollo], who professed soothsaying, convicted himself of lying. He pursued Daphne, but did not gain possession of her; and to Hyacinthus, [2499] who loved him, he did not foretell his death. And I say nothing of the masculine character of Minerva, nor of the feminine nature of Bacchus, nor of the fornicating disposition of Venus. Read to Jupiter, ye Greeks, the law against parricides, and the penalty of adultery, and the ignominy of pæderasty. Teach Minerva and Diana the works of women, and Bacchus the works of men. What seemliness is there in a woman's girding herself with armour, or in a man's decorating himself with cymbals, and garlands, and female attire, and accompanied by a herd of bacchanalian women?

Chapter III - Follies of the Greek mythology

For Hercules, celebrated by his three nights, [2500] sung by the poets for his successful labours, the son of Jupiter, who slew the lion and destroyed the many-headed hydra; who put to death the fierce and mighty boar, and was able to kill the fleet man-eating birds, and brought up from Hades the three-headed dog; who effectually cleansed the huge Augean building from its dung, and killed the bulls and the stag whose nostrils breathed fire, and plucked the golden fruit from the tree, and slew the poisonous serpent (and for some reason, which it is not lawful to utter, killed Achelous, and the guest-slaying Busiris), and crossed the mountains that he might get water which gave forth an articulate speech, as the story goes: he who was able to do so many and such like and so great deeds as these, how childishly he was delighted to be stunned by the cymbals of the satyrs, and to be conquered by the love of woman, and to be struck on the hips by the laughing Lyda! And at last, not being able to put off the tunic of Nessus, himself kindling his own funeral pile, so he died. Let Vulcan lay aside his envy, and not be jealous if he is hated because he is old and club-footed, and Mars loved, because young and beautiful. Since, therefore, ye Greeks, your gods are convicted of intemperance, and your heroes are effeminate, as the histories on which your dramas are founded have declared, such as the curse of Atreus, the bed of Thyestes [2501] and the taint in the house of Pelops, and Danaus murdering through hatred and making Ægyptus childless in the intoxication of his rage, and the Thyestean banquet spread by the Furies. [2502] And Procne is to this day flitting about, lamenting; and her sister of Athens shrills with her tongue cut out. For what need is there of speaking of the goad [2503] of OEdipus, and the murder of Laius, and the marrying his mother, and the mutual slaughter of those who were at once his brothers and his sons?

Chapter IV - Shameless practices of the Greeks

And your public assemblies I have come to hate. For there are excessive banquetings, and subtle flutes which provoke to lustful movements, and useless and luxurious anointings, and crowning with garlands. With such a mass of evils do you banish shame; and ye fill your minds with them, and are carried away by intemperance, and indulge as a common practice in wicked and insane fornication. And this further I would say to you, why are you, being a Greek, indignant at your son when he imitates Jupiter, and rises against you and defrauds you of your own wife? Why do you count him your enemy, and yet worship one that is like him? And why do you blame your wife for living in unchastity, and yet honour Venus with shrines? If indeed these things had been related by others, they would have seemed to be mere slanderous accusations, and not truth. But now your own poets sing these things, and your histories noisily publish them.

Chapter V - Closing appeal

Henceforth, ye Greeks, come and partake of incomparable wisdom, and be instructed by the Divine Word, and acquaint yourselves with the King immortal; and do not recognise those men as heroes who slaughter whole nations. For our own Ruler, [2504] the Divine Word, who even now constantly aids us, does not desire strength of body and beauty of feature, nor yet the high spirit of earth's nobility, but a pure soul, fortified by holiness, and the watchwords of our King, holy actions, for through the Word power passes into the soul. O trumpet of peace to the soul that is at war! O weapon that puttest to flight terrible passions! O instruction that quenches the innate fire of the soul! The Word exercises an influence which does not make poets: it does not equip philosophers nor skilled orators, but by its instruction it makes mortals immortal, mortals gods; and from the earth transports them to the realms above Olympus. Come, be taught; become as I am, for I, too, was as ye are. [2505] These have conquered me--the divinity of the instruction, and the power of the Word: for as a skilled serpent-charmer lures the terrible reptile from his den and causes it to flee, so the Word drives the fearful passions of our sensual nature from the very recesses of the soul; first driving forth lust, through which every ill is begotten--hatreds, strife, envy, emulations, anger, and such like. Lust being once banished, the soul becomes calm and serene. And being set free from the ills in which it was sunk up to the neck, it returns to Him who made it. For it is fit that it be restored to that state whence it departed, whence every soul was or is. [2506]

Footnotes:

2493. Potter would here read λιπαροῦ, "elegant" ironically for effeminate.; but the above reading is defended by Sylburg, on the ground that shepherds were so greatly despised, that this is not too hard an epithet to apply to Paris.

2494. Of the many attempts to amend this clause, there seems to be none satisfactory.

2495. Or, won the reputation of the virtue of wisdom by the vice of deceit.

2496. That is, the manner in which he did it, stopping his companions' ears with wax, and having himself bound to the mast of his ship.

2497. Or, Saturn son of Heaven.

2498. In the mysteries of Eleusis, the return of Proserpine from the lower world was celebrated.

2499. Apollo accidentally killed Hyacinthus by striking him on the head with a quoit.

2500. Τριέσπερον, so called, as some think, from his origin: "ex concubitu trium noctium.".

2501. Thyestes seduced the wife of his brother Atreus, whence the tragic career of the family.

2502. There is no apodosis in the Greek.

2503. Not, as the editors dispute, either the tongue of the buckle with which he put out his eyes, nor the awl with which his heels were bored through, but the goad with which he killed his father.

2504. Αὐτὸς γὰρ ἡμῶν.

2505. He seems to quote Gal. iv. 12.

2506. N. B. --It should be stated that modern critics consider this work as not improbably by another author.

Justin's Hortatory Address to the Greeks
[Translated by the Rev. M. Dods, M.A.]

Chapter I - Reasons for addressing the Greeks

As I begin this hortatory address to you, ye men of Greece, I pray God that I may know what I ought to say to you, and that you, shaking off your habitual [2507] love of disputing, and being delivered from the error of your fathers, may now choose what is profitable; not fancying that you commit any offence against your forefathers, though the things which you formerly considered by no means salutary should now seem useful to you. For accurate investigation of matters, putting truth to the question with a more searching scrutiny, often reveals that things which have passed for excellent are of quite another sort. Since, then, we propose to discourse of the true religion (than which, I think, there is nothing which is counted more valuable by those who desire to pass through life without danger, on account of the judgment which is to be after the termination of this life, and which is announced not only by our forefathers according to God, to wit the prophets and lawgivers, but also by those among yourselves who have been esteemed wise, not poets alone, but also philosophers, who professed among you that they had attained the true and divine knowledge), I think it well first of all to examine the teachers of religion, both our own and yours, who they were, and how great, and in what times they lived; in order that those who have formerly received from their fathers the false religion, may now, when they perceive this, be extricated from that inveterate error; and that we may clearly and manifestly show that we ourselves follow the religion of our forefathers according to God.

Chapter II - The poets are unfit to be religious teachers

Whom, then, ye men of Greece, do ye call your teachers of religion? The poets? It will do your cause no good to say so to men who know the poets; for they know how very ridiculous a theogony they have composed,--as we can learn from Homer, your most distinguished and prince of poets. For he says, first, that the gods were in the beginning generated from water; for he has written thus: [2508] --

"Both ocean, the origin of the gods, and their mother Tethys"

And then we must also remind you of what he further says of him whom ye consider the first of the gods, and whom he often calls "the father of gods and men;" for he said: [2509] --

"Zeus, who is the dispenser of war to men."

Indeed, he says that he was not only the dispenser of war to the army, but also the cause of perjury to the Trojans, by means of his daughter; [2510] and Homer introduces him in love, and bitterly complaining, and bewailing himself, and plotted against by the other gods, and at one time exclaiming concerning his own son: [2511] --

"Alas! he falls, my most beloved of men!
Sarpedon, vanquished by Patroclus, falls.
So will the fates."

And at another time concerning Hector: [2512] --

"Ah! I behold a warrior dear to me
Around the walls of Ilium driven, and grieve
For Hector."

And what he says of the conspiracy of the other gods against Zeus, they know who read these words: [2513] "When the other Olympians--Juno, and Neptune, and Minerva --wished to bind him." And unless the blessed gods had feared him whom gods call Briareus, Zeus would have been bound by them. And what Homer says of his intemperate loves, we must remind you in the very words he used. For he said that Zeus spake thus to Juno: [2514] --

"For never goddess pour'd, nor woman yet,
So full a tide of love into my breast;
I never loved Ixion's consort thus,
Nor sweet Acrisian Danaë, from whom
Sprang Perseus, noblest of the race of man;
Nor Phoenix' daughter fair, of whom were born
Minos, unmatch'd but by the powers above,

And Rhadamanthus; nor yet Semele,
Nor yet Alcmene, who in Thebes produced
The valiant Hercules; and though my son
By Semele were Bacchus, joy of man;
Nor Ceres golden-hair'd, nor high-enthron'd
Latona in the skies; no--nor thyself
As now I love thee, and my soul perceive
O'erwhelm'd with sweetness of intense desire."

It is fit that we now mention what one can learn from the work of Homer of the other gods, and what they suffered at the hands of men. For he says that Mars and Venus were wounded by Diomed, and of many others of the gods he relates the sufferings. For thus we can gather from the case of Dione consoling her daughter; for she said to her: [2515] --

"Have patience, dearest child; though much enforc'd
Restrain thine anger: we, in heav'n who dwell,
Have much to bear from mortals; and ourselves
Too oft upon each other suff'rings lay:
Mars had his suff'rings; by Alöeus' sons,
Otus and Ephialtes, strongly bound,
He thirteen months in brazen fetters lay:
Juno, too, suffer'd, when Amphitryon's son
Thro' her right breast a three-barb'd arrow sent:
Dire, and unheard of, were the pangs she bore,
Great Pluto's self the stinging arrow felt,
When that same son of Ægis-bearing Jove
Assail'd him in the very gates of hell,
And wrought him keenest anguish; pierced with pain,
To high Olympus, to the courts of Jove,
Groaning, he came; the bitter shaft remain'd
Deep in his shoulder fix'd, and griev'd his soul."

But if it is right to remind you of the battle of the gods, opposed to one another, your own poet himself will recount it, saying: [2516] --

"Such was the shock when gods in battle met;
For there to royal Neptune stood oppos'd
Phoebus Apollo with his arrows keen;
The blue-eyed Pallas to the god of war;
To Juno, Dian, heav'nly archeress,
Sister of Phoebus, golden-shafted queen.
Stout Hermes, helpful god, Latona fac'd."

These and such like things did Homer teach you; and not Homer only, but also Hesiod. So that if you believe your most distinguished poets, who have given the genealogies of your gods, you must of necessity either suppose that the gods are such beings as these, or believe that there are no gods at all.

Chapter III - Opinions of the school of Thales

And if you decline citing the poets, because you say it is allowable for them to frame myths, and to relate in a mythical way many things about the gods which are far from true, do you suppose you have some others for your religious teachers, or how do you say that they themselves [2517] have learned this religion of yours? For it is impossible that any should know matters so great and divine, who have not themselves learned them first from the initiated. [2518] You will no doubt say, "The sages and philosophers." For to them, as to a fortified wall, you are wont to flee, when any one quotes the opinions of your poets about the gods. Therefore, since it is fit that we commence with the ancients and the earliest, beginning thence I will produce the opinion of each, much more ridiculous as it is than the theology of the poets. For Thales of Miletus, who took the lead in the study of natural philosophy, declared that water was the first principle of all things; for from water he says that all things are, and that into water all are resolved. And after him Anaximander, who came from the same Miletus, said that the infinite was the first principle of all things; for that from this indeed all things are produced, and into this do all decay. Thirdly, Anaximenes--and he too was from Miletus--says that air is the first principle of all things; for he says that from this all things are produced, and into this all are resolved. Heraclitus and Hippasus, from Metapontus, say that fire is the first principle of all things; for from fire all things proceed, and in fire do all things terminate. Anaxagoras of Clazomenæ said that the homogeneous parts are the first principles of all things. Archelaus, the son of Apollodorus, an Athenian, says that the infinite air and its density and rarity are the first principle of all things. All these, forming a succession from Thales, followed the philosophy called by themselves physical.

Chapter IV - Opinions of Pythagoras and Epicurus

Then, in regular succession from another starting-point, Pythagoras the Samian, son of Mnesarchus, calls numbers, with their proportions and harmonies, and the elements composed of both, the first principles; and he includes also unity and the indefinite binary. [2519] Epicurus, an Athenian, the son of Neocles, says that the first principles of the things that exist are bodies perceptible by reason, admitting no vacuity, [2520] unbegotten, indestructible, which can neither be broken, nor admit of any formation of their parts, nor alteration, and are therefore perceptible by reason. Empedocles of Agrigentum, son of Meton, maintained that there were four elements--fire, air, water, earth; and two elementary powers --love and hate, [2521] of which the former is a power of union, the latter of separation. You see, then, the confusion of those who are considered by you to have been wise men, whom you assert to be your teachers of religion: some of them declaring that water is the first principle of all things; others, air, others, fire; and others, some other of these fore-mentioned elements; and all of them employing persuasive arguments for the establishment of their own errors, and attempting to prove their own peculiar dogma to be the most valuable. These things were said by them. How then, ye men of Greece, can it be safe for those who desire to be saved, to fancy that they can learn the true religion from these philosophers, who were neither able so to convince themselves as to prevent sectarian wrangling with one another, and not to appear definitely opposed to one another's opinions?

Chapter V - Opinions of Plato and Aristotle

But possibly those who are unwilling to give up the ancient and inveterate error, maintain that they have received the doctrine of their religion not from those who have now been mentioned, but from those who are esteemed among them as the most renowned and finished philosophers, Plato and Aristotle. For these, they say, have learned the perfect and true religion. But I would be glad to ask, first of all, from those who say so, from whom they say that these men have learned this knowledge; for it is impossible that men who have not learned these so great and divine matters from some who knew them, should either themselves know them, or be able correctly to teach others; and, in the second place, I think we ought to examine the opinions even of these sages. For we shall see whether each of these does not manifestly contradict the other. But if we find that even they do not agree with each other, I think it is easy to see clearly that they too are ignorant. For Plato, with the air of one that has descended from above, and has accurately ascertained and seen all that is in heaven, says that the most high God exists in a fiery substance. [2522] But Aristotle, in a book addressed to Alexander of Macedon, giving a compendious explanation of his own philosophy, clearly and manifestly overthrows the opinion of Plato, saying that God does not exist in a fiery substance: but inventing, as a fifth substance, some kind of ætherial and unchangeable body, says that God exists in it. Thus, at least, he wrote: "Not, as some of those who have erred regarding the Deity say, that God exists in a fiery substance." Then, as if he were not satisfied with this blasphemy against Plato, he further, for the sake of proving what he says about the ætherial body, cites as a witness him whom Plato had banished from his republic as a liar, and as being an imitator of the images of truth at three removes, [2523] for so Plato calls Homer; for he wrote: "Thus at least did Homer speak, [2524] And Zeus obtained the wide heaven in the air and the clouds,' " wishing to make his own opinion appear more worthy of credit by the testimony of Homer; not being aware that if he used Homer as a witness to prove that he spoke truth, many of his tenets would be proved untrue. For Thales of Miletus, who was the founder of philosophy among them, taking occasion from him, [2525] will contradict his first opinions about first principles. For Aristotle himself, having said that God and matter are the first principles of all things, Thales, the eldest of all their sages, says that water is the first principle of the things that exist; for he says that all things are from water, and that all things are resolved into water. And he conjectures this, first, from the fact that the seed of all living creatures, which is their first principle, is moist; and secondly, because all plants grow and bear fruit in moisture, but when deprived of moisture, wither. Then, as if not satisfied with his conjectures, he cites Homer as a most trustworthy testimony, who speaks thus:--

"Ocean, who is the origin of all." [2526]

May not Thales, then, very fairly say to him, "What is the reason, Aristotle, why you give heed to Homer, as if he spoke truth, when you wish to demolish the opinions of Plato; but when you promulgate an opinion contrary to ours, you think Homer untruthful?"

Chapter VI - Further disagreements between Plato and Aristotle

And that these very wonderful sages of yours do not even agree in other respects, can be easily learned from this. For while Plato says that there are three first principles of all things, God, and matter, and form,--God, the maker of all; and matter, which is the subject of the first production of all that is produced, and affords to God opportunity for His workmanship; and form, which is the type of each of the things produced,-- Aristotle makes no mention at all of form as a first principle, but says that there are two, God and matter. And again, while Plato says that the highest God and the ideas exist in the first place of the highest heavens, and in fixed sphere, Aristotle says that, next to the most high God, there are, not ideas, but certain gods, who can be perceived by the mind. Thus, then, do they differ concerning things heavenly. So that one can see that they not only are unable to understand our earthly matters, but also, being at variance among themselves regarding these things, they will appear unworthy of credit when they treat of things heavenly. And that even their doctrine regarding the human soul as it now is does not harmonize, is manifest from what has been said by each of them concerning it. For Plato says that it is of three parts, having the faculty of reason, of affection, and of appetite. [2527] But Aristotle says that the soul is not so comprehensive as to include also corruptible parts, but only reason. And Plato loudly maintains that "the whole soul is immortal." But Aristotle, naming it "the actuality," [2528] would have it to be mortal, not immortal. And the former says it is always in motion; but Aristotle says that it is immoveable, since it must itself precede all motion.

Chapter VII - Inconsistencies of Plato's doctrine

But in these things they are convicted of thinking in contradiction to each other. And if any one will accurately criticise their writings, they have chosen to abide in harmony not even with their own opinions. Plato, at any rate, at one time says that there are three first principles of the universe--God, and matter, and form; but at another time four, for he adds the universal soul. And again, when he has already said that matter is eternal, [2529] he afterwards says that it is produced; and when he has first given to form its peculiar rank as a first principle, and has asserted for its self-subsistence, he afterwards says that this same thing is among the things perceived by the understanding. Moreover, having first declared that everything that is made is mortal [2530] he afterwards states that some of the things that are made are indestructible and immortal. What, then, is the cause why those who have been esteemed wise among you disagree not only with one another but also with themselves? Manifestly, their unwillingness to learn from those who know, and their desire to attain accurate knowledge of things heavenly by their own human excess of wisdom though they were able to understand not even earthly matters. Certainly some of your philosophers say that the human soul is in us; others, that it is around us. For not even in this did they choose to agree with one another, but, distributing, as it were, ignorance in various ways among themselves, they thought fit to wrangle and dispute with one another even about the soul. For some of them say that the soul is fire, and some that it is the air; and others, the mind; and others, motion; and others, an exhalation; and certain others say that it is a power flowing from the stars; and others, number capable of motion; and others, a generating water. And a wholly confused and inharmonious opinion has prevailed among them, which only in this one respect appears praiseworthy to those who can form a right judgment, that they have been anxious to convict one another of error and falsehood.

Chapter VIII - Antiquity, inspiration, and harmony of Christian teachers

Since therefore it is impossible to learn anything true concerning religion from your teachers, who by their mutual disagreement have furnished you with sufficient proof of their own ignorance, I consider it reasonable to recur to our progenitors, who both in point of time have by a great way the precedence of your teachers, and who have taught us nothing from their own private fancy, nor differed with one another, nor attempted to overturn one another's positions, but without wrangling and contention received from God the knowledge which also they taught to us. For neither by nature nor by human conception is it possible for men to know things so great and divine, but by the gift which then descended from above upon the holy men, who had no need of rhetorical art, [2531] nor of uttering anything in a contentious or quarrelsome manner, but to present themselves pure [2532] to the energy of the Divine Spirit, in order that the divine plectrum itself, descending from heaven, and using righteous men as an instrument like a harp or lyre, might reveal to us the knowledge of things divine and heavenly. Wherefore, as if with one mouth and one tongue, they have in succession, and in harmony with one another, taught us both concerning God, and the creation of the world, and the formation of man, and concerning the immortality of the human soul, and the judgment which is to be after this life, and concerning all things which it is needful for us to know, and thus in divers times and places have afforded us the divine instruction. [2533]

Chapter IX - The antiquity of Moses proved by Greek writers

I will begin, then, with our first prophet and lawgiver, Moses; first explaining the times in which he lived, on authorities which among you are worthy of all credit. For I do not propose to prove these things only from our own divine histories, which as yet you are unwilling to credit on account of the inveterate error of your forefathers, but also from your own histories, and such, too, as have no reference to our worship, that you may know that, of all your teachers, whether sages, poets, historians, philosophers, or lawgivers, by far the oldest, as the Greek histories show us, was Moses, who was our first religious teacher. [2534] For in the times of Ogyges and Inachus, whom some of your poets suppose to have been earth-born, [2535] Moses is mentioned as the leader and ruler of the Jewish nation. For in this way he is mentioned both by Polemon in the first book of his Hellenics, and by Apion son of Posidonius in his book against the Jews, and in the fourth book of his history, where he says that during the reign of Inachus over Argos the Jews revolted from Amasis king of the Egyptians, and that Moses led them. And Ptolemæus the Mendesian, in relating the history of Egypt, concurs in all this. And those who write the Athenian history, Hellanicus and Philochorus (the author of The Attic History), Castor and Thallus, and Alexander Polyhistor, and also the very well informed writers on Jewish affairs, Philo and Josephus, have mentioned Moses as a very ancient and time-honoured prince of the Jews. Josephus, certainly, desiring to signify even by the title of his work the antiquity and age of the history, wrote thus at the commencement of the history: "The Jewish antiquities [2536] of Flavius Josephus,"--signifying the oldness of the history by the word "antiquities." And your most renowned historian Diodorus, who employed thirty whole years in epitomizing the libraries, and who, as he himself wrote, travelled over both Asia and Europe for the sake of great accuracy, and thus became an eye-witness of very many things, wrote forty entire books of his own history. And he in the first book, having said that he had learned from the Egyptian priests that Moses was an ancient lawgiver, and even the first, wrote of him in these very words: "For subsequent to the ancient manner of living in Egypt which gods and heroes are fabled to have regulated, they say that Moses [2537] first persuaded the people to use written laws, and to live by them; and he is recorded to have been a man both great of soul and of great faculty in social matters." Then, having proceeded a little further, and wishing to mention the ancient lawgivers, he mentions Moses first. For he spoke in these words: "Among the Jews they say that Moses ascribed his laws [2538] to that God who is called Jehovah, whether because they judged it a marvellous and quite divine conception which promised to benefit a multitude of men, or because they were of opinion that the people would be the more obedient when they contemplated the majesty and power of those who were said to have invented the laws. And they say that Sasunchis was the second Egyptian legislator, a man of excellent understanding. And the third, they say, was Sesonchosis the king, who not only performed the most brilliant military exploits of any in Egypt, but also consolidated that warlike race by legislation. And the fourth lawgiver, they say, was Bocchoris the king, a wise and surpassingly skilful man. And after him it is said that Amasis the king acceded to the government, whom they relate to have regulated all that pertains to the rulers of provinces, and to the general administration of the government of Egypt. And they say that Darius, the father of Xerxes, was the sixth who legislated for the Egyptians."

Chapter X - Training and inspiration of Moses [2539]

These things, ye men of Greece, have been recorded in writing concerning the antiquity of Moses by those who were not of our religion; and they said that they learned all these things from the Egyptian priests, among whom Moses was not only born, but also was thought worthy of partaking of all the education of the Egyptians, on account of his being adopted by the king's daughter as her son; and for the same reason was thought worthy of great attention, as the wisest of the historians relate, who have chosen to record his life and actions, and the rank of his descent, --I speak of Philo and Josephus. For these, in their narration of the history of the Jews, say that Moses was sprung from the race of the Chaldæans, and that he was born in Egypt when his forefathers had migrated on account of famine from Phoenicia to that country; and him God chose to honour on account of his exceeding virtue, and judged him worthy to become the leader and lawgiver of his own race, when He thought it right that the people of the Hebrews should return out of Egypt into their own land. To him first did God communicate that divine and prophetic gift which in those days descended upon the holy men, and him also did He first furnish that he might be our teacher in religion, and then after him the rest of the prophets, who both obtained the same gift as he, and taught us the same doctrines concerning the same subjects. These we assert to have been our teachers, who taught us nothing from their own human conception, but from the gift vouchsafed to them by God from above.

Chapter XI - Heathen oracles testify of Moses

But as you do not see the necessity of giving up the ancient error of your forefathers in obedience to these teachers [of ours], what teachers of your own do you maintain to have lived worthy of credit in the matter of religion? For, as I have frequently said, it is impossible that those who have not themselves learned these so great and divine things from such persons as are acquainted with them, should either themselves know them, or be able rightly to teach others. Since, therefore, it has been sufficiently proved that the opinions of your philosophers are obviously full of all ignorance and deceit, having now perhaps wholly abandoned the philosophers as formerly you abandoned the poets, you will turn to the deceit of the oracles; for in this style I have heard some speaking. Therefore I think it fit to tell you at this step in our discourse what I formerly heard among you concerning their utterances. For when one inquired at your oracle--it is your own story--what religious men had at any time happened to live, you say that the oracle answered thus: "Only the Chaldæans have obtained wisdom, and the Hebrews, who worship God Himself, the self-begotten King."

Since, therefore, you think that the truth can be learned from your oracles, when you read the histories and what has been written regarding the life of Moses by those who do not belong to our religion, and when you know that Moses and the rest of the prophets were descended from the race of the Chaldæans and Hebrews, do not think that anything incredible has taken place if a man sprung from a godly line, and who lived worthily of the godliness of his fathers, was chosen by God to be honoured with this great gift and to be set forth as the first of all the prophets.

Chapter XII - Antiquity of Moses proved

And I think it necessary also to consider the times in which your philosophers lived, that you may see that the time which produced them for you is very recent, and also short. For thus you will be able easily to recognise also the antiquity of Moses. But lest, by a complete survey of the periods, and by the use of a greater number of proofs, I should seem to be prolix, I think it may be sufficiently demonstrated from the following. For Socrates was the teacher of Plato, and Plato of Aristotle. Now these men flourished in the time of Philip and Alexander of Macedon, in which time also the Athenian orators flourished, as the Philippics of Demosthenes plainly show us. And those who have narrated the deeds of Alexander sufficiently prove that during his reign Aristotle associated with him. From all manner of proofs, then, it is easy to see that the history of Moses is by far more ancient than all profane [2540] histories. And, besides, it is fit that you recognise this fact also, that nothing has been accurately recorded by Greeks before the era of the Olympiads, and that there is no ancient work which makes known any action of the Greeks or Barbarians. But before that period existed only the history of the prophet Moses, which he wrote in the Hebrew character by the divine inspiration. For the Greek character was not yet in use, as the teachers of language themselves prove, telling us that Cadmus first brought the letters from Phoenicia, and communicated them to the Greeks. And your first of philosophers, Plato, testifies that they were a recent discovery. For in the Timæus [2541] he wrote that Solon, the wisest of the wise men, on his return from Egypt, said to Critias that he had heard this from a very aged Egyptian priest, who said to him, "O Solon, Solon, you Greeks are ever children, and aged Greek there is none." Then again he said, "You are all youths in soul, for you hold no ancient opinion derived through remote tradition, nor any system of instruction hoary with time; but all these things escape your knowledge, because for many generations the posterity of these ancient ages died mute, not having the use of letters." It is fit, therefore, that you understand that it is the fact that every history has been written in these recently-discovered Greek letters; and if any one would make mention of old poets, or legislators, or historians, or philosophers, or orators, he will find that they wrote their own works in the Greek character.

Chapter XIII - History of the Septuagint

But if any one says that the writings of Moses and of the rest of the prophets were also written in the Greek character, let him read profane histories, and know that Ptolemy, king of Egypt, when he had built the library in Alexandria, and by gathering books from every quarter had filled it, then learnt that very ancient histories written in Hebrew happened to be carefully preserved; and wishing to know their contents, he sent for seventy wise men from Jerusalem, who were acquainted with both the Greek and Hebrew language, and appointed them to translate the books; and that in freedom from all disturbance they might the more speedily complete the translation, he ordered that there should be constructed, not in the city itself, but seven stadia off (where the Pharos was built), as many little cots as there were translators, so that each by himself might complete his own translation; and enjoined upon those officers who were appointed to this duty, to afford them all attendance, but to prevent communication with one another, in order that the accuracy of the translation might be discernible even by their agreement. And when he ascertained that the seventy men had not only given the same meaning, but had employed the same words, and had failed in agreement with one another not even to the extent of one word; but had written the same things, and concerning the same things, he was struck with amazement, and believed that the translation had been written by divine power, and perceived that the men were worthy of all honour, as beloved of God; and with many gifts ordered them to return to their own country. And having, as was natural, marvelled at the books, and concluded them to be divine, he consecrated them in that library. These things, ye men of Greece, are no fable, nor do we narrate fictions; but we ourselves having been in Alexandria, saw the remains of the little cots at the Pharos still preserved, and having heard these things from the inhabitants, who had received them as part of their country's tradition, [2542] we now tell to you what you can also learn from others, and specially from those wise and esteemed men who have written of these things, Philo and Josephus, and many others. But if any of those who are wont to be forward in contradiction should say that these books do not belong to us, but to the Jews, and should assert that we in vain profess to have learnt our religion from them, let him know, as he may from those very things which are written in these books, that not to them, but to us, does the doctrine of them refer. That the books relating to our religion are to this day preserved among the Jews, has been a work of Divine Providence on our behalf; for lest, by producing them out of the Church, we should give occasion to those who wish to slander us to charge us with fraud, we demand that they be produced from the synagogue of the Jews, that from the very books still preserved among them it might clearly and evidently appear, that the laws which were written by holy men for instruction pertain to us.

Chapter XIV - A warning appeal to the Greeks

It is therefore necessary, ye Greeks, that you contemplate the things that are to be, and consider the judgment which is predicted by all, not only by the godly, but also by those who are irreligious, that ye do not without investigation commit yourselves to the error of your fathers, nor suppose that if they themselves have been in error, and have transmitted it to you, that this which they have taught you is true, but looking to the danger of so terrible a mistake, inquire and investigate carefully into those things which are, as you say, spoken of even by your own teachers. For even unwillingly they were on your account forced to say many things by the Divine regard for mankind, especially those of them who were in Egypt, and profited by the godliness of Moses and his ancestry. For I think that some of you, when you read even carelessly the history of Diodorus, and of those others who wrote of these things, cannot fail to see that both Orpheus, and Homer, and Solon, who wrote the laws of the Athenians, and Pythagoras, and Plato, and some others, when they had been in Egypt, and had taken advantage of the history of Moses, afterwards published doctrines concerning the gods quite contrary to those which formerly they had erroneously promulgated.

Chapter XV - Testimony of Orpheus to monotheism

At all events, we must remind you what Orpheus, who was, as one might say, your first teacher of polytheism, latterly addressed to his son Musæus, and to the other legitimate auditors, concerning the one and only God. And he spoke thus:--

"I speak to those who lawfully may hear:
All others, ye profane, now close the doors,
And, O Musæus! hearken thou to me,
Who offspring art of the light-bringing moon:
The words I utter now are true indeed;
And if thou former thoughts of mine hast seen,
Let them not rob thee of the blessed life,
But rather turn the depths of thine own heart
Unto the place where light and knowledge dwell.
Take thou the word divine to guide thy steps,
And walking well in the straight certain path,
Look to the one and universal King--
One, self-begotten, and the only One,
Of whom all things and we ourselves are sprung.
All things are open to His piercing gaze,
While He Himself is still invisible.
Present in all His works, though still unseen,
He gives to mortals evil out of good,
Sending both chilling wars and tearful griefs;
And other than the great King there is none.
The clouds for ever settle round His throne,
And mortal eyeballs in mere mortal eyes

Are weak, to see Jove reigning over all.
He sits established in the brazen heavens
Upon His golden throne; under His feet
He treads the earth, and stretches His right hand
To all the ends of ocean, and around
Tremble the mountain ranges and the streams,
The depths, too, of the blue and hoary sea."

And again, in some other place he says:--

"There is one Zeus alone, one sun, one hell,
One Bacchus; and in all things but one God;
Nor of all these as diverse let me speak."

And when he swears he says:--

"Now I adjure thee by the highest heaven,
The work of the great God, the only wise;
And I adjure thee by the Father's voice,
Which first He uttered when He stablished
The whole world by His counsel."

What does he mean by "I adjure thee by the Father's voice, which first He uttered?" It is the Word of God which he here names "the voice," by whom heaven and earth and the whole creation were made, as the divine prophecies of the holy men teach us; and these he himself also paid some attention to in Egypt, and understood that all creation was made by the Word of God; and therefore, after he says, "I adjure thee by the Father's voice, which first He uttered," he adds this besides, "when by His counsel He established the whole world." Here he calls the Word "voice," for the sake of the poetical metre. And that this is so, is manifest from the fact, that a little further on, where the metre permits him, he names it "Word." For he said:--

"Take thou the Word divine to guide thy steps."

Chapter XVI - Testimony of the Sibyl

We must also mention what the ancient and exceedingly remote Sibyl, whom Plato and Aristophanes, and others besides, mention as a prophetess, taught you in her oracular verses concerning one only God. And she speaks thus:--

"There is one only unbegotten God,
Omnipotent, invisible, most high,
All-seeing, but Himself seen by no flesh."

Then elsewhere thus:--

"But we have strayed from the Immortal's ways,
And worship with a dull and senseless mind
Idols, the workmanship of our own hands,
And images and figures of dead men."

And again somewhere else:--

"Blessed shall be those men upon the earth
Who shall love the great God before all else,
Blessing Him when they eat and when they drink;
Trusting in this their piety alone.
Who shall abjure all shrines which they may see,
All altars and vain figures of dumb stones,
Worthless and stained with blood of animals,
And sacrifice of the four-footed tribes,
Beholding the great glory of One God."

These are the Sibyl's words.

Chapter XVII - Testimony of Homer

And the poet Homer, using the license of poetry, and rivalling the original opinion of Orpheus regarding the plurality of the gods, mentions, indeed, several gods in a mythical style, lest he should seem to sing in a different strain from the poem of Orpheus, which he so distinctly proposed to rival, that even in the first line of his poem he indicated the relation he held to him. For as Orpheus in the beginning of his poem had said, "O goddess, sing the wrath of Demeter, who brings the goodly fruit," Homer began thus, "O goddess, sing the wrath of Achilles, son of Peleus," preferring, as it seems to me, even to violate the poetical metre in his first line, than that he should seem not to have remembered before all else the names of the gods. But shortly after he also clearly and explicitly presents his own opinion regarding one God only, somewhere [2543] saying to Achilles by the mouth of Phoenix, "Not though God Himself were to promise that He would peel off my old age, and give me the vigour of my youth," where he indicates by the pronoun the real and true God. And somewhere [2544] he makes Ulysses address the host of the Greeks thus: "The rule of many is not a good thing; let there be one ruler." And that the rule of many is not a good thing, but on the contrary an evil, he proposed to evince by fact, recounting the wars which took place on account of the multitude of rulers, and the fights and factions, and their mutual counterplots. For monarchy is free from contention. So far the poet Homer.

Chapter XVIII - Testimony of Sophocles

And if it is needful that we add testimonies concerning one God, even from the dramatists, hear even Sophocles speaking thus:--

"There is one God, in truth there is but one,
Who made the heavens and the broad earth beneath,
The glancing waves of ocean and the winds
But many of us mortals err in heart,
And set up for a solace in our woes
Images of the gods in stone and wood,
Or figures carved in brass or ivory,
And, furnishing for these our handiworks,
Both sacrifice and rite magnificent,
We think that thus we do a pious work."

Thus, then, Sophocles.

Chapter XIX - Testimony of Pythagoras

And Pythagoras, son of Mnesarchus, who expounded the doctrines of his own philosophy, mystically by means of symbols, as those who have written his life show, himself seems to have entertained thoughts about the unity of God not unworthy of his foreign residence in Egypt. For when he says that unity is the first principle of all things, and that it is the cause of all good, he teaches by an allegory that God is one, and alone. [2545] And that this is so, is evident from his saying that unity and one differ widely from one another. For he says that unity belongs to the class of things perceived by the mind, but that one belongs to numbers. And if you desire to see a clearer proof of the opinion of Pythagoras concerning one God, hear his own opinion, for he spoke as follows: "God is one; and He Himself does not, as some suppose, exist outside the world, but in it, He being wholly present in the whole circle, and beholding all generations; being the regulating ingredient of all the ages, and the administrator of His own powers and works, the first principle of all things, the light of heaven, and Father of all, the intelligence and animating soul of the universe, the movement of all orbits." Thus, then, Pythagoras.

Chapter XX - Testimony of Plato

But Plato, though he accepted, as is likely, the doctrine of Moses and the other prophets regarding one only God, which he learned while in Egypt, yet fearing, on account of what had befallen Socrates, lest he also should raise up some Anytus or Meletus against himself, who should accuse him before the Athenians, and say, "Plato is doing harm, and making himself mischievously busy, not acknowledging the gods recognised by the state;" in fear of the hemlock-juice, contrives an elaborate and ambiguous discourse concerning the gods, furnishing by his treatise gods to those who wish them, and none for those who are differently disposed, as may readily be seen from his own statements. For when he has laid down that everything that is made is mortal, he afterwards says that the gods were made. If, then, he would have God and matter to be the origin of all things, manifestly it is inevitably necessary to say that the gods were made of matter; but if of matter, out of which he said that evil also had its origin, he leaves right-thinking persons to consider what kind of beings the gods should be thought who are produced out of matter. For, for this very reason did he say that matter was eternal, [2546] that he might not seem to say that God is the creator of evil. And regarding the gods who were made by God, there is no doubt he said this: "Gods of gods, of whom I am the creator." And he manifestly held the correct opinion concerning the really existing God. For having heard in Egypt that God had said to Moses, when He was about to send him to the Hebrews, "I am that I am," [2547] he understood that God had not mentioned to him His own proper name.

Chapter XXI - The namelessness of God

For God cannot be called by any proper name, for names are given to mark out and distinguish their subject-matters, because these are many and diverse; but neither did any one exist before God who could give Him a name, nor did He Himself think it right to name Himself, seeing that He is one and unique, as He Himself also by His own prophets testifies, when He says, "I God am the first," and after this, "And beside me there is no other God." [2548] On this account, then, as I before said, God did not, when He sent Moses to the Hebrews, mention any name, but by a participle He mystically teaches them that He is the one and only God. "For," says He; "I am the Beingi;" manifestly contrasting Himself, "the Being," with those who are not, [2549] that those who had hitherto been deceived might see that they were attaching themselves, not to beings, but to those who had no being. Since, therefore, God knew that the first men remembered the old delusion of their forefathers, whereby the misanthropic demon contrived to deceive them when he said to them, "If ye obey me in transgressing the commandment of God, ye shall be as gods," calling those gods which had no being, in order that men, supposing that there were other gods in existence, might believe that they themselves could become gods. On this account He said to Moses, "I am the Being," that by the participle "being" He might teach the difference between God who is and those who are not. [2550] Men, therefore, having been duped by the deceiving demon, and having dared to disobey God, were cast out of Paradise, remembering the name of gods, but no longer being taught by God that there are no other gods. For it was not just that they who did not keep the first commandment, which it was easy to keep, should any longer be taught, but should rather be driven to just punishment. Being therefore banished from Paradise, and thinking that they were expelled on account of their disobedience only, not knowing that it was also because they had believed in the existence of gods which did not exist, they gave the name of gods even to the men who were afterwards born of themselves. This first false fancy, therefore, concerning gods, had its origin with the father of lies. God, therefore, knowing that the false opinion about the plurality of gods was burdening the soul of man like some disease, and wishing to remove and eradicate it, appeared first to Moses, and said to him, "I am He who is." For it was necessary, I think, that he who was to be the ruler and leader of the Hebrew people should first of all know the living God. Wherefore, having appeared to him first, as it was possible for God to appear to a man, He said to him, "I am He who is;" then, being about to send him to the Hebrews, He further orders him to say, "He who is hath sent me to you."

Chapter XXII - Studied ambiguity of Plato

Plato accordingly having learned this in Egypt, and being greatly taken with what was said about one God, did indeed consider it unsafe to mention the name of Moses, on account of his teaching the doctrine of one only God, for he dreaded the Areopagus; but what is very well expressed by him in his elaborate treatise, the Timæus, he has written in exact correspondence with what Moses said regarding God, though he has done so, not as if he had learned it from him, but as if he were expressing his own opinion. For he said, "In my opinion, then, we must first define what that is which exists eternally, and has no generation, [2551] and what that is which is always being generated, but never really is." Does not this, ye men of Greece, seem to those who are able to understand the matter to be one and the same thing, saving only the difference of the article? For Moses said, "He who is," and Plato, "That which is." But either of the expressions seems to apply to the ever-existent God. For He is the only one who eternally exists, and has no generation. What, then, that other thing is which is contrasted with the ever-existent, and of which he said, "And what that is which is always being generated, but never really is," we must attentively consider. For we shall find him clearly and evidently saying that He who is unbegotten is eternal, but that those that are begotten and made are generated and perish [2552] --as he said of the same class, "gods of gods, of whom I am maker"--for he speaks in the following words: "In my opinion, then, we must first define what that is which is always existent and has no birth, and what that is which is always being generated but never really is. The former, indeed, which is apprehended by reflection combined with reason, always exists in the same way; [2553] while the latter, on the other hand, is conjectured by opinion formed by the perception of the senses unaided by reason, since it never really is, but is coming into being and perishing." These expressions declare to those who can rightly understand them the death and destruction of the gods that have been brought into being. And I think it necessary to attend to this also, that Plato never names him the creator, but the fashioner [2554] of the gods, although, in the opinion of Plato, there is considerable difference between these two. For the creator creates the creature by his own capability and power, being in need of nothing else; but the fashioner frames his production when he has received from matter the capability for his work.

Chapter XXIII - Plato's self-contradiction

But, perhaps, some who are unwilling to abandon the doctrines of polytheism, will say that to these fashioned gods the maker said, "Since ye have been produced, ye are not immortal, nor at all imperishable; yet shall ye not perish nor succumb to the fatality of death, because you have obtained my will, [2555] which is a still greater and mightier bond." Here Plato, through fear of the adherents of polytheism, introduces his "maker" uttering words which contradict himself. For having formerly stated that he said that everything which is produced is perishable, he now introduces him saying the very opposite; and he does not see that it is thus absolutely impossible for him to escape the charge of falsehood. For he either at first uttered what is false when he said that everything which is produced is perishable, or now, when he propounds the very opposite to what he had formerly said. For if, according to his former definition, it is absolutely necessary that every created thing be perishable, how can he consistently make that possible which is absolutely impossible? So that Plato seems to grant an empty and impossible prerogative to his "maker," when he propounds that those who were once perishable because made from matter should again, by his intervention, become imperishable and enduring. For it is quite natural that the power of matter, which, according to Plato's opinion, is uncreated, and contemporary and coæval with the maker, should resist his will. For he who has not created has no power, in respect of that which is uncreated, so that it is not possible that it (matter), being free, can be controlled by any external necessity. Wherefore Plato himself, in consideration of this, has written thus: "It is necessary to affirm that God cannot suffer violence."

Chapter XXIV - Agreement of Plato and Homer

How, then, does Plato banish Homer from his republic, since, in the embassy to Achilles, he represents Phoenix as saying to Achilles, "Even the gods themselves are not inflexible," [2556] though Homer said this not of the king and Platonic maker of the gods, but of some of the multitude whom the Greeks esteem as gods, as one can gather from Plato's saying, "gods of gods?" For Homer, by that golden chain, [2557] refers all power and might to the one highest God. And the rest of the gods, he said, were so far distant from his divinity, that he thought fit to name them even along with men. At least he introduces Ulysses saying of Hector to Achilles, "He is raging terribly, trusting in Zeus, and values neither men nor gods." [2558] In this passage Homer seems to me without doubt to have learnt in Egypt, like Plato, concerning the one God, and plainly and openly to declare this, that he who trusts in the really existent God makes no account of those that do not exist. For thus the poet, in another passage, and employing another but equivalent word, to wit, a pronoun, made use of the same participle employed by Plato to designate the really existent God, concerning whom Plato said, "What that is which always exists, and has no birth." For not without a double sense does this expression of Phoenix seem to have been used: "Not even if God Himself were to promise me, that, having burnished off my old age, He should set me forth in the flower of youth." For the pronoun "Himself" signifies the really existing God. For thus, too, the oracle which was given to you concerning the Chaldæans and Hebrews signifies. For when some one inquired what men had ever lived godly, you say the answer was:--

"Only the Chaldæans and the Hebrews found wisdom,
Worshipping God Himself, the unbegotten King."

Chapter XXV - Plato's knowledge of God's eternity

How, then, does Plato blame Homer for saying that the gods are not inflexible, although, as is obvious from the expressions used, Homer said this for a useful purpose? For it is the property of those who expect to obtain mercy by prayer and sacrifices, to cease from and repent of their sins. For those who think that the Deity is inflexible, are by no means moved to abandon their sins, since they suppose that they will derive no benefit from repentance. How, then, does Plato the philosopher condemn the poet Homer for saying, "Even the gods themselves are not inflexible," and yet himself represent the maker of the gods as so easily turned, that he sometimes declares the gods to be mortal, and at other times declares the same to be immortal? And not only concerning them, but also concerning matter, from which, as he says, it is necessary that the created gods have been produced, he sometimes says that it is uncreated, and at other times that it is created; and yet he does not see that he himself, when he says that the maker of the gods is so easily turned, is convicted of having fallen into the very errors for which he blames Homer, though Homer said the very opposite concerning the maker of the gods. For he said that he spoke thus of himself:--

"For ne'er my promise shall deceive, or fail,
Or be recall'd, if with a nod confirm'd." [2559]

But Plato, as it seems, unwillingly entered not these strange dissertations concerning the gods, for he feared those who were attached to polytheism. And whatever he thinks fit to tell of all that he had learned from Moses and the prophets concerning one God, he preferred delivering in a mystical style, so that those who desired to be worshippers of God might have an inkling of his own opinion. For being charmed with that saying of God to Moses, "I am the really existing," and accepting with a great deal of thought the brief participial expression, he understood that God desired to signify to Moses His eternity, and therefore said, "I am the really existing;" for this word "existing" expresses not one time only, but the three--the past, the present, and the future. For when Plato says, "and which never really is," he uses the verb "is" of time indefinite. For the word "never" is not spoken, as some suppose, of the past, but of the future time. And this has been accurately understood even by profane writers. And therefore, when Plato wished, as it were, to interpret to the uninitiated what had been mystically expressed by the participle concerning the eternity of God, he employed the following language: "God indeed, as the old tradition runs, includes the beginning, and end, and middle of all things." In this sentence he plainly and obviously names the law of Moses "the old tradition," fearing, through dread of the hemlock-cup, to mention the name of Moses; for he understood that the teaching of the man was hateful to the Greeks; and he clearly enough indicates Moses by the antiquity of the tradition. And we have sufficiently proved from Diodorus and the rest of the historians, in the foregoing chapters, that the law of Moses is not only old, but even the first. For Diodorus says that he was the first of all lawgivers; the letters which belong to the Greeks, and which they employed in the writing of their histories, having not yet been discovered.

Chapter XXVI - Plato indebted to the prophets

And let no one wonder that Plato should believe Moses regarding the eternity of God. For you will find him mystically referring the true knowledge of realities to the prophets, next in order after the really existent God. For, discoursing in the Timæus about certain first principles, he wrote thus: "This we lay down as the first principle of fire and the other bodies, proceeding according to probability and necessity. But the first principles of these again God above knows, and whosoever among men is beloved of Him." [2560] And what men does he think beloved of God, but Moses and the rest of the prophets? For their prophecies he read, and, having learned from them the doctrine of the judgment, he thus proclaims it in the first book of the Republic: "When a man begins to think he is soon to die, fear invades him, and concern about things which had never before entered his head. And those stories about what goes on in Hades, which tell us that the man who has here been unjust must there be punished, though formerly ridiculed, now torment his soul with apprehensions that they may be true. And he, either through the feebleness of age, or even because he is now nearer to the things of the other world, views them more attentively. He becomes, therefore, full of apprehension and dread, and begins to call himself to account, and to consider whether he has done any one an injury. And that man who finds in his life many iniquities, and who continually starts from his sleep as children do, lives in terror, and with a forlorn prospect. But to him who is conscious of no wrong-doing, sweet hope is the constant companion and good nurse of old age, as Pindar says. [2561] For this, Socrates, he has elegantly expressed, that whoever leads a life of holiness and justice, him sweet hope, the nurse of age, accompanies, cheering his heart, for she powerfully sways the changeful mind of mortals.' " [2562] This Plato wrote in the first book of the Republic.

Chapter XXVII - Plato's knowledge of the judgment

And in the tenth book he plainly and manifestly wrote what he had learned from the prophets about the judgment, not as if he had learned it from them, but, on account of his fear of the Greeks, as if he had heard it from a man who had been slain in battle--for this story he thought fit to invent-- and who, when he was about to be buried on the twelfth day, and was lying on the funeral pile, came to life again, and described the other world. The following are his very words: [2563] "For he said that he was present when one was asked by another person where the great Ardiæus was. This Ardiæus had been prince in a certain city of Pamphylia, and had killed his aged father and his elder brother, and done many other unhallowed deeds, as was reported. He said, then, that the person who was asked said: He neither comes nor ever will come hither. For we saw, among other terrible sights, this also. When we were close to the mouth [of the pit], and were about to return to the upper air, and had suffered everything else, we suddenly beheld both him and others likewise, most of whom were tyrants. But there were also some private sinners who had committed great crimes. And these, when they thought they were to ascend, the mouth would not permit, but bellowed when any of those who were so incurably wicked attempted to ascend, unless they had paid the full penalty. Then fierce men, fiery to look at, stood close by, and hearing the din, [2564] took some and led them away; but Ardiæus and the rest, having bound hand and foot, and striking their heads down, and flaying, they dragged to the road outside, tearing them with thorns, and signifying to those who were present the cause of their suffering these things, and that they were leading them away to cast them into Tartarus. Hence, he said, that amidst all their various fears, this one was the greatest, lest the mouth should bellow when they ascended, since if it were silent each one would most gladly ascend; and that the punishments and torments were such as these, and that, on the other hand, the rewards were the reverse of these." Here Plato seems to me to have learnt from the prophets not only the doctrine of the judgment, but also of the resurrection, which the Greeks refuse to believe. For his saying that the soul is judged along with the body, proves nothing more clearly than that he believed the doctrine of the resurrection. Since how could Ardiæus and the rest have undergone such punishment in Hades, had they left on earth the body, with its head, hands, feet, and skin? For certainly they will never say that the soul has a head and hands, and feet and skin. But Plato, having fallen in with the testimonies of the prophets in Egypt, and having accepted what they teach concerning the resurrection of the body, teaches that the soul is judged in company with the body.

Chapter XXVIII - Homer's obligations to the sacred writers

And not only Plato, but Homer also, having received similar enlightenment in Egypt, said that Tityus was in like manner punished. For Ulysses speaks thus to Alcinous when he is recounting his divination by the shades of the dead: [2565] --

"There Tityus, large and long, in fetters bound,
O'erspread nine acres of infernal ground;
Two ravenous vultures, furious for their food,
Scream o'er the fiend, and riot in his blood,
Incessant gore the liver in his breast,
Th' immortal liver grows, and gives th' immortal feast."

For it is plain that it is not the soul, but the body, which has a liver. And in the same manner he has described both Sisyphus and Tantalus as enduring punishment with the body. And that Homer had been in Egypt, and introduced into his own poem much of what he there learnt, Diodorus, the most esteemed of historians, plainly enough teaches us. For he said that when he was in Egypt he had learnt that Helen, having received from Theon's wife, Polydamna, a drug, "lulling all sorrow and melancholy, and causing forgetfulness of all ills," [2566] brought it to Sparta. And Homer said that by making use of that drug Helen put an end to the lamentation of Menelaus, caused by the presence of Telemachus. And he also called Venus "golden," from what he had seen in Egypt. For he had seen the temple which in Egypt is called "the temple of golden Venus," and the plain which is named "the plain of golden Venus." And why do I now make mention of this? To show that the poet transferred to his own poem much of what is contained in the divine writings of the prophets. And first he transferred what Moses had related as the beginning of the creation of the world. For Moses wrote thus: "In the beginning God created the heaven and the earth," [2567] then the sun, and the moon, and the stars. For having learned this in Egypt, and having been much taken with what Moses had written in the Genesis of the world, he fabled that Vulcan had made in the shield of Achilles a kind of representation of the creation of the world. For he wrote thus: [2568] --

"There he described the earth, the heaven, the sea,
The sun that rests not, and the moon full-orb'd;
There also, all the stars which round about,
As with a radiant frontlet, bind the skies."

And he contrived also that the garden of Alcinous should preserve the likeness of Paradise, and through this likeness he represented it as ever-blooming and full of all fruits. For thus he wrote:[2569] --

"Tall thriving trees confess'd the fruitful mould;
The reddening apple ripens here to gold.
Here the blue fig with luscious juice o'erflows,
With deeper red the full pomegranate glows;
The branch here bends beneath the weighty pear,
And verdant olives flourish round the year.
The balmy spirit of the western gale
Eternal breathes on fruits, untaught to fail;
Each dropping pear a following pear supplies,
On apples apples, figs on figs arise.
The same mild season gives the blooms to blow,
The buds to harden, and the fruits to grow.
Here order'd vines in equal ranks appear,
With all th' united labours of the year.
Some to unload the fertile branches run,
Some dry the blackening clusters in the sun,
Others to tread the liquid harvest join.
The groaning presses foam with floods of wine.
Here are the vines in early flower descry'd

Here grapes discoloured on the sunny side,
And there in autumn's richest purple dy'd."

Do not these words present a manifest and clear imitation of what the first prophet Moses said about Paradise? And if any one wish to know something of the building of the tower by which the men of that day fancied they would obtain access to heaven, he will find a sufficiently exact allegorical imitation of this in what the poet has ascribed to Otus and Ephialtes. For of them he wrote thus: [2570] --

"Proud of their strength, and more than mortal size,
The gods they challenge, and affect the skies.
Heav'd on Olympus tottering Ossa stood;
On Ossa, Pelion nods with all his wood."

And the same holds good regarding the enemy of mankind who was cast out of heaven, whom the Sacred Scriptures call the Devil, [2571] a name which he obtained from his first devilry against man; and if any one would attentively consider the matter, he would find that the poet, though he certainly never mentions the name of "the devil," yet gives him a name from his wickedest action. For the poet, calling him Ate, [2572] says that he was hurled from heaven by their god, just as if he had a distinct remembrance of the expressions which Isaiah the prophet had uttered regarding him. He wrote thus in his own poem: [2573] --

"And, seizing by her glossy locks
The goddess Ate, in his wrath he swore
That never to the starry skies again,
And the Olympian heights, he would permit
The universal mischief to return.
Then, whirling her around, he cast her down
To earth. She, mingling with all works of men,
Caused many a pang to Jove."

Chapter XXIX - Origin of Plato's doctrine of form

And Plato, too, when he says that form is the third original principle next to God and matter, has manifestly received this suggestion from no other source than from Moses, having learned, indeed, from the words of Moses the name of form, but not having at the same time been instructed by the initiated, that without mystic insight it is impossible to have any distinct knowledge of the writings of Moses. For Moses wrote that God had spoken to him regarding the tabernacle in the following words: "And thou shalt make for me according to all that I show thee in the mount, the pattern of the tabernacle." [2574] And again: "And thou shalt erect the tabernacle according to the pattern of all the instruments thereof, even so shalt thou make it." [2575] And again, a little afterwards: "Thus then thou shalt make it according to the pattern which was showed to thee in the mount." [2576] Plato, then, reading these passages, and not receiving what was written with the suitable insight, thought that form had some kind of separate existence before that which the senses perceive, and he often calls it the pattern of the things which are made, since the writing of Moses spoke thus of the tabernacle: "According to the form showed to thee in the mount, so shalt thou make it."

Chapter XXX - Homer's knowledge of man's origin

And he was obviously deceived in the same way regarding the earth and heaven and man; for he supposes that there are "ideas" of these. For as Moses wrote thus, "In the beginning God created the heaven and the earth," and then subjoins this sentence, "And the earth was invisible and unfashioned," he thought that it was the pre-existent earth which was spoken of in the words, "The earth was," because Moses said, "And the earth was invisible and unfashioned;" and he thought that the earth, concerning which he says, "God created the heaven and the earth," was that earth which we perceive by the senses, and which God made according to the pre-existent form. And so also, of the heaven which was created, he thought that the heaven which was created--and which he also called the firmament--was that creation which the senses perceive; and that the heaven which the intellect perceives is that other of which the prophet said, "The heaven of heavens is the Lord's, but the earth hath He given to the children of men." [2577] And so also concerning man: Moses first mentions the name of man, and then after many other creations he makes mention of the formation of man, saying, "And God made man, taking dust from the earth." [2578] He thought, accordingly, that the man first so named existed before the man who was made, and that he who was formed of the earth was afterwards made according to the pre-existent form. And that man was formed of earth, Homer, too, having discovered from the ancient and divine history which says, "Dust thou art, and unto dust shalt thou return," [2579] calls the lifeless body of Hector dumb clay. For in condemnation of Achilles dragging the corpse of Hector after death, he says somewhere: [2580] --

"On the dumb clay he cast indignity,

Blinded with rage."

And again, somewhere else, [2581] he introduces Menelaus, thus addressing those who were not accepting Hector's challenge to single combat with becoming alacrity,--

"To earth and water may you all return,"--

resolving them in his violent rage into their original and pristine formation from earth. These things Homer and Plato, having learned in Egypt from the ancient histories, wrote in their own words.

Chapter XXXI - Further proof of Plato's acquaintance with Scripture

For from what other source, if not from his reading the writings of the prophets, could Plato have derived the information he gives us, that Jupiter drives a winged chariot in heaven? For he knew this from the following expressions of the prophet about the cherubim: "And the glory of the Lord went out from the house and rested on the cherubim; and the cherubim lift up their wings, and the wheels beside them; and the glory of the Lord God of Israel was over them above." [2582] And borrowing this idea, the magniloquent Plato shouts aloud with vast assurance, "The great Jove, indeed, driving his winged chariot in heaven." For from what other source, if not from Moses and the prophets, did he learn this and so write? And whence did he receive the suggestion of his saying that God exists in a fiery substance? Was it not from the third book of the history of the Kings, where it is written, "The Lord was not in the wind; and after the wind an earthquake, but the Lord was not in the earthquake; and after the earthquake a fire, but the Lord was not in the fire; and after the fire a still small voice?" [2583] But these things pious men must understand in a higher sense with profound and meditative insight. But Plato, not attending to the words with the suitable insight, said that God exists in a fiery substance.

Chapter XXXII - Plato's doctrine of the heavenly gift

And if any one will attentively consider the gift that descends from God on the holy men, -- which gift the sacred prophets call the Holy Ghost,--he shall find that this was announced under another name by Plato in the dialogue with Meno. For, fearing to name the gift of God "the Holy Ghost," lest he should seem, by following the teaching of the prophets, to be an enemy to the Greeks, he acknowledges, indeed, that it comes down from God, yet does not think fit to name it the Holy Ghost, but virtue. For so in the dialogue with Meno, concerning reminiscence, after he had put many questions regarding virtue, whether it could be taught or whether it could not be taught, but must be gained by practice, or whether it could be attained neither by practice nor by learning, but was a natural gift in men, or whether it comes in some other way, he makes this declaration in these very words: "But if now through this whole dialogue we have conducted our inquiry and discussion aright, virtue must be neither a natural gift, nor what one can receive by teaching, but comes to those to whom it does come by divine destiny." These things, I think, Plato having learned from the prophets regarding the Holy Ghost, he has manifestly transferred to what he calls virtue. For as the sacred prophets say that one and the same spirit is divided into seven spirits, so he also, naming it one and the same virtue, says this is divided into four virtues; wishing by all means to avoid mention of the Holy Spirit, but clearly declaring in a kind of allegory what the prophets said of the Holy Spirit. For to this effect he spoke in the dialogue with Meno towards the close: "From this reasoning, Meno, it appears that virtue comes to those to whom it does come by a divine destiny. But we shall know clearly about this, in what kind of way virtue comes to men, when, as a first step, we shall have set ourselves to investigate, as an independent inquiry, what virtue itself is." You see how he calls only by the name of virtue, the gift that descends from above; and yet he counts it worthy of inquiry, whether it is right that this [gift] be called virtue or some other thing, fearing to name it openly the Holy Spirit, lest he should seem to be following the teaching of the prophets.

Chapter XXXIII - Plato's idea of the beginning of time drawn from Moses

And from what source did Plato draw the information that time was created along with the heavens? For he wrote thus: "Time, accordingly, was created along with the heavens; in order that, coming into being together, they might also be together dissolved, if ever their dissolution should take place." Had he not learned this from the divine history of Moses? For he knew that the creation of time had received its original constitution from days and months and years. Since, then, the first day which was created along with the heavens constituted the beginning of all time (for thus Moses wrote, "In the beginning God created the heavens and the earth," and then immediately subjoins, "And one day was made," as if he would designate the whole of time by one part of it), Plato names the day "time," lest, if he mentioned the "day," he should seem to lay himself open to the accusation of the Athenians, that he was completely adopting the expressions of Moses. And from what source did he derive what he has written regarding the dissolution of the heavens? Had he not learned this, too, from the sacred prophets, and did he not think that this was their doctrine?

Chapter XXXIV - Whence men attributed to God human form

And if any person investigates the subject of images, and inquires on what ground those who first fashioned your gods conceived that they had the forms of men, he will find that this also was derived from the divine history. For seeing that Moses's history, speaking in the person of God, says, "Let Us make man in our image and likeness," these persons, under the impression that this meant that men were like God in form, began thus to fashion their gods, supposing they would make a likeness from a likeness. But why, ye men of Greece, am I now induced to recount these things? That ye may know that it is not possible to learn the true religion from those who were unable, even on those subjects by which they won the admiration of the heathen, [2584] to write anything original, but merely propounded by some allegorical device in their own writings what they had learned from Moses and the other prophets.

Chapter XXXV - Appeal to the Greeks

The time, then, ye men of Greece, is now come, that ye, having been persuaded by the secular histories that Moses and the rest of the prophets were far more ancient than any of those who have been esteemed sages among you, abandon the ancient delusion of your forefathers, and read the divine histories of the prophets, and ascertain from them the true religion; for they do not present to you artful discourses, nor speak speciously and plausibly--for this is the property of those who wish to rob you of the truth--but use with simplicity the words and expressions which offer themselves, and declare to you whatever the Holy Ghost, who descended upon them, chose to teach through them to those who are desirous to learn the true religion. Having then laid aside all false shame, and the inveterate error of mankind, with all its bombastic parade and empty noise, though by means of it you fancy you are possessed of all advantages, do you give yourselves to the things that profit you. For neither will you commit any offence against your fathers, if you now show a desire to betake yourselves to that which is quite opposed to their error, since it is likely enough that they themselves are now lamenting in Hades, and repenting with a too late repentance; and if it were possible for them to show you thence what had befallen them after the termination of this life, ye would know from what fearful ills they desired to deliver you. But now, since it is not possible in this present life that ye either learn from them, or from those who here profess to teach that philosophy which is falsely so called, it follows as the one thing that remains for you to do, that, renouncing the error of your fathers, ye read the prophecies of the sacred writers, [2585] not requiring from them unexceptionable diction (for the matters of our religion lie in works, [2586] not in words), and learn from them what will give you life everlasting. For those who bootlessly disgrace the name of philosophy are convicted of knowing nothing at all, as they are themselves forced, though unwillingly, to confess, since not only do they disagree with each other, but also expressed their own opinions sometimes in one way, sometimes in another.

Chapter XXXVI - True knowledge not held by the philosophers

And if "the discovery of the truth" be given among them as one definition of philosophy, how are they who are not in possession of the true knowledge worthy of the name of philosophy? For if Socrates, the wisest of your wise men, to whom even your oracle, as you yourselves say, bears witness, saying, "Of all men Socrates is the wisest"--if he confesses that he knows nothing, how did those who came after him profess to know even things heavenly? For Socrates said that he was on this account called wise, because, while other men pretended to know what they were ignorant of, he himself did not shrink from confessing that he knew nothing. For he said, "I seem to myself to be wisest by this little particular, that what I do not know, I do not suppose I know." Let no one fancy that Socrates ironically feigned ignorance, because he often used to do so in his dialogues. For the last expression of his apology which he uttered as he was being led away to the prison, proves that in seriousness and truth he was confessing his ignorance: "But now it is time to go away, I indeed to die, but you to live. And which of us goes to the better state, is hidden to all but God." Socrates, indeed, having uttered this last sentence in the Areopagus, departed to the prison, ascribing to God alone the knowledge of those things which are hidden from us; but those who came after him, though they are unable to comprehend even earthly things, profess to understand things heavenly as if they had seen them. Aristotle at least--as if he had seen things heavenly with greater accuracy than Plato--declared that God did not exist, as Plato said, in the fiery substance (for this was Plato's doctrine) but in the fifth element, air. And while he demanded that concerning these matters he should be believed on account of the excellence of his language, he yet departed this life because he was overwhelmed with the infamy and disgrace of being unable to discover even the nature of the Euripus in Chalcis. [2587] Let not any one, therefore, of sound judgment prefer the elegant diction of these men to his own salvation, but let him, according to that old story, stop his ears with wax, and flee the sweet hurt which these sirens would inflict upon him. For the above-mentioned men, presenting their elegant language as a kind of bait, have sought to seduce many from the right religion, in imitation of him who dared to teach the first men polytheism. Be not persuaded by these persons, I entreat you, but read the prophecies of the sacred writers.[2588] And if any slothfulness or old hereditary superstition prevents you from reading the prophecies of the holy men through which you can be instructed regarding the one only God, which is the first article of the true religion, yet believe him who, though at first he taught you polytheism, yet afterwards preferred to sing a useful and necessary recantation--I mean Orpheus, who said what I quoted a little before; and believe the others who wrote the same things concerning one God. For it was the work of Divine Providence on your behalf, that they, though unwillingly, bore testimony that what the prophets said regarding one God was true, in order that, the doctrine of a plurality of gods being rejected by all, occasion might be afforded you of knowing the truth.

Chapter XXXVII - Of the Sibyl [2589]

And you may in part easily learn the right religion from the ancient Sibyl, who by some kind of potent inspiration teaches you, through her oracular predictions, truths which seem to be much akin to the teaching of the prophets. She, they say, was of Babylonian extraction, being the daughter of Berosus, who wrote the Chaldæan History; and when she had crossed over (how, I know not) into the region of Campania, she there uttered her oracular sayings in a city called Cumæ, six miles from Baiæ, where the hot springs of Campania are found. And being in that city, we saw also a certain place, in which we were shown a very large basilica [2590] cut out of one stone; a vast affair, and worthy of all admiration. And they who had heard it from their fathers as part of their country's tradition, told us that it was here she used to publish her oracles. And in the middle of the basilica they showed us three receptacles cut out of one stone, in which, when filled with water, they said that she washed, and having put on her robe again, retires into the inmost chamber of the basilica, which is still a part of the one stone; and sitting in the middle of the chamber on a high rostrum and throne, thus proclaims her oracles. And both by many other writers has the Sibyl been mentioned as a prophetess, and also by Plato in his Phædrus. And Plato seems to me to have counted prophets divinely inspired when he read her prophecies. For he saw that what she had long ago predicted was accomplished; and on this account he expresses in the Dialogue with Meno his wonder at and admiration of prophets in the following terms: "Those whom we now call prophetic persons we should rightly name divine. And not least would we say that they are divine, and are raised to the prophetic ecstasy by the inspiration and possession of God, when they correctly speak of many and important matters, and yet know nothing of what they are saying," --plainly and manifestly referring to the prophecies of the Sibyl. For, unlike the poets who, after their poems are penned, have power to correct and polish, specially in the way of increasing the accuracy of their verse, she was filled indeed with prophecy at the time of the inspiration, but as soon as the inspiration ceased, there ceased also the remembrance of all she had said. And this indeed was the cause why some only, and not all, the metres of the verses of the Sibyl were preserved. For we ourselves, when in that city, ascertained from our cicerone, who showed us the places in which she used to prophesy, that there was a certain coffer made of brass in which they said that her remains were preserved. And besides all else which they told us as they had heard it from their fathers, they said also that they who then took down her prophecies, being illiterate persons, often went quite astray from the accuracy of the metres; and this, they said, was the cause of the want of metre in some of the verses, the prophetess having no remembrance of what she had said, after the possession and inspiration ceased, and the reporters having, through their lack of education, failed to record the metres with accuracy. And on this account, it is manifest that Plato had an eye to the prophecies of the Sibyl when he said this about prophets, for he said, "When they correctly speak of many and important matters, and yet know nothing of what they are saying."

Chapter XXXVIII - Concluding appeal

But since, ye men of Greece, the matters of the true religion lie not in the metrical numbers of poetry, nor yet in that culture which is highly esteemed among you, do ye henceforward pay less devotion to accuracy of metres and of language; and giving heed without contentiousness to the words of the Sibyl, recognise how great are the benefits which she will confer upon you by predicting, as she does in a clear and patent manner, the advent of our Saviour Jesus Christ; [2591] who, being the Word of God, inseparable from Him in power, having assumed man, who had been made in the image and likeness of God, restored to us the knowledge of the religion of our ancient forefathers, which the men who lived after them abandoned through the bewitching counsel of the envious devil, and turned to the worship of those who were no gods. And if you still hesitate and are hindered from belief regarding the formation of man, believe those whom you have hitherto thought it right to give heed to, and know that your own oracle, when asked by some one to utter a hymn of praise to the Almighty God, in the middle of the hymn spoke thus, "Who formed the first of men, and called him Adam." And this hymn is preserved by many whom we know, for the conviction of those who are unwilling to believe the truth which all bear witness to. If therefore, ye men of Greece, ye do not esteem the false fancy concerning those that are no gods at a higher rate than your own salvation, believe, as I said, the most ancient and time-honoured Sibyl, whose books are preserved in all the world, and who by some kind of potent inspiration both teaches us in her oracular utterances concerning those that are called gods, that have no existence; and also clearly and manifestly prophesies concerning the predicted advent of our Saviour Jesus Christ, and concerning all those things which were to be done by Him. For the knowledge of these things will constitute your necessary preparatory training for the study of the prophecies of the sacred writers. And if any one supposes that he has learned the doctrine concerning God from the most ancient of those whom you name philosophers, let him listen to Ammon and Hermes: [2592] to Ammon, who in his discourse concerning God calls Him wholly hidden; and to Hermes, who says plainly and distinctly, "that it is difficult to comprehend God, and that it is impossible even for the man who can comprehend Him to declare Him to others." From every point of view, therefore, it must be seen that in no other way than only from the prophets who teach us by divine inspiration, is it at all possible to learn anything concerning God and the true religion. [2593]

Footnotes:

2507. Literally, "former."

2508. Iliad, xiv. 302.

2509. Iliad, xix. 224.

2510. That is, Venus, who, after Paris had sworn that the war should be decided by single combat between himself and Menelaus, carried him off, and induced him, though defeated, to refuse performance of the articles agreed upon.

2511. Iliad, xvi. 433. Sarpedon was a son of Zeus.

2512. Iliad, xxii. 168.

2513. Iliad, i. 399, etc.

2514. Iliad, xiv. 315. (The passage is here given in full from Cowper's translation. In Justin's quotation one or two lines are omitted.)

2515. Iliad, v. 382 (from Lord Derby's translation).

2516. Iliad, xx. 66 (from Lord Derby's translation).

2517. i.e., these teachers.

2518. Literally, "those who knew."

2519. μονάδα καὶ τὴν ἀόριστον δυάδα. One, or unity, was considered by Pythagoras as the essence of number, and also as God. Two, or the indefinite binary, was the equivalent of evil. So Plutarch, De placit. philosoph., c. 7; from which treatise the above opinions of the various sects are quoted, generally verbatim.

2520. ἀμέτοχα κενοῦ: the void being that in which these bodies move, while they themselves are of a different nature from it.

2521. Or, accord and discord, attraction and repulsion.

2522. Or, "is of a fiery nature."

2523. See the Republic, x. 2. By the Platonic doctrine, the ideas of things in the mind of God were the realities; the things themselves, as seen by us, were the images of these realities; and poetry, therefore, describing the images of realities, was only at the third remove from nature. As Plato puts it briefly in this same passage, "the painter, the bed-maker, God--these three are the masters of three species of beds."

2524. Iliad, xv. 192.

2525. i.e., from Homer; using Homer's words as suggestive and confirmatory of his doctrine.

2526. Iliad, xiv. 246.

2527. τὸ λογικόν τὸ θυμικόν, τὸ ἐπιθυμητικόν, --corresponding to what we roughly speak of as reason, the heart, and the appetites.

2528. ἐντελέχεια, --the completion or actuality to which each thing, by virtue of its peculiar nature (or potentiality, δύναμις), can arrive.

2529. Literally, "unbegotten."

2530. Or, "liable to destruction."

2531. Literally, "the art of words."

2532. Literally, "clean," free from other influences.

2533. The diversities of Christian theology are to be regretted; but Justin here shows the harmony and order of truths, such as are everywhere received by Christians, to be an inestimable advantage.

2534. The incongruity in this sentence is Justin's.

2535. Autochthones. That is, sprung from the soil; and hence the oldest inhabitants, the aborigines.

2536. Literally, archæology.

2537. Unfortunately, Justin here mistook Menes for Moses. But he may have so read the name in his copy. See Grabe's note on Diodorus, and the quotation following in another note.

2538. This sentence must be so completed from the context in Diodorus. See the note of Maranus.

2539. Consult the ponderous learning of Warburton's Divine Legation, passim.

2540. Literally, "without," not belonging to the true faith.
2541. C. 3.
2542. Doubtless Justin relates the tradition as he received it. Consult Dr. Selwyn's full account of the fables concerning the LXX., in Smith's Dict. of the Bible, iii. p. 1203 ff.
2543. Iliad, ix. 445.
2544. Iliad, ii. 204.
2545. Has no fellow.
2546. Or, "uncreated."
2547. ὁ ὤν, "He who is; the Being."
2548. Isa. xliv. 6.
2549. Literally, "with the not-beings."
2550. Literally, "between the God being and not-beings."
2551. That is, "is not produced or created; has no birth."
2552. Or, "are born and die."
2553. κατὰ ταὐτά "according to the same things," i.e., in eternal immutability.
2554. Or, "demiurge or maker."
2555. That is, "my will to the contrary." See Plato, Tim., p. 41 cap 13.
2556. Iliad, ix. 497.
2557. That is, by the challenge of the chain introduced--Iliad, viii. 18.
2558. Iliad, ix. 238.
2559. Iliad, i. 526.
2560. Plato, Tim., p. 53 D, cap. 20.
2561. Pind., Fr., 233, a fragment preserved in this place.
2562. Plato, Rep., p. 330 D.
2563. Plato, Rep., p. 615, lib. x. p. 325. Ed. Bipont, 1785.
2564. The bellowing of the mouth of the pit.
2565. Odyssey, xi, 576 (Pope's translation, line 709).
2566. Odyssey, iv. 221; Milton's Comus, line 675.
2567. Gen. i. 1.
2568. Iliad, xviii. 483.
2569. Odyssey, vii. 114 (Pope's translation, line 146.).
2570. Odyssey, xi. 312 (Pope's translation, line 385).
2571. The false accuser; one who does injury by slanderous accusations.
2572. Ἄτη, the goddess of mischief, from whom spring all rash, blind deeds and their results.
2573. Iliad, xix. 126.
2574. Ex. xxv.
2575. Ex. xxv. 9.
2576. Ex. xxv. 40.
2577. Ps. cxv. 16.
2578. Gen. ii. 7.
2579. Gen. iii. 19.
2580. Iliad, xxii.
2581. Iliad, vii. 99.
2582. Ezek. xi. 22.
2583. 1 Kings xix. 11, 12.
2584. Literally, "those without."
2585. Literally, "sacred men."
2586. A noteworthy apology for early Christian writers.
2587. This is now supposed to be fable.
2588. Literally, "sacred men."
2589. In Grabe's edition consult notes of Lang and Kortholt, ii. p. 45.
2590. Travellers must recognise the agreement of Justin's story with the traditional cave still shown in this region.
2591. The fascinating use made of this by Virgil must not be overlooked:-- "Ultima Cumæi venit jam carminis ætas," etc. Ecl., iv. (Pollio) 4.
2592. Hermes Trismegistus. Milton (Penseroso, line 88,) translates this name.
2593. N.B.-- This work is not supposed to be Justin's by modern critics.

Justin on the Sole Government of God [2594]
[Translated by the Rev. G. Reith, M.A.]

Chapter I - Object of the author
Although human nature at first received a union of intelligence and safety to discern the truth, and the worship due to the one Lord of all, yet envy, insinuating the excellence of human greatness, turned men away to the making of idols; and this superstitious custom, after continuing for a long period, is handed down to the majority as if it were natural and true. It is the part of a lover of man, or rather of a lover of God, to remind men who have neglected it of that which they ought to know. For the truth is of itself sufficient to show forth, by means of those things which are contained under the pole of heaven, the order [instituted by] Him who has created them. But forgetfulness having taken possession of the minds of men, through the long-suffering of God, has acted recklessly in transferring to mortals the name which is applicable to the only true God; and from the few the infection of sin spread to the many, who were blinded by popular usage to the knowledge of that which was lasting and unchangeable. For the men of former generations, who instituted private and public rites in honour of such as were more powerful, caused forgetfulness of the Catholic [2595] faith to take possession of their posterity; but I, as I have just stated, along with a God-loving mind, shall employ the speech of one who loves man, and set it before those who have intelligence, which all ought to have who are privileged to observe the administration of the universe, so that they should worship unchangeably Him who knows all things. This I shall do, not by mere display of words, but by altogether using demonstration drawn from the old poetry in Greek literature, [2596] and from writings very common amongst all. For from these the famous men who have handed down idol-worship as law to the multitudes, shall be taught and convicted by their own poets and literature of great ignorance.

Chapter II - Testimonies to the unity of God
First, then, Æschylus, [2597] in expounding the arrangement of his work, [2598] expressed himself also as follows respecting the only God:--

"Afar from mortals place the holy God,
Nor ever think that He, like to thyself,
In fleshly robes is clad; for all unknown
Is the great God to such a worm as thou.
Divers similitudes He bears; at times
He seems as a consuming fire that burns
Unsated; now like water, then again
In sable folds of darkness shrouds Himself.
Nay, even the very beasts of earth reflect
His sacred image; whilst the wind, clouds, rain,
The roll of thunder and the lightning flash,
Reveal to men their great and sovereign Lord.
Before Him sea and rocks, with every fount,
And all the water floods, in reverence bend;
And as they gaze upon His awful face,
Mountains and earth, with the profoundest depths
Of ocean, and the highest peaks of hills,
Tremble: for He is Lord Omnipotent;
And this the glory is of God Most High."

But he was not the only man initiated in the knowledge of God; for Sophocles also thus describes the nature of the only Creator of all things, the One God:--

"There is one God, in truth there is but one,
Who made the heavens and the broad earth beneath,
The glancing waves of ocean, and the winds;
But many of us mortals err in heart,
And set up, for a solace in our woes,
Images of the gods in stone and brass,

Or figures carved in gold or ivory;
And, furnishing for these, our handiworks,
Both sacrifice and rite magnificent,
We think that thus we do a pious work."

And Philemon also, who published many explanations of ancient customs, shares in the knowledge of the truth; and thus he writes:--

"Tell me what thoughts of God we should conceive?
One, all things seeing, yet Himself unseen."

Even Orpheus, too, who introduces three hundred and sixty gods, will bear testimony in my favour from the tract called Diathecæ, in which he appears to repent of his error by writing the following:--

"I'ΛΛ speak to those who lawfully may hear;
All others, ye profane, now close the doors!
And, O Musæus, hearken thou to me,
Who offspring art of the light-bringing moon.
The words I tell thee now are true indeed,
And if thou former thoughts of mine hast seen,
Let them not rob thee of the blessed life;
But rather turn the depths of thine own heart
Unto that place where light and knowledge dwell.
Take thou the word divine to guide thy steps;
And walking well in the straight certain path,
Look to the one and universal King,
One, self-begotten, and the only One
Of whom all things, and we ourselves, are sprung.
All things are open to His piercing gaze,
While He Himself is still invisible;
Present in all His works, though still unseen,
He gives to mortals evil out of good,
Sending both chilling wars and tearful griefs;
And other than the Great King there is none.
The clouds for ever settle round His throne;
And mortal eyeballs in mere mortal eyes
Are weak to see Jove, reigning over all.
He sits established in the brazen heavens
Upon His throne; and underneath His feet
He treads the earth, and stretches His right hand
To all the ends of ocean, and around
Tremble the mountain ranges, and the streams,
The depths, too, of the blue and hoary sea."

He speaks indeed as if he had been an eyewitness of God's greatness. And Pythagoras [2599] agrees with him when he writes:--

"Should one in boldness say, Lo, I am God!
Besides the One--Eternal--Infinite,
Then let him from the throne he has usurped
Put forth his power and form another globe,
Such as we dwell in, saying, This is mine.
Nor only so, but in this new domain
For ever let him dwell. If this he can,
Then verily he is a god proclaimed."

Chapter III - Testimonies to a future judgment

Then further concerning Him, that He alone is powerful, both to institute judgment on the deeds performed in life, and on the ignorance of the Deity [displayed by men], I can adduce witnesses from your own ranks; and first Sophocles, [2600] who speaks as follows:--

"That time of times shall come, shall surely come,
When from the golden ether down shall fall
Fire's teeming treasure, and in burning flames
All things of earth and heaven shall be consumed;
And then, when all creation is dissolved,
The sea's last wave shall die upon the shore,
The bald earth stript of trees, the burning air

No winged thing upon its breast shall bear.
There are two roads to Hades, well we know; [2601]
By this the righteous, and by that the bad,
On to their separate fates shall tend; and He,
Who all things had destroyed, shall all things save."
And Philemon [2602] again:--
"Think'st thou, Nicostratus, the dead, who here
Enjoyed whate'er of good life offers man,
Escape the notice of Divinity,
As if they might forgotten be of Him?
Nay, there's an eye of Justice watching all;
For if the good and bad find the same end,
Then go thou, rob, steal, plunder, at thy will,
Do all the evil that to thee seems good.
Yet be not thou deceived; for underneath
There is a throne and place of judgment set,
Which God the Lord of all shall occupy;
Whose name is terrible, nor shall I dare
To breathe it forth in feeble human speech."
And Euripides: [2603] --
"Not grudgingly he gives a lease of life,
That we the holders may be fairly judged;
And if a mortal man doth think to hide
His daily guilt from the keen eye of God,
It is an evil thought; so if perchance
He meets with leisure-taking Justice, she
Demands him as her lawful prisoner:
But many of you hastily commit
A twofold sin, and say there is no God.
But, ah! there is; there is. Then see that he
Who, being wicked, prospers, may redeem
The time so precious, else hereafter waits
For him the due reward of punishment."

Chapter IV - God desires not sacrifices, but righteousness

And that God is not appeased by the libations and incense of evil-doers, but awards vengeance in righteousness to each one, Philemon [2604] again shall bear testimony to me:--
"If any one should dream, O Pamphilus,
By sacrifice of bulls or goats--nay, then,
By Jupiter--of any such like things;
Or by presenting gold or purple robes,
Or images of ivory and gems;
If thus he thinks he may propitiate God,
He errs, and shows himself a silly one.
But let him rather useful be, and good,
Committing neither theft nor lustful deeds,
Nor murder foul, for earthly riches' sake.
Let him of no man covet wife or child,
His splendid house, his wide-spread property,
His maiden, or his slave born in his house,
His horses, or his cattle, or his beeves,
Nay, covet not a pin, O Pamphilus,
For God, close by you, sees whate'er you do.
He ever with the wicked man is wroth,
But in the righteous takes a pleasure still,
Permitting him to reap fruit of his toil,
And to enjoy the bread his sweat has won.
But being righteous, see thou pay thy vows,
And unto God the giver offer gifts.
Place thy adorning not in outward shows,
But in an inward purity of heart;
Hearing the thunder then, thou shalt not fear,

Nor shalt thou flee, O master, at its voice,
For thou art conscious of no evil deed,
And God, close by you, sees whate'er you do."

Again, Plato, in Timæus, [2605] says: "But if any one on consideration should actually institute a rigid inquiry, he would be ignorant of the distinction between the human and the divine nature; because God mingles many [2606] things up into one, [and again is able to dissolve one into many things,] seeing that He is endued with knowledge and power; but no man either is, or ever shall be, able to perform any of these."

Chapter V - *The vain pretensions of false gods*

But concerning those who think that they shall share the holy and perfect name, which some have received by a vain tradition as if they were gods, Menander in the Auriga says:--

"If there exists a god who walketh out
With an old woman, or who enters in
By stealth to houses through the folding-doors,
He ne'er can please me; nay, but only he
Who stays at home, a just and righteous God,
To give salvation to His worshippers."

The same Menander, in the Sacerdos, says:--

"There is no God, O woman, that can save
One man by another; if indeed a man,
With sound of tinkling cymbals, charm a god
Where'er he listeth, then assuredly
He who doth so is much the greater god.
But these, O Rhode, are but the cunning schemes
Which daring men of intrigue, unabashed,
Invent to earn themselves a livelihood,
And yield a laughing-stock unto the age."

Again, the same Menander, stating his opinion about those who are received as gods, proving rather that they are not so, says:--

"Yea, if I this beheld, I then should wish
That back to me again my soul returned.
For tell me where, O Getas, in the world
'Tis possible to find out righteous gods?"

And in the Depositum:--

"There's an unrighteous judgment, as it seems,
Even with the gods."

And Euripides the tragedian, in Orestes, says:--

"Apollo having caused by his command
The murder of the mother, knoweth not
What honesty and justice signify.
We serve the gods, whoever they may be;
But from the central regions of the earth
You see Apollo plainly gives response
To mortals, and whate'er he says we do.
I him obeyed, when she that bore me fell
Slain by my hand: he is the wicked man.
Then slay him, for 'twas he that sinned, not I.
What could I do? Think you not that the god
Should free me from the blame which I do bear?"

The same also in Hippolytus:--

"But on these points the gods do not judge right."

And in Ion:--

"But in the daughter of Erechtheus
What interest have I? for that pertains
Not unto such as me. But when I come
With golden vessels for libations, I
The dew shall sprinkle, and yet needs must warn
Apollo of his deeds; for when he weds
Maidens by force, the children secretly
Begotten he betrays, and then neglects
When dying. Thus not you; but while you may

Always pursue the virtues, for the gods
Will surely punish men of wickedness.
How is it right that you, who have prescribed
Laws for men's guidance, live unrighteously?
But ye being absent, I shall freely speak,
And ye to men shall satisfaction give
For marriage forced, thou Neptune, Jupiter,
Who over heaven presides. The temples ye
Have emptied, while injustice ye repay.
And though ye laud the prudent to the skies,
Yet have ye filled your hands with wickedness.
No longer is it right to call men ill
If they do imitate the sins [2607] of gods; [2608]
Nay, evil let their teachers rather be."
And in Archelaus:--
"Full oft, my son, do gods mankind perplex."
And in Bellerophon:--
"They are no gods, who do not what is right."
And again in the same:--
"Gods reign in heaven most certainly, says one;
But it is false,---yea, false, -and let not him
Who speaks thus, be so foolish as to use
Ancient tradition, or to pay regard
Unto my words: but with unclouded eye
Behold the matter in its clearest light.
Power absolute, I say, robs men of life
And property; transgresses plighted faith;
Nor spares even cities, but with cruel hand
Despoils and devastates them ruthlessly.
But they that do these things have more success
Than those who live a gentle pious life;
And cities small, I know, which reverence gods,
Submissive bend before the many spears
Of larger impious ones; yea, and methinks
If any man lounge idly, and abstain
From working with his hands for sustenance,
Yet pray the gods; he very soon will know
If they from him misfortunes will avert."
And Menander in Diphilus: [2609] --
"Therefore ascribe we praise and honour great
To Him who Father is, and Lord of all;
Sole maker and preserver of mankind,
And who with all good things our earth has stored."
The same also in the Piscatores:--
"For I deem that which nourishes my life
Is God; but he whose custom 'tis to meet
The wants of men,--He needs not at our hands
Renewed supplies, Himself being all in all." [2610]
The same in the Fratres:--
"God ever is intelligence to those
Who righteous are: so wisest men have thought."
And in the Tibicinæ:--
"Good reason finds a temple in all things
Wherein to worship; for what is the mind,
But just the voice of God within us placed?"
And the tragedian in Phrixus:--
"But if the pious and the impious
Share the same lot, how could we think it just,
If Jove, the best, judges not uprightly?"
In Philoctetes:--
"You see how honourable gain is deemed
Even to the gods; and how he is admired

Whose shrine is laden most with yellow gold.
What, then, doth hinder thee, since it is good
To be like gods, from thus accepting gain?"
In Hecuba:--
"O Jupiter! whoever thou mayest be,
Of whom except in word all knowledge fails;"
and,--
"Jupiter, whether thou art indeed
A great necessity, or the mind of man,
I worship thee!"

Chapter VI - We should acknowledge one only God

Here, then, is a proof of virtue, and of a mind loving prudence, to recur to the communion of the unity, [2611] and to attach one's self to prudence for salvation, and make choice of the better things according to the free-will placed in man; and not to think that those who are possessed of human passions are lords of all, when they shall not appear to have even equal power with men. For in Homer, [2612] Demodocus says he is self-taught --

"God inspired me with strains"--

though he is a mortal. Æsculapius and Apollo are taught to heal by Chiron the Centaur,--a very novel thing indeed, for gods to be taught by a man. What need I speak of Bacchus, who the poet says is mad? or of Hercules, who he says is unhappy? What need to speak of Mars and Venus, the leaders of adultery; and by means of all these to establish the proof which has been undertaken? For if some one, in ignorance, should imitate the deeds which are said to be divine, he would be reckoned among impure men, and a stranger to life and humanity; and if any one does so knowingly, he will have a plausible excuse for escaping vengeance, by showing that imitation of godlike deeds of audacity is no sin. But if any one should blame these deeds, he will take away their well-known names, and not cover them up with specious and plausible words. It is necessary, then, to accept the true and invariable Name, not proclaimed by my words only, but by the words of those who have introduced us to the elements of learning, in order that we may not, by living idly in this present state of existence, not only as those who are ignorant of the heavenly glory, but also as having proved ourselves ungrateful, render our account to the Judge. [2613]

Footnotes:

2594. Θεοῦ is omitted in mss., but μοναρχία of itself implies it.

2595. i.e., the doctrine that God only is to be worshipped.

2596. Literally, "history."

2597. Grotius supposes this to be Æschylus the younger in some prologue.

2598. This may also be translated: "expounding the set of opinions prevalent in his day."

2599. "Pythagorei cujusdam fetus."-- Otto, after Goezius.

2600. Langus compares 2 Pet. iii. 7.

2601. Some propose to insert these three lines in the centre of the next quotation from Philemon, after the line, "Nay, there's an eye," etc.

2602. Some say Diphilus.

2603. Grotius joins these lines to the preceding. Clement of Alexandria assigns them, and the others, which are under the name of Euripides, to Diphilus.

2604. Some attribute these lines to Menander, others regard them as spurious.

2605. P. 68, D, cap. 30.

2606. The mss. are corrupt here. They seem to read, and one actually does read, "all" for "many." "Many" is in Plato, and the clause in brackets is taken from Plato to fill up the sense.

2607. κακά in Euripedes, καλά in text.

2608. See Warburton's Divine Legation (book ii. § 4), vol. ii. p. 20. Ed. London, 1811.

2609. These lines are assigned to Diphilus.

2610. The words from "but" to "all" are assigned by Otto to Justin, not to Menander.

2611. See chap. i., the opening sentence.

2612. Odyssey, xxii. 347.

2613. N. B.--This tractate is probably the genuine work of Justin.

Fragments of the Lost Work of Justin on the Resurrection

[Translated by the Rev. M. Dods, M.A.]

Chapter I - The self-evidencing power of truth

The word of truth is free, and carries its own authority, disdaining to fall under any skilful argument, or to endure the logical scrutiny of its hearers. But it would be believed for its own nobility, and for the confidence due to Him who sends it. Now the word of truth is sent from God; wherefore the freedom claimed by the truth is not arrogant. For being sent with authority, it were not fit that it should be required to produce proof of what is said; since neither is there any proof beyond itself, which is God. For every proof is more powerful and trustworthy than that which it proves; since what is disbelieved, until proof is produced, gets credit when such proof is produced, and is recognised as being what it was stated to be. But nothing is either more powerful or more trustworthy than the truth; so that he who requires proof of this is like one who wishes it demonstrated why the things that appear to the senses do appear. For the test of those things which are received through the reason, is sense; but of sense itself there is no test beyond itself. As then we bring those things which reason hunts after, to sense, and by it judge what kind of things they are, whether the things spoken be true or false, and then sit in judgment no longer, giving full credit to its decision; so also we refer all that is said regarding men and the world to the truth, and by it judge whether it be worthless or no. But the utterances of truth we judge by no separate test, giving full credit to itself. And God, the Father of the universe, who is the perfect intelligence, is the truth. And the Word, being His Son, came to us, having put on flesh, revealing both Himself and the Father, giving to us in Himself resurrection from the dead, and eternal life afterwards. And this is Jesus Christ, our Saviour and Lord. He, therefore, is Himself both the faith and the proof of Himself and of all things. Wherefore those who follow Him, and know Him, having faith in Him as their proof, shall rest in Him. But since the adversary does not cease to resist many, and uses many and divers arts to ensnare them, that he may seduce the faithful from their faith, and that he may prevent the faithless from believing, it seems to me necessary that we also, being armed with the invulnerable doctrines of the faith, do battle against him in behalf of the weak.

Chapter II - Objections to the resurrection of the flesh

They who maintain the wrong opinion say that there is no resurrection of the flesh; giving as their reason that it is impossible that what is corrupted and dissolved should be restored to the same as it had been. And besides the impossibility, they say that the salvation of the flesh is disadvantageous; and they abuse the flesh, adducing its infirmities, and declare that it only is the cause of our sins, so that if the flesh, say they, rise again, our infirmities also rise with it. And such sophistical reasons as the following they elaborate: If the flesh rise again, it must rise either entire and possessed of all its parts, or imperfect. But its rising imperfect argues a want of power on God's part, if some parts could be saved, and others not; but if all the parts are saved, then the body will manifestly have all its members. But is it not absurd to say that these members will exist after the resurrection from the dead, since the Saviour said, "They neither marry, nor are given in marriage, but shall be as the angels in heaven?" [2614] And the angels, say they, have neither flesh, nor do they eat, nor have sexual intercourse; therefore there shall be no resurrection of the flesh. By these and such like arguments, they attempt to distract men from the faith. And there are some who maintain that even Jesus Himself appeared only as spiritual, and not in flesh, but presented merely the appearance of flesh: these persons seek to rob the flesh of the promise. First, then, let us solve those things which seem to them to be insoluble; then we will introduce in an orderly manner the demonstration concerning the flesh, proving that it partakes of salvation.

Chapter III - If the members rise, must they discharge the same functions as now?

They say, then, if the body shall rise entire, and in possession of all its members, it necessarily follows that the functions of the members shall also be in existence; that the womb shall become pregnant, and the male also discharge his function of generation, and the rest of the members in like manner. Now let this argument stand or fall by this one assertion. For this being proved false, their whole objection will be removed. Now it is indeed evident that the members which discharge functions discharge those functions which in the present life we see, but it does not follow that they necessarily discharge the same functions from the beginning. And that this may be more clearly seen, let us consider it thus. The function of the womb is to become pregnant; and of the member of the male to impregnate. But as, though these members are destined to discharge such functions, it is not therefore necessary that they from the beginning discharge them (since we see many women who do not become pregnant, as those that are barren, even though they have wombs), so pregnancy is not the immediate and necessary consequence of having a womb; but those even who are not barren abstain from sexual intercourse, some being virgins from the first, and others from a certain time. And we see men also keeping themselves virgins, some from the first, and some from a certain time; so that by their means, marriage, made lawless through lust, is destroyed. [2615] And we find that some even of the lower animals, though possessed of wombs, do not bear, such as the mule; and the male mules do not beget their kind. So that both in the case of men and the irrational animals we can see sexual intercourse abolished; and this, too, before the future world. And our Lord Jesus Christ was born of a virgin, for no other reason than that He might destroy the begetting by lawless desire, and might show to the ruler [2616] that the formation of man was possible to God without human intervention. And when He had been born, and had submitted to the other conditions of the flesh,--I mean food, drink, and clothing,--this one condition only of discharging the sexual function He did not submit to; for, regarding the desires of the flesh, He accepted some as necessary, while others, which were unnecessary, He did not submit to. For if the flesh were deprived of food, drink, and clothing, it would be destroyed; but being deprived of lawless desire, it suffers no harm. And at the same time He foretold that, in the future world, sexual intercourse should be done away with; as He says, "The children of this world marry, and are given in marriage; but the children of the world to come neither marry nor are given in marriage, but shall be like the angels in heaven." [2617] Let not, then, those that are unbelieving marvel, if in the world to come He do away with those acts of our fleshly members which even in this present life are abolished.

Chapter IV - Must the deformed rise deformed?

Well, they say, if then the flesh rise, it must rise the same as it falls; so that if it die with one eye, it must rise one-eyed; if lame, lame; if defective in any part of the body, in this part the man must rise deficient. How truly blinded are they in the eyes of their hearts! For they have not seen on the earth blind men seeing again, and the lame walking by His word. All things which the Saviour did, He did in the first place in order that what was spoken concerning Him in the prophets might be fulfilled, "that the blind should receive sight, and the deaf hear," [2618] and so on; but also to induce the belief that in the resurrection the flesh shall rise entire. For if on earth He healed the sicknesses of the flesh, and made the body whole, much more will He do this in the resurrection, so that the flesh shall rise perfect and entire. In this manner, then, shall those dreaded difficulties of theirs be healed.

Chapter V - The resurrection of the flesh is not impossible

But again, of those who maintain that the flesh has no resurrection, some assert that it is impossible; others that, considering how vile and despicable the flesh is, it is not fit that God should raise it; and others, that it did not at the first receive the promise. First, then, in respect of those who say that it is impossible for God to raise it, it seems to me that I should show that they are ignorant, professing as they do in word that they are believers, yet by their works proving themselves to be unbelieving, even more unbelieving than the unbelievers. For, seeing that all the heathen believe in their idols, and are persuaded that to them all things are possible (as even their poet Homer says,[2619] "The gods can do all things, and that easily;" and he added the word "easily" that he might bring out the greatness of the power of the gods), many do seem to be more unbelieving than they. For if the heathen believe in their gods, which are idols ("which have ears, and they hear not; they have eyes, and they see not" [2620]), that they can do all things, though they be but devils, as saith the Scripture, "The gods of the nations are devils," [2621] much more ought we, who hold the right, excellent, and true faith, to believe in our God, since also we have proofs [of His power], first in the creation of the first man, for he was made from the earth by God; and this is sufficient evidence of God's power; and then they who observe things can see how men are generated one by another, and can marvel in a still greater degree that from a little drop of moisture so grand a living creature is formed. And certainly if this were only recorded in a promise, and not seen accomplished, this too would be much more incredible than the other; but it is rendered more credible by accomplishment.[2622] But even in the case of the resurrection the Saviour has shown us accomplishments, of which we will in a little speak. But now we are demonstrating that the resurrection of the flesh is possible, asking pardon of the children of the Church if we adduce arguments which seem to be secular [2623] and physical: [2624] first, because to God nothing is secular, not even the world itself, for it is His workmanship; and secondly, because we are conducting our argument so as to meet unbelievers. For if we argued with believers, it were enough to say that we believe; but now we must proceed by demonstrations. The foregoing proofs are indeed quite sufficient to evince the possibility of the resurrection of the flesh; but since these men are exceedingly unbelieving, we will further adduce a more convincing argument still, --an argument drawn not from faith, for they are not within its scope, but from their own mother unbelief,--I mean, of course, from physical reasons. For if by such arguments we prove to them that the resurrection of the flesh is possible, they are certainly worthy of great contempt if they can be persuaded neither by the deliverances of faith nor by the arguments of the world.

Chapter VI - The resurrection consistent with the opinions of the philosophers

Those, then, who are called natural philosophers, say, some of them, as Plato, that the universe is matter and God; others, as Epicurus, that it is atoms and the void; [2625] others, like the Stoics, that it is these four--fire, water, air, earth. For it is sufficient to mention the most prevalent opinions. And Plato says that all things are made from matter by God, and according to His design; but Epicures and his followers say that all things are made from the atom and the void by some kind of self-regulating action of the natural movement of the bodies; and the Stoics, that all are made of the four elements, God pervading them. But while there is such discrepancy among them, there are some doctrines acknowledged by them all in common, one of which is that neither can anything be produced from what is not in being, nor anything be destroyed or dissolved into what has not any being, and that the elements exist indestructible out of which all things are generated. And this being so, the regeneration of the flesh will, according to all these philosophers, appear to be possible. For if, according to Plato, it is matter and God, both these are indestructible and God; and God indeed occupies the position of an artificer, to wit, a potter; and matter occupies the place of clay or wax, or some such thing. That, then, which is formed of matter, be it an image or a statue, is destructible; but the matter itself is indestructible, such as clay or wax, or any other such kind of matter. Thus the artist designs in the clay or wax, and makes the form of a living animal; and again, if his handiwork be destroyed, it is not impossible for him to make the same form, by working up the same material, and fashioning it anew. So that, according to Plato, neither will it be impossible for God, who is Himself indestructible, and has also indestructible material, even after that which has been first formed of it has been destroyed, to make it anew again, and to make the same form just as it was before. But according to the Stoics even, the body being produced by the mixture of the four elementary substances, when this body has been dissolved into the four elements, these remaining indestructible, it is possible that they receive a second time the same fusion and composition, from God pervading them, and so re-make the body which they formerly made. Like as if a man shall make a composition of gold and silver, and brass and tin, and then shall wish to dissolve it again, so that each element exist separately, having again mixed them, he may, if he pleases, make the very same composition as he had formerly made. Again, according to Epicurus, the atoms and the void being indestructible, it is by a definite arrangement and adjustment of the atoms as they come together, that both all other formations are produced, and the body itself; and it being in course of time dissolved, is dissolved again into those atoms from which it was also produced. And as these remain indestructible, it is not at all impossible, that by coming together again, and receiving the same arrangement and position, they should make a body of like nature to what was formerly produced by them; as if a jeweller should make in mosaic the form of an animal, and the stones should be scattered by time or by the man himself who made them, he having still in his possession the scattered stones, may gather them together again, and having gathered, may dispose them in the same way, and make the same form of an animal. And shall not God be able to collect again the decomposed members of the flesh, and make the same body as was formerly produced by Him?

Chapter VII - The body valuable in God's sight

But the proof of the possibility of the resurrection of the flesh I have sufficiently demonstrated, in answer to men of the world. And if the resurrection of the flesh is not found impossible on the principles even of unbelievers, how much more will it be found in accordance with the mind of believers! But following our order, we must now speak with respect to those who think meanly of the flesh, and say that it is not worthy of the resurrection nor of the heavenly economy, [2626] because, first, its substance is earth; and besides, because it is full of all wickedness, so that it forces the soul to sin along with it. But these persons seem to be ignorant of the whole work of God, both of the genesis and formation of man at the first, and why the things in the world were made. [2627] For does not the word say, "Let Us make man in our image, and after our likeness?"[2628] What kind of man? Manifestly He means fleshly man, For the word says, "And God took dust of the earth, and made man." [2629] It is evident, therefore, that man made in the image of God was of flesh. Is it not, then, absurd to say, that the flesh made by God in His own image is contemptible, and worth nothing? But that the flesh is with God a precious possession is manifest, first from its being formed by Him, if at least the image is valuable to the former and artist; and besides, its value can be gathered from the creation of the rest of the world. For that on account of which the rest is made, is the most precious of all to the maker.

Chapter VIII - Does the body cause the soul to sin?

Quite true, say they; yet the flesh is a sinner, so much so, that it forces the soul to sin along with it. And thus they vainly accuse it, and lay to its charge alone the sins of both. But in what instance can the flesh possibly sin by itself, if it have not the soul going before it and inciting it? For as in the case of a yoke of oxen, if one or other is loosed from the yoke, neither of them can plough alone; so neither can soul or body alone effect anything, if they be unyoked from their communion. And if it is the flesh that is the sinner, then on its account alone did the Saviour come, as He says, "I am not come to call the righteous, but sinners to repentance." [2630] Since, then, the flesh has been proved to be valuable in the sight of God, and glorious above all His works, it would very justly be saved by Him.

We must meet, therefore, those who say, that even though it be the special handiwork of God, and beyond all else valued by Him, it would not immediately follow that it has the promise of the resurrection. Yet is it not absurd, that that which has been produced with such circumstance, and which is beyond all else valuable, should be so neglected by its Maker, as to pass to nonentity? Then the sculptor and painter, if they wish the works they have made to endure, that they may win glory by them, renew them when they begin to decay; but God would so neglect His own possession and work, that it becomes annihilated, and no longer exists. Should we not call this labour in vain? As if a man who has built a house should forthwith destroy it, or should neglect it, though he sees it falling into decay, and is able to repair it: we would blame him for labouring in vain; and should we not so blame God? But not such an one is the Incorruptible,--not senseless is the Intelligence of the universe. Let the unbelieving be silent, even though they themselves do not believe.

But, in truth, He has even called the flesh to the resurrection, and promises to it everlasting life. For where He promises to save man, there He gives the promise to the flesh. For what is man but the reasonable animal composed of body and soul? Is the soul by itself man? No; but the soul of man. Would the body be called man? No, but it is called the body of man. If, then, neither of these is by itself man, but that which is made up of the two together is called man, and God has called man to life and resurrection, He has called not a part, but the whole, which is the soul and the body. Since would it not be unquestionably absurd, if, while these two are in the same being and according to the same law, the one were saved and the other not? And if it be not impossible, as has already been proved, that the flesh be regenerated, what is the distinction on the ground of which the soul is saved and the body not? Do they make God a grudging God? But He is good, and will have all to be saved. And by God and His proclamation, not only has your soul heard and believed on Jesus Christ, and with it the flesh, [2631] but both were washed, and both wrought righteousness. They make God, then ungrateful and unjust, if, while both believe on Him, He desires to save one and not the other. Well, they say, but the soul is incorruptible, being a part of God and inspired by Him, and therefore He desires to save what is peculiarly His own and akin to Himself; but the flesh is corruptible, and not from Him, as the soul is. Then what thanks are due to Him, and what manifestation of His power and goodness is it, if He purposed to save what is by nature saved and exists as a part of Himself? For it had its salvation from itself; so that in saving the soul, God does no great thing. For to be saved is its natural destiny, because it is a part of Himself, being His inspiration. But no thanks are due to one who saves what is his own; for this is to save himself. For he who saves a part himself, saves himself by his own means, lest he become defective in that part; and this is not the act of a good man. For not even when a man does good to his children and offspring, does one call him a good man; for even the most savage of the wild beasts do so, and indeed willingly endure death, if need be, for the sake of their cubs. But if a man were to perform the same acts in behalf of his slaves, that man would justly be called good. Wherefore the Saviour also taught us to love our enemies, since, says He, what thank have ye? So that He has shown us that it is a good work not only to love those that are begotten of Him, but also those that are without. And what He enjoins upon us, He Himself first of all does. [2632]

Chapter IX - The resurrection of Christ proves that the body rises

If He had no need of the flesh, why did He heal it? And what is most forcible of all, He raised the dead. Why? Was it not to show what the resurrection should be? How then did He raise the dead? Their souls or their bodies? Manifestly both. If the resurrection were only spiritual, it was requisite that He, in raising the dead, should show the body lying apart by itself, and the soul living apart by itself. But now He did not do so, but raised the body, confirming in it the promise of life. Why did He rise in the flesh in which He suffered, unless to show the resurrection of the flesh? And wishing to confirm this, when His disciples did not know whether to believe He had truly risen in the body, and were looking upon Him and doubting, He said to them, "Ye have not yet faith, see that it is I;" [2633] and He let them handle Him, and showed them the prints of the nails in His hands. And when they were by every kind of proof persuaded that it was Himself, and in the body, they asked Him to eat with them, that they might thus still more accurately ascertain that He had in verity risen bodily; and He did eat honey-comb and fish. And when He had thus shown them that there is truly a resurrection of the flesh, wishing to show them this also, that it is not impossible for flesh to ascend into heaven (as He had said that our dwelling-place is in heaven), "He was taken up into heaven while they beheld," [2634] as He was in the flesh. If, therefore, after all that has been said, any one demand demonstration of the resurrection, he is in no respect different from the Sadducees, since the resurrection of the flesh is the power of God, and, being above all reasoning, is established by faith, and seen in works.

Chapter X - The body saved, and will therefore rise

The resurrection is a resurrection of the flesh which died. For the spirit dies not; the soul is in the body, and without a soul it cannot live. The body, when the soul forsakes it, is not. For the body is the house of the soul; and the soul the house of the spirit. These three, in all those who cherish a sincere hope and unquestioning faith in God, will be saved. Considering, therefore, even such arguments as are suited to this world, and finding that, even according to them, it is not impossible that the flesh be regenerated; and seeing that, besides all these proofs, the Saviour in the whole Gospel shows that there is salvation for the flesh, why do we any longer endure those unbelieving and dangerous arguments, and fail to see that we are retrograding when we listen to such an argument as this: that the soul is immortal, but the body mortal, and incapable of being revived? For this we used to hear from Pythagoras and Plato, even before we learned the truth. If then the Saviour said this, and proclaimed salvation to the soul alone, what new thing, beyond what we heard from Pythagoras and Plato and all their band, did He bring us? But now He has come proclaiming the glad tidings of a new and strange hope to men. For indeed it was a strange and new thing for God to promise that He would not keep incorruption in incorruption, but would make corruption incorruption. But because the prince of wickedness could in no other way corrupt the truth, he sent forth his apostles (evil men who introduced pestilent doctrines), choosing them from among those who crucified our Saviour; and these men bore the name of the Saviour, but did the works of him that sent them, through whom the name itself has been spoken against. But if the flesh do not rise, why is it also guarded, and why do we not rather suffer it to indulge its desires? Why do we not imitate physicians, who, it is said, when they get a patient that is despaired of and incurable, allow him to indulge his desires? For they know that he is dying; and this indeed those who hate the flesh surely do, casting it out of its inheritance, so far as they can; for on this account they also despise it, because it is shortly to become a corpse. But if our physician Christ, God, having rescued us from our desires, regulates our flesh with His own wise and temperate rule, it is evident that He guards it from sins because it possesses a hope of salvation, as physicians do not suffer men whom they hope to save to indulge in what pleasures they please. [2635]

Footnotes:

2614. Mark xii. 25.

2615. That is to say, their lives are a protest against entering into marriage for any other purpose than that of begetting children.

2616. i.e., to the devil. St. John xii. 31, John xiv. 30, John xvi. 11.

2617. Luke xx. 34, 35.

2618. Isa. xxxv. 5.

2619. Odyssey, ii. 304.

2620. Ps. cxv. 5.
2621. Ps. xcvi. 5.
2622. i.e., by actually happening under our observation.
2623. ἔξωθεν, "without" or "outside," to which reference is made in the next clause, which may be translated, "because nothing is outside God," or, "because to God nothing is without.' "
2624. κοσμικῶν, arguments drawn from the laws by which the world is governed.
2625. τὸ κενόν, the void of space in which the infinity of atoms moved.
2626. Or, "citizenship."
2627. This might also be rendered, "and the things in the world, on account of which he was made;" but the subsequent argument shows the propriety of the above rendering.
2628. Gen. i. 26.
2629. Gen. ii. 7.
2630. Mark ii. 17.
2631. Migne proposes to read here καὶ οὐ σὺν αὐτῇ, "without the flesh," which gives a more obvious meaning. The above reading is, however, defensible. Justin means that the flesh was not merely partaking of the soul's faith and promise, but had rights of its own.
2632. It is supposed that a part of the treatise has been here dropped out.
2633. Comp. Luke xxiv. 32, etc.
2634. Acts i. 9.
2635. N.B.--These fragments are probably genuine.

Other Fragments from the Lost Writings of Justin

[Translated by the Rev. A. Roberts, D.D.]

I

The most admirable Justin rightly declared that the aforesaid demons [2636] resembled robbers.--Tatian's Address to the Greeks, chap. xviii.

II

And Justin well said in his book against Marcion, that he would not have believed the Lord Himself, if He had announced any other God than the Fashioner and Maker [of the world], and our Nourisher. But since, from the one God, who both made this world and formed us, and contains as well as administers all things, there came to us the only-begotten Son, summing up His own workmanship in Himself, my faith in Him is stedfast, and my love towards the Father is immoveable, God bestowing both upon us.--Irenæus: Heresies, iv. 6.

III

Justin well said: Before the advent of the Lord, Satan never ventured to blaspheme God, inasmuch as he was not yet sure of his own damnation, since that was announced concerning him by the prophets only in parables and allegories. But after the advent of the Lord, learning plainly from the discourses of Christ and His apostles that eternal fire was prepared for him who voluntarily departed from Godi, and for all who, without repentance, persevere in apostasy, then, by means of a man of this sort, he, as if already condemned, blasphemes that God who inflicts judgment upon him, and imputes the sin of his apostasy to his Maker, instead of to his own will and predilection.--Irenæus: Heresies, v. 26.

IV

Expounding the reason of the incessant plotting of the devil against us, he declares: Before the advent of the Lord, the devil did not so plainly know the measure of his own punishment, inasmuch as the divine prophets had but enigmatically announced it; as, for instance, Isaiah, who in the person of the Assyrian tragically revealed the course to be followed against the devil. But when the Lord appeared, and the devil clearly understood that eternal fire was laid up and prepared for him and his angels, he then began to plot without ceasing against the faithful, being desirous to have many companions in his apostasy, that he might not by himself endure the shame of condemnation, comforting himself by this cold and malicious consolation.--From the writings of John of Antioch.

V

And Justin of Neapolis, a man who was not far separated from the apostles either in age or excellence, says that that which is mortal is inherited, but that which is immortal inherits; and that the flesh indeed dies, but the kingdom of heaven lives.--From Methodius On the Resurrection, in Photius.

VI

Neither is there straitness with God, nor anything that is not absolutely perfect.--From manuscript of the writings of Justin.

VII

We shall not injure God by remaining ignorant of Him, but shall deprive ourselves of His friendship.

VIII

The unskilfulness of the teacher proves destructive to his disciples, and the carelessness of the disciples entails danger on the teacher, and especially should they owe their negligence to his want of knowledge.

IX

The soul can with difficulty be recalled to those good things from which it has fallen, and is with difficulty dragged away from those evils to which it has become accustomed. If at any time thou showest a disposition to blame thyself, then perhaps, through the medicine of repentance, I should cherish good hopes regarding thee. But when thou altogether despisest fear, and rejectest with scorn the very faith of Christ, it were better for thee that thou hadst never been born from the womb.--From the writings of John of Damascus.

X

By the two birds [2637] Christ is denoted, both dead as man, and living as God. He is likened to a bird, because He is understood and declared to be from above, and from heaven. And the living bird, having been dipped in the blood of the dead one, was afterwards let go. For the living and divine Word was in the crucified and dead temple [of the body], as being a partaker of the passion, and yet impassible to God.

By that which took place in the running [2638] water, in which the wood and the hyssop and the scarlet were dipped, is set forth the bloody passion of Christ on the cross for the salvation of those who are sprinkled with the Spirit, and the water, and the blood. Wherefore the material for purification was not provided chiefly with reference to leprosy, but with regard to the forgiveness of sins, that both leprosy might be understood to be an emblem of sin, and the things which were sacrificed an emblem of Him who was to be sacrificed for sins.

For this reason, consequently, he ordered that the scarlet should be dipped at the same time in the water, thus predicting that the flesh should no longer possess its natural [evil] properties. For this reason, also, were there the two birds, the one being sacrificed in the water, and the other dipped both in the blood and in the water and then sent away, just as is narrated also respecting the goats.

The goat that was sent away presented a type of Him who taketh away the sins of men. But the two contained a representation of the one economy of God incarnate. For He was wounded for our transgressions, and He bare the sins of many, and He was delivered for our iniquities.--From manuscript of writings of Justin.

XI

When God formed man at the beginning, He suspended the things of nature on his will, and made an experiment by means of one commandment. For He ordained that, if he kept this, he should partake of immortal existence; but if he transgressed it, the contrary should be his lot. Man having been thus made, and immediately looking towards transgression, naturally became subject to corruption. Corruption then becoming inherent in nature, it was necessary that He who wished to save should be one who destroyed the efficient cause of corruption. And this could not otherwise be done than by the life which is according to nature being united to that which had received the corruption, and so destroying the corruption, while preserving as immortal for the future that which had received it. It was therefore necessary that the Word should become possessed of a body, that He might deliver us from the death of natural corruption. For if, as ye [2639] say, He had simply by a nod warded off death from us, death indeed would not have approached us on account of the expression of His will; but none the less would we again have become corruptible, inasmuch as we carried about in ourselves that natural corruption.--Leontius against Eutychians, etc., book ii.

XII

As it is inherent in all bodies formed by God to have a shadow, so it is fitting that God, who is just, should render to those who choose what is good, and to those who prefer what is evil, to every one according to his deserts.--From the writings of John of Damascus.

XIII

He speaks not of the Gentiles in foreign lands, but concerning [the people] who agree with the Gentiles, according to that which is spoken by Jeremiah: "It is a bitter thing for thee, that thou hast forsaken me, saith the Lord thy God, that of old thou hast broken thy yoke, and torn asunder thy bands, and said, I will not serve Thee, but will go to every high hill, and underneath every tree, and there shall I become dissolute in my fornication." [2640] --From manuscript of the writings of Justin.

XIV

Neither shall light ever be darkness as long as light exists, nor shall the truth of the things pertaining to us be controverted. For truth is that than which nothing is more powerful. Every one who might speak the truth, and speaks it not, shall be judged by God.--Manuscript and works of John of Damascus.

XV

And the fact that it was not said of the seventh day equally with the other days, "And there was evening, and there was morning," is a distinct indication of the consummation which is to take place in it before it is finished, as the fathers declare, especially St. Clement, and Irenæus, and Justin the martyr and philosopher, who, commenting with exceeding wisdom on the number six of the sixth day, affirms that the intelligent soul of man and his five susceptible senses were the six works of the sixth day. Whence also, having discoursed at length on the number six, he declares that all things which have been framed by God are divided into six classes,--viz., into things intelligent and immortal, such as are the angels; into things reasonable and mortal, such as mankind; into things sensitive and irrational, such as cattle, and birds, and fishes; into things that can advance, and move, and are insensible, such as the winds, and the clouds, and the waters, and the stars; into things which increase and are immoveable, such as the trees; and into things which are insensible and immoveable, such as the mountains, the earth, and such like. For all the creatures of God, in heaven and on earth, fall under one or other of these divisions, and are circumscribed by them.-- From the writings of Anastasius.

XVI

Sound doctrine does not enter into the hard and disobedient heart; but, as if beaten back, enters anew into itself.

XVII

As the good of the body is health, so the good of the soul is knowledge, which is indeed a kind of health of soul, by which a likeness to God is attained.--From the writings of John of Damascus.

XVIII

To yield and give way to our passions is the lowest slavery, even as to rule over them is the only liberty.

The greatest of all good is to be free from sin, the next is to be justified; but he must be reckoned the most unfortunate of men, who, while living unrighteously, remains for a long time unpunished.

Animals in harness cannot but be carried over a precipice by the inexperience and badness of their driver, even as by his skilfulness and excellence they will be saved.

The end contemplated by a philosopher is likeness to God, so far as that is possible.--From the writings of Antonius Melissa.

XIX

[The words] of St. Justin, philosopher and martyr, from the fifth part of his Apology: [2641] --I reckon prosperity, O men, to consist in nothing else than in living according to truth. But we do not live properly, or according to truth, unless we understand the nature of things.

It escapes them apparently, that he who has by a true faith come forth from error to the truth, has truly known himself, not, as they say, as being in a state of frenzy, but as free from the unstable and (as to every variety of error) changeable corruption, by the simple and ever identical truth.--From the writings of John of Damascus.

Footnotes:

2636. See, on the Resurrection, cap. vi.; and compare, --
"And of those demons that are found
In fire, air, flood, or under ground,"
etc. Milton, Pens., line 93.

2637. See Lev. xiv. 49-53.

2638. Literally, "living."

2639. The Gentiles are here referred to, who saw no necessity for the incarnation.

2640. Jer. ii. 19, etc. (LXX.)

2641. It is doubtful if these words are really Justin's, or, if so, from which, or what part, of his Apologies they are derived.

Introductory Note to the Martyrdom of Justin Martyr

Crescens, a cynic, has the ill-renown of stirring up the persecution in which Justin and his friends suffered for Christ. The story that he died by the hemlock seems to have originated among the Greeks, who naturally gave this turn to the sufferings of a philosopher. The following Introductory Notice of the translator supplies all that need be added.

Though nothing is known as to the date or authorship of the following narrative, it is generally reckoned among the most trustworthy of the Martyria. An absurd addition was in some copies made to it, to the effect that Justin died by means of hemlock. Some have thought it necessary, on account of this story, to conceive of two Justins, one of whom, the celebrated defender of the Christian faith whose writings are given in this volume, died through poison, while the other suffered in the way here described, along with several of his friends. But the description of Justin given in the following account, is evidently such as compels us to refer it to the famous apologist and martyr of the second century. [2642]

The Martyrdom of the Holy Martyrs Justin, Chariton, Charites, Pæon, and Liberianus, who Suffered at Rome

[Translated by the Rev. M. Dods, M.A.]

Chapter I - Examination of Justin by the prefect

In the time of the lawless partisans of idolatry, wicked decrees were passed against the godly Christians in town and country, to force them to offer libations to vain idols; and accordingly the holy men, having been apprehended, were brought before the prefect of Rome, Rusticus by name. And when they had been brought before his judgment-seat, Rusticus the prefect said to Justin, "Obey the gods at once, and submit to the kings." [2643] Justin said, "To obey the commandments of our Saviour Jesus Christ is worthy neither of blame nor of condemnation." Rusticus the prefect said, "What kind of doctrines do you profess?" Justin said, "I have endeavoured to learn all doctrines; but I have acquiesced at last in the true doctrines, those namely of the Christians, even though they do not please those who hold false opinions." Rusticus the prefect said, "Are those the doctrines that please you, you utterly wretched man?" Justin said, "Yes, since I adhere to them with right dogma." [2644] Rusticus the prefect said, "What is the dogma?" Justin said, "That according to which we worship the God of the Christians, whom we reckon to be one from the beginning, the maker and fashioner of the whole creation, visible and invisible; and the Lord Jesus Christ, the Son of God, who had also been preached beforehand by the prophets as about to be present with the race of men, the herald of salvation and teacher of good disciples. And I, being a man, think that what I can say is insignificant in comparison with His boundless divinity, acknowledging a certain prophetic power, [2645] since it was prophesied concerning Him of whom now I say that He is the Son of God. For I know that of old the prophets foretold His appearance among men."

Chapter II - Examination of Justin continued

Rusticus the prefect said, "Where do you assemble?" Justin said, "Where each one chooses and can: for do you fancy that we all meet in the very same place? Not so; because the God of the Christians is not circumscribed by place; but being invisible, fills heaven and earth, and everywhere is worshipped and glorified by the faithful." Rusticus the prefect said, "Tell me where you assemble, or into what place do you collect your followers?" Justin said, "I live above one Martinus, at the Timiotinian Bath; and during the whole time (and I am now living in Rome for the second time) I am unaware of any other meeting than his. And if any one wished to come to me, I communicated to him the doctrines of truth." Rusticus said, "Are you not, then, a Christian?" Justin said, "Yes, I am a Christian."

Chapter III - Examination of Chariton and others

Then said the prefect Rusticus to Chariton, "Tell me further, Chariton, are you also a Christian?" Chariton said, "I am a Christian by the command of God." Rusticus the prefect asked the woman Charito, "What say you, Charito?" Charito said, "I am a Christian by the grace of God." Rusticus said to Euelpistus, "And what are you?" Euelpistus, a servant of Cæsar, answered, "I too am a Christian, having been freed by Christ; and by the grace of Christ I partake of the same hope." Rusticus the prefect said to Hierax, "And you, are you a Christian?" Hierax said, "Yes, I am a Christian, for I revere and worship the same God." Rusticus the prefect said, "Did Justin make you Christians?" Hierax said, "I was a Christian, and will be a Christian." And Pæon stood up and said, "I too am a Christian." Rusticus the prefect said, "Who taught you?" Pæon said, "From our parents we received this good confession." Euelpistus said, "I willingly heard the words of Justin. But from my parents also I learned to be a Christian." Rusticus the prefect said, "Where are your parents?" Euelpistus said, "In Cappadocia." Rusticus says to Hierax, "Where are your parents?" And he answered, and said, "Christ is our true father, and faith in Him is our mother; and my earthly parents died; and I, when I was driven from Iconium in Phrygia, came here." Rusticus the prefect said to Liberianus, "And what say you? Are you a Christian, and unwilling to worship [the gods]?" Liberianus said, "I too am a Christian, for I worship and reverence the only true God."

Chapter IV - Rusticus threatens the Christians with death

The prefect says to Justin, "Hearken, you who are called learned, and think that you know true doctrines; if you are scourged and beheaded, do you believe you will ascend into heaven?" Justin said, "I hope that, if I endure these things, I shall have His gifts. [2646] For I know that, to all who have thus lived, there abides the divine favour until the completion of the whole world." Rusticus the prefect said, "Do you suppose, then, that you will ascend into heaven to receive some recompense?" Justin said, "I do not suppose it, but I know and am fully persuaded of it." Rusticus the prefect said, "Let us, then, now come to the matter in hand, and which presses. Having come together, offer sacrifice with one accord to the gods." Justin said, "No right-thinking person falls away from piety to impiety." Rusticus the prefect said, "Unless ye obey, ye shall be mercilessly punished." Justin said, "Through prayer we can be saved on account of our Lord Jesus Christ, even when we have been punished, [2647] because this shall become to us salvation and confidence at the more fearful and universal judgment-seat of our Lord and Saviour." Thus also said the other martyrs: "Do what you will, for we are Christians, and do not sacrifice to idols."

Chapter V - Sentence pronounced and executed

Rusticus the prefect pronounced sentence, saying, "Let those who have refused to sacrifice to the gods and to yield to the command of the emperor be scourged, [2648] and led away to suffer the punishment of decapitation, according to the laws." The holy martyrs having glorified God, and having gone forth to the accustomed place, were beheaded, and perfected their testimony in the confession of the Saviour. And some of the faithful having secretly removed their bodies, laid them in a suitable place, the grace of our Lord Jesus Christ having wrought along with them, to whom be glory for ever and ever. Amen.

Footnotes:

2642. See Cave, Lives of the Fathers, i. 243. Epiphanius, by fixing the martyrdom under the prefecture of Rusticus, seems to identify this history; but, then, he also connects it with the reign of Hadrian. Ed. Oehler, tom ii. 709. Berlin, 1859.

2643. i.e., the emperors.

2644. Μετὰ δόγματος ὀρθοῦ, orthodoxy.

2645. That is, that a prophetic inspiration is required to speak worthily of Christ.

2646. Another reading is δόγματα, which may be translated, "I shall have what He teaches us to expect."

2647. This passage admits of another rendering. Lord Hailes, following the common Latin version, thus translates: "It was our chief wish to endure tortures for the sake of our Lord Jesus Christ, and so to be saved."

2648. This wholesale sentence implies a great indifference to the probable Roman citizenship of some of them, if not our heroic martyr himself; but Acts xxii. 25-29 seems to allow that the condemned were not protected by the law.

www.ingramcontent.com/pod-product-compliance
Lightning Source LLC
Chambersburg PA
CBHW031309150426
43191CB00005B/138